gente
GENTE
gente
gente
Gente
Gente
gente
Gente
gente
gente
gente
GENTE
gente
gente
Gente
gente
Gente
gente
gente
Gente
Gente
GENTE
gente
gente
gente
Gente
gente
gente

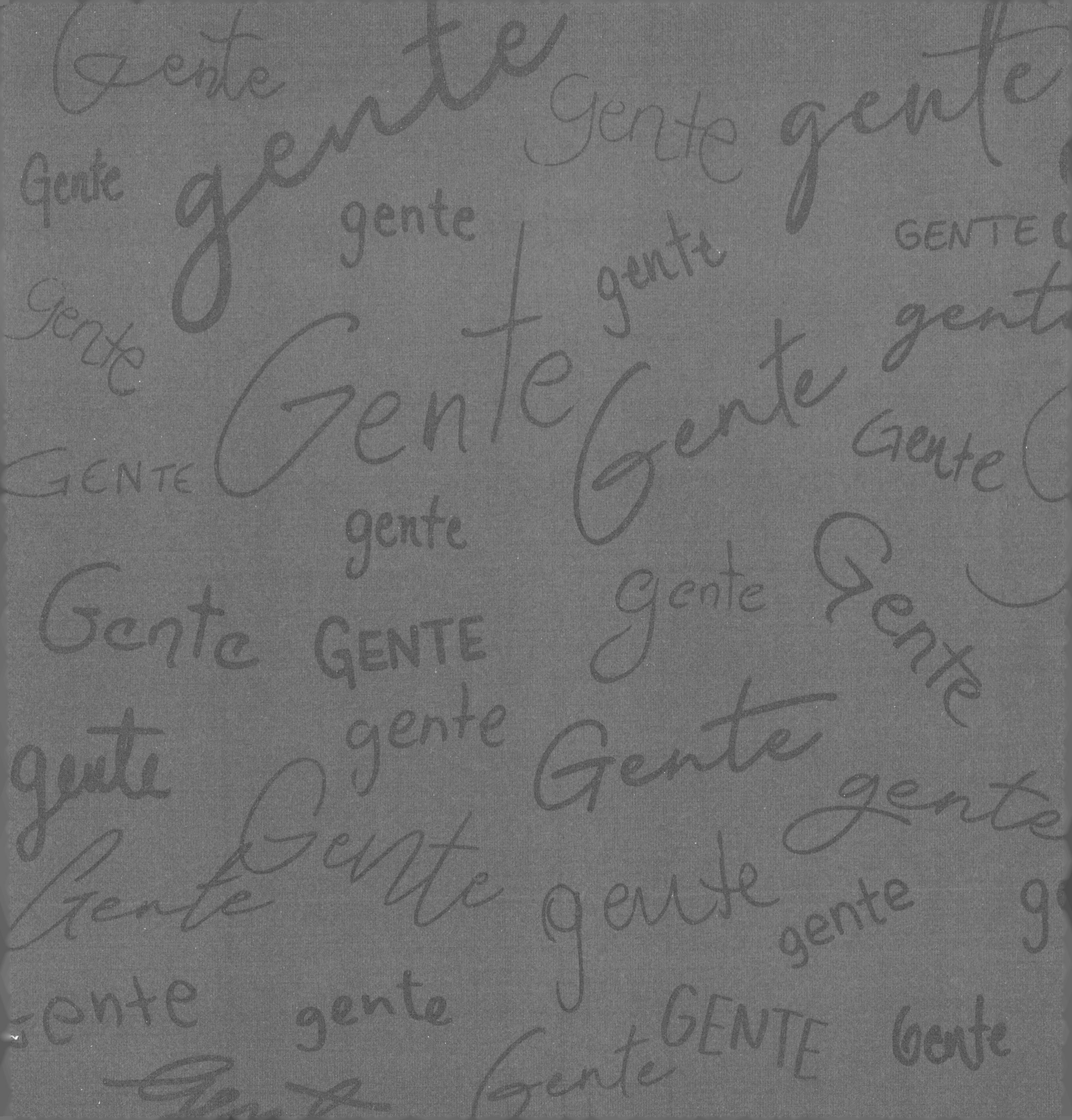

The closer we get to other people, the closer we get to ourselves.

*I am an expression of what we are.*

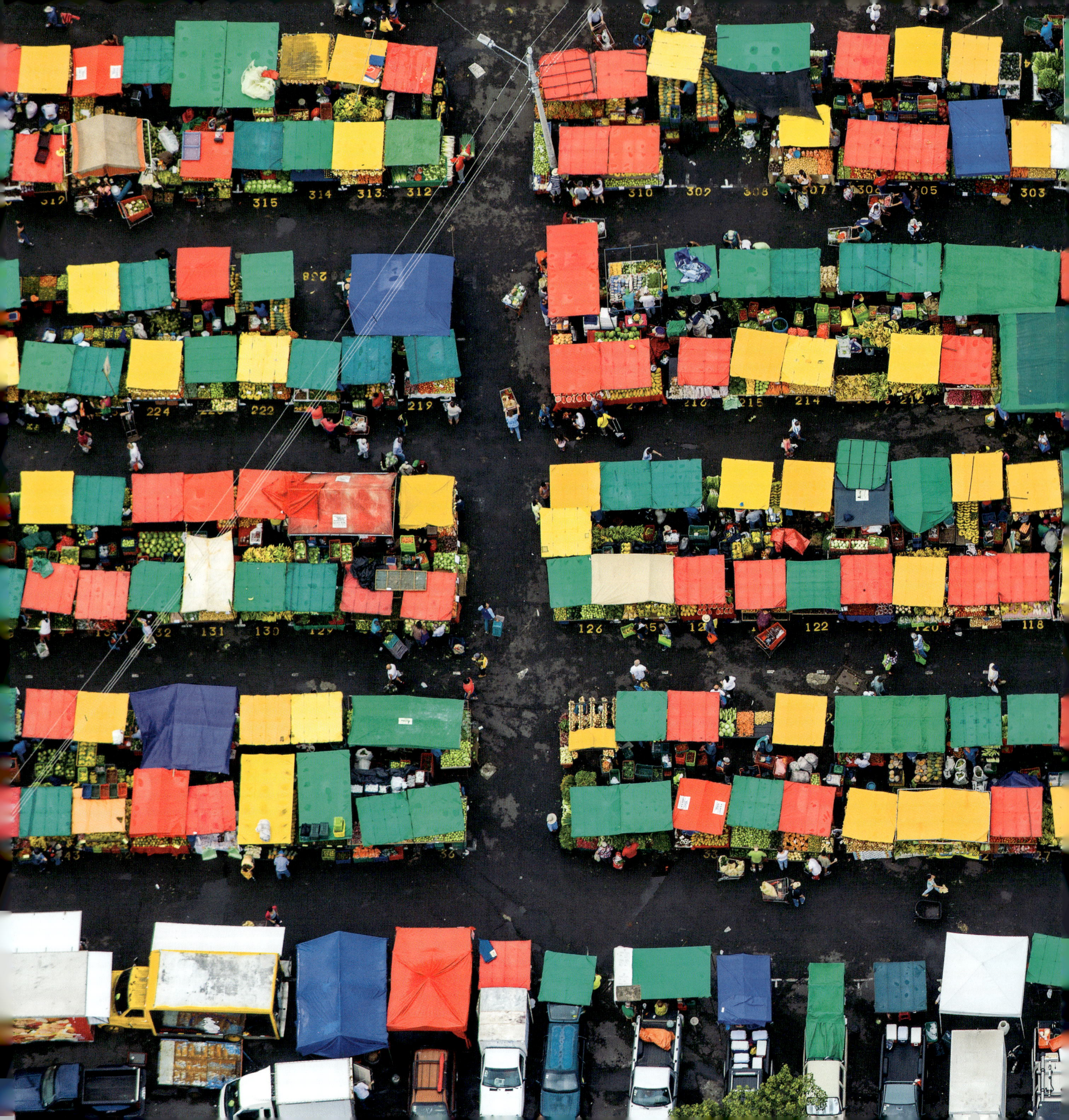

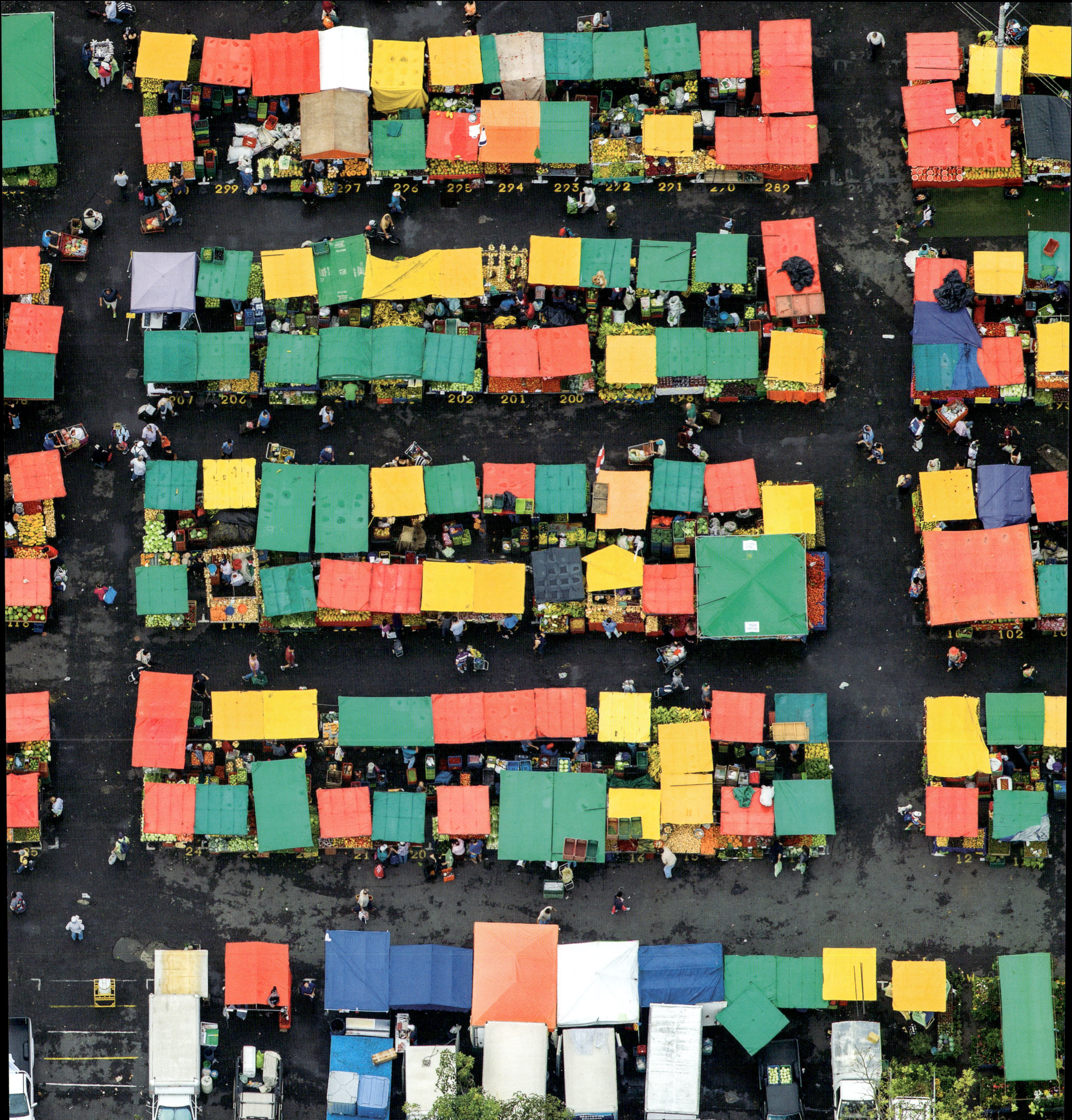

F

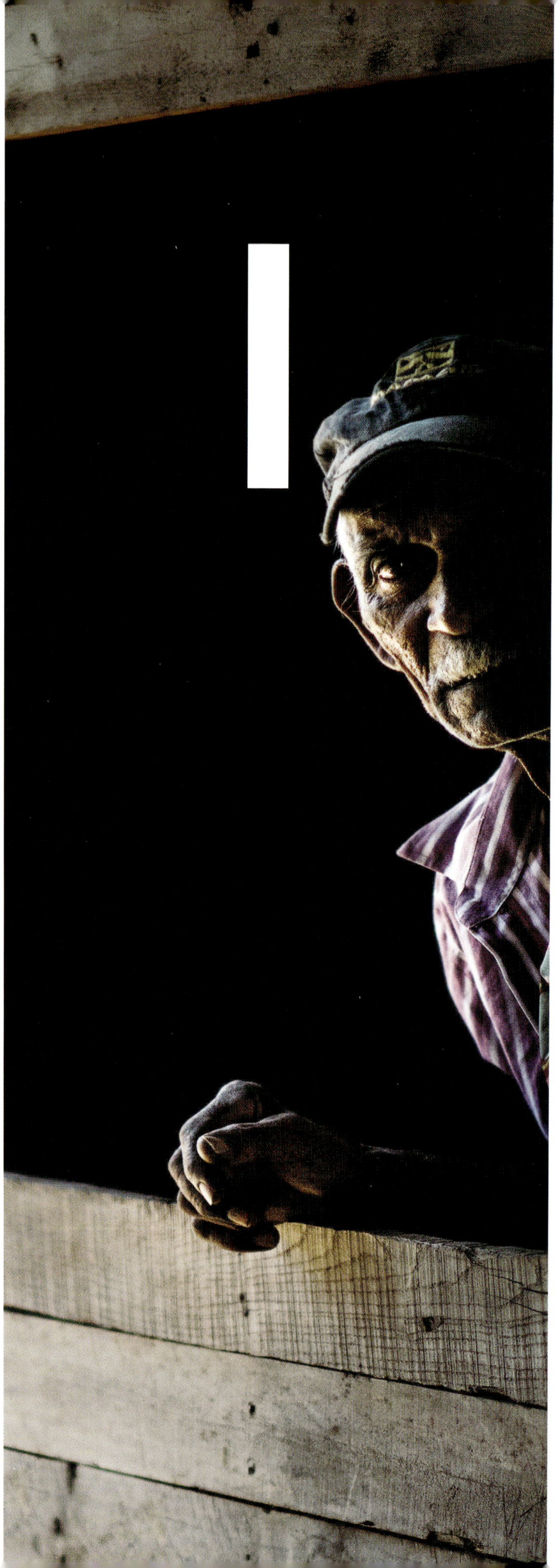

V E

# MILLION AND COUNTING...

Who are we, 200 years after gaining our independence? What do we look forward to? What worries, surprises, excites us? How do we remember our lives and how do we imagine the future?

There's no doubt that these questions have 5 million-plus answers, and it's also a certainty that there's no way of knowing them all. At most, throughout our lives we become familiar with the way of being, the points of view and the life stories of a few dozen people.

This book, more than an exhaustive effort to take "portraits" of who we are, is an open window on slightly more than 50 faces. A lens that gives us a brief but up-close look at the lives and memories of dozens of Ticos and Ticas. It's only a fragment of the impressive mosaic that makes up the Costa Rican nation as we celebrate our country's bicentennial.

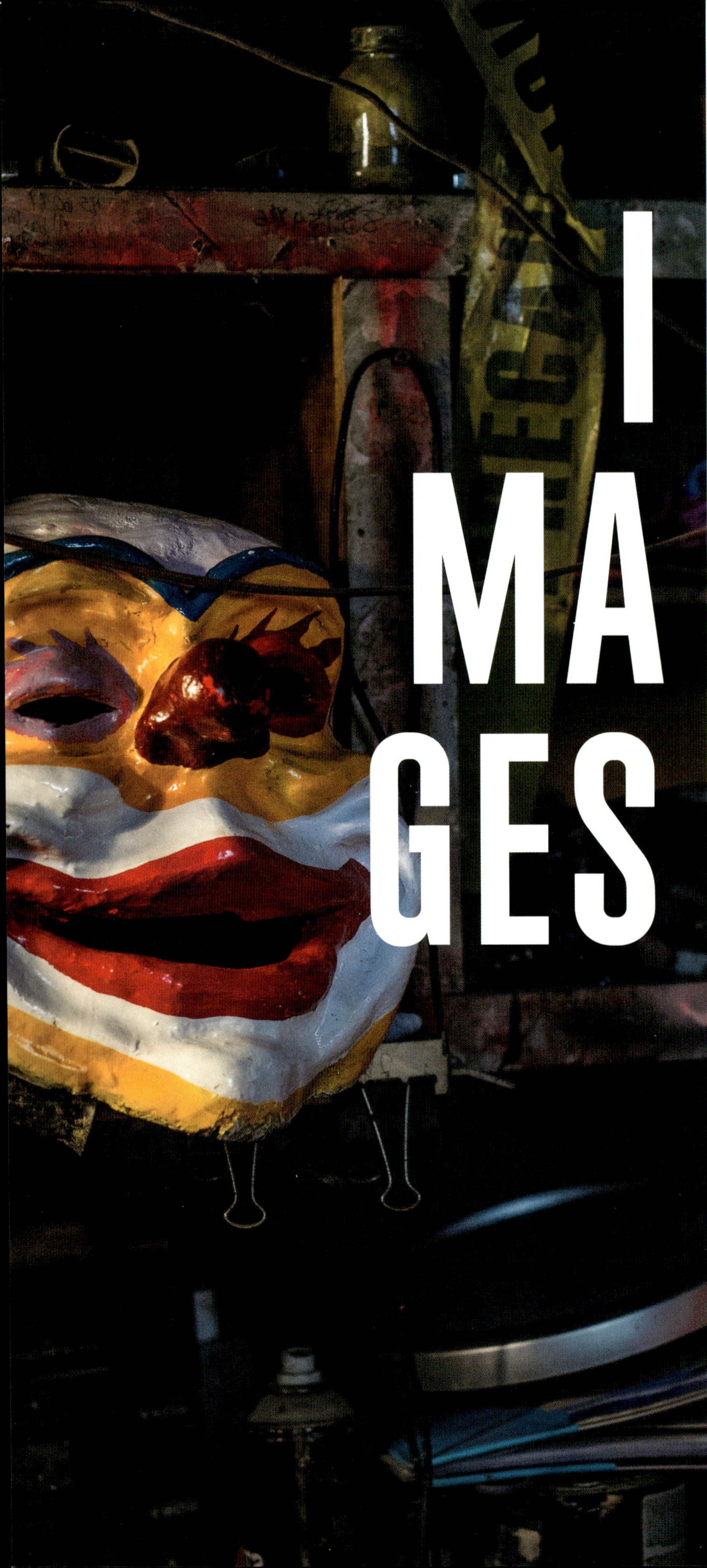

# IMAGES AND WORDS

*Costa Ricans: Pura Gente, Pura Vida*, then, is part testimonial document, part kaleidoscope, part mirror.

But after all, what are mirrors if not objects that return an imperfect, ever-changing image? The book-mirror, by offering two distinct images together (one visual and one textual), seeks to create a three-dimensional image of the people portrayed that's warmer, closer and we hope profoundly human.

Because the words and images complement each other, they overlap. They speak to each other and to us at the same time, helping us to understand things that otherwise we couldn't: where that expression came from; how many roads that smile walked before being captured in a photo; what memories dwell in those bright eyes when they're beneath closed eyelids at night.

The photographs in the book make a statement that's separate from the reporting. They are deliberate, produced with great effort and full of detail, made for the purpose of shining light on the character of each person — to deliver intense visual poetry that delights the eyes again and again and always delivers a sense of wonder.

At the same time, the text has been through a long process of distillation, from the interview on location to the final edits of a select group of authors, who have deliberately added their own literary intentions, their filter of facts and memories, to craft stories that have value in and of themselves, but which placed alongside the photos build new meanings that transcend both the visual and the literary.

Word and image combine in an imaginary equation that excites and seduces, that invites us to think and to love. Not to love or desire something, just to love. To love ourselves.

What other mission could this book have, other than to invoke the primordial affection that unites us all?

# LANDSCAPES WITH FACES

This is also a variation on the visual narrative history of the Pucci family. Juan José, Giancarlo and Sergio, who with so much clarity have shown us the undiscovered landscapes of this country, are recognizable this time in the faces of those who inhabit these landscapes.

In this book there are no "personalities," just persons, people with a story to tell. In other words, basically any person who has loved, dreamed and lived long enough to remember. Nothing more. And that's what's so beautiful, because it's enough.

There was no search for the hero or the martyr, but for the human being, with his nature, culture, upbringing, disappointments and triumphs. This is the book of the centenarian from the Blue Zone who only hopes that life will allow him to see his centenarian lady friend come to visit him one more time. It's a book about hopes and small miracles, like the kind you experience sitting quietly on a surfboard, waiting for the wind to whip up the waves so you can flow with them toward the shore, enjoying the illusion of being one with the sea.

These are the great stories that fill the heart of this book: the stories of "pure people" with their pure lives, in which the purity has no moral burden, but a sense of simplicity: It's pure life, nothing more, that resonates in the pages of this book.

And this is the invitation we offer: to see and to read like someone who's present, captivated by the humanity that surrounds us. Enjoying the fact that we're human in a country with 5 million-plus stories like these.

The closer we get to other people, the closer we get to ourselves. I am an expression of what we are.

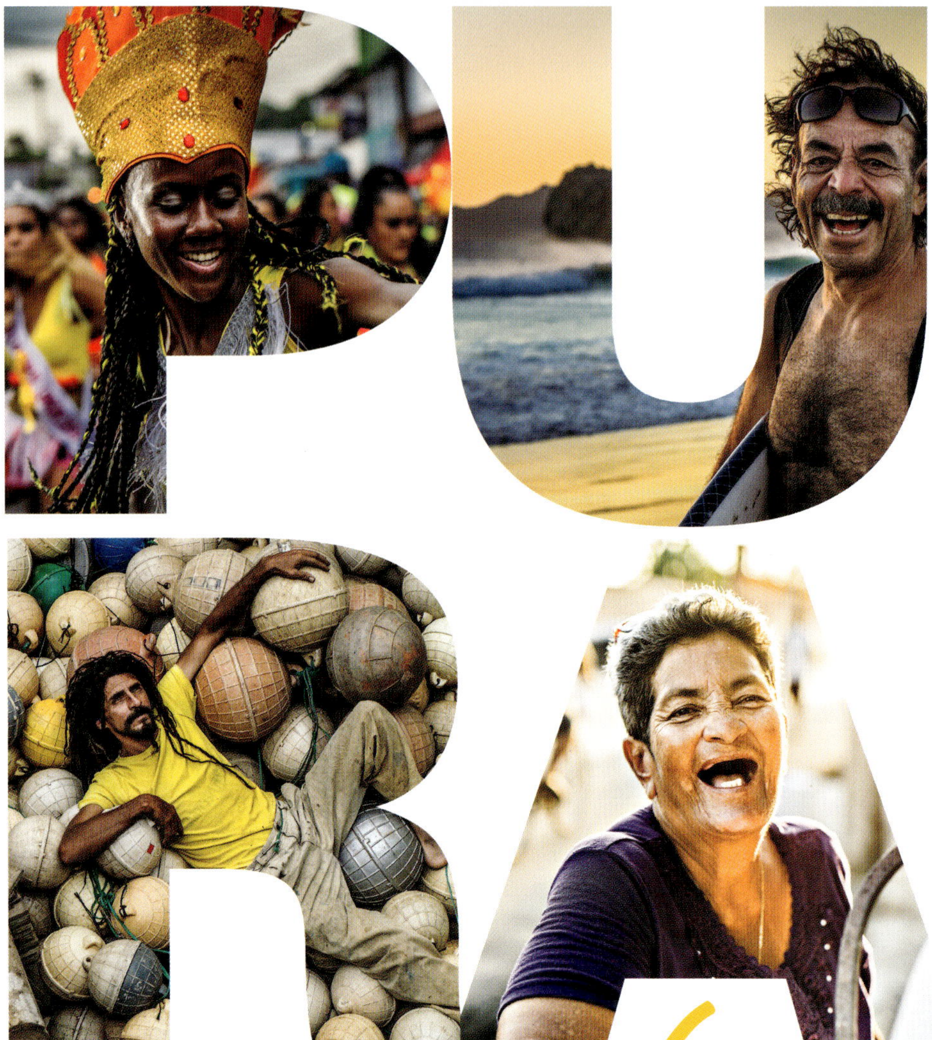

# PURA gente

The phrase "Costa Rica is its people" is well-worn for a reason: This isn't just a coast rich in nature, but also in humanity. "Pura vida" ("pure life") is also overused, although sometimes it's a shield to avoid delving deeper into what we think or feel. But it's no lie — we are "pura vida"! A fuller life, with many facets and perspectives.

"Pura vida" doesn't mean we aren't complex. There are many layers of our humanity still to be discovered, and conflicts force us to look where we don't want to. To look at us is to recognize us. It's curiosity that makes us believe.

Through the years, our adventures have been full of sunsets and magical places, but in the company of the storekeeper, the lady at the little restaurant, the buddies, the tour guide, the park ranger, the mentor, the boatman, the family, the entrepreneurial people, scientists and explorers. People full of stories.

A strong curiosity arose in us, a calling to listen to and get to know the Ticos even better. This has been a journey of over two years, not only throughout the seven provinces but also through our own hopes and fears.

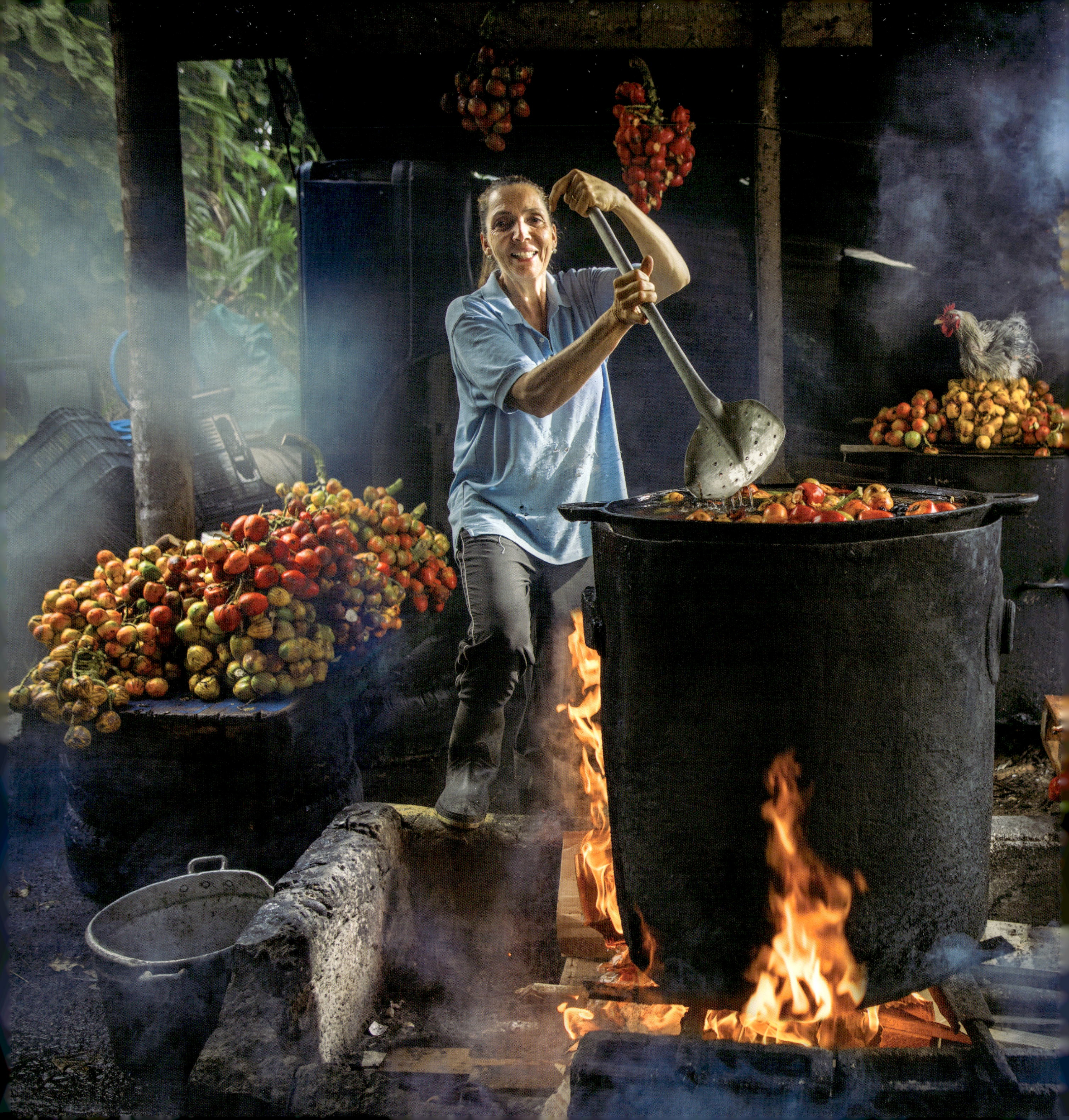

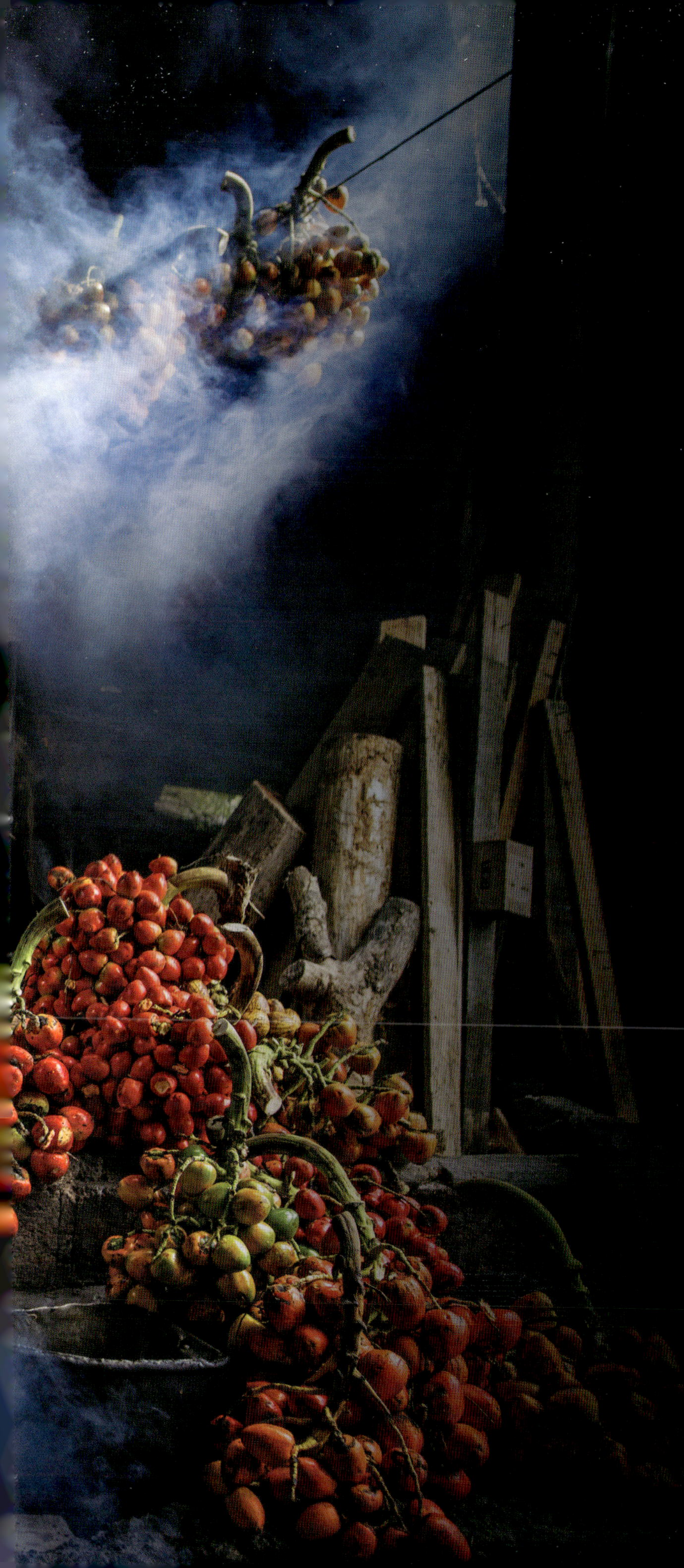

# BOUGAINVILLEA

At Magda's house, everyone is special. She doesn't have "fancy" dishes that she saves for visitors; she always uses the same nice dinner set because family is the center of her life. The table occupies a place of great importance in her heart; there she works, but also gathers loved ones there to share, because there's nothing more important than being together. Maybe that idea is rooted in a memory: One day when she was 10 years old, her father came home with a bag of tilapia, a memorable meal for a family of scant resources, consisting of a day laborer, a coffee picker and four small children. "My father was a loving man, simple, humble. He never drank, never ran around with women.

# AT MAGDA'S HOUSE, EVERYONE IS SPECIAL

For him, life was us, his family." The tilapias were a great novelty, and they magically turned into an unforgettable story. Don Juan Rafael dug a hole in the yard, filled it with water and put the fish in it so that the kids could go "fishing." Magda doesn't like the smell of fish much, but tilapia is a freshwater fish and has a lighter flavor. And that tilapia from her childhood, the one she "caught" before eating it that day her father let them go fishing, is so symbolic that it occupies a giant place in her childhood memories. "One holds onto things, smells and colors that you don't forget," and the lunch that day is one of those treasures saved in her memory: rice, beans, parboiled bananas and fried tilapia. A feast in a house where chayote hash was more common, and where the special dinner on Sunday was a big pot of rice "with the smell of a can of tuna."

Magda plants *pejibaye* on the farm she inherited from her father, the man from whom she learned the importance of a relationship with the earth, a grumpy day laborer who was sometimes in a bad mood because he worried about supporting his family with a low-paying, exhausting job. She couldn't go to high school, and for years that was a big concern. It's hard to get ahead without studying. But she taught herself to make bread, and now she goes to open-air markets selling innovative products derived from *pejibaye*: eggnog, sweets, pastries and other baked goods...
Magda never stops innovating. "I'm going to retire the day the *pejibayes* stop bearing fruit." She has no interest in abandoning a business that brings her income and satisfaction. She tirelessly divides her days between growing and cooking. Looking at her, you really start to think that the *pejibayes* will probably stop bearing fruit before she decides to stop working.

In Magda's memory there's a summer day full of purple flowers under which, one day during Holy Week, after eating golden tilapias brought home so happily by her father, they lay in silence looking for a cool place to enjoy the afternoon. How to forget that content, unexpected moment, resting her head on her father's chest? It was hot, the sky was blue, the light filtered through the summer bunches of bougainvillea, and the breeze felt wonderful after a delicious lunch. There was no hurry. For a while there was no need to run off to attend to the endless chores of life in the country; for a while everything was great and there were no worries. That sums up the personality of Magda: in the ability to find enchantment in the simplest things, to find the greatest happiness in the smallest details. "It feels so nice to be here, there's nothing more beautiful than being with your family," were her thoughts that day, looking at the blue sky, building a memory that would be with her for the rest of her life.

**Written by: Adriana Sánchez**

**Magda del Carmen Araya Brenes**
Tucurrique
Born Feb. 20, 1963

Magda produces *pejibayes* (peach palm fruit) in a farm she inherited from her father at Las Vueltas de Tucurrique. She is the owner of the bakery Repostería Magdalena, she has participated in food fairs around the country since the 1990s, and she never misses the famous Pejibaye Fair of Tucurrique. She's a homebody — hard-working, simple and generous —, and she believes fervently that there's nothing more important than family. She runs an innovative business, preparing many dishes out of *pejibaye*, from eggnog to pastries, tamales, sweets and popsicles, as well as flours with which she bakes cakes and empanadas. All the recipes are her own, a product of her talent and creativity, and from the years of research she's put into preparing *pejibaye*.

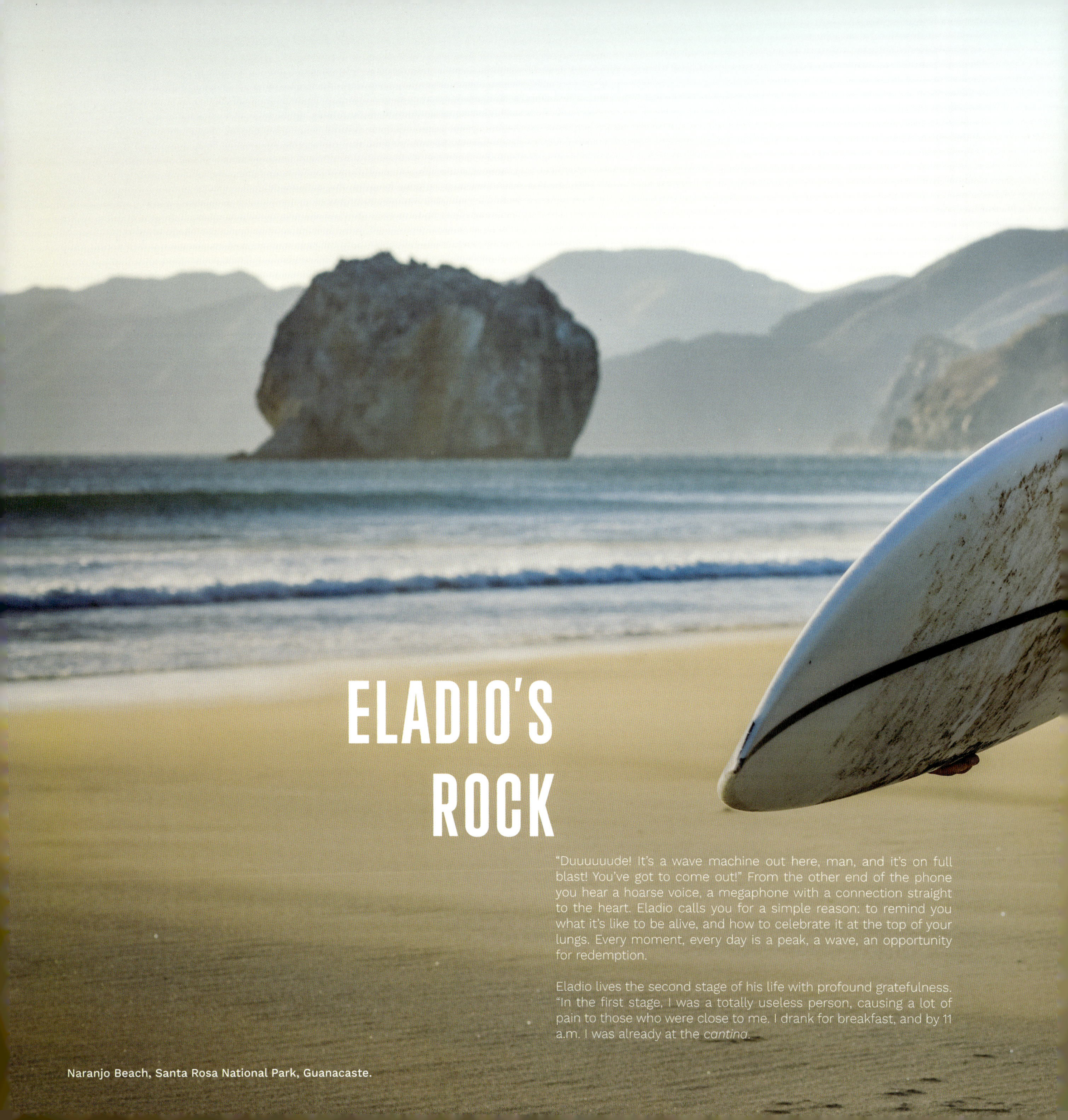

# ELADIO'S ROCK

"Duuuuuude! It's a wave machine out here, man, and it's on full blast! You've got to come out!" From the other end of the phone you hear a hoarse voice, a megaphone with a connection straight to the heart. Eladio calls you for a simple reason: to remind you what it's like to be alive, and how to celebrate it at the top of your lungs. Every moment, every day is a peak, a wave, an opportunity for redemption.

Eladio lives the second stage of his life with profound gratefulness. "In the first stage, I was a totally useless person, causing a lot of pain to those who were close to me. I drank for breakfast, and by 11 a.m. I was already at the *cantina*.

Naranjo Beach, Santa Rosa National Park, Guanacaste.

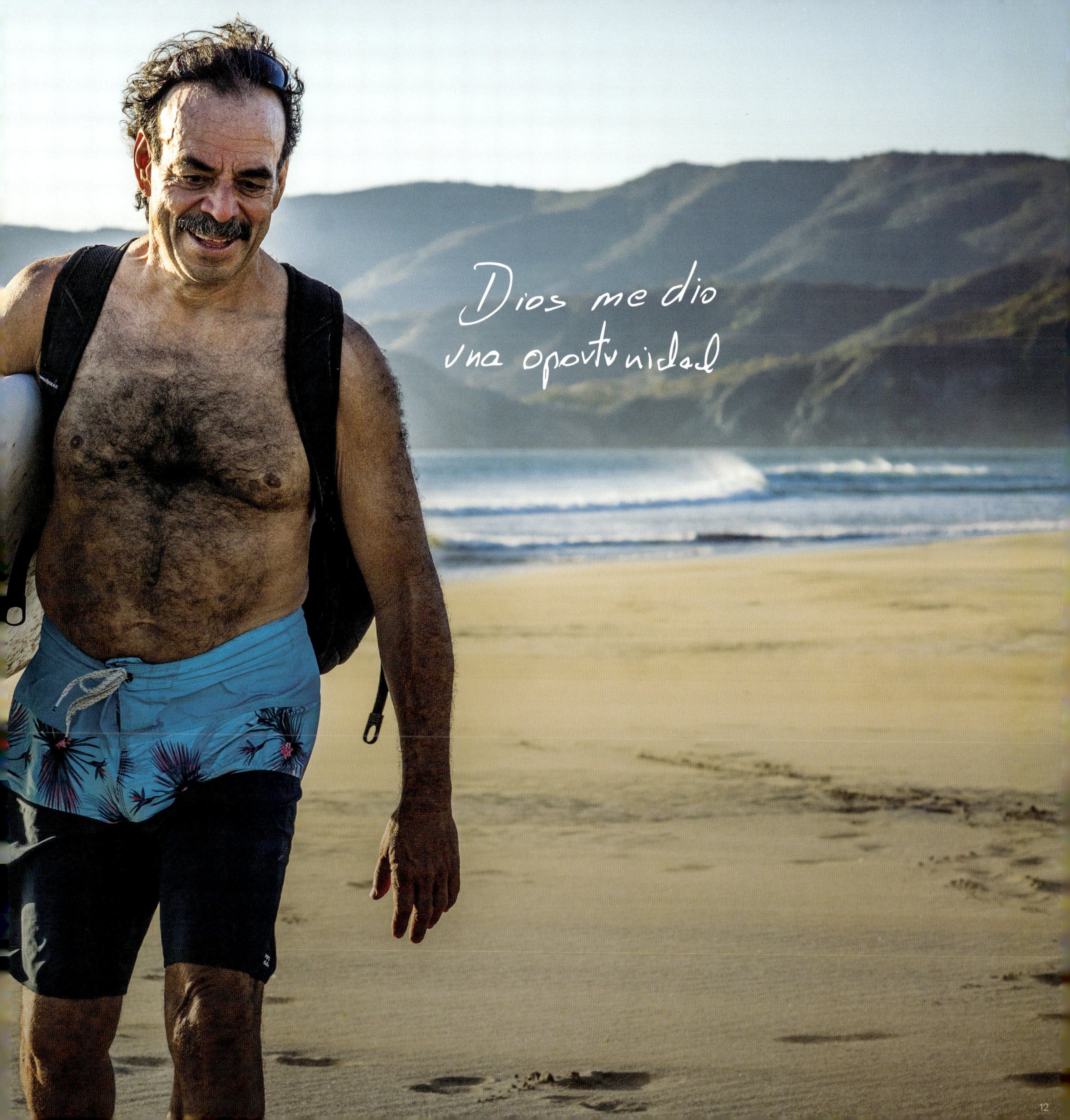
Dios me dio
una oportunidad

## IT WAS UNCERTAIN WHETHER HE WOULD BE ABLE TO WALK AGAIN

"My dad took care of me, and I drank in front of him. So stupid, right?" His hard-working father pushed on against all odds. For years, he ran a hardware store, where he gave his son some space. But Eladio, in a drunken moment, sold it — or practically gave it away. Eladio still recalls that memory with great pain.

"I had children with three women, and I didn't make any of them happy." With pain and genuine repentance, he talks about how he would have liked to be there for his kids, and to have been less violent with his girlfriends.

"God gave me an opportunity." Some 25 years ago at a festival in Liberia, he had a fight with his girlfriend, Vanessa. She wanted to stop partying and he wanted to keep drinking. He angrily forced her to get off his motorcycle. Five minutes later, he jumped a red light and a car ran over his leg. He had five operations, and it was uncertain whether he would be able to walk again or — even worse for him — to surf. Dr. Sperling Vetik not only saved his leg, but seeing his parents' pain, he offered not to charge for his rehabilitation if he would give up drugs and alcohol. Then and there, Eladio stopped drinking and doing drugs.

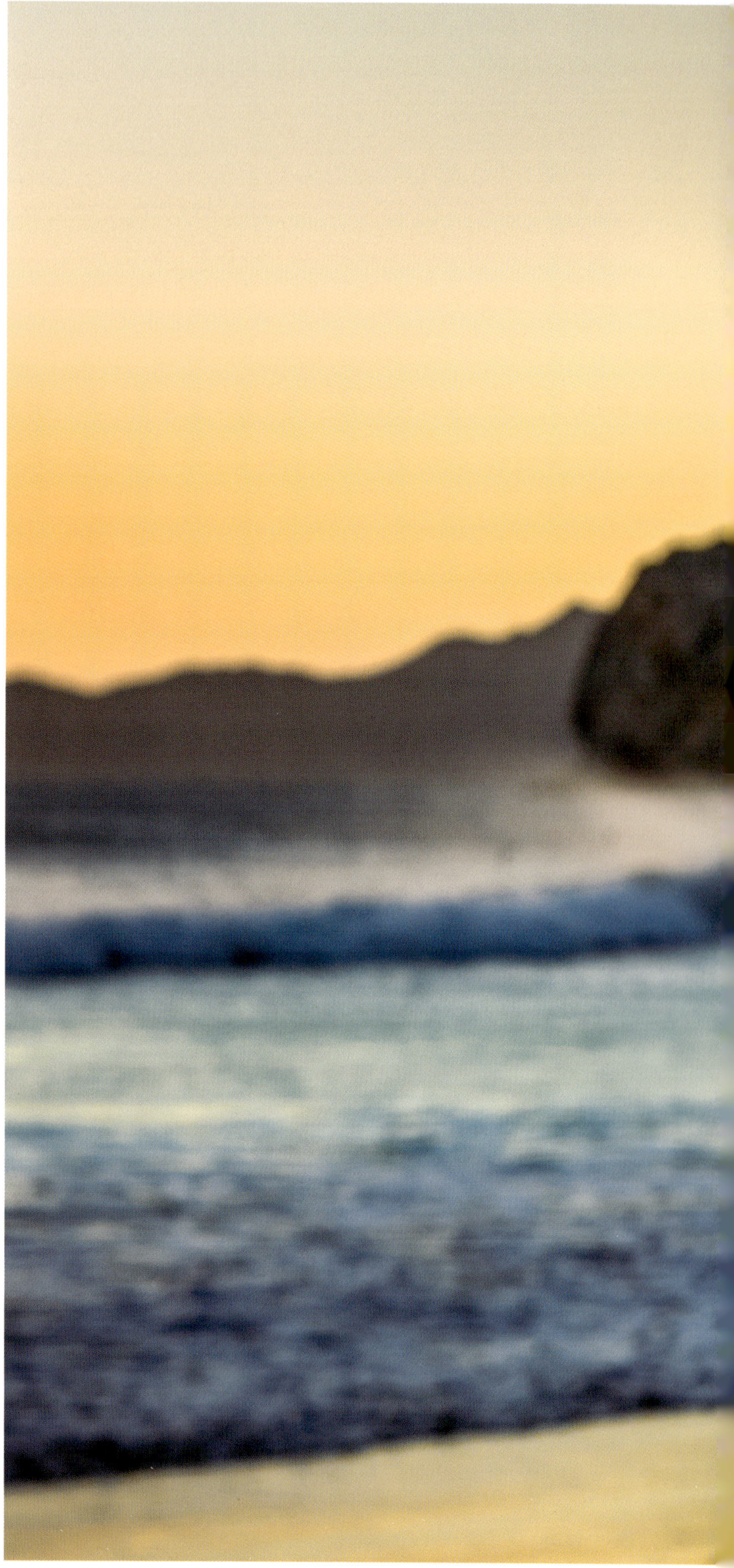

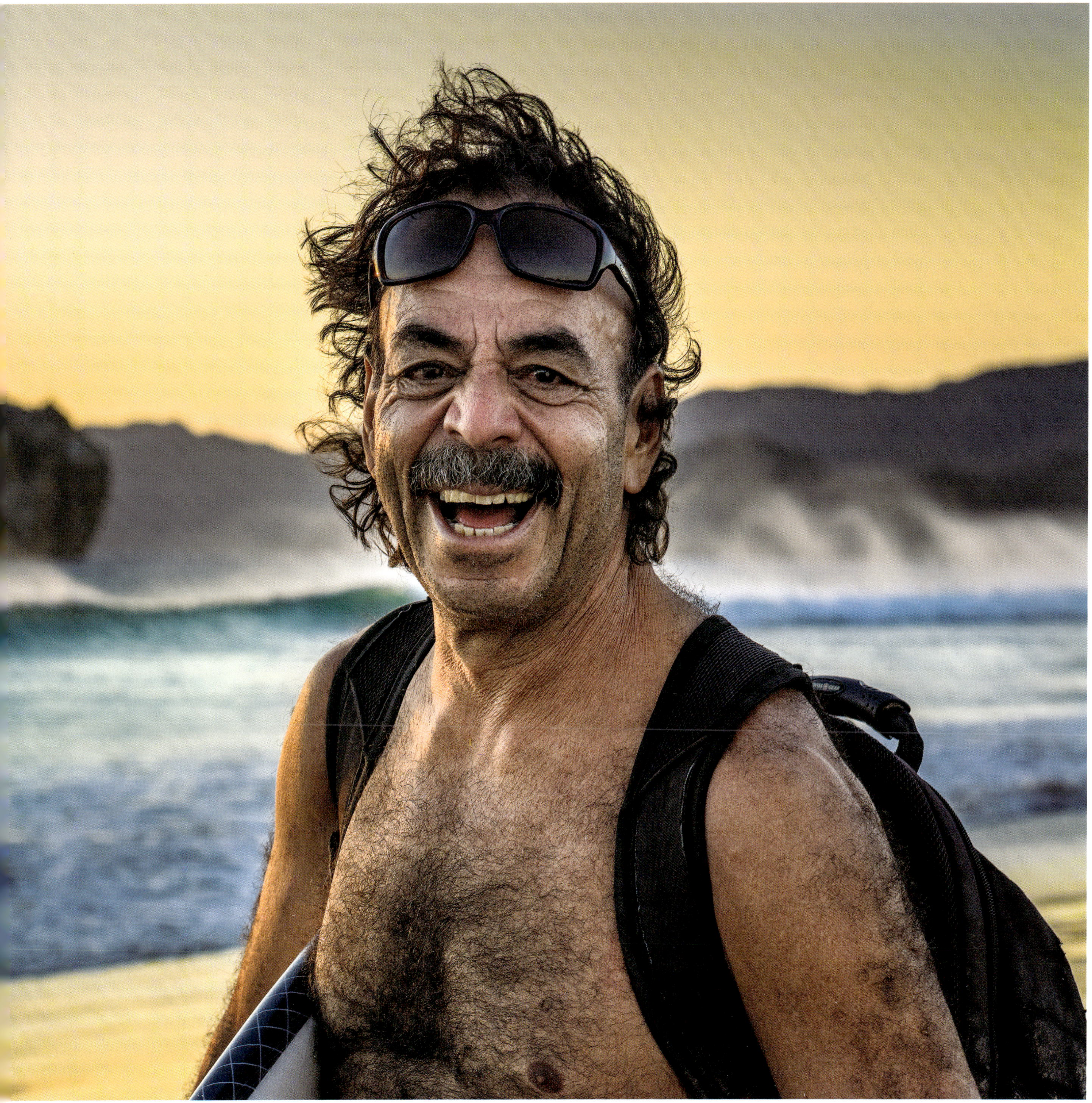

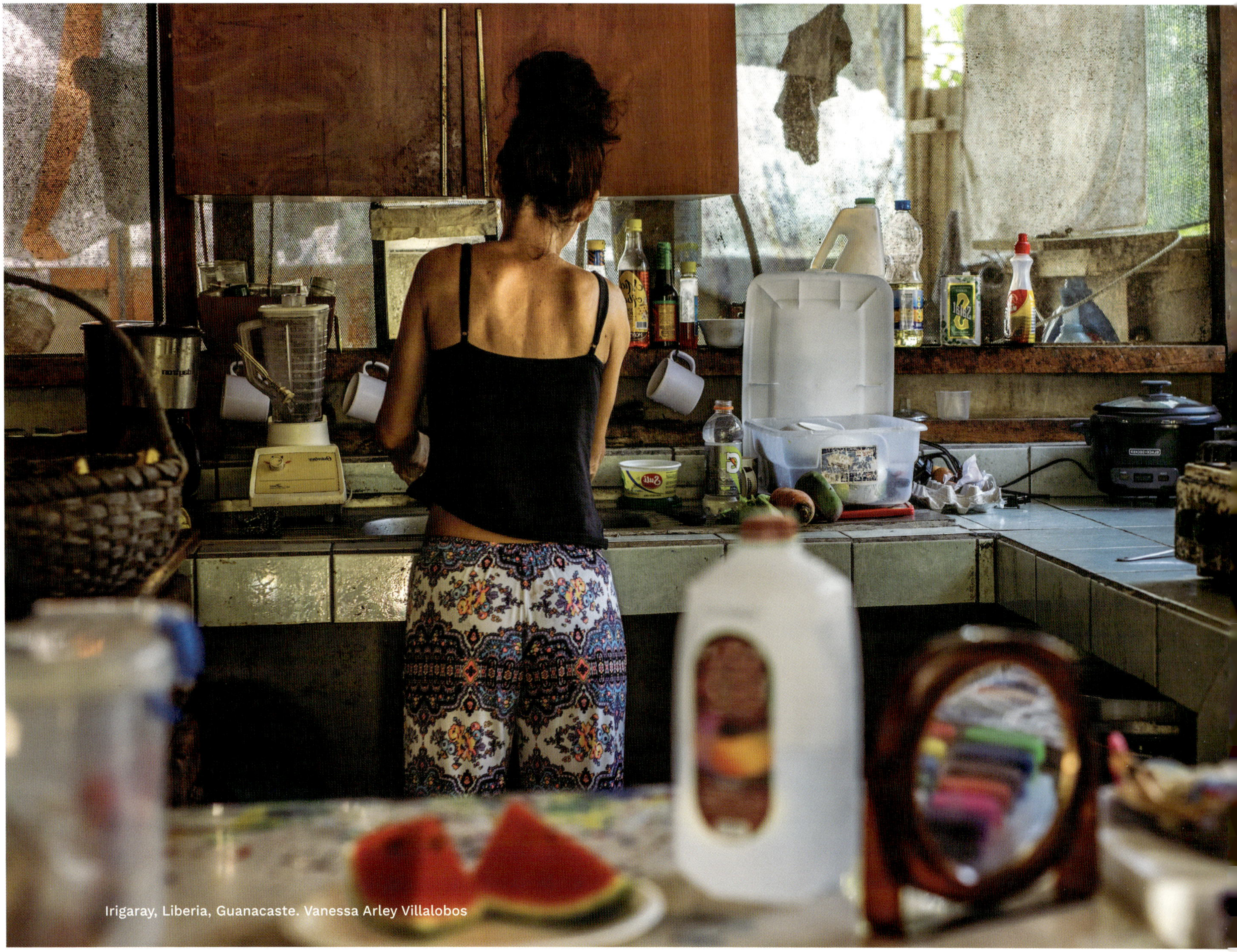

Irigaray, Liberia, Guanacaste. Vanessa Arley Villalobos

**Eladio Castro Mora**
Irigaray, Liberia
Born May 7, 1958

Eladio is an entrepreneur, tourism guide and owner of Eladio's Place, located outside Santa Rosa National Park. He's been linked to that place for so long that the locals recognize him as an icon. A nature lover and a passionate surfer, he's gotten ahead in life with great effort, guiding tourists to surf at Witch's Rock and to explore the beauty of the park. Language hasn't limited him much — when he started out working in tourism, he communicated with foreigners using "pure sign language," but now he holds his own in English. His outgoing and passionate personality is part of why clients like him. "Witch's Rock gives me life, makes me happy," he says. "Surfing is infinite, and I want to surf until the last day of my life."

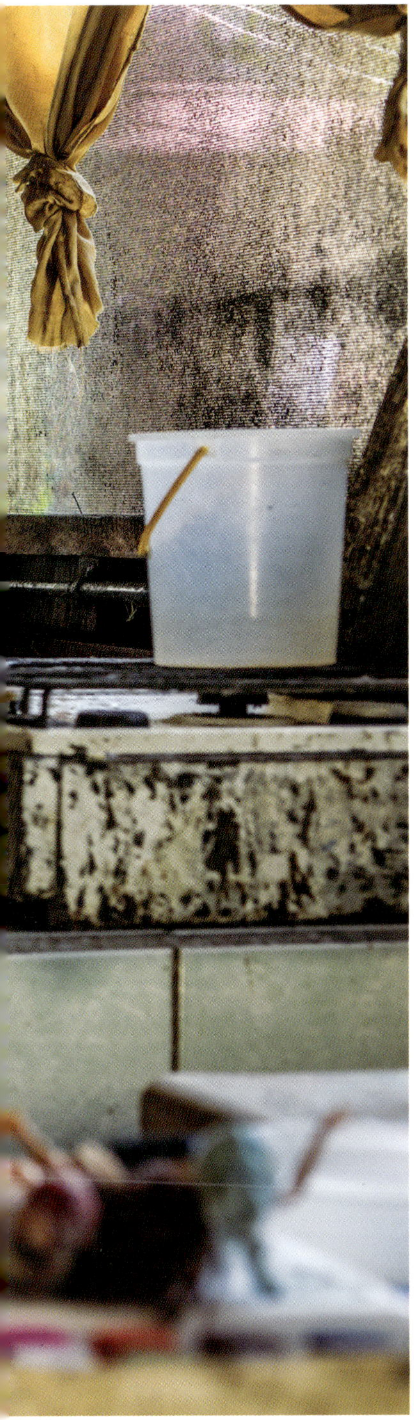

He escaped from the noisy city and went to live with Vanessa at Witch's Rock. They camped for three years below an enormous tamarind tree that's still there. Hugging the tree, he pleaded desperately, "God, if you exist, please help me!!" Little by little, he developed a different relationship with his demons, he hiked the trails of the dry tropical forest, and he slept under the starriest sky he had ever seen in his life. But more than anything, with all his soul he paddled a wave that traveled thousands of miles to crash furiously on that Costa Rican beach, letting himself be swept along with his last breath until the final crash — that's what cured him.

Today Eladio has been clean for 25 years, and he's a tourism entrepreneur. Part guide, part biology instructor, he inspires everyone with his contagious passion. "This place gives me clarity to confront the problems in my life... It's a health clinic. I've hosted groups from Google who came to stay 10 days and left this place transformed."

**Written by: Giancarlo Pucci Golcher**

Vanessa continues to be his partner in adventure, and the mother of his youngest children. Gabrielito, 7, and Ana Lucía, 9, have a father who is present, loving, and very, very hard-working. "I'm so happy I learned to be a dad! It's a blessing, dude." For many years, Eladio was profoundly hurt by something that someone told him during his drunken years in his native Plaza Víquez. "Eladio, you're just a *pachucazo*" — referring to his crude style of speaking, but also suggesting he was just a rude, boorish street person.

Recently a professor from the University of Georgia who stayed at Eladio's Place with his students told him that the reason he came back year after year was actually his style of being and speaking, the way he used words, his street English, his contagious authenticity, and his ability to make people happy. That was his redemption. "Time heals all."

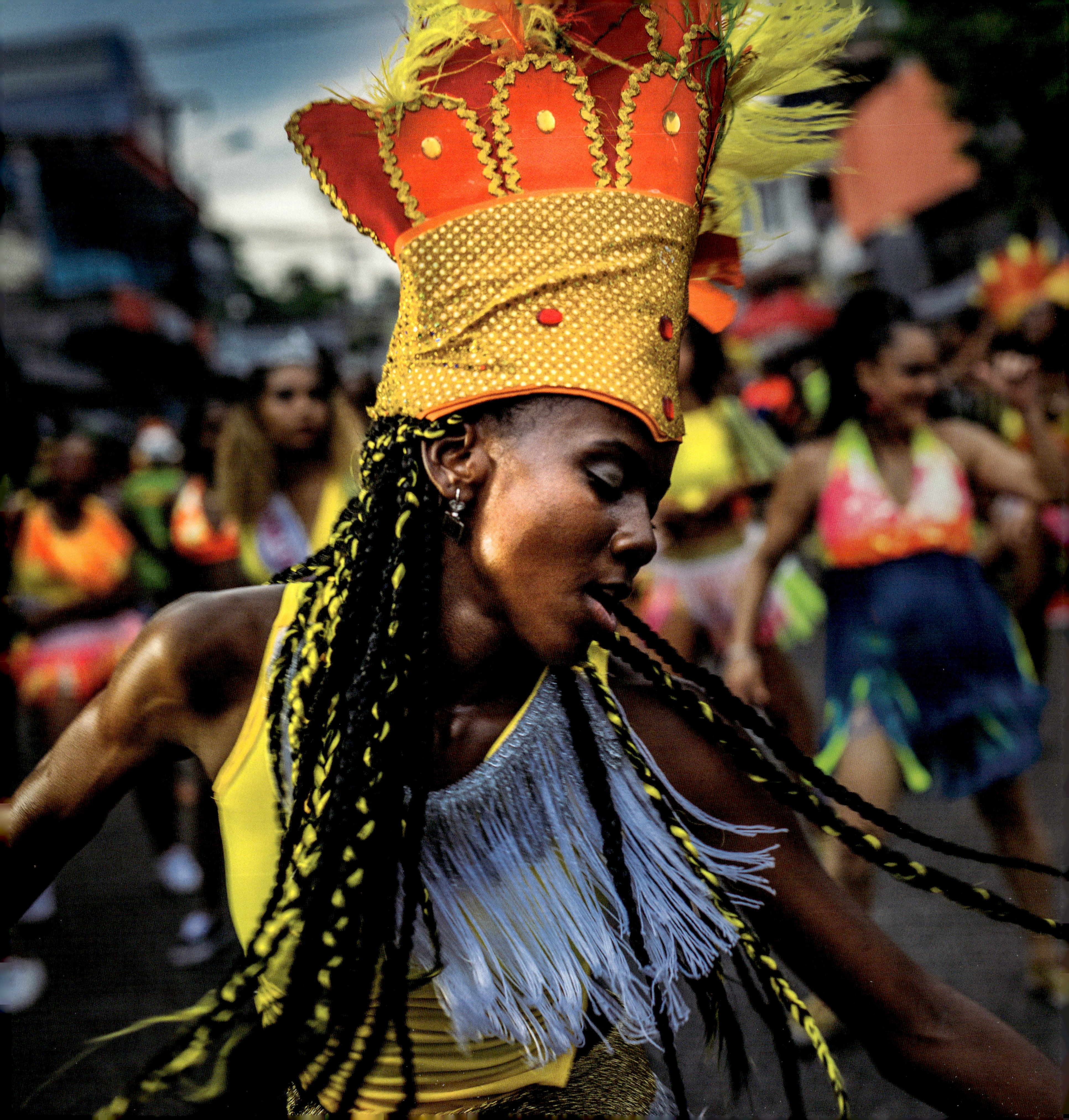

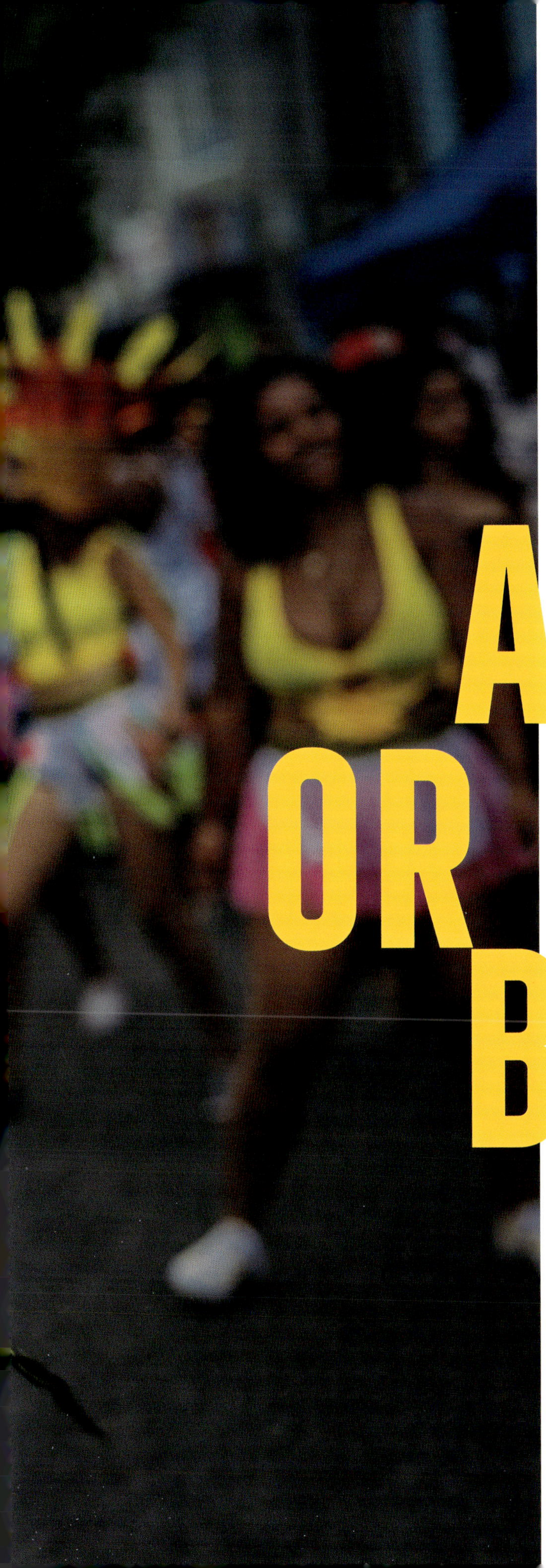

# A positive OR B negative?

Angeline runs along the inside track. They reach the final stretch and she's almost certain to win second place. Running in front of her is the woman who always beats her, and she knows that in this straightaway her rival will probably stretch out the distance by even more. But this time she notices that the leader isn't getting away from her, and she thinks, "Today is the day." She closes with all her strength, and after years of running an unwinnable race, she wins!

With a side glance, she looks at the spectators to confirm what she already knows: Neither her father nor her mother came to watch her run.

Her friend from the track team congratulates her enthusiastically: "Angeline! You won!" She replies, "I won, my twin, I won!" She calls her friend her "twin" because when they comb their hair the same way, straight and loose, they look almost identical.

"We get along really well," says Angeline. "She's younger than me and she runs hurdles."

It's easy to understand what this victory means to Angeline when she talks about how as a child she felt intimidated, like an ugly duckling — introverted, quiet, always looking down. She finds it easy to recall painful stories, like when she was invited to be in a dance troupe and the leader sent her to the end of the line, but not before making fun of her in front of everyone else.

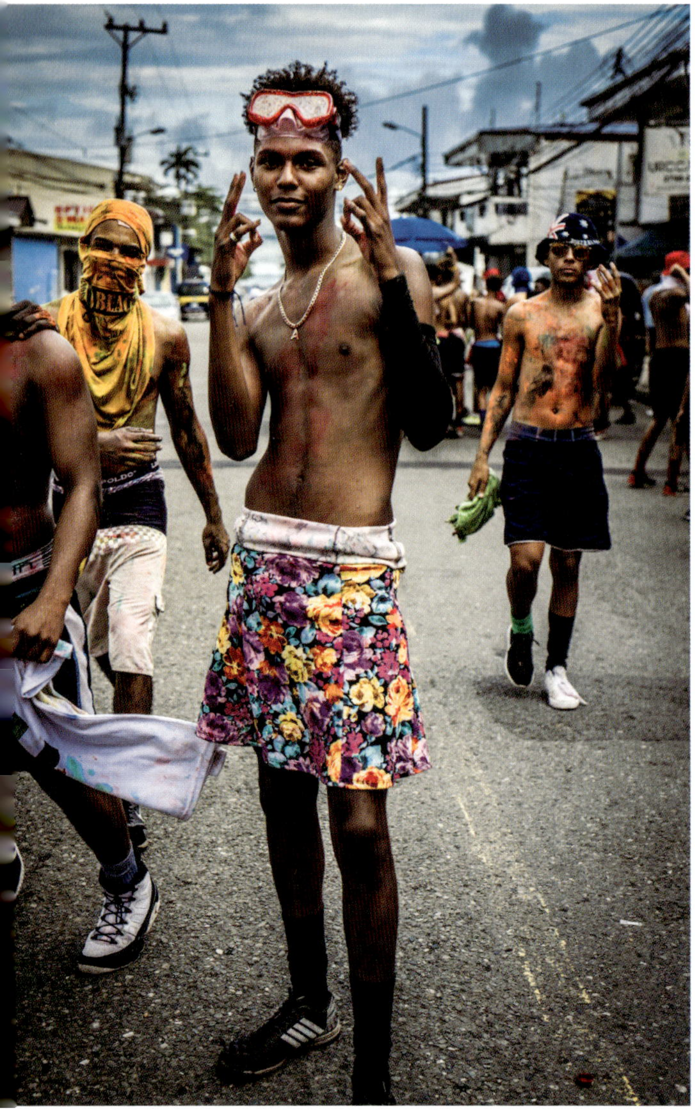

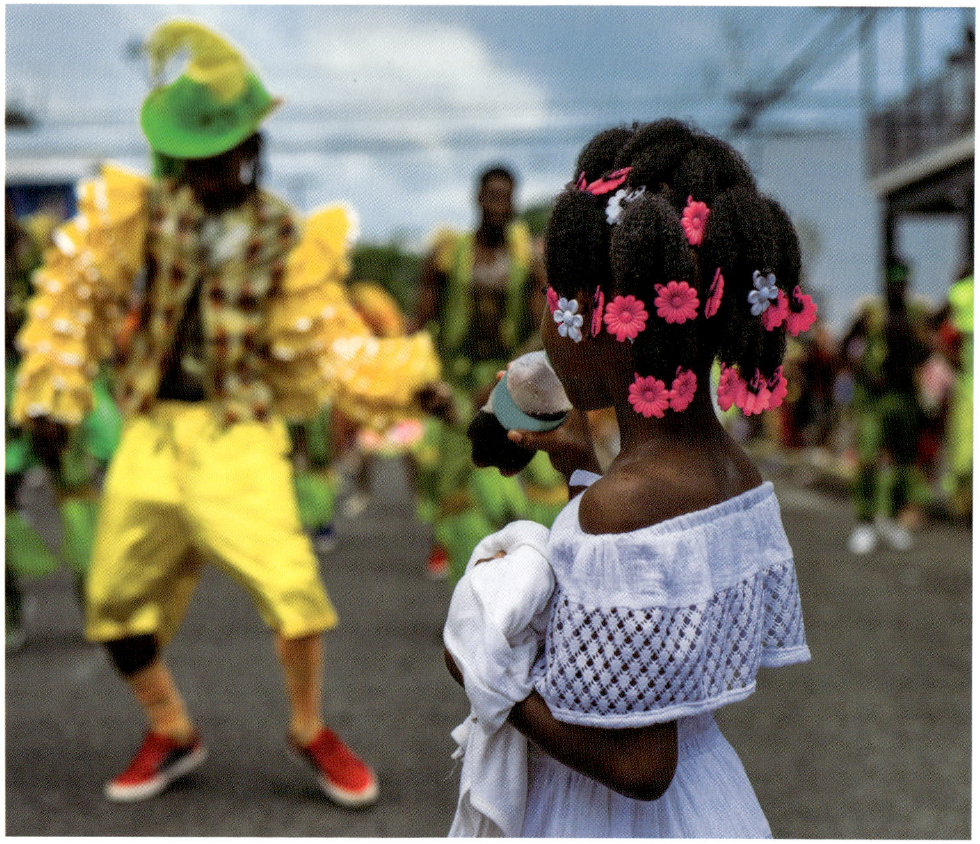

## IF IT WEREN'T FOR HIM, I DON'T KNOW IF I'D BE STUDYING

When she was about to turn 18, her father asked her to do a DNA test. She asked, "How could my father be asking for this?" Her mother answered, "Your father doesn't love you, obviously: You're going to a public school and all your siblings are in private schools."

In school she didn't want to play, dance or do anything else. During recess she talked to her teacher about biology. "We sat down and talked during the entire recess," she said. "If it weren't for him, I don't know if I'd be studying. He admired me because he said that despite everything that was happening to me, I wasn't getting into drugs, I wasn't dead, and I wasn't pregnant."

One day after biology class, she came straight from school to ask her father what blood type he had. At first, there was total silence. Her father was a nurse, so he definitely knew what she was talking about. After a long pause, he said his blood type was A. "That's impossible,"

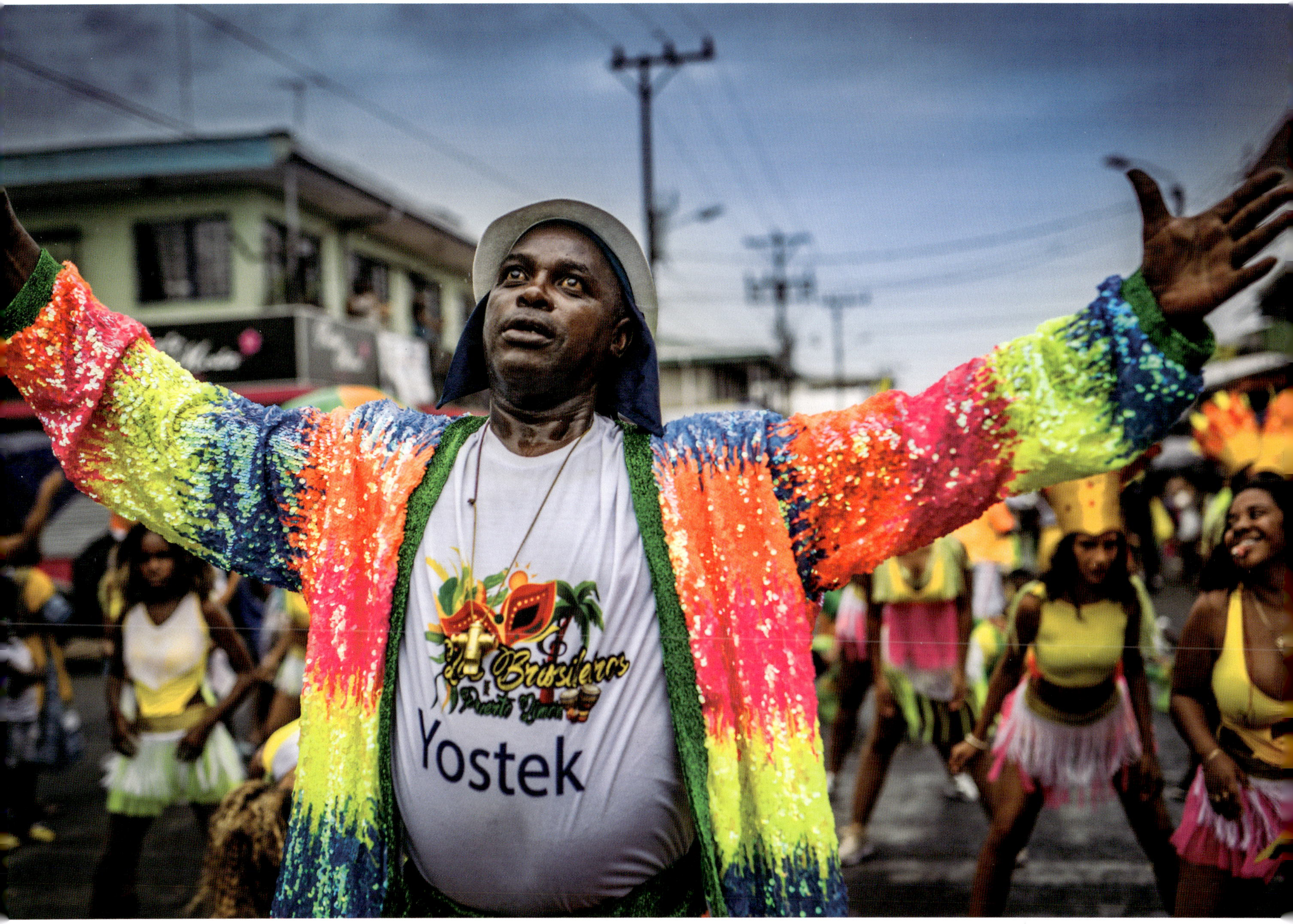


Carnival 2019, Limón. Los Brasileiros comparsa.

## WHEN SHE DANCES, SHE GOES INTO A TRANCE...

Angeline said. "My mother is type O, my father is type A, so how can I be type B?"

Angeline left her house for six months.

"I started asking my mom's friends — I couldn't stand this intrigue. One day I ran into her first boyfriend, and I was talking to him and he confessed to me that she called him when I left the house, to tell him I had left. And I'm thinking, why is she calling him if he's not my father? So we started talking, and I started to connect the dots."

In those six months, Angeline started dancing.

"I want to know! Even though I think I already know," she says. "They won't tell me the truth like I want to hear it. I asked a laboratory how much a DNA test costs, but it's really expensive, like 500 dollars."

One day after a rehearsal, she saw a post from her athlete friend, the one she called her "twin," who looked so much like her, posing in a photo next to her mom's first boyfriend. "I didn't know that man was her father," she says.

Angeline greatly enjoys dancing with her troupe, now first in line, during the five hours of the Carnaval festival in Limón. When she dances, she goes into a trance, the world stops, and she forgets everything. She is liberated and passionate, and she gives her all to every movement.

**Written by: Sergio Pucci Golcher**

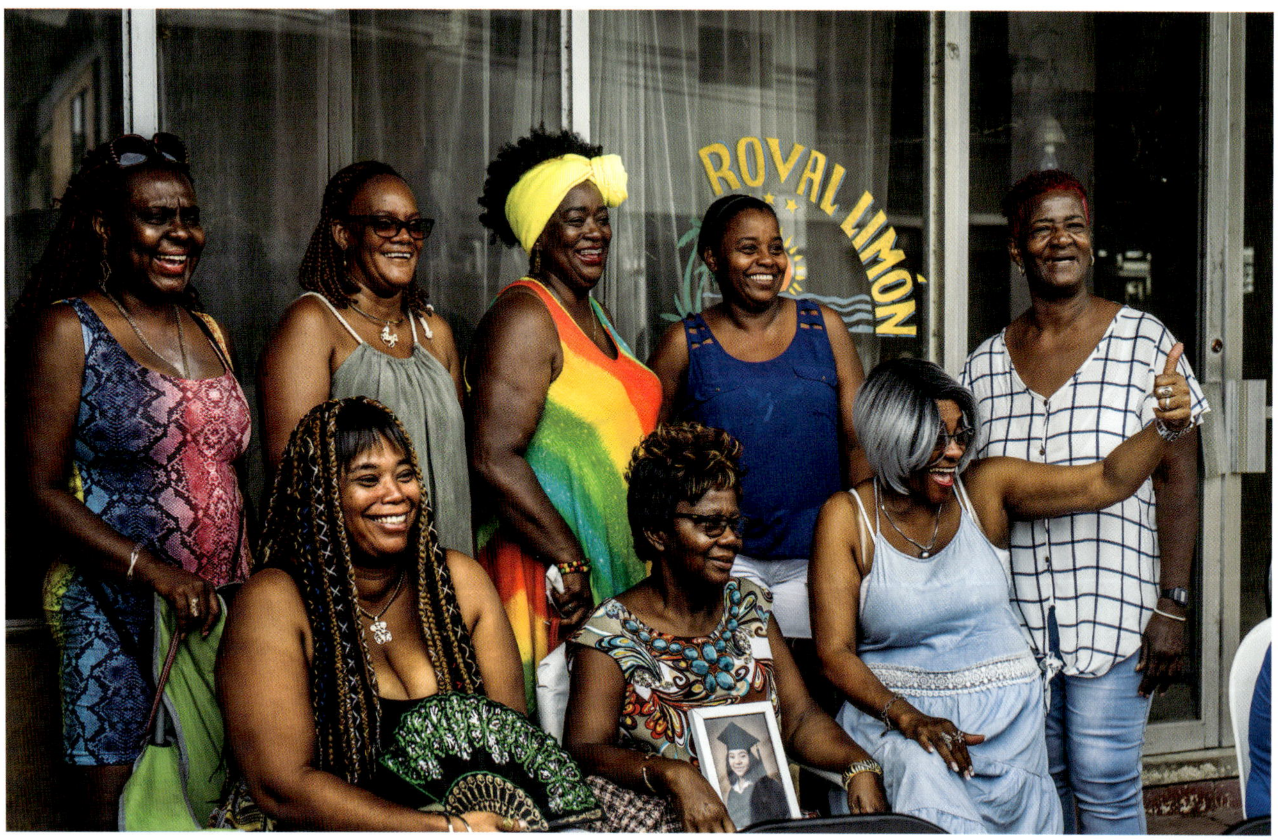

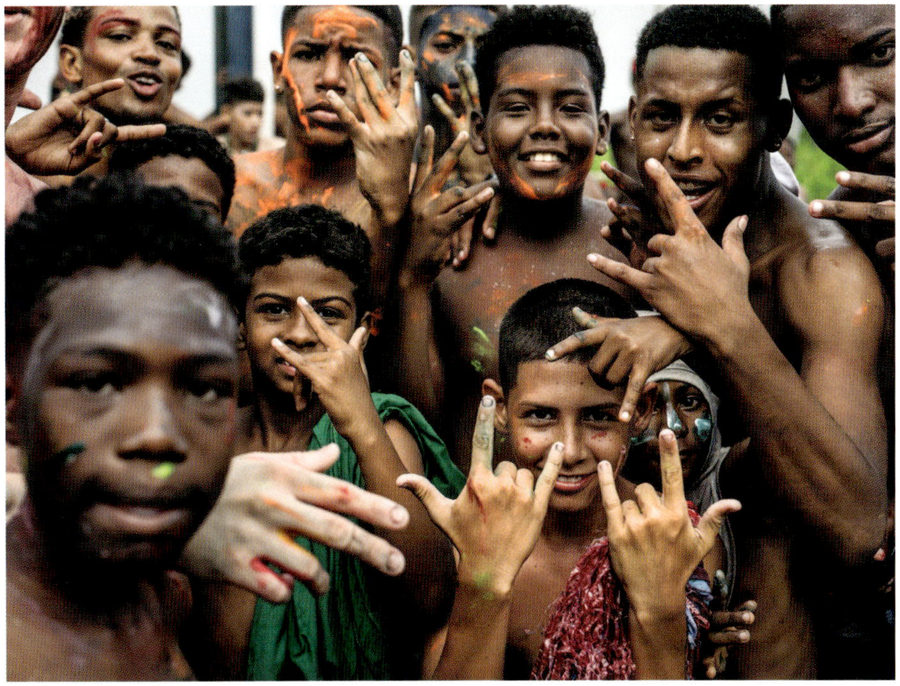

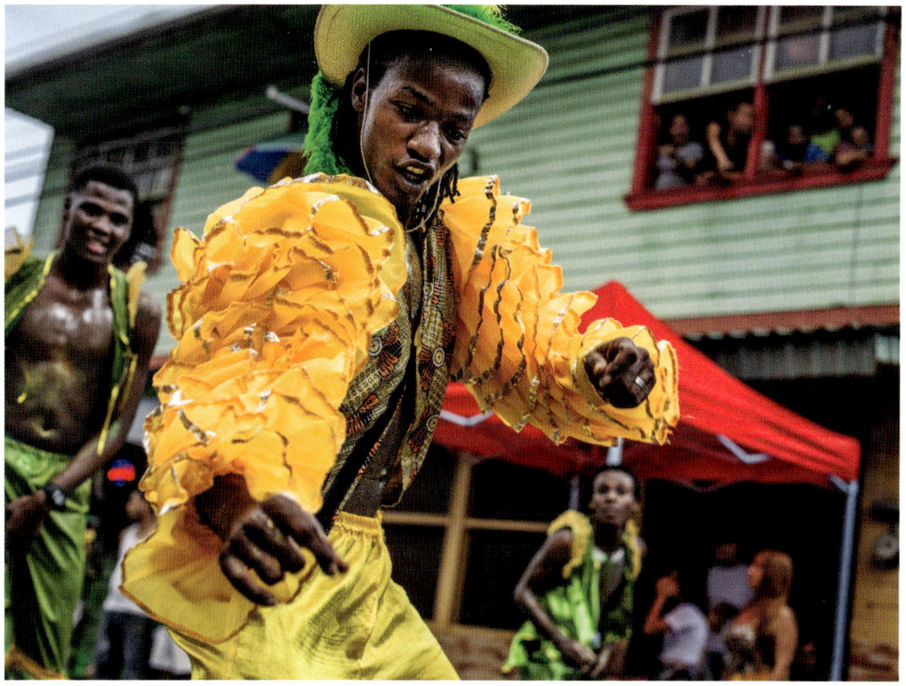

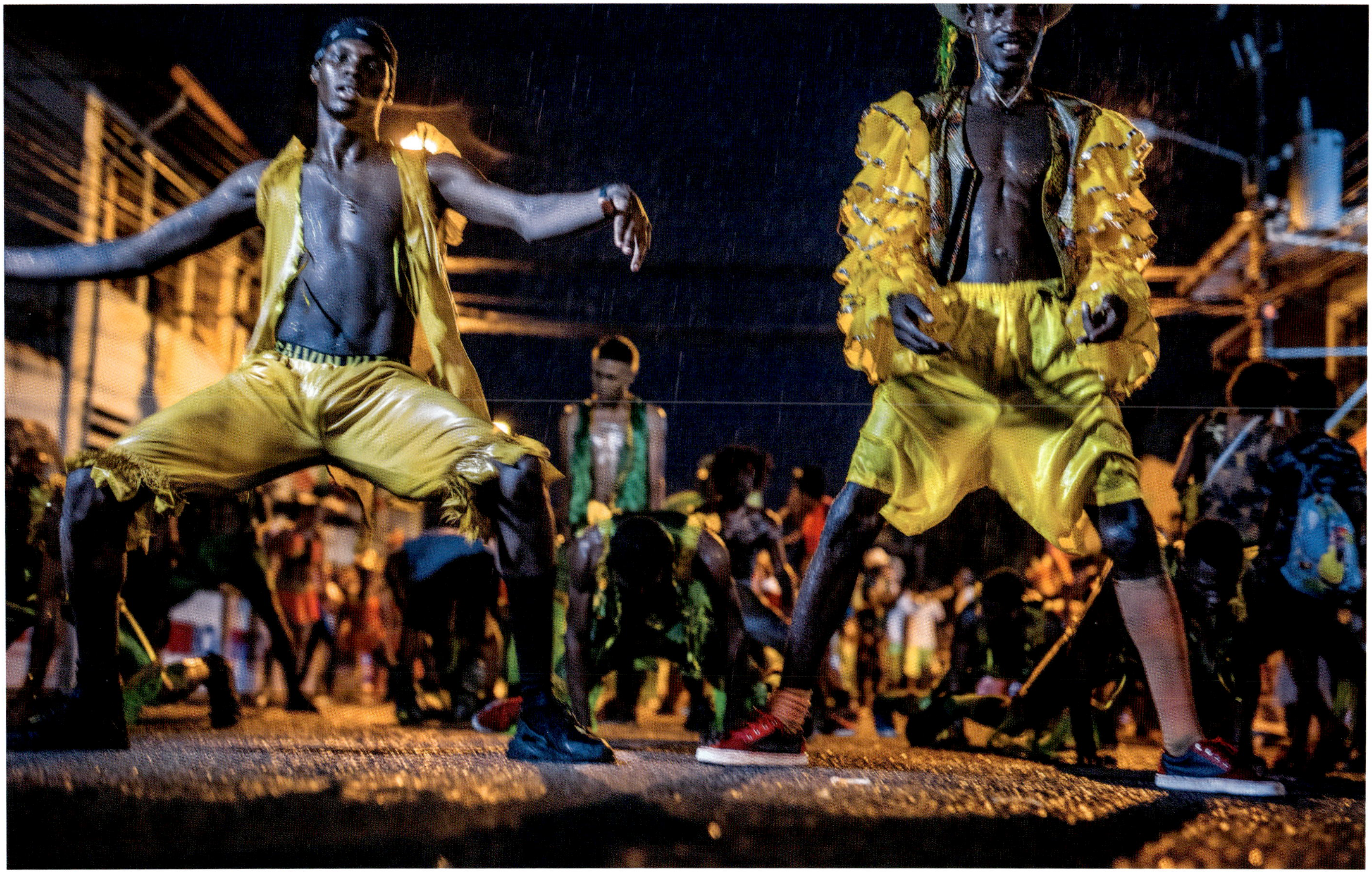

**Angeline Pondler Estrada**
Limón
Born April 6, 1999

Angeline is an athlete, dedicating most of her effort, concentration, and discipline to sports. That's where she's pinned her hopes for personal growth and professional success. Even though she can't count on her parents' support, thanks to her athletic skills she has an opportunity to study English and improve her communication abilities. At the same time, English is a language that can help her fulfill her dream of living and training in another country and improving as an athlete. Angeline is also a member of a dance troupe. She shares this passion with her mother and her siblings. Dancing runs in her blood — it's effortless, fun, enjoyable, and relaxing. Thanks to dancing, Angeline was able to heal her self-esteem. Before she arrived at this consciousness and this connection to music, she felt ashamed to be seen, feeling "too skinny to be a woman from Limón," along with other beliefs that kept her from shining. The process of self-discovery that she has found through dance has liberated her from a lot of judgment, and now she enjoys herself freely, leading a female dance crew at the Carnaval festival.

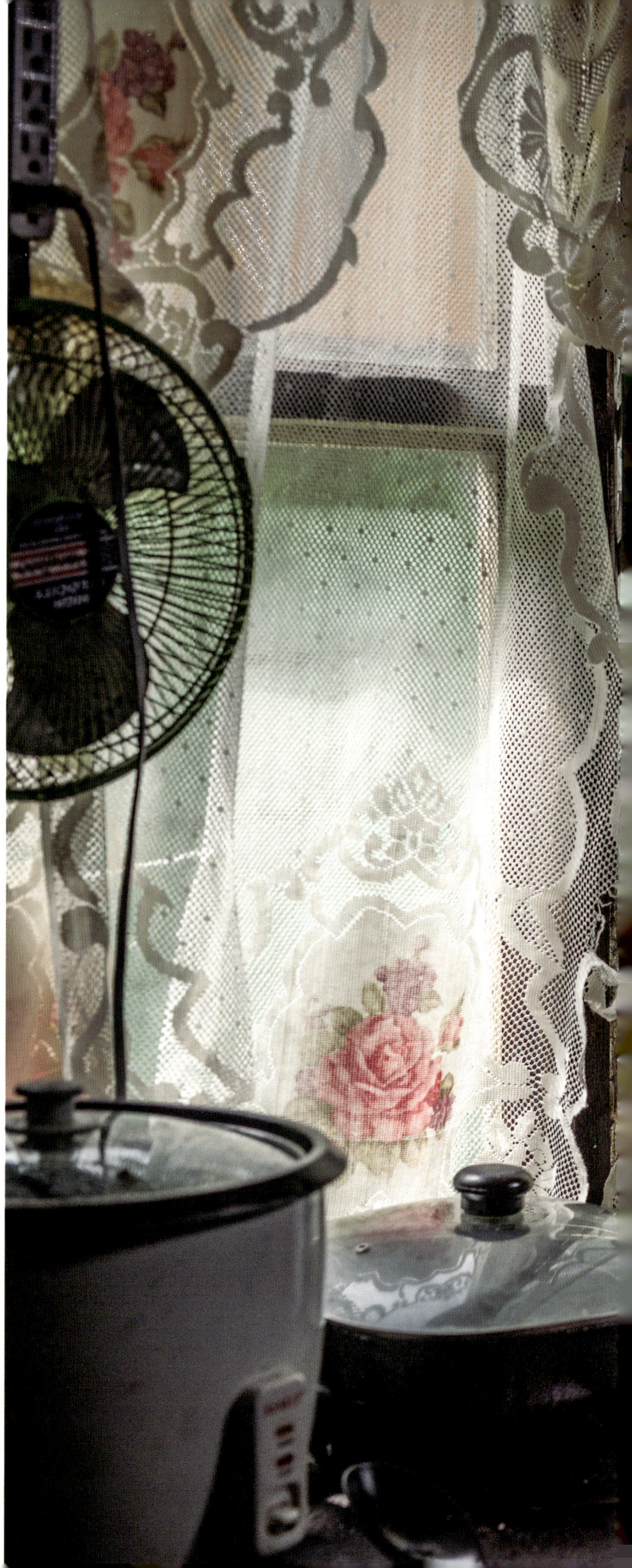

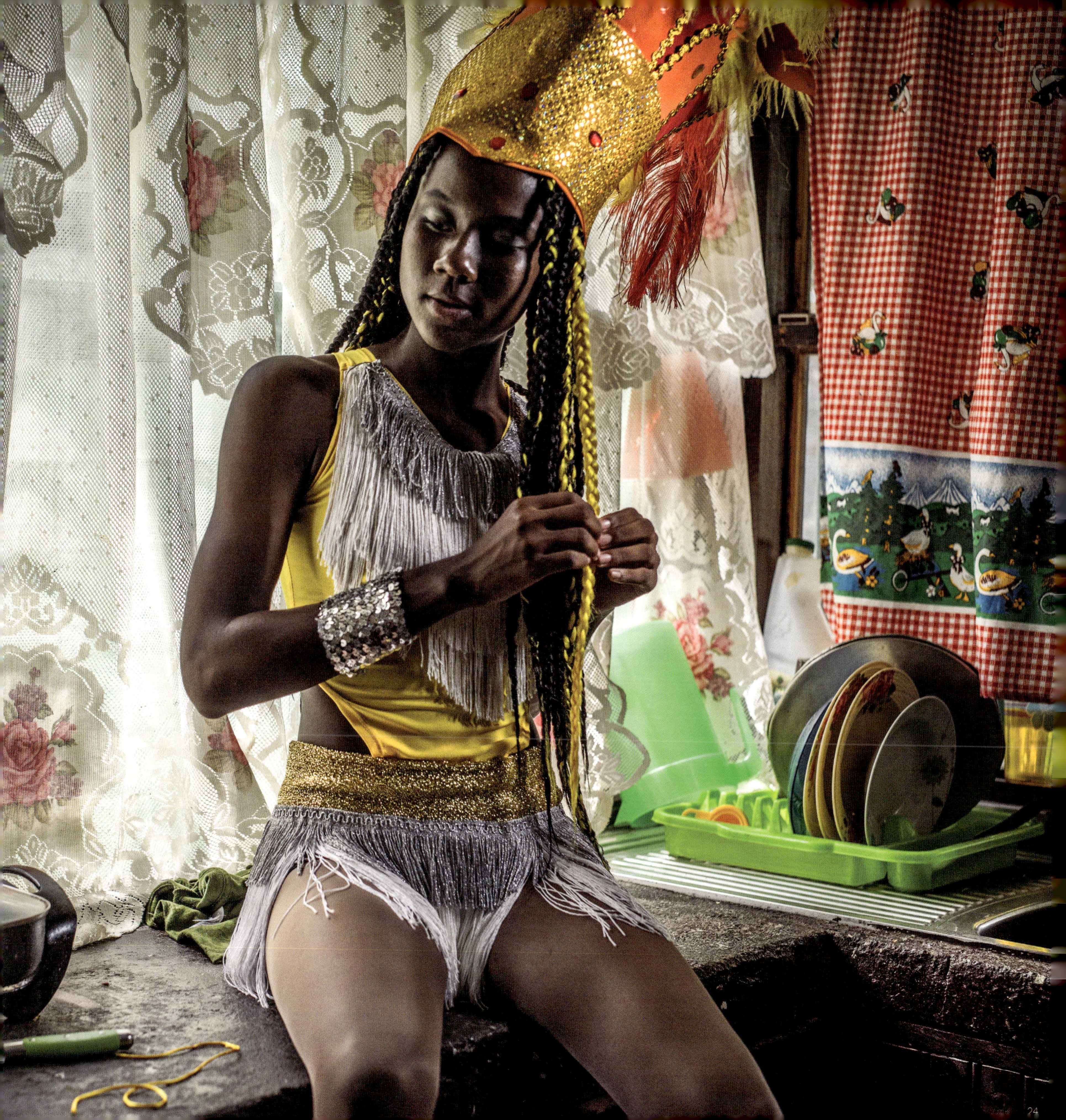

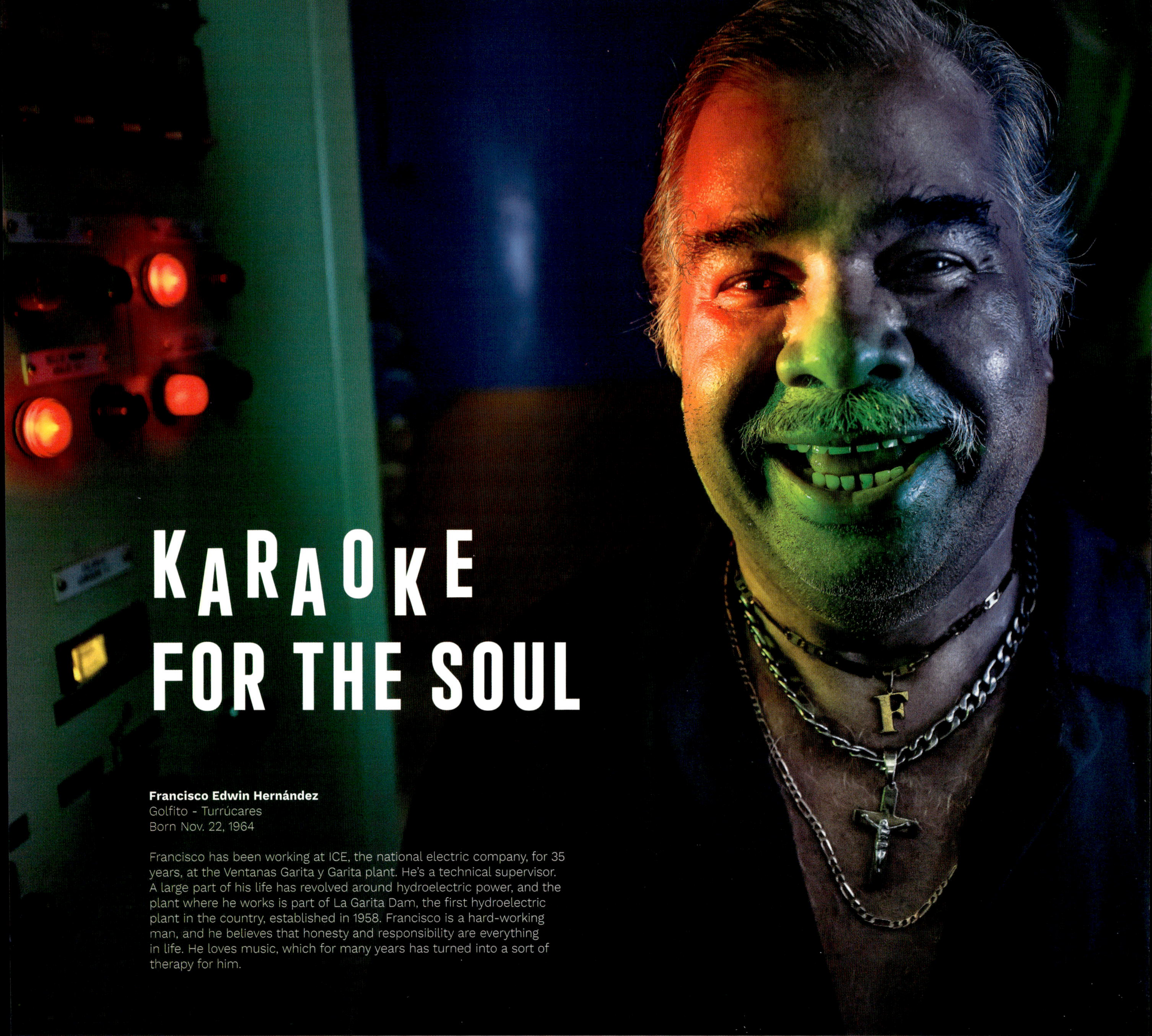

# KARAOKE FOR THE SOUL

**Francisco Edwin Hernández**
Golfito - Turrúcares
Born Nov. 22, 1964

Francisco has been working at ICE, the national electric company, for 35 years, at the Ventanas Garita y Garita plant. He's a technical supervisor. A large part of his life has revolved around hydroelectric power, and the plant where he works is part of La Garita Dam, the first hydroelectric plant in the country, established in 1958. Francisco is a hard-working man, and he believes that honesty and responsibility are everything in life. He loves music, which for many years has turned into a sort of therapy for him.

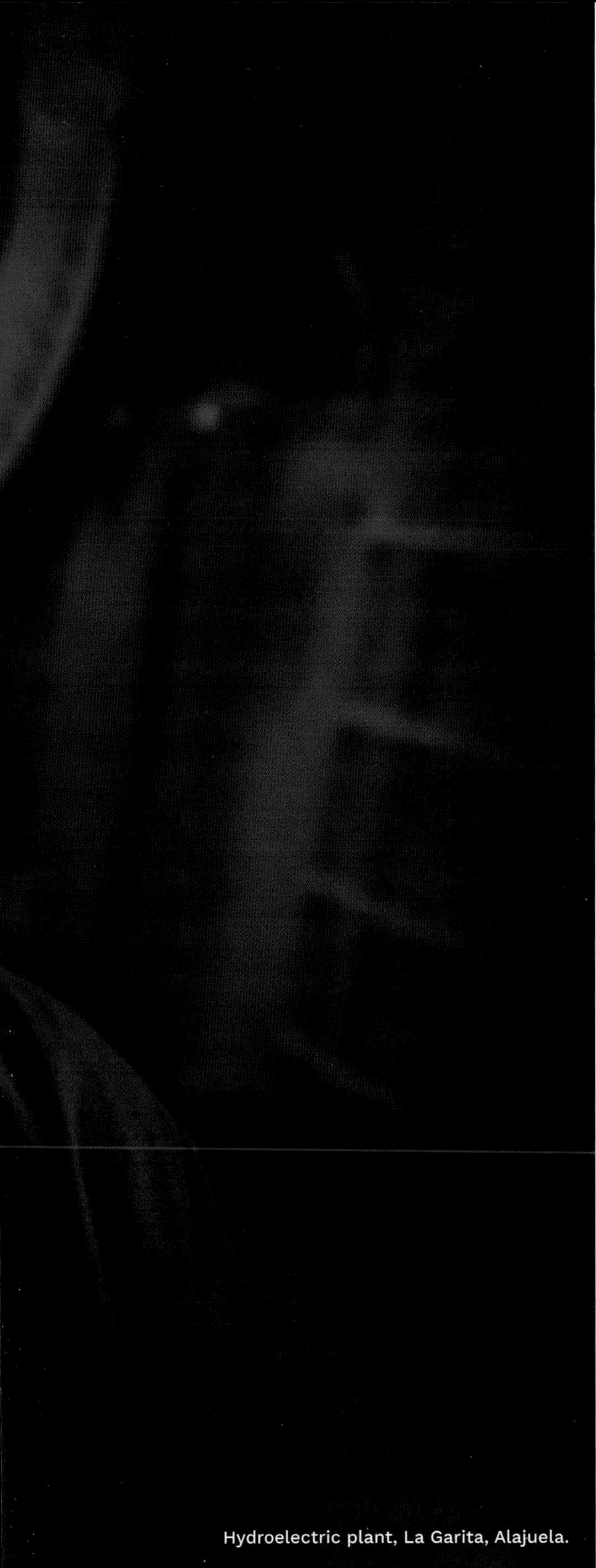

Hydroelectric plant, La Garita, Alajuela.

Francisco Edwin Hernández graduated in 1984 from the vocational school in Alajuela, and by January he was already working at the ICE plant at Ventanas de la Garita. He lives 500 meters away, and every day he goes from the plant to his house and from his house to the plant. "My family is my life, my work is my life and that's my circuit, a very small one, but it makes me happy."

For 35 years he's been locked into this routine. "When there's an earthquake, I think about my family, but I can't leave the plant, it's a very big responsibility." When the Cinchona earthquake struck, they evacuated everyone, but he stayed behind. Edwin's job is not for the claustrophobic. "I'm an ICE man. At least 80 coworkers and I have been working here for over 20 years, including three brothers.... The death of my sister-in-law's husband, a coworker, is one of those little things that mark you.... When something at the plant goes bad, we all go bad."

For over three decades, Edwin has been incapacitated only three times, but about 10 years ago he started to get depressed. One day he felt his temperature rise, he got dizzy, and that kept happening: His face got hot and he felt like he was suffocating, so he started to worry. In the mornings he isolated himself so that his co-workers wouldn't notice — he went to the sink and threw water on his face because he felt like he was drowning. He went to his main doctor and started spending his money on tests. He started to get tense and anxious. They couldn't find a problem anywhere. The cardiologist had to throw him out of his office one day: "I did all the tests and you're fine, give thanks to God and get out of here."

One day, to distract himself, he went with a colleague to Karaoke La Laguna, very close to his house. Edwin was really interested in this activity. He had always liked live music, and besides he liked the way people applauded even for someone who sang terribly. Even though he didn't dare to sing, he forgot about his troubles for a while. Maybe his doctor was right, he thought, when he said that his problem was that he spent his life competing with himself.

Today Edwin is well-known at three karaoke bars — they greet him by name, from the doorman to the DJ, at La Laguna, Bar Nachos in Los Ángeles de Atenas, and Los Almendros in Cebadilla.

"Now I'm brave enough to try to sing, and they applaud me. I've been sort of rehearsing the song." He goes alone, he doesn't drink, and he eats dinner before he goes out, because the white rice Gabriela makes is second to none. He has his phone in his hand, and he always tells his wife the same thing: If you need me, call me. When the big dance starts up at the bar, he goes home.

He's decided to dedicate more time to his son (Edwin Francisco, instead of Francisco Edwin, like him). "The boy is quiet but really dependent on me. Sometimes when I went to work in the early morning he would call at 11 and ask me, 'What time do you get off, Dad?' I wouldn't even tell him.... He was quiet a few seconds and then he would say, 'Ah ... well, take care of yourself.'"

Today, he's still a man committed to his job, only he's a bit wiser about finding a balance.

*"I gave her my soul, and I didn't bet that one day she would leave, without one regret,"* says one of his favorites, "Beautiful Lies" by Diego Verdaguer. At home, he turns on the microphone he bought and refines his technique. He analyzes concerts by Marco Antonio Solís, and as soon as he leaves for work, he turns up the volume.

Edwin's gaze demonstrates the beauty of simplicity. He's understood something important — it's the simple moments that mark the rhythm of the song.

**Written by: Sergio Pucci Golcher**

# FROM MASS TO CHOCOLITO

"Go get ready, we have to go to Mass!" shouts my grandmother from the kitchen. Elizabeth doesn't want to stop drawing but she has no choice: Every Saturday the family attends the 4 o'clock Mass religiously at the church in San Juan de Naranjo.

"Go now!"

She obeys. Not with the kind of enthusiasm that would make her rise to her feet to applaud. When she remembers that today she has to serve as an altar girl, she hurries up. Entering the sacristy and touching the sacred objects is a privilege granted to few children.

Once at church, she doesn't pay much attention to the liturgy. She can't stop thinking that every Saturday when Mass is over, they would give her money to buy a Chocolito candy. And if there aren't any strawberry Chocolitos this week, she'll choose a Tutto. Because there isn't enough money for a Choys.

When Mass is over, she takes off running. The little store is near the church. A few blocks away. You have to cross the main highway, the one that goes to Zarcero and ends up in San Carlos.

"Cross carefully! Look both ways!"

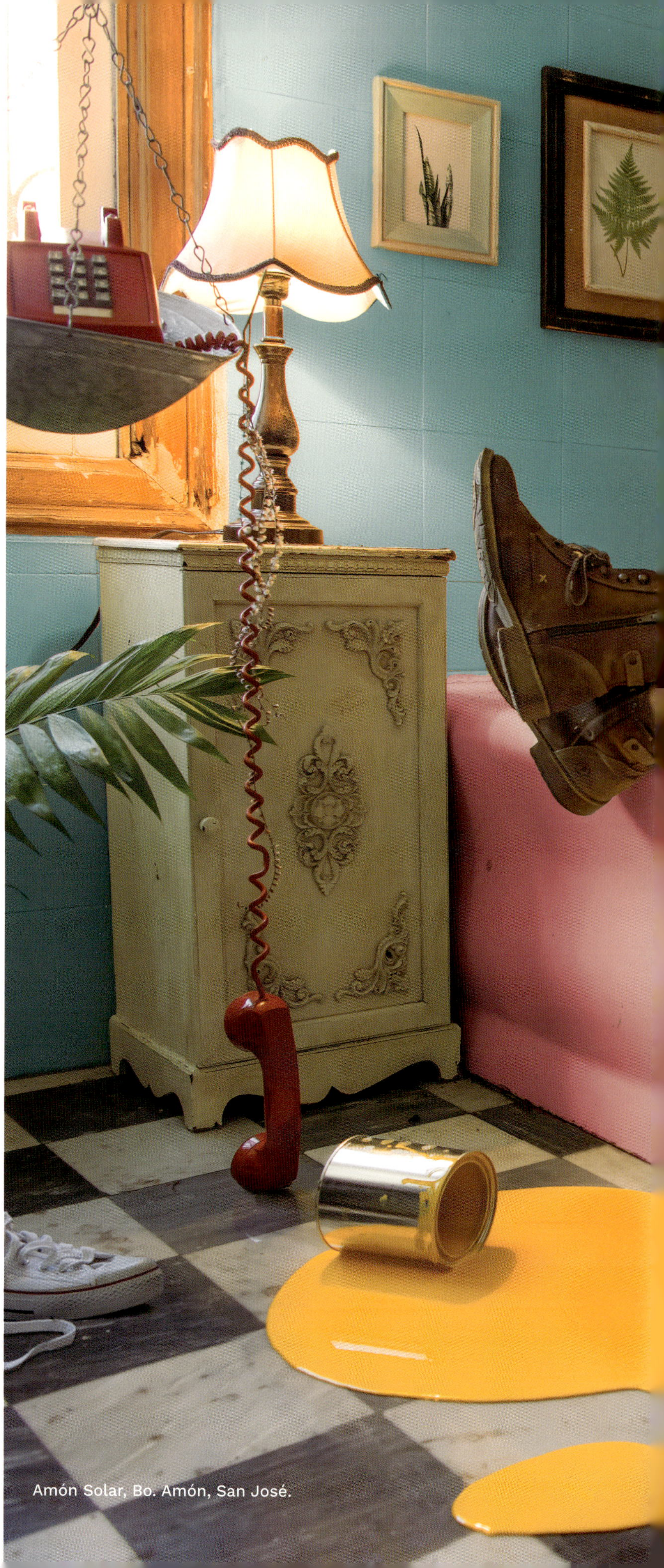

Amón Solar, Bo. Amón, San José.

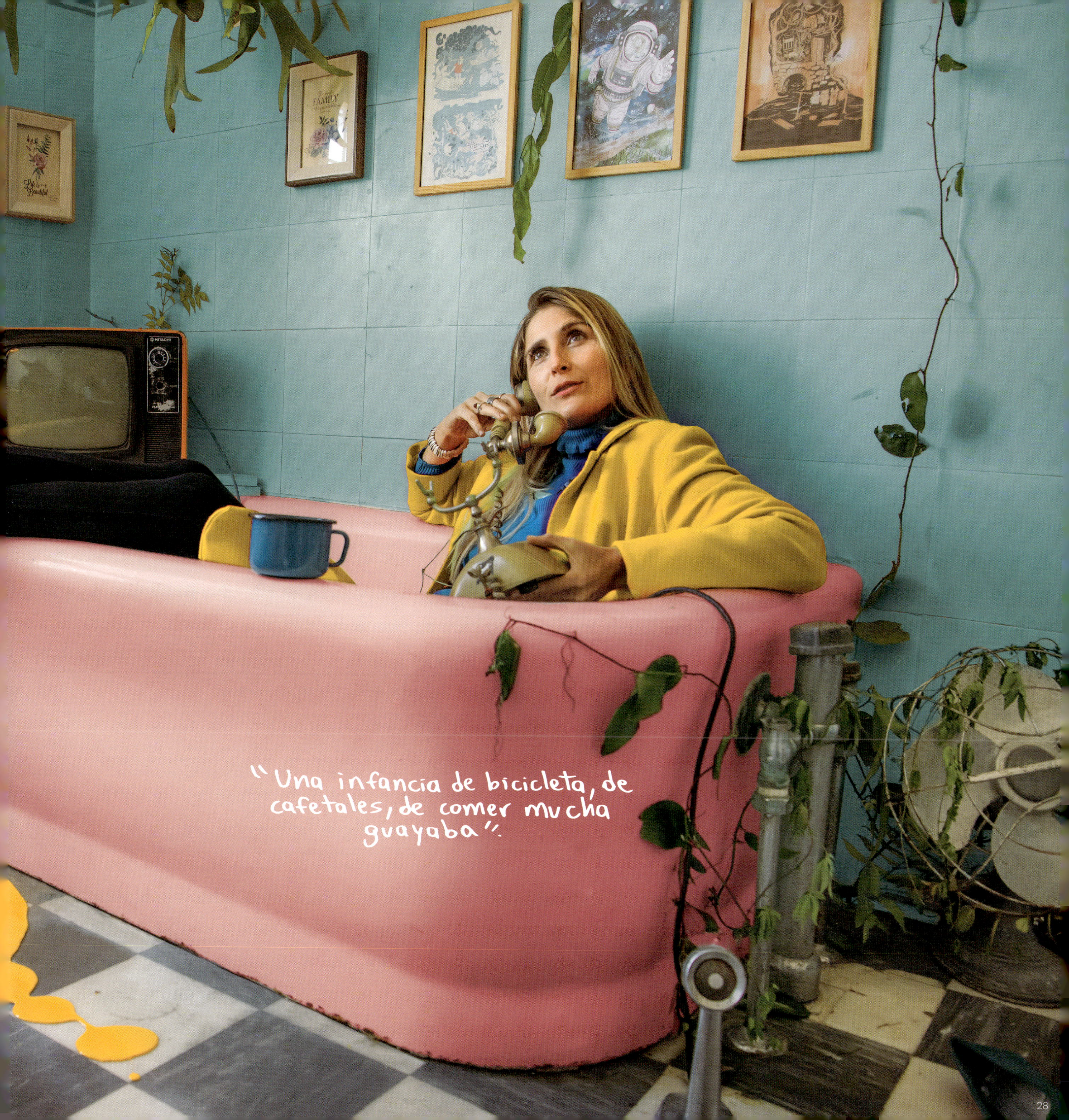
"Una infancia de bicicleta, de cafetales, de comer mucha guayaba".

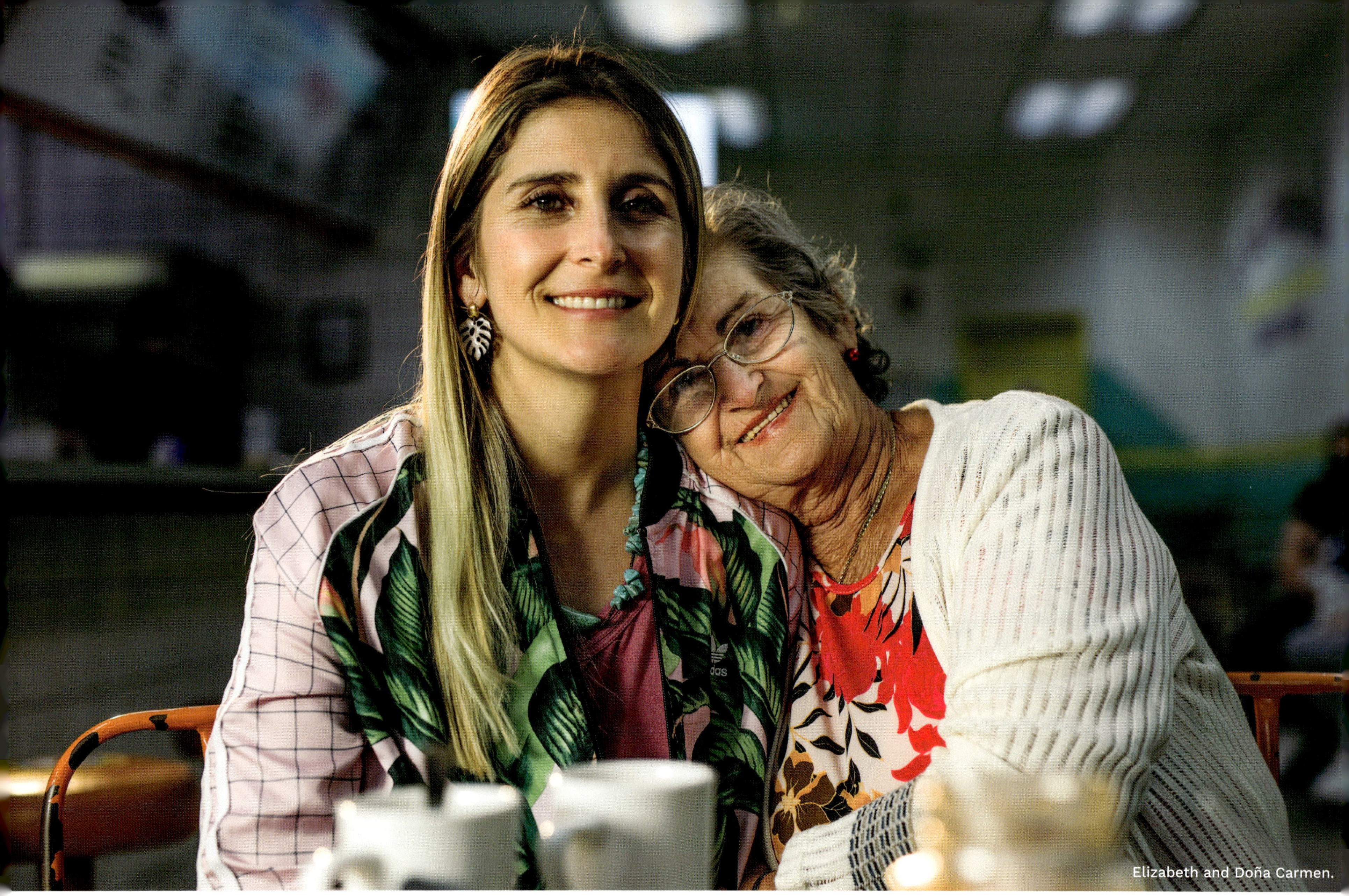

Elizabeth and Doña Carmen.

## "HOW'S THE LITTLE GIRL?"

Her mother's voice resonates in her head each time she crosses. Elizabeth looks both ways and spots her friend Cristina talking to Doña Ruth near the little store. Excited, she decides to sneak up on her from behind, cover her eyes with her hands and with a disguised voice ask the familiar question, "Guess who?"

She hurries over. Halfway across the road, she thinks she's making too much noise, that Cristina is about to turn around and ruin her game. She slows down. At that moment she feels a blow and falls to the ground.

"My God!"

Doña Ruth's cry opens her eyes. She's sprawled on the blue-gray asphalt. Understanding that she's not dead, but dying of embarrassment, Elizabeth gets up with as much dignity as she can muster, brushes off her clothes and tries to walk.

She falls to the ground again. Don Helio, Ruth's husband, appears out of nowhere, picks her up in his arms and takes her immediately to their home. There Doña Ruth examines her and gives her sugar water.

She hears when Don Helio decides to call an ambulance. Elizabeth feels panicked. She doesn't care if her brain burst open or if she broke a bone — she knows that her grandmother and mother are going to give her a stern scolding. She jumps and moves her legs, trying to convince Don Helio and Doña Ruth that she's fine, that there's no need to call an ambulance.

When they take her home, Elizabeth hopes to enter stealthily, saving herself a scolding. It's useless. Her family already knows all about it, and they've gone from anguish to relief to learn that she's OK. But her grandmother still scolds her:

"How is it possible that you got run over by a VW?"

"A VW?" Elizabeth realizes that she doesn't know who or what hit her. Nor does she remember when Cristina appeared.

The next day, Elizabeth learned from Don Helio that the driver of the VW, a chubby, nearly bald man, parked on the side of the highway, gathered his strength to approach Doña Ruth's house, and with a wispy voice asked from the doorway:

"How's the little girl?"

When Don Helio assured him that Elizabeth was fine, the man went back to the highway and kneeled in the middle, blocking traffic, and thanked God repeatedly, drowning in tears.

And Cristina? Though terrified, she had vanished immediately from the scene of the accident. On Monday, before going into class, and despite Elizabeth's embarrassment, she related what happened to all her little sixth grade friends, with a wealth of details. As if she had been the star of the story!

**Written by: Claudia Barrionuevo**

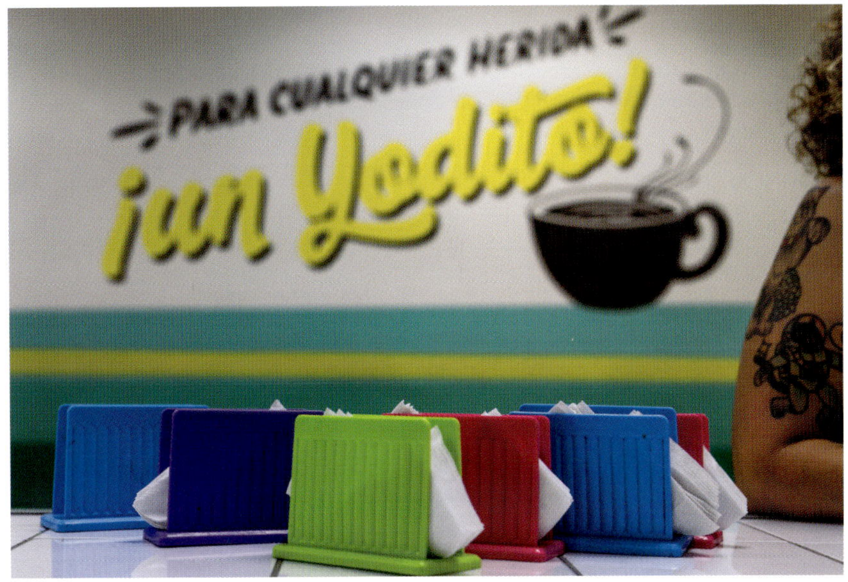


Soda Yogui's, Los Yoses, San Pedro.

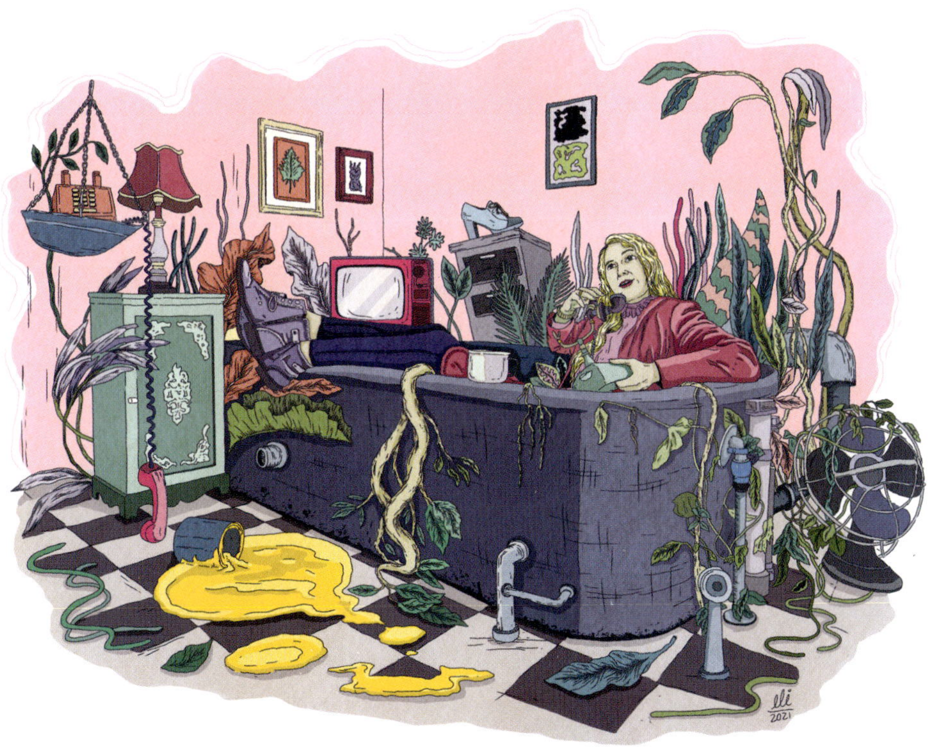

**Elizabeth Arguello Miranda**
Naranjo
Born Aug. 21, 1986

Elizabeth is an audiovisual artist, illustrator, and muralist. She believes in public art and has painted murals all over this country, as well as in other countries. She grew up in San Juan de Naranjo with her grandmother and mother, who is deaf. Since she was a girl, she liked to draw. She spent a lot of time drawing and talking while she drew, as if the personalities she drew had voices, so she would speak to herself in different voices for hours. The neighbors would pass by and see her talking to herself. As an adult, sometimes she catches herself talking out loud while alone, and she's discovered it's at moments where she's trying to tap her creativity. At 17, she migrated to San José, where she studied graphic design.

# BROUGHT TOGETHER BY AN EARTHQUAKE

Sometimes a century goes by in a breath, and at other times a breath lasts an eternity, like love. Do you know that instant when an earthquake begins? You only know it if you've lived it. Or better said, if you've survived it, because not everyone has been so fortunate, as with love. You hear the rumbling first, like a distant galloping that's growing intimately close. Those experienced in earthquakes know you feel them in the chest before you hear them. It's a premonition of uncertainty, because it's true of every earthquake that you never know how long it will last until it's over. In wooden buildings, or those with metal roofs, the creaking is intense, as if you were traveling in a mechanical ship, a species of giant robot that's walking in a hurry with some difficulty toward who knows where. *It took Costa Rica almost a century, since the creation of the Civil Registry in 1864, to reach 1 million inhabitants in 1956*. Some tectonic faults

## THEY SAW FRIENDS DISAPPEAR, SWALLOWED FOREVER BY A LANDSLIDE

are continental. Some are activated when the bottom of the ocean rises up, as happened with the earthquakes in Limón or Nicoya. Those are felt all over the country. Local faults sometimes cause more damage in a single community. Communities impacted by earthquakes along local faults sometimes experience natural catastrophes that the rest of the population doesn't even notice. That's how the Cinchona earthquake was, along a local fault. *Then 19 years went by to reach 2 million inhabitants in 1975*. Do you remember where you were that day? Four hours after the event, authorities in the capital were ignorant of the magnitude of the disaster, but not Twitter, which by that time already knew everything. Through that medium the first cries for help arrived. The survivors saw walls crumble, furniture and appliances fall over and deep, intimidating trenches open up in fields and highways. They attended to bleeding people and saw friends disappear, swallowed forever by a landslide rushing toward

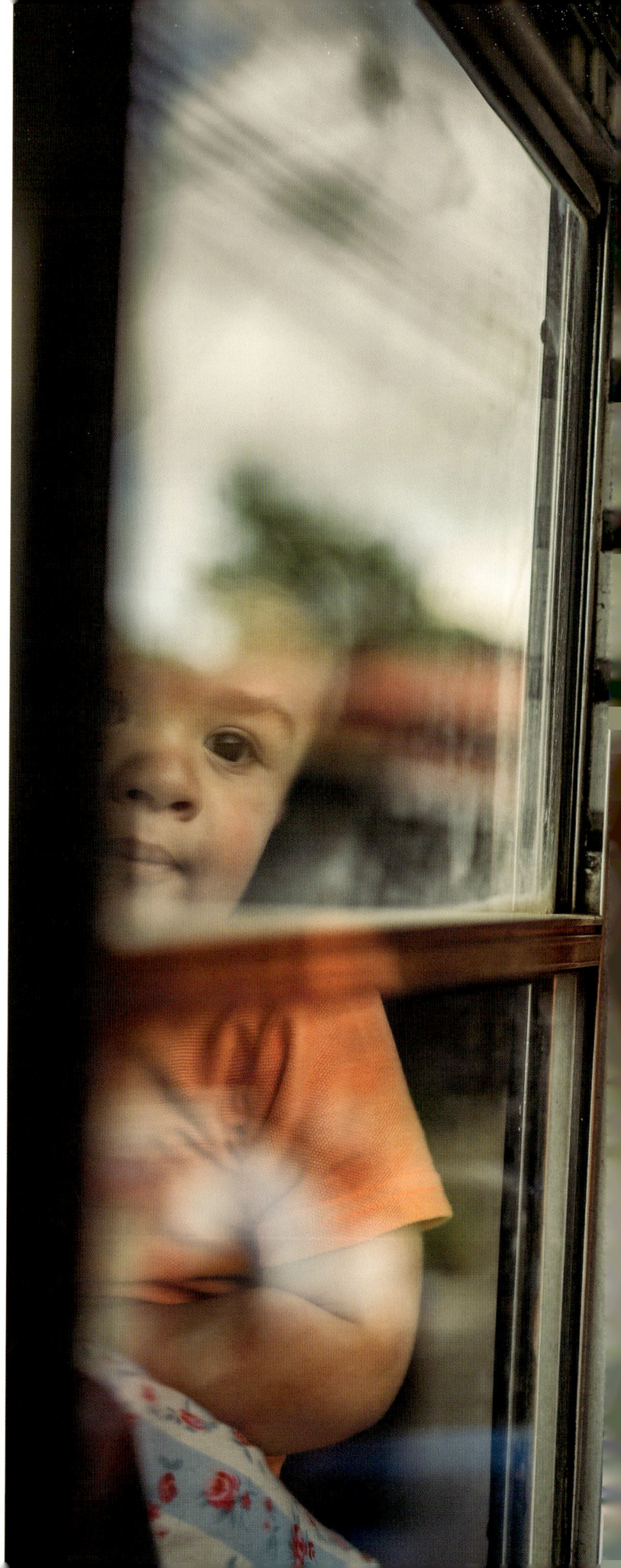

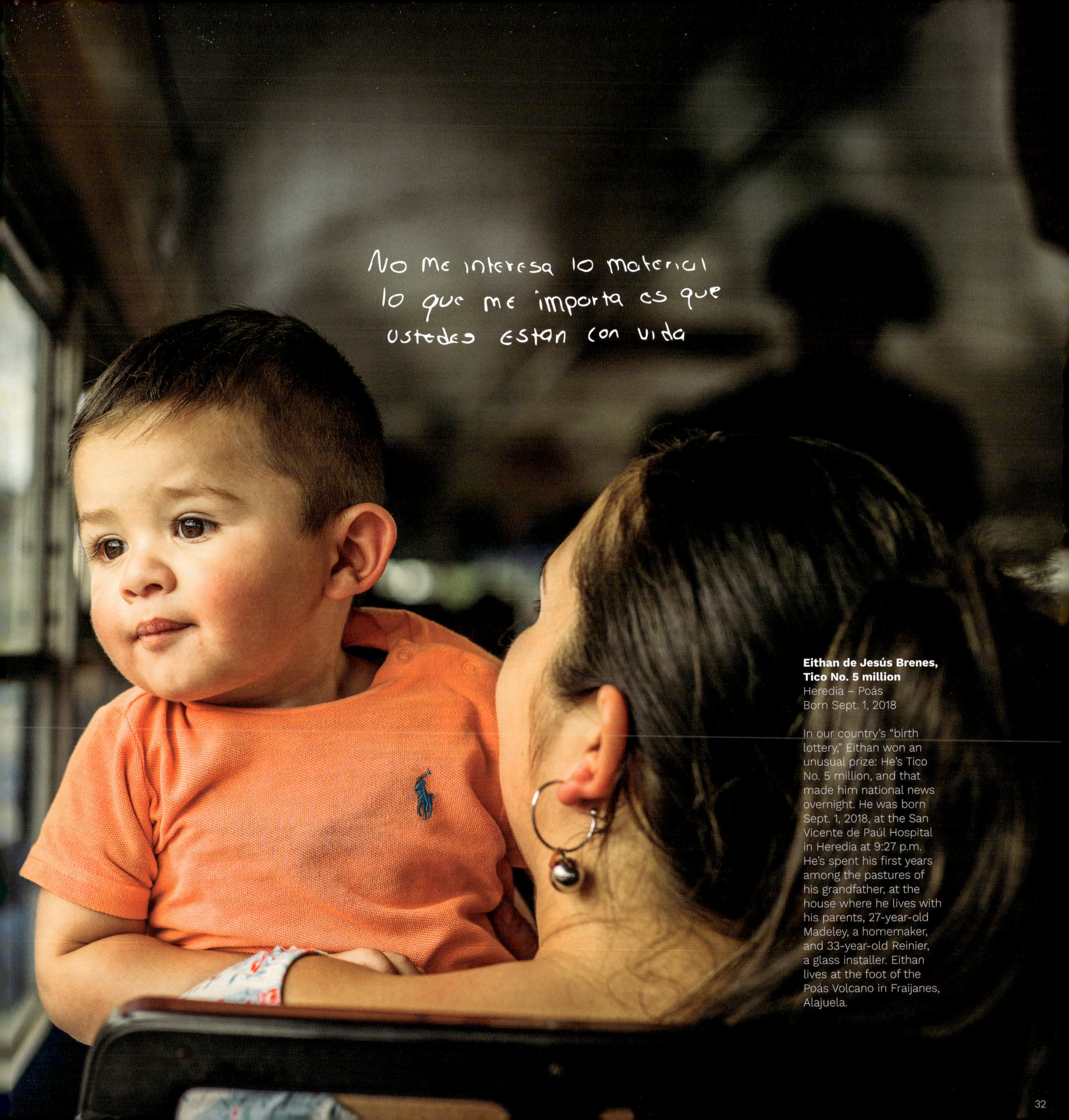


**Eithan de Jesús Brenes, Tico No. 5 million**
Heredia – Poás
Born Sept. 1, 2018

In our country's "birth lottery," Eithan won an unusual prize: He's Tico No. 5 million, and that made him national news overnight. He was born Sept. 1, 2018, at the San Vicente de Paúl Hospital in Heredia at 9:27 p.m. He's spent his first years among the pastures of his grandfather, at the house where he lives with his parents, 27-year-old Madeley, a homemaker, and 33-year-old Reinier, a glass installer. Eithan lives at the foot of the Poás Volcano in Fraijanes, Alajuela.

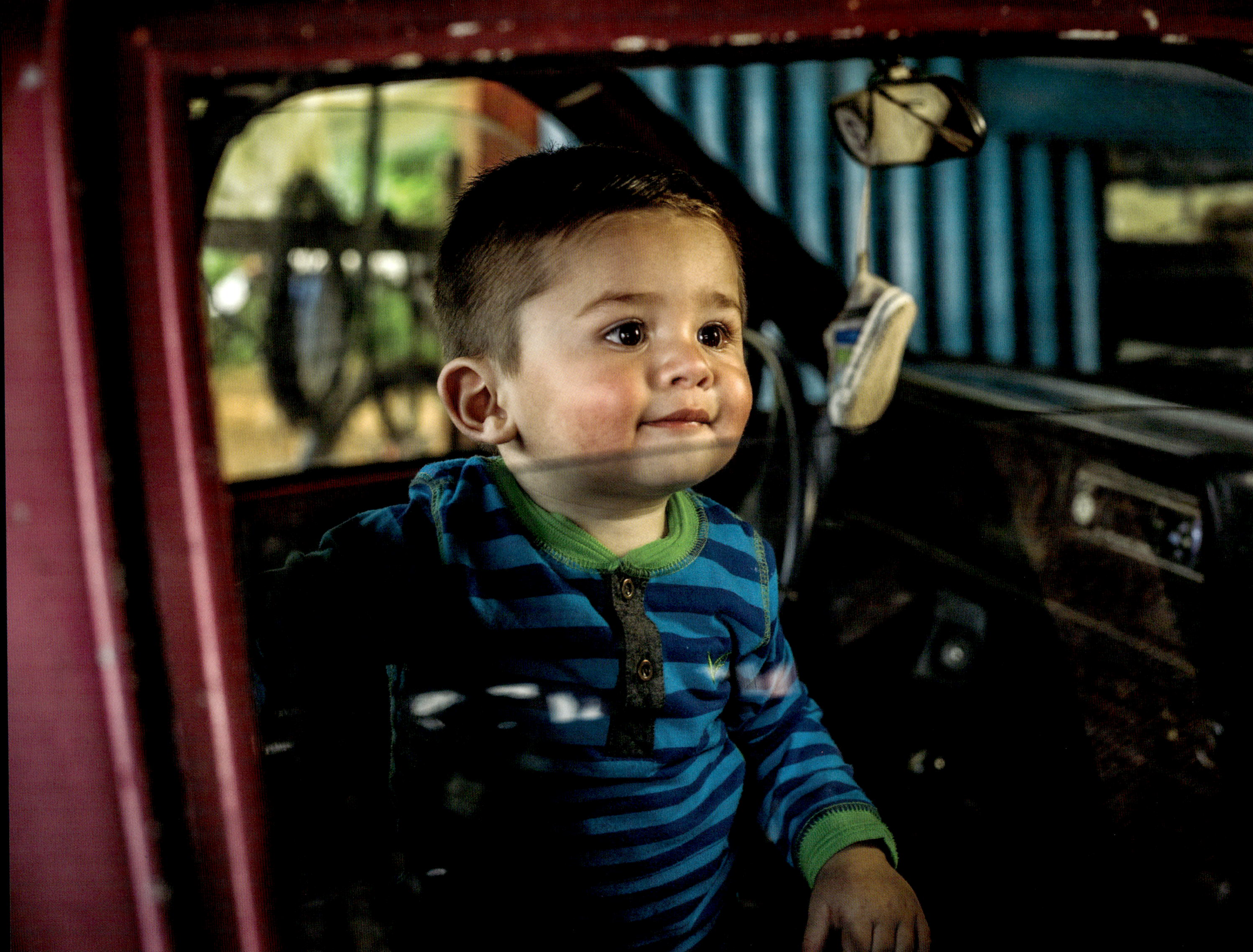

the Sarapiquí River. *Fifteen more years went by before reaching 3 million Costa Ricans, in 1990*. But there's no bad thing that doesn't bring some good. The collapsed homes had to be rebuilt. Reinier was a hardworking entrepreneur who changed the dairy industry by installing glass, and the earthquake opened up a big opportunity for him. One of the destroyed homes that needed his attention was that of Madeley, a girl who was left traumatized by the tragic power of nature. The violent shaking of the walls, roofs and windows of the home destroyed by the quake — with her, her mother and her sisters inside — is a distressing reminder that still makes her jump with every tremor. One day she saw Reinier come and she took a good look at him. Her uncle was the

## FROM THAT NIGHT FORWARD, HE ARRIVED TO VISIT HER WITH MORE FREQUENCY

master builder, and she confided in him that the glass guy was good-looking. Each time Reinier appeared to install glass, the uncle would announce him by saying "Pure yogurt!" — code for very good, healthy, appetizing. All the workers knew what that signal meant and they would all tease her. *After 11 years the country reached 4 million inhabitants in 2001.* Although they grew up living very close together, they had never met, even though he worked with cattle with Madeley's uncle by marriage. One year later, serendipity brought them together when Reinier went with some of Madeley's cousins to the Festival of Light, which she was attending too with other cousins. There they spoke for the first time, and after that they were inseparable. From that night forward, he arrived to visit her with more frequency until, five years later, love joined them in matrimony. *And that's the story of how Eithan de Jesús, the 5 millionth Costa Rican, was born in September 2018 to parents who were brought together by the earthquake in Cinchona.*

Written by: Alvaro Cedeño

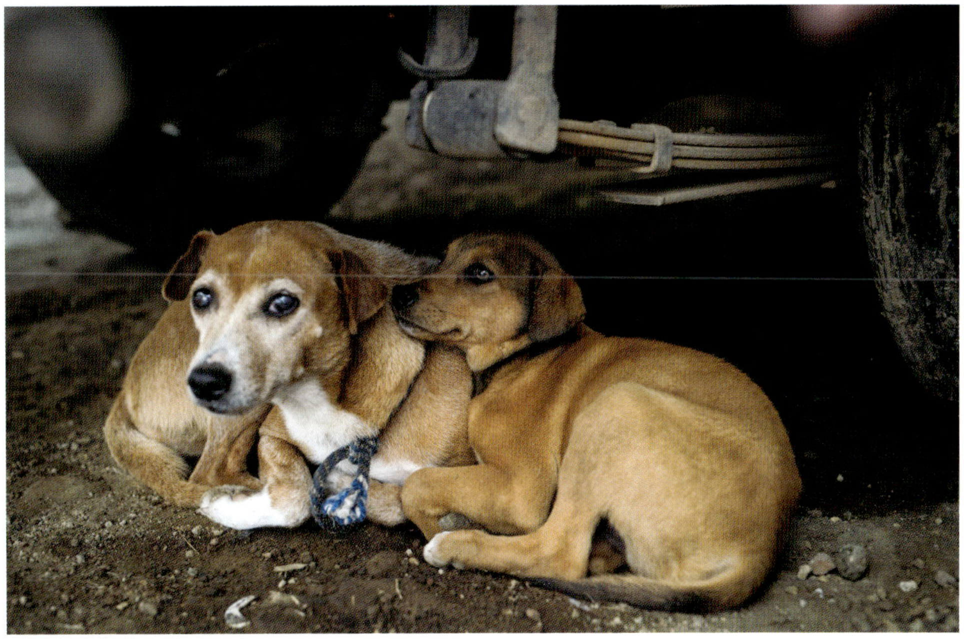

Fraijanes, Alajuela.

# THE DOCTOR WHO FELL IN LOVE IN JAPAN

María Amalia Matamoros listed agronomy as one of three options to apply to the University of Costa Rica, since she really didn't know what she wanted to do with the rest of her life. Without deep convictions and just in case, she also listed medicine.

With the same indecisiveness, she jumped over a couple of other options a few years later, when she had to choose her major and decided on pediatric surgery. But she felt like she wanted to live a bit longer and learn more, and she thought about continuing her training in the United States. But, again, she had no clear idea what she wanted to do.

One day she saw a notice in the newspaper about a scholarship from the government of Japan, but she thought little of it. A day later, she remembered the ad when she walked in front of the Japanese Embassy. Without giving it much thought, she rang the bell. She put the application in her back seat and forgot about it again. Finally, after washing her car and finding this piece of paper again, she embarked on a race against time. The world was a bigger place back then, the distances longer, and the biggest technological advance was a fax machine at Radiográfica Costarricense, the X-ray lab. Thanks to being given a three-day grace period, she was able to fulfill the requirements in the nick of time, while asking herself why she was exerting

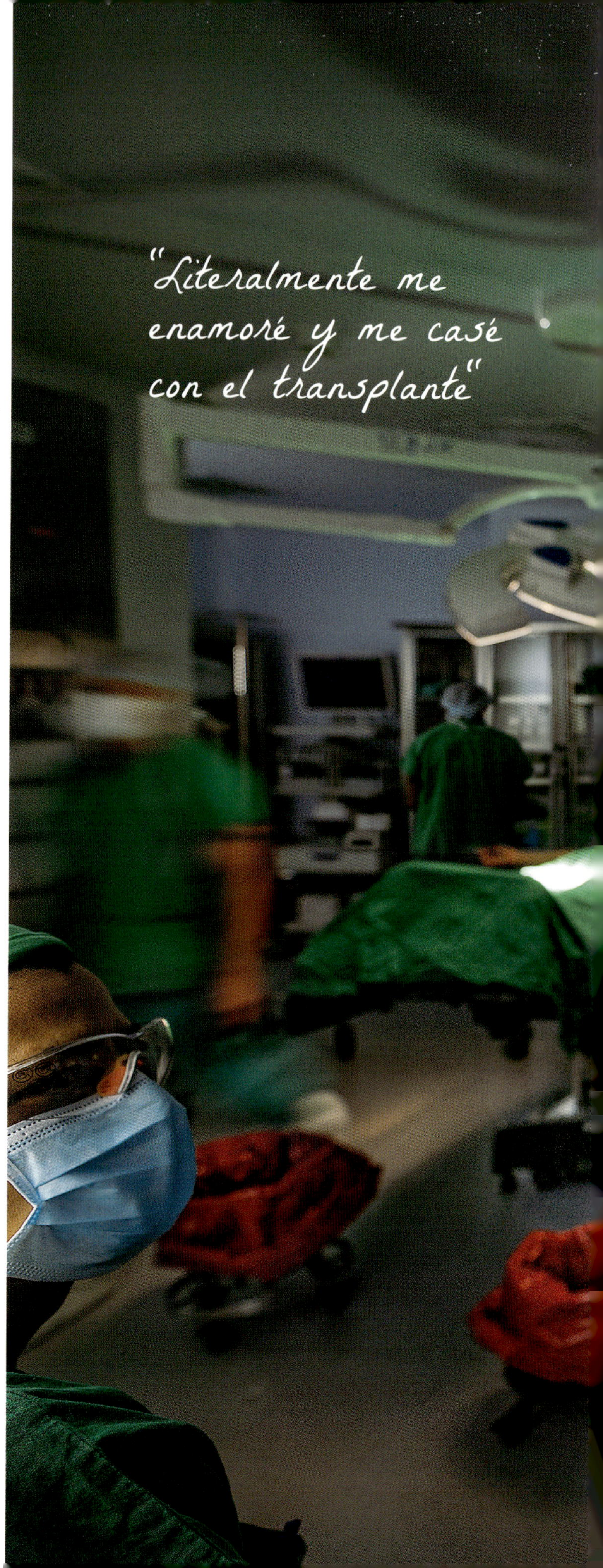

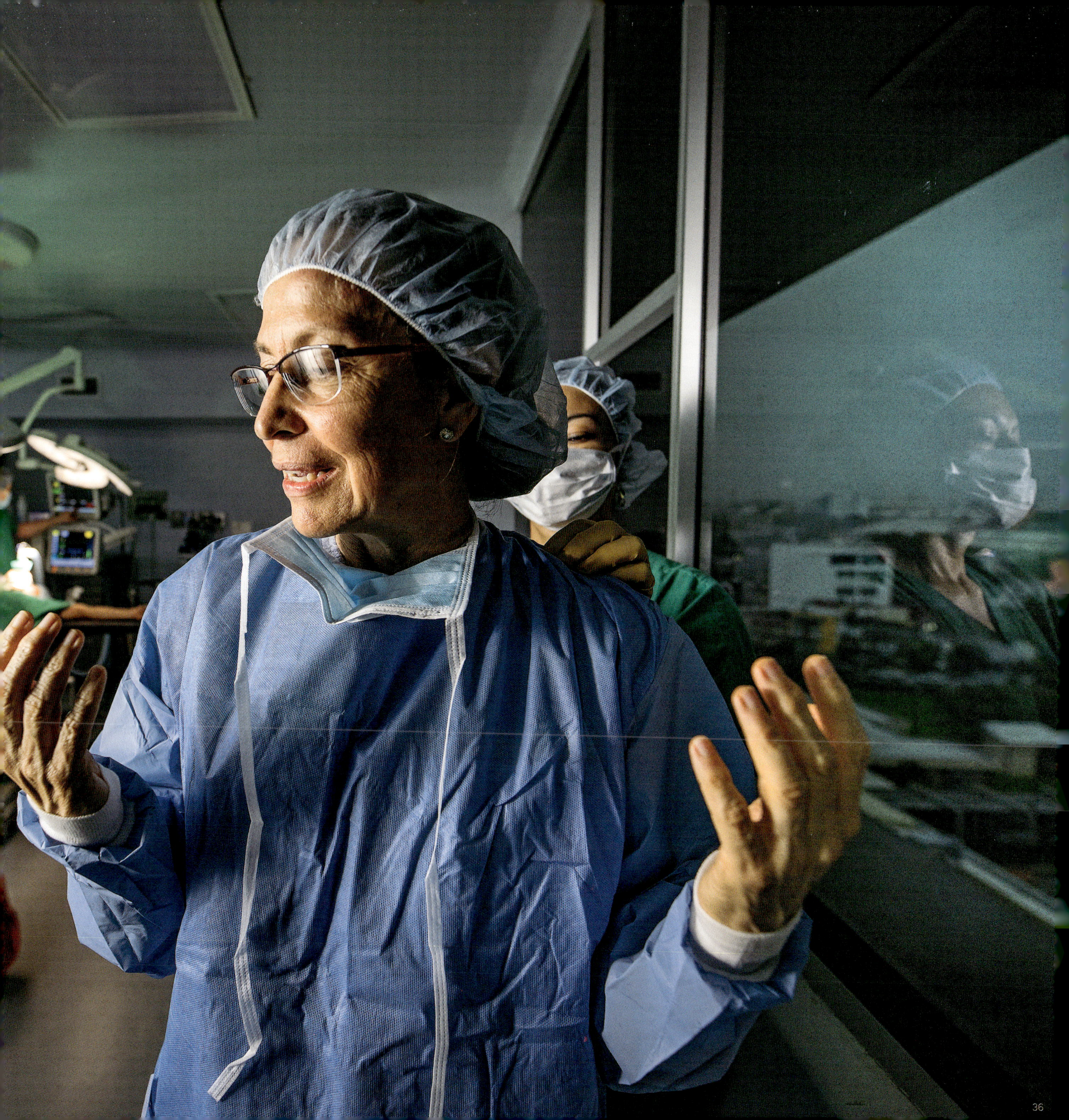

## THE ANSWER WOULD ARRIVE FROM JAPAN IN AN UNEXPECTED MANNER

so much effort to go to a place that was never in her plans.

The answer would arrive from Japan in an unexpected manner.

One cold night in December, a physician/musician invited her to a party at the home of the director of the Osaka orchestra. The young doctor still didn't speak much Japanese, she didn't understand the social niceties, and she couldn't play any musical instruments. She felt like a fish out of water. Until, by total surprise, a Japanese person spoke to her in Spanish. Double surprise: This Japanese person not only knew Costa Rica, but had Costa Rican nieces. Triple surprise: One of these nieces had been María Amalia's classmate in her first year in college. The man, a surgeon from Kyoto who was also not a musician, saved the evening.

Also, curiously, and not because she had shown any interest in this specialty, the doctor really wanted to introduce her to an expert in liver transplants. And that's how, less than a week later, thinking she would be introduced to another ordinary physician, she was presented to Dr. Koichi Tanaka. The instant he met her, the world-famous doctor knew why María Amalia Matamoros, who grew up amid coffee farms in Naranjo, Alajuela, had come to Japan: "You're here because of children who die from the blockage of bile ducts in your country. You want to change that. Welcome to Kyoto."

While she was still trying to make sense of this unexpected prophecy, Dr. Tanaka ordered his team of doctors to teach her everything. And so it went. In Japan, the hierarchies are very clear; the one who knows the most gives the orders, and the others comply.

She learned that in order to fit in, she had to erase herself, to unlearn all her customs and her Western outlook. She became Japanese, and Dr. Tanaka became her teacher. She obeyed him without question in the middle of the night when, after many hours of surgery and without explanation, he told her to leave the operating room at 3 a.m. and accompany him on a long trip to the distant city of Kyushu to attend a conference. The speaker was Nancy Ascher, the first woman who ever transplanted a liver, and the head of the transplant program at the University of California in San Francisco. With no explanation from Tanaka, María Amalia got the message: You could be this same woman in your own country.

A few years later, she founded a company that established a nationwide protocol for transplanting livers in Costa Rica. She also became friends with Dr. Ascher, and they still collaborate to this day. And that's how Dr. Matamoros devoted her career to liver transplants, and finally decided what she wanted to do with the rest of her life.

**Written by: Abril Gordienko López**

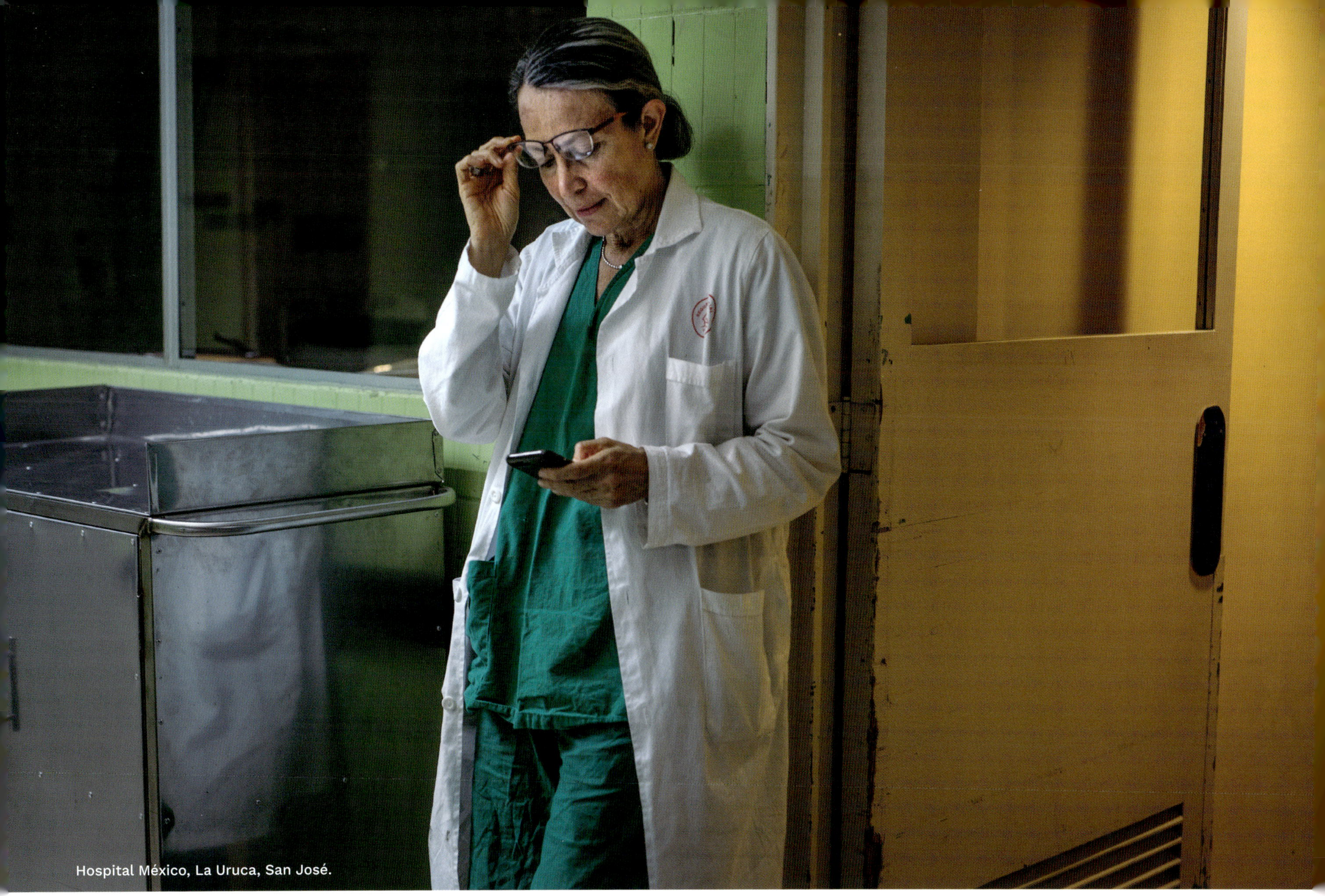
Hospital México, La Uruca, San José.

**María Amalia Matamoros Ramírez**
Naranjo - San José
Born April 30, 1966

María Amalia is a medical surgeon, a specialist in pediatric surgery and a graduate of the University of Costa Rica. She also specializes in transplant surgery, of livers and bile ducts — she is an expert in organ transplants — and if we tried to list all her skills, we would run out of space. She is one of the most accomplished liver surgeons in Latin America, and as of 2019 it's been 20 years since she started the Pediatric Liver Transplant Program that she still directs. She started the program after training in Japan for three years. María Amalia grew up in Naranjo, with two brothers and two sisters and her parents, Don Adrián (a coffee grower) and Doña María Julia (a retired teacher). Japan changed her life: "I came to Kyoto, and I literally fell in love and got married to the idea of transplants."

• Some 70% of medical specialists work for the CCSS government health care system.

# HAIL ON THE LAKE

I remember being enclosed in my room and feeling the sadness come. After a day full of activities that kept me distracted, I saw it coming, entering that spiral that broke me down, returning to my real life, where every day was a bad day. In the maelstrom of feelings, I ended up crying, sitting on my doorstep. I cried so hard I couldn't even hear my own thoughts anymore. I felt broken, overwhelmed, lost.

I left my room without thinking about it much, as if I was being led by the hand. The storm drenched me in a second. I walked down the trails looking for the lake. I could hear the cracking sound of the hailstones falling on the zinc roof as I left the house. I walked among giant trees, invisible animals and infinite rain. In a few minutes I reached the lake, and I plunged in. It was the first time in years that hail had fallen at the San Carlos dock.

I was working as a guide for a family of foreigners that had organized a trip to help their mother, a delightful older woman, to feel alive again. She had recently lost her husband, and her children wanted to take her to a new place, so they chose Costa Rica. A tourism company offered me the job. It was a big responsibility at an inconvenient moment, but I accepted the challenge.

It was Christmas, and there I was working, far from my family and my son. A few months before, I had suffered an accident that prevented me from working in the high season, and I had no insurance or savings. Besides my financial problems, I carried a huge pain in my self-esteem because I couldn't provide for my little boy or get along with my ex — the world was falling in on me.

That's why that night I left my room, annoyed with the universe, with life, with nature. When I reached the lake, I took my clothes off and got into the warm water in a hailstorm without a second thought. I sat down, almost completely covered by the warm water. I dunked my head. Below the surface, a profound silence. I was overcome by a feeling of humility. Nature has that magic: making you feel tiny and also enormous, part of something bigger than yourself. I felt calm, breathing, and the energy was healing me. Little by little, the anxiety that was tormenting me washed away and I understood that I was one with the universe.

"The river runs from Turrialba to Siquirres," said a friend. "How we get there is our business, but the river always ends up there."

We climbed trees with the old woman, we walked through the forest, and little by little I felt my confidence restored. We even got to the point where she agreed to run the rapids, even though she was terrified by the water. Her bravery was so obvious that it was impossible not to be moved. She came to trust me so much that she started saying she would do whatever I said.

That tour, that night of hailstones at the lake, that woman who came to Costa Rica to change her life and ended up changing mine, gave me the strength to start a new project close to nature, where I belong.

Since that magical tour, every time I have a birthday I receive an envelope containing $10 from that woman, just like that, like a grandmother who has adopted a grandson and is betting on his destiny.

**Written by: Alonso Muñoz**

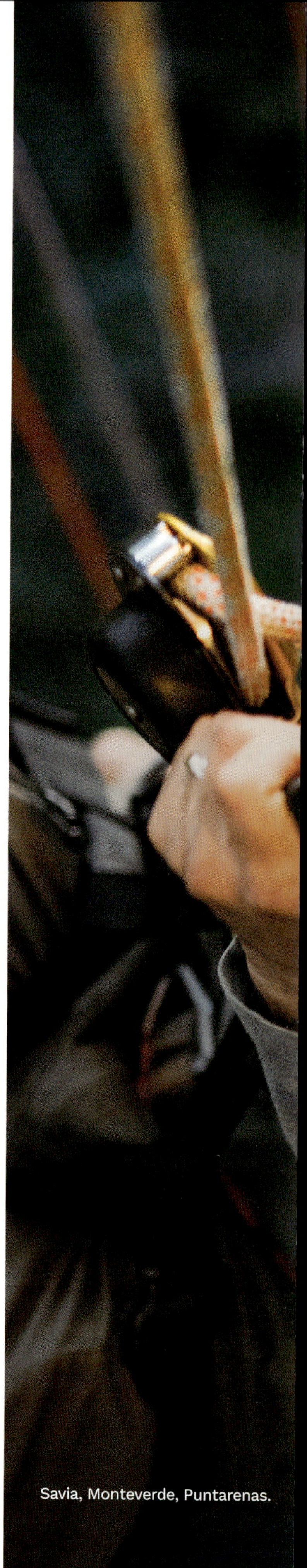

Savia, Monteverde, Puntarenas.

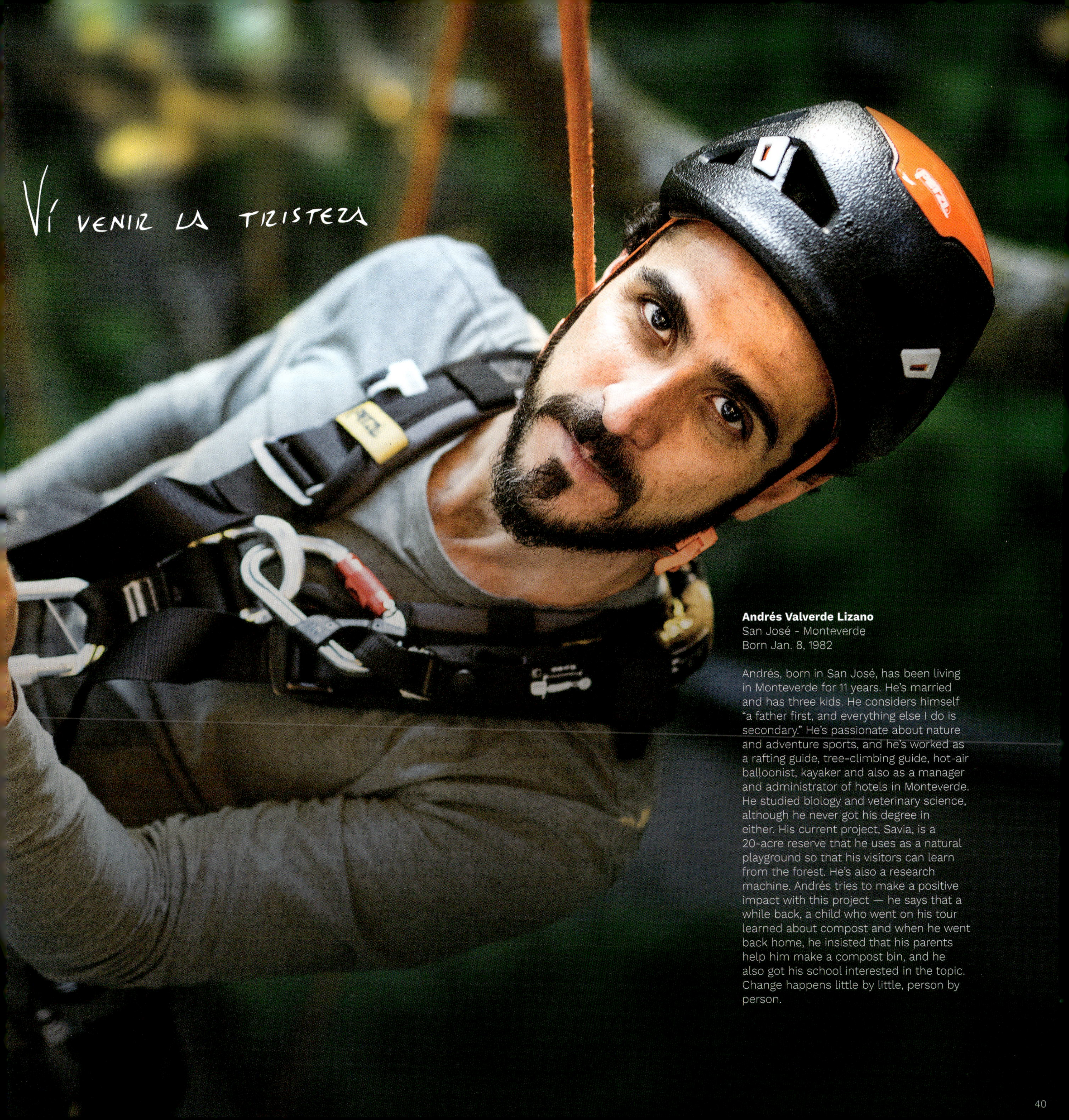

Ví venir la tristeza

**Andrés Valverde Lizano**
San José - Monteverde
Born Jan. 8, 1982

Andrés, born in San José, has been living in Monteverde for 11 years. He's married and has three kids. He considers himself "a father first, and everything else I do is secondary." He's passionate about nature and adventure sports, and he's worked as a rafting guide, tree-climbing guide, hot-air balloonist, kayaker and also as a manager and administrator of hotels in Monteverde. He studied biology and veterinary science, although he never got his degree in either. His current project, Savia, is a 20-acre reserve that he uses as a natural playground so that his visitors can learn from the forest. He's also a research machine. Andrés tries to make a positive impact with this project — he says that a while back, a child who went on his tour learned about compost and when he went back home, he insisted that his parents help him make a compost bin, and he also got his school interested in the topic. Change happens little by little, person by person.

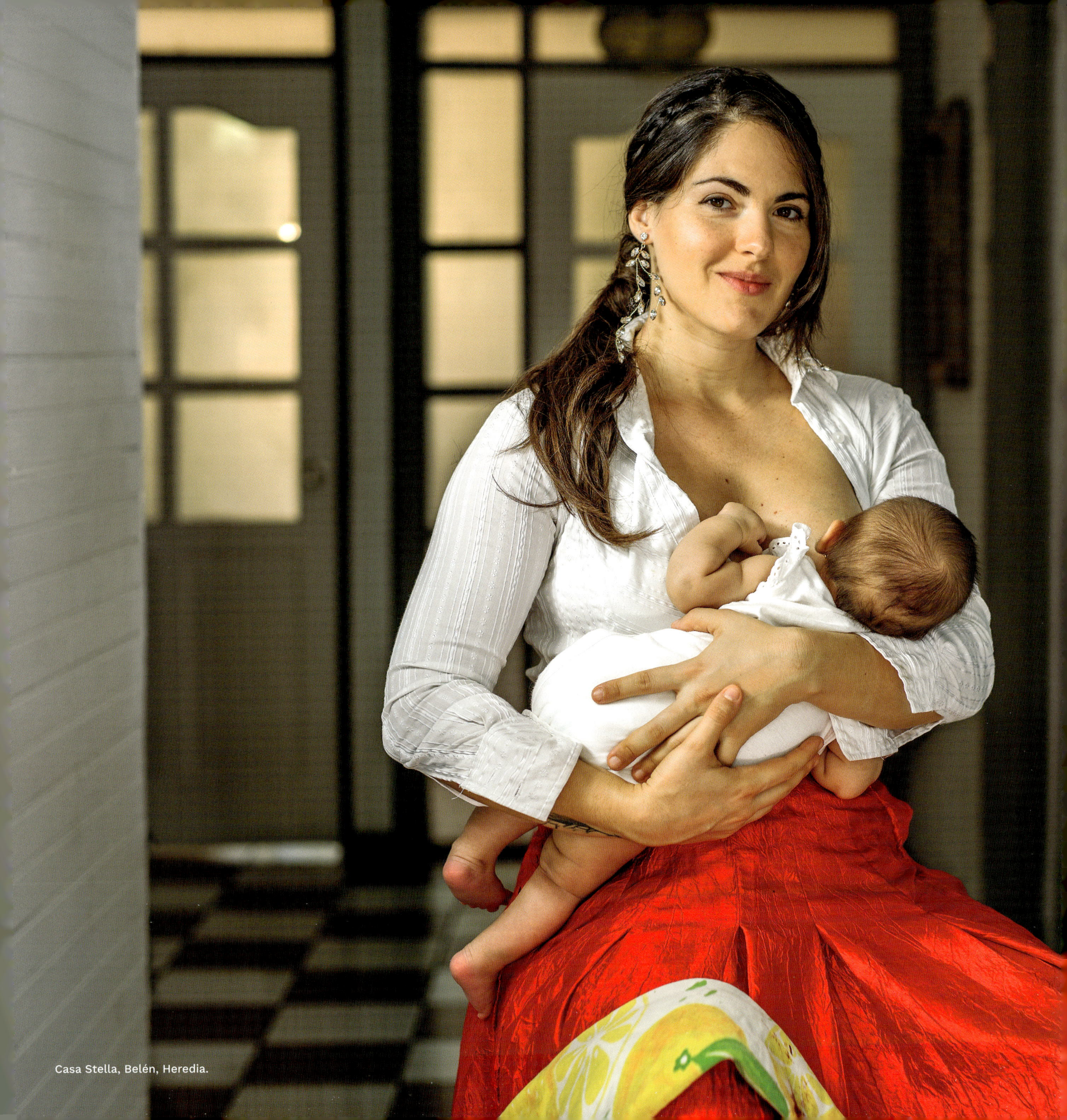

Casa Stella, Belén, Heredia.

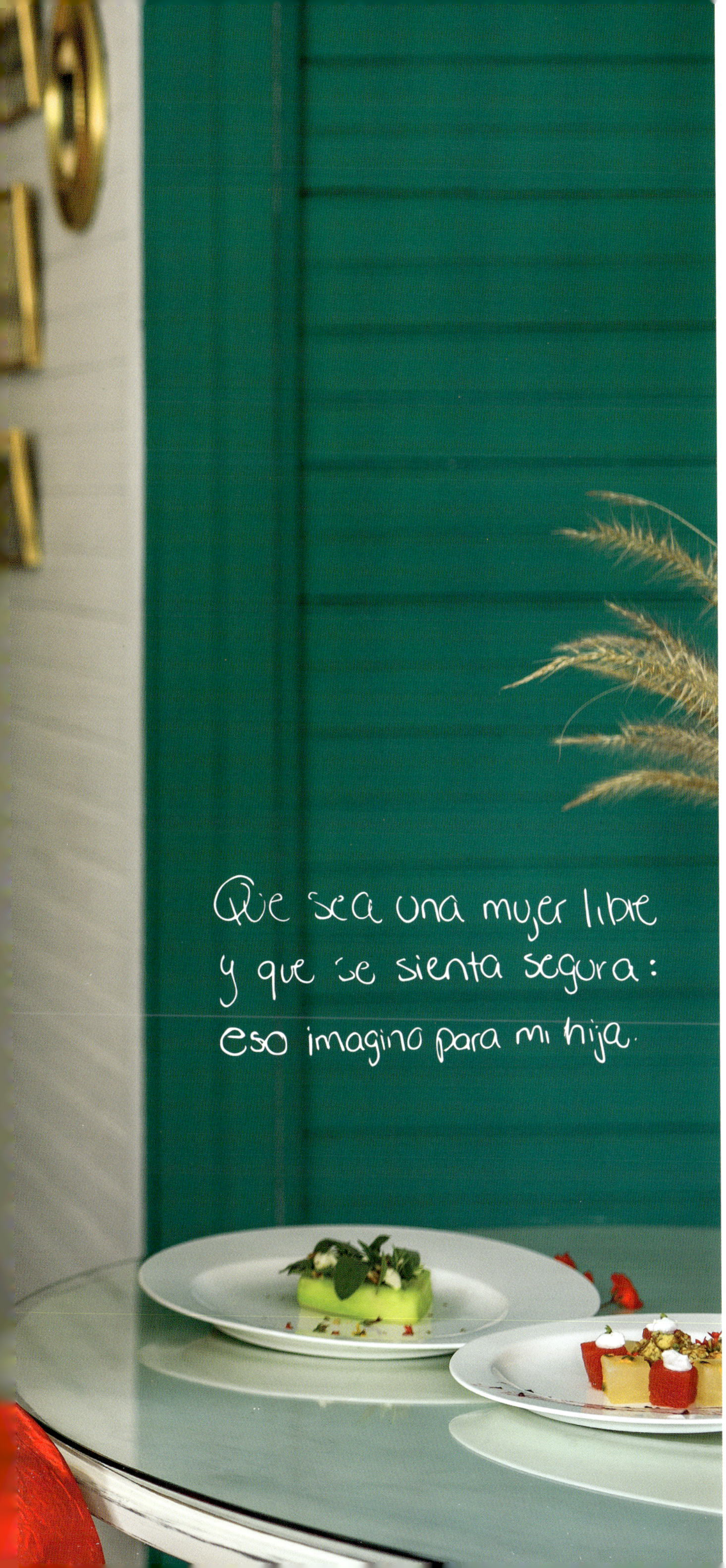


# A BIG HOUSE FULL OF PEOPLE

The house was very large and had an enormous yard, with a terrace, fruit trees and pets of all kinds. The turtle is still there.

I had a neighborhood and a park. We skated and played hide-and-seek. There were lots of us!

We are nine siblings. My twin and I were the last to arrive, 16 years after the oldest. My parents had to do without the terrace in front of their room to make a room for Mauricio and me. We were inseparable from a very early age. They always put us to sleep separately, but we woke up together. Not in our beds, but in the beds of our other siblings. First I would move to another bed, and then he would.

When you belong to a family with so many kids, you don't know what silence is. There's always a fight. You can always hear "Mom!" from some corner of the house. Also, someone is always sick.

We all had assigned chores. We worked as a team. There was constant movement in the kitchen. It wasn't easy to feed so many people. We bought a lot of things in bulk. I remember a bucket full of beans between the kitchen and the yard, ready to be cleaned.

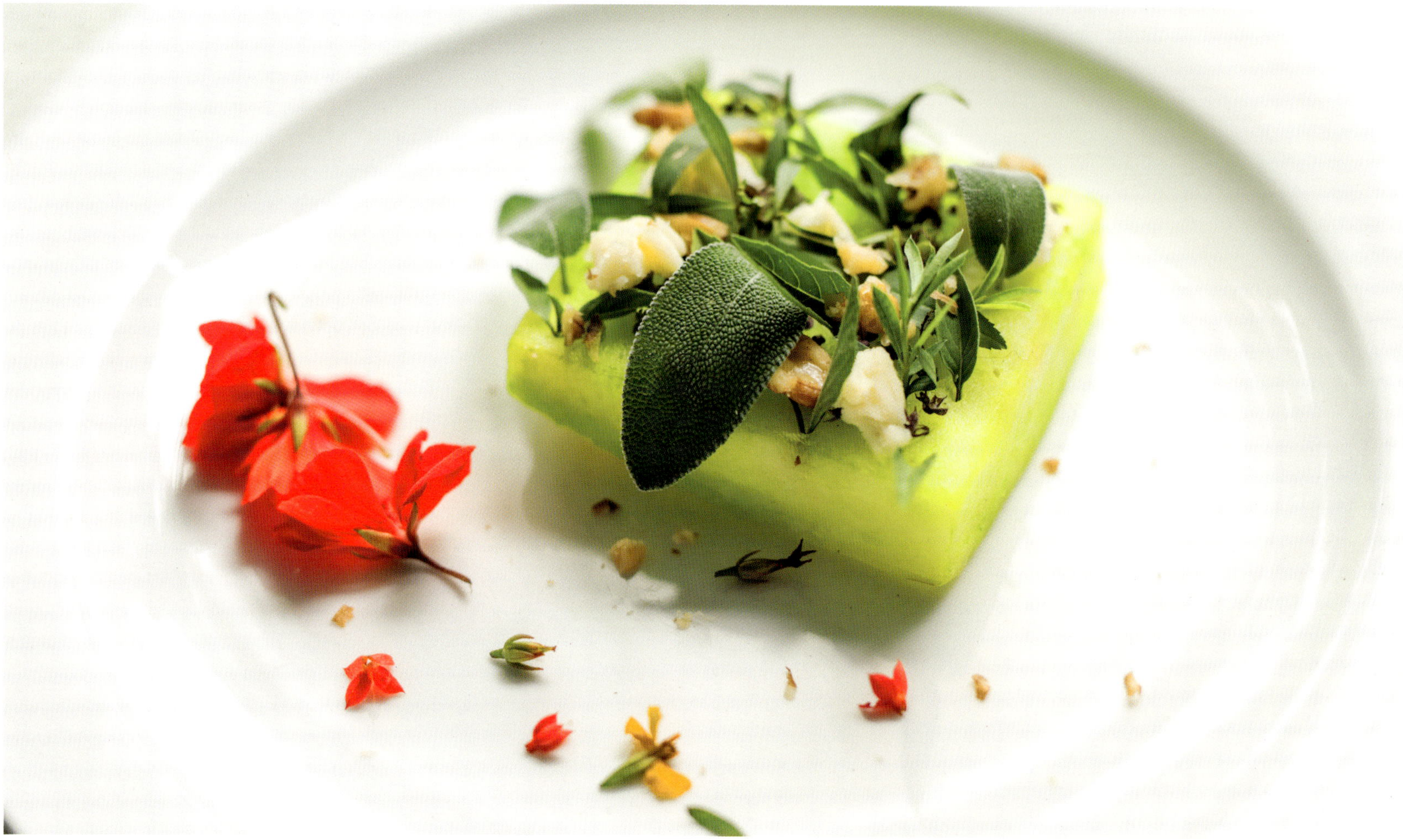

Privacy was an unknown privilege. It didn't exist. You couldn't shut yourself in your room, because you always shared it with somebody. And also, if you ever managed to shut yourself in, you would immediately hear Mom's voice: "Why do you shut the door??"

My parents came from large families, so they were used to it. Mom would go swimming and she would leave us in baby strollers alongside the pool. The gentlemen of the club suffered. They didn't understand our mom's tranquility. And Dad would take us on outings in a yellow van. Everyone, including my maternal grandparents. Listening to children's Topo Gigio music along the road.

I don't understand how my mother managed to take care of all nine of us. The older ones had to take care of the younger ones. And although among so many people you were never alone, sometimes someone managed to evade the surveillance. In those moments of solitude, anything could happen. One time, one of my brothers lit his bed on fire and almost burned down the house. Another, tired of hearing me cry when I was a baby, left me on the roof.

When I turned 5, they gave me some little ducklings. They were in a cardboard box. I was alone when I thought it would be a great idea to get into the bathtub with them. So that's what I did, I took a bath with the little ducklings. I put a lot of shampoo on them, and they started fading and died. In those days my grandfather was very sick, and I thought he too had been washed in shampoo.

In another solitary moment, I did something that had smelly consequences. One day I started to smell bad. Very bad. I was very small and nobody understood why I smelled so bad. Each day it got worse. Amid the constant hustle and bustle of our house, one night my worried parents finally took me to a doctor. At first I was happy because they put a Hello Kitty jacket on me. But at the doctor's office this issue stopped being amusing when the doctor put some pliers in one of my nostrils. From there, he removed a germinated bean. With a little twig and small leaves. That's why I smelled so bad. I don't know how much time went by from when I put a bean up my nose until they took it out of me. I had grabbed it out of the bucket of beans when nobody was watching me.

Now I'm a mother. Shortly after Antonia was born, I had a very difficult first week, and I thought of my parents. How can anyone have more than three kids?

I went back to living in a very big house. The one that used to belong to my paternal grandmother. Where my father grew up with his eight siblings. Where Antonia and I are still getting to know each other.

**Written by: Claudia Barrionuevo**

**María Laura Zamora**
San Antonio de Belén
Born Sept. 23, 1987

María Laura is a chef, and cooking is her profession and passion. A passion that has carried her to many corners of the planet but always brings her back to Costa Rica, the place that has the best ingredients and where she has learned the most about cooking. She is one of nine siblings and she was a twin brother, whom she "bossed around" when they were small. She grew up in Belén but she's of Lebanese ancestry, and although she grew up surrounded by a lot of people, now she lives alone with her daughter Antonia. The experience of being a mother has left her really happy. Her business, Deliarte Catering Service, offers all kinds of gastronomic consultations and menus for events, which usually take place at Casa Stella, a place that has belonged to her family for more than 115 years and which she's now in charge of managing.

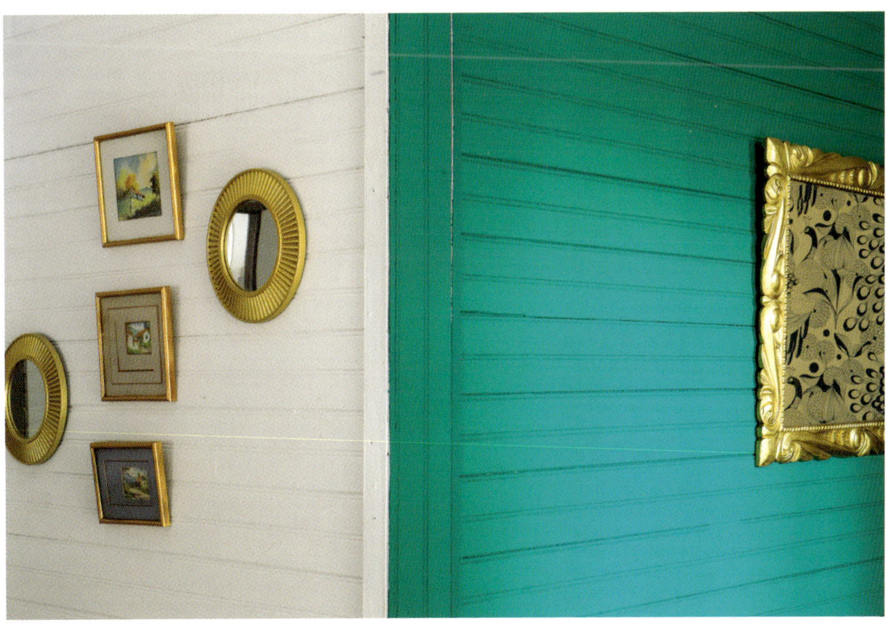

Casa Stella, Belén, Heredia.

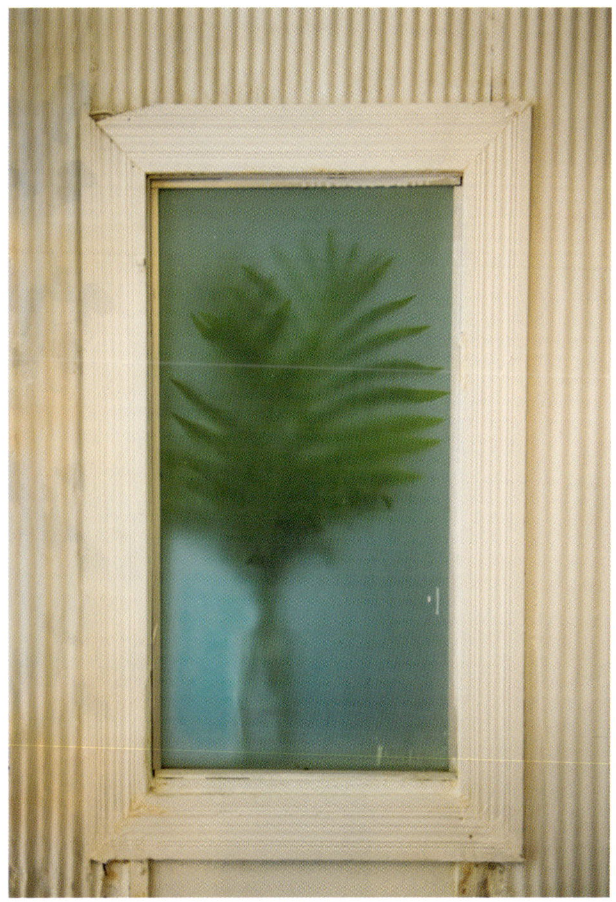

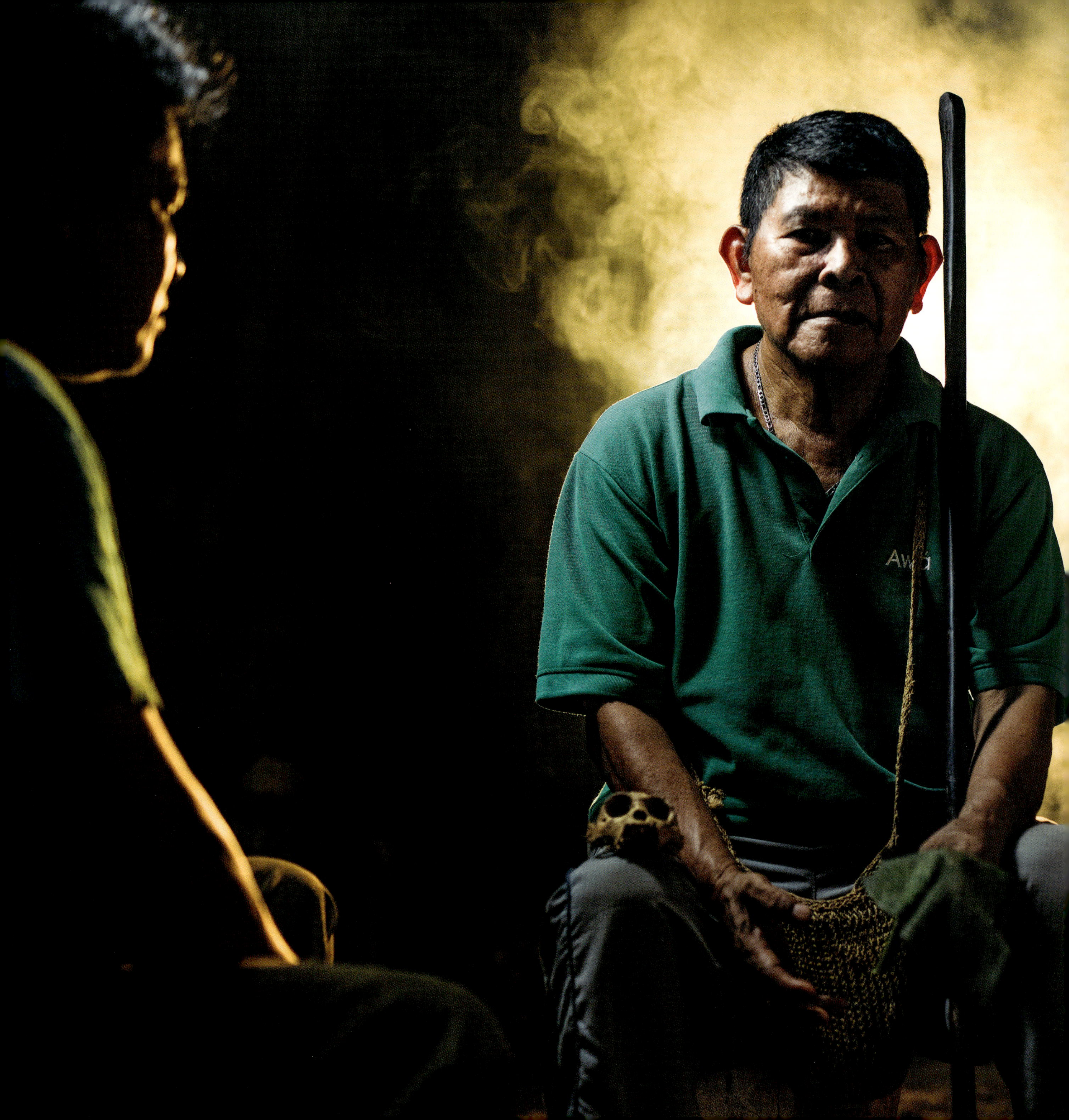

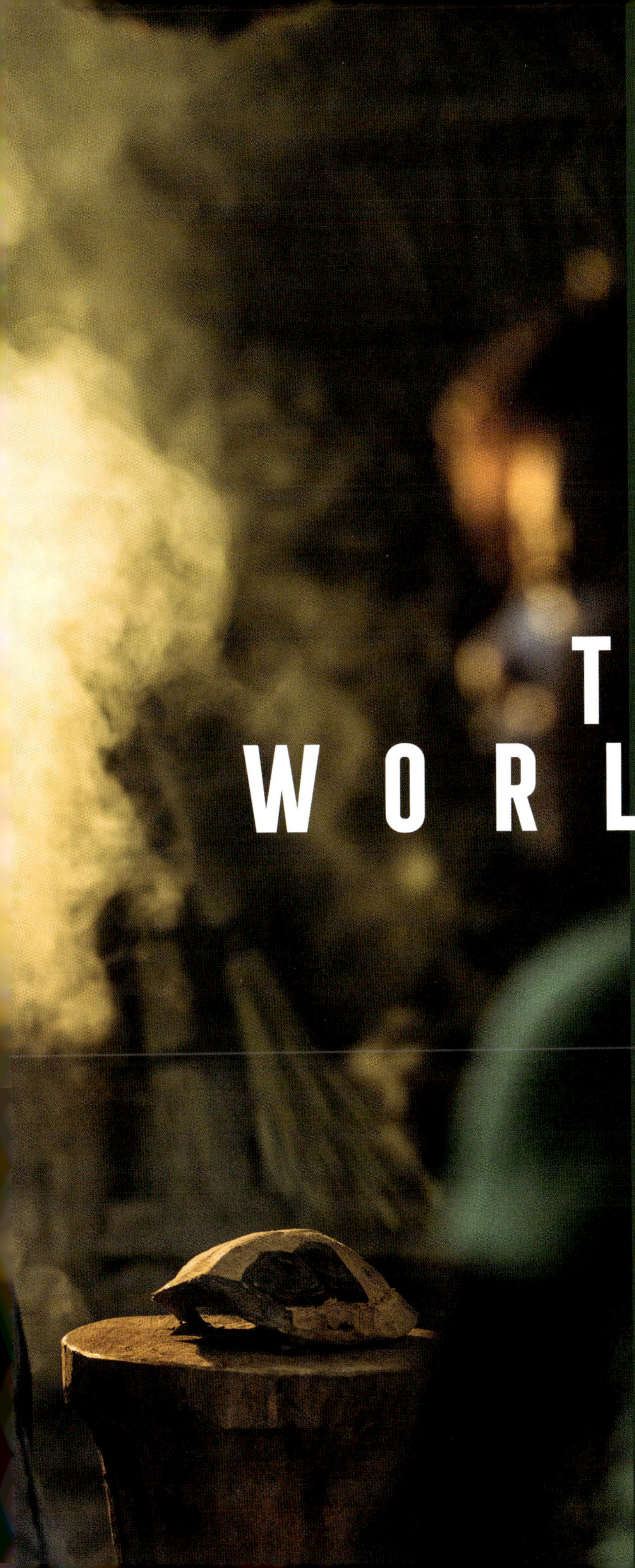

# TWO WORLDS

The descent begins, and Lisandro can't help thinking, "I'm going to die on this plane."

"Are they descending or are we falling? What's going on?" he asks his friend Leila, the *sicua* (white) woman who is married to an indigenous Boruca man, who invited them to this ceremony of Latin American shamans.

In the 30 minutes that pass before they touch ground, looking at the city of Barcelona through the window, a couple of memories come to mind.

Lisandro was 18, they had gone out at 4 a.m. and they were deep in the mountain. They had a wild pig surrounded. He ran through the dense forest at top speed, to keep it from getting away, while his father and other members of the tribe did the same, forming a circle. Finally, accompanied by a shriek, came the fatal thrust. It was a good-sized peccary that would be enough to feed lots of people in the village. But an instant later, there was a second shriek. A fer-de-lance disappeared into the brush, but its fangs had left their mark in his father's bare foot.

The boar became unimportant, as they knew where it was and someone could pick it up later.

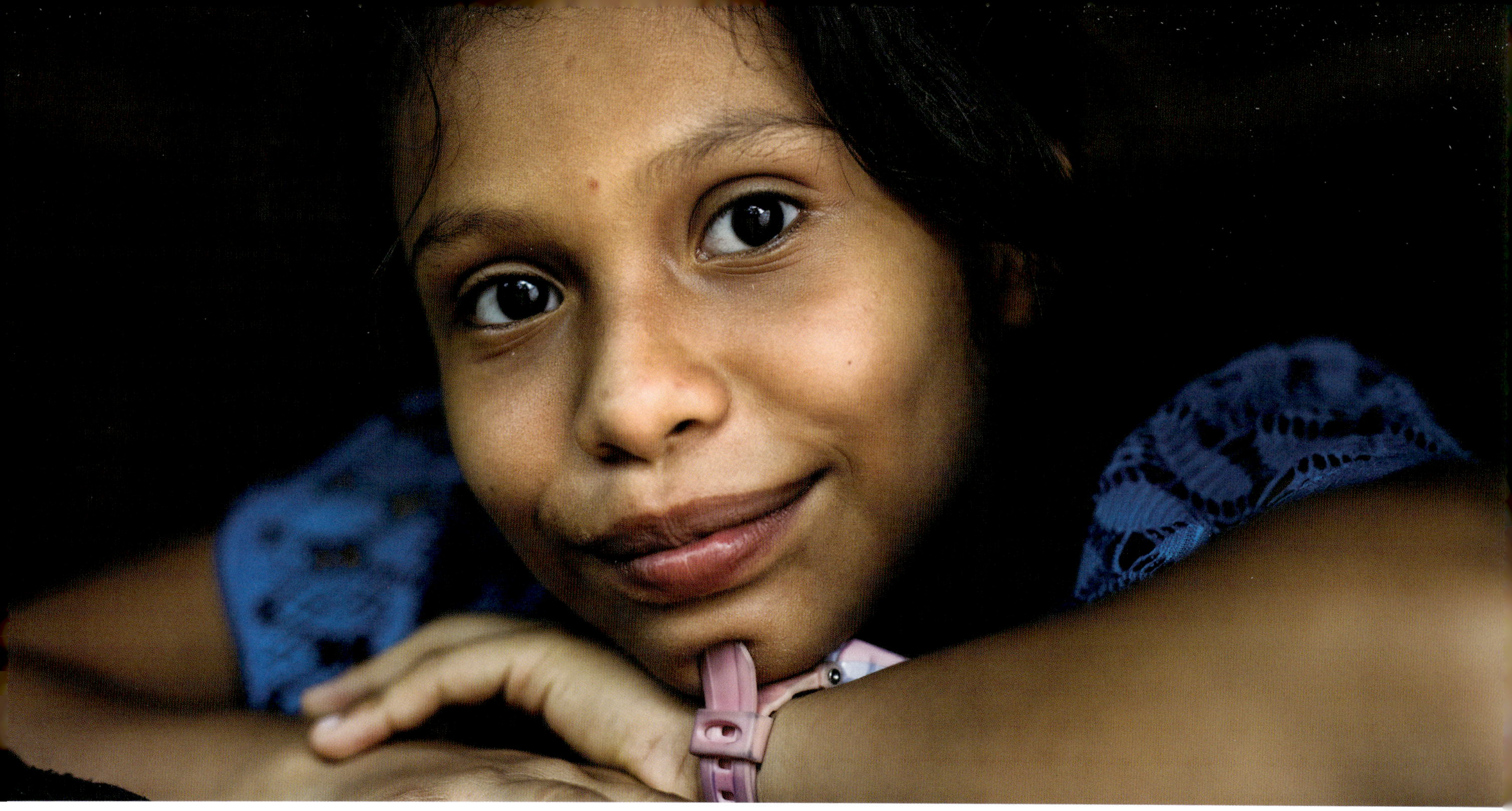

**Lisandro Porras**
Talamanca. 58 years old

Lisandro is one of the 48 *awá* (indigenous doctors) who live in Talamanca. To become a doctor, he spent 10 years studying, from the age of 12 to 22. During that time, he dedicated himself exclusively to his studies, as Sibú needs a mind that's totally open to receive knowledge. For *kíkipa awá* (grandfather doctors), the most important thing in life is to transmit their oral tradition to new generations, preventing the disappearance of ancestral knowledge. Lisandro has five children, and two of his grandchildren are currently studying medicine as apprentices of *awá*. This profession is essentially masculine, and doctors like Lisandro are responsible for preserving the knowledge of their communities through song. They sing at purification ceremonies when new members of the community are born, and they sing to treat ailments of the body. Lisandro advises that you plant during the new moon, and he prefers dark earth to red, as the latter is "bad for planting."

But they were many hours from the village, and the time it would take to treat the bite would mean the difference between life and death for his father.

Lisandro had already been studying for six years to become an *awá*, a Bribri doctor. His grandfather trained him, according to tradition, from the age of 12 to 22. While they walked, helping his father hobble along, he debated with himself. Lisandro knew something the others didn't, and he preferred not to reveal it until they reached the village: The plant they used as a remedy against fer-de-lance venom, which had saved his father's life on four previous occasions, was scarce at that time and might not be enough for the months of treatment he would need.

That adventure, which now seemed so long ago, had ended in an encounter with a *sicua* doctor at the Tony Facio Hospital in Limón who couldn't understand how his father had survived four fer-de-lance bites without antivenin, ironically in one of the countries that produces the largest quantity and exports it to the world.

While his father recovered, the doctor showed great curiosity about their ancestral practices, and this awoke in him a curiosity about the world of *sicua* medicine.

After that encounter they never met again, but it was enough that Lisandro still remembers him as a friend.

• **Indigenous people make up 2.4% of Costa Rica's population.**

Then he remembered an incident when he turned 28. All the *kíkipa* (grandfather *awá*) in Talamanca gathered at the Association of Indigenous People in Cachabri to discuss a communique from the Ministry of Health that prohibited the practice of natural medicine without a degree that accredited them as doctors.

They invited outside doctors to listen to the words of the *kíkipa*. The encounter was initially tense, as the Bribri refused to speak Spanish, because to speak their truth it had to be in the Bribri language.

The translators explained to the *sicua* doctors about plants, about the cycles of the moon and the rain. They explained why it's more effective to plant in the forest than in a garden; they told them how much to cut and how much to plant; they related how their knowledge isn't written down anywhere, but exists in the hearts and minds of the awá, in part because many didn't know how to write, and in part because it implied a connection with the environment.

Lisandro tried to make them see that their knowledge comes from observation, or in other words, from Sibú, the Bribri god, just as the information and ultimately the health of the *sicua* people are in the hands of the *sicua* god.

The *sicua* doctors offered the *awá* doctors an opportunity to come and work in their clinics. "That won't work," they answered. "A *sicua* doctor heals in a clinic, and an *awá* heals in his home."

At the end of the meeting, the doctors proposed that if the indigenous people couldn't cure a patient, they could send him to a hospital. The *awá* community returned the suggestion: If they couldn't cure a patient, the *awá* would be happy to receive him. The exchange set a historic precedent for the Bribri community and for the country.

When they arrive at the airport in Barcelona, his bag full of medicinal plants emerges on a conveyor belt, just as his friend Leila had promised.

**Written by: Sergio Pucci Golcher**

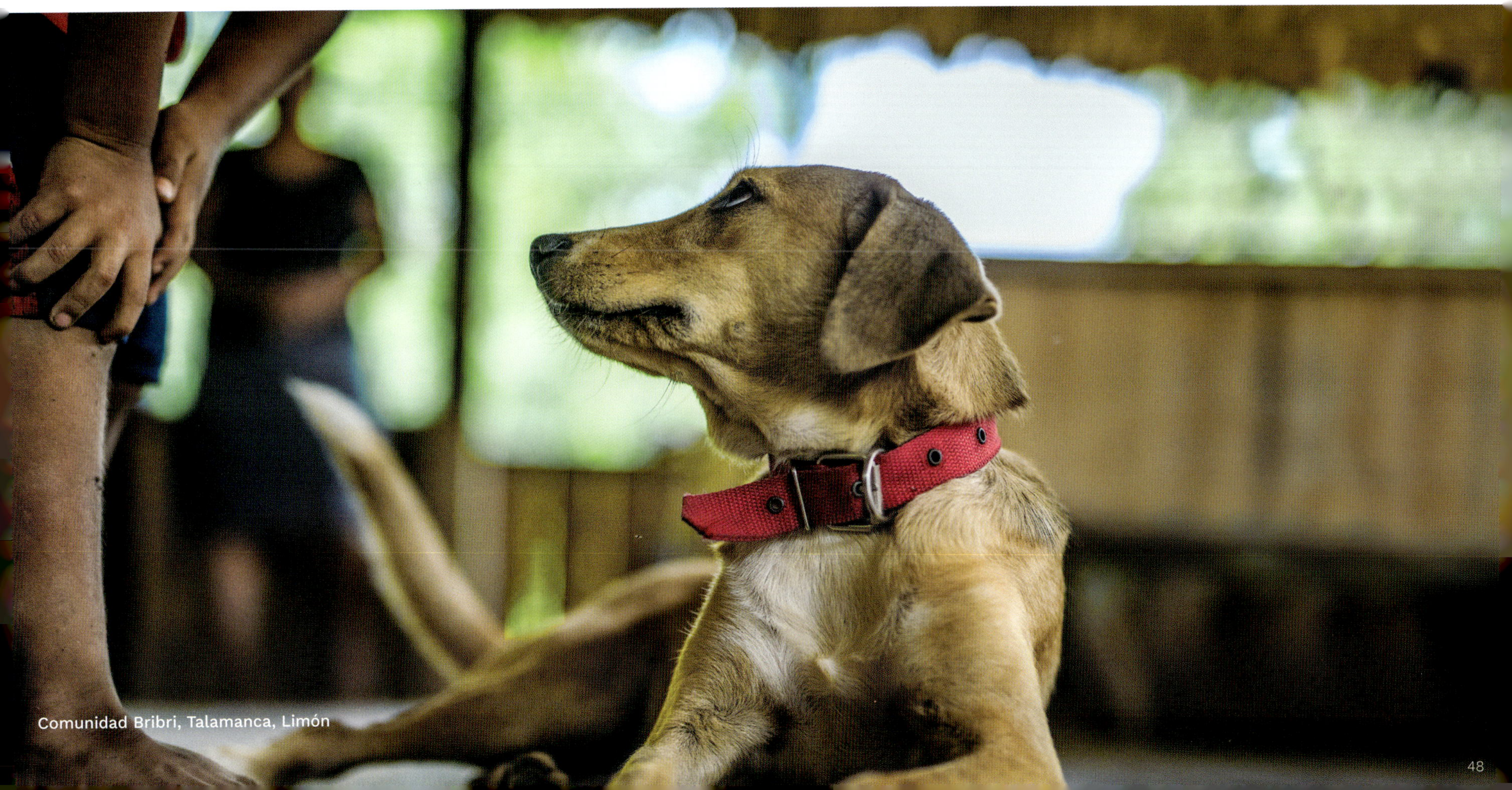

Comunidad Bribri, Talamanca, Limón

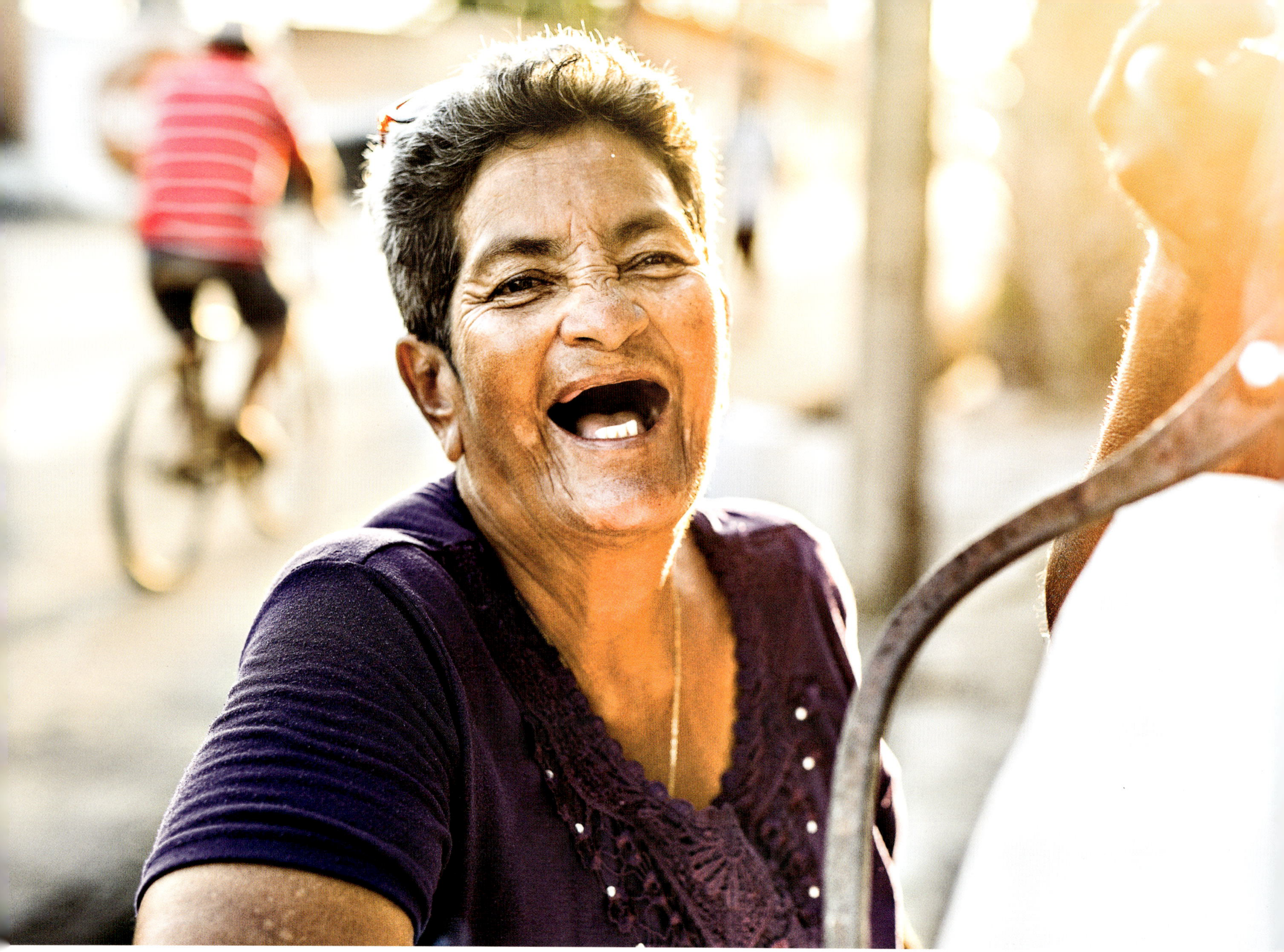

# THE NIGHT I DANCED THE BOLERO

They say that one time two lovers went into the ocean and came out with only one leg each. There were a lot of sharks here. That's why people preferred to go swimming in the Baths, because it had a fence.

By day, the Baths was a spa, but at night it turned into a dancehall. The dance floor was the only part that had a roof, and the rest was pure sun and sand, all surrounded by a fence reaching all the way into the sea. If you can imagine, it's where the big sign is today that says "Puntarenas." It was huge — almost the whole town could fit in there. I can tell you that confidently, because there they did the

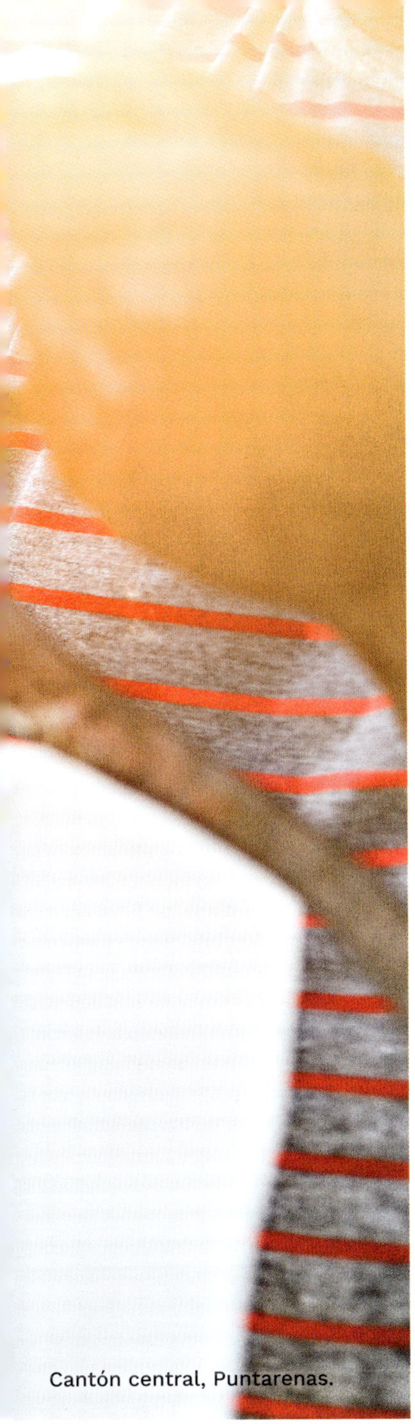

Cantón central, Puntarenas.

## MY MOTHER WAS WAITING FOR ME WITH THE CORD OF AN ELECTRIC IRON

"Oldies Dance" every year, and all of us went.

That dance happened once a year, and we all looked forward to it. The first band started playing at 7 p.m. and the last one finished at 6 a.m. All the greatest bands came: the Billos Caracas Boys, the Sonora Santanera, and Gilberto Hernández himself. I knew them all, especially Gilberto Hernández, who was a native of Puntarenas. He was a childhood friend of my father's. Once they were adults, he would always look for my father to go out and party. I called him "Uncle", like he was part of the family. When he played at the Oldies Dance, I was allowed to get in free.

When I was 17, I went out every weekend dancing with my friends. There were 12 of us, all living on the same street.

We always dressed up nice. No pants, no torn tennis shoes. To go to the dance? We always wore dresses and high-heeled shoes. And the men wore shirts with buttons and leather shoes, well polished! The shine on those shoes was what drove you crazy.

We went down the street picking each other up. I was the first to leave my house because I lived the farthest away. When we were outside the house of one of our friends, we'd give them a shout to come on out. When they did, each of the mothers would say, "You go there alone, you come home alone." Period. Besides, there was a firm curfew: 11 at night. We always obeyed.

We would arrive and push three tables together to sit down and wait for men to ask us to dance. There was one group of 12 boys who also went dancing every weekend. I liked one of them, but he never asked me to dance.

When it was almost 11, to get away from the boys and get home on time, we would give each other a sign and pretend to go to the bathroom. But in fact, we jumped over the fence and went running along the sand of the beach. We had so much fun on the way home, everybody running.

Until the Oldies Dance. One year, some boys came from the capital. Between them and the dozen boys who always went, they competed to get us to dance, and I'm sure that was why the boy I liked finally asked me. It was almost 11 p.m. and Gilberto Hernández was playing. When he saw me dancing with the boy, he started playing my favorite "bolerito," a classic love song.

That night I left at 6 a.m., and I stepped on a little rock and felt a sharp pain. When I took off my shoe, I saw that it had a hole in it! I had not only danced the night away, I had danced my shoe away.

When I got home, my mother was waiting for me with the cord of an electric iron. "Get ready for this, little lady!" But it was worth it, because that boy was the one I married.

**Written by: Libertad Sobrado**

**María Cecilia Cantillo Cantillo**
Puntarenas
Born April 5, 1954

María Cecilia is a street vendor who has always lived in downtown Puntarenas. Even though she was born in Guanacaste, she's never gone to visit that place — the day after she was born, she came to Puntarenas, the town in which she spent her life. There she married (her husband has since died), and they had three children. She works in one of the port town's most important and iconic jobs: selling snow cones. She's a great dancer who spent much of her youth in the dance halls. She still loves to dance.

**María Elena Rivera Garita**
Cartago – Moravia
Born Oct. 13, 1991

María Elena was born in Cartago, studied tourism and worked in hotels for a while. She's one of the new representatives of the local gastronomy scene, and working as a coffee barista, she's in one of the most important emerging professions in this country. She's currently head barista at the Restaurante Franco in Barrio Escalante, and she competes at a national and international level. She was the national barista champion in 2019, and she competed in Boston for the world championship with baristas from about 60 countries, qualifying for the semifinals. She comes from a family of coffee growers, and the product runs in her veins: "Coffee reminds me of my grandmother." Sometimes she breaks down in tears after a competition.

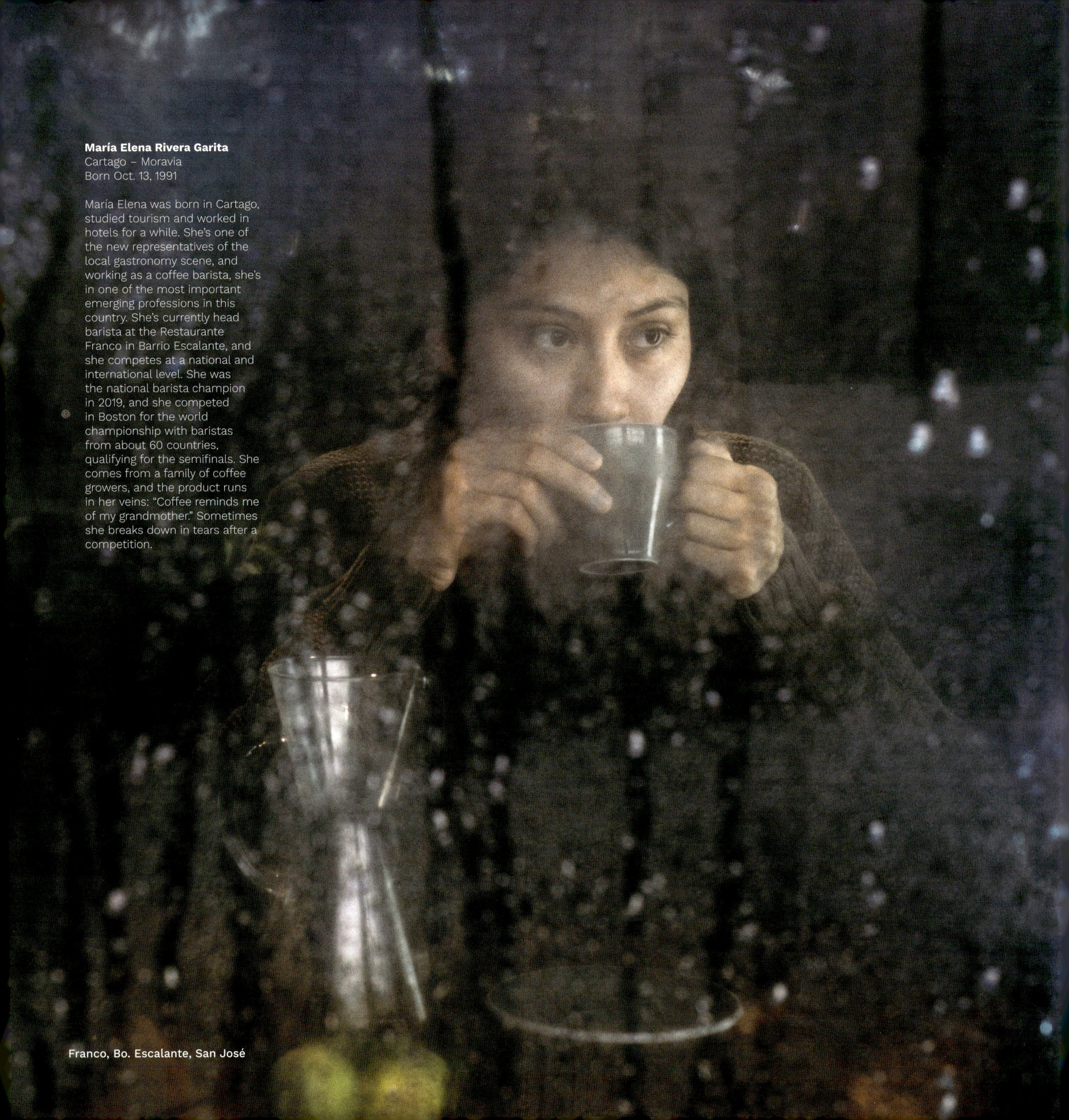

Franco, Bo. Escalante, San José

# THE MOUNTAIN

Like a single organism, the group accommodates itself to the lack of benches on the plaza. It's 7 a.m. at the Plaza de la Cultura. What they don't know about hiking, they make up for in enthusiasm and in the instructions of the more experienced: To climb the Pico Blanco hill, you have to arrive early and climb aboard a pickup truck, making room for the bicycle someone brought, and once on top of the hill, you have to carefully crawl through the barbed-wire fence and start making your descent down the slope.

María Elena is pretty cautious, and she's the last to squeeze through the little gap. Her grandfather taught her a fundamental respect for the mountain. With one hand she holds the barbed wire for the others, and with the other she holds some coffee she bought on the road, which she can't help comparing to the coffee her grandfather brewed on a wood stove, which she carries in a plastic bottle.

Up in the mountain, there's a group of people having a picnic, there are cows and there are also signs of civilization on the river they crossed with the water up to their knees, until they arrived at a beautiful waterfall.

Or at least that's what María Elena would later repeat in her head. She was used to trusting in her feelings, living largely from intuition, in which she can distinguish the aroma of a Caracolillo coffee from the Tarrazú region and a less floral variety from the Naranjo region. She has confidence in the intuitive knowledge passed down by her grandfather.

Three hours have passed since they started descending the mountain and the trail smells different — it smells like the *lack* of a trail — and the closer the sun is to setting, the more it illuminates what everyone in the group is thinking: They're lost.

The guy with the bicycle suggests that he ride ahead looking for a way out, and then return to the group, but he doesn't do it. María thinks, "He's got it easy, what a dummy!" But she holds her tongue for now, better not to get irritated or resentful with anybody. The mountain knows your intentions, her grandfather would say. "Grandpa, do you believe in goblins?" Elena once asked while she helped him remove weeds and prepare products for the farmers' market. "No, not really," he said, "but I do believe in the mountain."

The baby starts crying and the mother sings to her. María Elena puts on her headphones so as not to think about the stories of goblins who get people lost, tempting them, for example, by luring them to a waterfall. She also doesn't want to think about how you shouldn't follow their tracks because their feet are backwards, so when it looks like they're moving away, in fact they're getting closer.

"We shouldn't have brought a baby," she tells herself. "It's been six hours," she tells herself. "All that stuff about goblins is nonsense; everything I heard on my uncle's farm doesn't count, I was a small girl," she tries to tell herself.

"The mountain is getting revenge," thinks María Elena, "for that time I went to the beach when they told me my grandfather had died, he was gone, and I couldn't be with him. And now the mountain is getting us lost, and the closer you get to a tree, the farther away it looks." Her heart is beating fast and she feels like crying. But the feeling goes away when her headphones play a reggae song from Black Uhuru that she once played for her grandfather, and he started dancing, and suddenly she smells recently brewed coffee.

"Here it is, I found the fence!" says their friend with the bicycle. Elena sees some diminutive tracks on the ground heading toward the exit, but she knows to stay silent, she sees the mountain and she exhales loudly. Upon completing each barista test in the future she will feel an inexplicable need to cry, but that will come later, and for now she's just thinking about returning home and making the best coffee the world has ever smelled.

**Written by: Luis Salazar**

**• Of our export products, coffee is the only one that we have exported for more than 200 years.**

# METAL TEETH

"El vibráfono no es difícil de tocar, es difícil de jalar"

The Caribbean is a cauldron where the best seasonings on the planet are thrown into the stew. The Central American isthmus is a fundamental part of this setting, where the African population, the indigenous peoples and the European conquerors became one, for better and for worse. Our essence of diaspora, movement and contradiction was the soup that cooked the sound, the *guaguancó*, the *calypso*, the *murga*, the *palo de mayo* and the *punta* dance. Rhythm is in our DNA. His blood, inescapably faithful to his roots, was what set Felipe on a path, as if on a blimp traveling from San José to New York.

"Hello? Felipe, how are you? Come on over! We're having a party at the hotel. I've been talking about you for a half-hour to the other guys. Come! Residente and all its people are here!"

Felipe was in a taxi with his wife, Argelia, on the way to meet the girls of Mariachi Flor de Toloache to celebrate their surprising recent Grammy win, but on the other end of the phone, the "Poet of Salsa" was demanding his presence, so he asked the taxi driver to turn around, while he called the other people to let them know that they would arrive a bit later.

The streetlights illuminated the face of Felipe while he returned to the hotel where they awaited him anxiously. The way circumstances wove together to reach this point in his life were unforgettable. That concert with Son de Tikizia, when he delighted Cheo Feliciano with his style of playing the vibraphone, with his father and uncle crying tears of pride to see him playing next to a salsa master, was such a stroke of luck that years later, while he was studying in Puerto Rico, he was hired to record *"Eba Say Ajá,"* an album featuring Cheo and Rubén Blades.

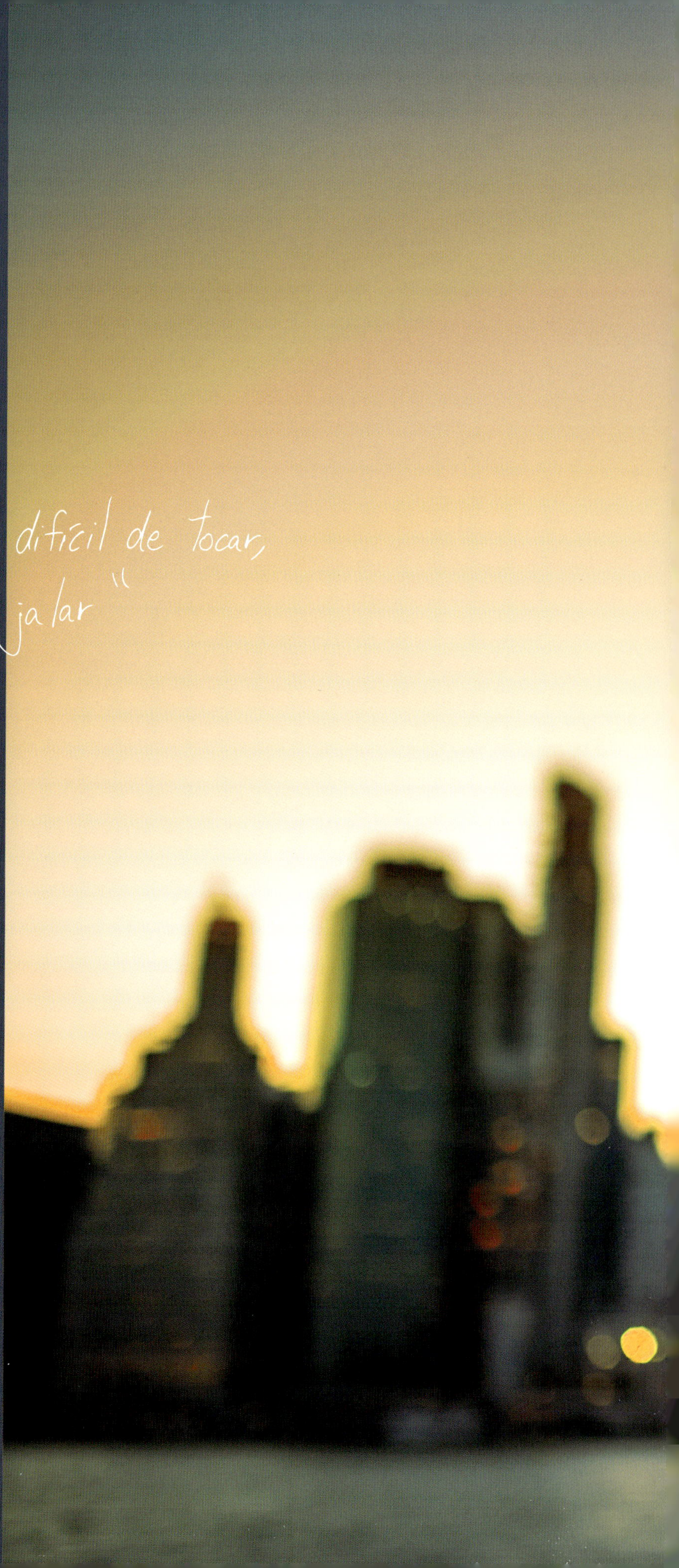

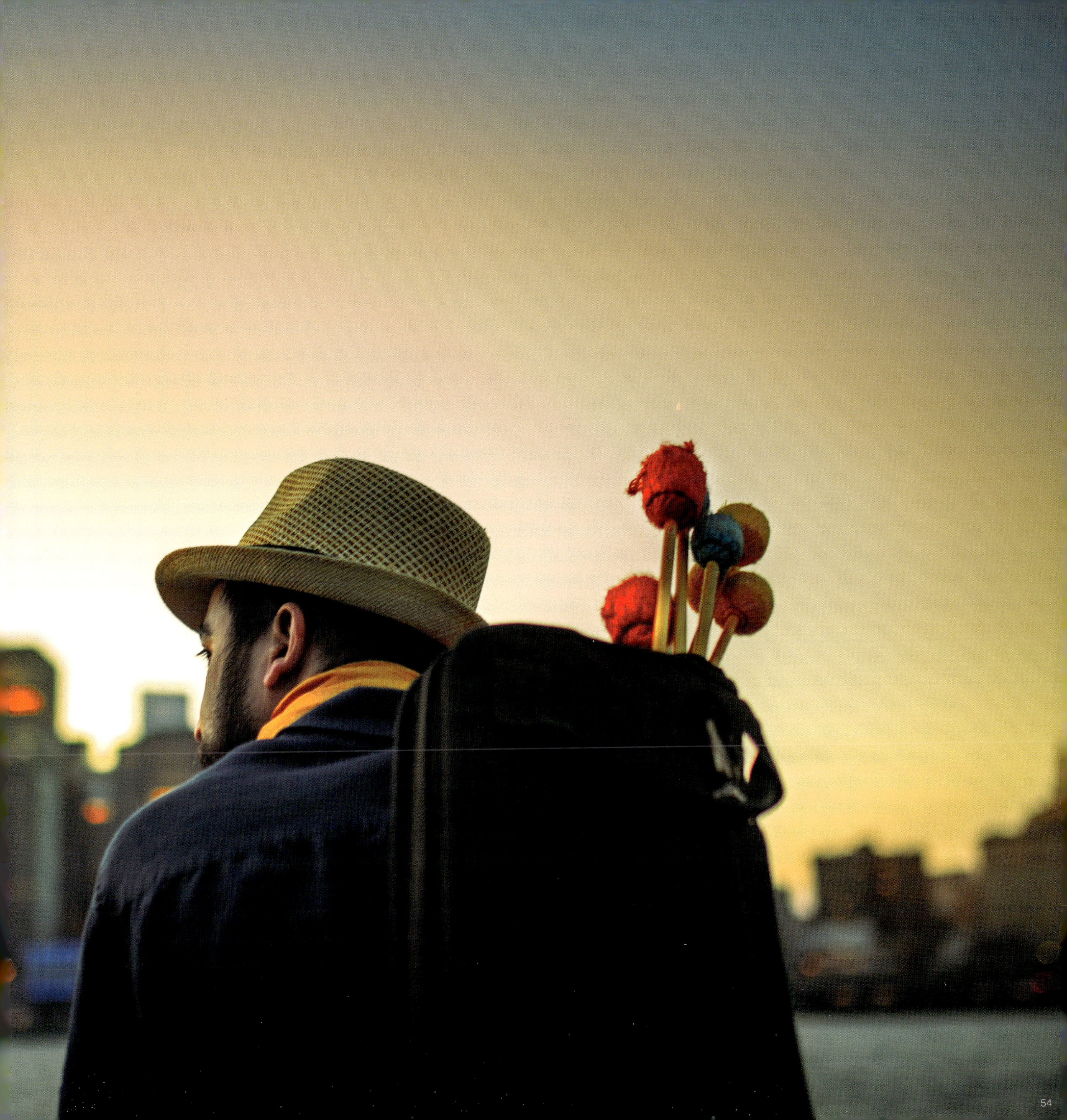

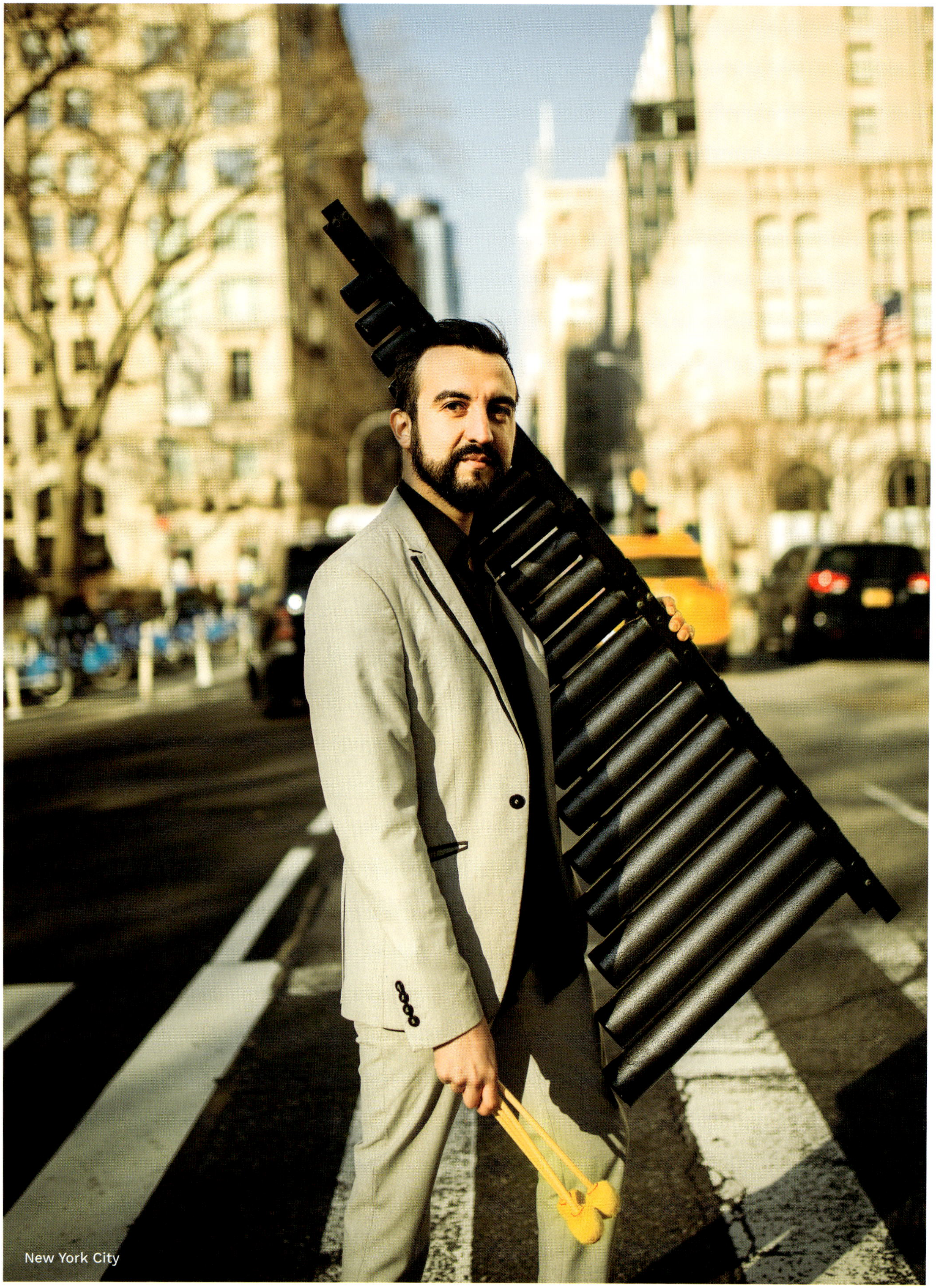
New York City

## DEDICATION AND HUMILITY

Once while he was in Mexico, he received a call from Daniel Aisemberg, who gave him some news that changed everything. He had shown Rubén Blades his arrangement for the song "Siembra," and with an impressed look on his face, he listened to the 11 minutes from beginning to end. He seemed to have a job offer for Felipe, which is why he and Argelia decided to go to New York. There wasn't enough work in Costa Rica, and he felt the Big Apple calling to him. After six months there, Felipe had a transcendental encounter with "El Flaco Navaja" ("the skinny knife"), a chameleonic New York artist, of the kind you don't know if they're coming or going.

"*Oye* you play the vibraphone, right? Look, I'm going to play this record — this vibraphonist is *cabrón*, one of the best I've ever heard. Do you know him?"

At that moment, the "metal teeth" of Felipe's vibraphone began to sound, like a boomerang, recalling that session with Cheo and Blades recorded a while back.

"Of course, man, that's me!"

"*Wat?* Are you *kiddin'* me? How can that be you? So you know Rubén, right'?"

"No, I don't know him. That was a recording I made on the recommendation of my piano teacher in Puerto Rico."

"No way! Let me call him!"

A meeting was set for the next day. Felipe showed up, barely believing what was happening. Rubén received him like someone he had known his whole life, and right there on his doorstep, he affirmed his intention of making him the musical director for his wife, Luba Mason, and he told him he was going to resolve his work visa immediately. They went into the living room and, with whiskey in hand, began a relationship that culminated in this moment, where Felipe was waiting outside the hotel room, about to be received at a grand Caribbean party. Between songs and merriment, Rubén spoke up and gave a speech in honor of Felipe. Relaxed and in the cadence he was known for, he spoke of effort, dedication and humility, of Central American brotherhood and mutual admiration.

Felipe sees New York as a big campus, where his spirit stays on earth but his music is pushed to the limits, alert to how the game is played, like that young man of 15 in front of a vibraphone at the Castella Conservatory, feeling love at first glance.

**Written by: Fabricio Walker**

**Felipe Fournier Soto**
Bronx, New York, USA
Born Sept. 22, 1985

A Latin Grammy-winning producer, vibraphone player, percussionist, arranger and educator. A graduate in Caribbean jazz and music from the Music Conservatory of Puerto Rico, he also studied percussion and education at the National University of Costa Rica. In 2017, he won the Latin Grammy for Best Mariachi/Ranchero Album for producing "Las caras lindas" ("The Beautiful Faces") by Mariachi Flor de Toloache. He was nominated for the Grammy and Latin Grammy with Charlie Sepúlveda, Néstor Torres, Rubén Blades and Cheo Feliciano. He's lived in New York since 2013 and is musical director of "Supermambo! A Vibes Tribute to Tito Puente," "Triangle" by Luba Mason, and the folkloric ballet NEPANTLA. He also plays with Luisito Quintero, Axel Tosca, Xiomara Laugart, Jarana Beat and the Consoul Big Band. Felipe is an "odd duck," as fame is not important to him and he doesn't feel special for knowing famous people. His most sincere relationship is with music and not with show business. He comes from a family of musicians; his great-grandfather was a circus musician. He studied music because of the influence of his father, Diego, who always insisted on the importance of academic training: "My father made me study because he felt like less of a musician because he couldn't read music, but to me he was a greater musician than many. He could play anything by ear, from Shakira to Beethoven."

- **Around 6% of Costa Ricans live outside the country.**

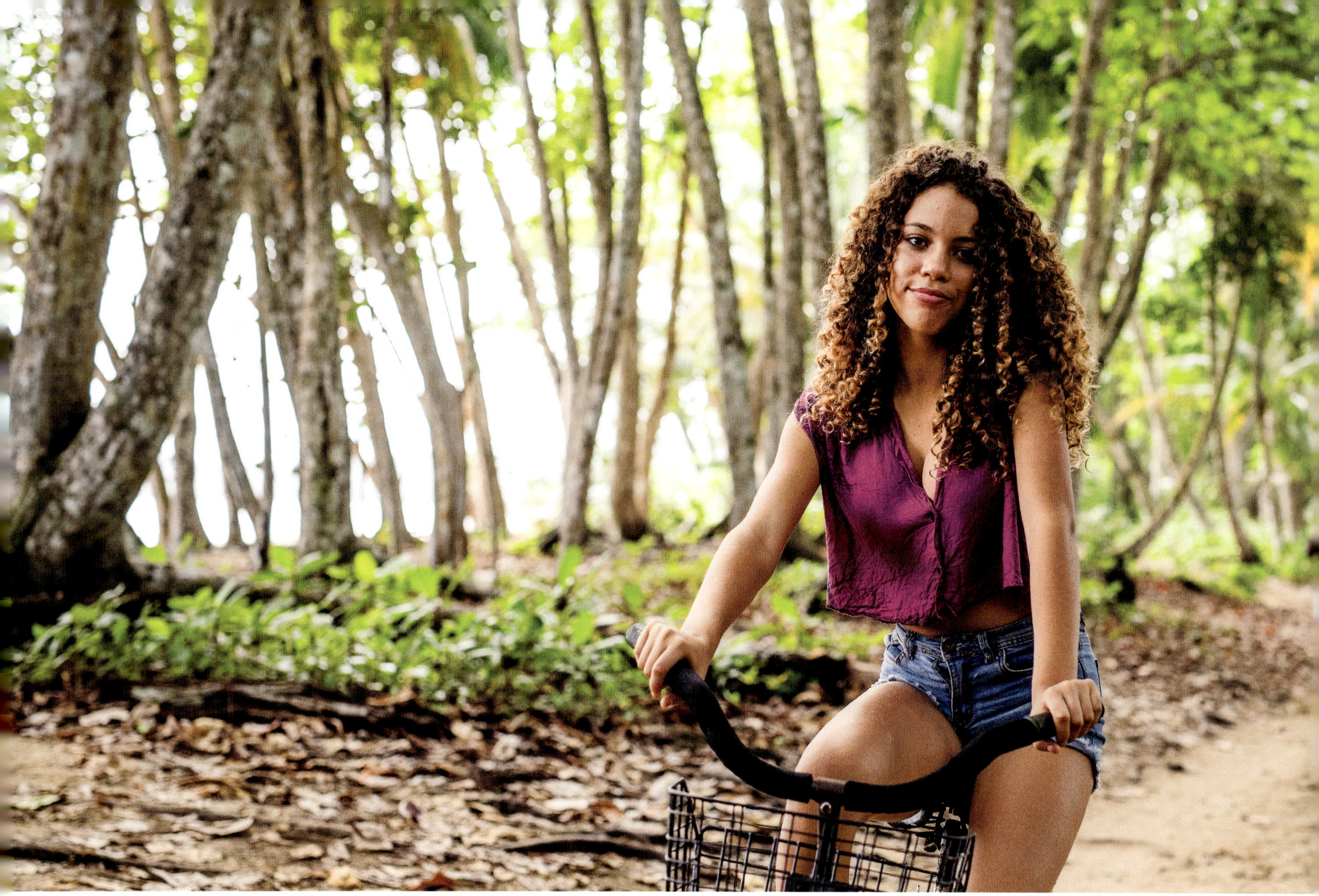

**Jubanel Taylor Larrauri**
Playa Chiquita
Born Oct. 7, 2005

Jubanel is the fencing champion of Central America in the "cadet" category (under 17). She has been national champion in the under-14 category and champion of the National Games in the under-14, cadet and major categories (all ages). The daughter of an African-Costa Rican man and a white Argentinian woman, Jubanel is from a region where people of different social classes mix with few distinctions, and she feels very proud of that. She's an animal lover who as a child was a big activist and a volunteer at the Puerto Viejo animal rescue center.

# HER NAME IS JUBANEL

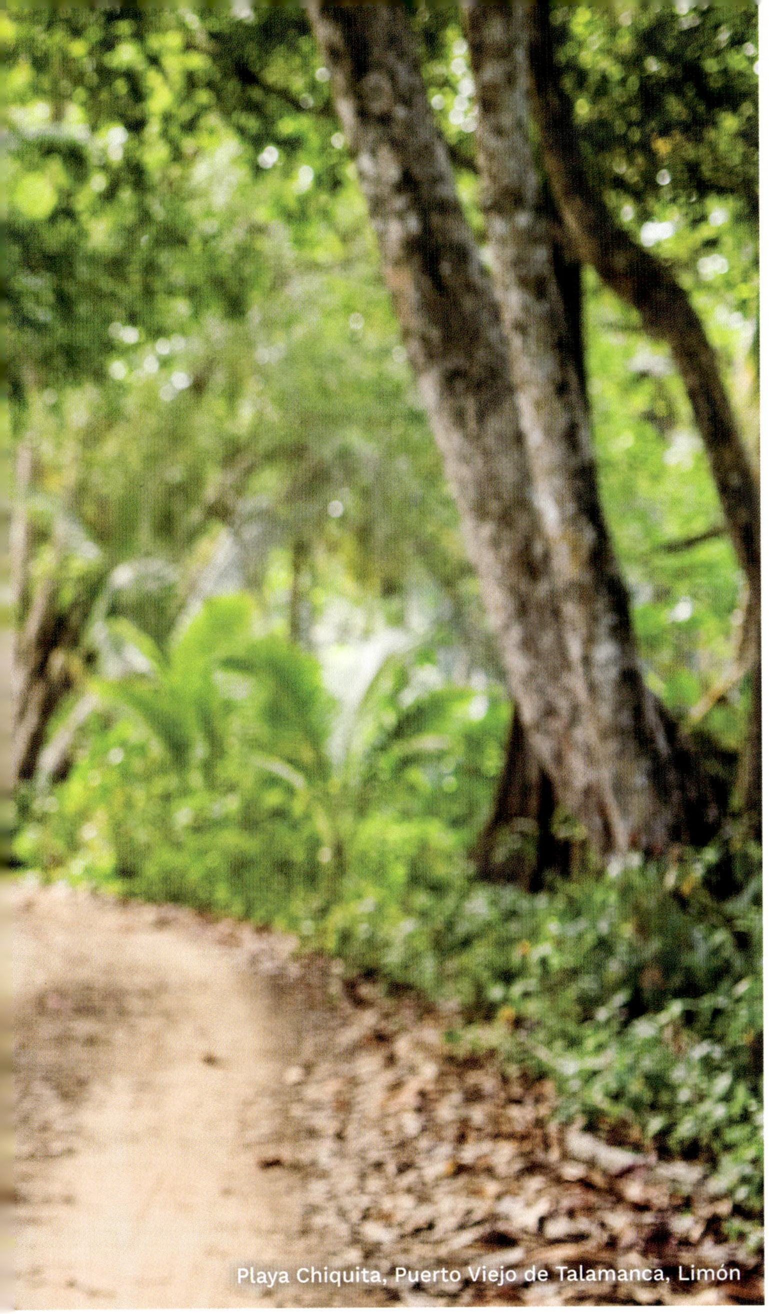

Playa Chiquita, Puerto Viejo de Talamanca, Limón

Her name isn't just a name. It's a vision. A way of understanding that which surrounds us. Ijuba Jubane means a butterfly of the night that moves toward the light. *Ijuba-Juba-Juba-Juba-Jubane*. A week before her birth, a nocturnal butterfly landed on the left shoulder of Silvestre, her father, and stayed there for the entire time it took him to descend a hill. The girl started to move her wings and to change the destiny of her life long before she entered this world. A seer had recommended to Maitena, her mother, that the name ended in "el" to take advantage of the vibration in pronouncing it.

The night before her birth, Maitena woke up to the sound of drums from the band Amon Zulú that was playing at Café Viejo. *Ijuba-Juba-Juba-Juba-Jubane*, and she decided to go dancing. That's how beneath the foliage made shiny by heavy showers, under the lights in a tree-covered bower full of tables and hammocks, with the people dancing to calypso under the palms and the banana fronds, with the sea in the background like an intermittent lullaby, Maitena's water broke and, without letting this rush her, kept dancing a while longer, until she decided to go to a friend's house, where at 5:05 in the morning, between the sounds of the howler monkeys and the smell of a joint, Ijuba Jubanel was born painlessly. Her birth brought the light of day.

Maitena is from Argentina, but she came to live in Costa Rica following the vision of a dream. Being a producer of a program of extreme sports, she did a feature on Edwin Salem, an Argentinian who surfed giant waves all over the world. He told her about Costa Rica, most of all about the sea, and about a small town full of black people. One night Maitena dreamed of some hot springs where Edwin Salem came looking for her on a bicycle to take her to a place called Punta Uva. From above, she saw the landscape, the bay, the cliff. She circled like a bird over that immense jungle she'd never seen before. The dream kept getting more intense: Maitena could enlarge the image, deepen the details. When she woke up, she turned on the television to a travel channel that was featuring Costa Rica. *Ijuba-Juba-Juba-Juba-Jubane*. All of this was too much coincidence, but ultimately it was the dream that propelled her to try her luck. When at last she arrived in Puerto Viejo for the first time, she had the impression that she had been there forever. And here she met Silvestre Taylor and knew immediately — with the intuition for which she is known — that this descendant of the Zulu tribe was the man who would be the father of her child.

*Ijuba-Juba-Juba-Juba-Jubane*. From childhood, Juba had great sensitivity toward living beings. She rescued mice that were used to feed snakes at an animal rescue center. One day Silvestre was cleaning two huge red snappers on the seashore, and one started to revive. So Maitena told him: "Get that one before it escapes!" When Silvestre raised the machete to finish killing it, Juba interrupted: "Nooooo, it has eyes, Daddy, it has eyes!" And never again did she want to eat anything with eyes. Another day she tried to glue a lizard's tail back on with a hibiscus flower.

Since she was little, she has moved with enviable skill and dexterity: She had good finger coordination from the time she was one, and she started walking at 10 months. She never crawled, and she cried when they put her on her stomach. Maitena took her to the beach every day. There Juba learned to swim and to walk at the same time. She also learned to grab little fish with her hands and let them slide on her like little acrobats, because she learned to see the beauty in the ephemeral, in that which continually changes, because long before entering this world, Juba could already hear the breathing of the sea: *Ijuba-Juba-Juba-Juba-Jubane*.

"The light flapping of a butterfly's wings can be felt on the other side of the world."
Chinese proverb

**Written by: Carla Pravisani**

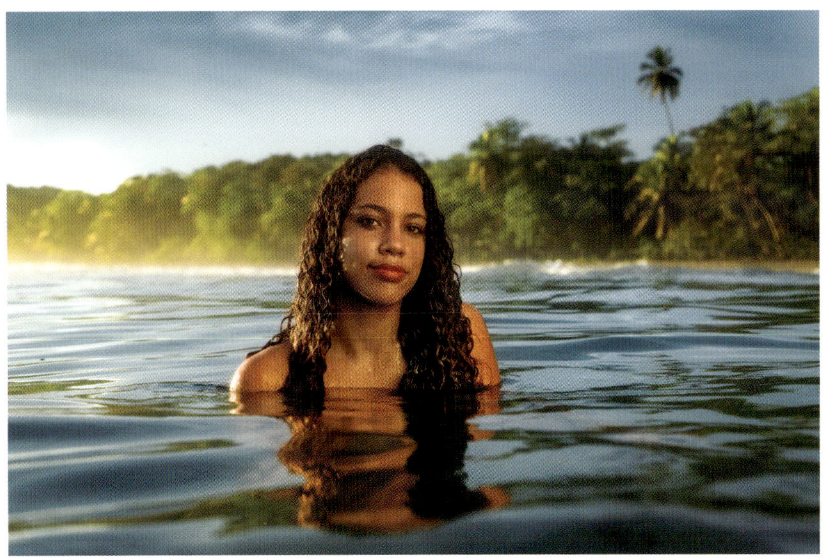

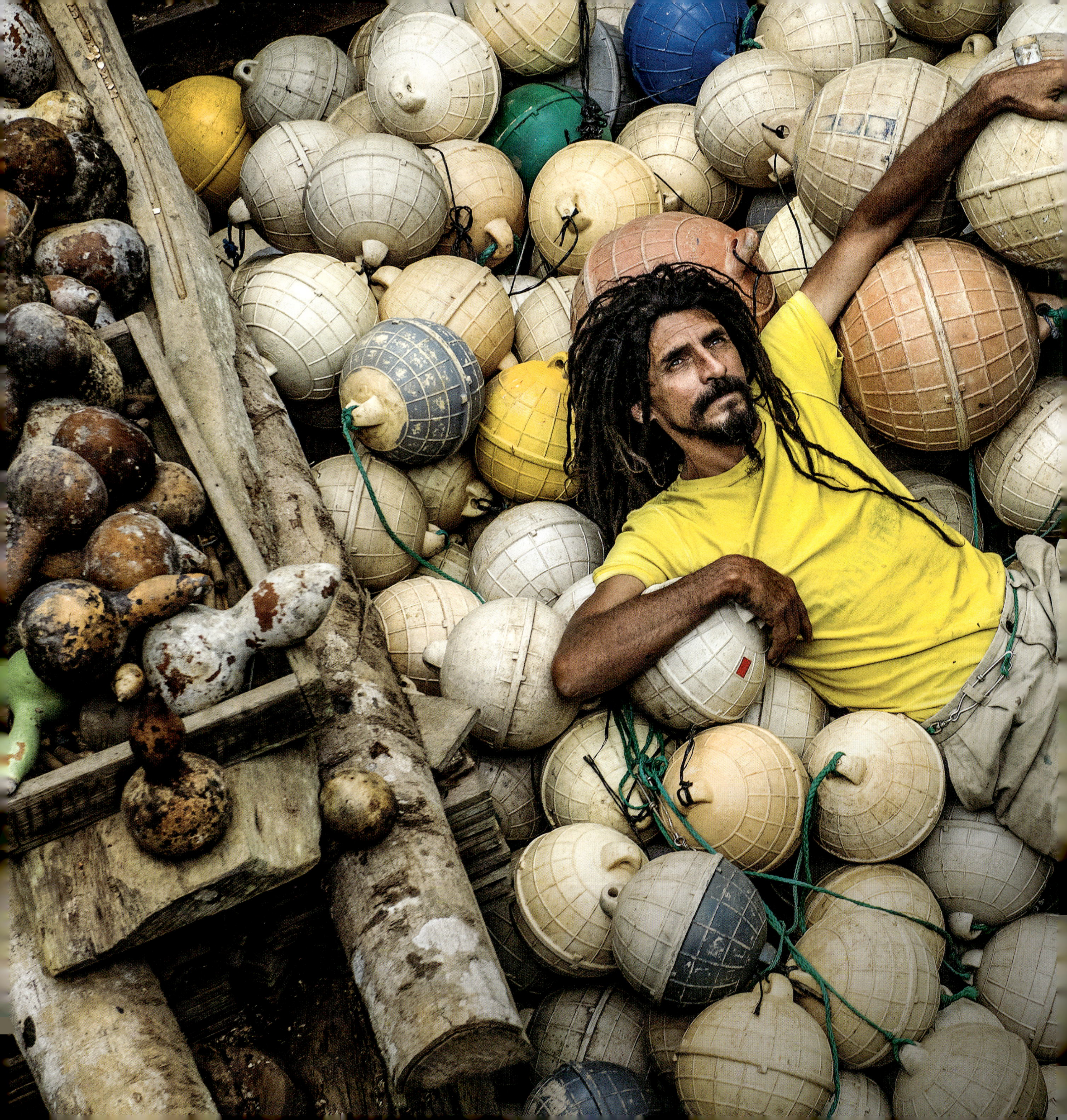

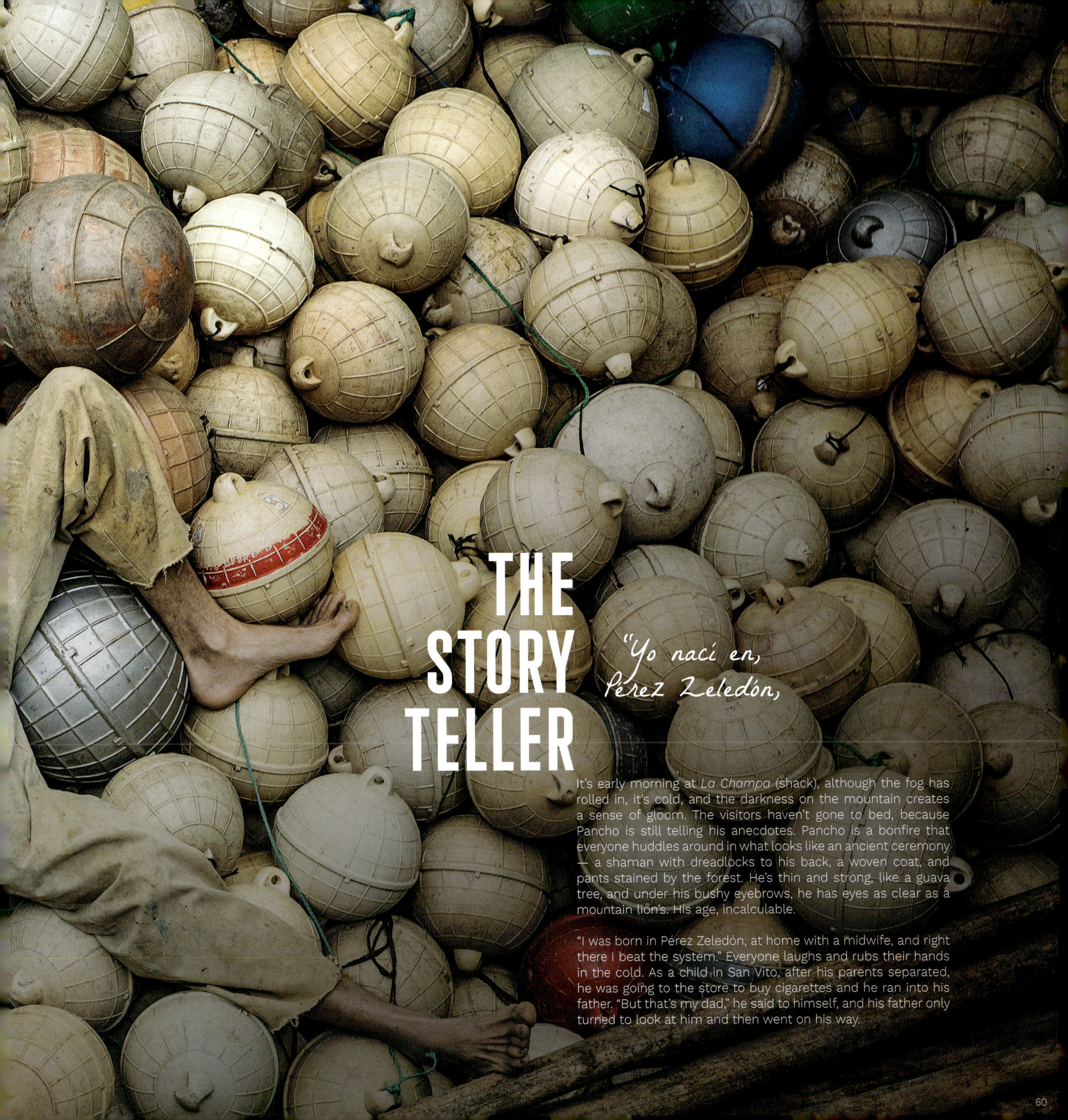

# THE STORY TELLER

*"Yo nací en, Pérez Zeledón,*

It's early morning at *La Champa* (shack), although the fog has rolled in, it's cold, and the darkness on the mountain creates a sense of gloom. The visitors haven't gone to bed, because Pancho is still telling his anecdotes. Pancho is a bonfire that everyone huddles around in what looks like an ancient ceremony — a shaman with dreadlocks to his back, a woven coat, and pants stained by the forest. He's thin and strong, like a guava tree, and under his bushy eyebrows, he has eyes as clear as a mountain lion's. His age, incalculable.

"I was born in Pérez Zeledón, at home with a midwife, and right there I beat the system." Everyone laughs and rubs their hands in the cold. As a child in San Vito, after his parents separated, he was going to the store to buy cigarettes and he ran into his father. "But that's my dad," he said to himself, and his father only turned to look at him and then went on his way.

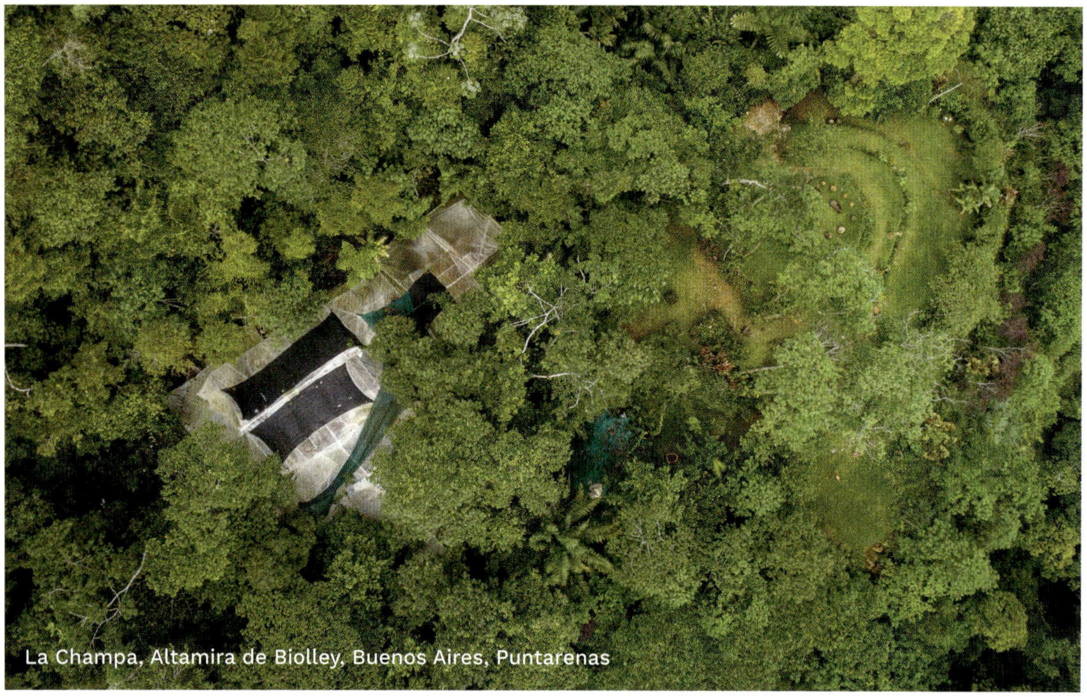

La Champa, Altamira de Biolley, Buenos Aires, Puntarenas

## A FROZEN GUST HIT US, AND WE ALL GOT GOOSEBUMPS

When he returned home from his errand, his mother said she had just been told that his father had died in an accident. For those of us sitting around, our blood runs cold.

I offer to make some coffee, and Pancho smiles, because he always wants coffee. I shake off the cold and go into *La Champa*. They say *La Champa* is an extension of Pancho's head — it's his masterpiece, an art installation. By day it's beautiful, but in the early morning its beauty blends with other sensations. The buoys and tree trunks with exposed roots hanging on the wall look like the faces of beings from another dimension. I make the coffee as fast as I can and return to the group. I find them hypnotized by another of Pancho's anecdotes:

"I had an opportunity to go to Isla del Coco back in the '90s. I was working at INBio, and I had a permit to go on the island, to explore and camp, a permission that nobody else had." He pauses, takes a sip of coffee and continues. "Coming down from Cerro Iglesias, I went to the Eugenio River, where there was a metal hanging bridge. On the other side of the bridge, I saw a man wearing a hat and clothes soiled by the mountain. I thought it was strange to see another person there, and dressed like me.

"I started to perceive his presence, and the guy didn't speak, but with a gesture he indicated that I can cross the bridge first. Crossing the bridge, I see that it's deteriorated, it creaked badly, like it was going to collapse, and as I approached the other side, the man's energy seemed to grow stronger. When I got there, he made room for me to pass, without speaking, but he greeted me with a gesture, and I kept walking. Later, I turned around to watch him cross the bridge, but he wasn't there anymore. Returning to the refuge, I asked about him, and nobody could explain. There were only three of us on the island." A frozen gust hit us, and we all got goosebumps.

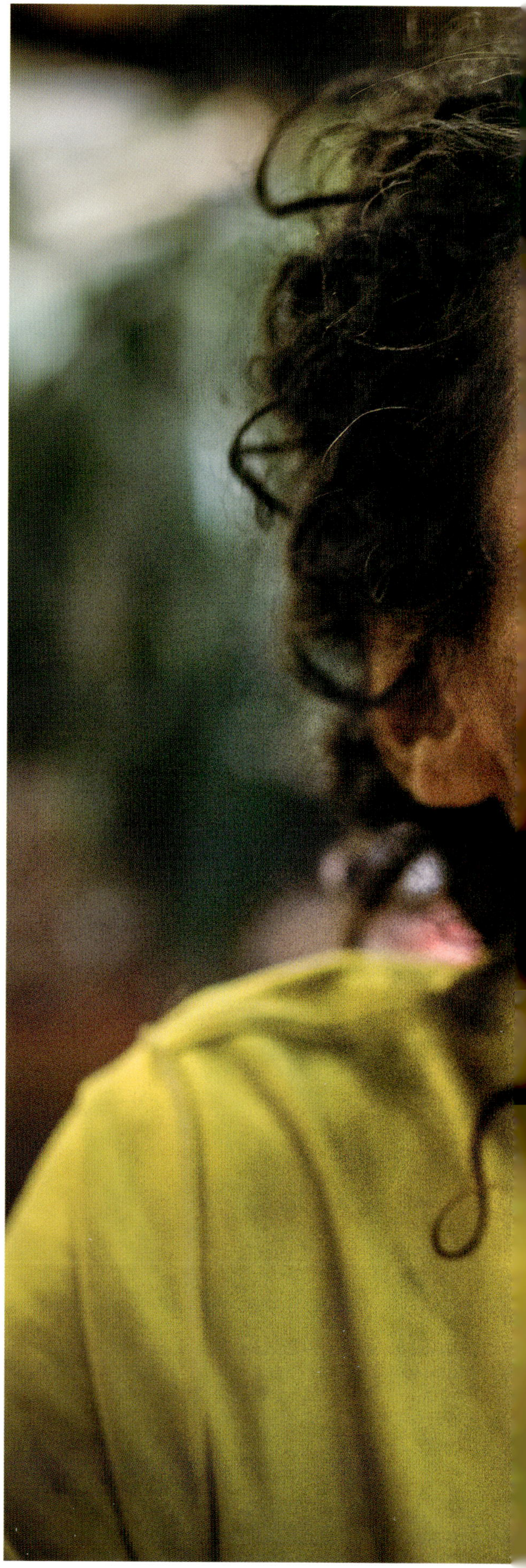

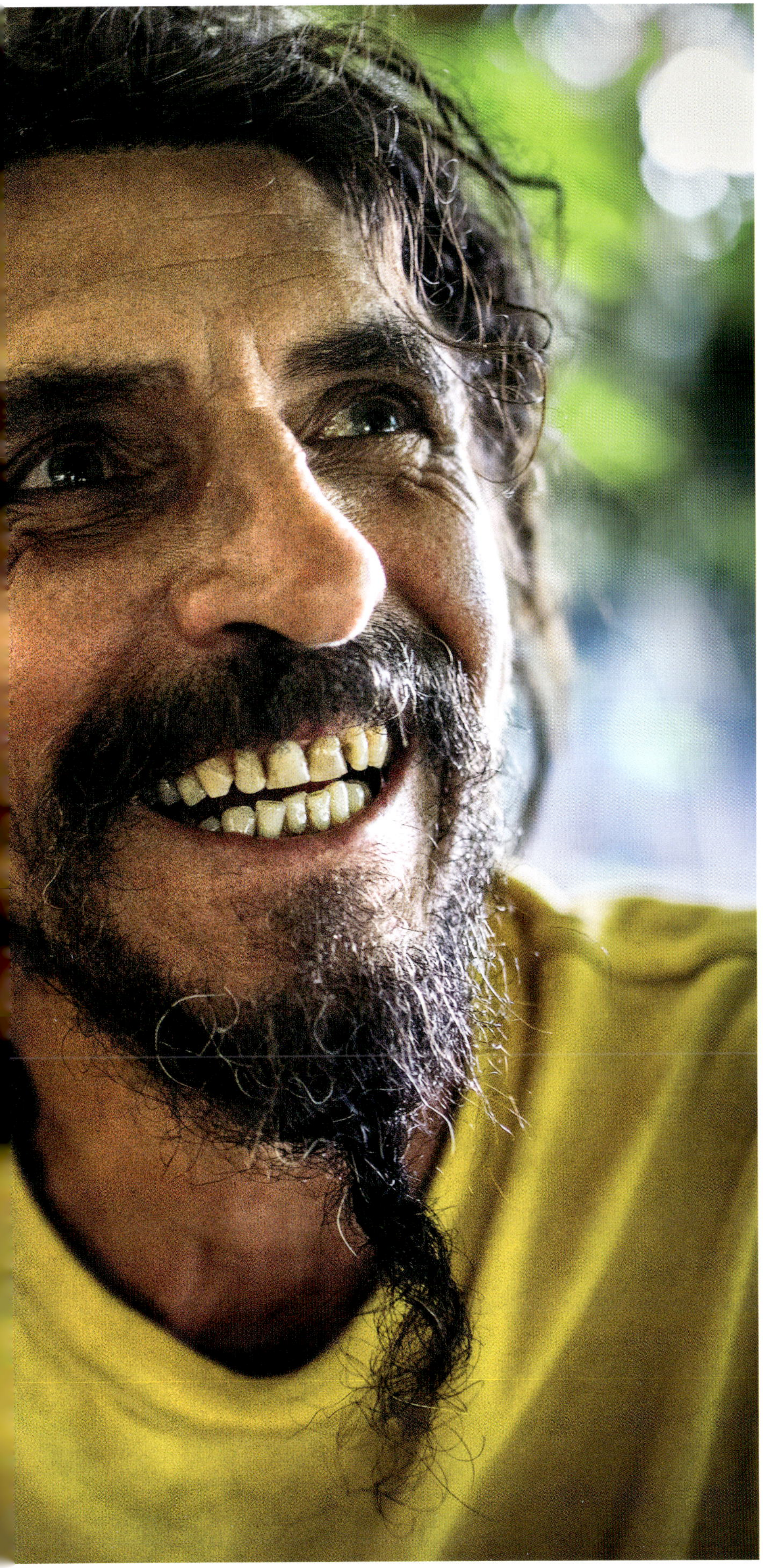

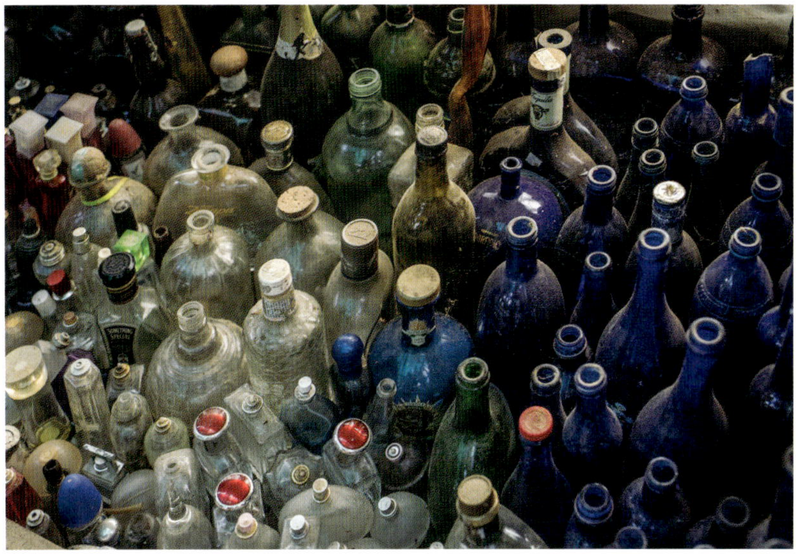

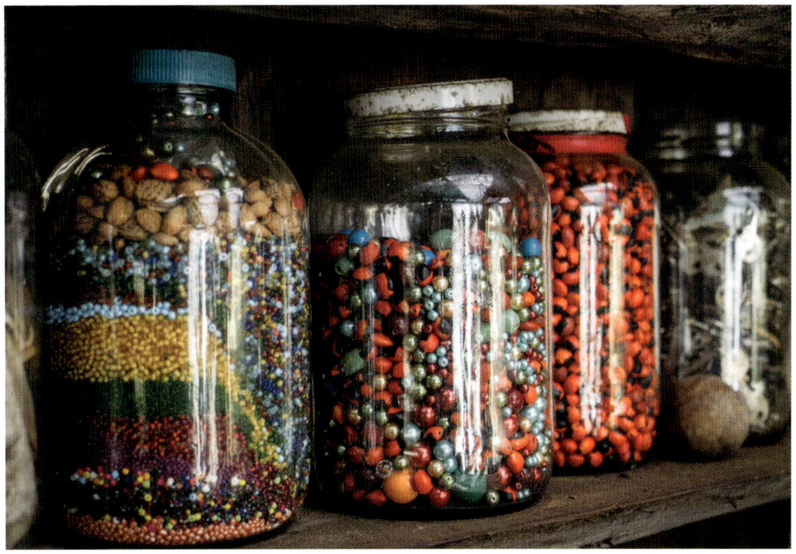

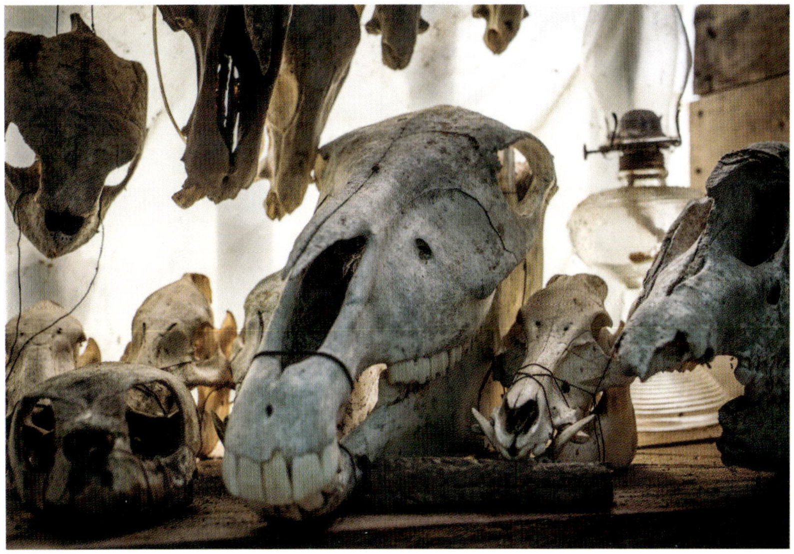

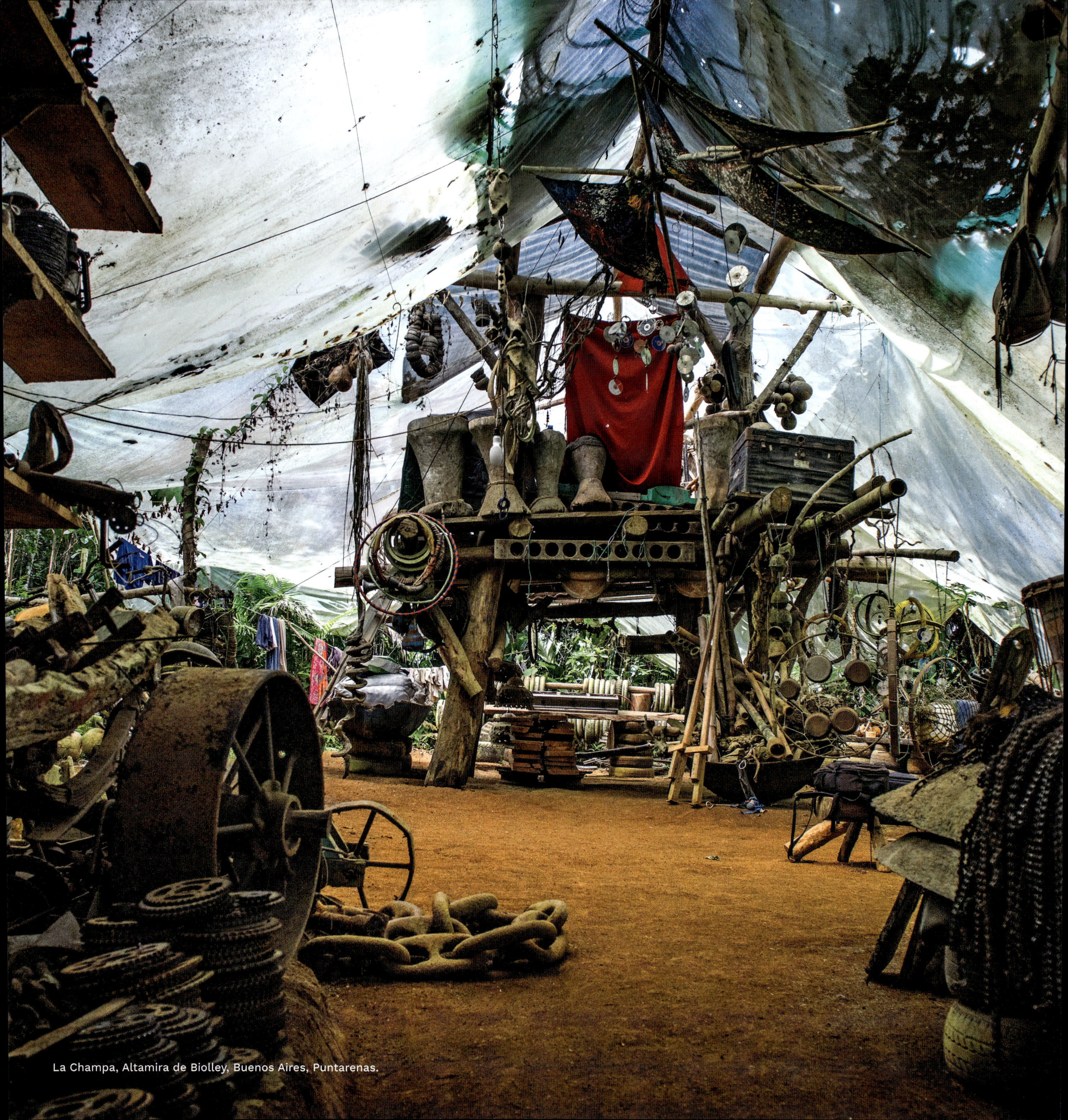

La Champa, Altamira de Biolley, Buenos Aires, Puntarenas.

Not long afterward, the river washed that bridge away. Pancho designed, engineered, and built a new one in the same place as that mysterious encounter, with recycled materials, fishing line, ropes, and buoys.

Maybe Pancho was commissioned to build that bridge by some supernatural means.

The Copey Bridge was named for one of the island's indigenous trees, which springs from its supports, putting down roots like a mangrove, in a fusion of nature and recycled waste materials.

There are some who think that Pancho is a direct connection with the universe, as his mountain lion eyes have seen things that no one else ever will, and in his mysticism he is open to realities hidden from less perceptive eyes.

**Written by: Jeison Herrera**

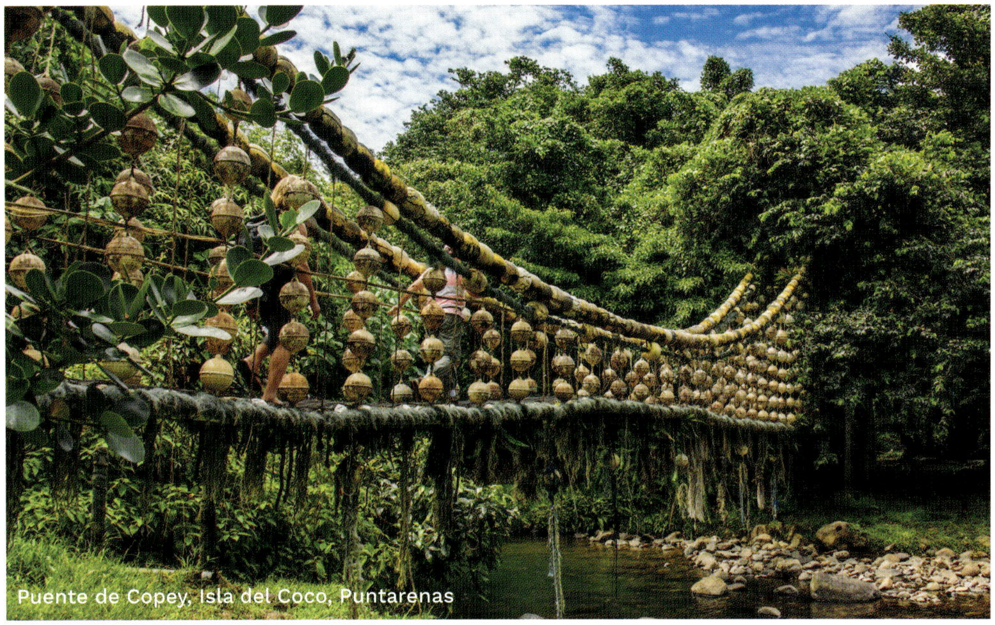
Puente de Copey, Isla del Coco, Puntarenas

**Francisco Javier Quesada Quesada, "Pancho"**
Altamira, La Amistad de Biolley
Born Dec. 17, 1964

A community activist and a mystic, Pancho "gamed the system" from birth, because he was born at home with the help of a midwife. He spent his first years in the country, but he migrated to San Isidro de El General in 1976 after the death of his father. There he became a musician and joined a choir, the school band, and a musical group called "Los Bruncas." But Pancho is into everything. He knows construction, ferrocement, drawing, Indian ink.... He studied for two years at a university, where he learned about the structure of drawing, and he was also involved in INBio, where he acquired knowledge of ecology and biology. He's the creator of various public works. He's also an artisan, and he grows materials for his colleagues. One of his greatest passions is the exchange of knowledge among the people he's involved with, and collectively building histories of things and the science behind them. For 26 years, he's lived in the mountains of Buenos Aires, Puntarenas, far from the city, studying, learning and sharing with anyone who comes near. Pancho has a daughter and is an avid reader.

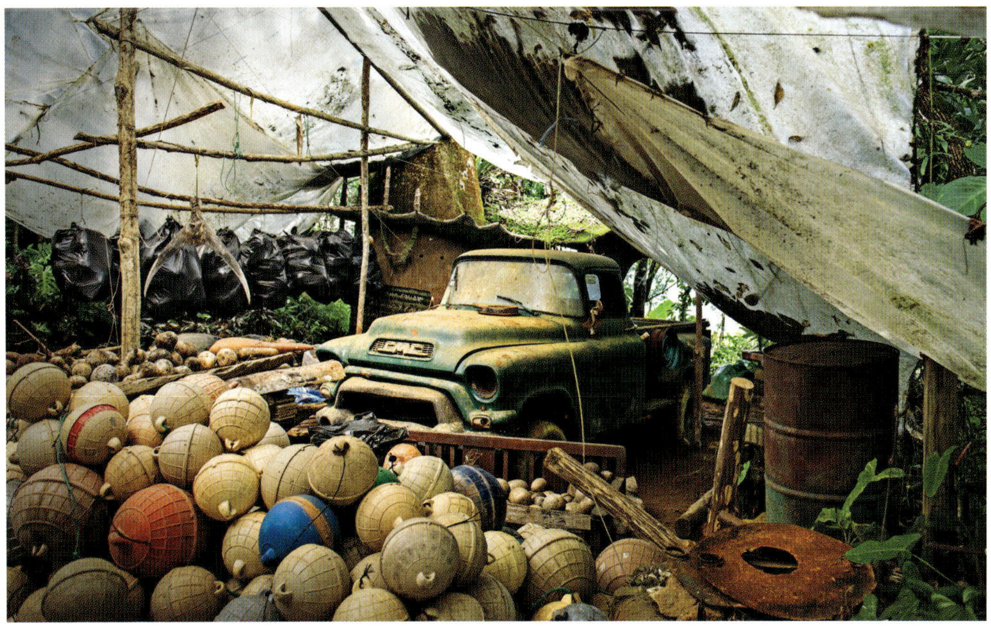

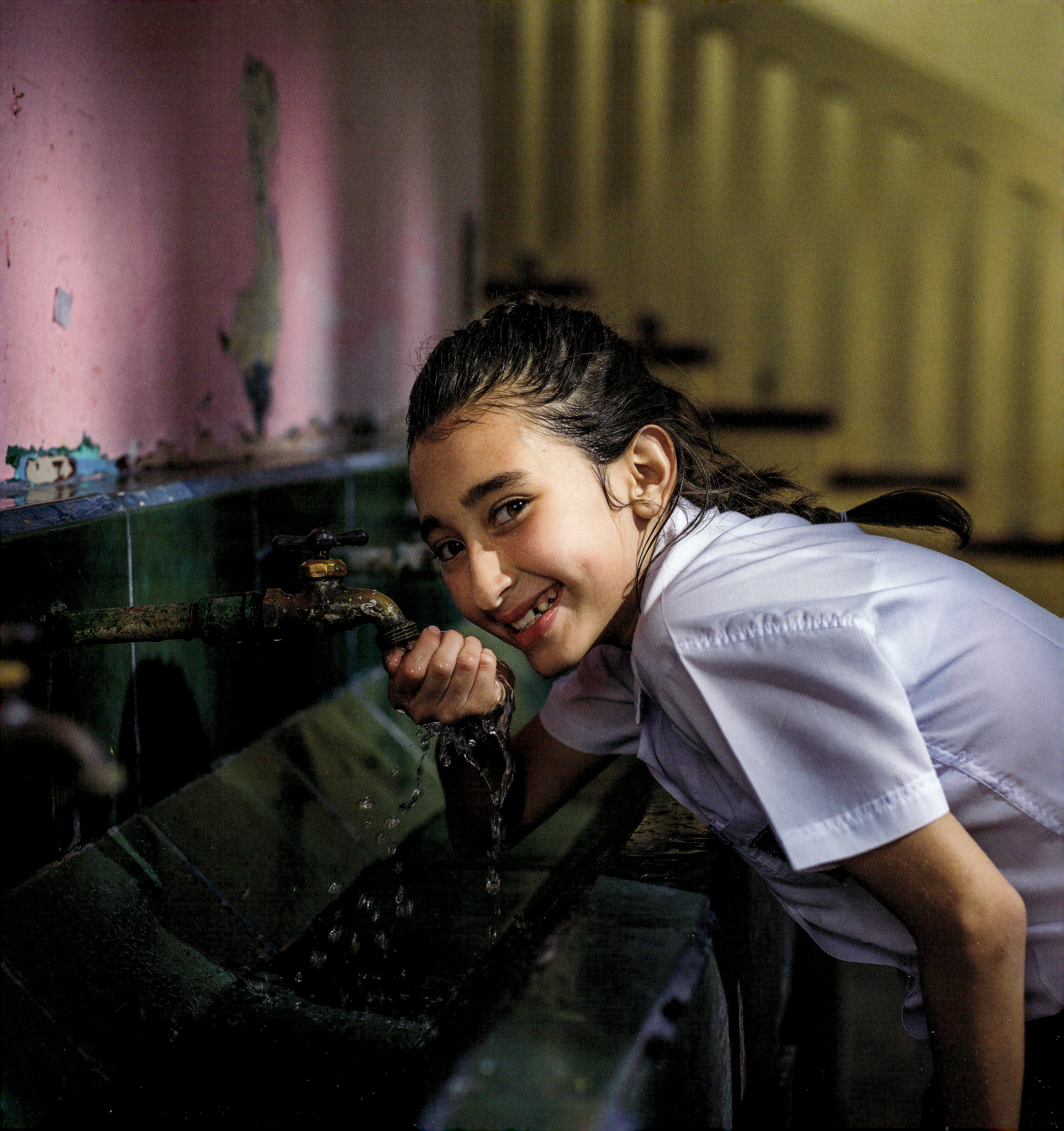

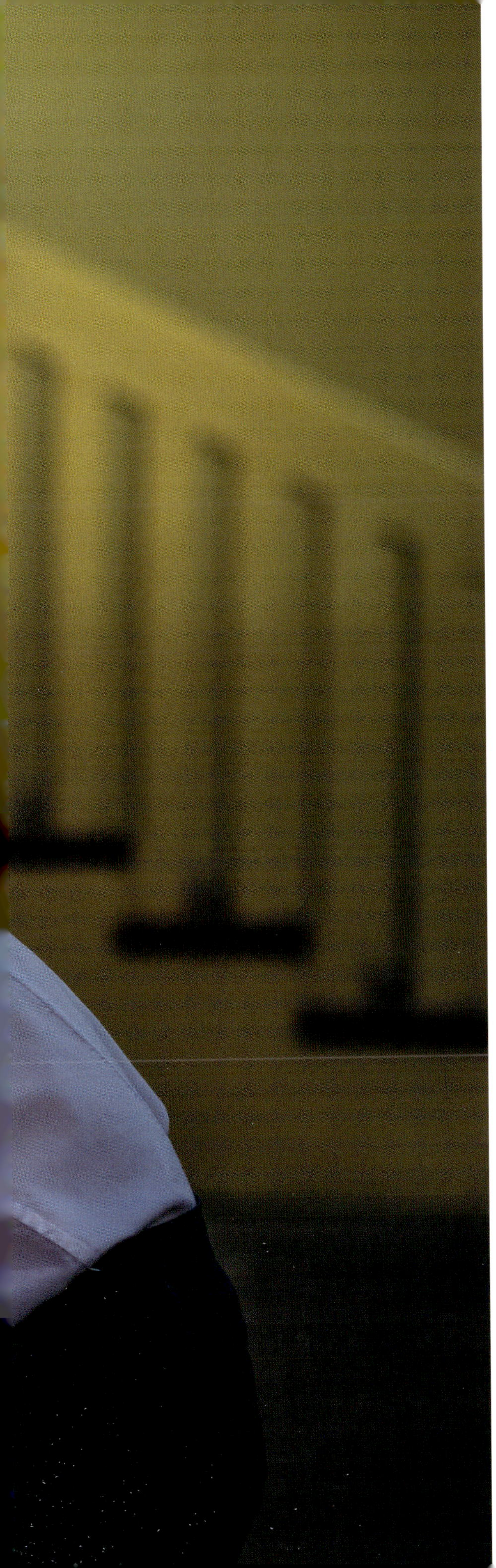

# THE TWO FACES OF A CLOUD

An airplane flies over the central volcanic mountain range. From above, the land looks like rumpled black cardboard with green sawdust sprinkled on top, like in a Nativity scene. Between the airplane and the ground there are thin clouds, and it feels strange to see clouds from above — they look the same as from below, except the background is different. From 30,000 feet, the cows look like grains of rice on a green background, and the trees look like broccoli. The cars are little rectangles and it looks like they're barely moving, although they're actually speeding down the highway. In the thick glass of the airplane window, she can see her own reflection. The girl who's traveling has her hair gathered in a ponytail, and her eyes are huge. It's like she's seeing things for the first time, and in fact she is — it's the first time she's returning to her country and she sees it from above. It's the first time she sees the clouds from the other side, with the earth in the background, and she smiles when she notices that they look the same as from below — the two faces of a cloud are the same.

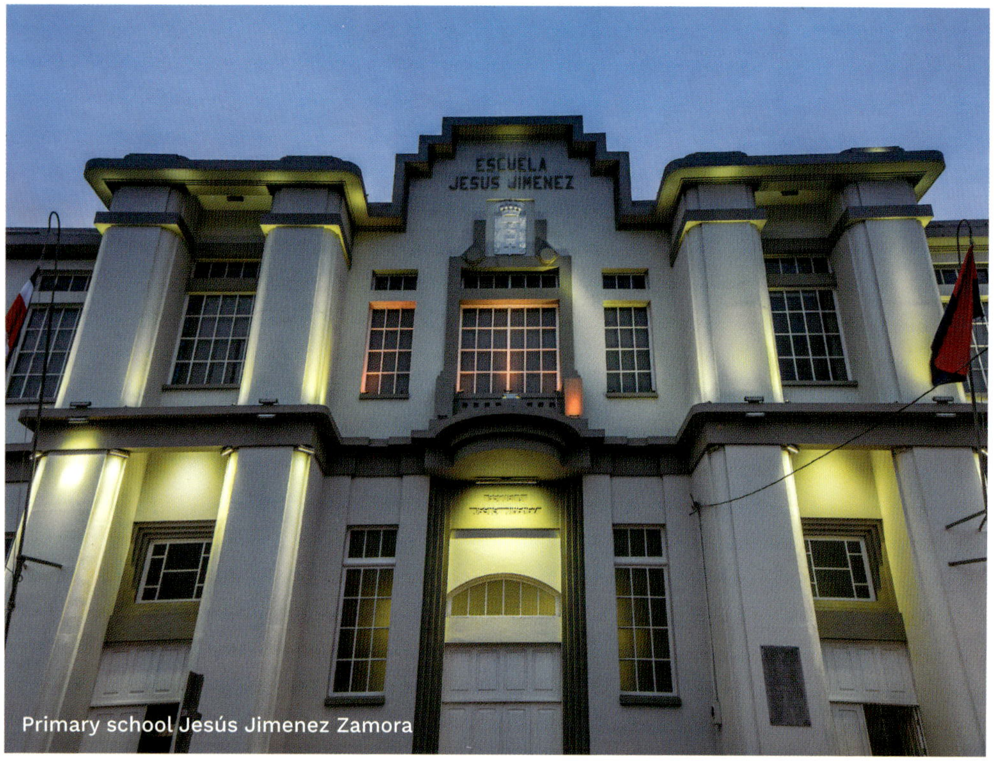


Primary school Jesús Jimenez Zamora

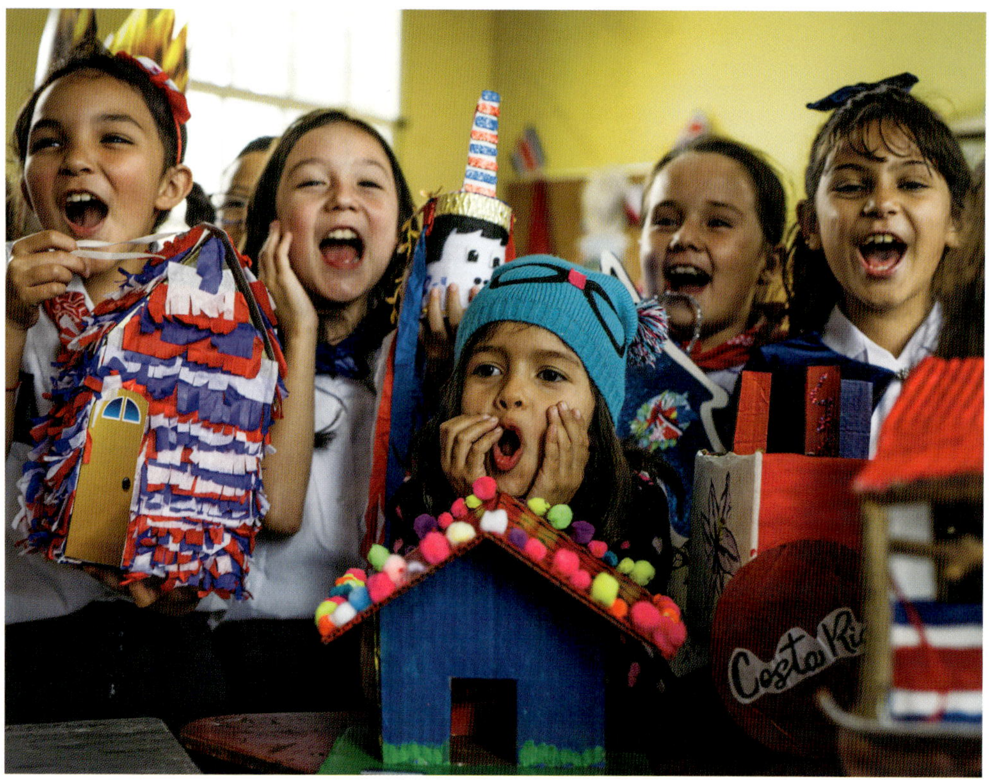


The child with the huge eyes is named Mariam, and she's returning home after spending several days in Houston, where along with six other children, she participated in a robotics program called First Lego League Jr. They were selected to attend after getting a perfect score on a project in which they explained how water is used and conserved at the Jesús Jiménez school in Cartago.

In her bag below the seat is her favorite book. ¨Good Night Stories For Rebel Girls", a volume in which the stories of marvelous women are told. Later that same day, her mother offered to take her to McDonald's as a reward, but she's tired and she wants "real food," cooked by her mother. That day she drinks some tea and sleeps until the next day.

This girl returning to her country for the first time will stay on her path, sticking with the robotics, cheerleading, and dance. She'll also keep participating in the political party she organized, whereby she ran for president of the student body to achieve things for her school and for her fellow students.

At night she still dreams about the time she was in the United States; she dreams about NASA, about indigestion-inducing hamburgers, about putting together a basketball team. But above all she dreams of that first time she saw everything from above; she dreams of seeing everything from 30,000 feet in the air. She dreams of that precious moment when she notices that the clouds look the same from the other side. She dreams of the cardboard mountains of the country of her birth, something you appreciate with your eyes only after having left it for a while, even if it was just a few days. She dreams about that country, not just any country, but the one that's hers.

**Written by: Diego Van der laat**

• Free, mandatory elementary education paid for by the state was declared under the government of Jesús Jiménez Zamora.

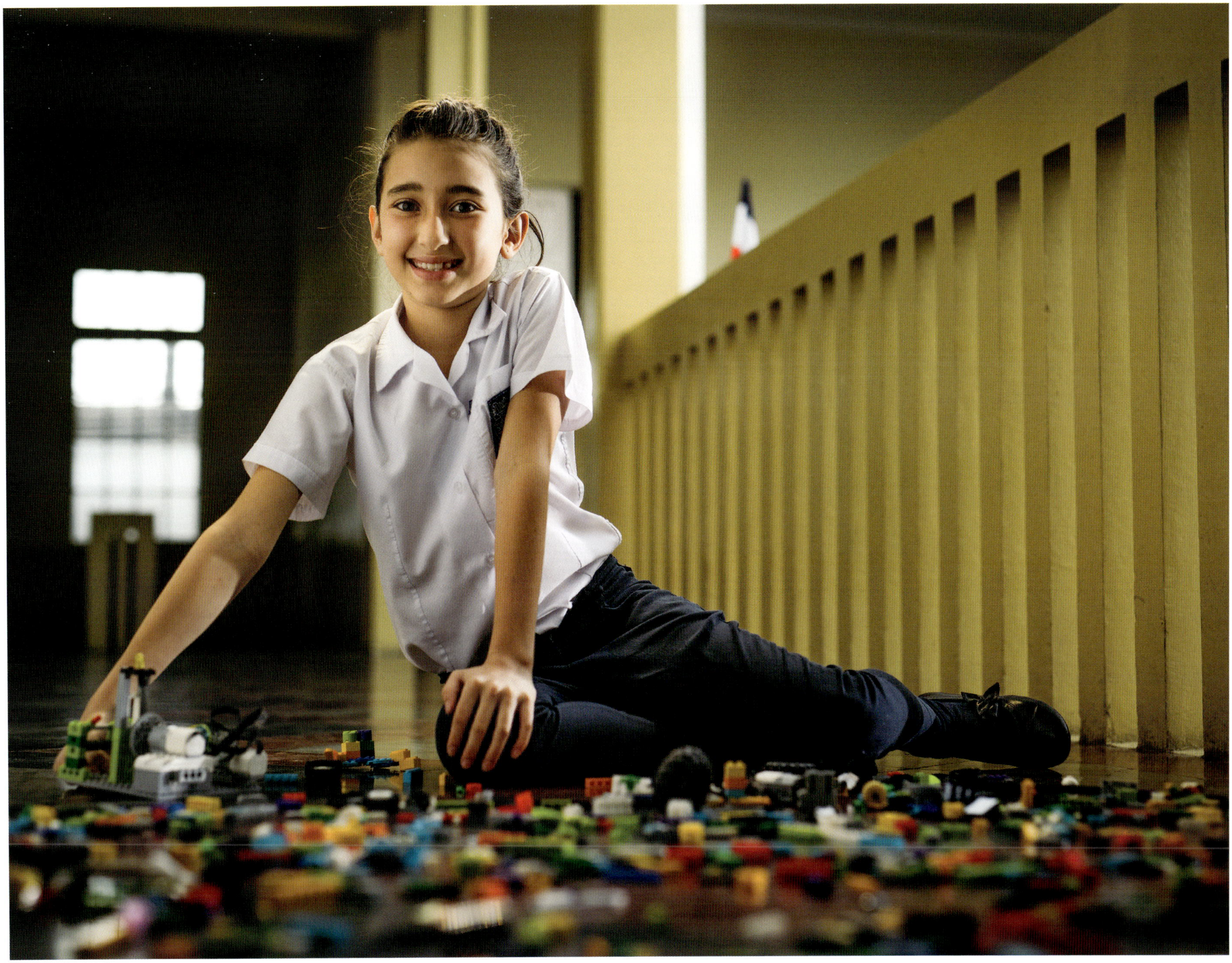

**Mariam Leiva Delgado**
Cartago
Born Sept. 7, 2009

Mariam belongs to a robotics club at the Jesús Jiménez school. Her mother, Johanna Delgado, graduated from the same school. Mariam is an extroverted girl, active and decisive — a young woman who fights to find a place in traditionally male pursuits like science, sports, and politics. She's a very good student, a member of the school cheerleading team, and she also does karate, basketball, and ballet. In 2020, she ran for president of the student body and came in second. She's very close to her mother, she's a swimmer, and she's talkative and friendly. Mariam considers Ticos and Ticas to be very good people, and she's happy to be from Costa Rica because it's such a friendly country.

# A BAGUETTE UNDER THE ARM

*esperaba que Papá me diera la carta de libertad*

There are some who grow up in a house behind a little convenience store, or on the second floor above a pharmacy. The home of Juan José in Rohrmoser was half house, half clinic. A full clinic with a waiting room, a doctor's office, and an operating room. A full house with a father, mother, and six children. And the third of them, Juan José.

The daily routine of the house-clinic had its oddities. Like when his parents sat down for dinner dressed in their blue surgery scrubs. Or knowing how to answer the second telephone, of a different color, the one from the clinic, like their mother had taught them:

"Dr. Manuel Enrique Chacón Bolaños' aesthetic surgery clinic. How can I help you?"
Always in the same tone of voice. He could also accurately describe all the services that were offered here. But there was always some caller who recognized a juvenile voice and asked how old the person answering the phone was.

The clinic provoked curiosity and morbid fascination. Juan José and his siblings once stood on a crowbar to spy through the window into the operating room. Oh, God, if their mother ever caught them!

But living in a home clinic had many advantages. Like that Sunday when, after a picnic, 7-year-old Juan José got stuck in a barbed-wire fence and suffered a long, deep cut in his calf. His mother wrapped a handkerchief around his leg, and where did they take him? They took him home, so his father could sew him up.

Juan José was born at Hospital México like his brother Manuel. Marco, the youngest, was born at a private clinic. But the other three children...

In 1968, in the remote Valle de la Estrella, his mother, an obstetric nurse, and his father, completing his medical training, were awaiting their firstborn daughter. The plan was to travel to San José by train. But they didn't have time. They took off, and in the middle of a banana plantation, Jenssie was born.

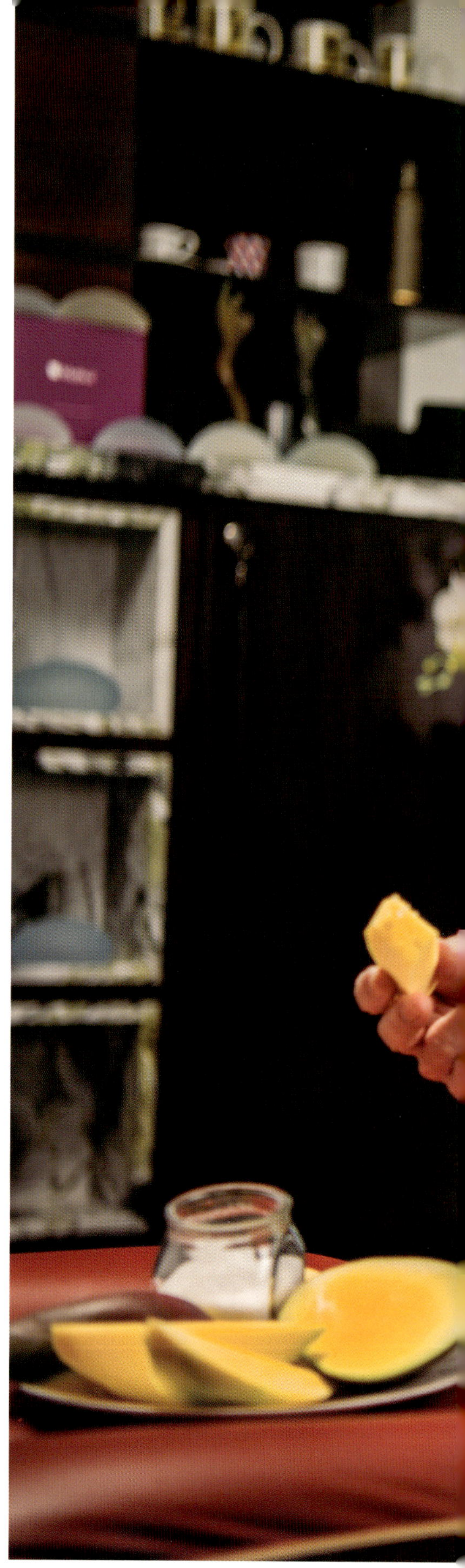

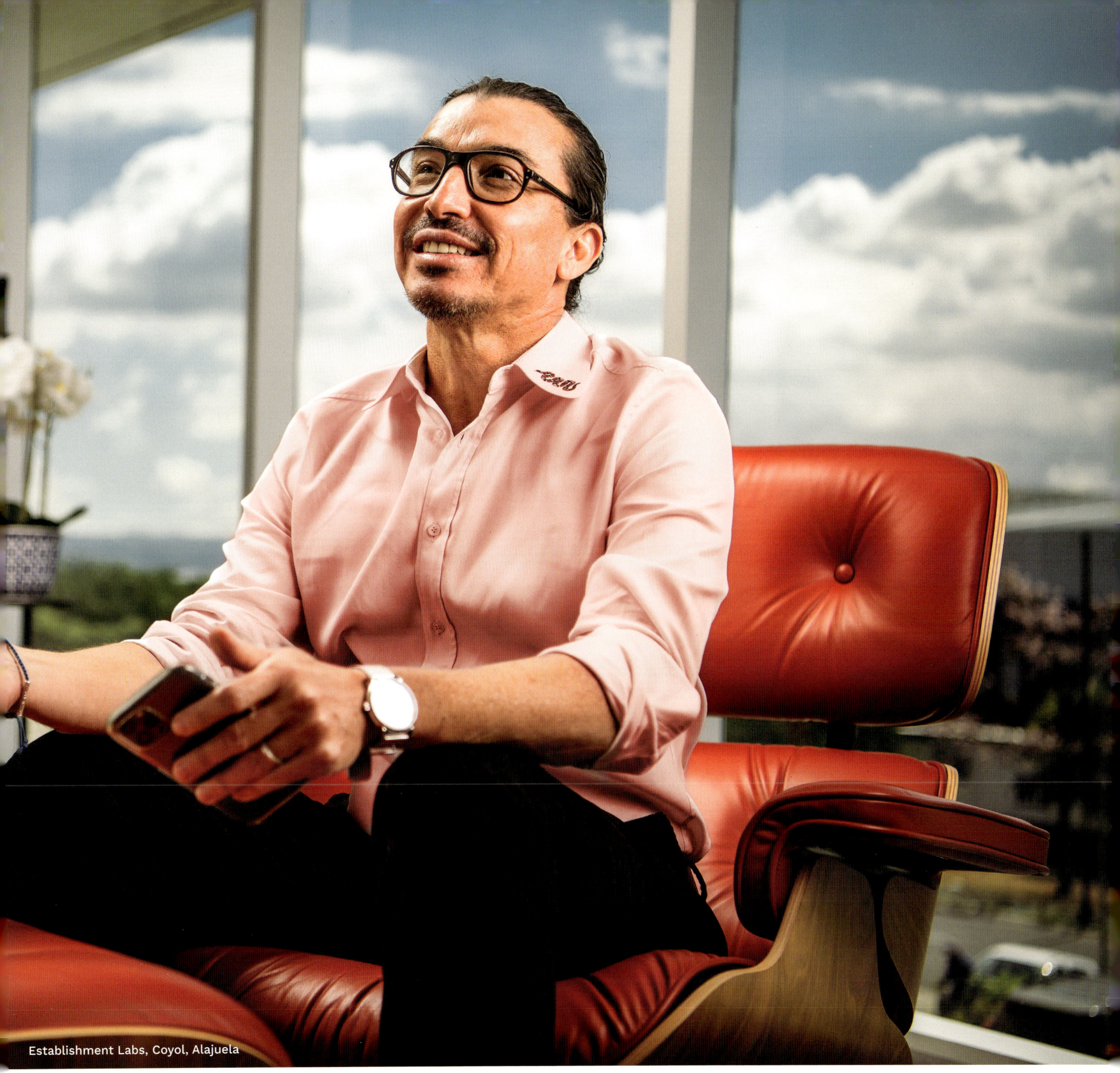
Establishment Labs, Coyol, Alajuela

• Medical devices are currently Costa Rica's primary export product.

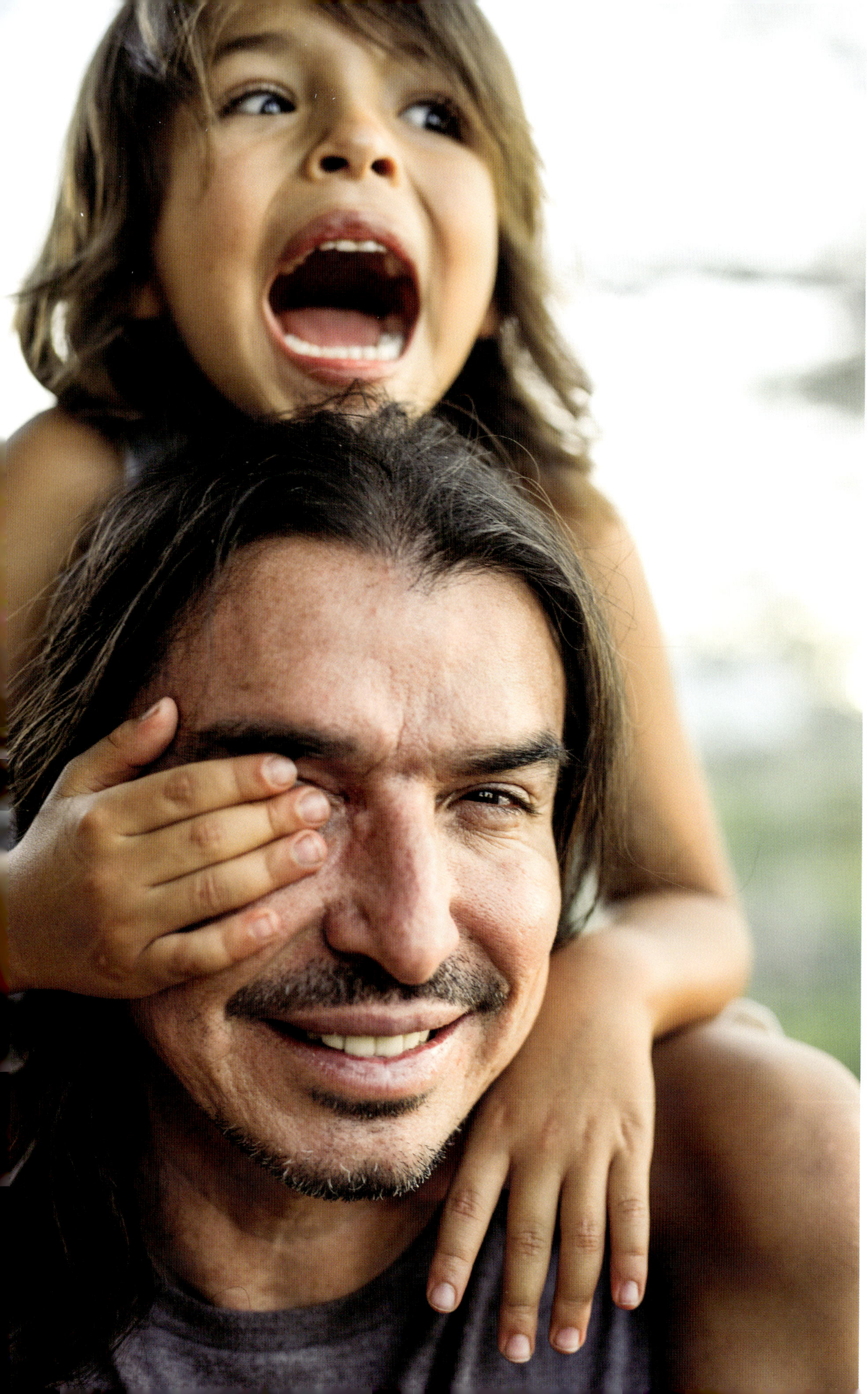

**Juan José Chacón Quirós**
Puriscal - Santa Ana
Born March 7, 1972

Growing up in a clinic turned the idea of surgery into part of his everyday life.
Juan José founded Establishment Labs in 2004 and has served as director and executive director of Establishment Labs Holdings Inc., the first Costa Rican business listed on international stock exchanges since its creation in 2013. He's been involved in various aspects of the aesthetics industry, and for almost a decade he's been general manager of a business that distributes aesthetic medical devices throughout Latin America. Before that, he was the development manager for a renowned plastic and reconstructive surgery clinic in Costa Rica. He is the co-holder of more than 45 patents that have helped to advance medical technology in areas such as implants, RFID tags, biosensors, 3D technology and surgical instruments. He was president of the Costa Rican Rugby Federation from 2009 to 2015. He studied economics at the Académie de Poitiers and attended the University of Massachusetts at Amherst. He holds an MIT Sloan Advanced Certificate for Executives (ACE) in Management, Innovation and Technology.
Juan José is married and has three children.

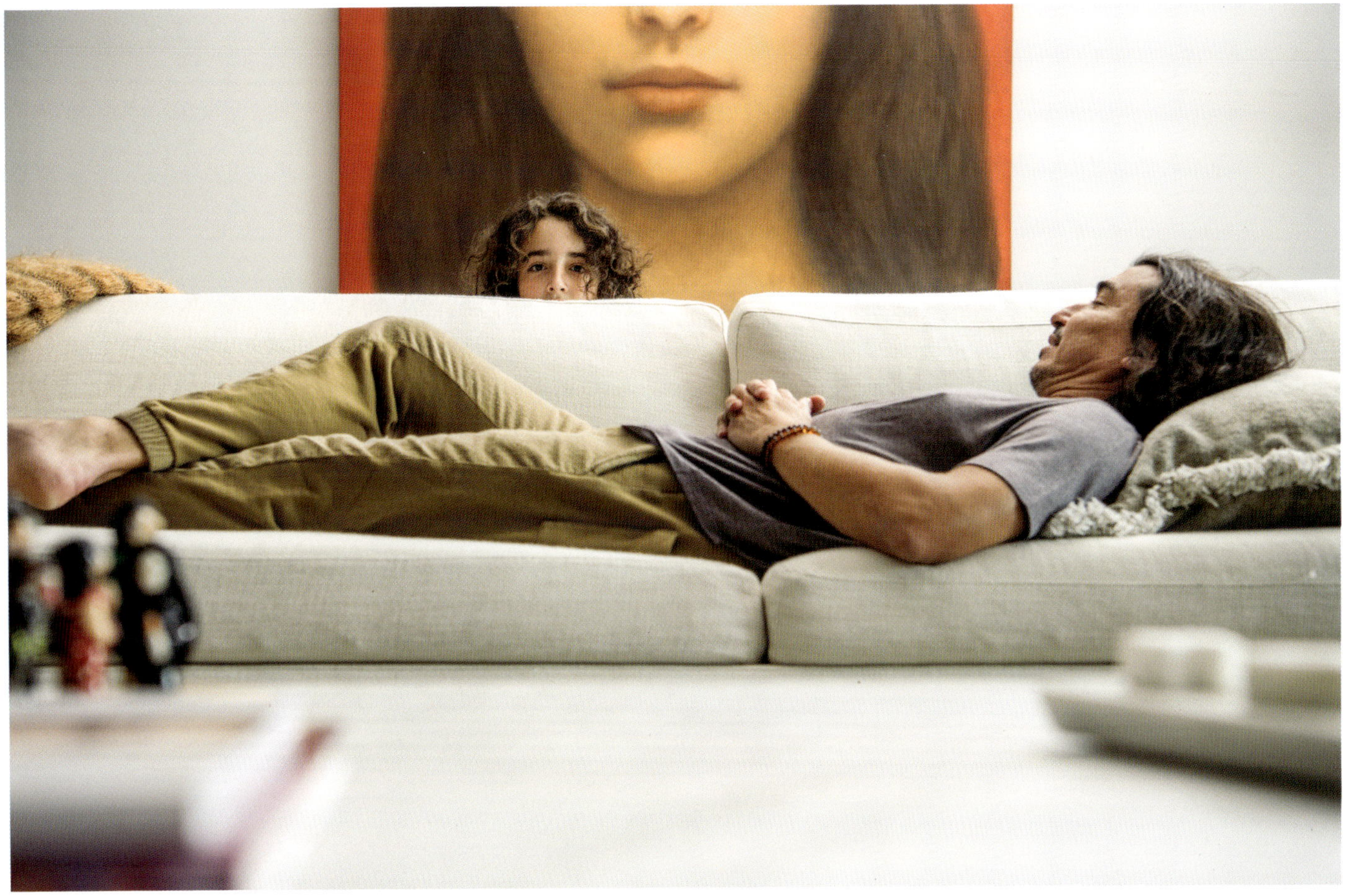

## THE PLAN WAS TO TRAVEL TO SAN JOSÉ BY TRAIN. BUT THEY DIDN'T HAVE TIME

Six years and two children later, his parents repeated the exercise — this time in the glamorous city of Paris. His father was doing his residency in aesthetic surgery, and his mother couldn't afford the luxury of staying in the hospital for a week after childbirth, as she was told would be necessary. Who would take care of Juan José and her other children? With the complicity of the nurses and doctors at the hospital, they collected the necessary supplies for the father to attend the birth at home. At the end of his workday, the father picked up the kids at their day care, and upon arriving at the apartment — a classic sixth-floor flat without an elevator — Gilles came into the world.

The third time his parents birthed a baby alone was in 1976, at the house-clinic in Rohrmoser. They had no time to go to the hospital. But at least they had a clinic at home! When Juan José came home from school, he was greeted by Odilie, the maid, who said

"Go buy bread — your little sister is already here!"

Returning from the Smith bakery, with the bread under his arm, Juan José found his siblings all around the bed where his mother was holding Francine. His smiling father told them in French, "all the little kids come with a baguette under the arm."

Juan José grew up and studied economics. One day his father called him from the operating room. The nurse had quit, and he needed someone to hand him the instruments during the operation. Although he had no training, Juan José was able to do it. His father asked him to keep on helping him after that. And two years went by like that. To Juan José, they seemed like a thousand.

Early one morning, sitting in front of his desk, trying to find a way to break free, he felt an animal moving inside his pants. He squeezed it until it stopped moving, and he discovered that it was a mouse. Juan José thought that was a sign, and he finally found the courage to quit his job, stand firm and start his own life.

**Written by: Claudia Barrionuevo**

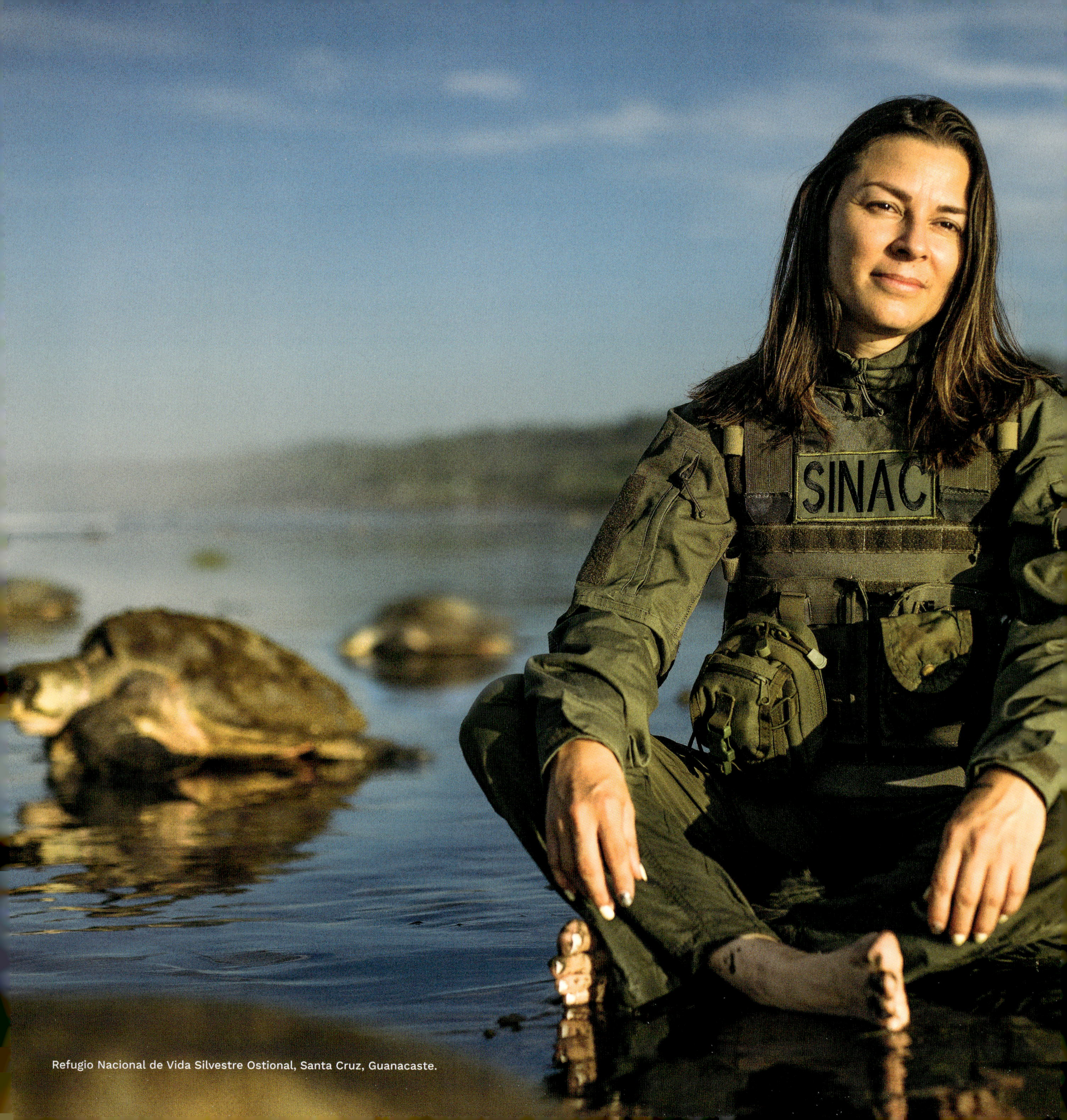

Refugio Nacional de Vida Silvestre Ostional, Santa Cruz, Guanacaste.

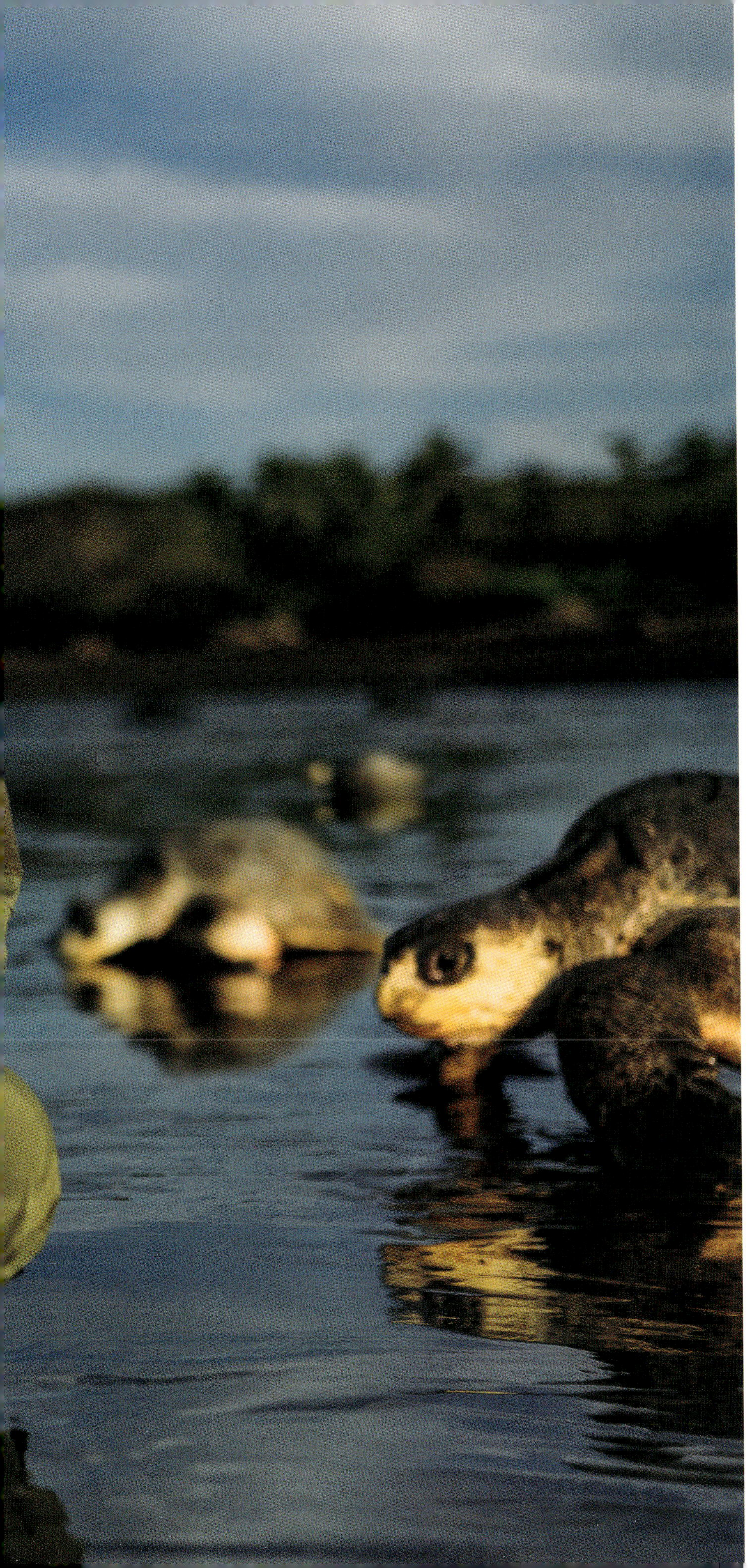

# LIKE FAMILY

Bye, Mom, see you later! I grab my purse, throw in my dress and high-heeled shoes, avoid visual contact with her and head for Los Colegios. I had a plan that night. I grew up on the streets of Moravia playing with my neighbors, skating at top speed, knees scraped, the booming music from my surfer brother's room, '80s rock and Madonna choreographies. That night a neighbor girl invited me to a 15th birthday dance party, and some older boys drove us in their car. The dance finished but we had plenty of energy to keep going. It was already late and since I had no way of telling my parents that I was fine, I decided to keep having fun.

Cartago, a distant province, at an age and a time of night when I wasn't allowed to be outside the house. My family was worried, which was uncommon for them. I didn't come home for dinner, but we ate fried chicken in front of the Basílica de los Ángeles. It hasn't been a restful night, but I played hide-and-seek in the park and laughed way too much. Dad can't sleep, and soon it's time to go to work. It's almost 5 a.m., and I'm feeling sweaty from nerves and the pit in my stomach as I enter the house.

I open the door and see the eyes of my mother, my father and my siblings. Seeing me is a relief, their souls return to their bodies, and nobody scolds me, but they aren't happy, either. My father goes to work after his sleepless night. It's a day to stay in my room, not even coming out to eat. The image of my disappointed father leaving for

## THEY ALSO PROTECT ME, LIKE BIG BROTHERS

work returns to mind. It's nighttime and the emotions inundate the house. It was the most heart-rending conversation I'd ever had with my father. He wasn't mad, he was actually afraid that something had happened to me; he was hurt, I had let him down, and he cried with me for the first time. I never imagined that something so innocent could turn into something so complicated. I felt morally destroyed, and I was punished for a month.

Dad wasn't afraid of life; his agility enabled him to build, fix, climb, and impress anyone with the Frankenstein scar on his arm. Under the fruit trees in the yard he revealed his secrets to me, about finances and matters of the heart. I saw my accomplice, example and dominant role model cry twice. The second time was dancing at my wedding, when he realized I wasn't his little girl anymore.

My brother left home to surf with foreigners for weeks. He had ways of surviving in the middle of nature. If he found a nest of turtle eggs, he only took eight, burying the rest and taking only what was necessary. I empathetically explained to him that in fact he was fouling the entire nest. When I go to visit him, he makes sure I'm first in line to see him catching air when he surfs. He's my big brother, although at times he feels like the little brother.

I left the city with the values, the advice and the mentality of perseverance that my family instilled in me. I landed at the park to expand my vision with a new family. My coworkers encourage me to take days off,

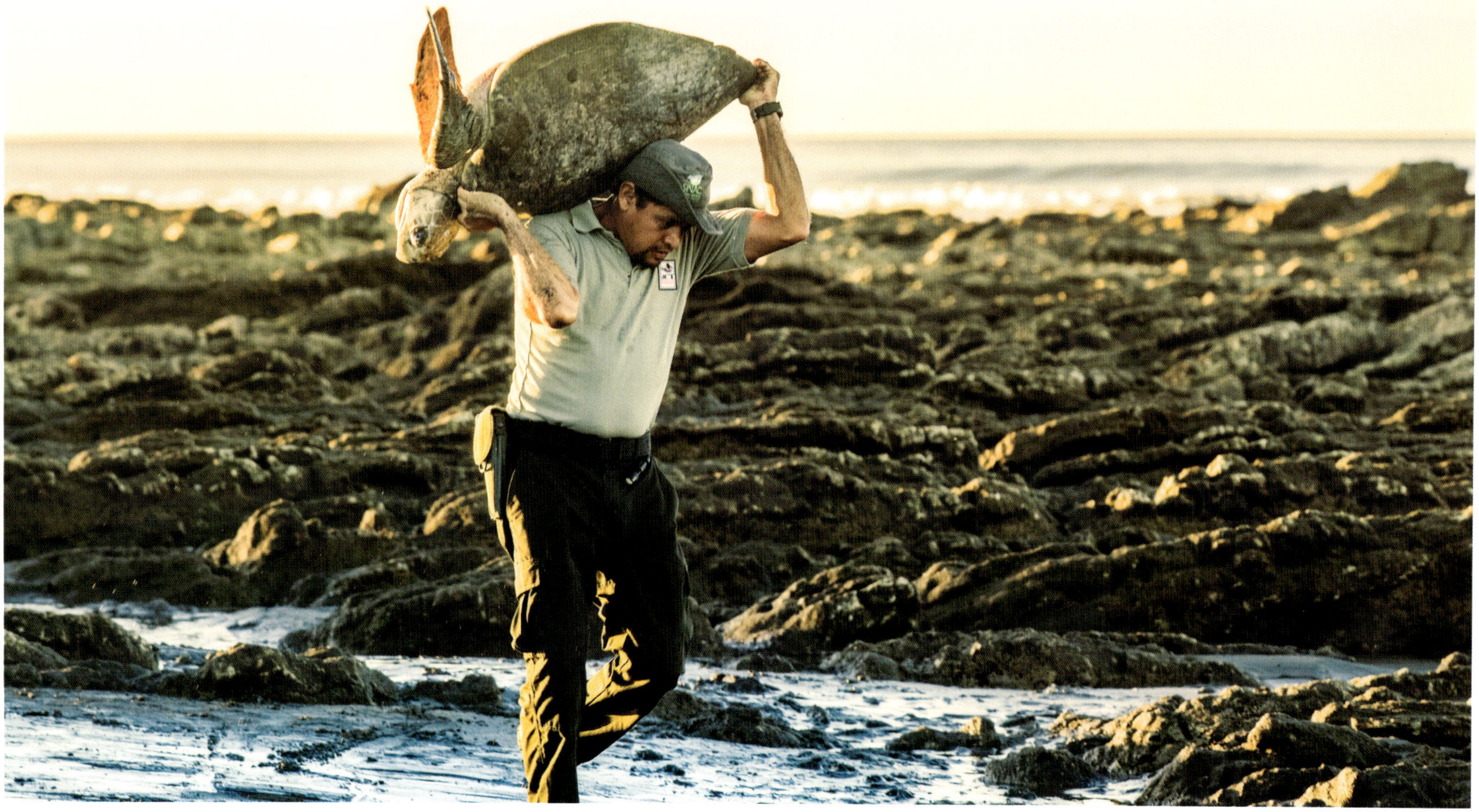

Rescuing a stranded turtle on the rocks. Official José Pablo Baltodano Díaz.

buying my bus ticket and making sure that I really leave and don't get off at the next stop. They feel my absence, although I scold them sometimes when they push my limits. We work as a team, pursuing egg poachers in the mangroves, at turtle arrivals or at community gatherings, and at the end of the day, we keep sharing the house and I remain the boss.

They recognize that I move forward without fear, and this empowers me not to restrain my impulses. Nature extends a special power to anyone who trusts in its strength and its sensibility. They also protect me, like big brothers, from the emotional trauma of seeing a family torn by pain and fury when they see an egg thief placed in a patrol car.

**Written by: María José Sosa**

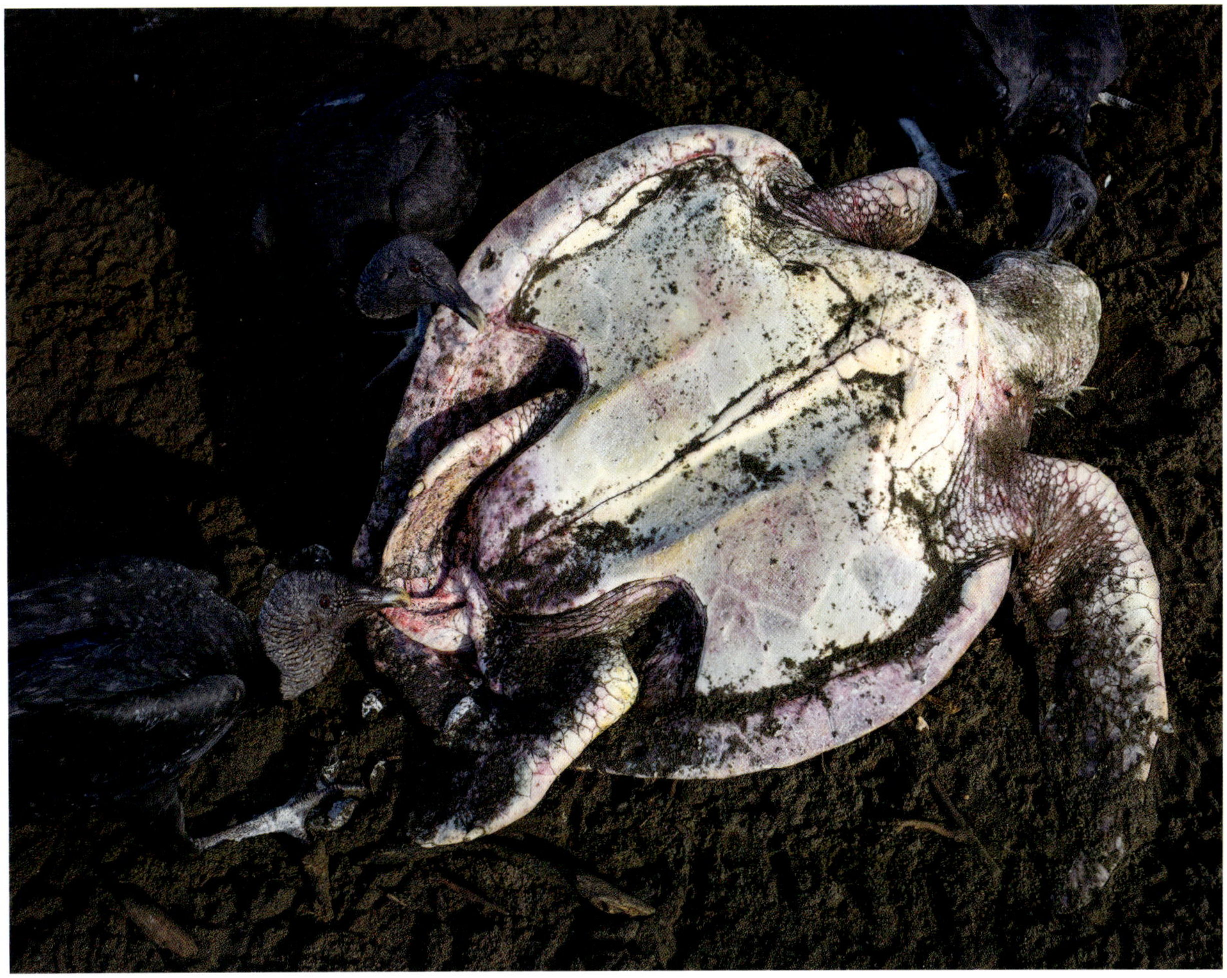

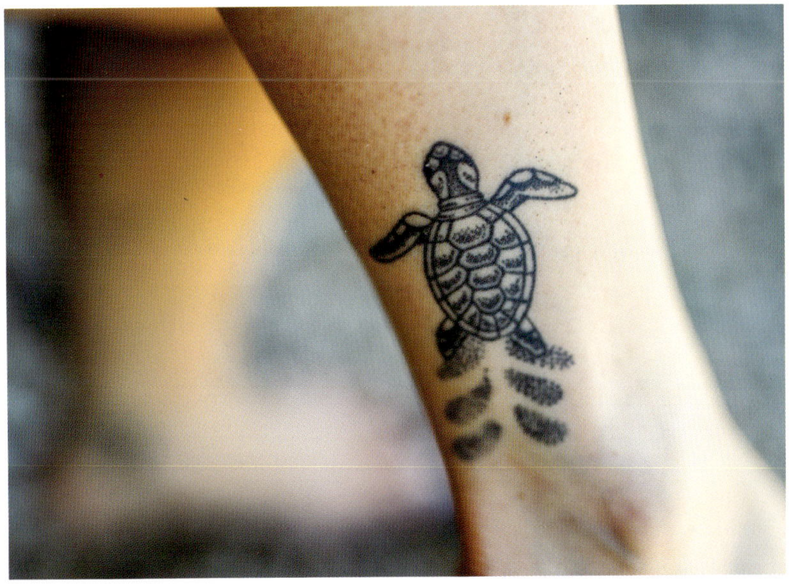

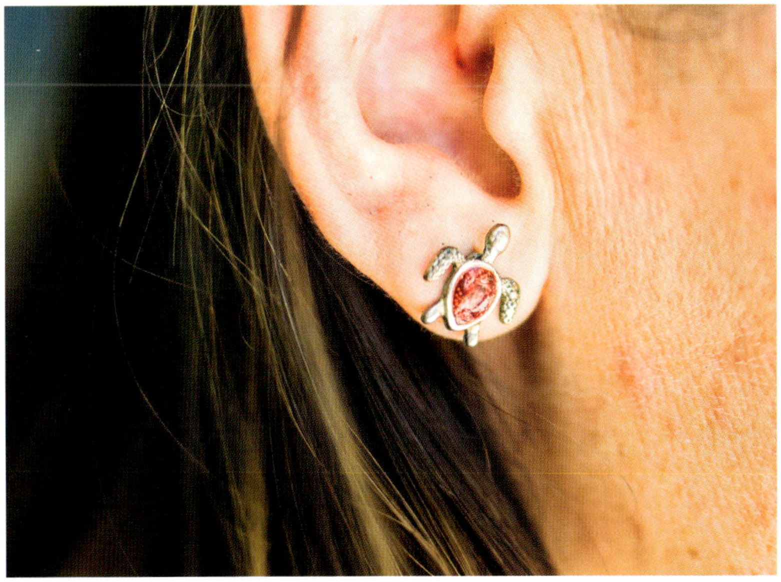

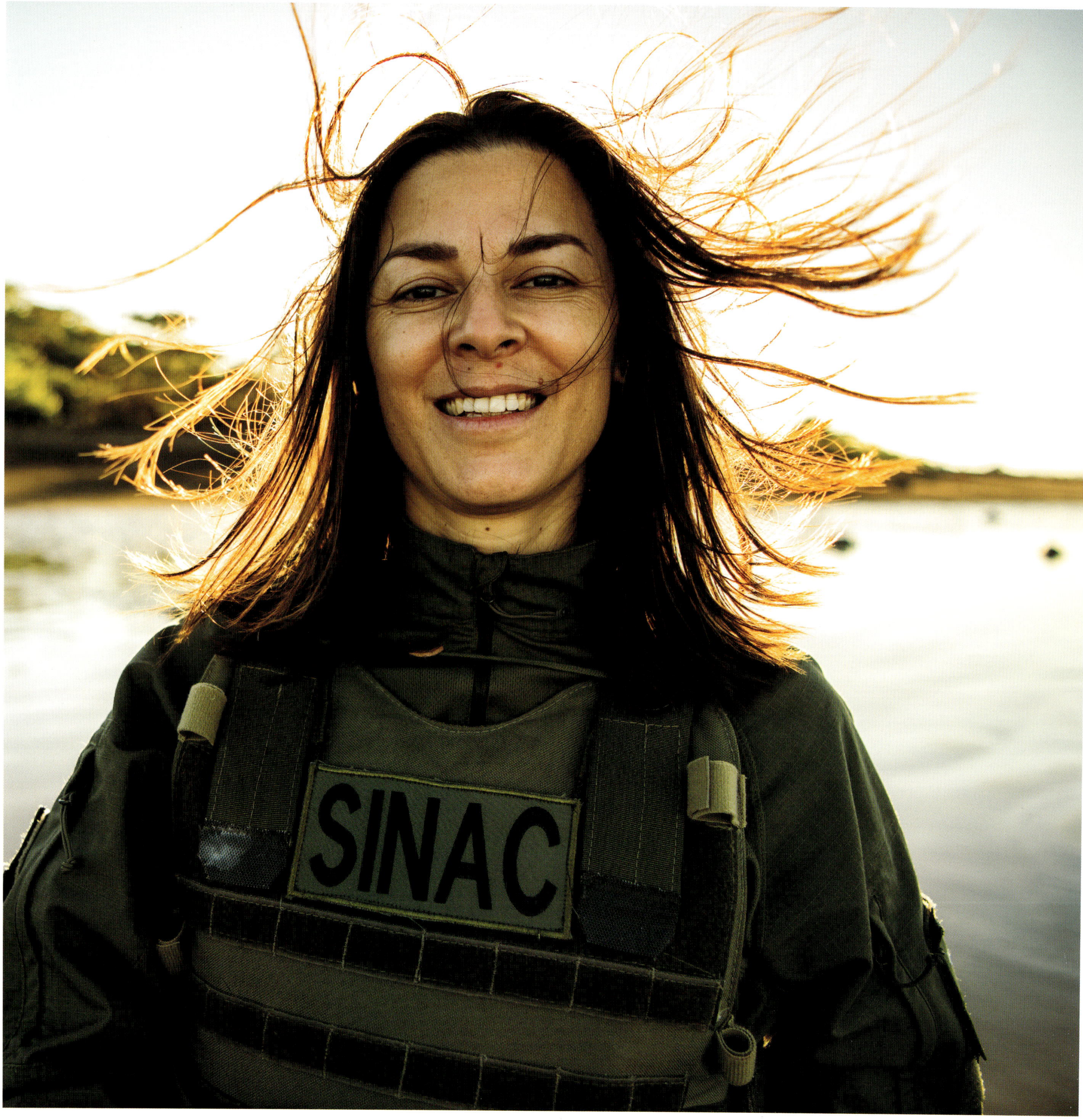
SINAC

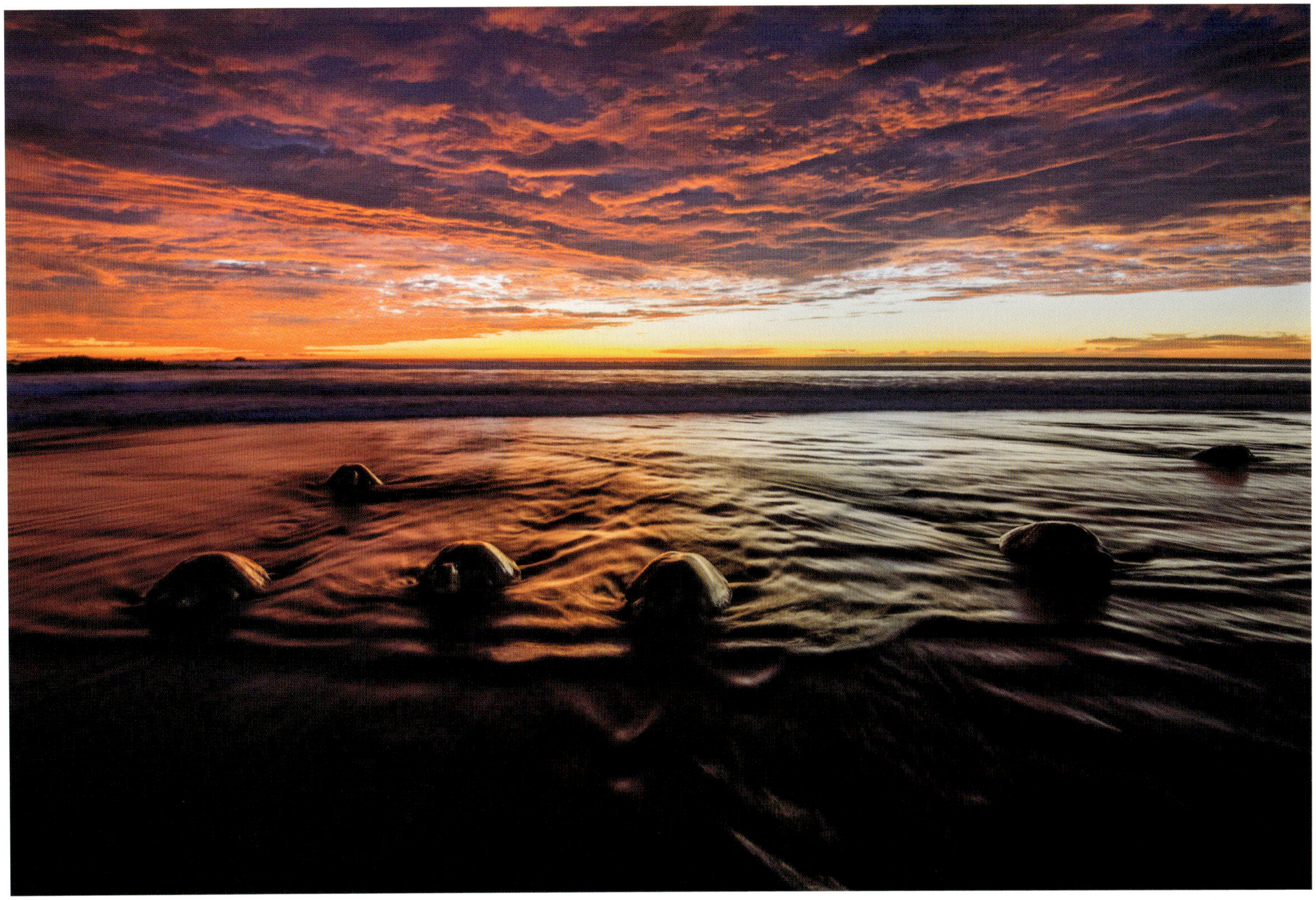

**Yeimy María Cedeño Solís**
San José – Ostional
Born Oct. 8, 1977

Tropical biologist and currently director of the Ostional National Wildlife Refuge, a protected zone that has a beautiful peculiarity: working hand in hand with the community. She started there in 2016 after working since 2008 on a team that created the wildlife management plans for protected areas of the Tempisque Conservation Area. A lover of sea turtles, Yeimy dedicates part of her time to sharing information with visitors that's more valuable than just pointing out nesting areas: "Leave your pet at home when you visit the beach. Especially dogs, which dig up the nests to eat the turtle eggs. Once a nest has been dug up, even though we rebury it, it's left damaged."

• **Women hold 16% of SINAC jobs in protected wilderness areas.**

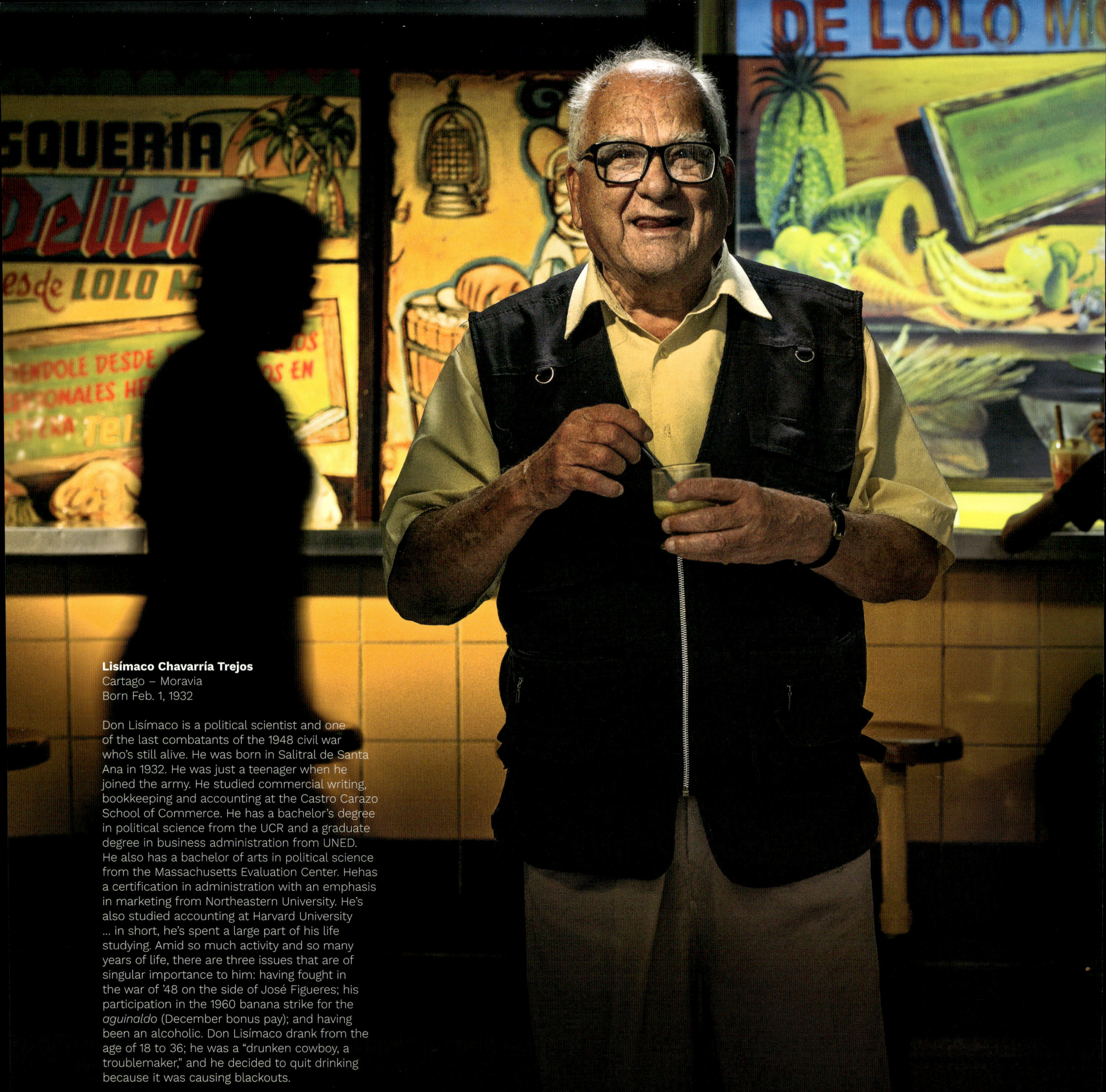

**Lisímaco Chavarría Trejos**
Cartago – Moravia
Born Feb. 1, 1932

Don Lisímaco is a political scientist and one of the last combatants of the 1948 civil war who's still alive. He was born in Salitral de Santa Ana in 1932. He was just a teenager when he joined the army. He studied commercial writing, bookkeeping and accounting at the Castro Carazo School of Commerce. He has a bachelor's degree in political science from the UCR and a graduate degree in business administration from UNED. He also has a bachelor of arts in political science from the Massachusetts Evaluation Center. Hehas a certification in administration with an emphasis in marketing from Northeastern University. He's also studied accounting at Harvard University ... in short, he's spent a large part of his life studying. Amid so much activity and so many years of life, there are three issues that are of singular importance to him: having fought in the war of '48 on the side of José Figueres; his participation in the 1960 banana strike for the *aguinaldo* (December bonus pay); and having been an alcoholic. Don Lisímaco drank from the age of 18 to 36; he was a "drunken cowboy, a troublemaker," and he decided to quit drinking because it was causing blackouts.

# THE LONG ROAD BACK

On the road between Santa Ana and Salitral lived his grandmother, Jesús, and his grandfather, Casiano. This home of open doors received family members, neighbors and anyone who needed a cup of coffee or a little push in life. Their kindness and spirit of solidarity built a legacy more powerful than any fortune. In the afternoons you could see Doña Jesús telling her grandchildren stories about her celebrated first cousin, the ex-president Juanito Mora. All these stories stayed in the memory of Lisímaco, who was one of her grandchildren and the main character in the story I'm about to tell you. It was the 1940s, and the drums of war were booming on every corner of the planet.

Lisímaco was 8 years old and was on an eternal search for adventure with his friends from the neighborhood. Just like you could see them running races or climbing trees, they would take up collections to buy a liter of guaro and orange juice. Alcohol sales weren't restricted like they are today, so boys and girls were more at risk of underage drinking.

Lisímaco's path took him to San Isidro de El General, to work at the pharmacy and the beehives of some family members. It was 1948 when the civil war broke out, and his thirst for adventure led him to side with the liberationists. He grabbed a Mauser and at the tender age of 15 he spent five weeks in battle, firing left and right, his only motive to stay alive. In his mind he remembers feeling like a hitman, the difference being he didn't know who he had shot. His nose was full of the smell of the charred bodies of the enemy, while his mouth was numb from the firewater he poured down his throat.

The liberationists won the war and Lisímaco kept working with his family, earning the money that would pay for his studies.

He worked at the customs office, and later as an inspector in the banana zone, coinciding with the strike for the *aguinaldo*.

His prominence in that successful battle, winning this right for the working people, put him on track to winning a scholarship to study unionism in New York. Later he traveled to Europe at his own expense to steep himself in the daily activities of an organized workers' movement.

A few years later, when he was working in the Interior Ministry, a man he didn't know from San Ignacio de Acosta asked him for a recommendation in order to get a job, since he had fallen on hard times. Faithful to the style of his grandmother Jesús, he agreed to help him without asking anything in return.

As he continued on his path, growing in experience, the drinking clouded his memory and cast a shadow over his actions.

Two years later, in the most decadent point of his alcohol addiction, he took the bus to San Ignacio de Acosta by mistake. He spent a week sleeping behind a church and drinking inconsolably, digging in his subconscious for a reason to keep living.

The seventh day of his bender, as if sent by supernatural forces, the man he had helped years ago appeared and found him lying on the ground. Astonished, the man picked him up and took him to his home in Sabanilla de Acosta. They spent four hours walking, during which his drunkenness subsided and he was overcome with shame. At the house, they received him happily, he bathed and they gave him something to eat. Ironically, that night he slept in an oxcart. The next day, overwhelmed by the love and humility of this family, he decided to stop drinking and at the age of 36 he joined Alcoholics Anonymous, to which he still belongs.

The long road is what gives you experience, and nobody ever said it would be easy to walk. Time gave him a wife and children, who in turn gave him grandchildren and great-grandchildren, for whom he has felt a love that surpasses time and space: that eternally remembered smell of brewed coffee, on the road between Santa Ana and Salitral.

**Written by: Fabricio Walker**

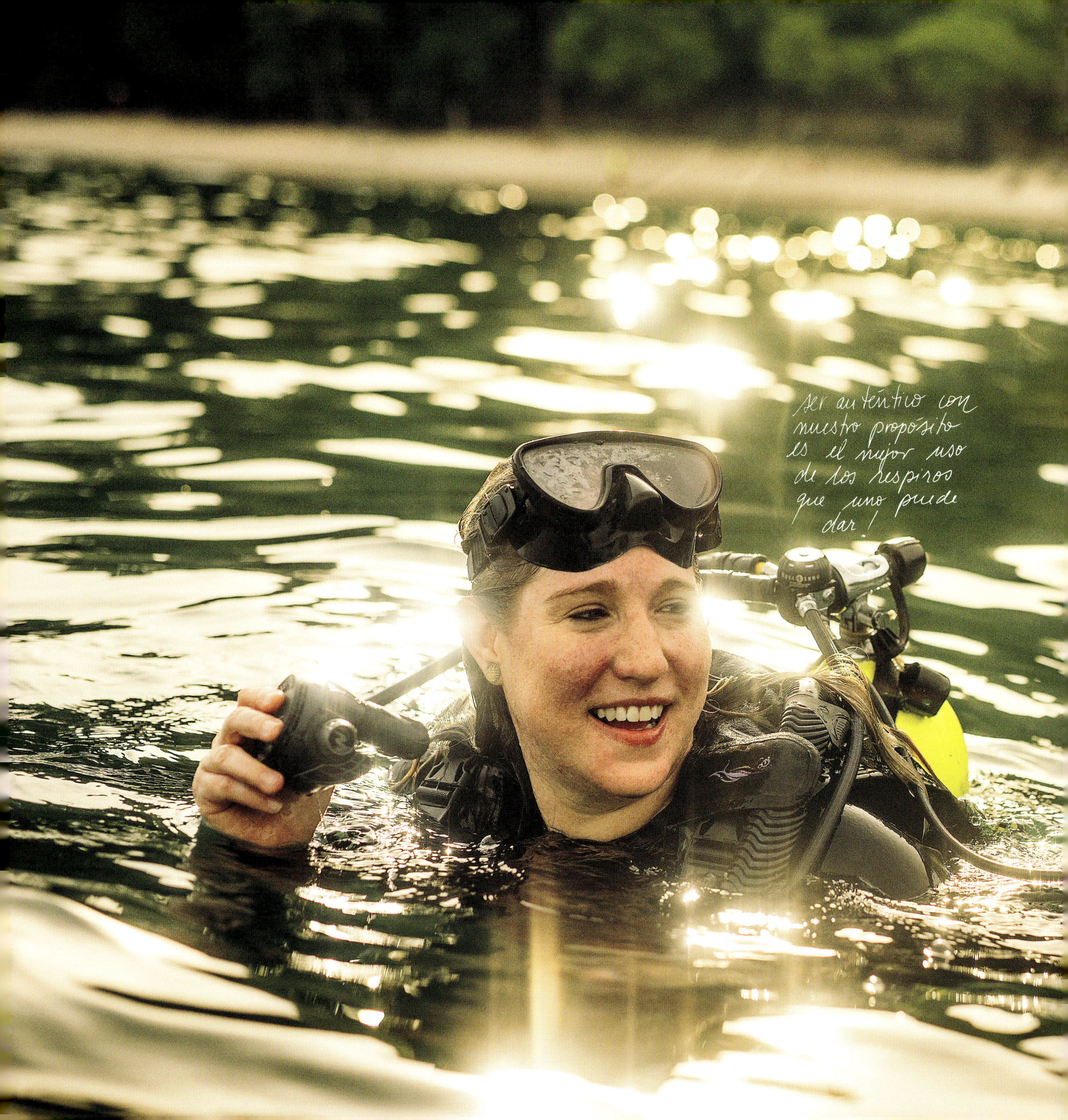
ser auténtico con
nuestro propósito
es el mejor uso
de los respiros
que uno puede
dar!

# STAR SHOWER

If I used to think the ocean was silent when I plunged into it, now I know it's just the opposite. The ocean is a habitat full of sounds that serve as communication networks for multiple life forms that live there. It's a loud, primordial life environment, and I find it fascinating to study.

Even though I've been on more than 100 dives in my 41 years of being Melania Guerra, the scenery before my eyes is always different. When I explore what happens below the waves, I imagine how Heinrich Schliemann may have felt upon discovering Troy. But my greatest inspiration was seeing Franklin Chang in space, and also the life of Jacques Cousteau. The sea of the blue planet was what I wanted to know. I observe it, explore it, study it with instruments and discover new things every time I dive.

Of course, there are always risks. Once, on a dock in San Diego, I was with a colleague who collected sea urchins, and since we had gone diving so many times together, we didn't check our equipment properly. We dove to 60 feet, and in the dim light I saw that the needle of my regulator was moving like crazy. I breathed several times, and suddenly there was no more air. Fortunately, I reacted by pushing myself against a rock toward my partner, grabbed him by the feet and pulled the regulator out of his mouth, though I had to blow water out of it before I could breathe again. I blew out with the last air I had in my lungs and managed to breathe again. It was a conscious breath, unforgettable, that restored oxygen to my body and my life.

## WHEN I RETURNED TO THE SURFACE, A BIGGER SURPRISE AWAITED

After that experience, it took a lot to get over my fear of diving again. But six years later, I was invited to Isla del Coco, and given the opportunity to dive there. I remembered my admiration for Cousteau and I got excited again. So this time, I trained hard to get over my trauma. It was only a matter of throwing myself into the water by night until I felt its magnitude all over again. Once underwater, I observed by the light of my lamp how the whitetip sharks fed, making waves with their rapid motions as if in a bustling Persian market.

Suddenly a space opened among the fish, and a big, beautiful tiger shark appeared, probably pregnant, and assumed leadership of the group. Life below the water continued to be an invaluable apprenticeship for me. That world deserves to be protected.

When I returned to the surface, a bigger surprise awaited: the shine of bioluminescent plankton all around me. I thought only of my gratefulness for being in the middle of that star shower. Because it felt like a little cosmos opened up in front of me, and I was a planet in the middle of the night floating in the Pacific Ocean.

When I returned from this trip, I received the news that my grandfather had fallen. He was 93 years old. When I visited him, he was lying in bed reading a report about my recent expedition. He commented on this with great pride to the people sharing the room with him. It was the last time I saw him.

With his death, I thought of his last breath, and about how life is a succession of unconscious breaths, so that except in extraordinary situations, we don't even notice that they keep us alive. Would my grandfather have been conscious of his last breath? I'll never know, just as I'll never know when my last breath will come. What I do know is that each breath is unique, and you have to make the most of it, trying to be conscious of the purpose we have before us. It's the best way to make use of the first breath you ever took, inhaling air for the first time, with that unique instinct that infants have when they emerge from the womb into the light.

**Written by: Dorelia Barahona**

10 times more marine area than land mass.

Playa Blanca, Punta Leona, Puntarenas

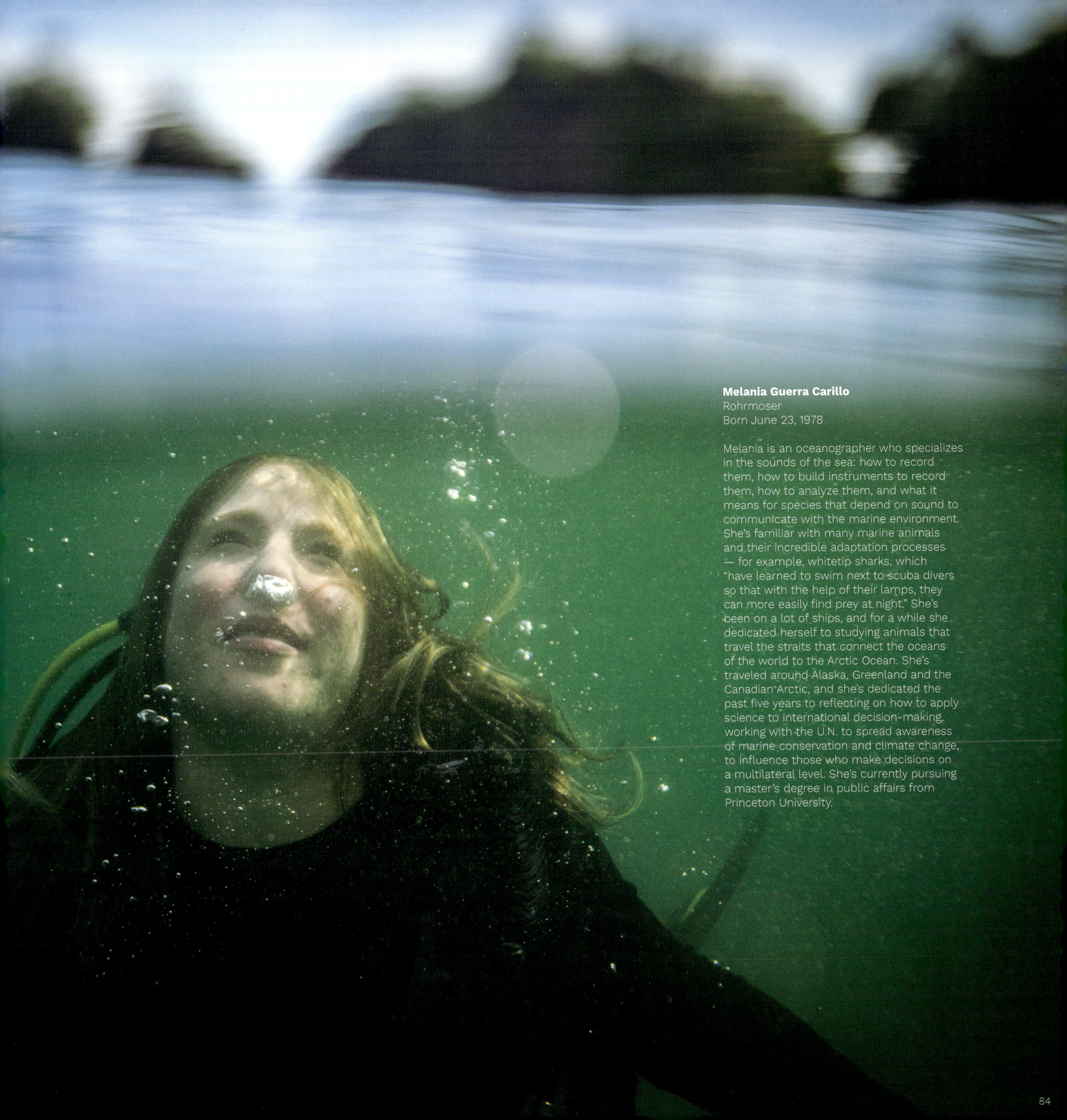

**Melania Guerra Carillo**
Rohrmoser
Born June 23, 1978

Melania is an oceanographer who specializes in the sounds of the sea: how to record them, how to build instruments to record them, how to analyze them, and what it means for species that depend on sound to communicate with the marine environment. She's familiar with many marine animals and their incredible adaptation processes — for example, whitetip sharks, which "have learned to swim next to scuba divers so that with the help of their lamps, they can more easily find prey at night." She's been on a lot of ships, and for a while she dedicated herself to studying animals that travel the straits that connect the oceans of the world to the Arctic Ocean. She's traveled around Alaska, Greenland and the Canadian Arctic, and she's dedicated the past five years to reflecting on how to apply science to international decision-making, working with the U.N. to spread awareness of marine conservation and climate change, to influence those who make decisions on a multilateral level. She's currently pursuing a master's degree in public affairs from Princeton University.

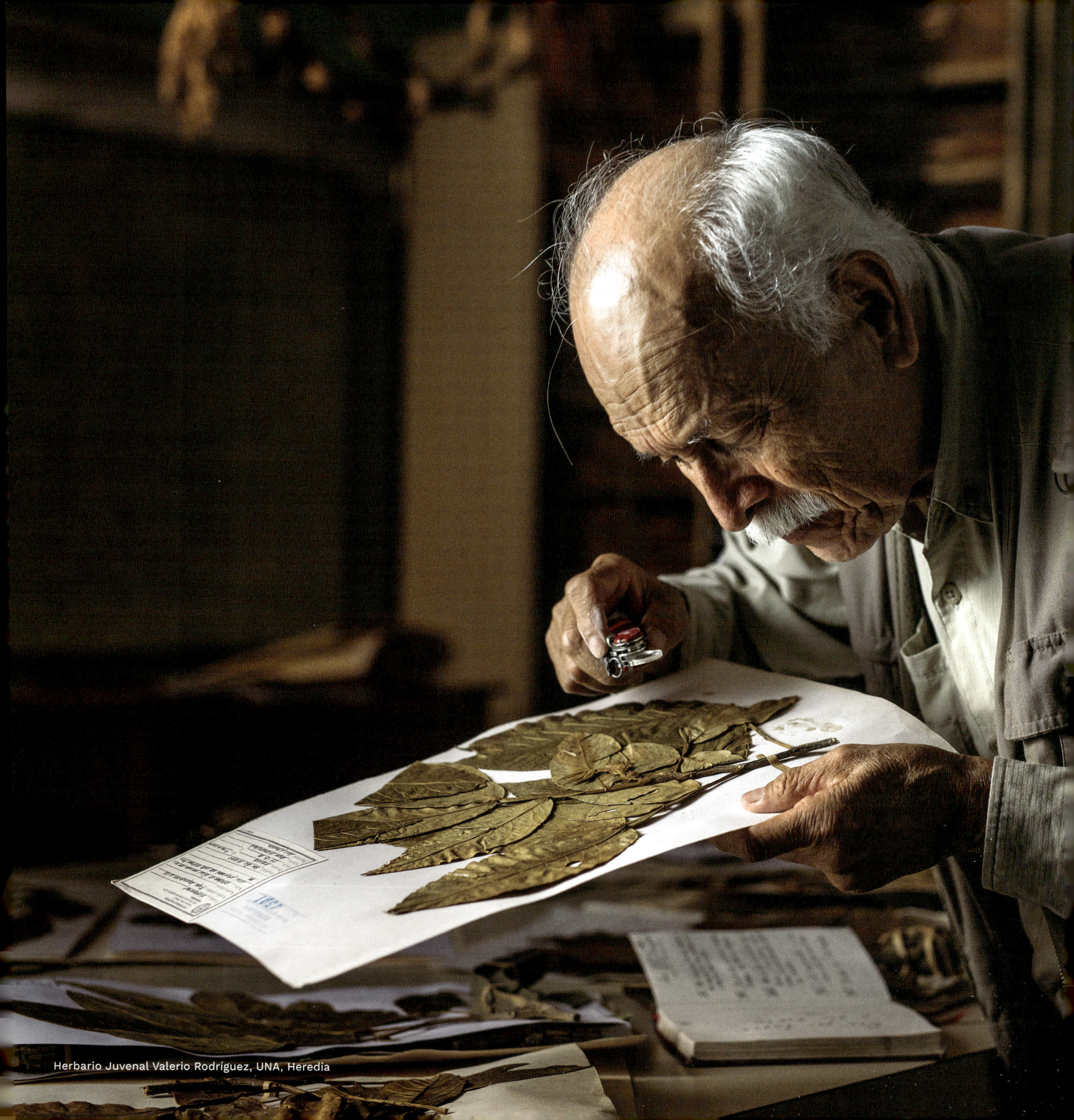

Herbario Juvenal Valerio Rodríguez, UNA, Heredia

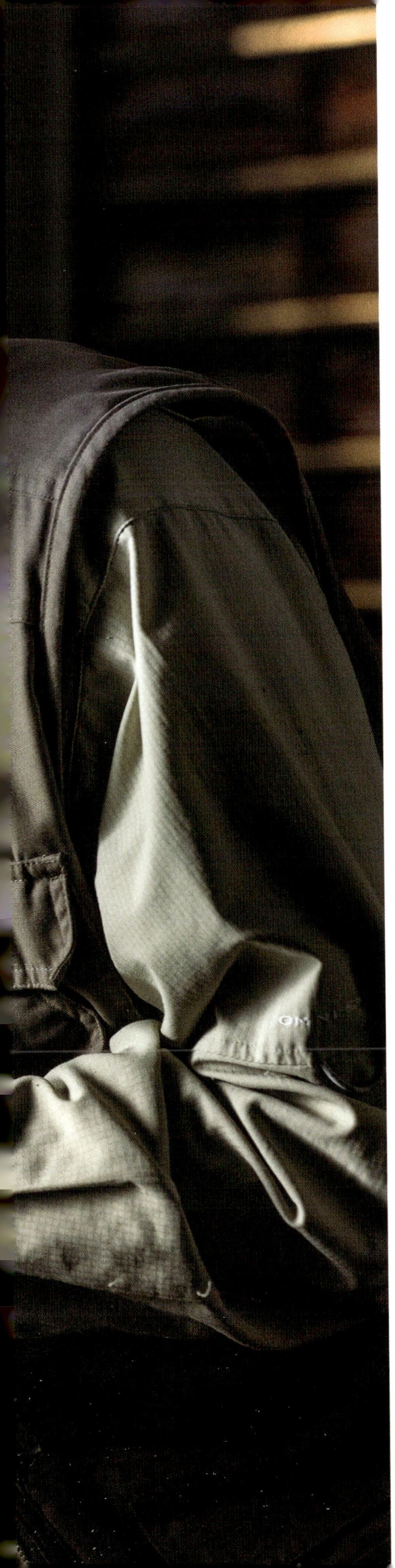

*A mi nadie me regaña ni yo regaño a nadie.*

# NINA'S HOUSE

It was in Turrialba at the end of the 1950s, or maybe it was the beginning of the '60s. The cement that covered the train station contrasted with the dirt streets of the neighborhood. Barefoot merchants went door to door offering food for barter in front of all the unfenced houses.

The Turrialba River, now badly contaminated, was then crystalline and full of fish and other creatures playing in the water, swimming with the current or jumping in from the banks. And right there, trying to dry himself off in the sun, we could have seen Luis Poveda as a little boy, not knowing that one day he would be a construction assistant, an aspiring teacher in Cimarrón and Peralta, and a biologist in love with the trees and the freedom of the forest. We could also see him sneaking away to Nina's house.

Being a woman in Latin America implies struggling constantly for rights that seem obvious and assuming clearly implied duties. In mid-century Turrialba, very few women finished high school, and far fewer went on to higher education. Also, there was a big number of girls migrating from the country to the city who ended up being sex workers, without economic independence, girls exploited by men, their partners or their pimps, who are notoriously aggressive. But Nina was different — she maintained strength and independence, and she always found a way to dignify her work, building her own house on the banks of the Turrialba River.

The fire burning within, like the sugarcane harvest in the middle of the day, and the hyperactivity of the trembling hand at midnight, turned into a long line outside her house. Nina, during the high holy days, entertained half the world and had to set up a strategic schedule: first the men from Tayutic, then from La Suiza, then from Atirro, then from Pavones, then from Aquiares and finally from downtown, so that nobody would miss the bus.

But on this day, there was no holy day, no saint and no money in the purse, but there was a gap in the wall that he could look through.

Through the spaces between the wooden boards, Luis could see Nina cleaning a young man's genitals with a lime. "You're more beautiful all the time," she told him. After a little foreplay, the boy became a victim of his own mind, with a bad outcome from the nerves of a vulnerable man. And there was Luis, spying and holding back his laughter. From afar, Nina scolded our friend with her eyes and silently suggested that he go away, while her client attempted a desperate maneuver with his hands, trying to resuscitate the dead.

In the middle of all this, Luis let out a little laugh, and the boy inside, finally noticing that he was there, took off running after him, but Luis was lost in a distant

## HE STARTED PRAYING TO ALL THE SAINTS HE COULD REMEMBER.

cloud of dust. That night Luis lay on his bed with his eyes wide open looking at the ceiling and laughing out loud.

A few days later he returned quietly to his home, as if nothing had happened. He came in thinking of maybe having lunch, going to a swimming hole, playing a soccer game, or whatever a boy might have in his head. When he opened the door, he saw a woman sitting next to his mother, looking splendid — Nina. Luis couldn't believe it, and all he could say was, "Good afternoon, *señora*."

He went to his room in a cold sweat and started praying to all the saints he could remember. He imagined the beating his mother would give him. Why was Nina there? Did she come here to accuse him? He's learned so much from Nina. ... She's always treated him with affection... He knew that spying on her wasn't good, but she knew he was just being naughty. He took a deep breath and went out again so as not to draw suspicion. "Thanks, Doña Chela, the dress fit perfectly. I'm going to leave you more fabric." His soul returned to his body. Nina's beautiful clothes were made by his mother.

**Written by: Fabricio Walker**

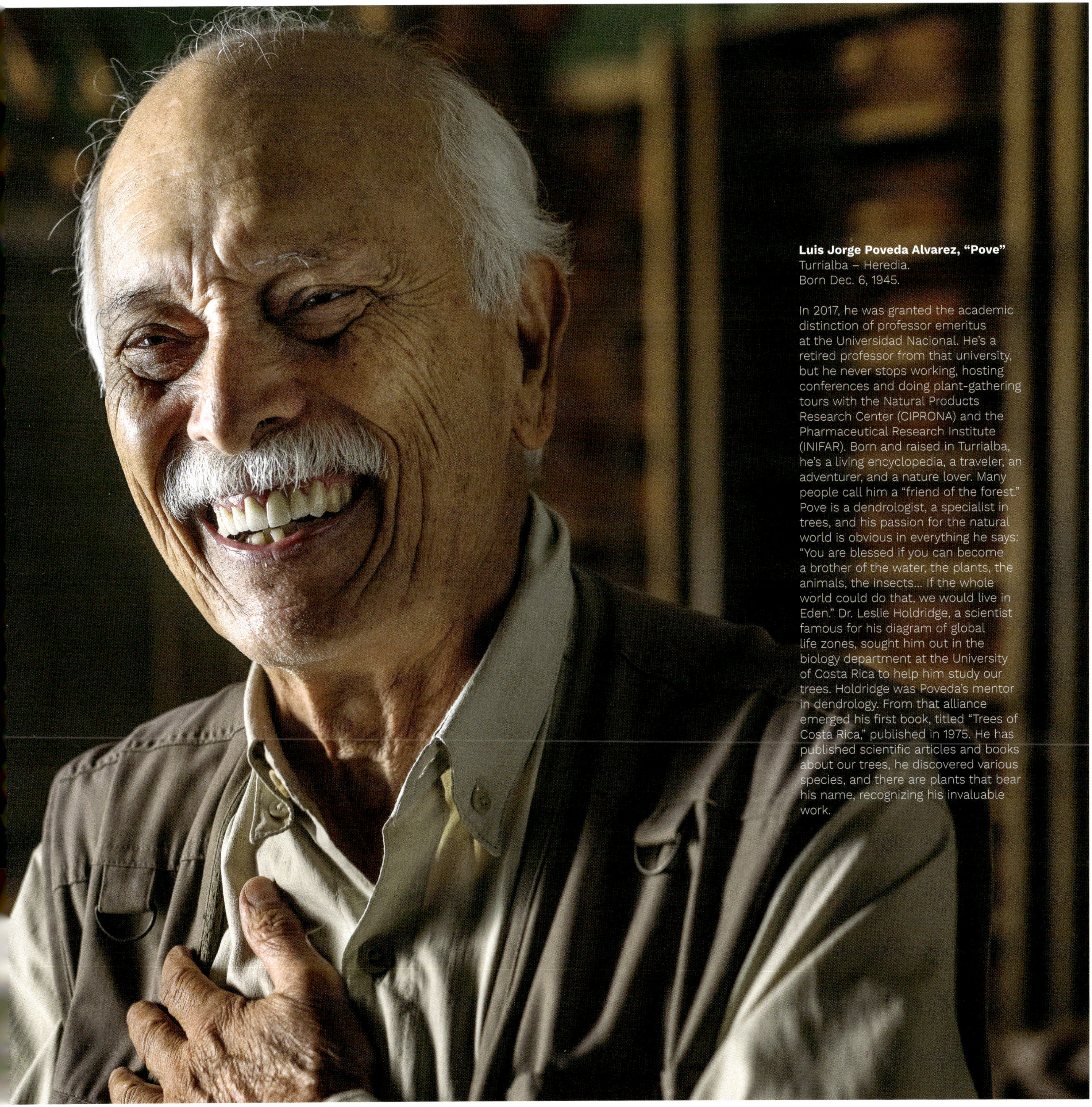

**Luis Jorge Poveda Alvarez, "Pove"**
Turrialba – Heredia.
Born Dec. 6, 1945.

In 2017, he was granted the academic distinction of professor emeritus at the Universidad Nacional. He's a retired professor from that university, but he never stops working, hosting conferences and doing plant-gathering tours with the Natural Products Research Center (CIPRONA) and the Pharmaceutical Research Institute (INIFAR). Born and raised in Turrialba, he's a living encyclopedia, a traveler, an adventurer, and a nature lover. Many people call him a "friend of the forest." Pove is a dendrologist, a specialist in trees, and his passion for the natural world is obvious in everything he says: "You are blessed if you can become a brother of the water, the plants, the animals, the insects... If the whole world could do that, we would live in Eden." Dr. Leslie Holdridge, a scientist famous for his diagram of global life zones, sought him out in the biology department at the University of Costa Rica to help him study our trees. Holdridge was Poveda's mentor in dendrology. From that alliance emerged his first book, titled "Trees of Costa Rica," published in 1975. He has published scientific articles and books about our trees, he discovered various species, and there are plants that bear his name, recognizing his invaluable work.

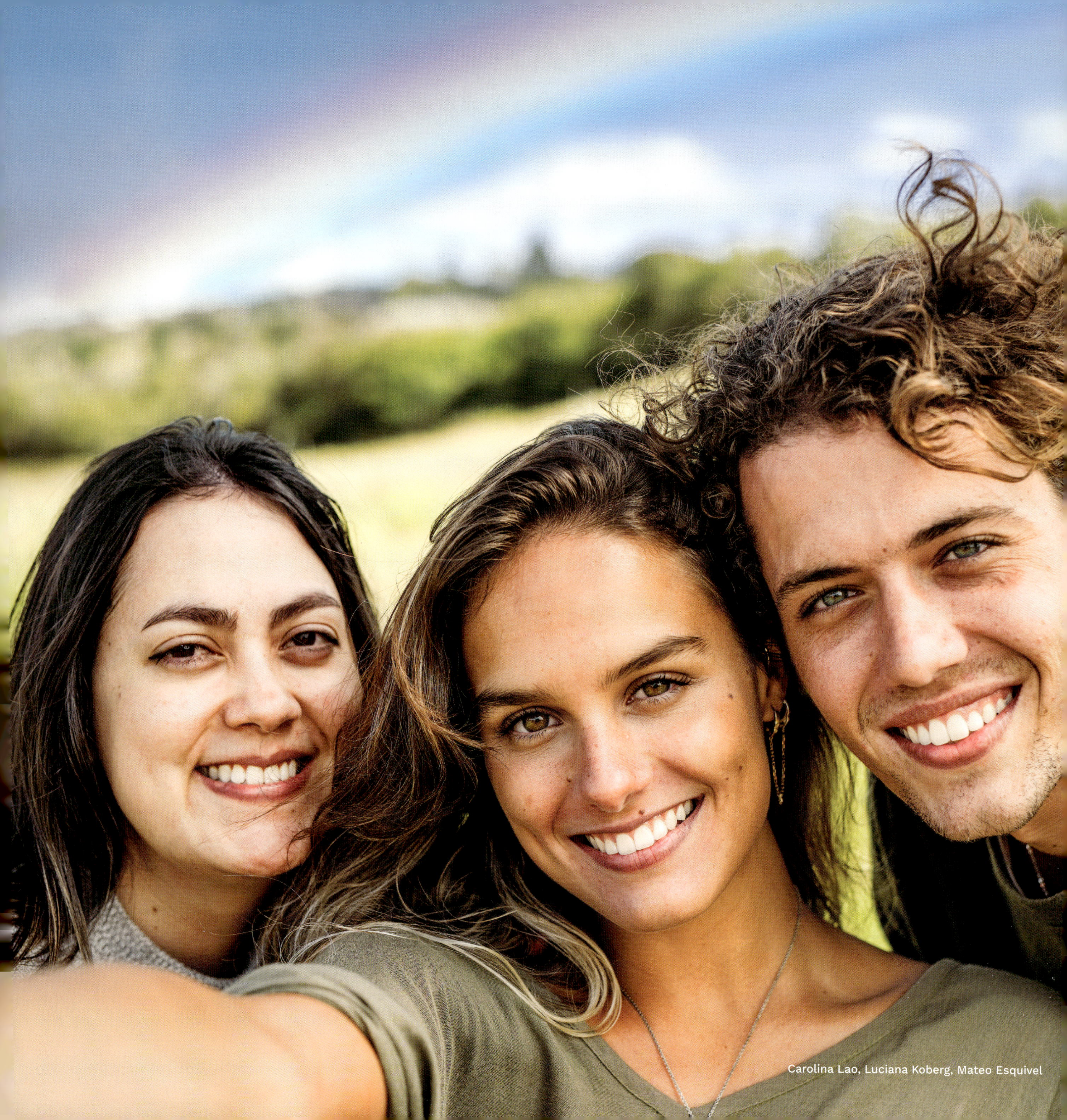
Carolina Lao, Luciana Koberg, Mateo Esquivel

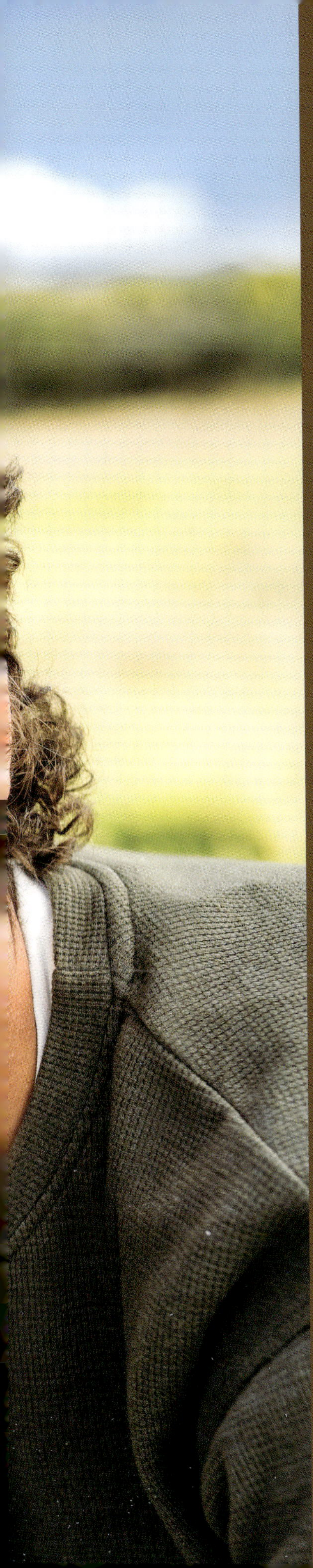

# FIREFLY

"My whole life passed before my eyes." We all know under what circumstances people say that.

In my case, it didn't happen because I was just 7 years old, and I guess you don't have much life behind you at that point.

There are younger generations that won't understand what it's like to return from the beach over the Aguacate hill: the curvy roads, getting carsick, the Sunday night traffic jams, but that's where it was. When you come back, sunburned, and you start feeling the cold wind, which at that moment feels so strange. We would take out the back seats, and my father would throw down a mattress and we would lie down the whole way home. Both of us face up, singing a made-up song, which we still remember and I don't know why: "There once was a fish that swam, that swam around and met a surfer...." Like we were lying on the beach, the roof of the car blocking the stars that started disappearing as we approached the city.

# LYING FACE UP ON THE SAND HERE

A little Honda came up driving like crazy, very fast, so my father made room, but his tires left the road. Suddenly up was down and down was up, and this happened once, twice, three times. We ended up overturned on a hillside, where a boulder stopped our car, breaking the windshield but preventing us from continuing to roll down the interminable hillside and saving our lives. Nobody got hurt — my sister and I were fine, as if nothing had happened, probably influenced by my father's calm. He carried us barefoot back up the hill, climbing the slope back to the road, where a lot of people approached to offer help.

I distinctly remember one man who gave me something to drink. I remember him although I probably never saw him again.

Lying face up on the sand here, at the end of the year in Playa Negra, is when my whole life really does pass before my eyes, not because anything tragic is happening, but because what are you without your memories? There's a meteor shower, and that will also turn into a memory. It's incredible! Sometimes there are two meteors at once, and some seem to last an eternity. Anyone who has seen one will know how hypnotic it is, that one feels privileged and at the same time very small.

And thinking of those lights I also remember how in the house of my best friend, Claudia, we used to go out and catch fireflies. We would trap them in a jar and we would set them free later. We went out in pajamas to catch them, and our mothers didn't like it because we would tromp through the mud, playing in a downpour. The pajamas would go in the trash.

# I TRY TO SHINE WITH MY OWN LIGHT

**Luciana Koberg Garrón**
Escazú
Born June 30, 2000

For almost 18 years, since her early childhood, she's been a classical ballet dancer. She trained in the classic Russian style of ballet. She thought she would dedicate her life to this, and she was very competitive, a trait she learned from her parents, who were athletes. In her adolescence she started having panic attacks, which she attributed to academic pressures and the fact that her body didn't match the "traditional" standards of the aesthetics of ballet. She decided to go to Germany, and in the year she was there, she abandoned the idea of becoming a professional ballerina. She studied German, and working as a babysitter she discovered her passion for working with children. Returning from Berlin, she started studying psychology. She also sells artisanal granola, and she recently started dancing again, now with different expectations. She has an intimate relationship with the natural environment: "I love nature and that's where I feel like the best version of myself."

This was in San Ramón de Tres Ríos, so the yard was a forest in which we would lose ourselves as if we were far from the city. I think we did it because afterwards we could bathe in hot water, which was the best feeling in the world.

My mom called me Luciérnaga, "Firefly," actually still does, instead of Luciana. She said it means a woman of light, and to tell the truth I liked the name. In fact, I try to shine with my own light, like fireflies. Like stars.

I remember spinning and spinning at another point in my life and not feeling the strange calm that I felt that night in the car. Spinning on a stage, dancing ballet, with all the stresses that this discipline, poorly managed, can cause women and their bodies. There was no calm there, only anxiety... Maybe that's also how the fireflies felt in the jar.

After the car crash, what I remember most is that the next day was Monday and we didn't have to go to school. That's what I remember, as well as the man whose identity I'll never know. Something made me get out of that car that kept rolling and rolling, with the same calm that it gives me to see the stars on the beach at this moment.

**Written by: Adrián Castro**

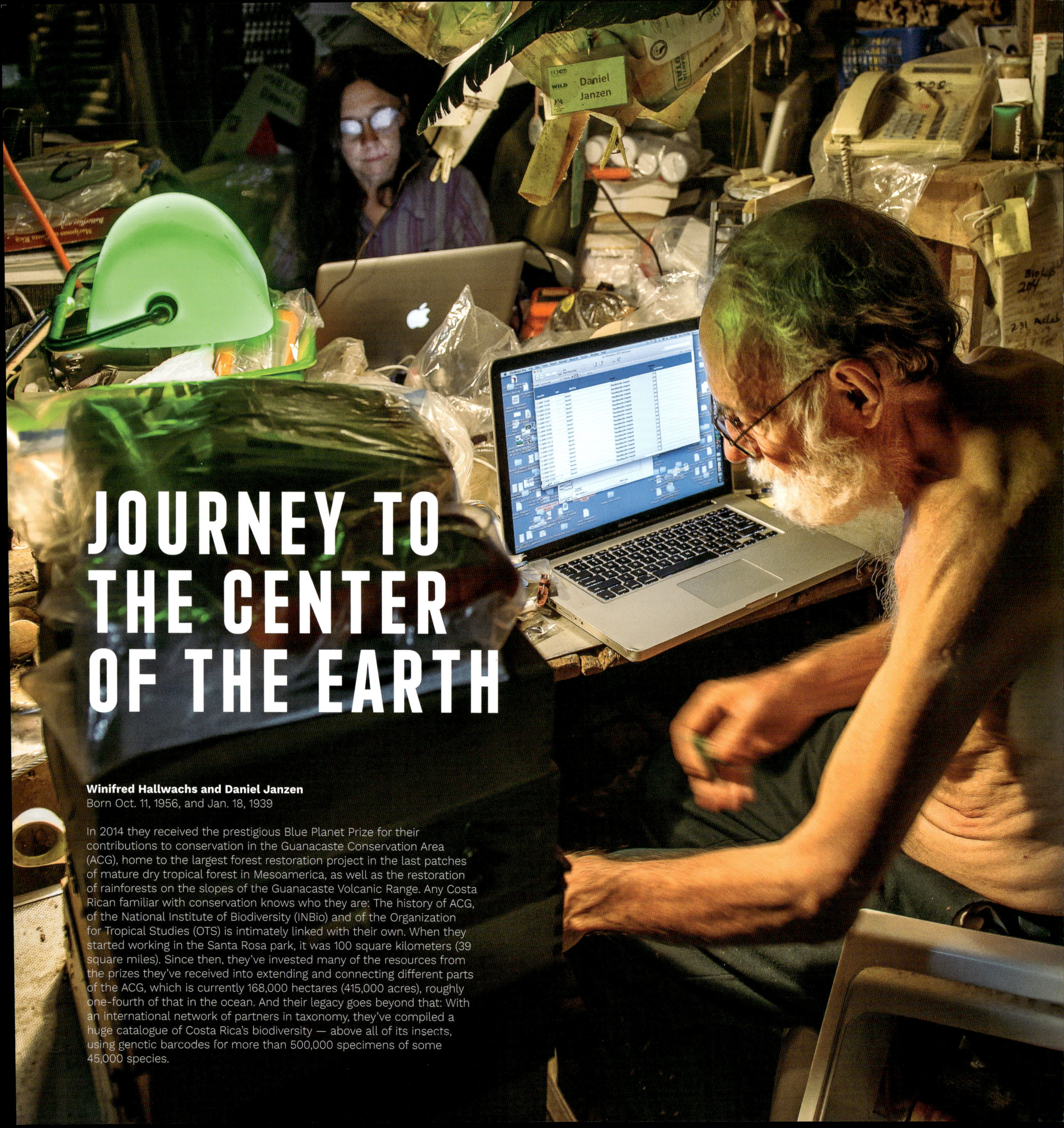


# JOURNEY TO THE CENTER OF THE EARTH

**Winifred Hallwachs and Daniel Janzen**
Born Oct. 11, 1956, and Jan. 18, 1939

In 2014 they received the prestigious Blue Planet Prize for their contributions to conservation in the Guanacaste Conservation Area (ACG), home to the largest forest restoration project in the last patches of mature dry tropical forest in Mesoamerica, as well as the restoration of rainforests on the slopes of the Guanacaste Volcanic Range. Any Costa Rican familiar with conservation knows who they are: The history of ACG, of the National Institute of Biodiversity (INBio) and of the Organization for Tropical Studies (OTS) is intimately linked with their own. When they started working in the Santa Rosa park, it was 100 square kilometers (39 square miles). Since then, they've invested many of the resources from the prizes they've received into extending and connecting different parts of the ACG, which is currently 168,000 hectares (415,000 acres), roughly one-fourth of that in the ocean. And their legacy goes beyond that: With an international network of partners in taxonomy, they've compiled a huge catalogue of Costa Rica's biodiversity — above all of its insects, using genetic barcodes for more than 500,000 specimens of some 45,000 species.

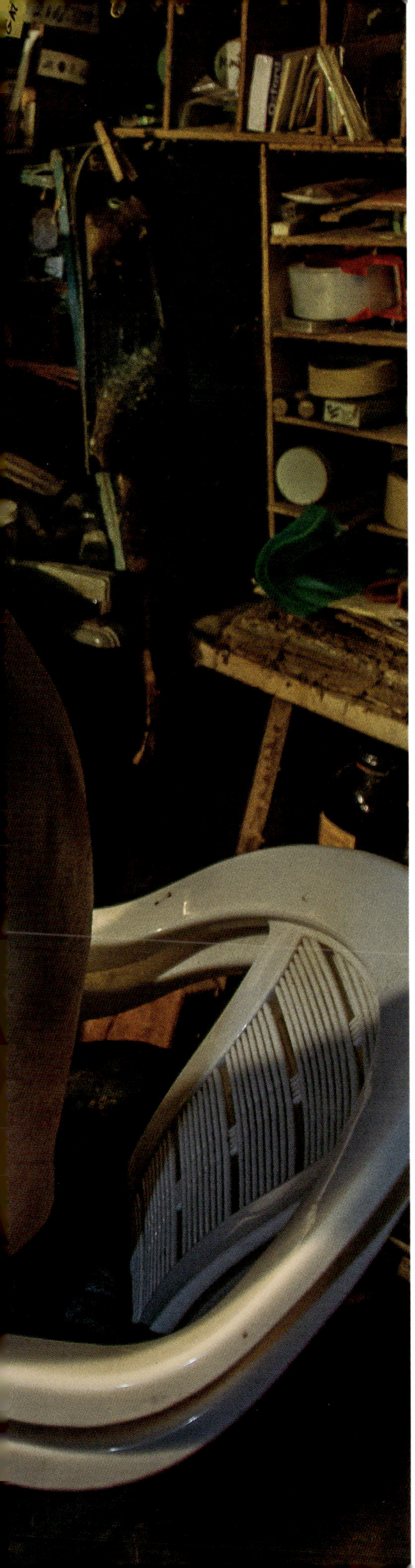

A long line of little green crickets born on a branch, their long antennas combed by the wind of Santa Rosa National Park. That's the moment Winnie can't forget, betraying her meticulous study of the natural world. You can't mention Dan without mentioning her, and vice versa. He speaks of her affectionately as an extension of himself: "She's more intelligent and curious. I talk, and she thinks." She chooses her words carefully to honor him: "He has a magnetic ability to speak from the heart." They call each other Win and Dan. And they would both fit perfectly as characters in a Jules Verne novel.

Their partnership started 42 years ago; she was a student in one of his taxonomy classes in Minnesota. She was 23, he was 39. "He was fascinated by these insects, and I was intrigued by his fascination," she says.

For their second act, they climbed on a Lacsa plane for the first of many shared adventures. Win remembers her nervousness: What would she talk about for so many hours with an expert like him? But the flight seemed short, as they didn't stop talking. That's how she learned about the origin of Dan's fascination with moths. At the age of 9 someone gave him a butterfly net. In very little time, he had caught all the butterflies that existed in the Minneapolis area, which wasn't exactly renowned for its biodiversity. But his world grew larger with a visit to the Museum of Natural History. Dan remembers an exhibit of tropical butterflies, where the butterflies were *blue* ! and came in hundreds of other colors, textures and shapes. That day he said to himself: I've got to see the place they came from! That's how he would come to Costa Rica, never to leave, and Winnie would follow him.

**THAT'S HOW HE WOULD COME TO COSTA RICA, NEVER TO LEAVE**

They landed by night in San José, which was sparsely populated and densely forested in 1978. That first trip together would take them to the Sirena station in the middle of Corcovado. "There were a lot of bugs, it was very romantic," she says with a smile. In those days, Dan still "hunted" with a net. At sunset they would go wait for nightfall in some ginger plants where their beloved *Nystalea* flew around. Dan would catch them at night using only his sense of hearing. He recognized their distinctive buzz, and his reflexes allowed him to capture them with a well-aimed thrust.

That voyage evokes the novel written almost 100 years earlier by Verne, *Journey to the Center of the Earth*. One night they walked to Llorona, a distant beach, famous for a waterfall that spills right on the beach. Their mission was to place some mousetraps alongside some 150-foot trees on the edge of the cliff. They were in an impressive primary forest that they describe as a formidable cathedral. Sadly, that was the last day those giants remained standing — that night a huge storm lashed the coast and knocked over these stately centenarians. "It was devastating to see so much destruction, not caused by humans. That day we understood how critical it was to protect big stretches of forest." That "Aha!" moment, years later, would benefit the Guanacaste Conservation Area, and with it all Costa Ricans.

Winnie relates that while they were crossing the Sirena River — full of caiman eyes — she lost her glasses, and without them she couldn't see for weeks; she needed Dan's hand to help her cross the streets of San José. With the passage of decades, it's been up to her to guide him, since Meniere's disease has affected his inner ear. Now she cares for Dan with the same affection he showed her when he led the hike where they fell in love with the nocturnal butterflies, with the forest, with each other and with Costa Rica, a country that would embrace them as natives on their own merits.

**Written by: Giancarlo Pucci Golcher**

# MY FAVORITE SWIMMING HOLE

I'm not afraid to jump in a spring, nor to open my eyes as soon as I'm underwater. This is my favorite swimming hole, and in fact I learned to swim here. As soon as I get out of school, the first thing I do is come here. But when my mom is not at home, they don't let me.

One time, I was alone at home, and I really wanted to go to the spring, but I couldn't. And so I had to wash clothes. I went to our laundry area. I climbed up onto the washing machine. I added water, added more water, and added still more water! It was like I did it just to hear the sound of the water. I felt like I was at the swimming hole. And I almost emptied the entire bag of powdered detergent into the water. And since I liked to play with foam, I started to throw all the foam up in the air, like this. The foam almost started spilling out of the laundry room. Nobody caught me. But when my mom returned from some errands in Orotina, she saw what I had done and she punished me. I can't use the washer anymore when she's not there.

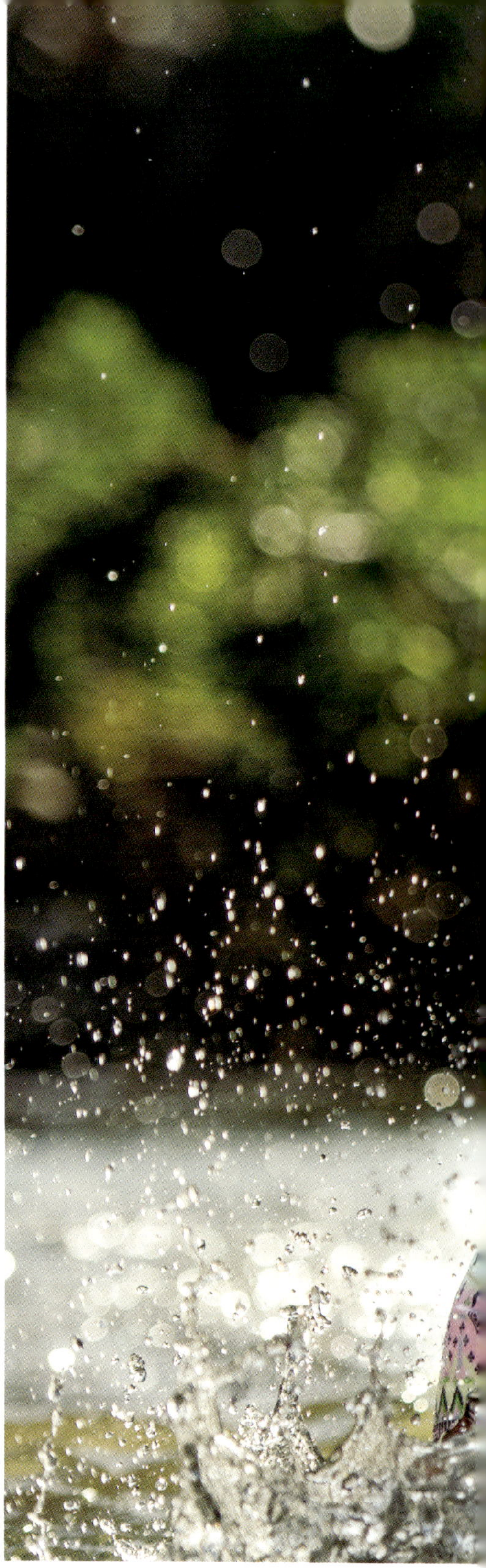

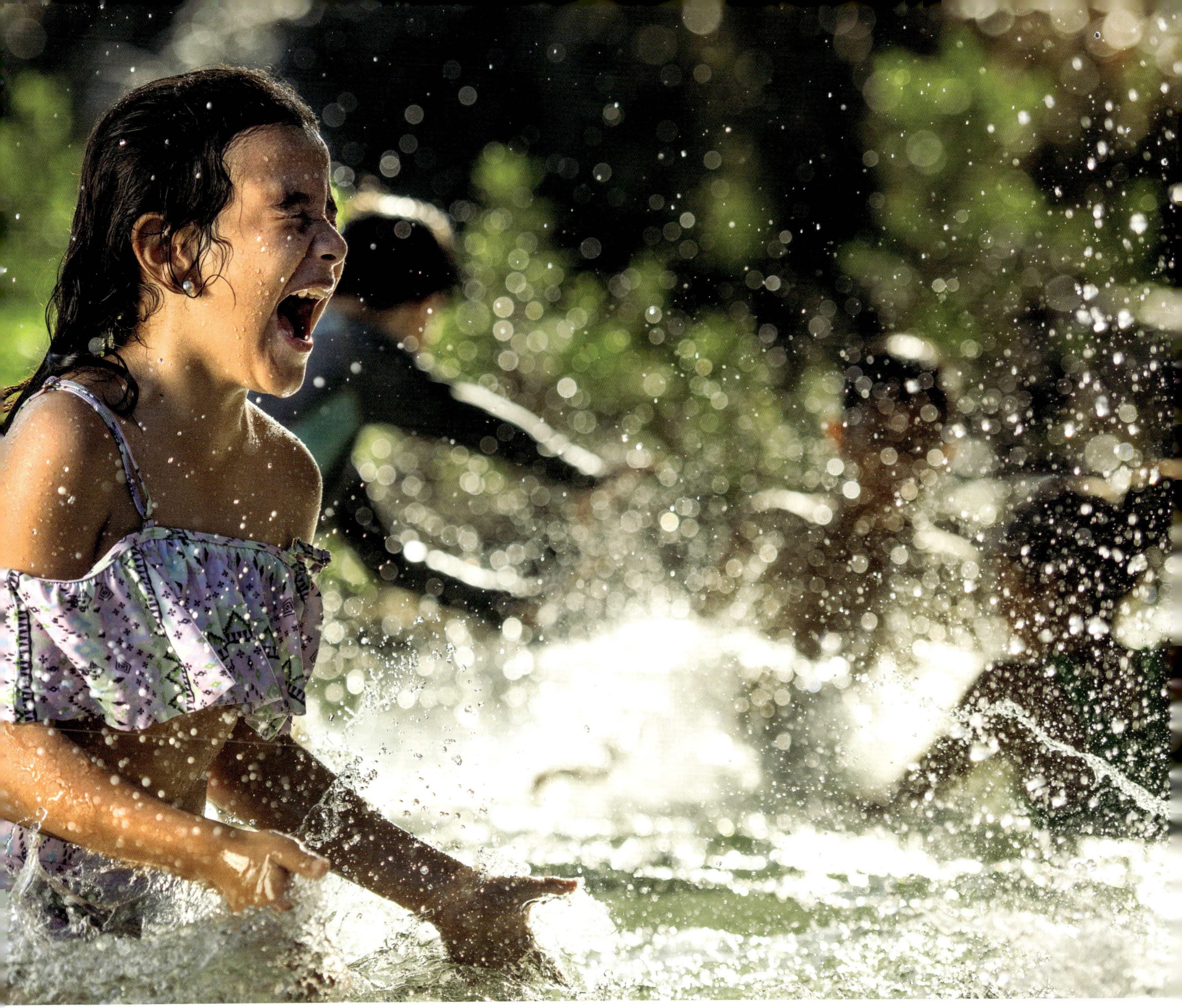

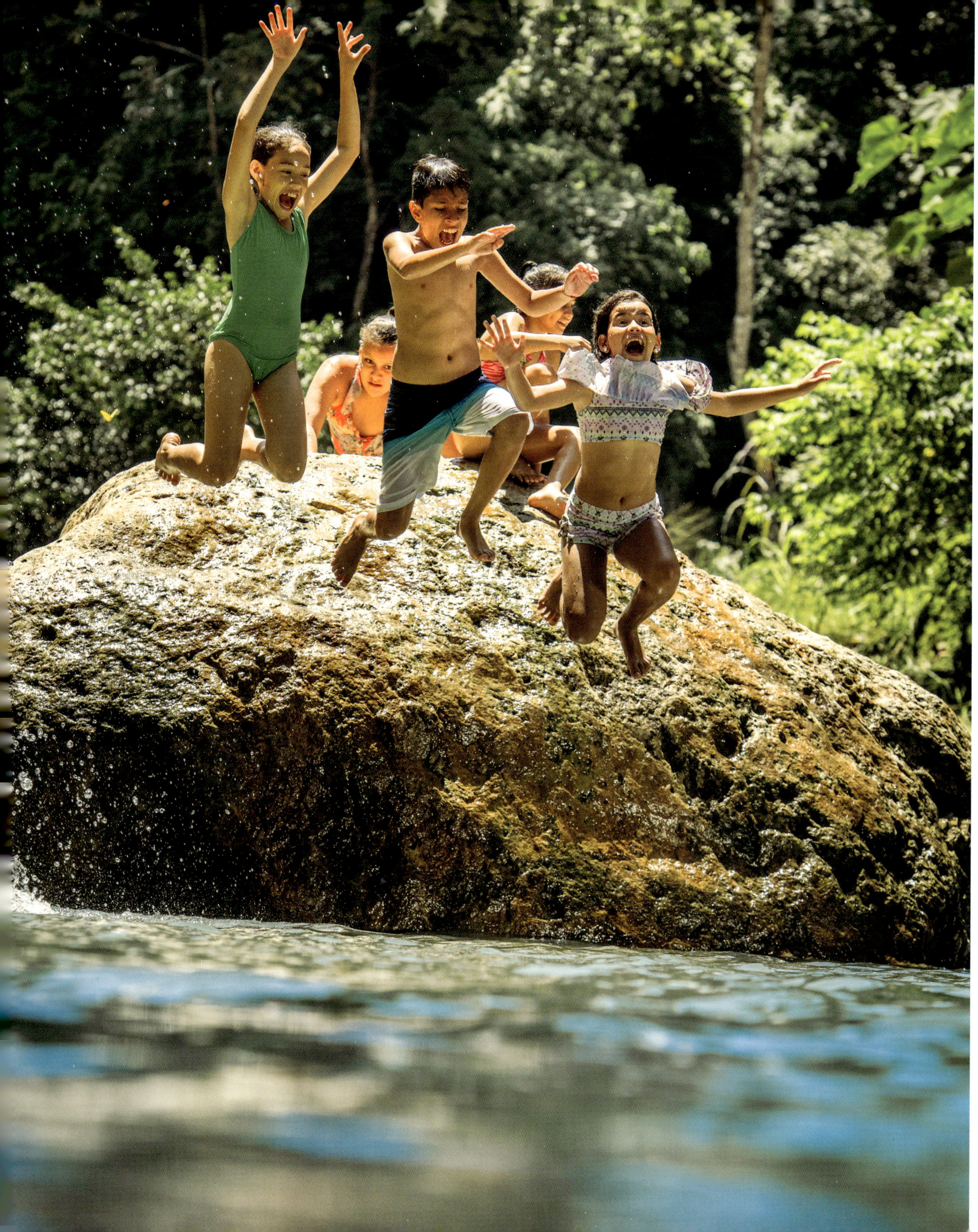

## I GET MAD, BECAUSE ALL OF THAT IS ULTIMATELY GOING TO END UP IN THE RIVER

But that was a long time ago — I was seven then, and I'm nine now. All that water I wasted, I could have used for other things. I don't like to play with foam anymore, nor to waste anything, because that just hurts nature. Both of my parents work at the little restaurant across the street from our house. We separate all our trash there. I help them haul bags from the kitchen to the street every Wednesday, when the recycling girl comes. And when I see people throwing trash on the streets, I scold them. I get mad, because all of that is ultimately going to end up in the river.

**Written by: Libertad Sobrado**

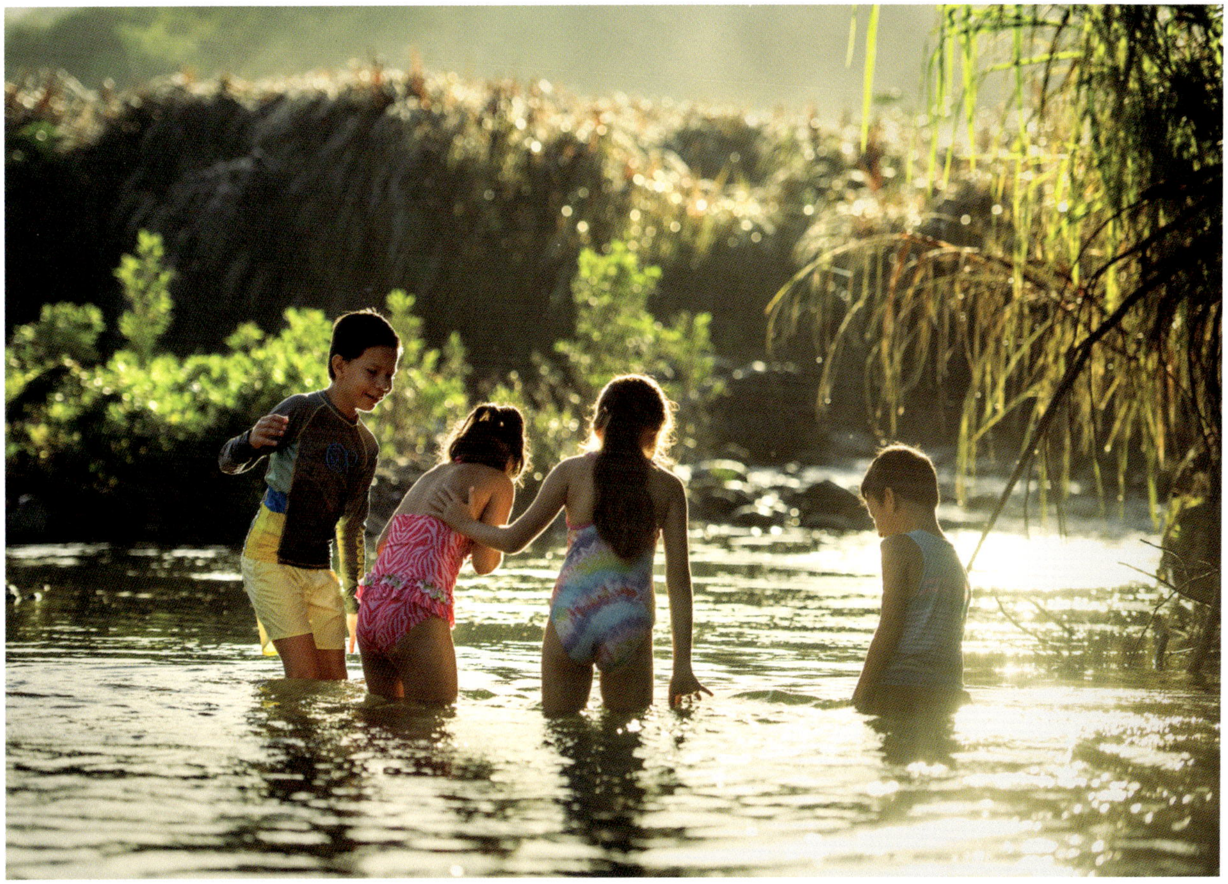

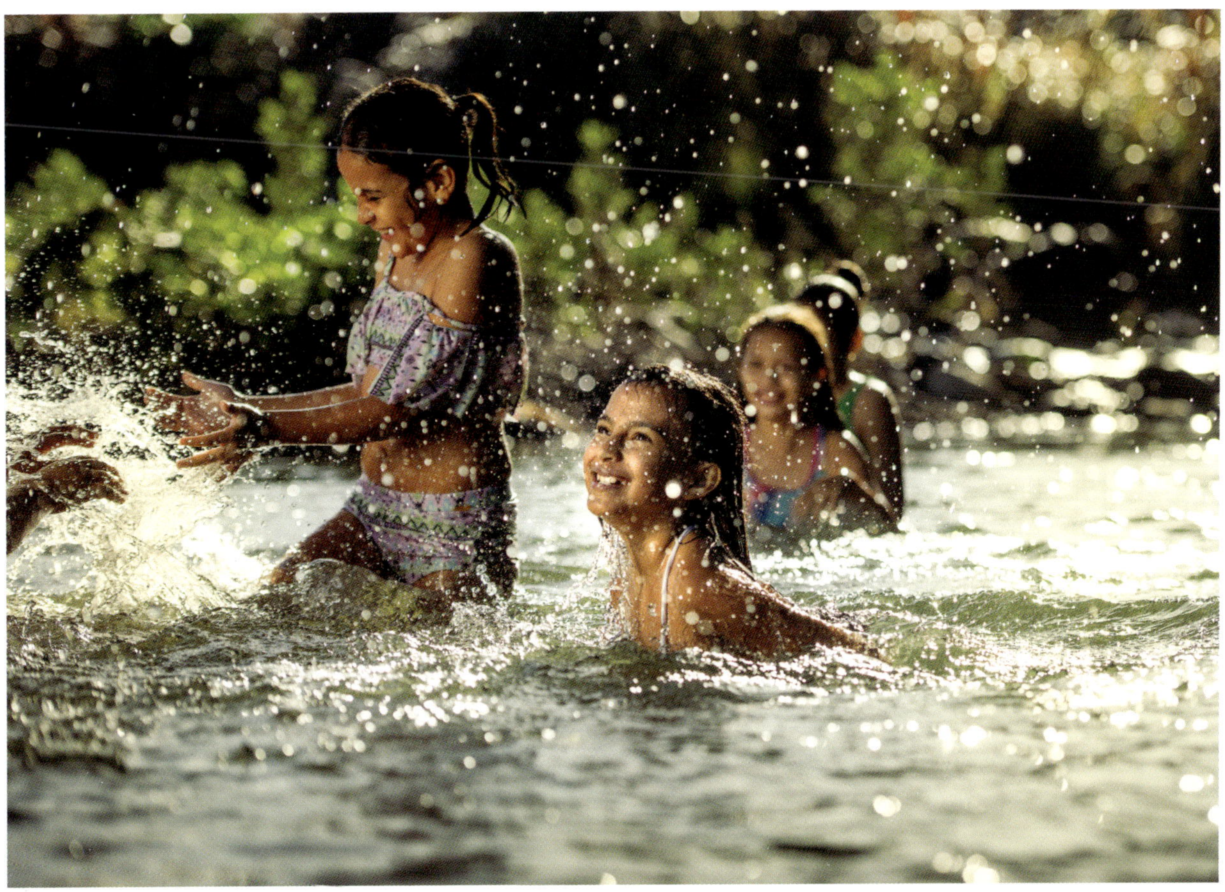

**Jimena Amador**
San Mateo
Born Dec. 10, 2009

Jimena is pure happiness: She loves to swim in freshwater springs. She's a free-spirited girl, a dreamer, concerned about the environment: "If I could, I would make clones of everybody in the world to go around picking up trash." If we were to speak of superpowers, that of Jimena would be to turn back time to prevent pollution. These are the kind of dreams that can change the world.

# THE END OF AN ERA

3:15 a.m. "Let them criticize, mama, all they want," sings an old radio that emits more static than anything else, whose antenna is barely held together with tape. Two guys approach who aren't from here.

"Buddy, give me four chicken wings and some fries with all the sauces. What kind of juices do you have?"

"Barley rice," the man says from the other side of the counter, wearing an apron that could tell some stories. In one pocket is a dishrag and in the other a wad of bills to make change.

"I'll have the same, Pop," says the other one.

"Man, Leo, today we win 2–0. If not, I'll buy you that clam ceviche."

"It's tough, man, the Puerto always screws us. Besides, you said the same thing last time, and you still owe me a Churchill."

A typical soccer conversation follows between friends seeking reconciliation with their bodies after what would appear to be a night of many drinks. In the background you can hear a concert of frying food and bubbling grease, with yellowed light bulbs to illuminate the scene for those "dying of hunger." All kinds of nocturnal characters come by this place: "pirate" taxi drivers, legitimate taxi drivers, drunks, prostitutes, workers, believers, churchgoers, and even atheists... All of them are looking for their piece of chicken to help them get to bed before dawn.

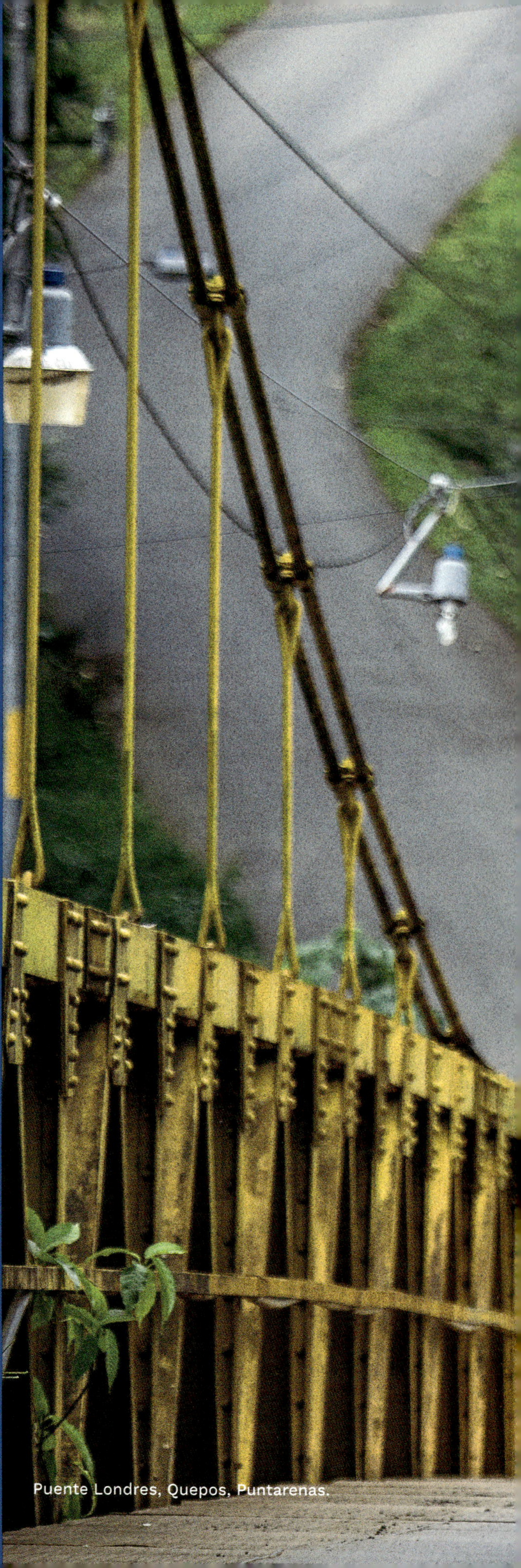

Puente Londres, Quepos, Puntarenas.

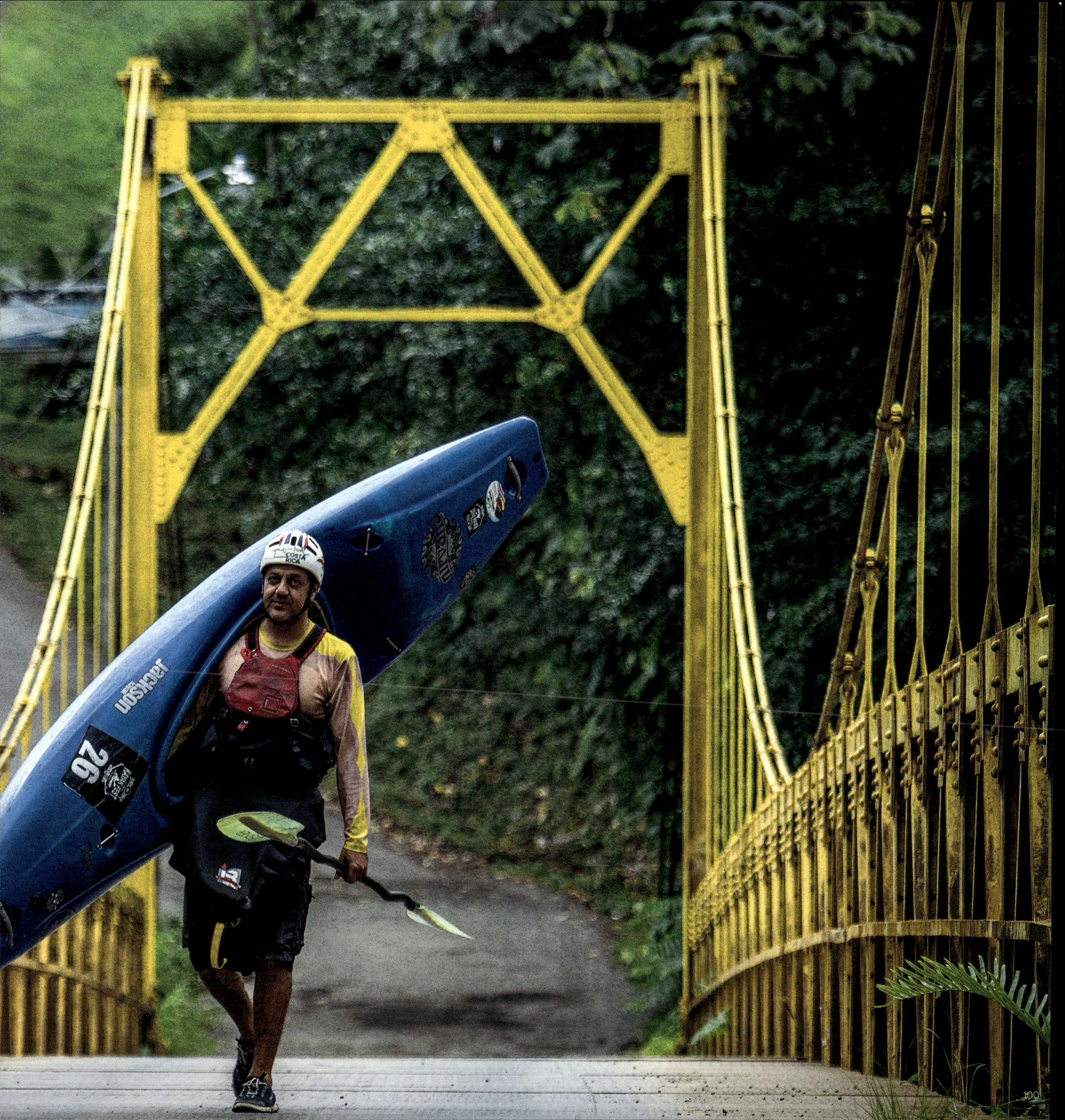
COSTA
RICA
jackson
26

## THE FOREST WITNESSED THAT LEO HAD NO OTHER OPTION

Months ago, there was a notice in the paper: "Seeking rafting guides." Leo didn't know much about that, but he decided to give it a try. He did speak English, and his brother had taught him a thing or two about first aid.

"Those in front, paddles up! Those in back, paddle hard! ... Good! That was a Class 4 rapid," commented the trainer of future guides. Leo was one of those paddling in back, but in his mind he was way in front, thinking and feeling at one with the river, his dreams flooded with water.

"Man, the rafting thing is on Sundays, so I don't think I'm going to be able to come as much to watch Saprissa play."
"Stupid referee! That's a foul!" says Leo's friend. ("He got no balls," replies an unfriendly voice from someone sitting on the stairs.) "Man, Evaristo just isn't getting it done today. That Devil Contreras is messing him up," says Leo's friend.

"Yes, yes, but be quiet because they could start throwing bags of pee at us." Leo meant to tell his buddy that maybe an era had come to an end. With a certain melancholy, he remembered some unique experiences, like when he invaded the goal during the finals and had to spend Father's Day in a paddy wagon...
"Goooooooooooal!!!" A magical opportunity opens up for two men to embrace with abandon in the middle of the crowd. At times a goal gets in the way of something you wanted to say, and this was one of those cases. Saprissa scored, and yet Leo once again had to go without his ceviche.

The man at the chicken shop approaches with his companion of a thousand battles: a dishrag that appears to have been used previously to clean up the filth of all the food joints in the province. "You don't see it yet," says the man, looking fixedly at Leo, "but I'm going to tell you something: that new kid with Saprissa, Fonseca, mark my words, that kid is going to be somebody."
There are situations that are made to convince you, if not define you.

"OK, guys, a deserved rest. Anyone who wants can jump in the water during this stretch, it's worth it." And so Leo did. He let himself go, like you let a soul go when it has decided to be free. He floated down the course of the river, even though it seemed that he was flying. He looked at the sky, drops of rain falling incessantly, carrying clairvoyant messages. Not every day did he get to explore a river canyon, surrounded by plants and trees of every shape and shade of green, looking on like gaping spectators. The forest witnessed that Leo had no other option. From this moment forward, Leo belonged to the river.

**Written by: Fernando Alvarado**

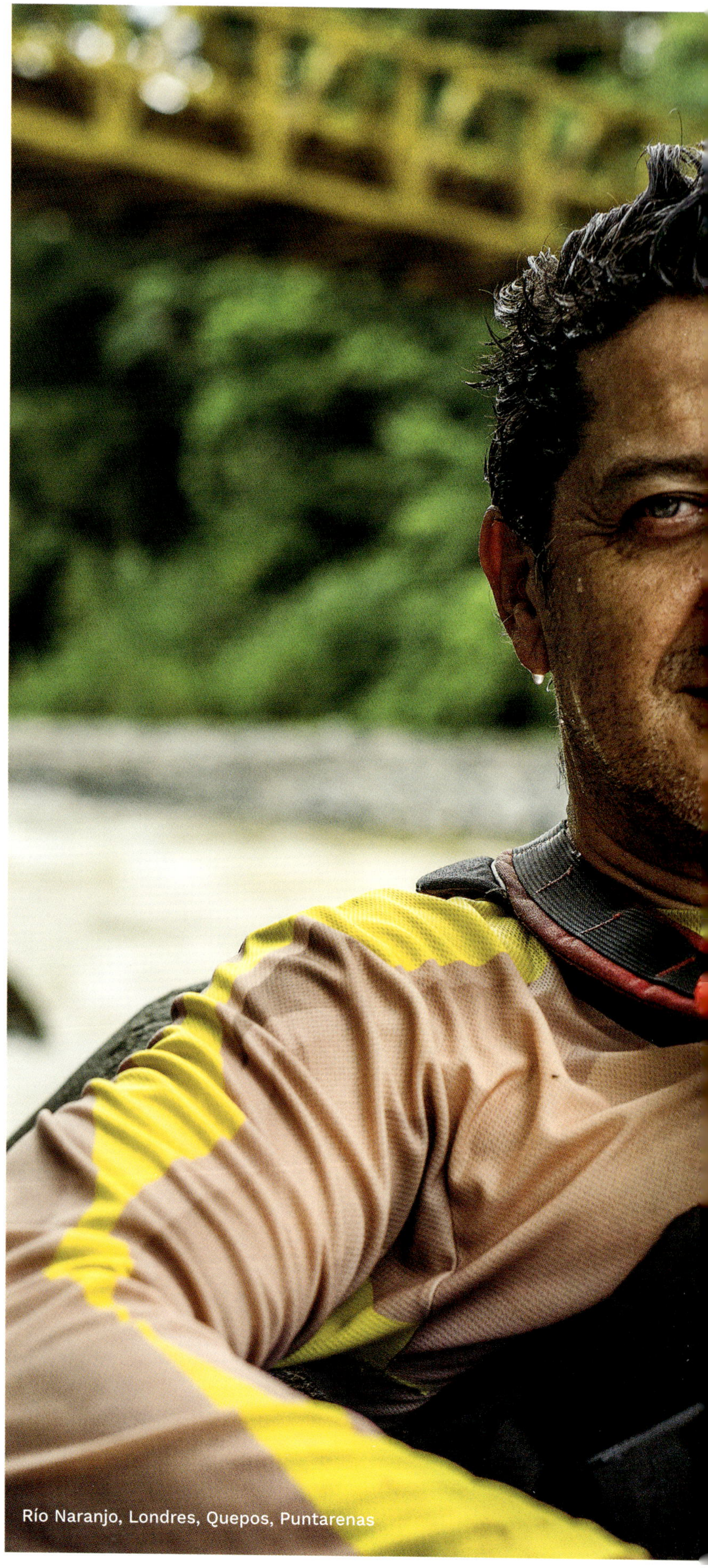

Río Naranjo, Londres, Quepos, Puntarenas

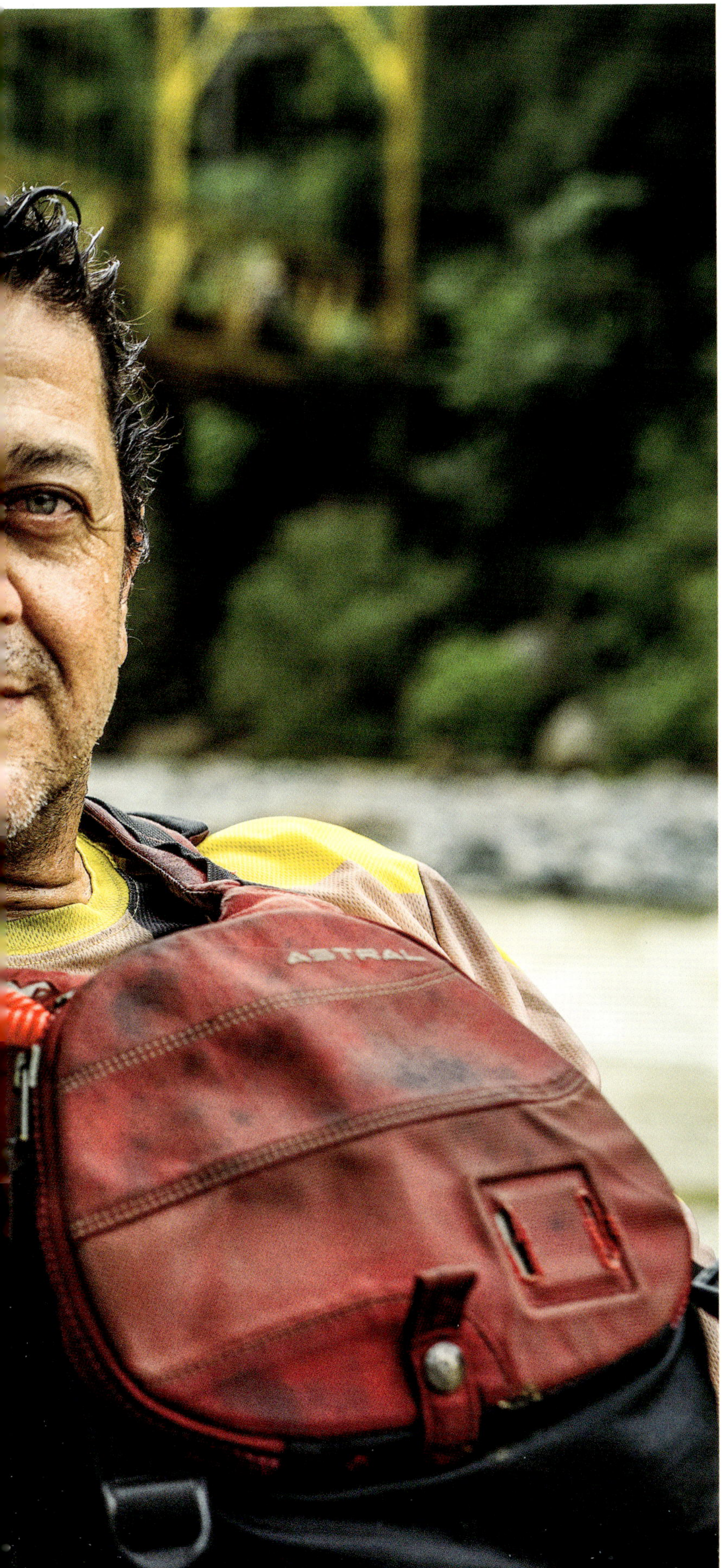

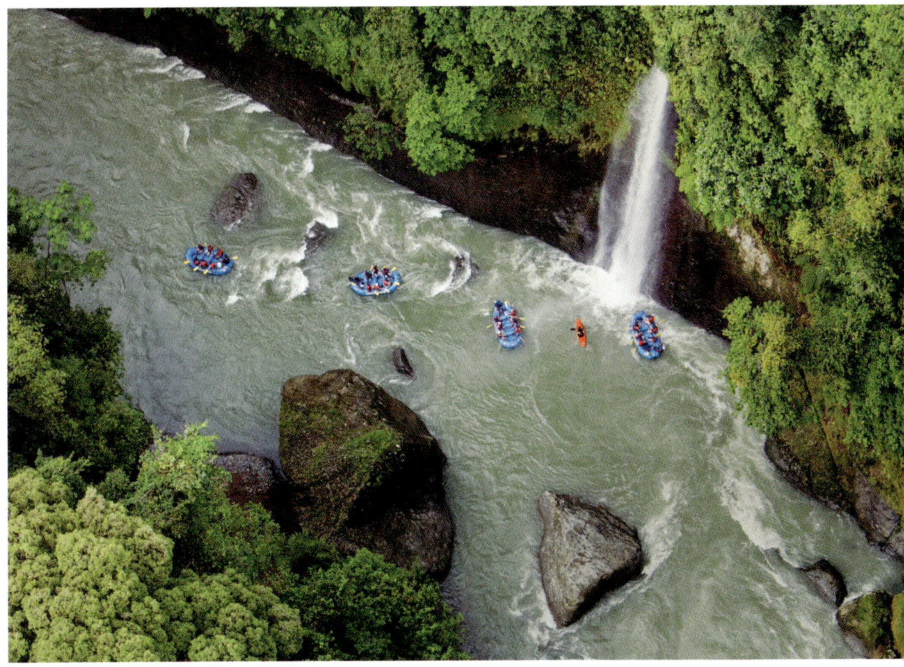

Bajo del Tigre, Siquirres, Limón.

**Leonardo Vásquez Boza**
San José – Quepos
Born Dec. 4, 1972

Leonardo never really settled down until he arrived in Quepos. He tried his luck in many corners of the country, including Turrialba and La Fortuna, and even lived in South Carolina, where he studied for a master's degree in natural resources. Although his working life started in his family business, since 1992 the story of Leonardo's life has been written by the rivers. That year he became certified as a rafting guide and started working at the iconic Ríos Tropicales, under the beloved Rafa Gallo. In 2002, he started his own business in adventure tourism and rafting along the central Pacific coast, called H2O. Leonardo is married and has two children, to whom he tries to impart a value of the highest importance: "What I try to teach my kids now is to be happy, to find happiness in your studies and in your work, and in everything you do, that's the mission."

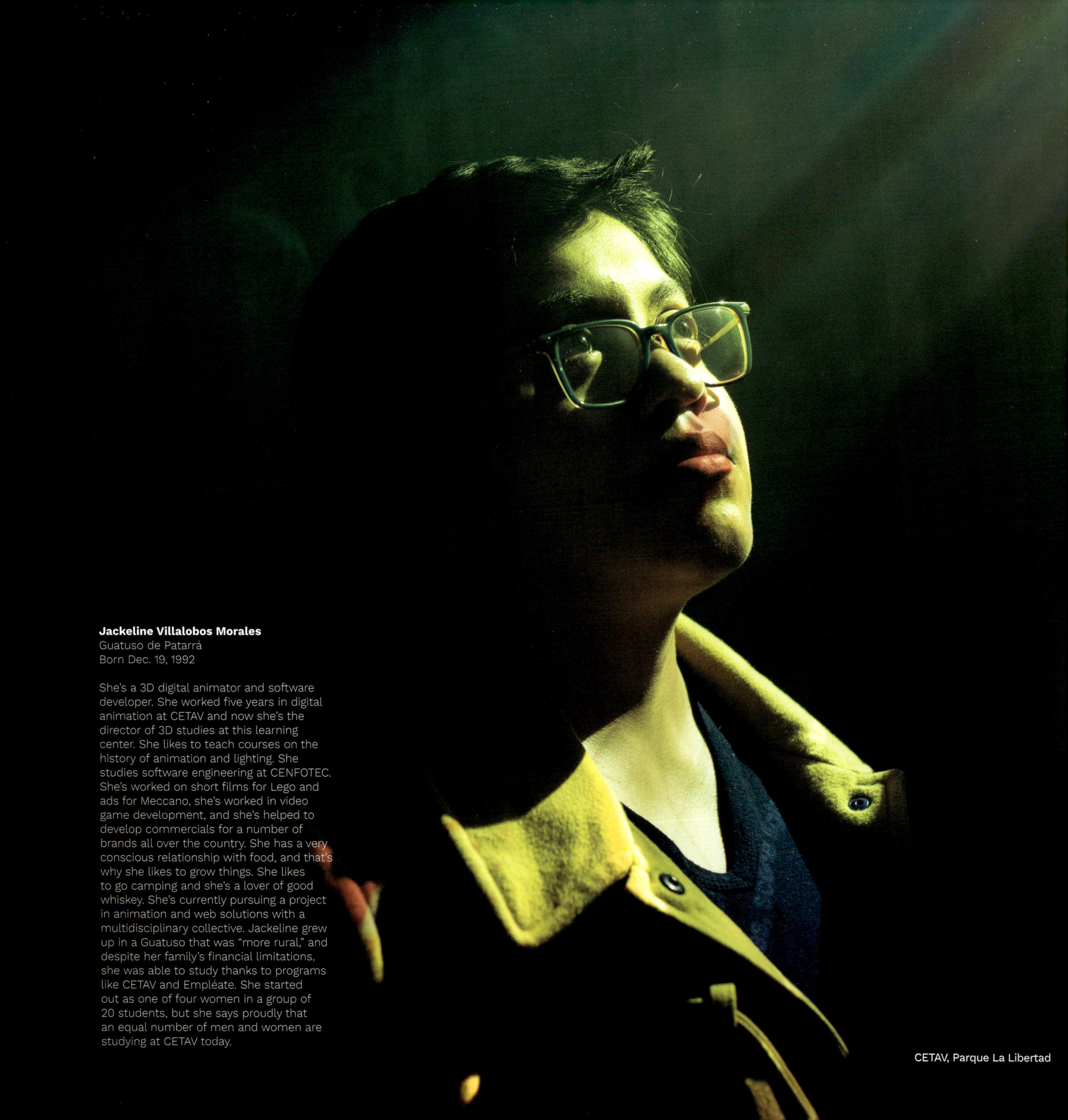

**Jackeline Villalobos Morales**
Guatuso de Patarrá
Born Dec. 19, 1992

She's a 3D digital animator and software developer. She worked five years in digital animation at CETAV and now she's the director of 3D studies at this learning center. She likes to teach courses on the history of animation and lighting. She studies software engineering at CENFOTEC. She's worked on short films for Lego and ads for Meccano, she's worked in video game development, and she's helped to develop commercials for a number of brands all over the country. She has a very conscious relationship with food, and that's why she likes to grow things. She likes to go camping and she's a lover of good whiskey. She's currently pursuing a project in animation and web solutions with a multidisciplinary collective. Jackeline grew up in a Guatuso that was "more rural," and despite her family's financial limitations, she was able to study thanks to programs like CETAV and Empléate. She started out as one of four women in a group of 20 students, but she says proudly that an equal number of men and women are studying at CETAV today.

CETAV, Parque La Libertad

# TEARS OF HAPPINESS

I'd seen him cry only once, when his mother died, but this was the first time I saw him cry from happiness. I was so touched to see tears on his face, just as he was feeling when the plane took off.

Dad was very calm and understanding, but I imagine it wasn't always like that. Growing up in Patarrá with alcoholic parents couldn't have been easy. At 11 years old, he had to start working to support the family.

He knocked on doors from one garage to the next offering to work, and between cars and trucks he learned to drive. When he married my mom, that was the only thing he knew how to do. He got a job driving trucks, distributing cleaning products.

I think he breaks the mold, and that's why it wasn't hard for him to get better jobs. His own boss advised him to start a delivery business, and the boss himself would use his services. In little time, he had already bought trucks and hired a staff. These were good years. He always advised me to study, to make something of my life, he said.... I feel that he said this so that I could please have an easier life than he did.

I was 14 years old when one day Dad came home and put a manila envelope full of money on the table. They had been forced to sell the farm in Siquirres to settle their debts. The business was bankrupt.

For them it was easy to live within these limits, but for my older brother and me, it was like watching our dreams die.

I didn't care that we wouldn't go to La Paella in San Francisco to eat on weekends anymore; the only thing that went through my head was: How will I pay for my education?

Dad was raised in a traditional macho environment, in which showing your feelings was an obstacle to moving forward. He said his children needed a mother at home and he didn't let her work. But with me it was different — he encouraged me to study.

I started working part-time with a photographer, looking for a way to finance a career in design. Just like Dad, I moved from job to job, until I went to a convention and approached a CETAV booth. I applied for a scholarship. The many hours of video games and my interest in logic, numbers and drawing bore fruit.

I went to school prepared to study, never imagining that I would end up being the coordinator of 3D digital animation studies.

After the family business failed, our life was much simpler. Although his lessons were many, what Dad enjoyed most was teaching me how to savor the woody flavor of a good whiskey. Without ice or water, that's how he drank it.

It didn't take much time for that seed to grow. As soon as I had the opportunity, I traveled to Scotland with my boyfriend to learn more about the culture of whiskey. Each region has its own whisky, and we did a tour that offered samples at each locale. When the time came to taste, I looked for the one that he would have liked most.

When I was a girl, the idea of traveling wasn't even an option, but at that moment I was toasting in his honor with an Argbeg.

Right there, I knew that I wanted to put my parents on a plane. Maybe Mexico isn't Scotland, but it's a shorter trip and they're older now. I don't know if they were from emotion or pride — we were just taking off — but those tears had already made the trip worthwhile.

**Written by: Michelle Macluf**

# ARISING FROM THE ASHES

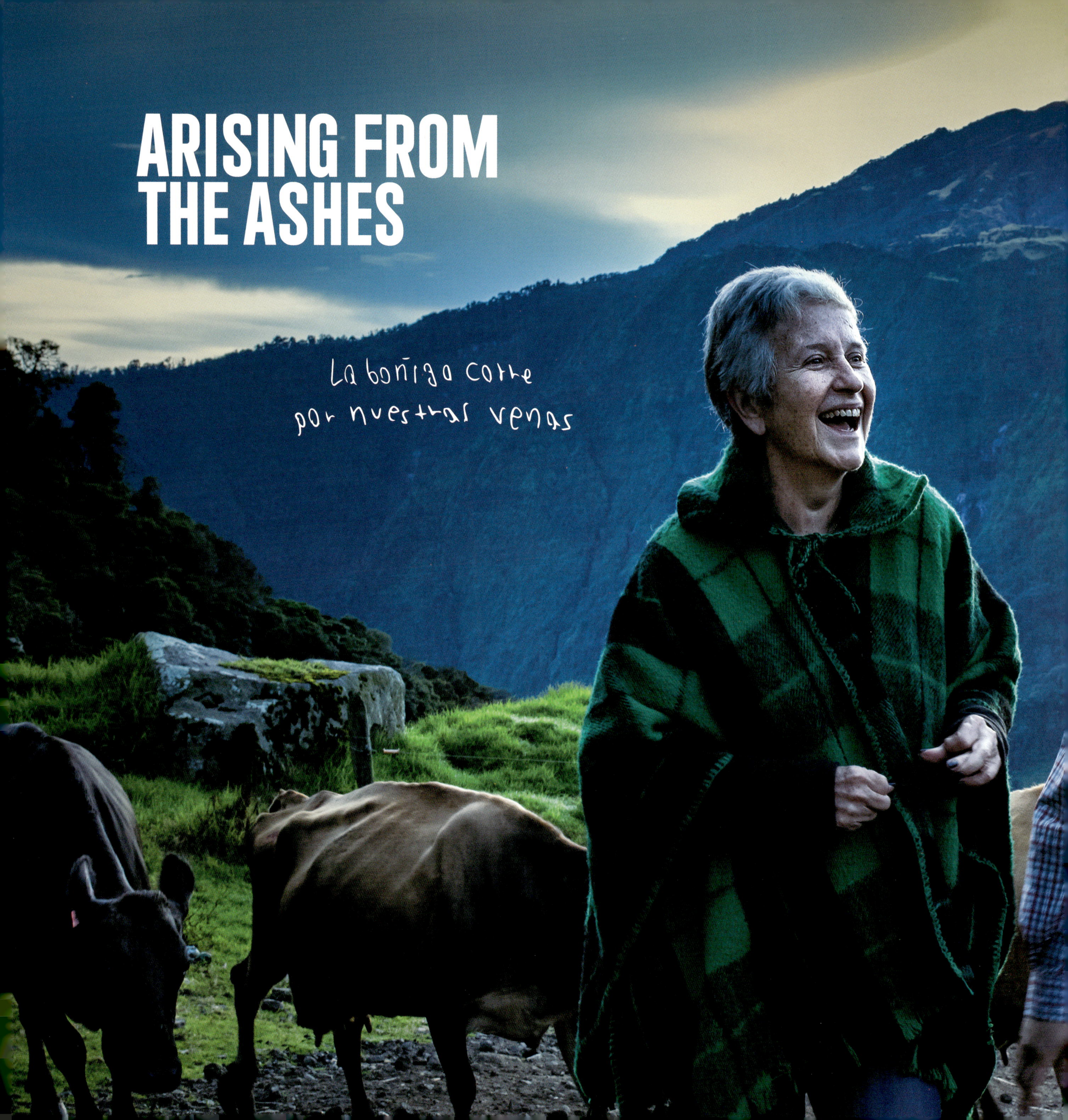

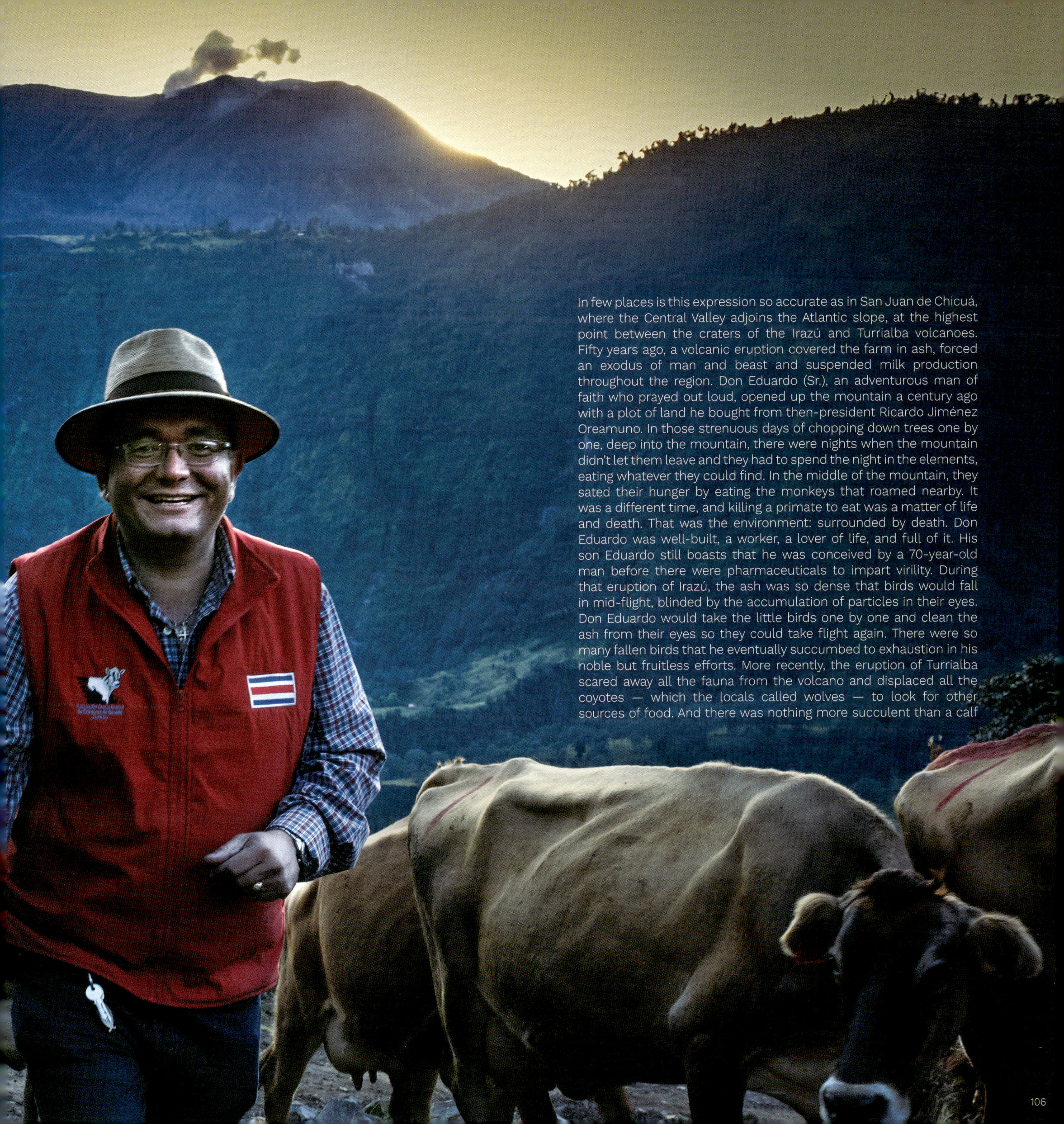

In few places is this expression so accurate as in San Juan de Chicuá, where the Central Valley adjoins the Atlantic slope, at the highest point between the craters of the Irazú and Turrialba volcanoes. Fifty years ago, a volcanic eruption covered the farm in ash, forced an exodus of man and beast and suspended milk production throughout the region. Don Eduardo (Sr.), an adventurous man of faith who prayed out loud, opened up the mountain a century ago with a plot of land he bought from then-president Ricardo Jiménez Oreamuno. In those strenuous days of chopping down trees one by one, deep into the mountain, there were nights when the mountain didn't let them leave and they had to spend the night in the elements, eating whatever they could find. In the middle of the mountain, they sated their hunger by eating the monkeys that roamed nearby. It was a different time, and killing a primate to eat was a matter of life and death. That was the environment: surrounded by death. Don Eduardo was well-built, a worker, a lover of life, and full of it. His son Eduardo still boasts that he was conceived by a 70-year-old man before there were pharmaceuticals to impart virility. During that eruption of Irazú, the ash was so dense that birds would fall in mid-flight, blinded by the accumulation of particles in their eyes. Don Eduardo would take the little birds one by one and clean the ash from their eyes so they could take flight again. There were so many fallen birds that he eventually succumbed to exhaustion in his noble but fruitless efforts. More recently, the eruption of Turrialba scared away all the fauna from the volcano and displaced all the coyotes — which the locals called wolves — to look for other sources of food. And there was nothing more succulent than a calf

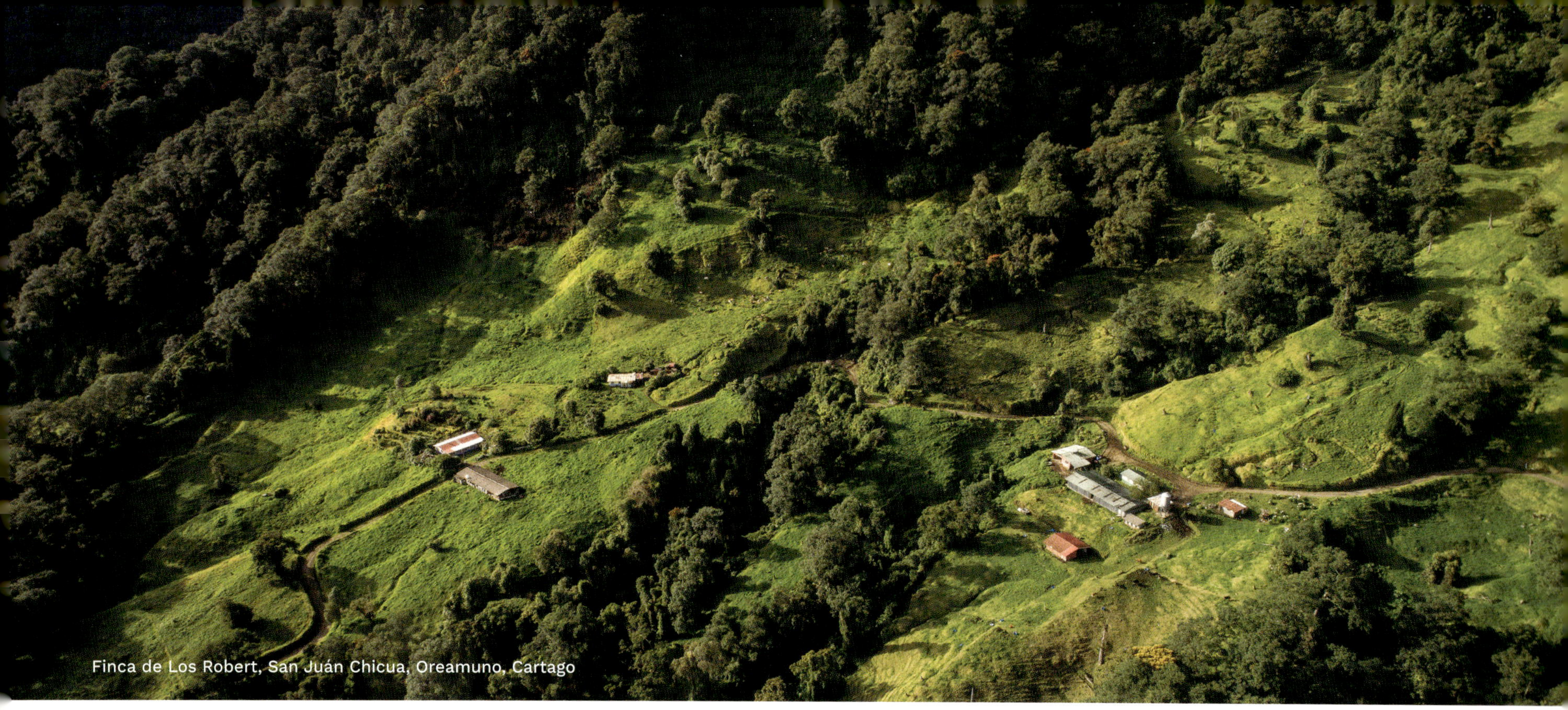

Finca de Los Robert, San Juán Chicua, Oreamuno, Cartago

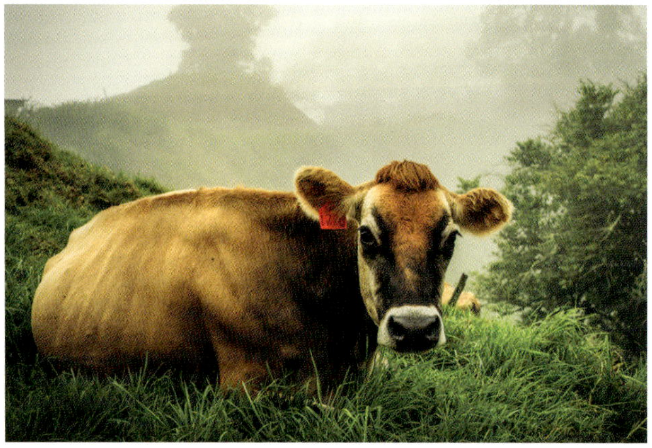

from the dairy farm. The people in charge of the cows liked the wolves, which they describe as large, hairy and blue-eyed. But losing calves is costly and must be avoided. Again, life or death. It's the same cycle as with the cows, that upon birth the Roberts greet with kisses, hugs, affection and baptism, and when it's time to take them away, they say goodbye with thankfulness and affection. The milk comes from a place of love, an inspired place. On a clear day, you can see the Atlantic from the Robert farm. The countryside here makes you pause and contemplate. But peace can be stolen by an underground river on any given day, like when the entire dairy farm vanished in seconds. "That's life, it's chaos, it's constant adaptation." The cerebral hemorrhage of Don Eduardo, the cancer of Doña Argentina, the debt of the lands after the eruptions, the hurricanes that knocked down the mountain.... "Here

**Eduardo Robert Ureña**
Cartago – Desamparados
Born Feb. 23, 1977

Eduardo grew up in the mountains, and the outdoors is an essential element of who he is. This agricultural engineer is owner of a milk farm called Lechería Villa Emilia, one of the 100-year-old businesses of the Robert family. He studied at the little school in La Finca, where his mother was a teacher. He went on to study at the Colegio Seminario, and his love for cows and farms led him to study agronomy in Santa Clara de San Carlos, where he met the mother of his son Emiliano. He has a niece who is 20 years older, Marlene Robert, who looks more like his aunt when you see them together. She studied hotel management in Mexico, and more than 40 years ago she married David, with whom she shares the work on the farms at Hacienda Los Gavilanes. She embraces the newborn calves, gives them first names and last names, and promises them that at her farm they'll have a good life. Eduardo's father married twice: Marlene is the granddaughter of his first wife, Argentina, and Eduardo is the son of the second, Doña Fulana. He's dedicated almost 25 years to dairy farming, and he's president of the Costa Rican Association of Jersey Cattle Breeders. His farm is right in the middle of two volcanoes, Irazú and Turrialba.

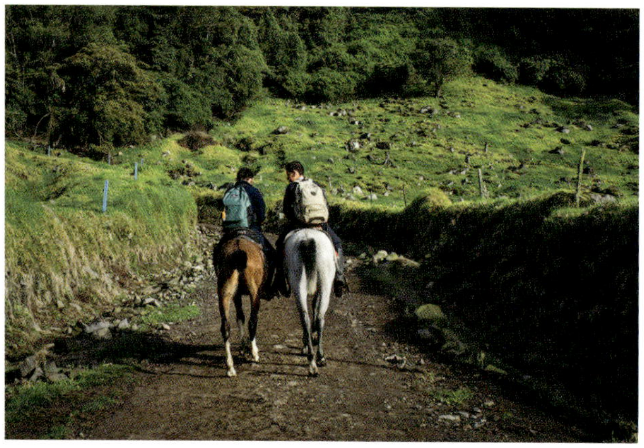

you have a front-row seat on the cycle of life." Like when the ash killed the spiders that eat the *Prosapia*, the plague that eats the grass that's eaten by the cows. This rumbling of the ground is from this volcano or that one. No way of knowing. What you do know is that when there's an eruption of ash and stone that changes your life and your business, it's time to suspend, to go away, to leave behind. You know that one day, calm will return, although it won't be permanent.

The day Don Eduardo died, 90 years old, a funeral carriage had never driven so far. Not even the Red Cross came here. They had to carry the coffin in a pickup, wrapped in blankets so that the ropes wouldn't stain it. The entire community followed on foot, on trucks or on horses. They said goodbye to a great one like great ones. Barely a month later, a truck came for the first time to pick up milk, and life changed for the better, at least a little.

**Written by: Alvaro Cedeño**

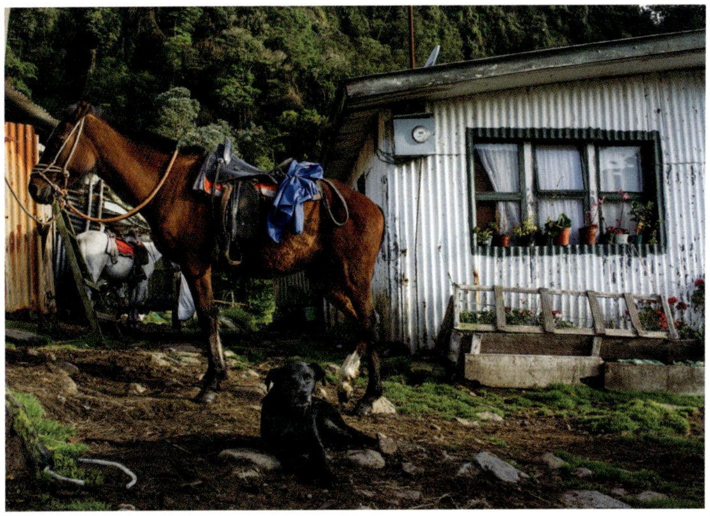

•Costa Ricans drink some 217 liters of milk per year per person.

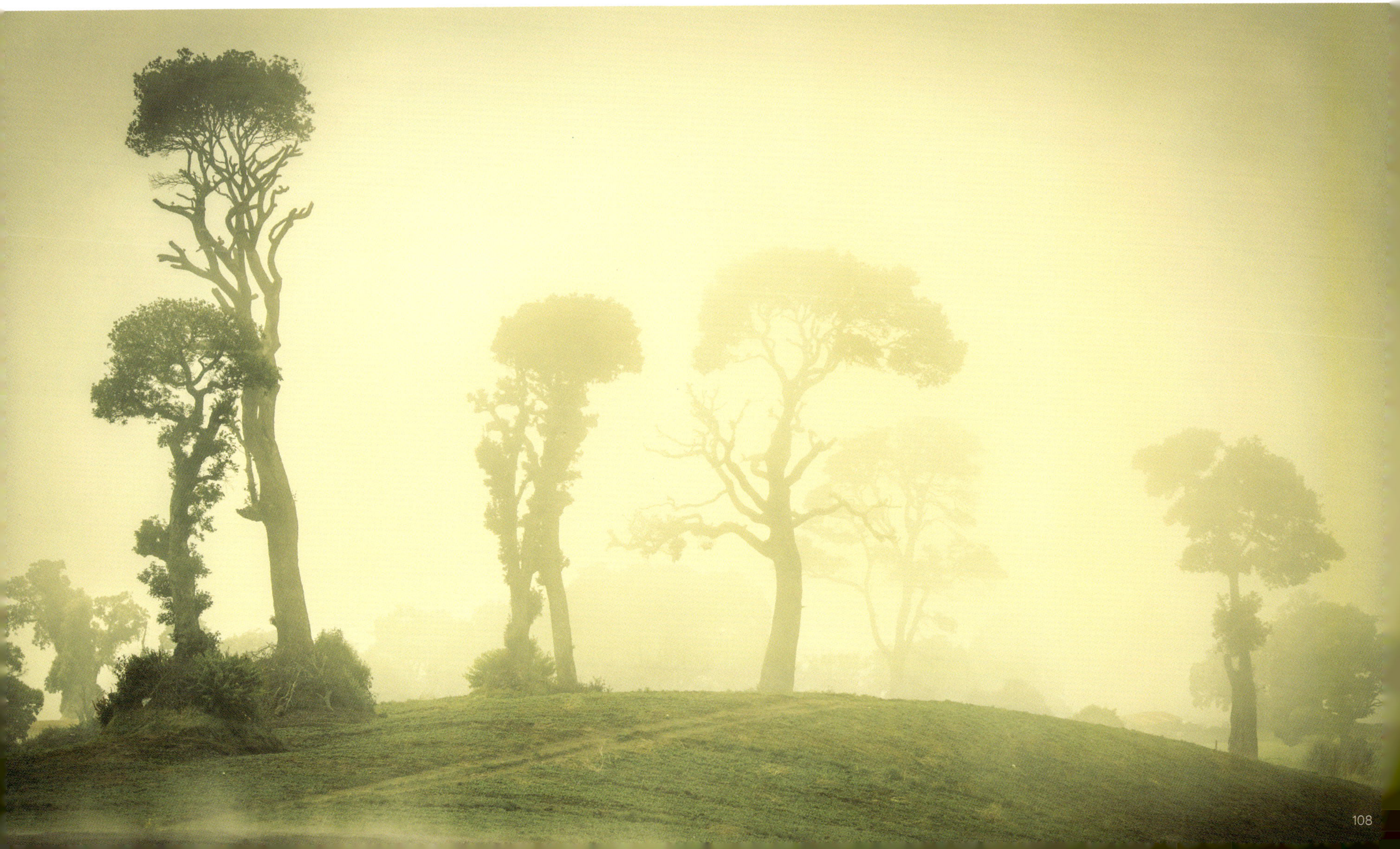

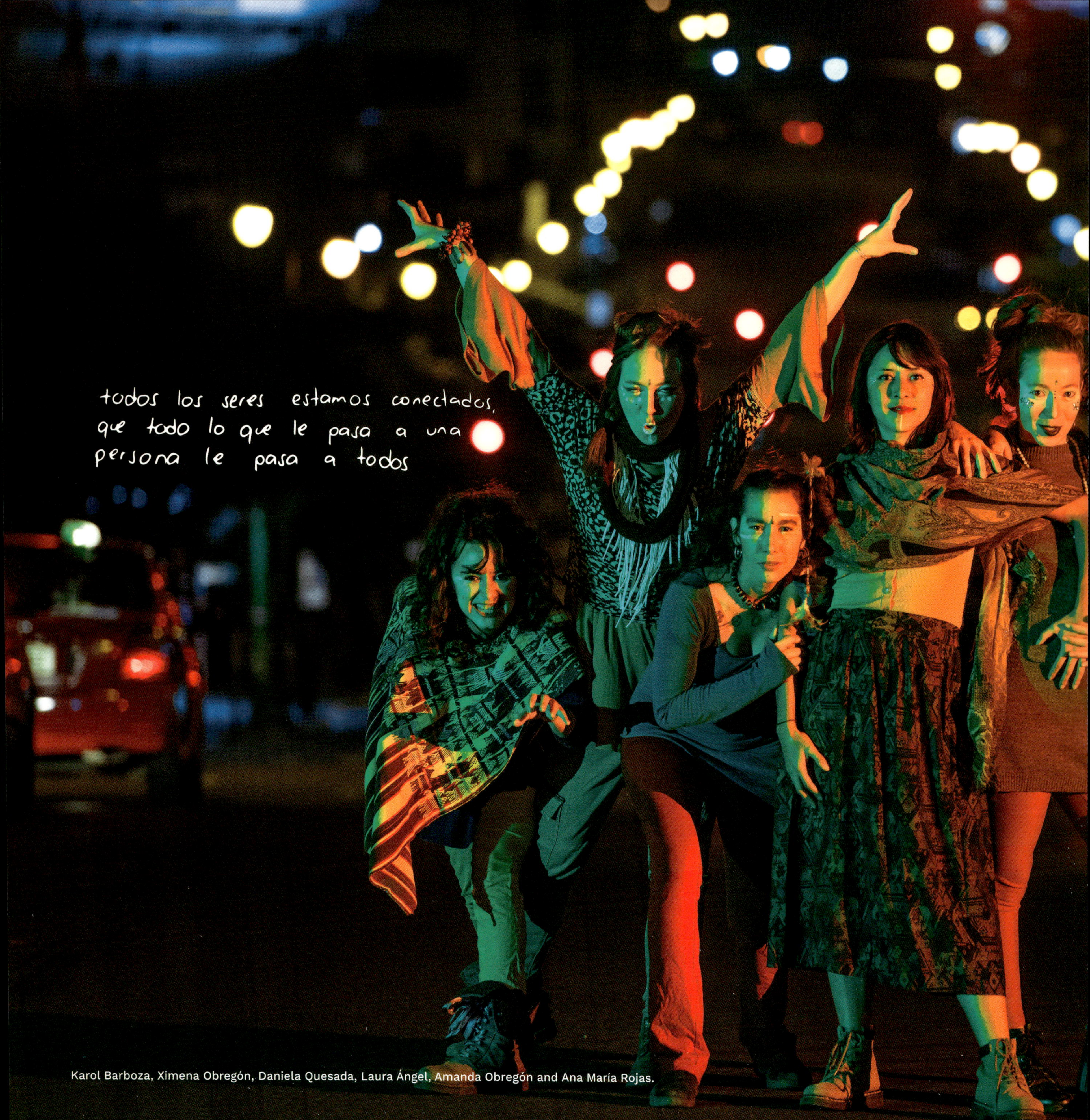


Karol Barboza, Ximena Obregón, Daniela Quesada, Laura Ángel, Amanda Obregón and Ana María Rojas.

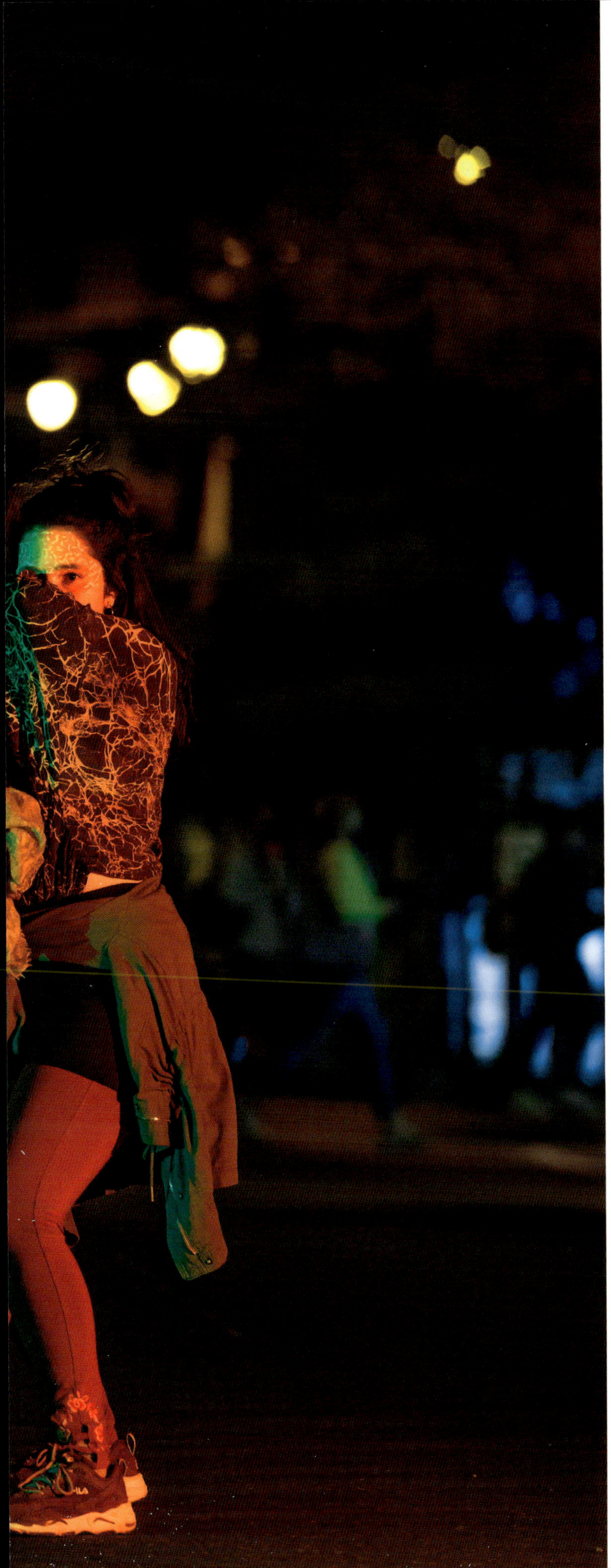

# STRA TE GY

In less than 24 hours, they had spread their voice all over Costa Rica. The interconnectivity and the power of broadcasting information over social networks demonstrated their ability to cross the pond in a matter of hours. Her grandmother in Italy had heard the news, and her brother in Poland too. In Brazil they were organizing collectives to pray for her, and in Costa Rica her photography was more powerful than any algorithm and was soon within reach of the entire population. Anyone who didn't use Facebook or Instagram would soon hear the news. She had been lifted up in prayers to all the angels and archangels in prayer chains by all the little old ladies in the country.

Meanwhile, Blu took advantage of the fact that her cellphone had no charge to disconnect herself from her hectic routine, while her image kept going more viral than any premeditated publicity campaign.

The contact number on the posters they had shared belonged to Fabi, another member of Viajo Sola, and although people were asked to call only with pertinent information, the phone never stopped ringing — friends, family, co-workers, and even total strangers.

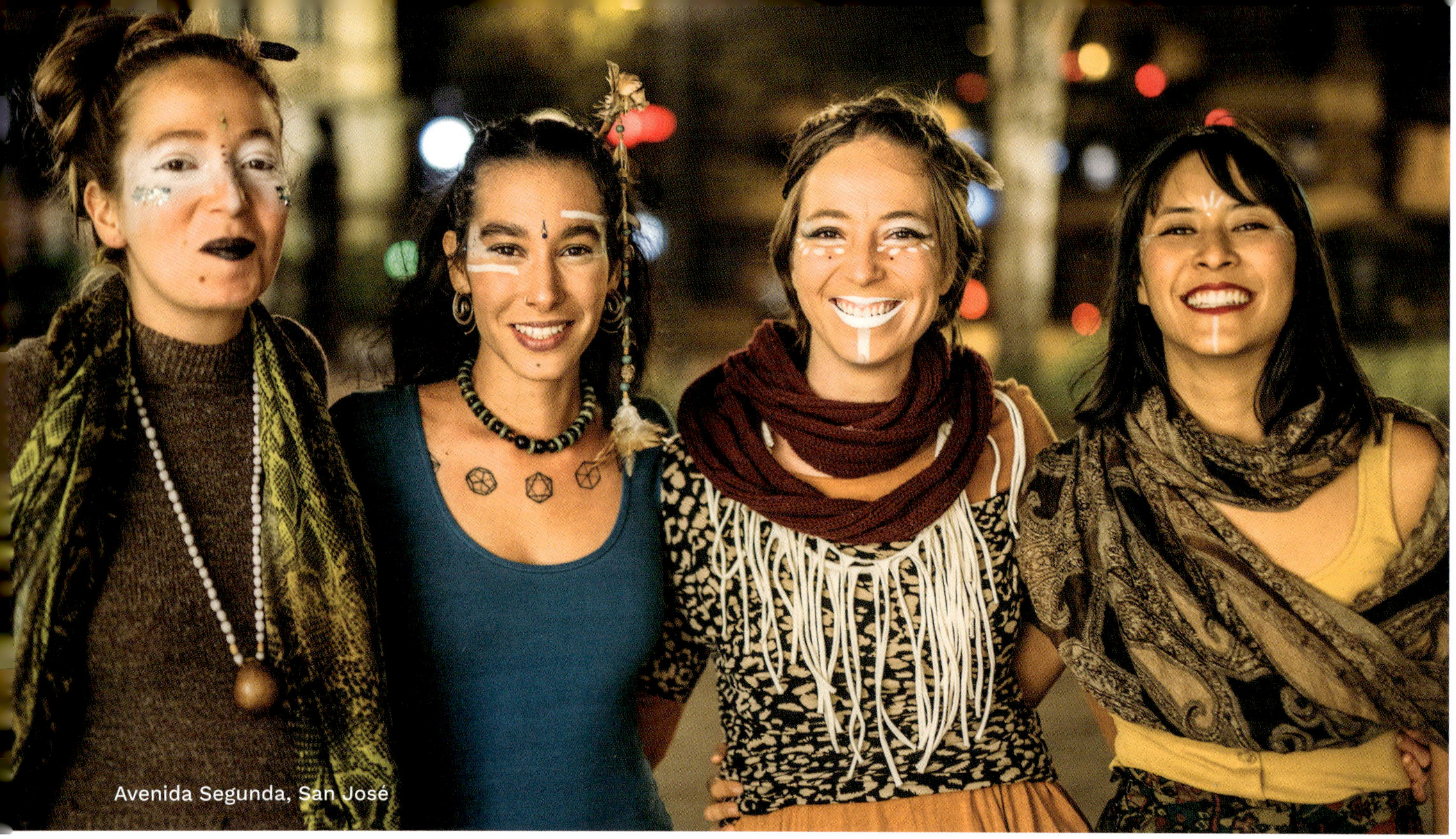

Avenida Segunda, San José

"Did you find her yet? What have you heard?"

Even students of metaphysics dialed in from whatever plane they were on.

"Hello, I was meditating, and I saw her near the Poás Volcano — you should go check over there."

A self-appointed investigative team had even taken upon itself to organize a search based on the last places she was seen.

Blu emerged from the rehearsal exhausted at 2:30 p.m., got on her motorcycle and headed toward Coronado from San José to deliver the tickets to the premiere of her next show to a good friend. After months of rehearsal, the tiredness and the cold of the mountain had gotten to her, so Blu thought the responsible thing to do was to look for a place to sleep. After all, she had fallen off her motorcycle on other occasions out of sheer exhaustion.

This, more than the profound conversation, made her forget to deliver another ticket, and she also missed a 6:30 p.m. work engagement, which she had never missed before.

When she didn't show up at work, an alarm was sounded among her colleagues in the collective, especially among the members of the stage group with whom she had organized the show called "Strategists," which used crude humor to demonstrate the state of alertness and the strategies that women had to develop to navigate this world, where claims of femicide and disappearances accumulate daily.

It was a lively topic, something they had developed in a campaign of powerful and striking expectations, yet paranoia and fear were now taking its place. That morning, after recovering her strength, she was woken up by the curiosity of a knock-knock on the door in such a remote place.

As soon as she opened the door, two good friends threw themselves upon her with tears in their eyes.

To understand the magnitude of what was happening was not an easy task. Months would go by before Blu lost her phobia of social networks.

Meanwhile, in the offices of the OIJ federal police, her mother could barely voice her anguish, waiting for them to formulate an action plan. Suddenly, the phone rang.
"Hello, Mom. I'm fine."
Even though the mom sounded very worried, the tranquility of her daughter's voice restored her calm. It took them a while to process everything. Blu's friends went on warning her what she would face as soon as she turned on her cellphone again.
She didn't know whether to feel embarrassment or gratitude, so she succumbed to both. In time, she realized everything that had transpired was an act of intense love acting out of fear. Blu was an instrument that demonstrated the functionality of social networks and their potential. At the end of the day, she *was* found. There was no shortage of people who believed that this was all a marketing strategy to promote her show. And even though this was a very embarrassing experience for Blu and her loved ones, the next weekend and for the entire season the theaters were full.

**Written by: Michelle Macluf**

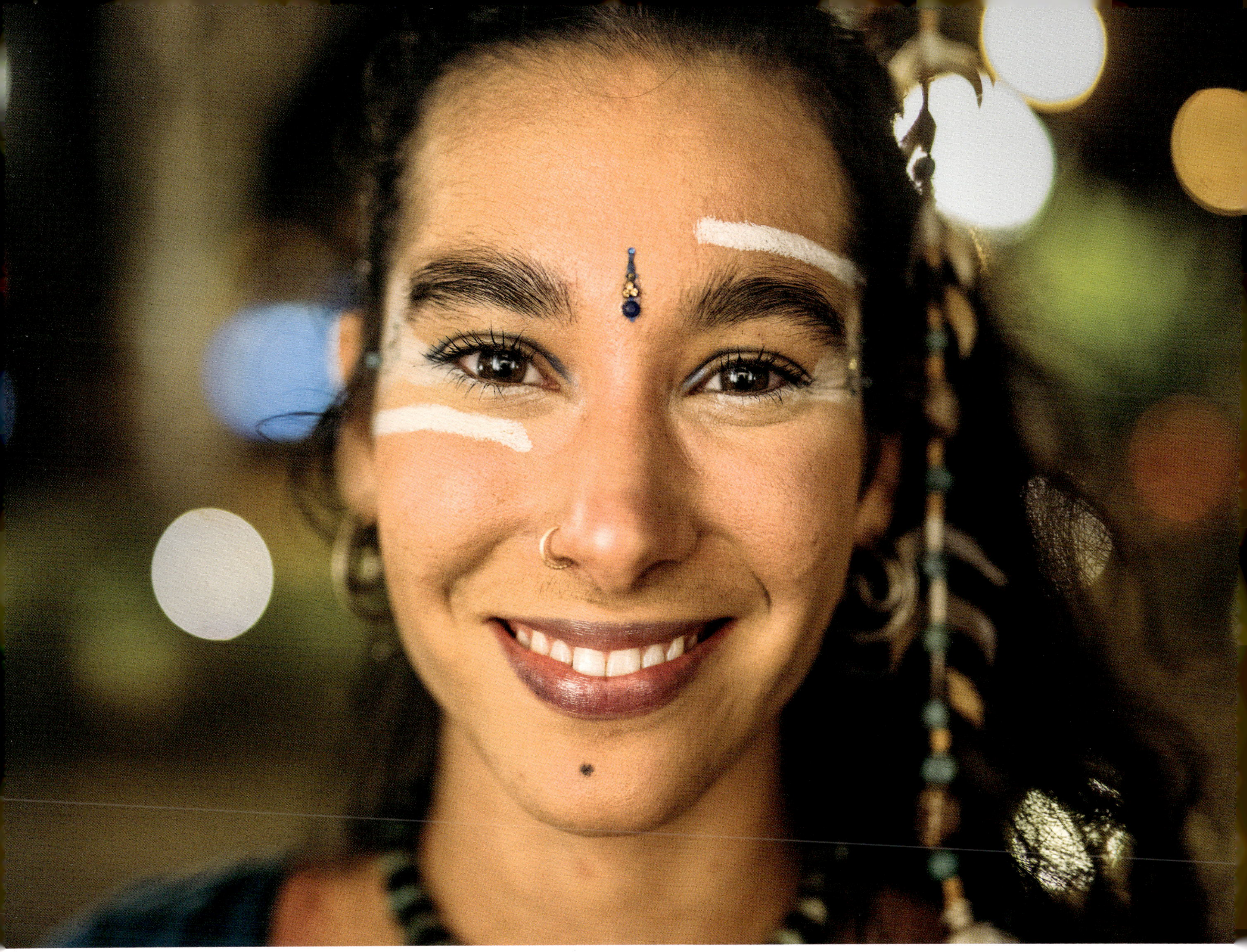

**Colectiva Viajo Sola- Blu Daniela Quesada Delgado**

11 members of a disruptive urban collective with a feminine voice: Amanda Obregón, Ana María Rojas , Berenice Jiménez, Carolina Sheridan, Daniela Isabel Quesada, Diana Avellán, Fabiola Brenes, Irene Gutiérrez, Karol Andrea Barboza, Laura Ángel and Ximena Obregón.
"Viajo Sola" ("I Travel Alone") was born in 2018 as a community of female artists in a constant state of collective creation and expression. They're called to express the need for freedom of movement without fear, raising awareness about the normalization of gender violence. Their mission entails an interdisciplinary spectacle; they facilitate artistic workshops, create interventions in public spaces, and through community interactions propose investigative avenues to mapping experiences related to traveling alone and how that impacts their realities. Daniela Isabel Quesada, "Blu," is a multidisciplinary artist and a member of the collective, a group of singer-songwriters, composers and performance artists.

# NOT GERARDO, JUST 'SELVA'

*There are stories where reality kidnaps the imagination. Truth actually makes fiction boring. When the Puccis asked me if I could write a story about Gerardo, I hesitated. I admit that I envisioned a man from the country, dignified but predictable. Later the story lived on a WhatsApp message that hadn't been listened to for weeks. When I finally played the interview, driving around on a bicycle on the streets of Escazú, the person speaking to me wasn't Gerardo. It was "Selva" ("Jungle"). And there's only one Selva.*

*In my notes I had to paraphrase to keep the train of thought going. "I was the poorest of the rich" / "If I fall down dead today, that's great! And if they burn down my house, then I'll watch the flames." / "I think I could fill a museum with my art." / "As a child I found some hallucinogenic mushrooms and I ate them for a week without stopping." / "So the guy hit me in the head with a machete."*

*Wow. It was overwhelming, but here goes my best effort, in two inadequate paragraphs.*

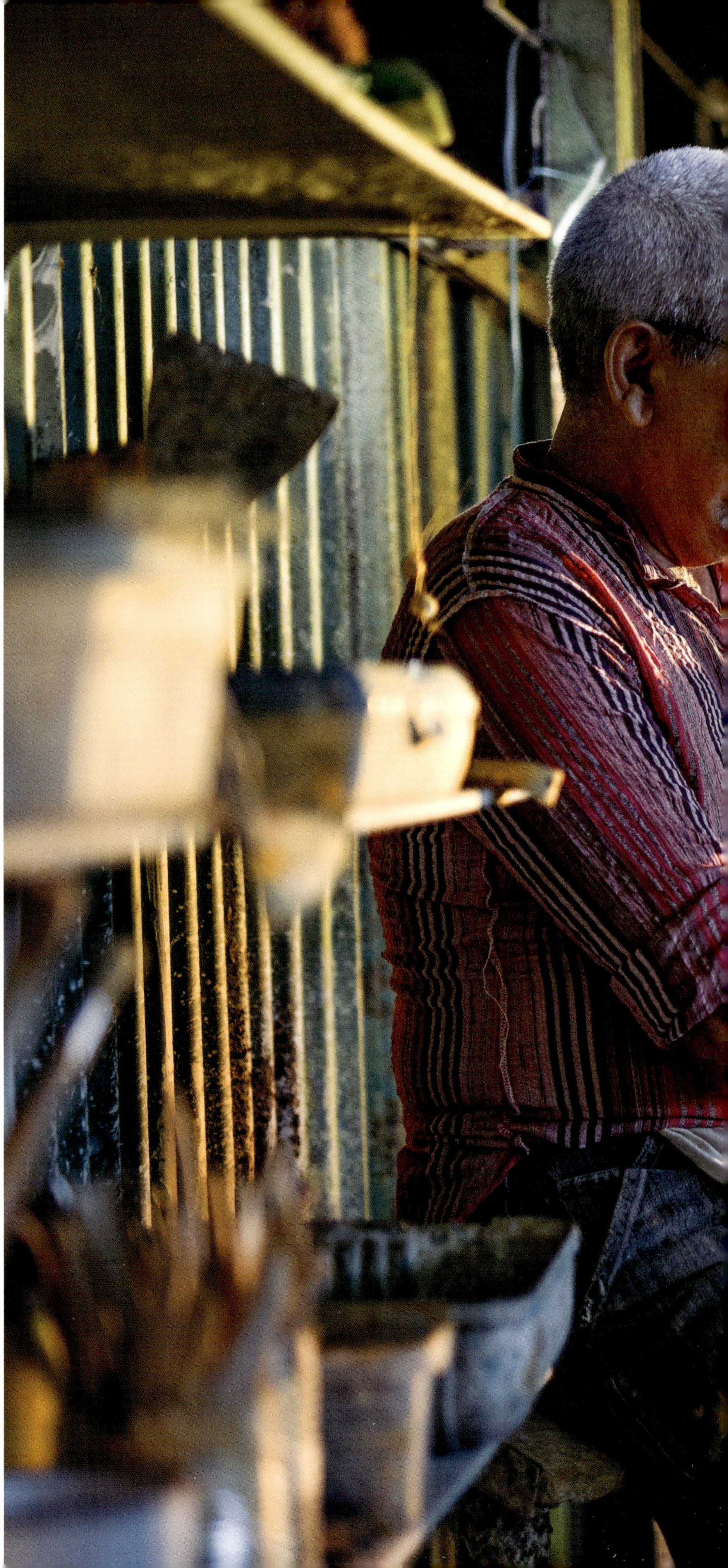

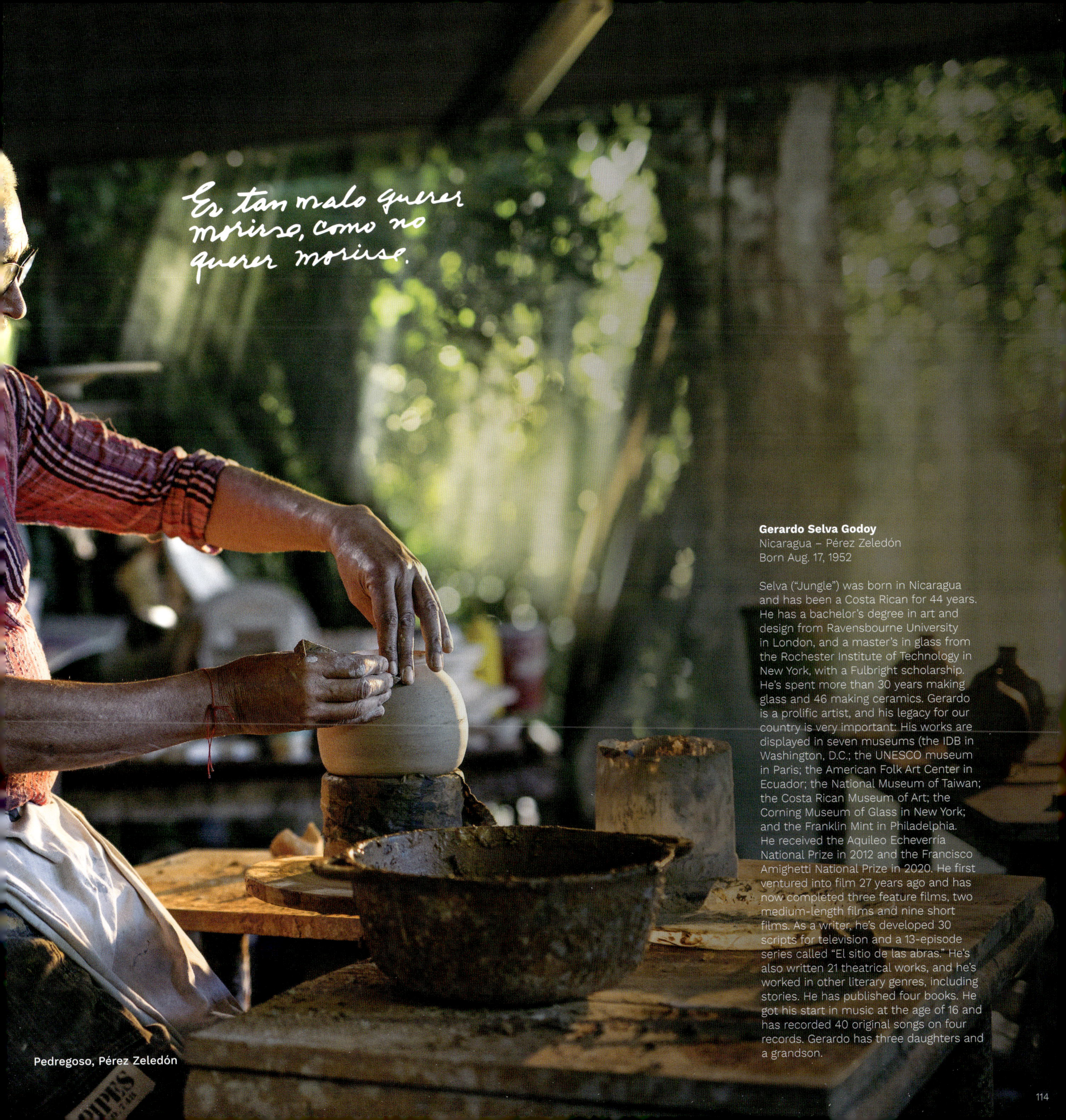

*Es tan malo querer morirse, como no querer morirse.*

**Gerardo Selva Godoy**
Nicaragua – Pérez Zeledón
Born Aug. 17, 1952

Selva ("Jungle") was born in Nicaragua and has been a Costa Rican for 44 years. He has a bachelor's degree in art and design from Ravensbourne University in London, and a master's in glass from the Rochester Institute of Technology in New York, with a Fulbright scholarship. He's spent more than 30 years making glass and 46 making ceramics. Gerardo is a prolific artist, and his legacy for our country is very important: His works are displayed in seven museums (the IDB in Washington, D.C.; the UNESCO museum in Paris; the American Folk Art Center in Ecuador; the National Museum of Taiwan; the Costa Rican Museum of Art; the Corning Museum of Glass in New York; and the Franklin Mint in Philadelphia. He received the Aquileo Echeverría National Prize in 2012 and the Francisco Amighetti National Prize in 2020. He first ventured into film 27 years ago and has now completed three feature films, two medium-length films and nine short films. As a writer, he's developed 30 scripts for television and a 13-episode series called "El sitio de las abras." He's also written 21 theatrical works, and he's worked in other literary genres, including stories. He has published four books. He got his start in music at the age of 16 and has recorded 40 original songs on four records. Gerardo has three daughters and a grandson.

Pedregoso, Pérez Zeledón

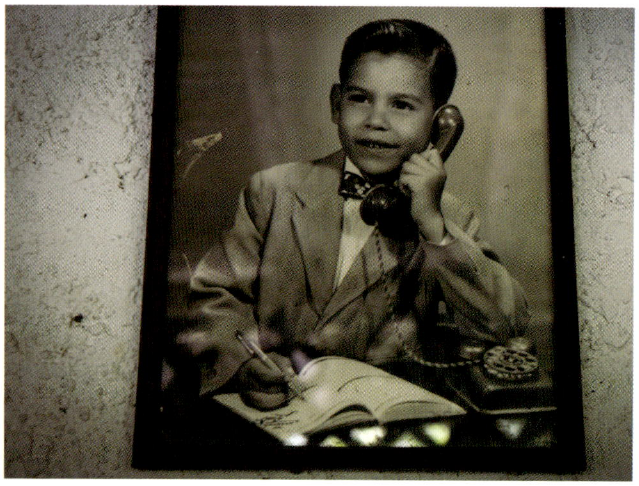

## I JUST DISSAPPOINTED THAT THEY NEVER TOOK ME OUT TO PLAY

Gerardo Selva had privileged blood in a complicated context. A diplomat father, an absent mother. A formula that resulted in a moment in his childhood that would cause him trauma for the rest of his life. It was 1960, and he was a young child. For those who weren't around at the time, that was the first, unsuccessful attempt of a Sandinista revolution against the dictatorship of Somoza in Nicaragua. When it retreated, a group of revolutionaries, understandably desperate in the face of a dark and imminent future in the hands of the dictatorship, decided to kidnap an entire boarding school — the same school where Selva had spent long and boring days after the semi-abandonment of his family, which was tired of raising so many kids. The image turns out to be representative of the man this boy would become. Machine gun in hand, partly thrilled and partly terrified, the revolutionaries had run into

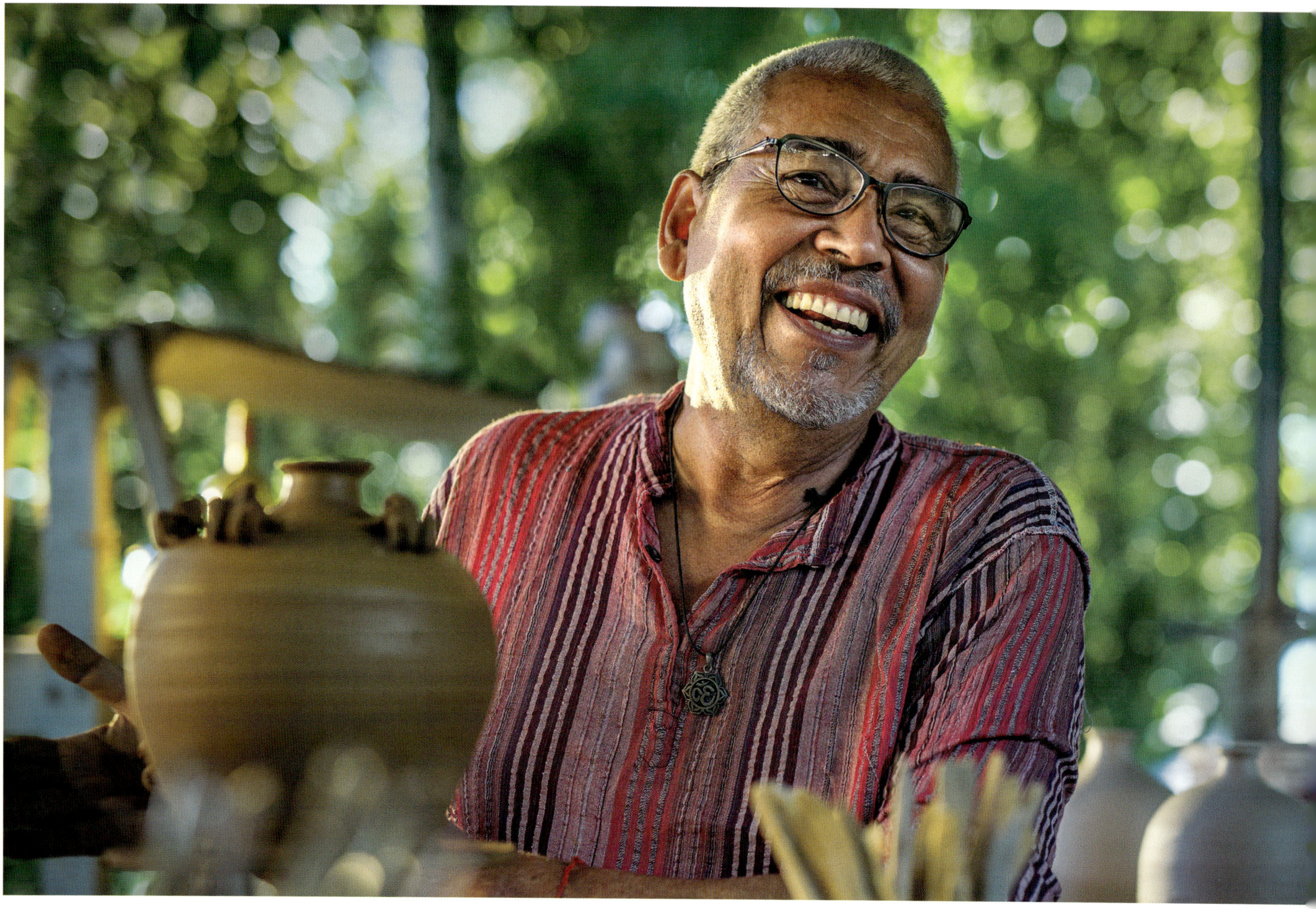

a difficult diplomatic problem: They had unknowingly kidnapped the son of a Somozista lawmaker. Facing the promise that "we're going to take you out to play," young Selva just waited anxiously, wanting to escape from what felt like a prison. "I never knew why they let me go. I just got disappointed that they never took me out to play."

What follows is worthy of a novel. Selva would go on to fall in love with Costa Rica (where he still lives today, in Pérez Zeledón), and here his adolescence would end, before he left for London, where when studying industrial design he learned about ceramics, his first artistic love. The first of many ... as evidenced by his 40 songs on four records, his four books, the six plays he wrote and the three films he wrote and directed.

The influence of having seen Pink Floyd or David Bowie live at Wembley, under the influence of LSD, yearning to import his psychedelic discoveries into the real world ... in a recurring manner backed by an insatiable curiosity. "In those days they sent us acid like it was candy." Words that only a person free of self-condemnation could pronounce so freely. And here's where the subtle magic of this man lies. Artist, head of a family, husband, homosexual ... his life renders these simplistic labels useless. Finding meaning without meaning to, just being, he confounds the wise. Having no mask to hide behind has given him genuine liberty to navigate his life, characterized initially by the purest chaos, and following the rhythm of fruitful years of well-being, stages clearly divided by the discovery of Zen meditation. A full and irreverent life, partly dedicated to his daughters, partly to his search for meaning in life.

And his greatest discovery? "Giving meaning to each action, you can find peace in the meaninglessness of life."

*Without even looking at Selva's portrait, I would bet that he has pronounced wrinkles around his mouth and eyes, from looking up so much, and from smiling.*

**Written by: Sebastián Castro**

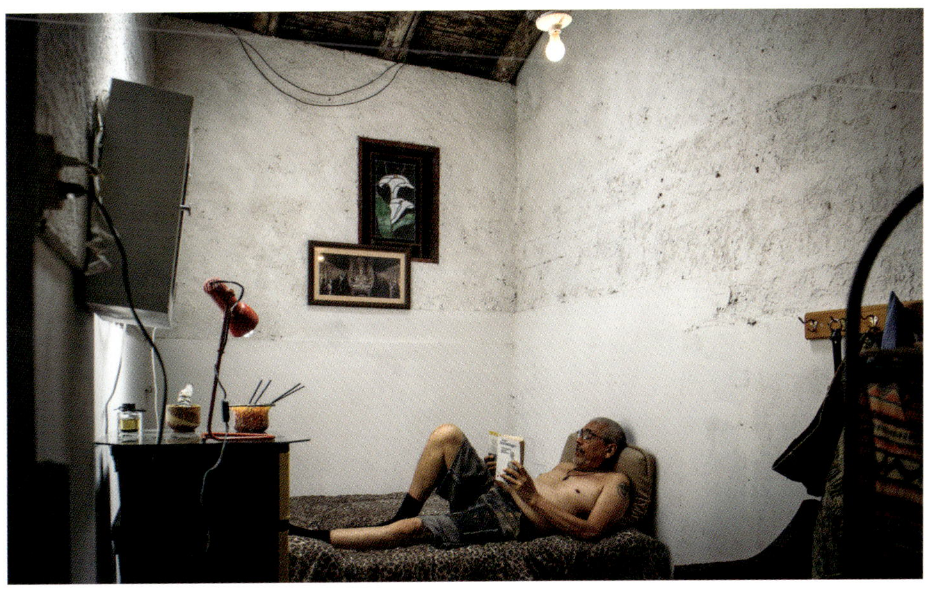

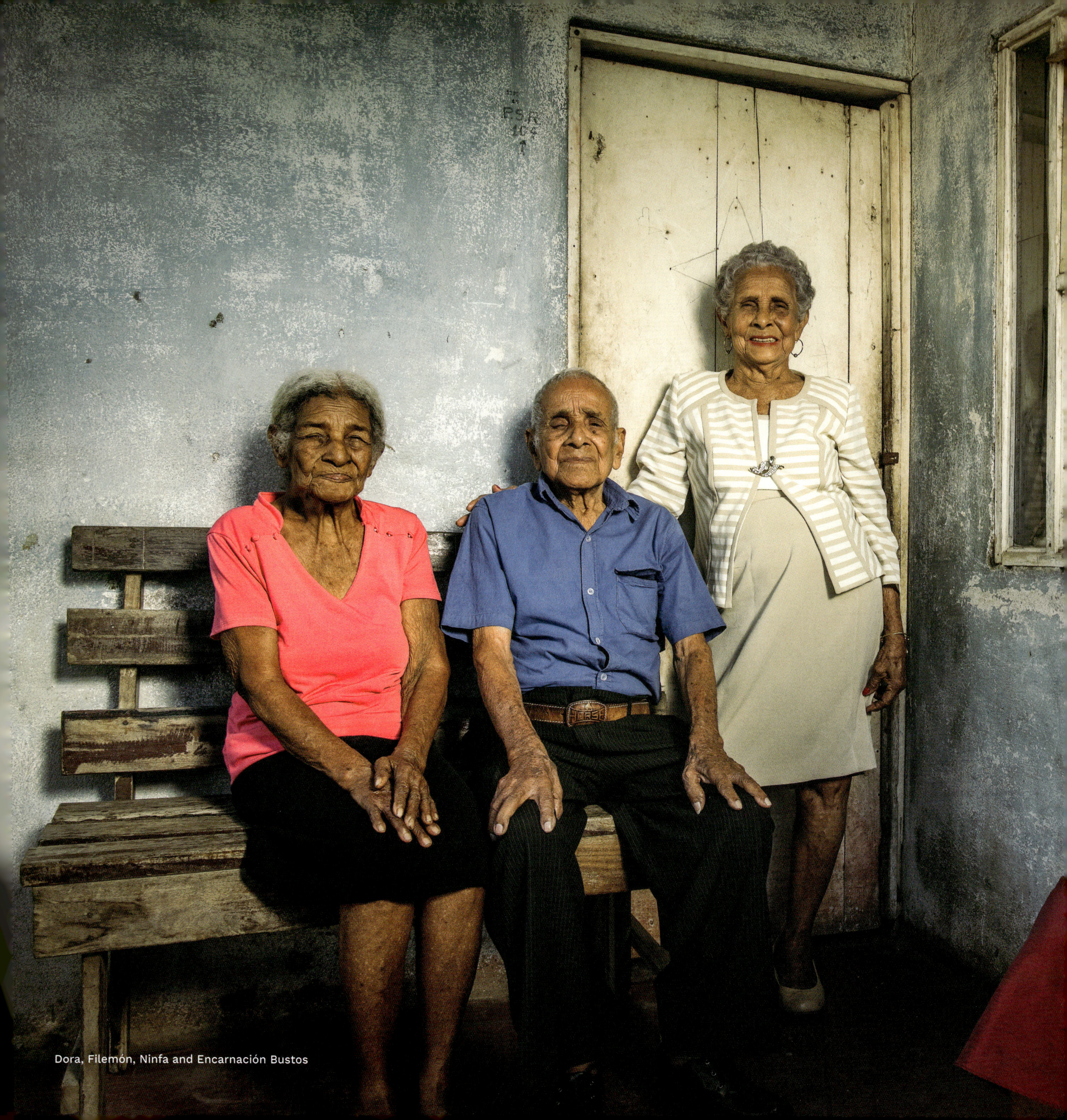

Dora, Filemón, Ninfa and Encarnación Bustos

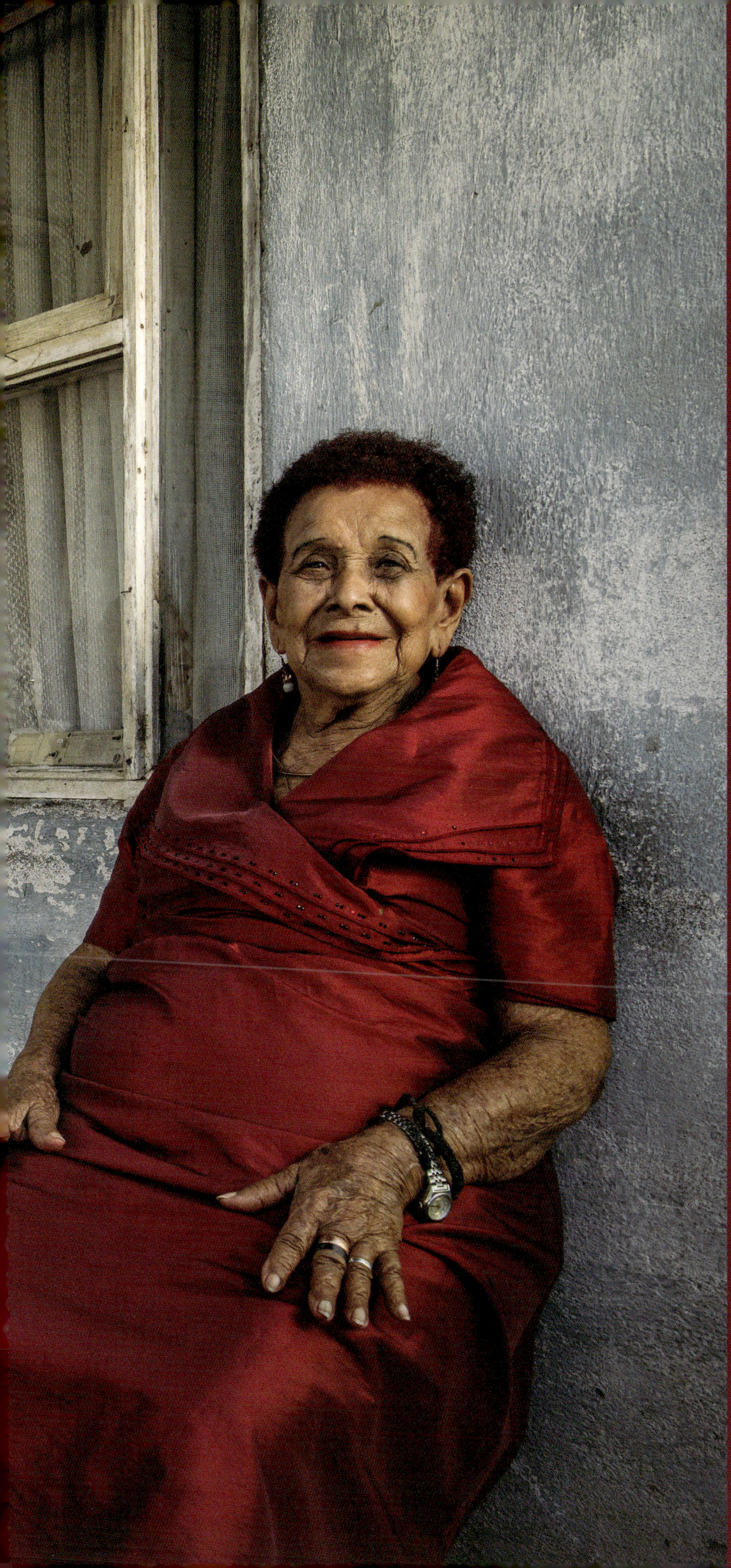

# THE FULL MOON OF MARCH

My grandmother had an onomatopoeia for everything. "Aha, I heard you there, *carrús, carrús*. How many ears of corn have you eaten, boy?" Or another, "No wonder you haven't done your homework, you spent all day *pleque, pleque*, talking nonsense!" That was how she spoke. But one of the sayings I liked most was the one she used to describe the slow passage of the oxcarts over the dusty roads. My grandmother said "In those days, from Guardia to Puerto Jesús, it took days, *gueré, gueré, gueré....*" And she would say these words with her eyes half-closed and her neck loose, simulating the balance of her body, sleepy because of the monotone sound of the rolling oxcart.

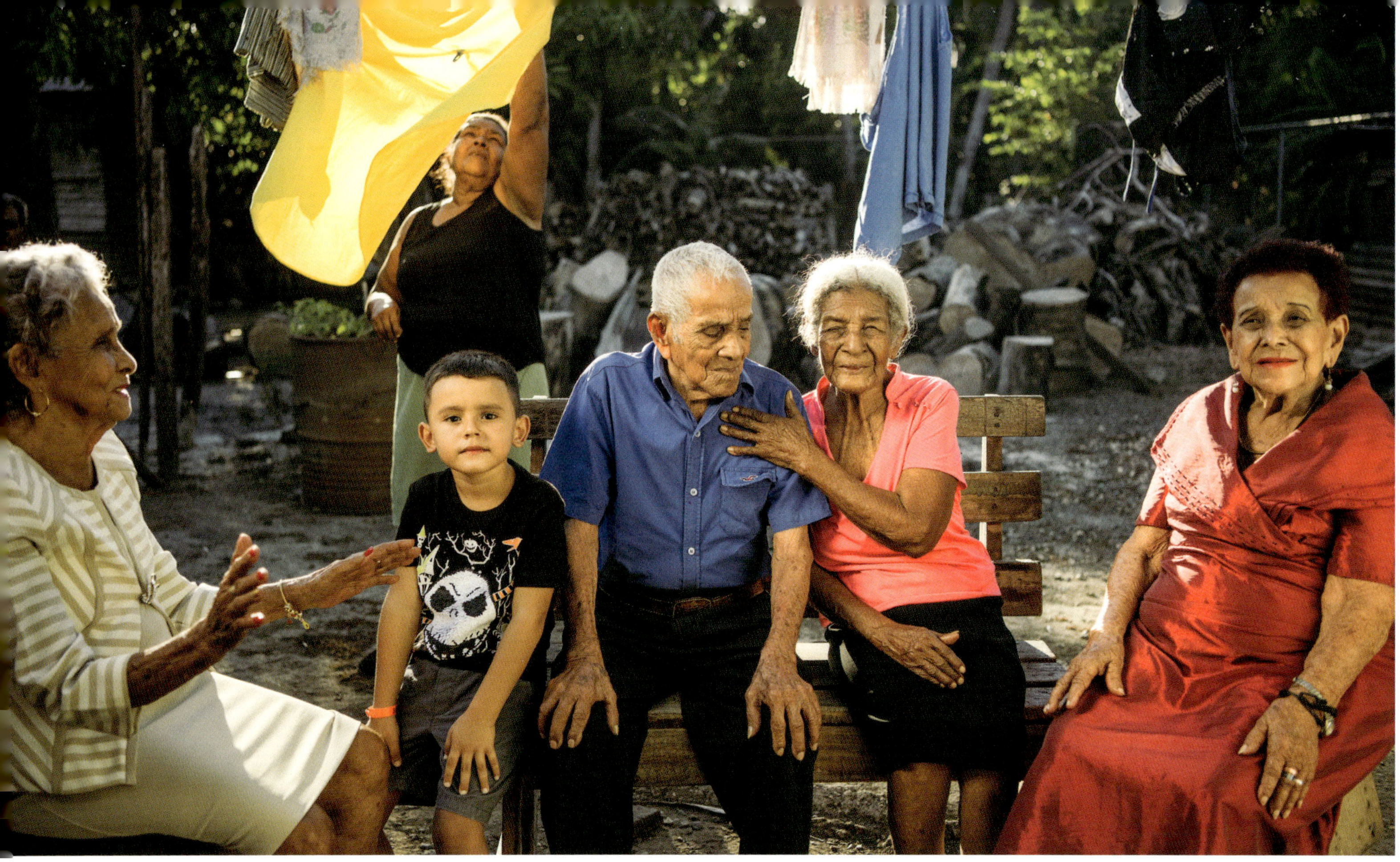

Ninfa, Santiago Vargas, Zaida, Filemón, Dora and Encarnación

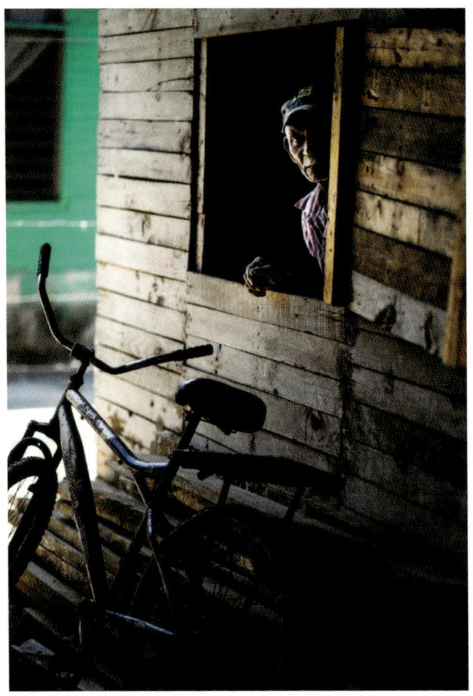

That's how I imagine her at the age of 14, traveling with her family to Playas del Coco in the days before the full moon of March. I imagine the preparations: chickens boiling in pots from the day before, corn to grind up, a little pot of corn pudding for dessert, and the oven smoking while the rosquillas cooked.

I see her tying back her braids and tying a handkerchief around her head so that the dust of the long road wouldn't ruin her hair, which with so much effort she kept healthy and shiny, free of lice and other pests.

On the oxcart rode her parents, herself, her brothers, and sisters. In the back were their bedrolls, and a sheet they tied to the branches to protect their food from bird droppings. On both sides of the cart, pots and pans of all sizes clattered, swinging just like them as the hours passed, as if they were also falling half-asleep with the interminable *gueré, gueré*.

As their paths crossed, oxcarts from all over the peninsula joined up to form a caravan that stretched to the horizon, raising a dust cloud you could see from Playa Hermosa. The traffic congestion allowed the families to greet each other and get into a festive mood. A guitar struck the spark and the entire caravan burst into cowboy-style cries.

Upon reaching the final stretch, my grandmother stood up on the cart and looked around until she spotted her friend "Dorita," Dora Amparo Bustos Duarte, a year younger than her. They had met two summers before and

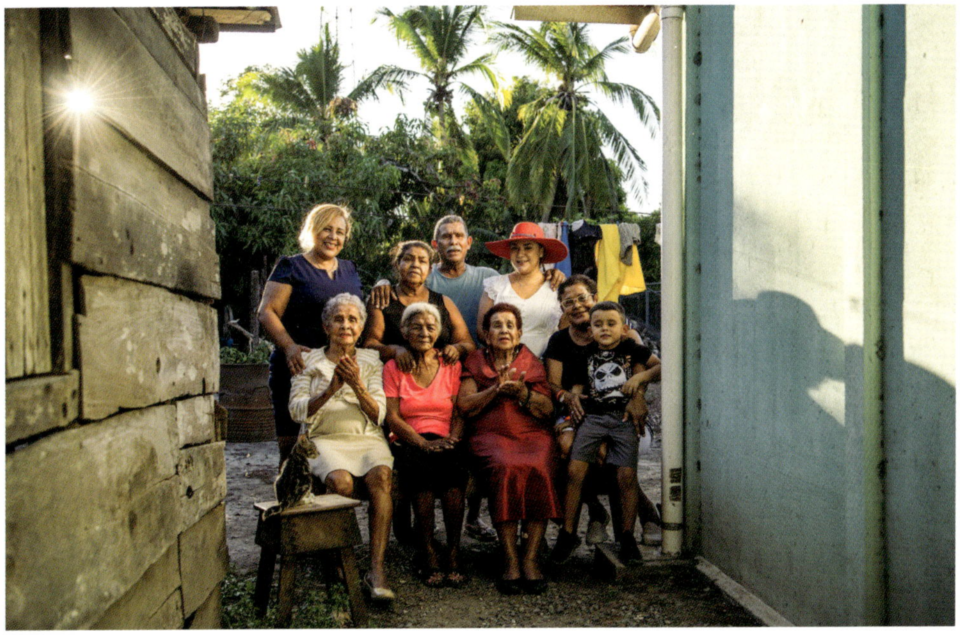

Bustos Family

had become close friends. Or as close as two people can be who only see each other once a year for three days, during the full moon of March.

As soon as they had unloaded the cart and made camp, my grandmother and Dorita would run off to the shade of some palm trees they had reserved, anxious to catch up: who was serenading whom, who was marrying whom, who was doing this or that... They had an agenda as long as the caravan that had brought them here. They would gossip until night fell, and then they got in trouble when their mothers found them there, *pleque, pleque*, at all hours.

My grandmother and Dorita didn't talk about misery, or about the hard work they had been required to do for as long as they could remember. They didn't talk about

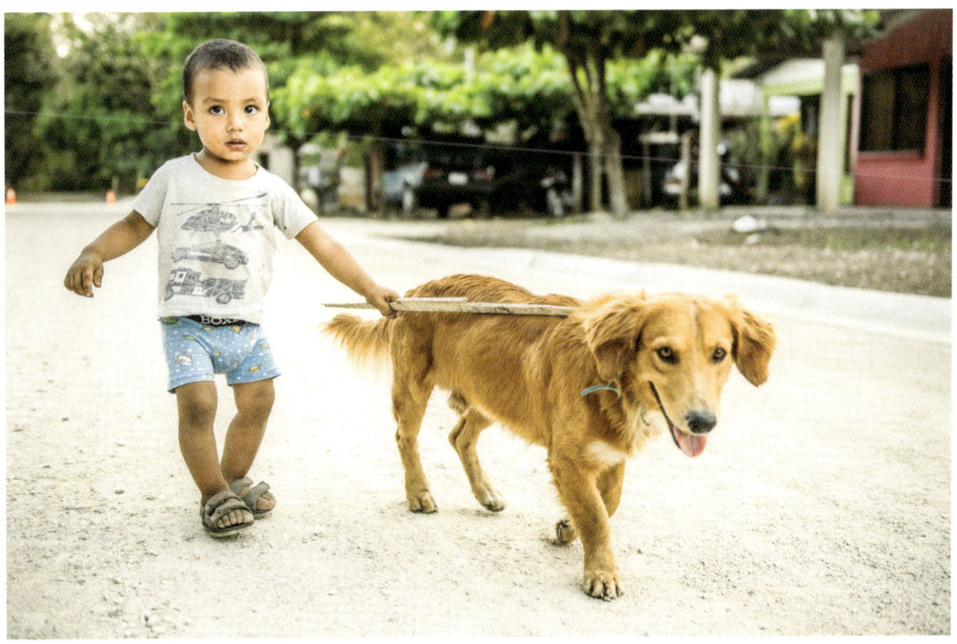

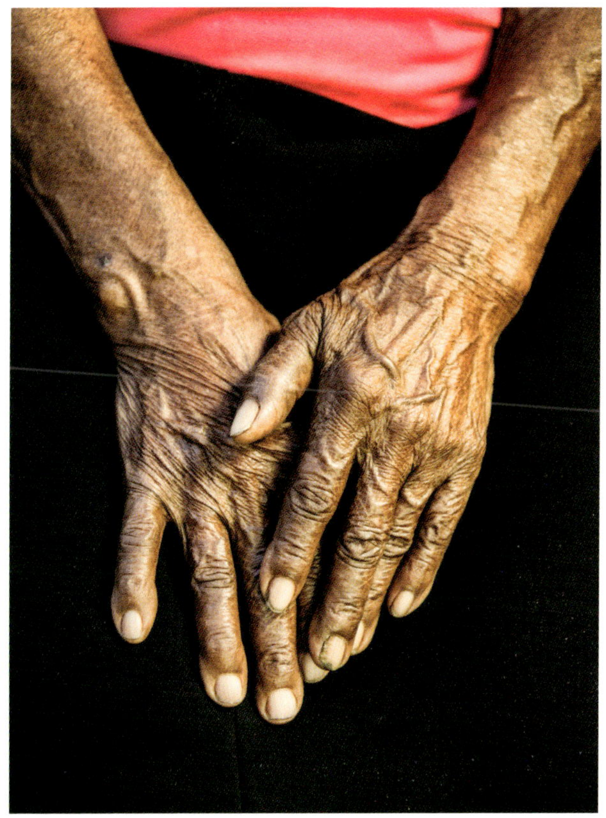

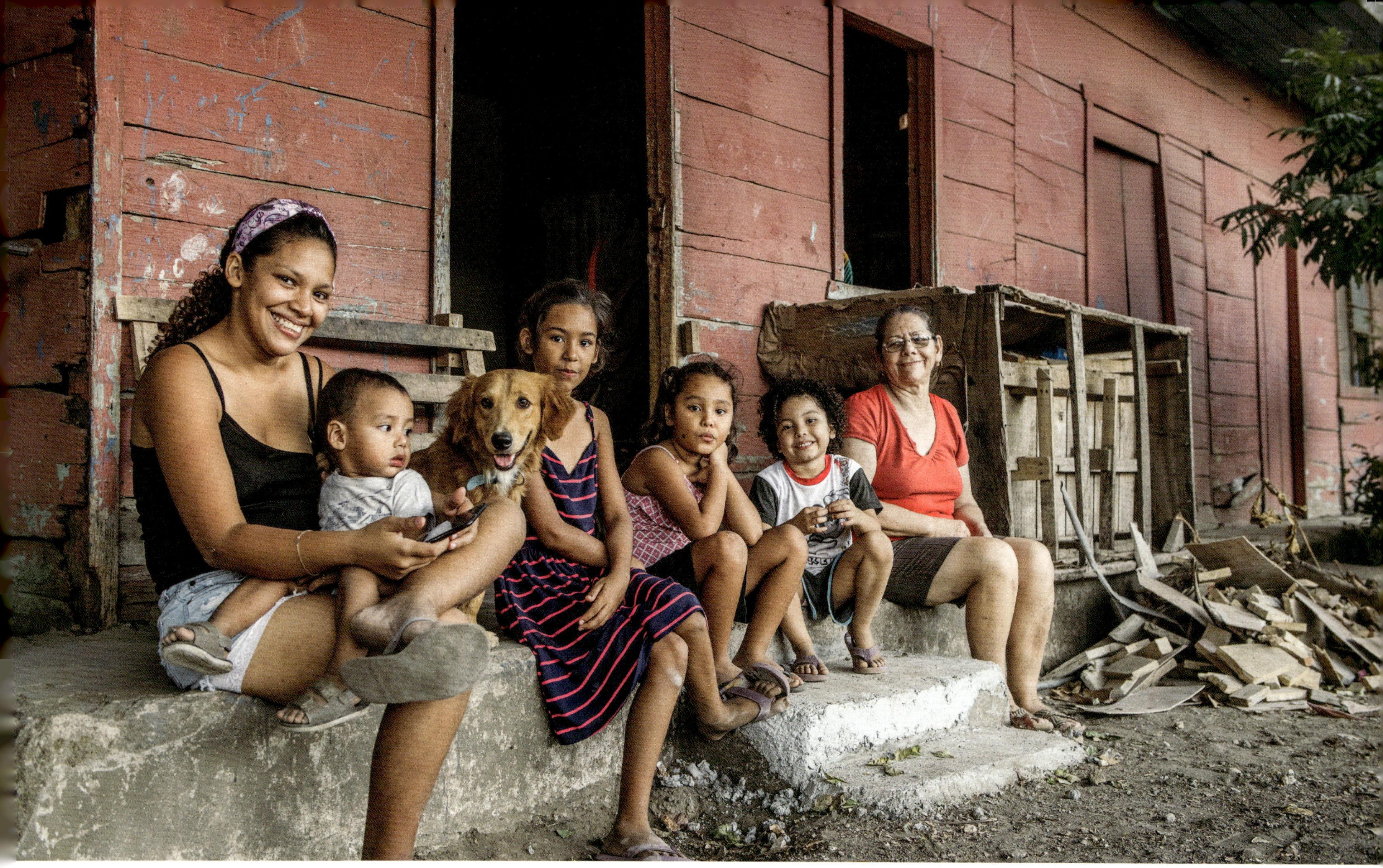

Navarrete - Herrera Family

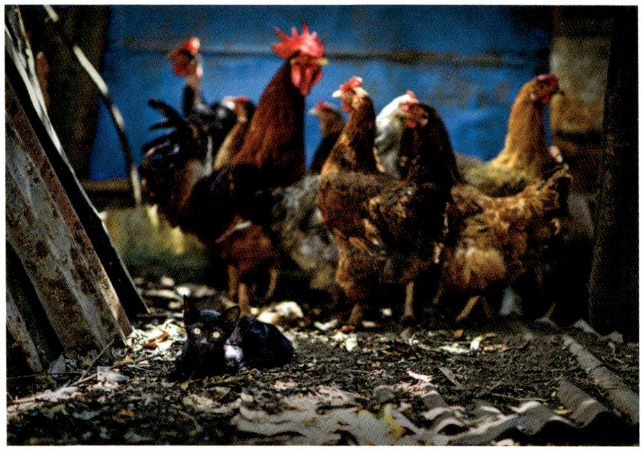

how difficult it was to live without electricity, lighting branches with wasp wax for light. They talked about girl stuff, about love and the lack thereof, while on the immense beach the bonfires burned, marimbas chimed, and guitars were plucked.

Both of them got married and had kids a few years later. Asphalt and internal combustion engines finally put an end to their pilgrimages by oxcart to Playas del Coco.

The full moon of March still arrives on time, but my grandmother and Dorita never met up again. At least not in this world.

**Written by: Jaime Gamboa**

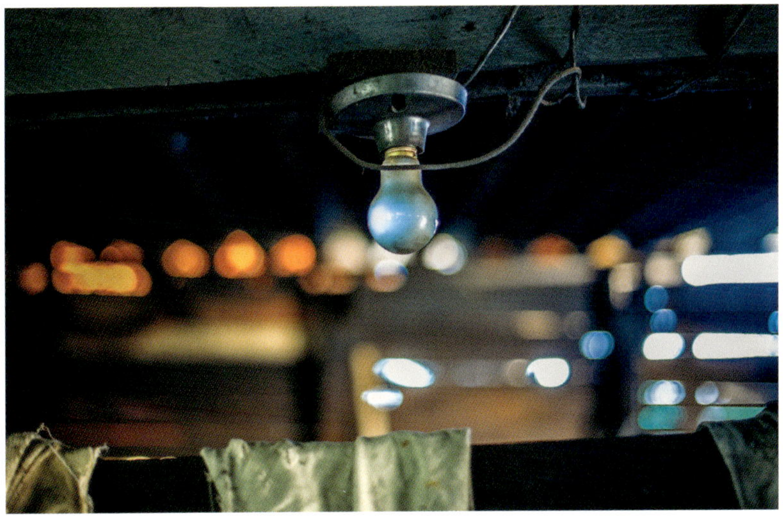

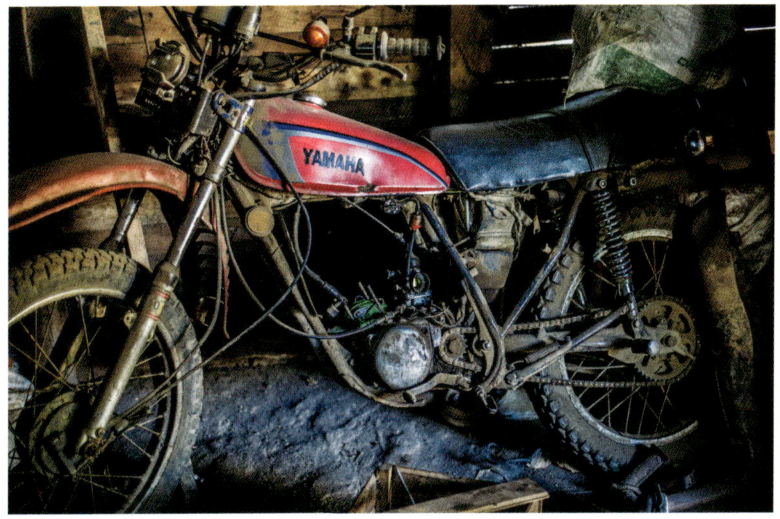


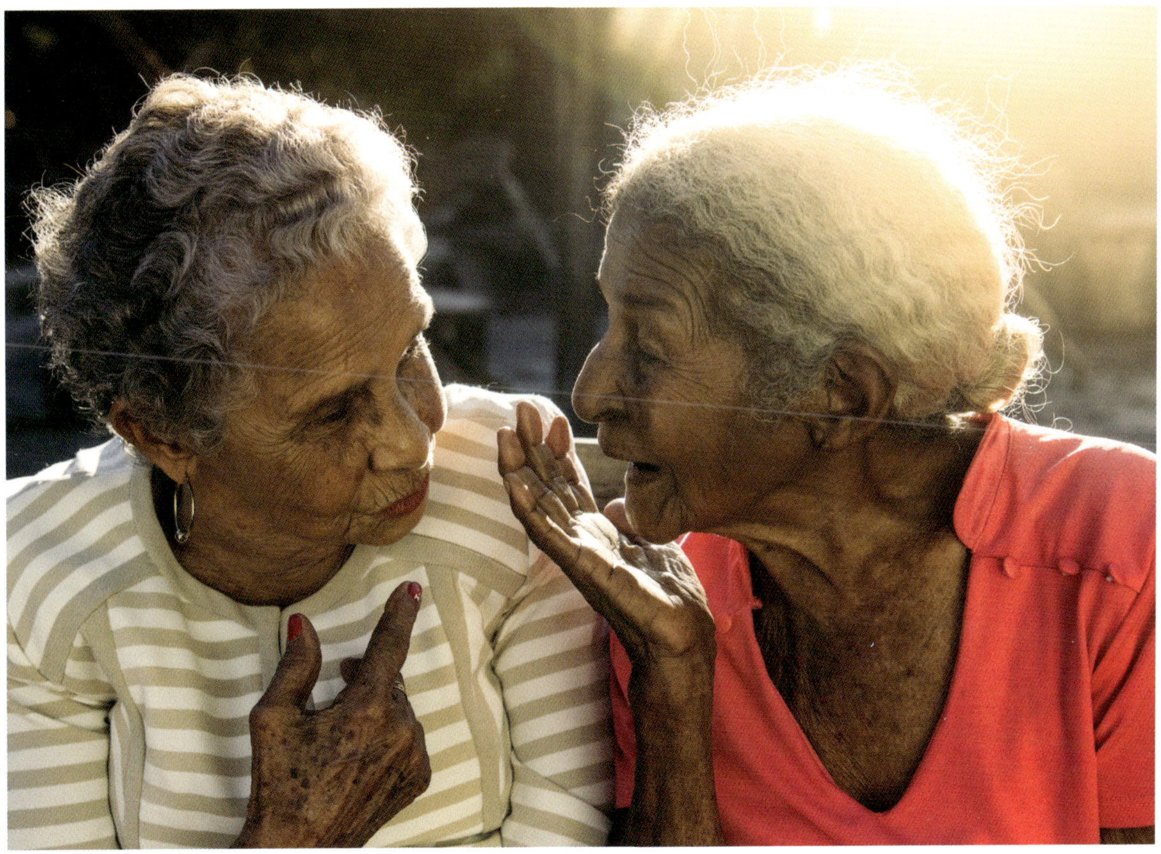

San Blas, Cardinal, Carrillo, Guanacaste

**Dora Amparo Bustos Duarte**
Nicoya
Born March 6, 1919

She loves to dance, and dancing was how she met her husband, whom she married at the age of 19. Dora became a widow with six children, and she washed clothes and sold pastries to support them. From childhood, she learned how to make pastries called "rosquillas," grinding corn and kneading tortillas with her mother. In her house there was no electricity, but they made candles in cans, with wax from wasps' nests. One of the most exciting moments of her life was when her children could finally work to help out with household expenses — she remembers them returning very happily from their first day at work. Her mother, Guadalupe, also had to raise seven children alone, because her husband left her. Although her younger siblings were able to study, Dora and the older ones had to leave school to help their mother make ends meet. They sold food door to door and worked as seamstresses. It was a hard life, and now Dora says she's tired and has insomnia, but she also maintains that "when you talk about bad things, either they get worse or they get better."

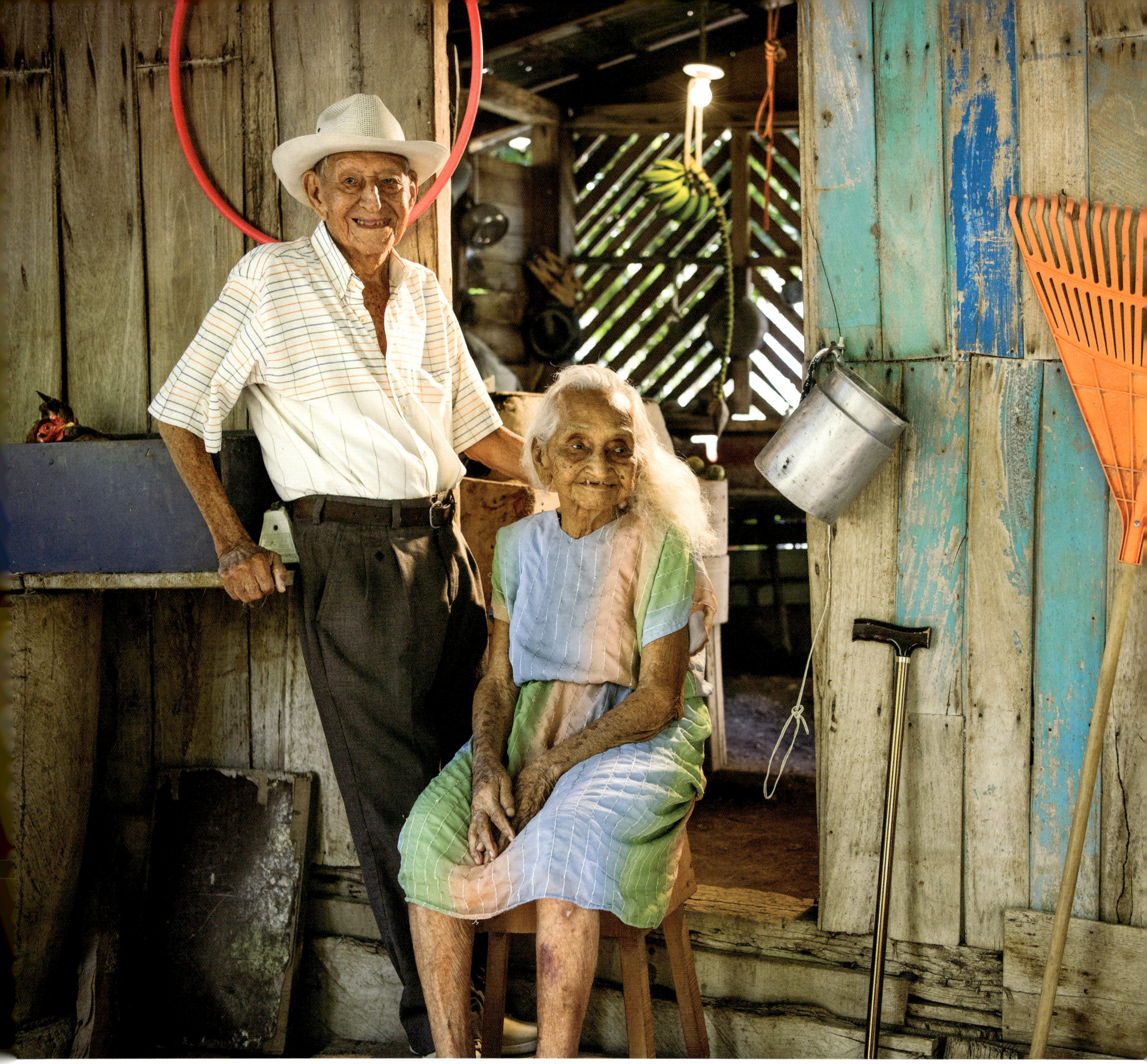

Pachito Villegas and Ma.Trinidad Espinoza

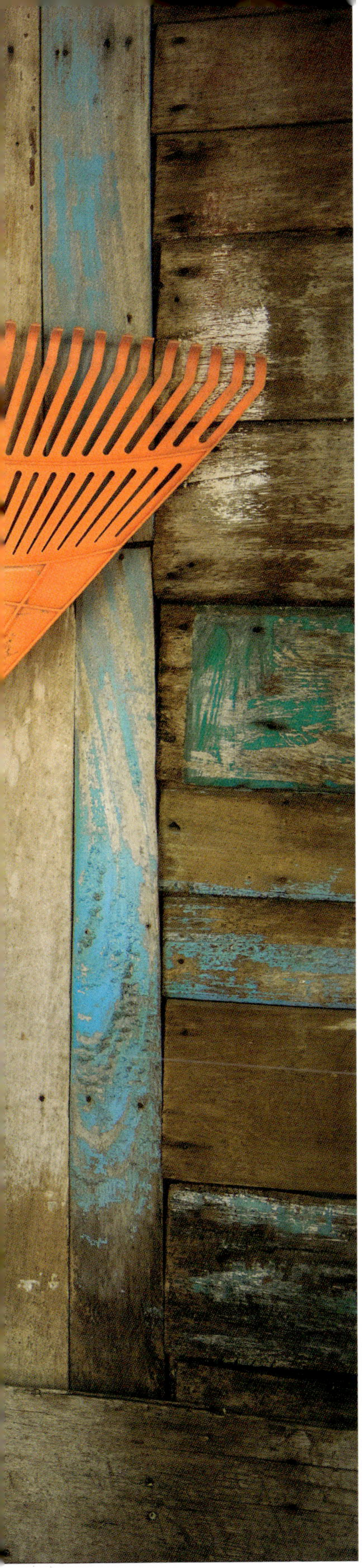

# A COWBOY FROM A BLUE ZONE

The dust cloud of the cattle drive boils up in Pachito's memory.

The images and faces from his life make a long line. Looking back on his 104 years is like contemplating the frescos in a cathedral. It's impossible to try to understand them. You can only try to imagine the trails of old Guanacaste, Quebrada Honda before asphalt, the plains trampled by the hordes of men and beasts who smashed their boots and hooves into the pastures where before there was nothing but primary forest.

Pachito was born in those long-ago times. He lost his mother before he can remember, and he spent his very short childhood on a horse. He grew up on the end of a lasso, a pike, some palm wine, and a lot of misery. He didn't even ponder what all that meant, about his luck or his destiny - he just kept riding his horse, like his father, like his beloved twin, who died one Christmas Day.

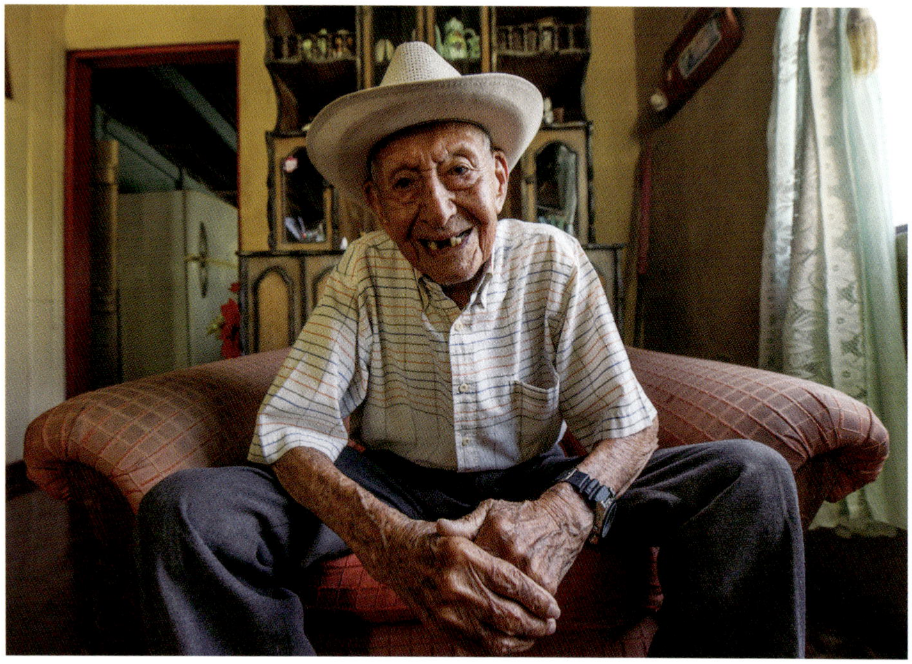

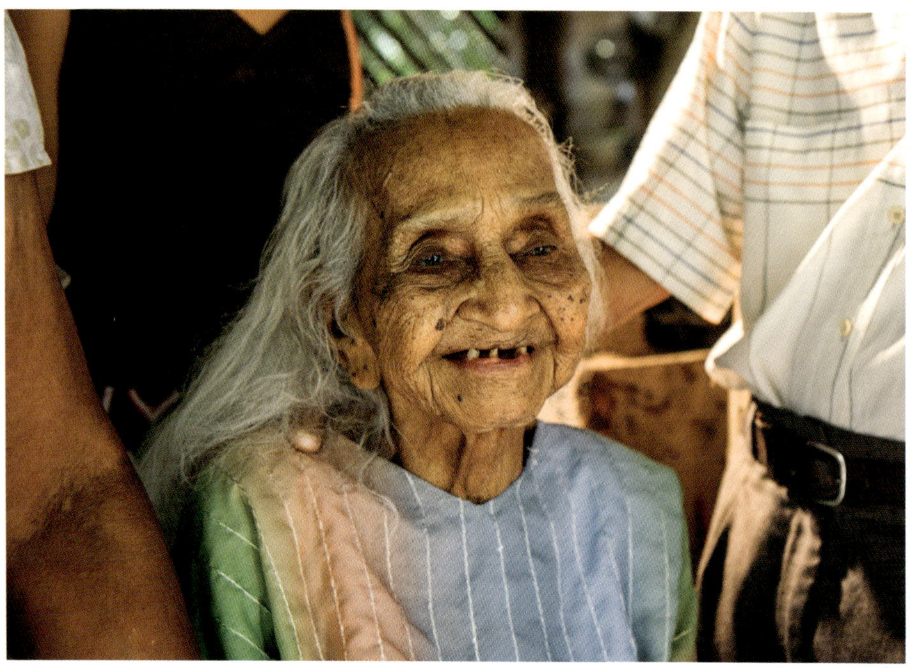

## HE SENT HIS SON TO LOOK FOR A HORSE TO TAKE HIS STEPMOTHER AWAY

His life feels like an endless cattle roundup that started when he was three, when his father put him on the back of a little horse guided by a rope. By the age of six, he was riding on his own, imitating the gestures and movements of the grown-ups.

Years before, his mother had died. He barely remembers that. But the one he does remember is his stepmother, a woman with a hard heart, who made life difficult for all the kids from "the other woman." Humiliation and exhausting chores made first his sister and then his brother look for a partner and leave the family home. So Pachito added to his sorrows a bitter loneliness that he tried to resolve with liquor, wine, and violence.

One day, encouraged by his uncle - the same one who had given him his first drink of liquor at the age of 10 — Pachito came out of the cantina intending to beat up his stepmother. They say that his father, Don Cástulo must have suspected, because he came home just in time to stop Pachito, now 20 years old, agitated and drunk, from carrying out his plan.

Don Cástulo, seeing Pachito's aggressiveness, sent his son to look for a horse to take his stepmother away. He made the woman get on the horse and ride to Puerto Jesús, a port town on the Nicoya Peninsula. Effectively, he was sending her away

• The Nicoya Peninsula is one of five Blue Zones in the world.

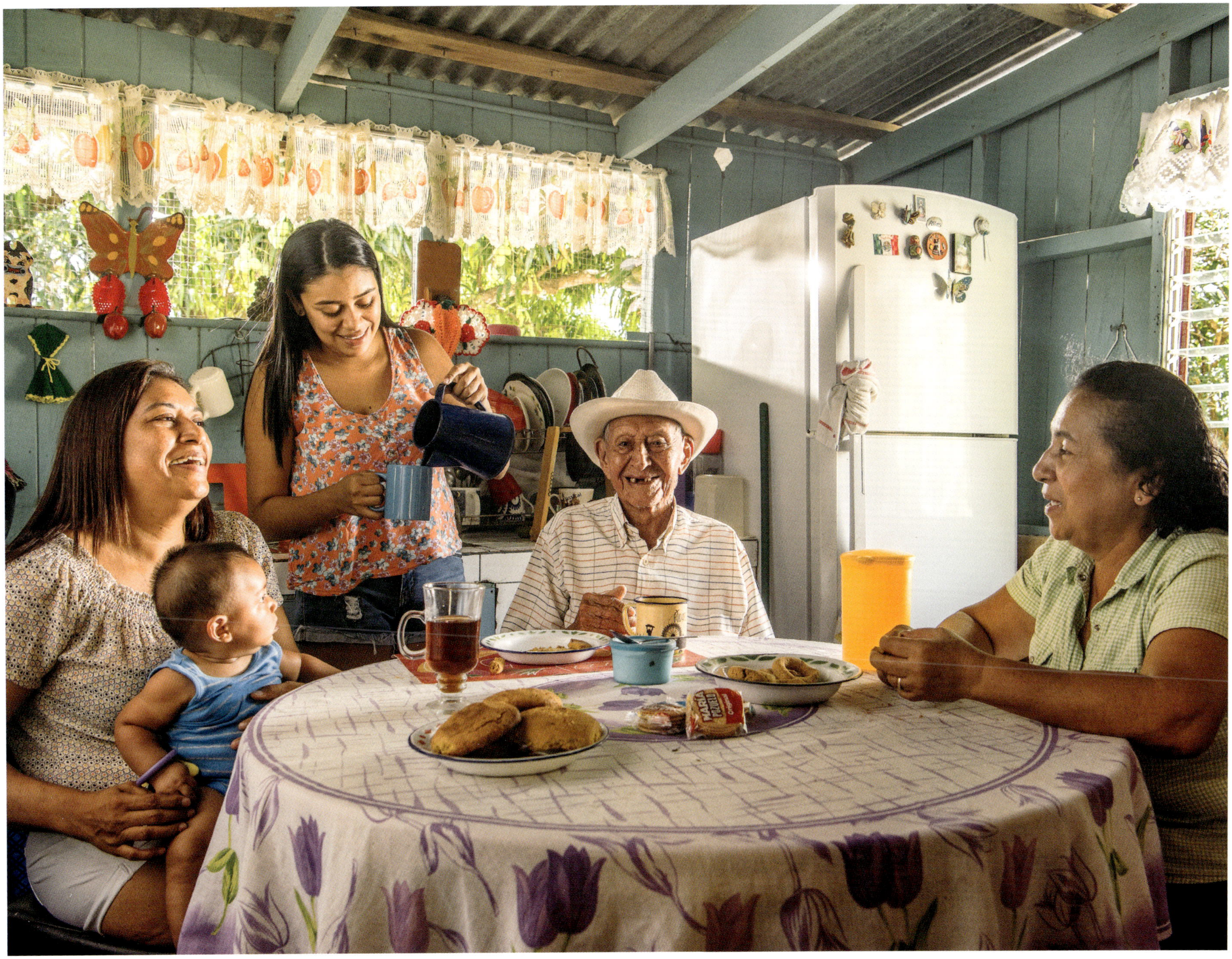

Ingrid Villegas, Mateo Fonseca, Alexa García, Pachito and Paulina Villegas

to San José. Months later, when Pachito wanted to get together with a woman, Don Cástulo stopped him in his tracks: "You left me without a woman, and now I'm leaving you without a woman." They agreed that the son would have to take care of the father until the day he died.

This pact didn't last long, because Don Cástulo died when Pachito was just 28 years old. And by the age of 30, he already had a family. At first it was a glance, later a smile, later a kiss. The rest was 66 years of marriage, eight children, and many grandchildren. Pachito was a dedicated husband, and he passed on to his children a lesson that he had engraved into his soul: "There's nothing worse than a stepmother."

Between cattle roundups, young Pachito had noticed that when he went to Bolsón to sell cows, he could buy things that weren't for sale in his town, and he could make a little profit. Slowly but surely, he made enough money to buy some land and find his own little

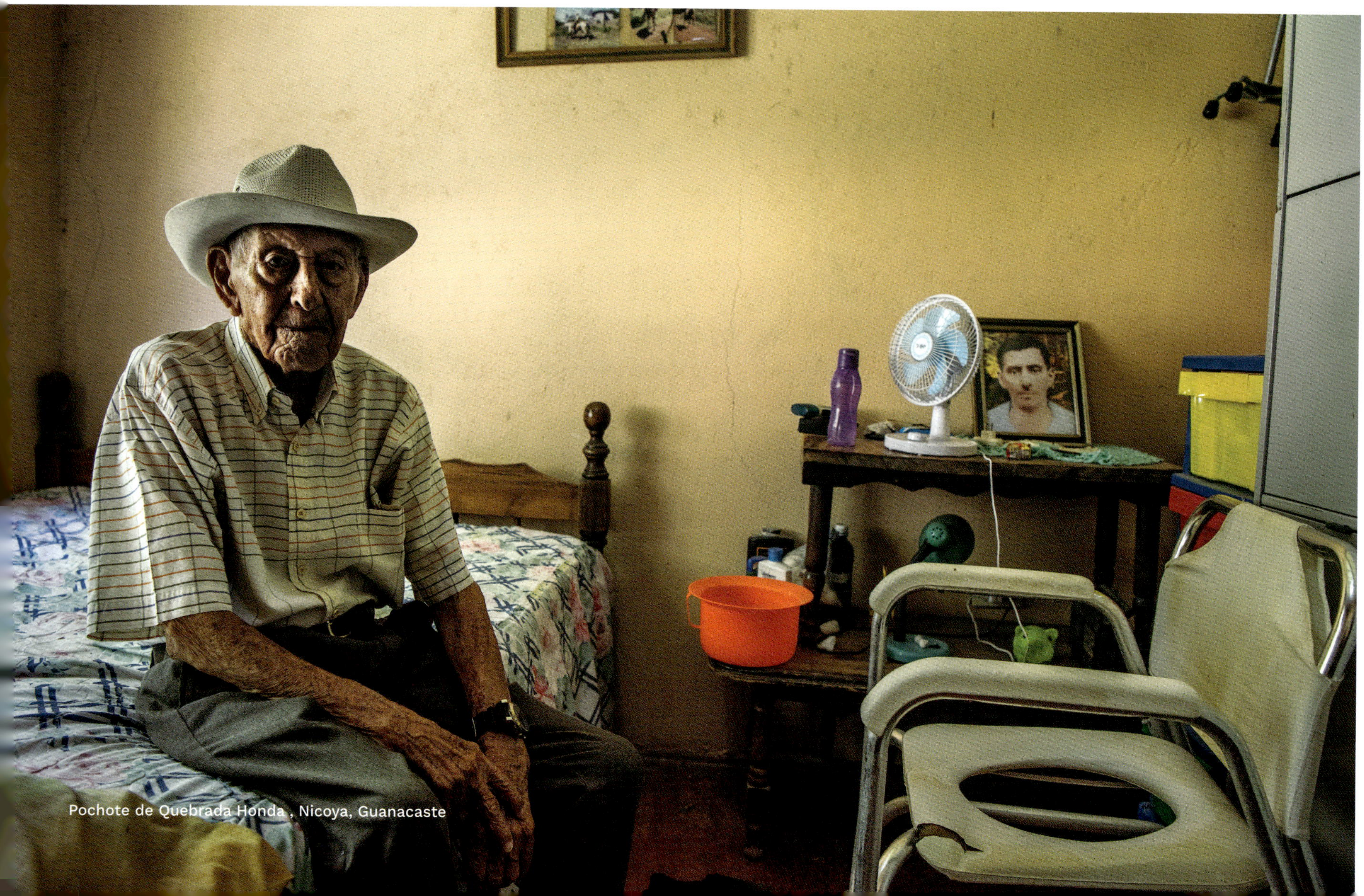

Pochote de Quebrada Honda , Nicoya, Guanacaste

"cash cow" to distribute to his children when the time was right.

He doesn't remember anymore when the time was right, but it was a while ago. It's not easy to live for more than a century. Few make it that far. But getting there is a party — although he can't get onto his horse Corazón anymore without help.

The days go by between the crowing of the roosters and the shouts of the little kids running around. Don Bonifacio Villegas, the tireless Pachito, waits in the hall for a visit from Trini, his friend of 90 years. But Trini is also a bit older. Maybe she won't come today.

**Written by: Jaime Gamboa**

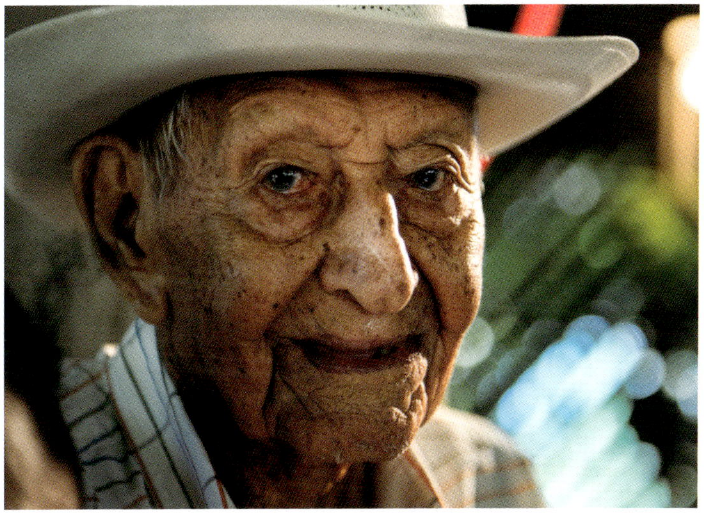

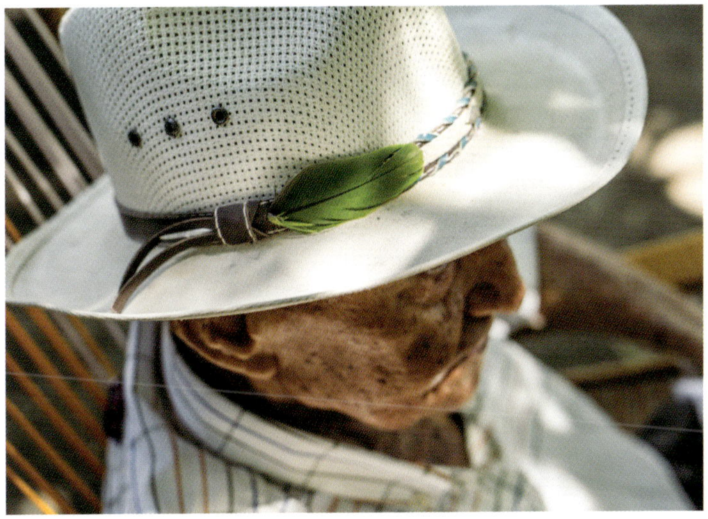

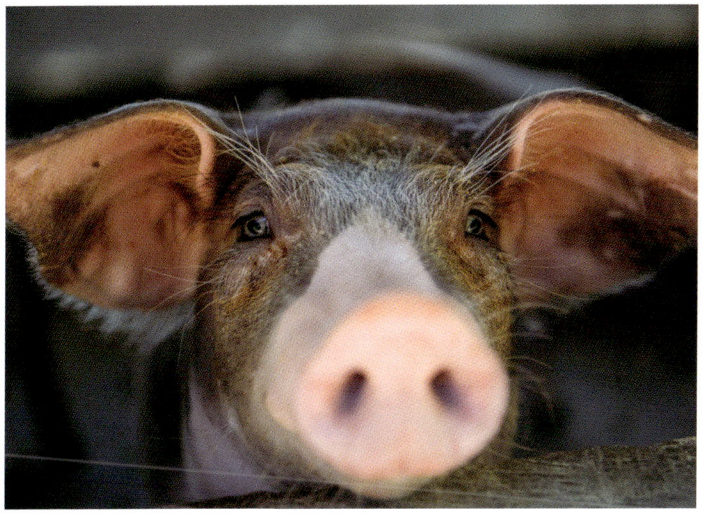

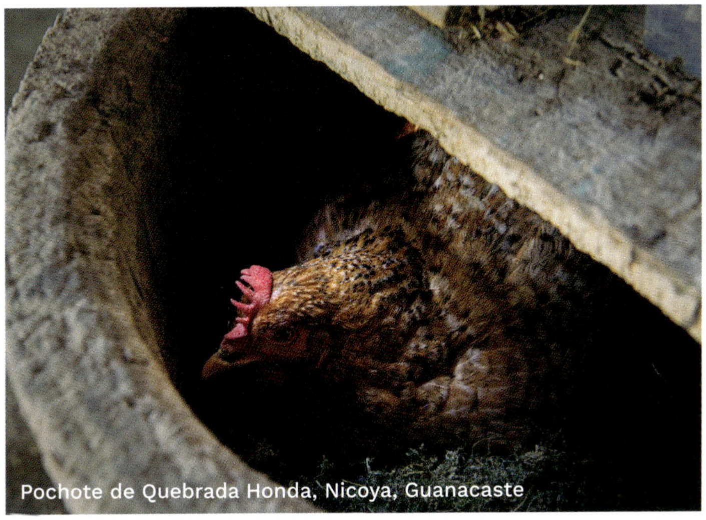

Pochote de Quebrada Honda, Nicoya, Guanacaste

**José Bonifacio Villegas Fonseca, "Pachito"**
Nicoya
Born May 14, 1917

By the age of six, he was already a horseman. He worked with his father as a cowboy. In time, he learned what he could buy on his travels, and later resell at a better price, and that's how he got his start in sales, and saved enough to buy 60 acres, of which he gave a piece to each of his eight children. He has a large family and a grandson that he likes to spoil. He met his best friend, Trini, more than 90 years ago, when his father took him to her house to buy some stuff. The reasons he thinks people live to be over 100 are: Food without pesticides that they grow themselves in soil rich in minerals and nutrients, daily exercise at work, a relaxed life with a lot of laughter, stress-free, social connections in a big family, being surrounded by people who love you, and even the affection of an old horse, like his beloved Corazón.

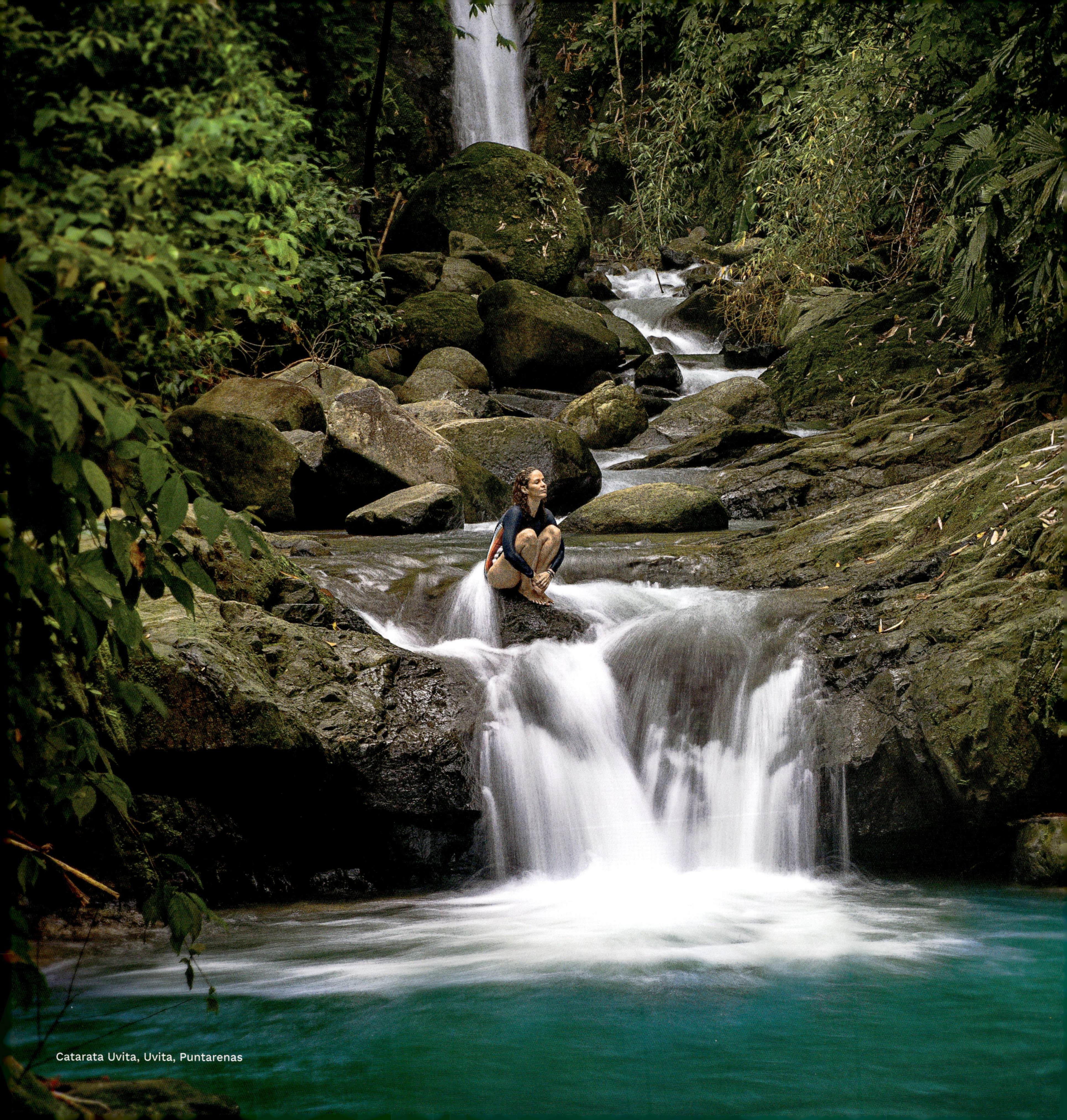

Catarata Uvita, Uvita, Puntarenas

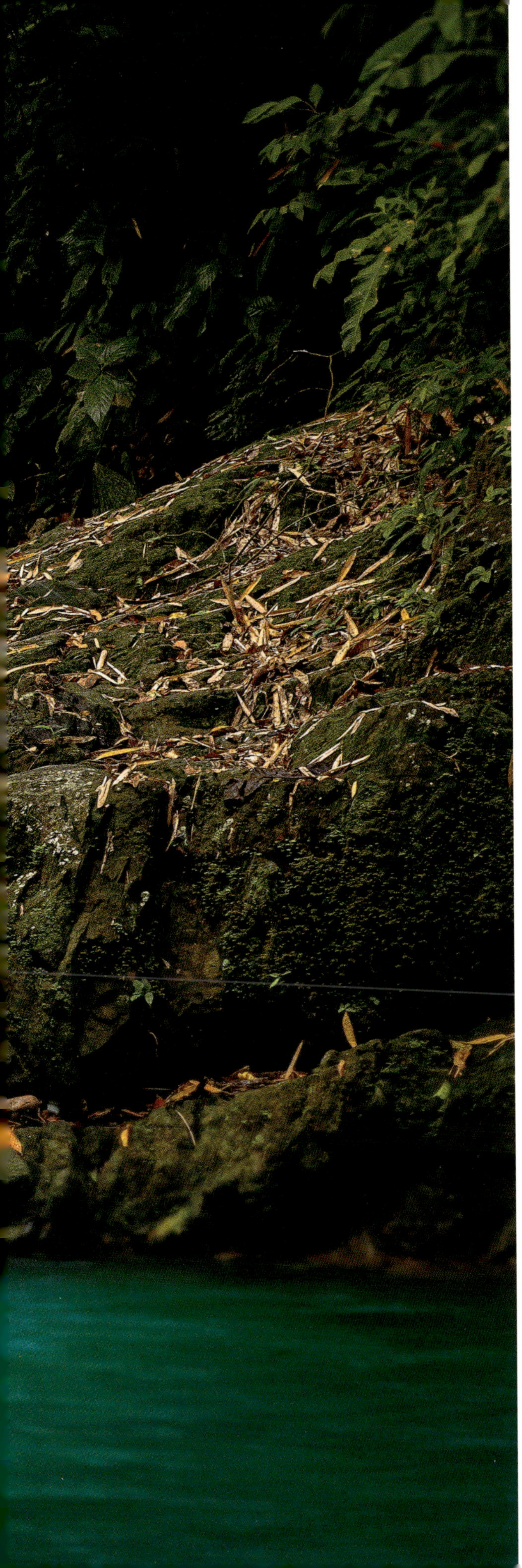

# JUMP INTO THE WATER

"What was it they told us? To the right or to the left?" says Nati, panting. Tiberias, the city we left behind three hours ago on a pair of bicycles, was no longer visible.

"I think it was the other way. ... What the hell, let's ride all the way around."

I don't know if it was the uphills, the 55° Celsius summer heat or the hangover, but I was starting to feel like I was dying. What was I doing here?

If I told my aunts that I decided to come to Israel in a filthy bar in Los Yoses, maybe they wouldn't be so happy. With each turn of the pedals, images came to my head of visiting them on Sunday afternoons in San Ramón de Alajuela. Between prayers, they would take out an album with black pages and old photos of their trips to Jerusalem. This was the birthplace of so many religions — the Holy Land.

I wasn't so holy, but I had a huge desire to travel. And the roads I've traveled have been full of gifts from life. Like the friend I ran into at a heavy metal concert. He told me he had been on a kibbutz, and he said they would pay you and house you if you worked there. At the time I thought traveling was only for gringos, not for me, a Tica with no money.

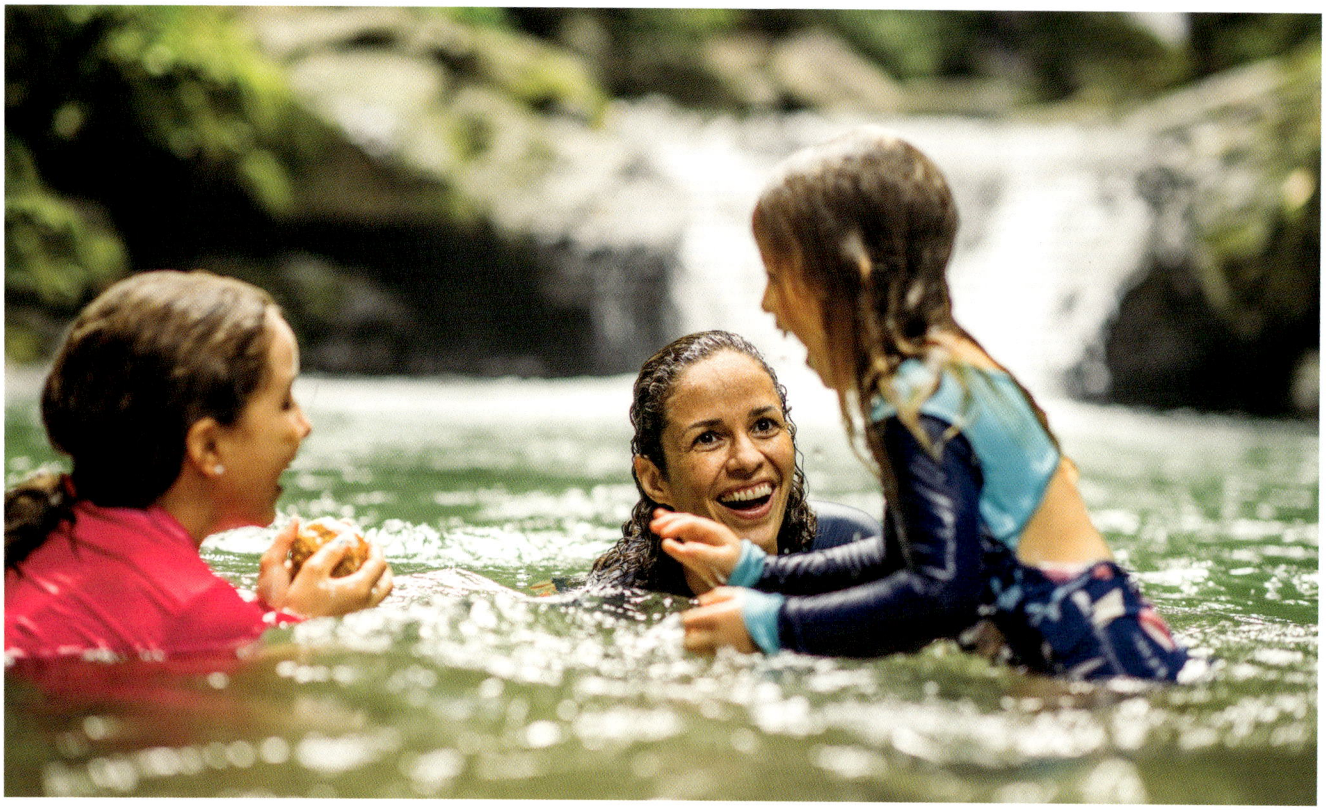

**Maya, Pilar and Clea**

I had dreamed of flying, looking out the window, the sovereignty of sea and sky, and imagining that I wasn't in a plane, but flying on the wings of a gliding seabird. It felt like my supreme flight. But the reality is that I flew economy seated in the middle, without knowing where I would live when we landed. That's where I met a Guatemalan man with tiny eyeglasses who was very nice.

"I live on a kibbutz," was the first thing he told me. As soon as we arrived in Tel Aviv, we called this kibbutz and they accepted us as volunteers. We had to take a bus to the north at the Tahana Merkazit, the Tel Aviv bus station. It was a huge building, much bigger than the San Pedro Mall, but half-empty and dark. It was Purim and I didn't know that, but that's why everyone was walking around in costumes.

Aside from the costumes, seeing so many weapons made an impact on me, coming from Costa Rica, where that would be unthinkable. Just like the Guatemalan man, none of my friends wanted to wage war, but military service was obligatory. Probably because of that, my entire family — except for my father — had opposed my trip. To the south, the Gaza Strip was exploding. And I, in the north, was working every day on a kibbutz.... Except on weekends, when I could go out and explore, like this day when we came to Tiberias.

There, circling the Sea of Galilee, with no trace of the swimming holes that we came to find, and thinking I was going to faint any minute ... an open-bed truck stopped, white, with no windows. *Let's go!* We know they were musicians because of the instruments, but we couldn't understand anything they were saying to us. We just asked them if we could ride in the bed to get back, and there we went, by the hand of God.

I must have fallen asleep, because soon they parked and told us in broken English and incomprehensible Hebrew that they were going swimming and we could go with them if we wanted. And so, in the most unexpected way, we arrived at the blessed swimming hole. I didn't even have the strength to move, but I jumped in the water.

Now that I'm 42 years old, sometimes I get a bit nervous when my husband takes our daughters surfing, but I remember that, of all the gifts I've received, the first was from my father, who in my brief 19 years taught me to trust in life.

**Written by: Libertad Sobrado**

**Pilar Salazar López**
San Ramón, Alajuela – Bahía Ballena, Osa
Born March 6, 1978

Pilar was born on March 6, the same day as her favorite writer, Gabriel García Márquez. The trip of her life took her from San Ramón to distant shores, including the United States, Israel and Greece, but fate brought her back to Costa Rica, to Uvita de Osa. She has a degree in administration with an emphasis in the business of tourism, and she has a sustainable Certified B Corporation, Bodhi Surf + Yoga, in which she combines her love of nature and family that are the source of her happiness and her reason for being. She runs the administrative end and the yoga. Pilar is a curious, creative woman, an avid reader and a lover of life, with a great interest in exploring and learning. She is married, has two daughters and loves people.

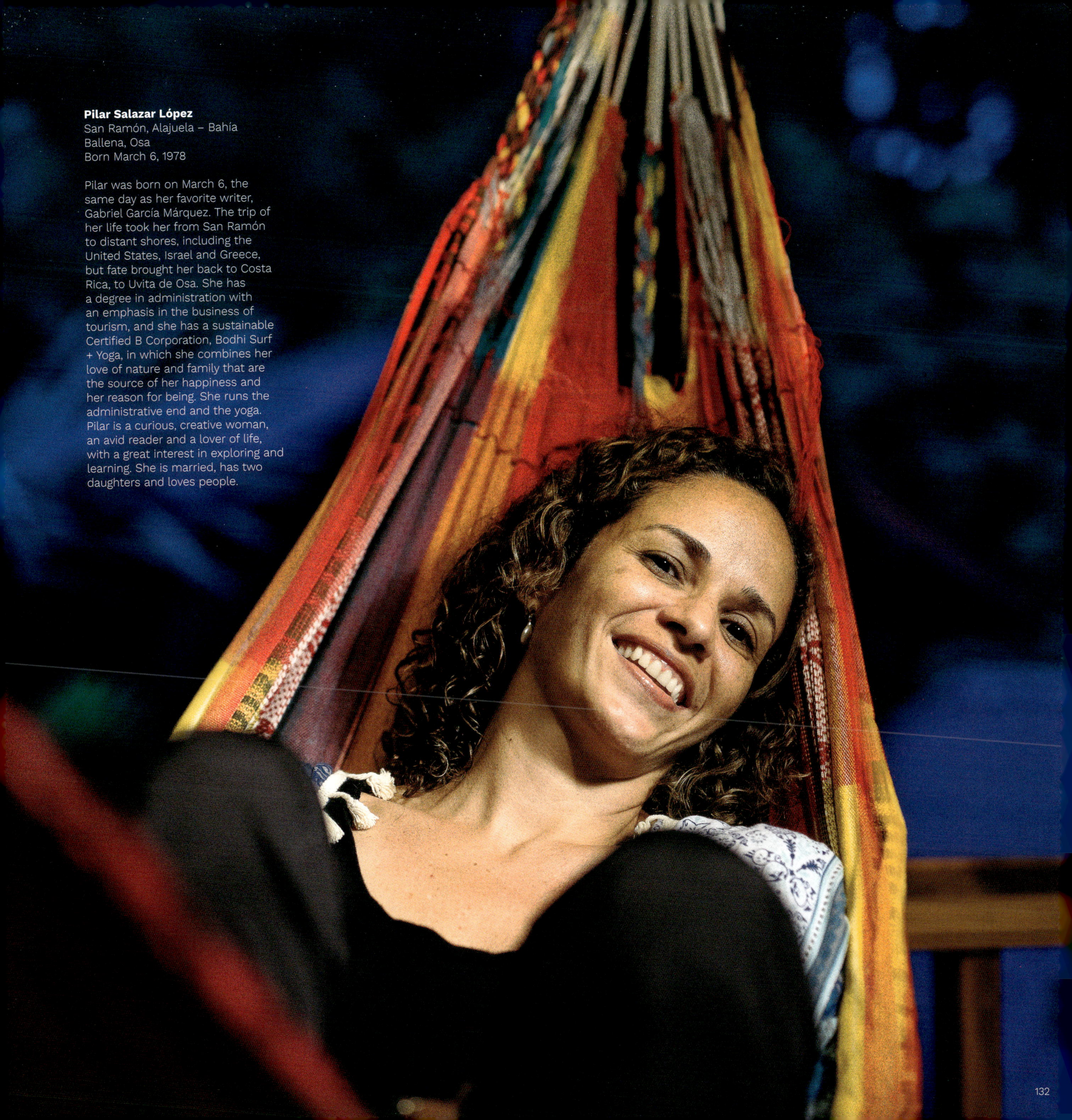

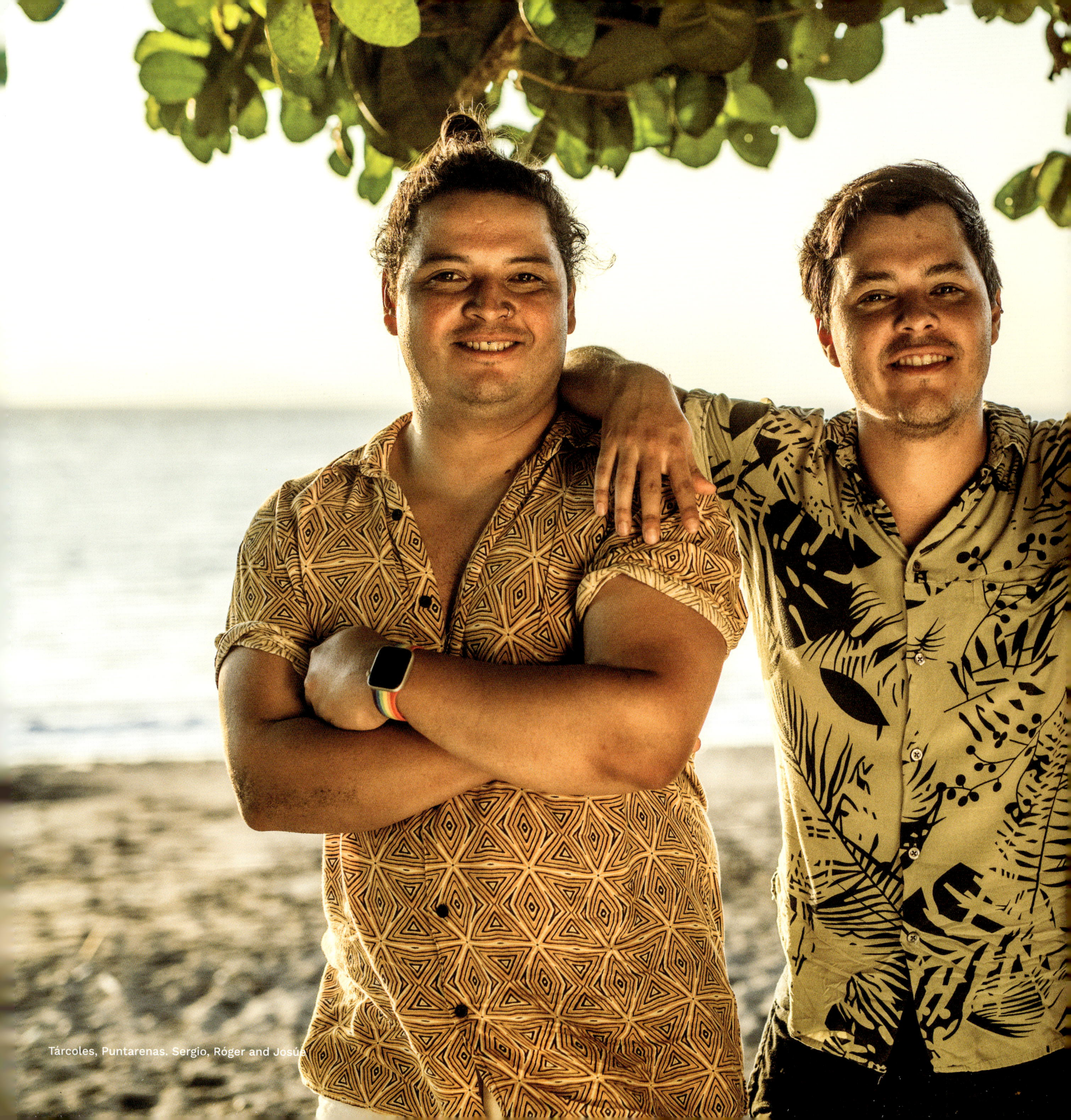

Tárcoles, Puntarenas. Sergio, Róger and Josúe

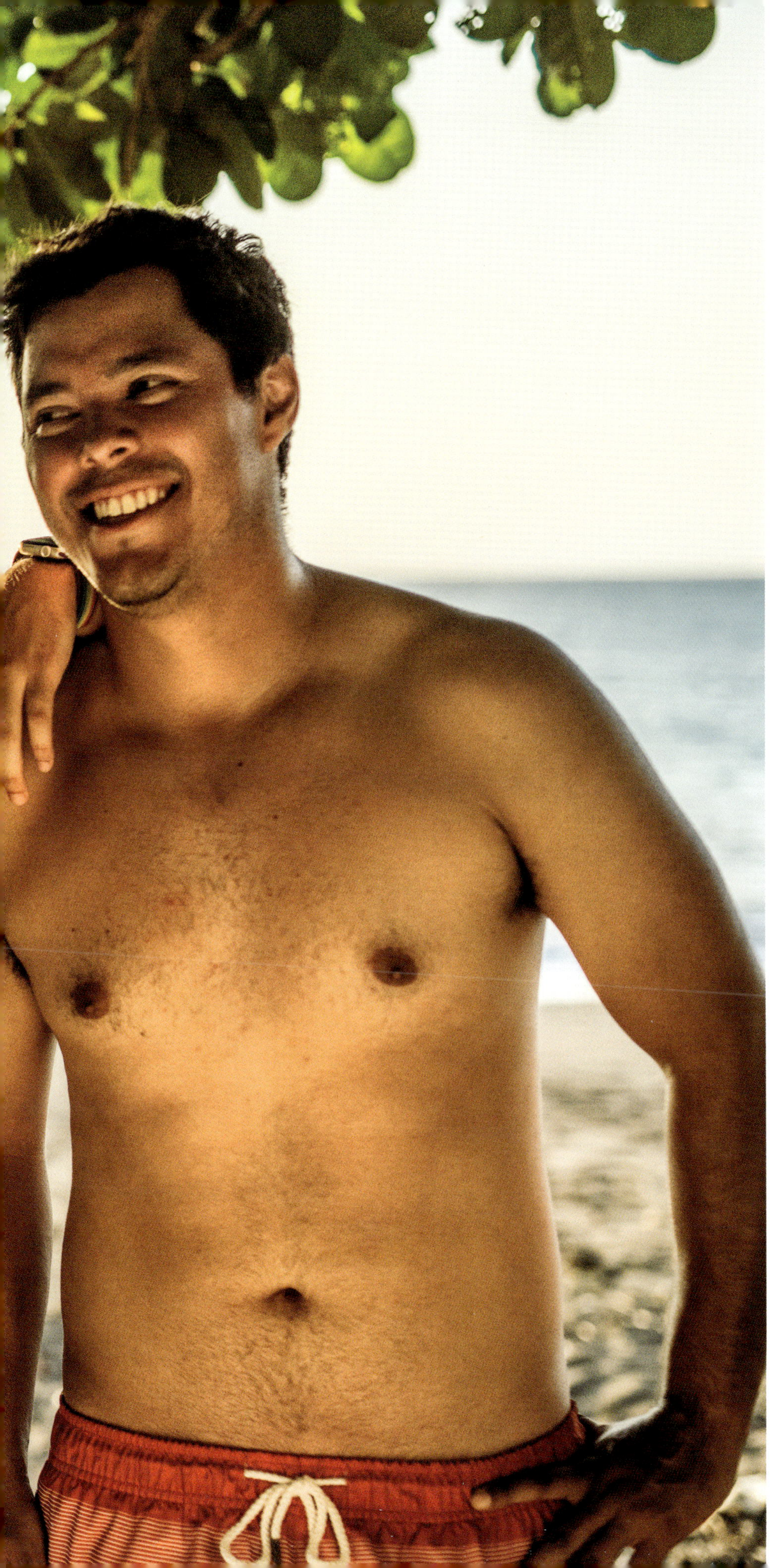

# PANCAKES, A PRELUDE TO LOVE

Twin brothers Róger and Josué share a room, but basically nothing else. They couldn't be more different. One night at the age of 18, Josué from his bed sees Róger half hidden in his sheets "sending little messages, with little laughs, and those revealing smiles." Róger tells him he met a girl. In terms of girls, as in other things, Josué and Róger are opposites. In high school, Róger had lots of female friends, as he found it easy to talk to women. To Josué not so much; he spent his time playing soccer, which didn't interest Róger.

Their mother, Rita, understands them. She's also a twin, and she says that for a long time she felt pressure to be like her sister. So she lets these two be different, be themselves.

For Róger it wasn't always so easy. Sometimes he thought it would be better to be like Josué, an athlete and a ladies' man.... "But in my heart I knew I wanted to be me."

One day, during that period of little messages, Róger decides to walk in the room and with little preamble and a mix of fear and anticipation, asks Josué: "Man, do you love me?" "Obviously, man, we're brothers." Roger insists, "But man, no matter what happens, will you keep loving me?" Josué insists again that he will. With that assurance, Roger tells him that he's homosexual.

Josué always defended his brother at school when he was picked on, but he had never allowed himself to believe

## "BUT MAN, NO MATTER WHAT HAPPENS, WILL YOU KEEP LOVING ME?"

that he didn't like girls. In tears, he embraced him and he said, "Man, you and I are one person. Everyone has his own tastes. You respect me and I respect you, and the love and regard will never be taken away."

Róger, flooded with relief, tells Josué that the person causing all those laughs and smiles every night was named Sergio. For their first date, Sergio came up with a plan. The neighbor girls would advise when Sergio's house was empty. Once they were together, some cousins released a dog that always came into their house, giving them a perfect excuse to close the door. Fourteen years later, they both agree that the plan worked.

Meeting Sergio, whose family knew about his sexual orientation, pushed Róger to take a step that for a long time he could barely contemplate. He went into the room where his parents were watching television, turned it off and started talking to them. "I consider myself a good son, I consider myself a good brother, a good student. I don't do any harm in society, but I have a different sexual preference."

Luis, his father, couldn't avoid crying and insisting that he give women a try, but his mother said she had known since he was a boy and she accepted it. He ended up telling them, "Don't waste money on a psychologist, because I am what I am and that's not going to change."

Just a couple of days later, Róger invited Sergio to dinner at his house, under the condition that there would be no displays of affection.
On one of his first visits, since Sergio lived in Cartago, he had to spend the night. Róger's father allowed it after making sure that Sergio's mother agreed. The next day he got up and made pancakes for his son and his boyfriend.

The pancakes, more than breakfast or a welcoming treat, were a prelude to love. As Luis tells it, his initial feelings turned into great esteem with the passage of time.

Today, when there's some family problem, Luis and Rita frequently call Sergio, who's more attentive than Róger. And Josué, who is a surveyor, has a leveling tool tattooed on each foot, one adjusted differently from the other one. They may be very different, but Róger and Josué love and support each other like two people who knew one another nine months before entering the world.

**Written by: Gloriana Sojo**

**Róger Alonso and Alonso Josué Durán Hernández and family**
San Francisco de Dos Ríos
Born Oct. 26, 1988

Róger Alonso and Alonso Josué are twin brothers, 32 years old. They have a big sister, Maricruz, who is an esthetician and an entrepreneur. Their mother, Rita, is a lawyer, and she also has a twin sister. Their father, Luis, is retired. Róger is an ad designer and Josué is a surveyor. Sergio Fernández, the son-in-law of Don Luis, has also been part of the family for 14 years (at this time he and Roger are building their own house). Don Luis remembers that one night, years ago, they called to tell him that his son had been detained at a bar in the capital for using fake IDs. At the moment, everyone was afraid, but he said that with time, this would turn into a funny story, just as it is today. Luis is a native of San José, and Rita is from Guanacaste. Together they've built a home full of love, where their pride in their children predominates. They face all challenges together, supporting and celebrating one another. They have a little dog, an important part of the family, named Clotilde.

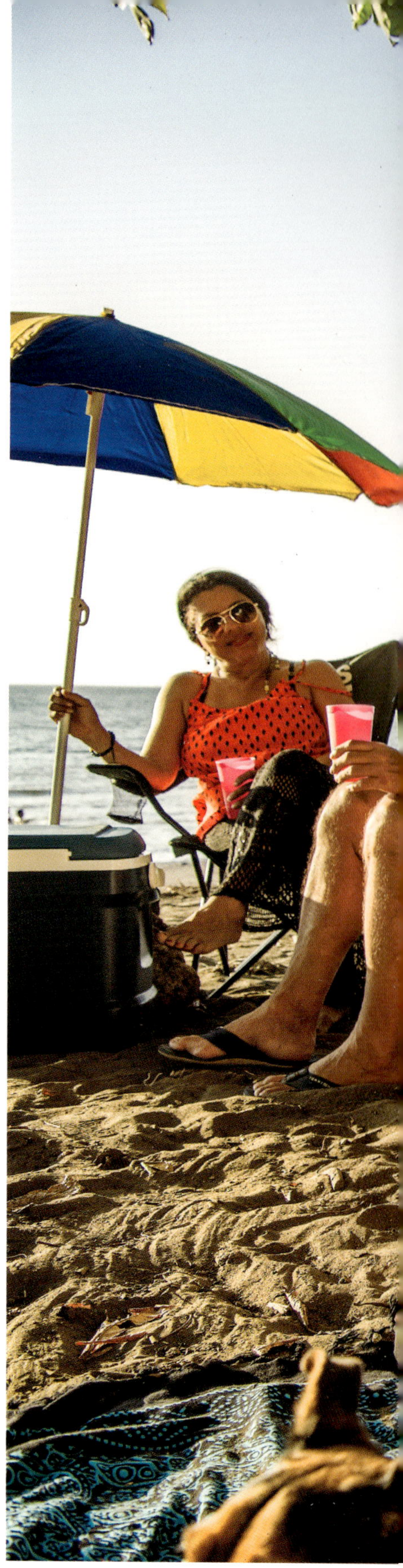

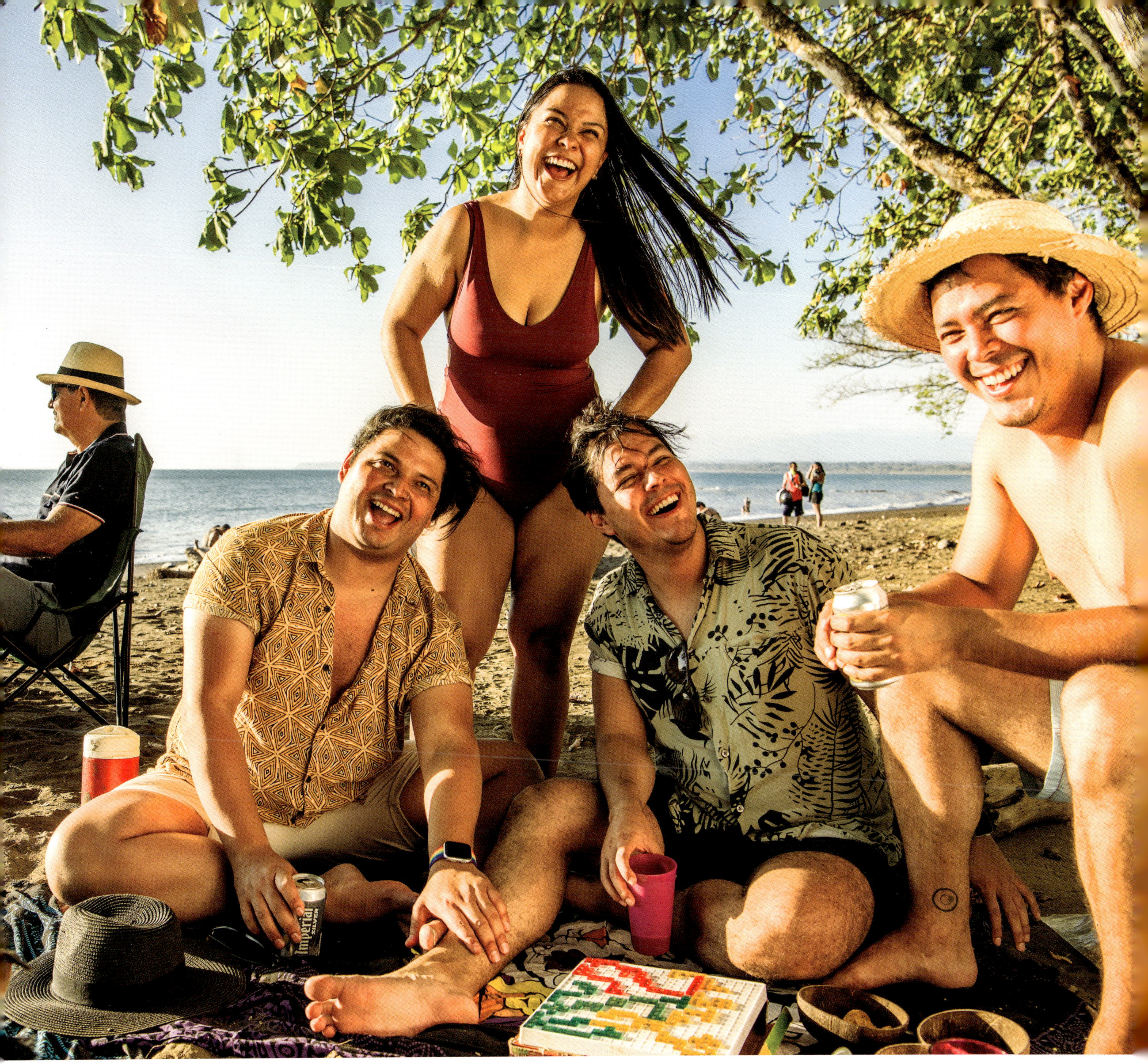

Rita Hernández, Luis Durán, Sergio Fernández,  Maricruz, Róger, and Josué Durán Hernández

# LITTLE GHOSTS

When the sun shines on him from in front and the glare of the light on the saltwater affects his eyes, Sebastián blinks. His pupils shrink, like a shutter that regulates the amount of light that reaches his brain. He's where he wants to be, sitting on his surfboard, surrounded by mountains of saltwater. The breeze is gentle, and from there he can hear the waves breaking on the beach. You could say that here in the water is where it all began. Many years ago he was right there with his first camera in his hands, taking pictures of his friends while they were surfing. At the time he was studying tourism, intending to spend most of his time in the water. And that's what he ended up doing.

When he looks back, his memory produces images that he has stored in his head, reminiscences like movies made of many frames per second. Little ghosts. He sees, for example, a naked boy running on the beach, followed by a man with a camera, and he recognizes himself and his father. He remembers that a few years later, in his adolescence, he liked to go to work with his father, and he was intrigued by how in the world of film production they could turn day into artificial night, or vice versa. The lights, the immense bulbs and the cables all caught his attention. From the water, he can see himself helping on the set, his teenage brain soaking it in, learning.

He remembers his mother too, and whenever he expresses gratitude for the place he's at, he mentions both of them, because they were equally important in shaping him.

In the movies that play in his head, sometimes things get mixed up, and some images are superimposed on others in the framework of the mechanisms of his memory. Sometimes he can see panthers and helicopters. He can see himself when he was younger, working in the United States. He can see himself working at his father's business, but also distancing himself from him and working for the competition. He can see something like a peace pipe and right beside it the word *reconciliation*. He also sees a herd of cows ambling down the highway and he remembers not being able to swerve in time to avoid them. He sees an accident in which a loved one dies, and he also sees the moment in which he had to make a decision: the moment of change.

All of that is in his head, projected constantly on an infinite loop, an eternal record. To access those images, all it takes is for the sun and the saltwater to conspire. All it takes is for his blinking to be involuntary.

When the sun shines on him from in front, Sebastián closes his eyes, and that's how he travels through time.

**Written by: Diego Vanderlaat**

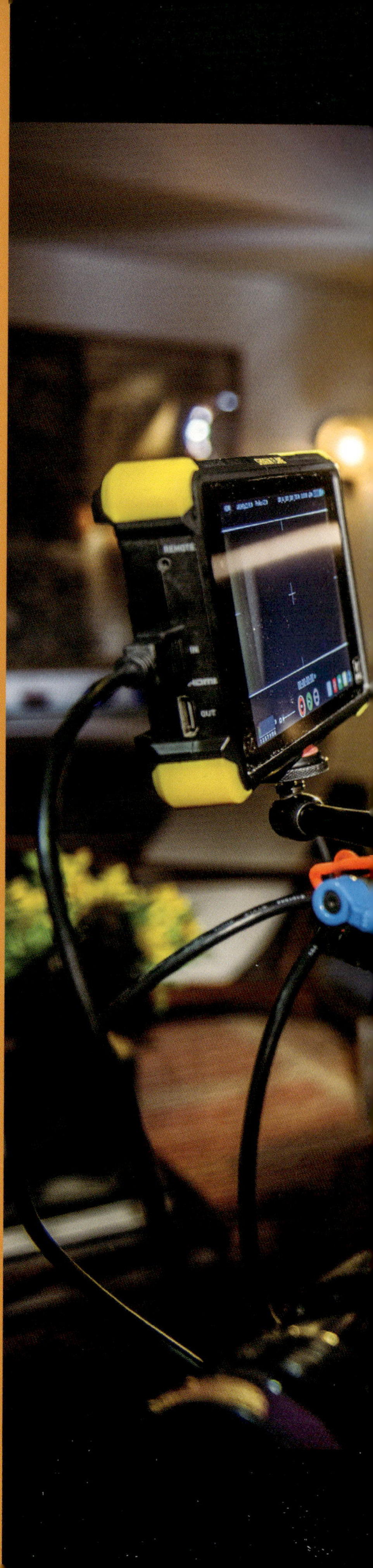

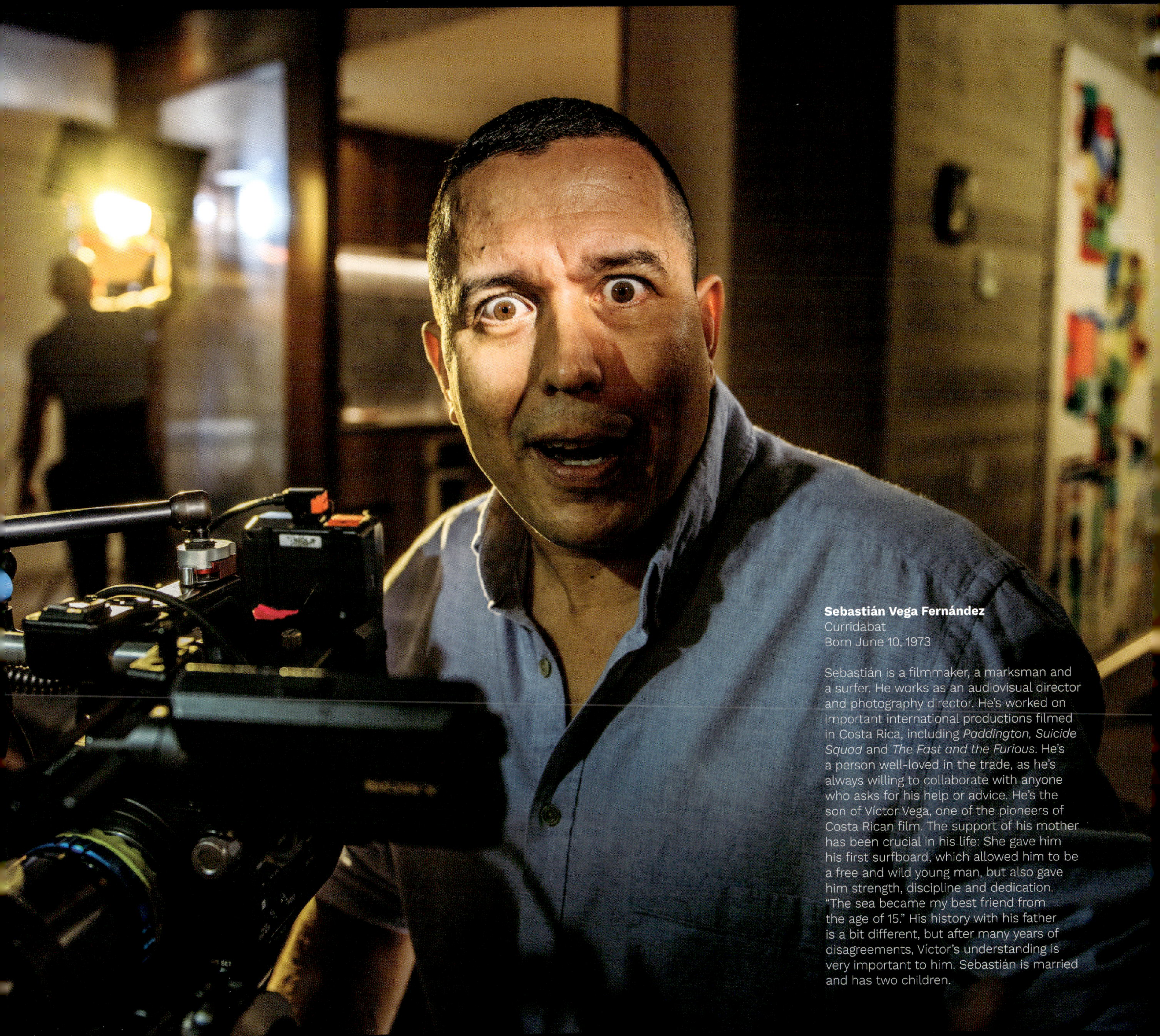

**Sebastián Vega Fernández**
Curridabat
Born June 10, 1973

Sebastián is a filmmaker, a marksman and a surfer. He works as an audiovisual director and photography director. He's worked on important international productions filmed in Costa Rica, including *Paddington*, *Suicide Squad* and *The Fast and the Furious*. He's a person well-loved in the trade, as he's always willing to collaborate with anyone who asks for his help or advice. He's the son of Víctor Vega, one of the pioneers of Costa Rican film. The support of his mother has been crucial in his life: She gave him his first surfboard, which allowed him to be a free and wild young man, but also gave him strength, discipline and dedication. "The sea became my best friend from the age of 15." His history with his father is a bit different, but after many years of disagreements, Víctor's understanding is very important to him. Sebastián is married and has two children.

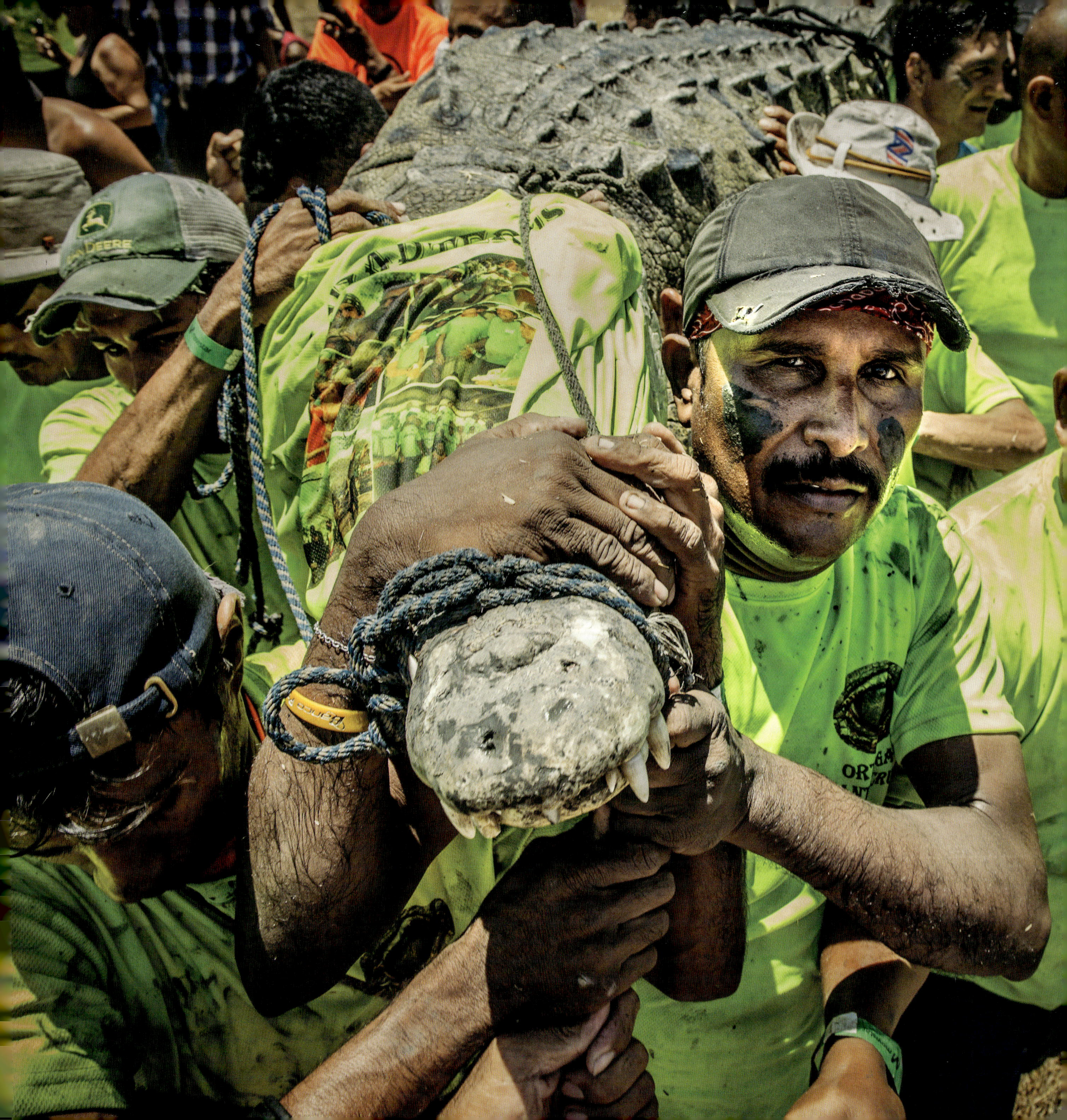

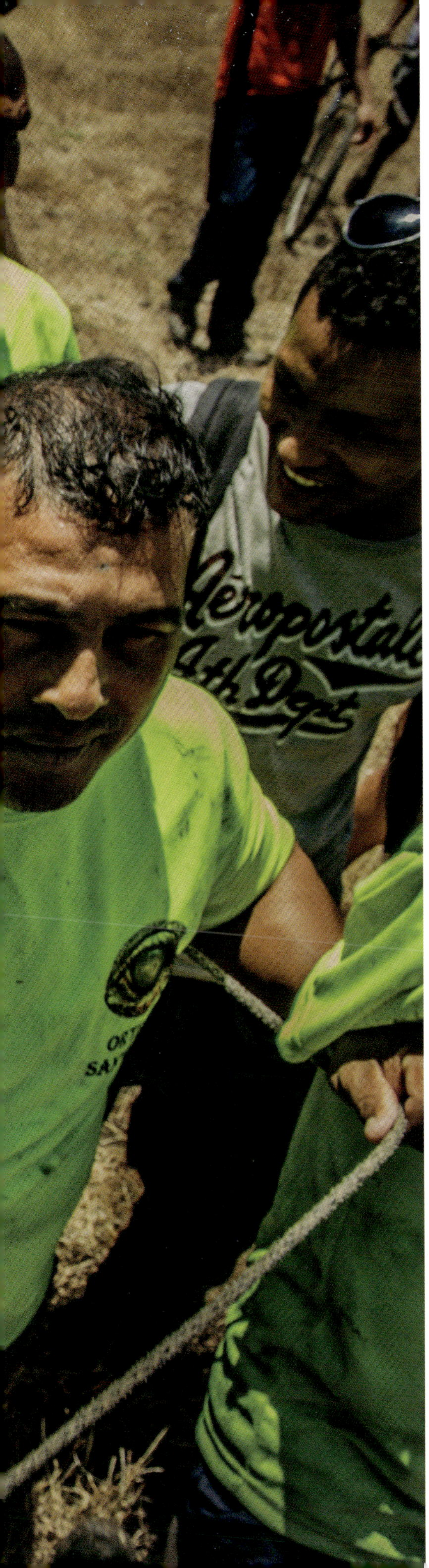

# THE NEXT GOOD FRIDAY

Ortega is a town with a river. Humberto remembers his father before Holy Week, negotiating the current of the Tempisque, the water up the chest, and he at the age of 9 on his father's shoulders, with a spear in his hand, performing a chore that probably predates the Spanish colonization. He still doesn't understand how his father knows where the fish will be, as he's totally blind, but the fact is that he always comes home with a "coat rack" full of good fish, already cleaned and ready to salt.

They say that Humberto's father went blind during a sugar harvest. They're not sure if it was so many years of carrying ashes, managing with his machete to cut the recently burned sugarcane, or if something else happened: a change of temperature, a mysterious "air" or just bad luck. Humberto learned through him that vision isn't everything, that there are lots of ways to see, because his father always knew what was going on around him. That's how he knew that his 11-year-old boy was desperate to get into the river with the men to *lagartear*, meaning to wrangle crocodiles.

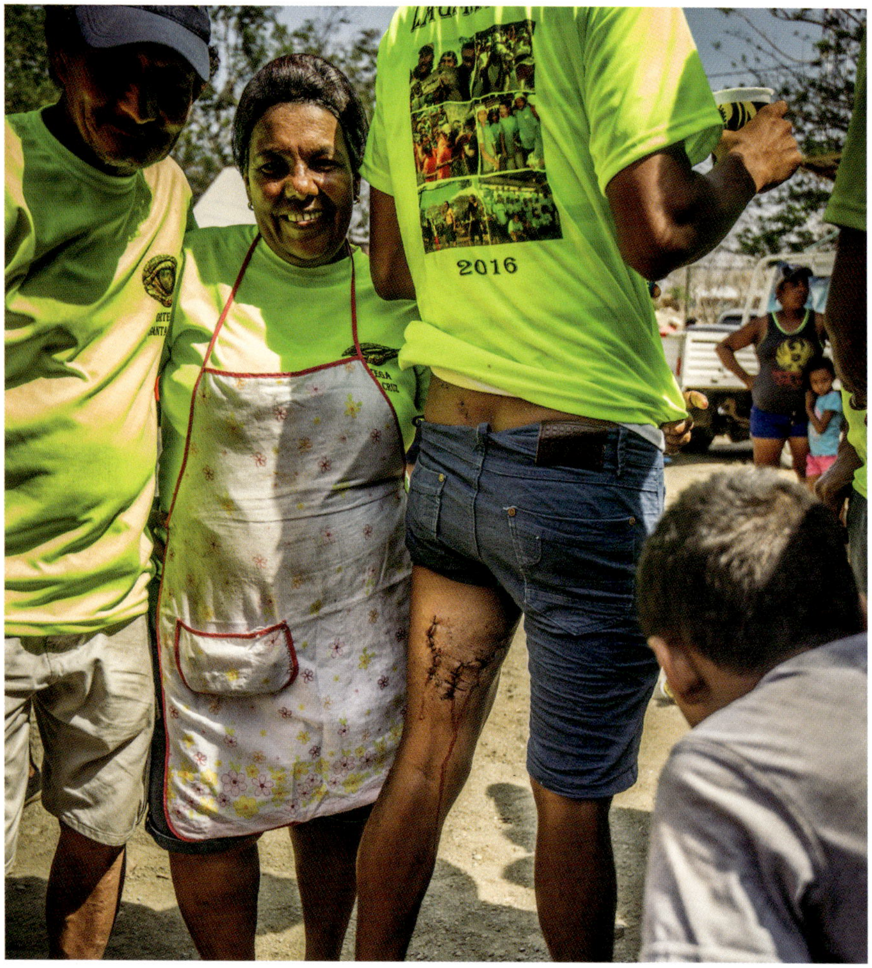


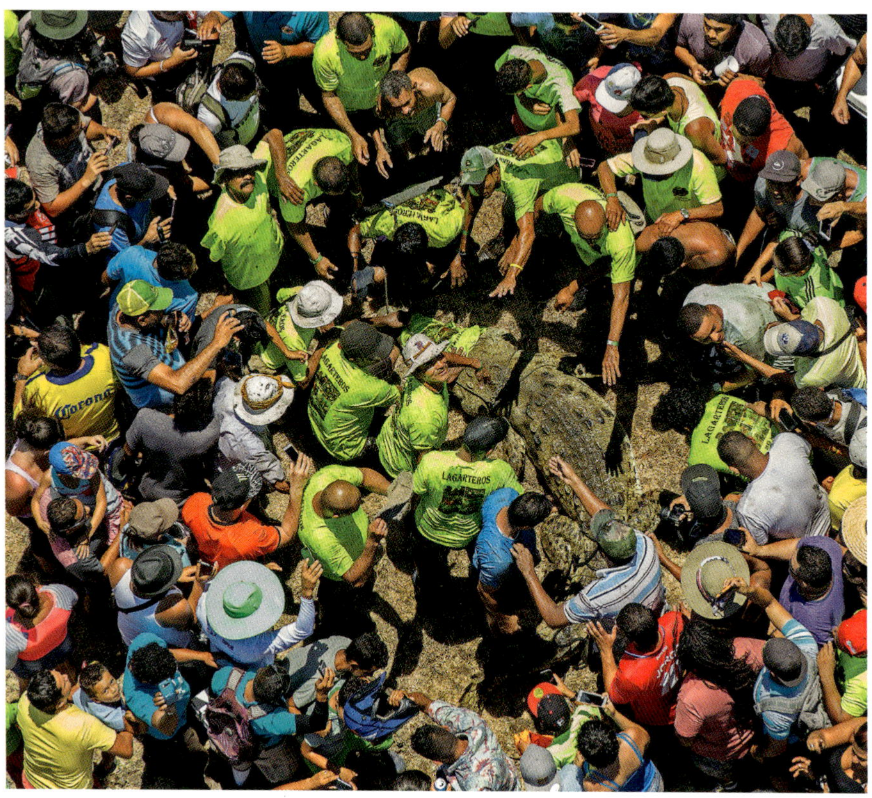

## UNCLE GÜICHO, WHO STILL WENT IN THE WATER AT THE AGE OF 90

In Ortega the mandates of tradition are deeply respected, including the fast, the authority of the father, and of course the custom of *lagartear* on Good Friday. The way they see things, having abandoned the old practice of killing the animal to take advantage of the "magic" qualities of its fat and its teeth, the *lagartos* ("lizards," as they call the crocodiles that live in the Tempisque) now have nothing to fear: They capture them, take them to an enclosure in town and set them free the next day, in the exact same place they found them.

It doesn't appear that Humberto and his friends have received a lot of information about how much a wild animal suffers when it's captured by force and removed from its habitat. For the men of Ortega it's a tradition, one that identifies them as inhabitants of this small town, the heirs of more than 200 years of croc wrangling and many more of veneration of the crocodile, symbol of fertility and death to the Chorotega tribes that prospered on the Tempisque many centuries before.

That was perhaps what the blind eyes of Humberto's father perceived the day he gave him permission to join the party that Good Friday. "You're going to go, but you're going to be the *tilichero*, nothing more." The *tilichero* was the "stuff watcher," the person who guarded the shoes, socks, leashes and other things the men had to leave on the shore of the river while they hunted the animal. "If you listen to me and everything goes well, next year I'll let you go in the river." Even though he was greatly disappointed at first, the boy obeyed his father to the letter and contented himself this time with being the *tilichero*.

One year later, Humberto returned home soaked in water and didn't have to say anything. Behind his blind eyes, his father knew perfectly that the boy had returned safe and sound, having become a *lagartero* crocodile wrangler at 12 years of age. He embraced him, water and all, and together they remembered Uncle Güicho, who still went in the water at the age of 90.

But all this was a while back. Today Humberto knows this tradition will disappear, just like the money earned from tourist visits in those days has disappeared, if they don't find a way to preserve it without removing the *lagarto* from the river. He and his buddies consider creative alternatives: What if on Good Friday we parade through town with a *lagarto* made of cement, or of wood?

Ortega is a town with a river. They'll find the answer soon.

**Written by: Jaime Gamboa**

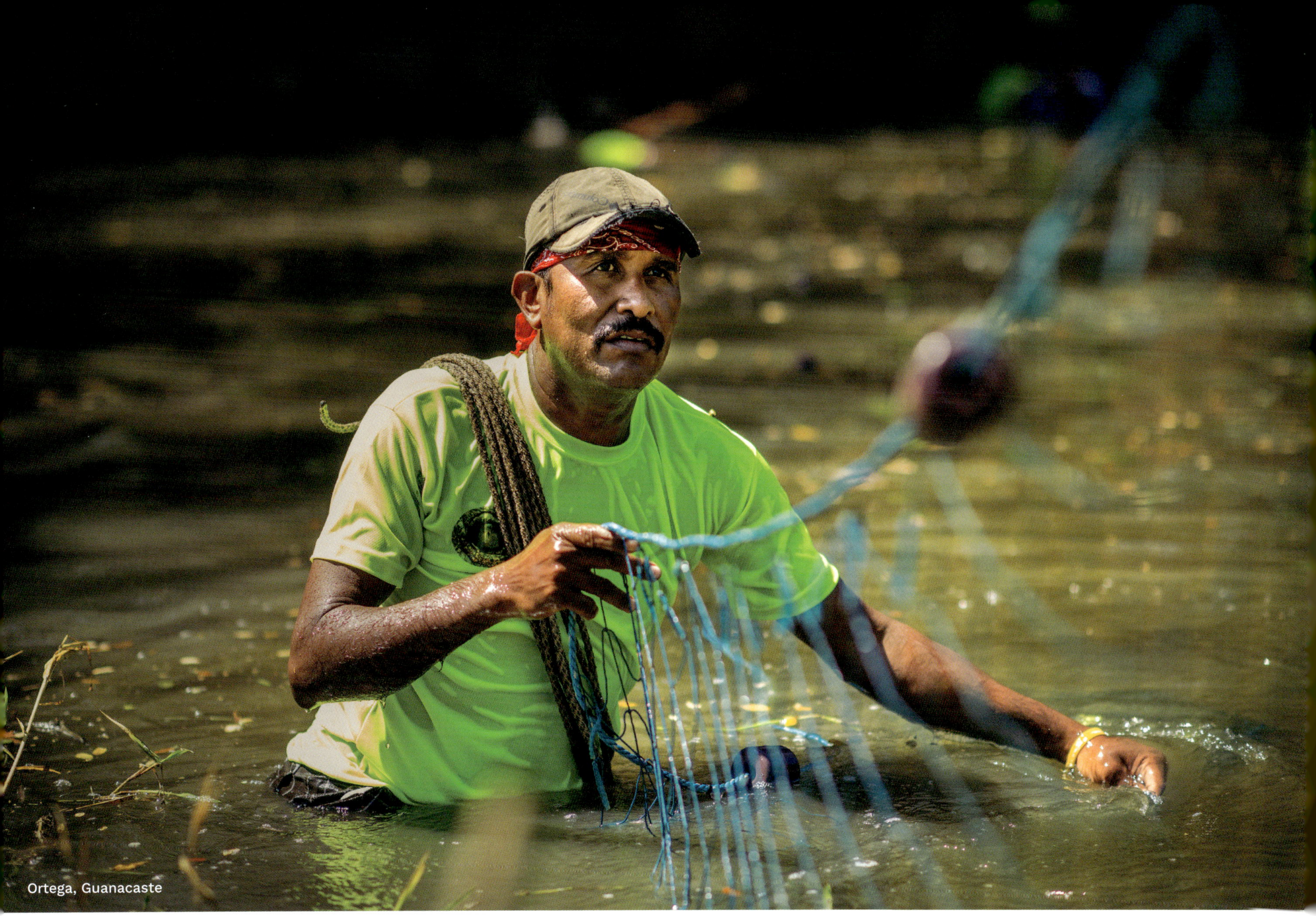

Ortega, Guanacaste

**Humberto Miguel Angulo Piña**
Ortega de Santa Cruz
Born Nov. 3, 1968

In winter, he plants corn and beans in the fields of his neighbors from the town, and in summer, he works for a business that grows cantaloupe and watermelon. But in his professional life he's done it all: He was a mechanic's helper, he was a cattle feeder, he harvested sugarcane, he drove a tractor, and he has worked in agriculture irrigation and night security. He was also a banana worker in Río Frío de Sarapiquí. Humberto finished only primary school because his family often had to choose between eating and other priorities. His father, Osberto, always gave him good advice about work: "Never lie — if they ask whether you know how to do something and you don't, say no." His daughter Tatiana is 4 years old and is his great source of pride: intelligent and a lover of animals, and when she grows up she wants to be a "doctor of little animals." Some things are hereditary, as Humberto would have liked to have a degree to do professional work in some area related to nature: "Here a jocote fruit falls to the ground, we clean it and eat it. We know how to appreciate what nature gives us. The big corporations put a lot of pressure on nature, and that's not good for it."

# SACRED SUNDAYS

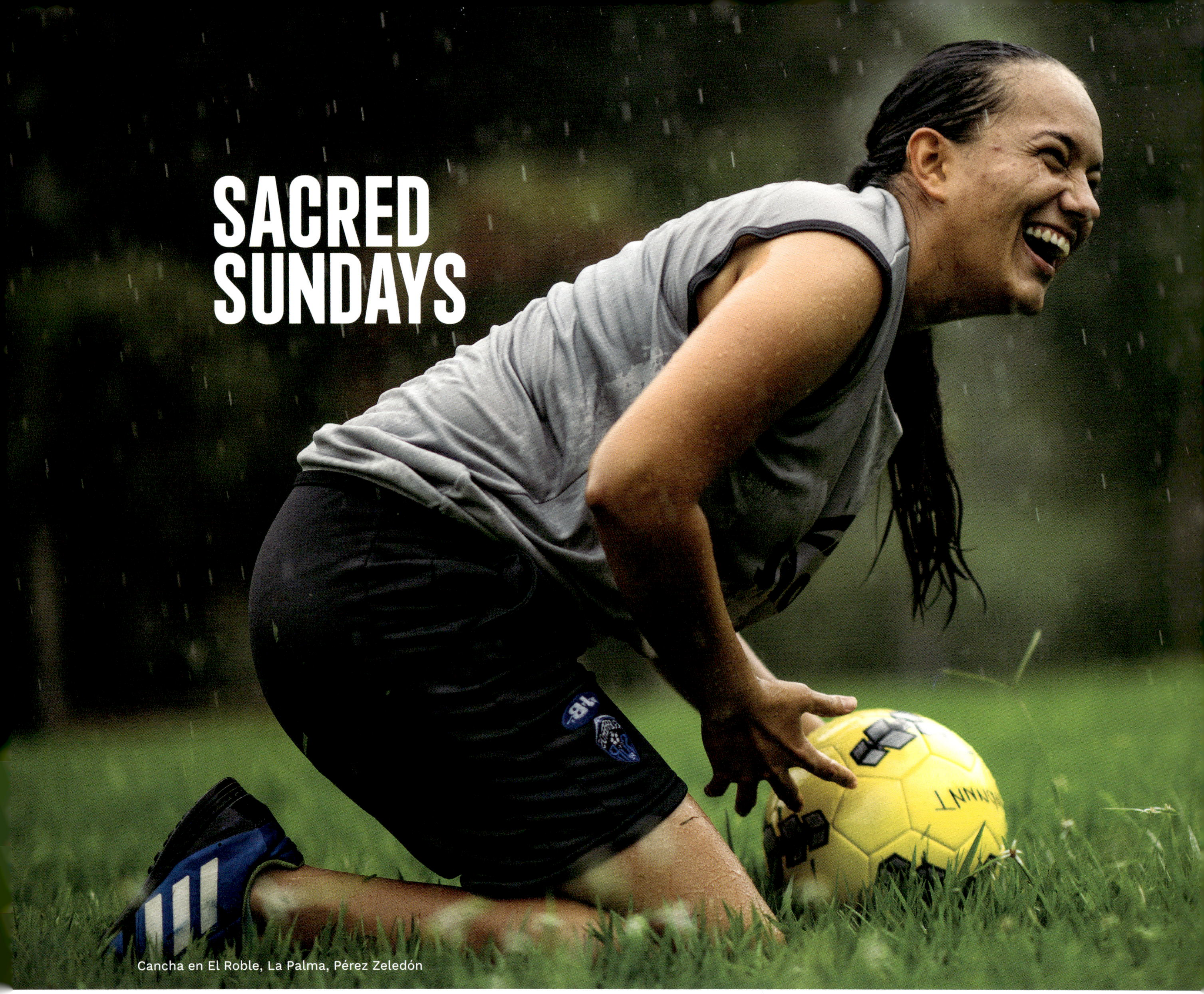

Cancha en El Roble, La Palma, Pérez Zeledón

**Verónica Acuña Navarro**
San Isidro de El General
Born Oct. 29, 1992

Verónica has a degree in business administration with a major in finance, and she's also a women's soccer coach. She works in the department that coordinates minor-league soccer for the municipality of Pérez Zeledón, scheduling training times, matches, and anything else that involves the minor leagues. For eight years, she's worked to popularize female soccer in the Southern Zone. Verónica is a woman who excels in a traditionally male role, dedicated to women's soccer teams, of which she is the technical director. "There are things that surprise me as a woman, because I've achieved things that men haven't," she says. "Every time something like that happens, I feel fulfilled, because every accomplishment for me isn't just for me, but for all the women dedicated to this discipline."

• One in three people in the country plays soccer, and female players represent 9% of the population.

"Here I come!" shouted Verónica, pedaling downhill, hoping her cousins would make room so she wouldn't run into the mango tree. The whole gang took turns blasting down the hill on a bicycle. It was a big group: 19 cousins got together almost every weekend at this magical house in the country that her grandfather had built with his own hands, about 20 minutes from downtown Pérez Zeledón.

Here she learned to play soccer, and to scrape the wax from her grandmother's floors to apply to the cardboard that they used to sled down the hill. Here her carpenter grandfather taught her how to use a saw, and how to make knots with ropes and wire. At the end of the year she went with him to kill a pig, and she also watched him give mouth-to-mouth resuscitation to a 3-year-old brother who almost died. The grandfather was always there, like the glue he used to hold wood together.

Every Sunday, the whole family gathered in front of the TV to watch a game, and they shouted, laughed, and joked. The grandfather got excited and even helped them build their homemade fly traps. With the same enthusiasm, the children started organizing soccer games in the yard, splitting into teams, everyone against everyone, and that's how Verónica learned to kick the ball when she was very young.

By the age of 19, Verónica was on the second-ranked team out of Pérez Zeledón. Her dream of becoming a professional player was within sight, but one day her coach quit and the team was about to break up in need of a trainer. Her next play would change her life completely. She decided to change positions, leave her post as goalie, and start directing her teammates from the bench. It was an act of solidarity, sacrificing her dreams in the face of the sudden possibility that her team could die.

## EVEN THOUGH HE WAS NO LONGER CONSCIOUS, HE WAITED FOR VERÓNICA'S VISIT TO SAY GOODBYE

Known as a little girl in a big family, but with the inspiration of a grandfather who always rallied the troops, Verónica found a new vocation as a technical director, and in her first season she led the team straight into the first division.
One sunny Sunday morning, Verónica addresses her team. They form a circle, holding hands, and she closes her eyes and goes back to the place where she grew up. She looks up to see that from the second floor of the house, her grandfather is looking down with a big smile. Nothing makes him happier than having his whole family together having a good time.

In Verónica's heart there's a sharp pain to remind her that her grandfather died many Sundays ago. She tries to focus on the present, on the match that's about to start, but she distracts herself for a few seconds more remembering that last Sunday when she spent the morning with her grandfather at the hospital. He had been pre-comatose for weeks, and she didn't want to visit him for fear that he would die in her presence. That same Sunday, he died. Even though he was no longer conscious, he waited for Verónica's visit to say goodbye.

Her team waits for her last words before running onto the field. She lowers her head and squeezes the players' hands, and she utters in a firm but affectionate voice the same prayer she says every Sunday:

*"May God and my grandfather guide you and keep you from any injury on the field."*

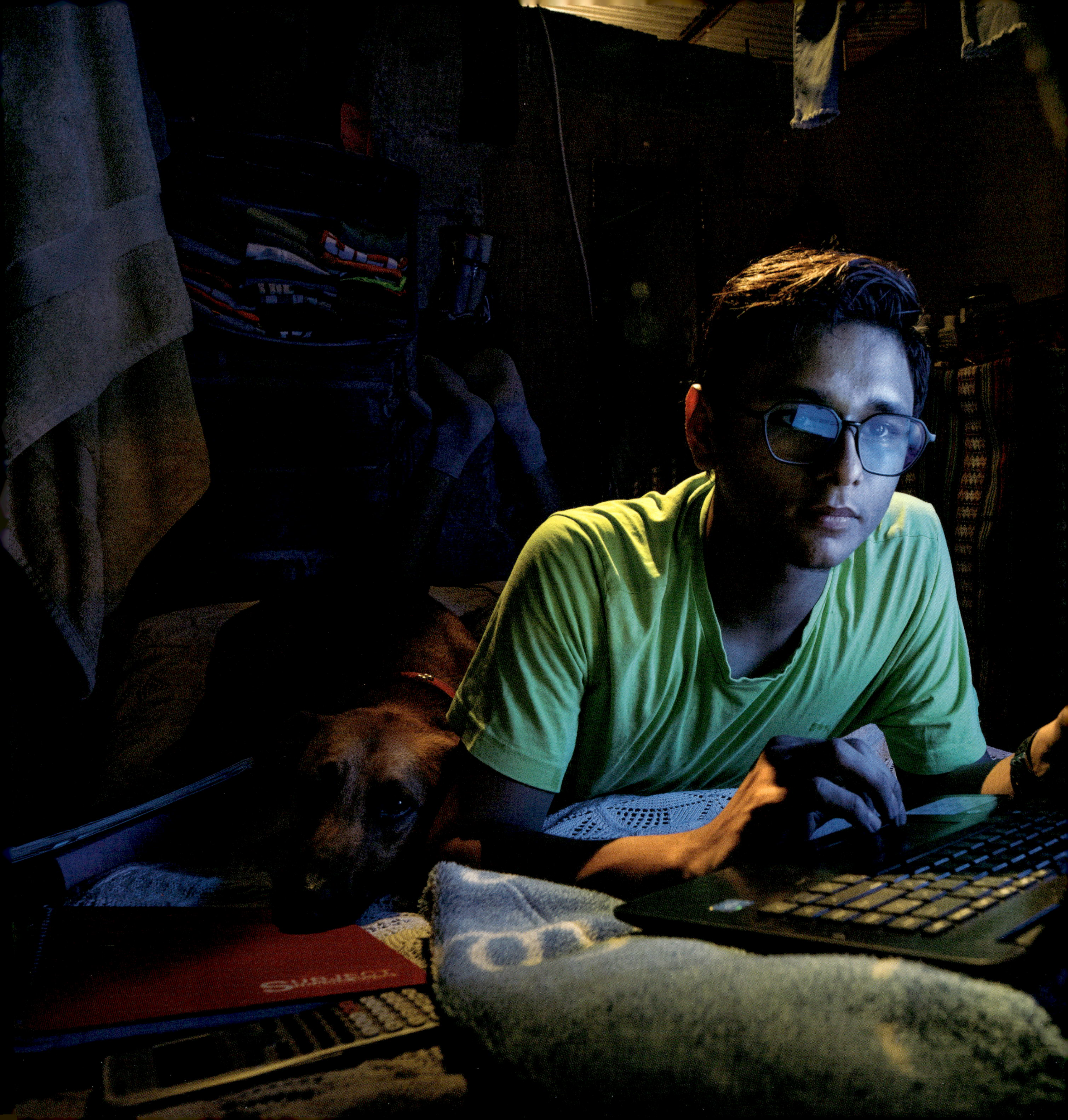
SUBJECT

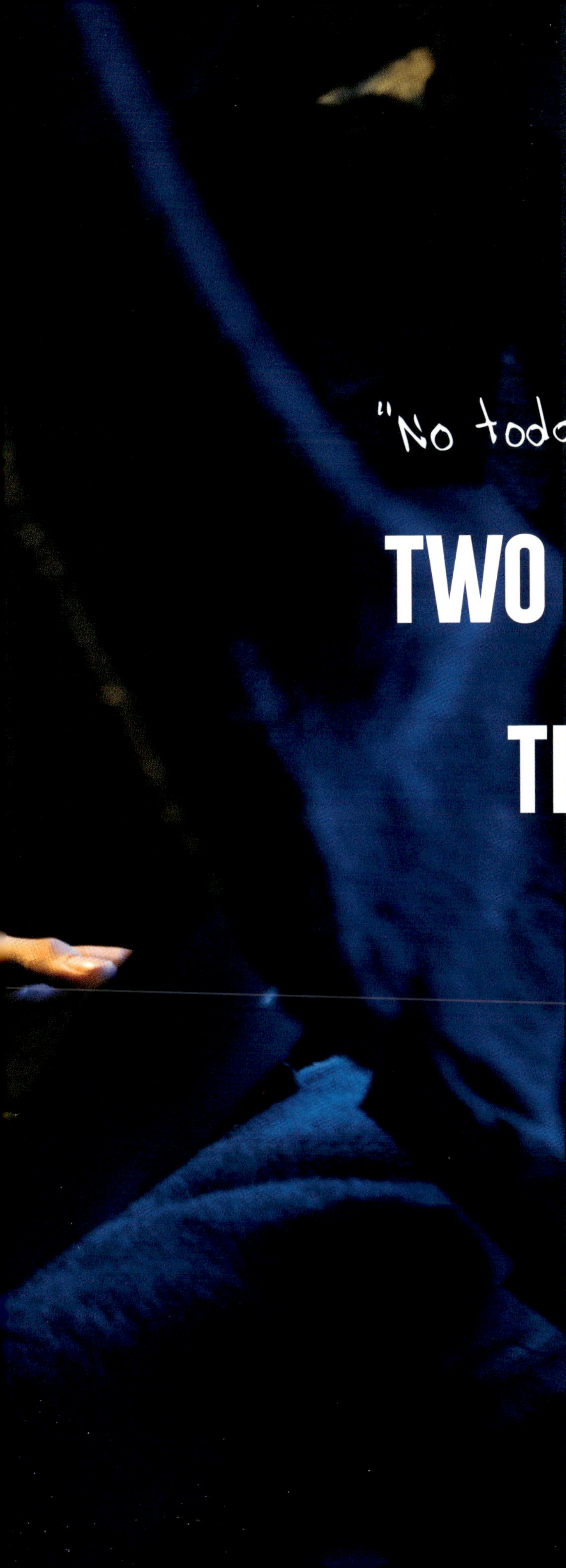

"No toda la gente de la Carpio es mala"

# TWO BLOCKS FROM THE TOAD CAVE

It was a Tuesday. My mom was at work as a maid; my brother and I were at home with Dad, because that day we didn't have to scrounge for work at the dump.
We were sitting down to eat lunch, when the first bite was interrupted by a loud noise.
"A thief," I thought, while Dad ran off to see what had happened.

"The house is burning!" he screamed, terrified. "Everyone outside! Run! Run!"

What happened next, I'll never forget: my father and our neighbors trying to rescue food, clothes, whatever, until the fire completely consumed that wooden house we were renting in Tres Ríos.

# I HAD NO WORDS TO ACCOMPANY THAT EMBRACE

I remember that night we slept at a neighbor's house, and the only things we had were donated by the neighborhood. I remembered when my mother noticed that the terrible fire she saw on the news had burned down the whole house and everything she had spent her life collecting.

But the most vivid memory is the face of my father, his countenance destroyed; and me, offering the strongest hug that a 6-year-old child can offer.

I had no words to accompany that embrace. I sincerely don't know if I would have the words today.

***

Amid the ashes, everything changed.

Jesús, my father, who really is my maternal grandfather, and Yadira, my mother, who is really my grandmother — left with nothing — took me to Nicaragua, where my biological mother lived with my five siblings in a zinc house that we shared with dogs, chickens and all the other animals on the farm. It had a mud floor, and it stank.

Two years later, we returned to Costa Rica, and shortly afterward I started high school. I spent the time between soccer games and video games, ignoring the voice of my father that echoed in my head: "Study — that's your only job."

I didn't feel like it.

"Mom, what is that?" I asked when I saw her calf, below her dress. "That's nothing, those are varicose veins," she said. "Did you do your homework yet, little guy?" Her voice tried to hide a great weariness.

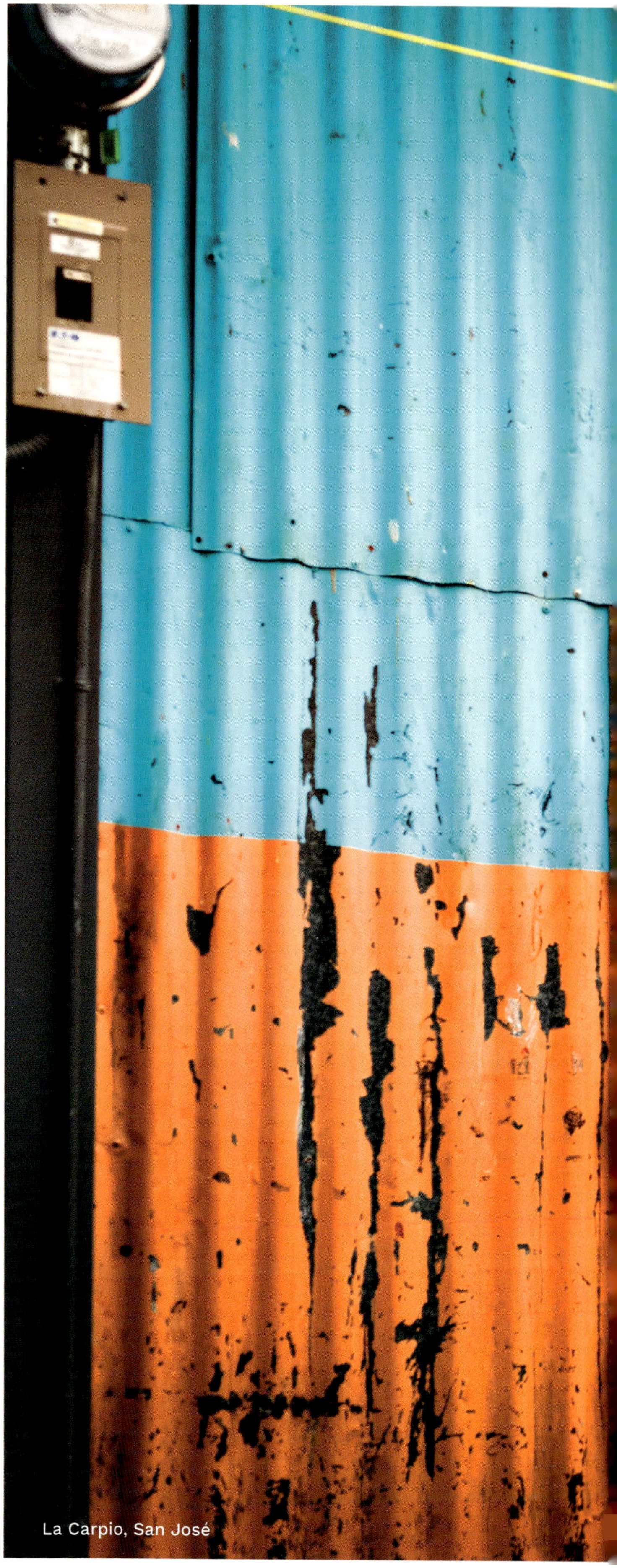

La Carpio, San José

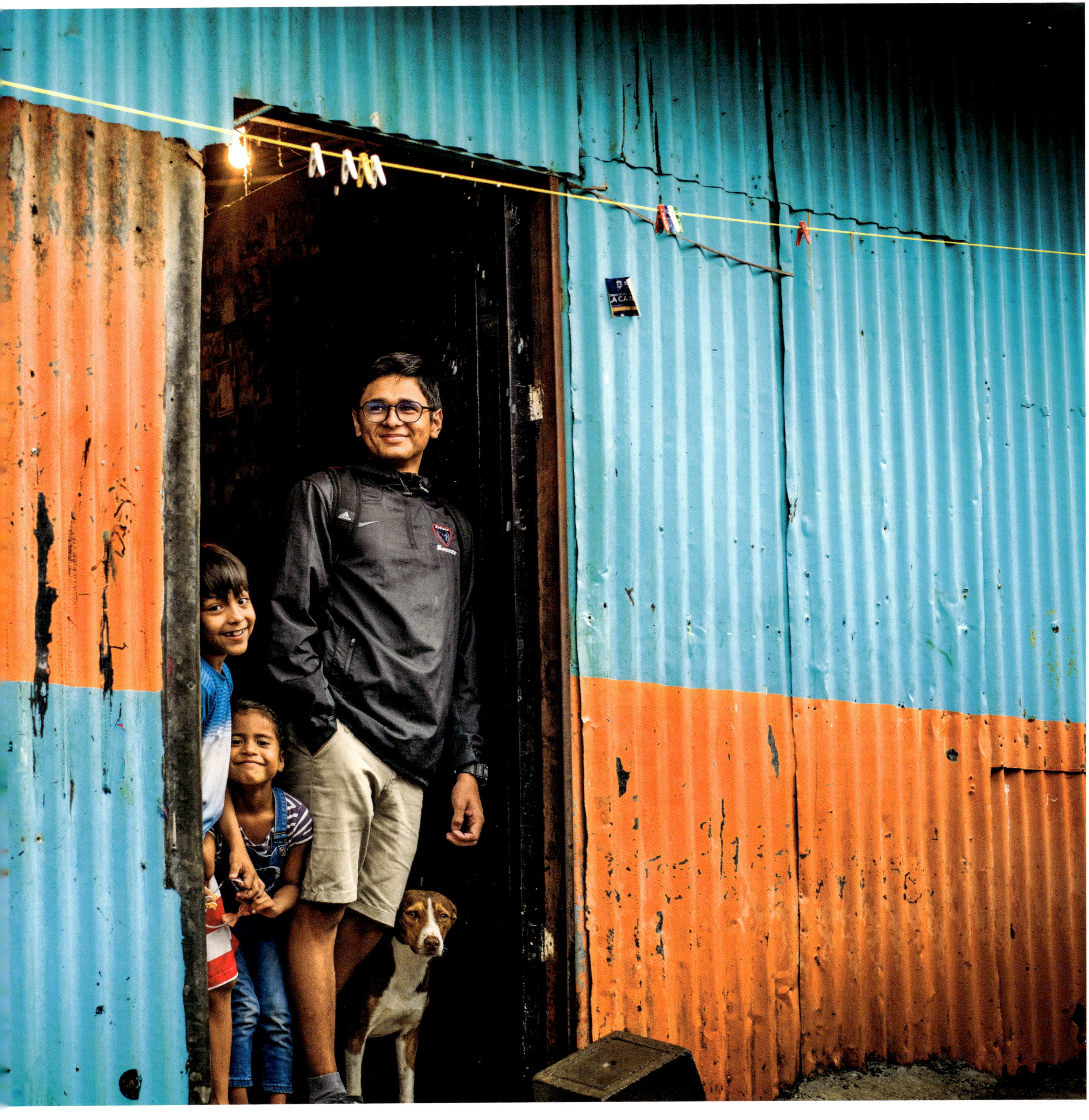

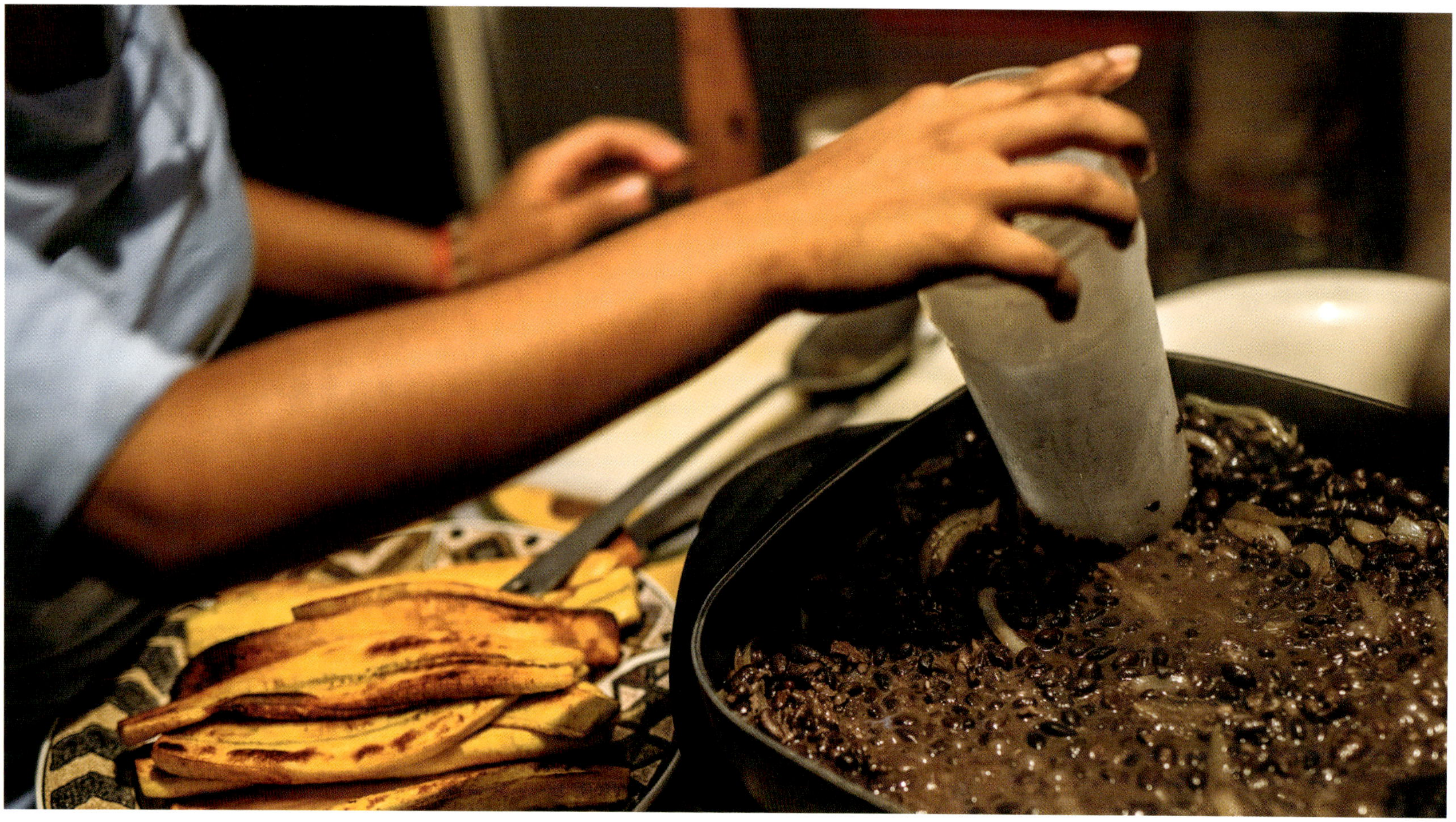

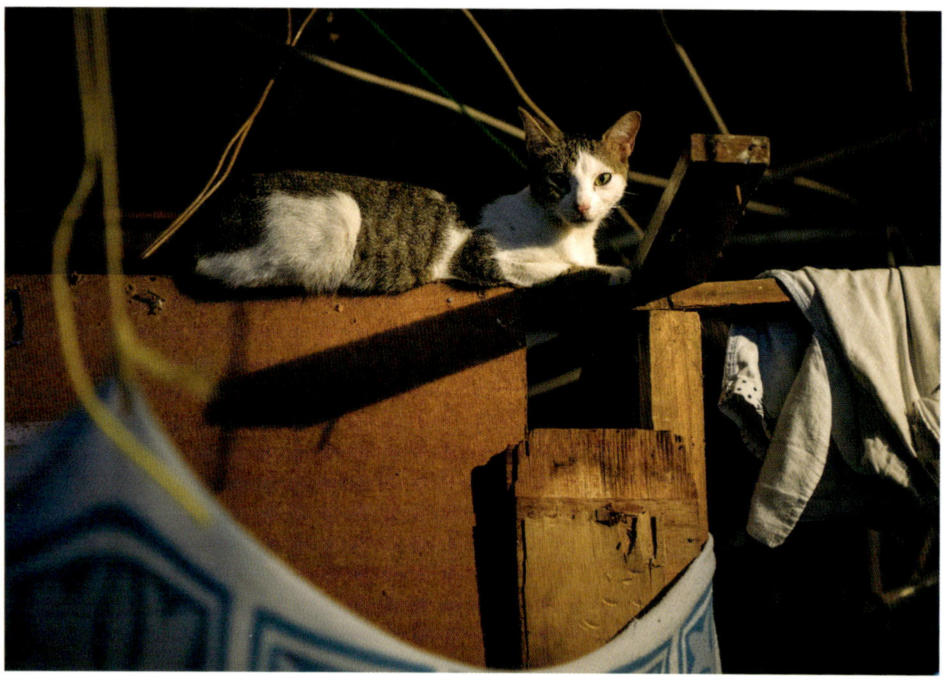

"I can't be such a lazy-ass!" I said to myself, egging myself on. "I can't be like that! My mom with varicose veins from working so hard as a maid to send me to school, and I'm just goofing off."

I decided to apply myself.

I started with mathematics, with a "chicken-pecking" calculator that sounded like a hen pecking at the ground — with its "click-clack-clack-click, it became the biggest joke in the class. I didn't care.

I was already in the 9th grade, and I had a girlfriend — oh my God!

Virginia and I started competing to see who could get the best grades. She almost always beat me, but I started to get grades in the 90s.

"Write to 'the Corner,'" she told me one day, sure that they could help me like they had helped her.

"Sorry, we're full," I heard for six months. But finally, I

don't know if it was because of merit or sheer persistence, they gave me an opportunity.

At the same time, my father took off for Spain to look for work, and my mom went to Nicaragua to take care of her great-grandmother. I was left alone, homeless, without a nickel. Virginia and her family opened their doors to me.

We lived two blocks from the "Cueva del Sapo," the "Toad Cave," a notorious drug den. In our house there were four rooms, all with cloth doors. Thirteen of us lived in 650 square feet, not counting the dogs. To say that we were a bit squeezed would be too kind.

From a young age I learned that life is not a bag of candy. The fire, the poverty of Nicaragua, and my abandonment at age 15; but I also learned to be grateful.

Thanks to Virginia and her family I have a roof. Thanks to La Esquina I have an opportunity to study at LEAD University. Thanks to my efforts, and those of my parents, I'm going to be an economist.

Soon I'm going to have the tools to help other kids like me, so that together we can show this country that in La Carpio, we are good people.

**Written by: Eugenio Desanti**

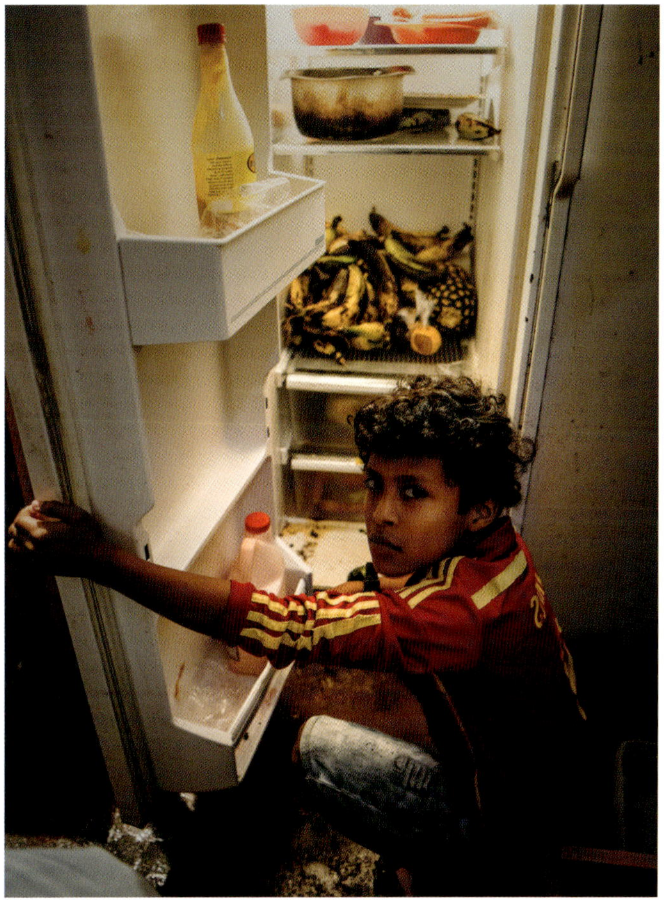

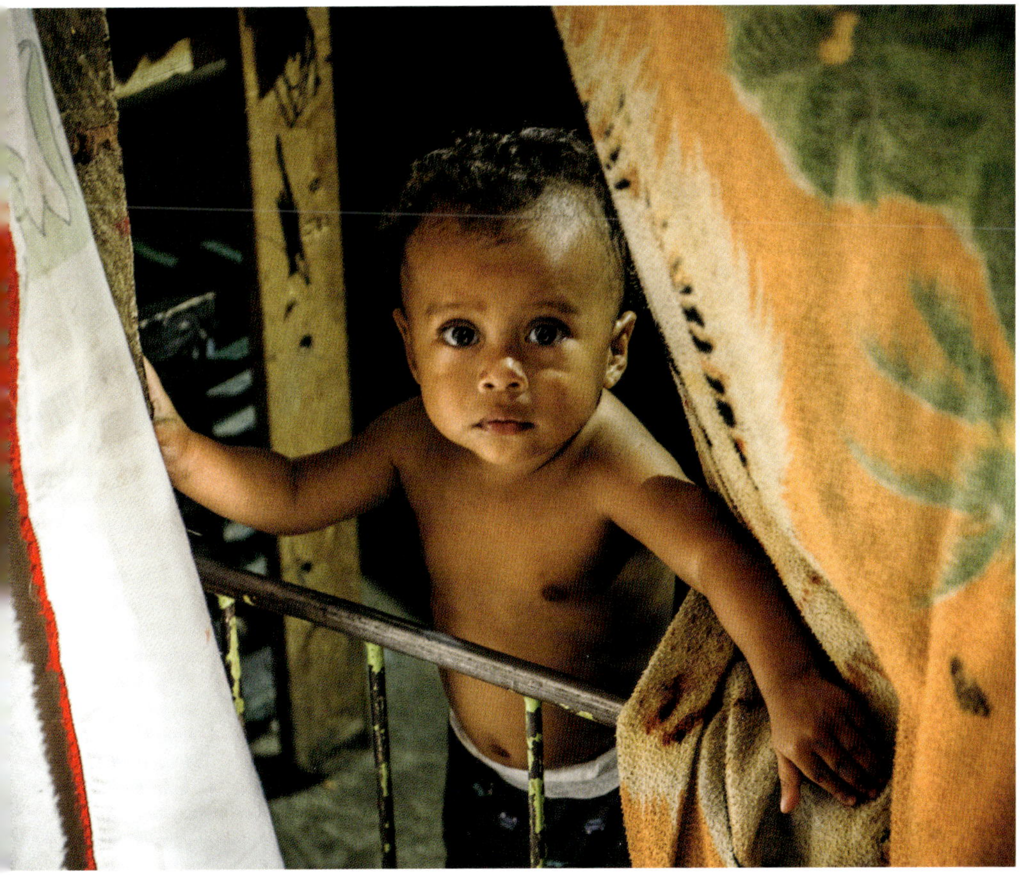

**Yilmer López Lacayo**
La Carpio. 19 years old

Yilmer comes from an immigrant family. They came to this country when he was young. When the family went back to Nicaragua, he stayed here with his girlfriend, and her family took him into their house — a space of 600 square feet where 13 people lived. Together they studied and they struggled to get ahead. After several months of effort, he was able to get into "La Esquina" ("The Corner"), a social enterprise dedicated to supporting high-risk youths, raising awareness of the conditions that drive young people to delinquency, and stressing the importance of prevention. He currently lives in La Carpio and studies economics at LEAD University. "Tell my story," he says. "Offer an example that not everyone in La Carpio is bad, that not everyone is looking for drugs."

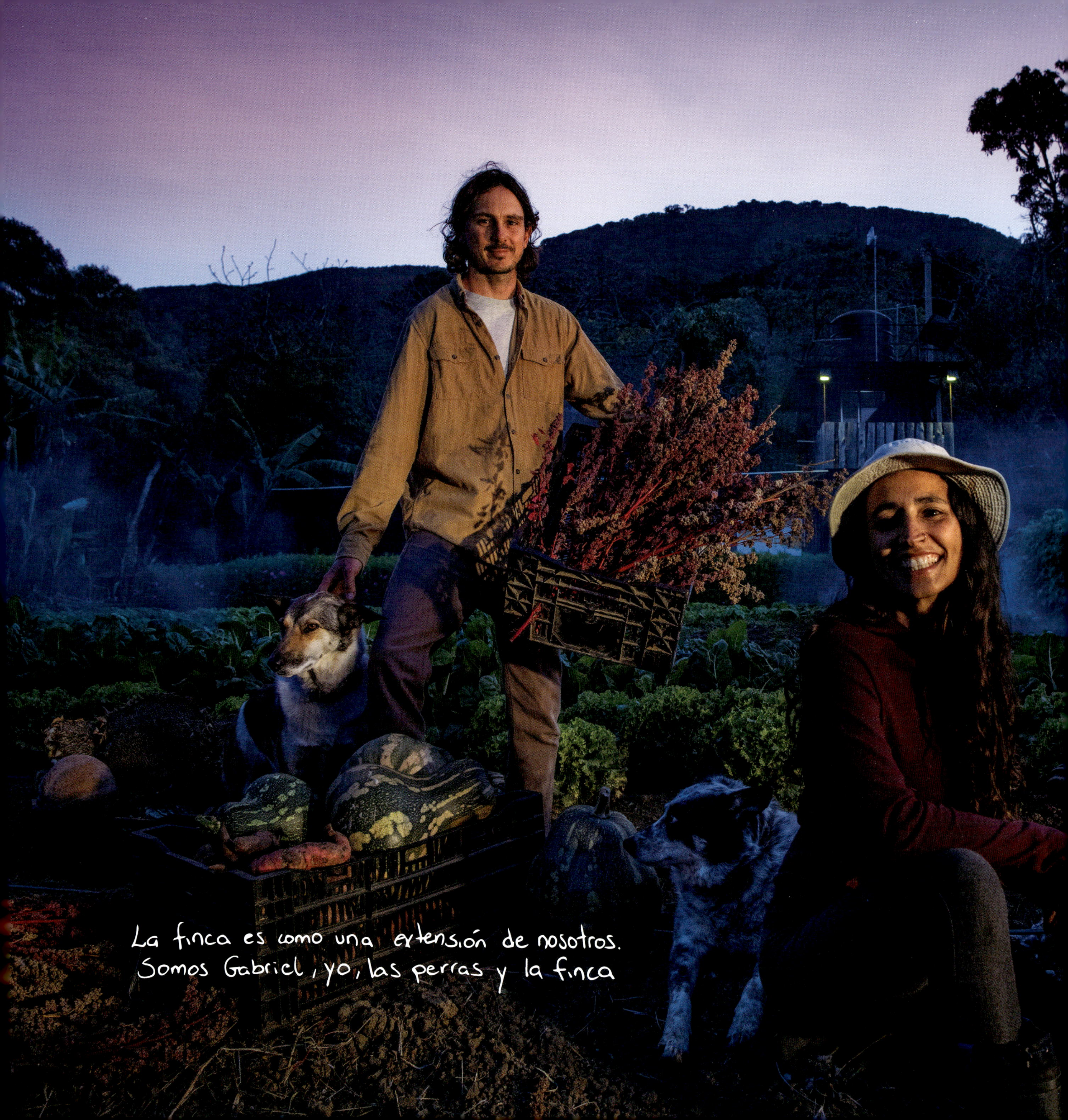

La finca es como una extensión de nosotros.
Somos Gabriel, yo, las perras y la finca

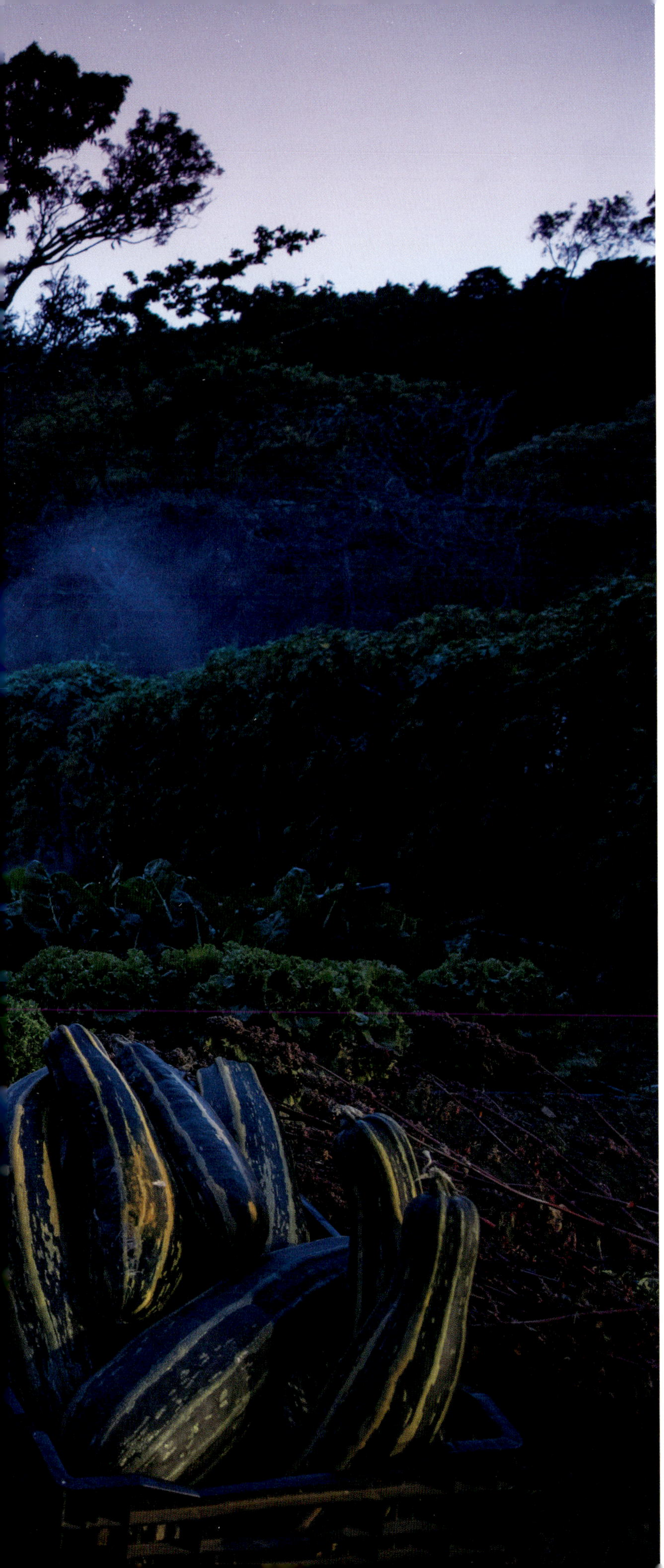

# OUR FARM

We were sitting outside the office, seated on chairs harder than the poverty that follows the holidays. Gabriel, my partner, sat there as if in a movie from a Central American David Lynch. I sat like the Colombian version of "Ugly Betty," fantasizing about the face of a boss whose name we had only heard mentioned.

It was getting late, and I looked at Gabriel, who was looking serious while trying not to fall asleep. I thought we were wasting our time, but he said, "Mima, we're not leaving this place until we get those light poles." Our project of acquiring a farm was collapsing, and we were playing our last card.

That dream of a farm had started a few years before. Gabo and I had visited several organic farms on a trip outside the country. One night, having a few beers, we started dreaming of having our own. On our return, we started searching for our own piece of land in Costa Rica, a search that ended up in Desamparados. The farm was already ours, but we had a big electricity problem. We wanted to put in solar panels, but it was too expensive.

We approached the offices of power and light, where they asked us for a ton of paperwork to satisfy their protocols. After months of tedious applications and countless rejections, they approved our application. But it turned out that to put in 300 meters of electricity, we had to pay 8 million colones ($13,000 today), and we almost fell over backwards. We played the lottery, we asked for loans, we prayed to the Negrita, but the money never arrived. It became so exhausting that we started to think our project would never succeed.

One day, as we were walking in frustration through the building of the electric company, we saw an office that looked important. We entered on a whim, with the hope that someone in power could literally give us some light. We asked to be attended, and it turned out to be nothing more and nothing less than the office of Don Fructuoso, the director of power and light, the big fish.

While Gabo and I were talking, the secretary called us. We got up quickly and entered the famous office of Don Fructuoso, a severe man with a big stomach and a very imposing, direct voice. He looked nothing like Don Armando, the insufferable boss in "Ugly Betty."

"What can I do for you?" he asked us very seriously. Gabriel started to explain with great passion our plans for our farm. The man started to get impatient. "OK, but what do you want?" So I looked him in the eyes and I told him: "We don't have enough money to put in the electricity that we need to work the farm." "And how much do you have?" he asked. Gabo and I looked at each other. I replied confidently, "600,000." "OK, you put up that and we'll put up the rest." That was it; he signed a paper and quickly invited us to leave his office. As we walked out, a huge smile broke onto our faces. Arriving at our car, we embraced and shouted in silence, the kind of shouts that come from the belly.

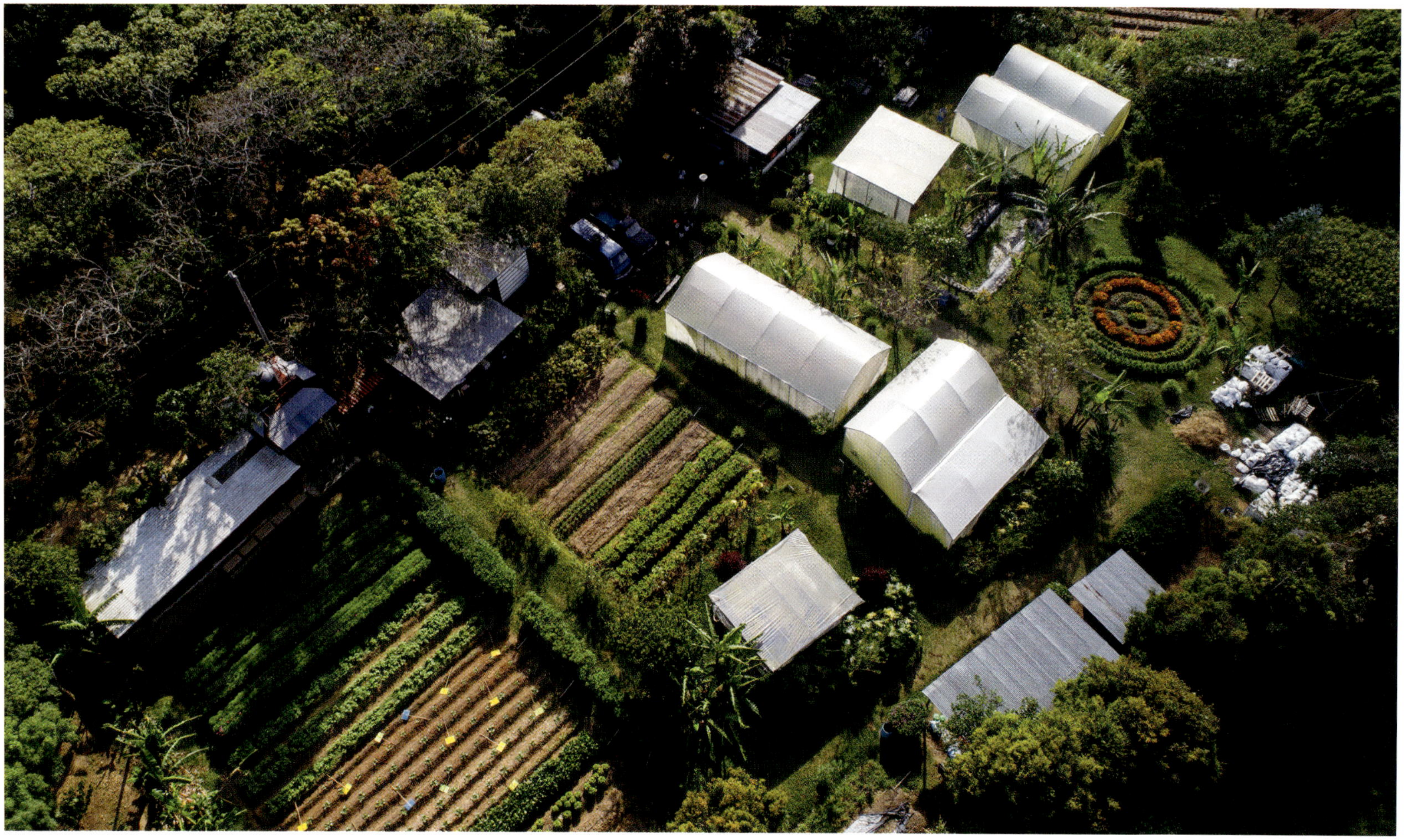

El Tablazo Agroecological Farm, San Miguel, Desamparados

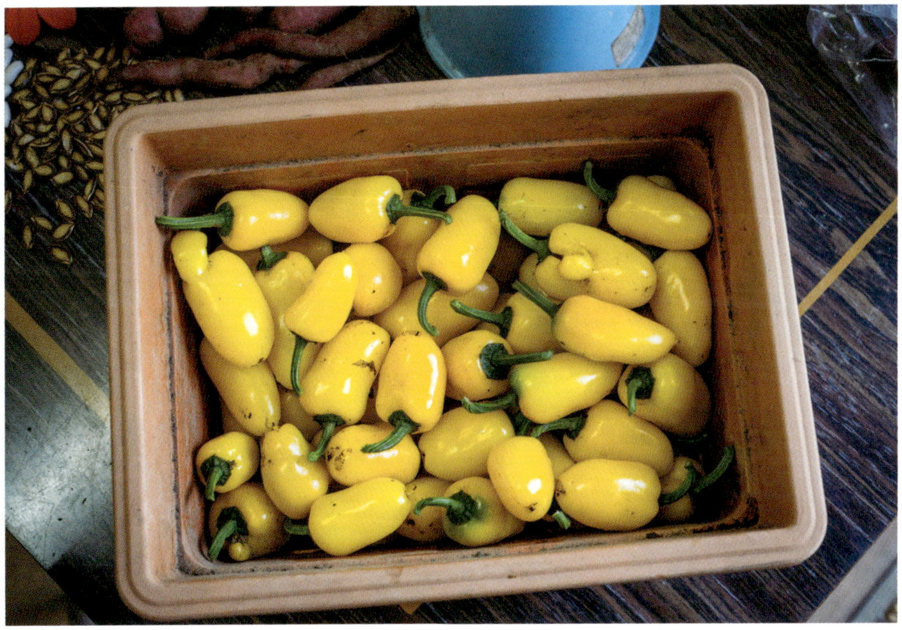

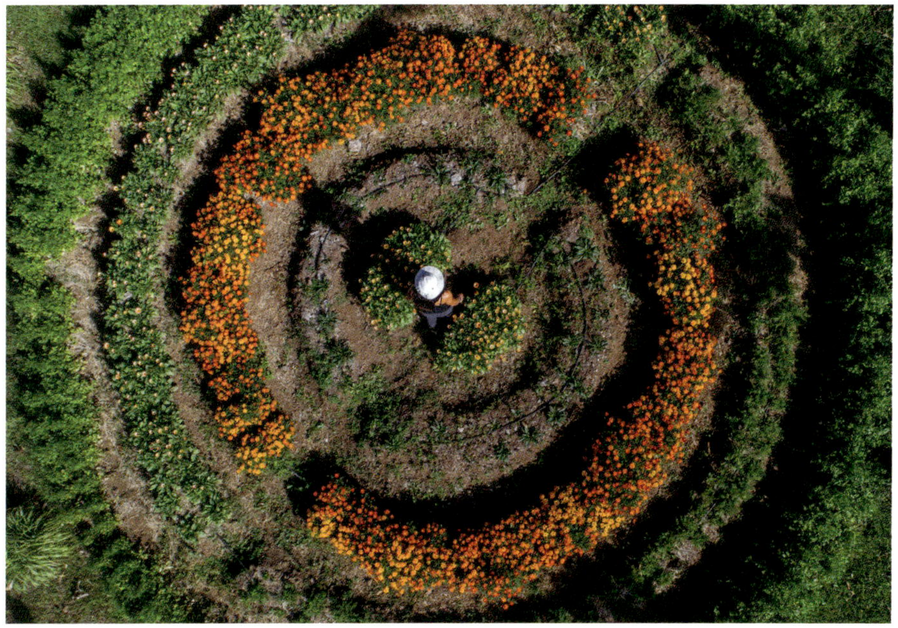

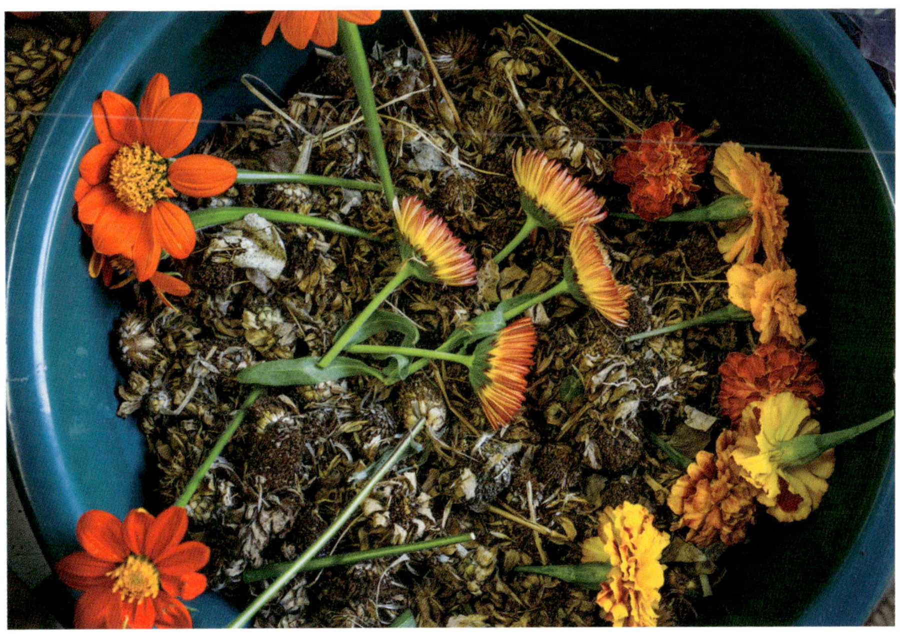

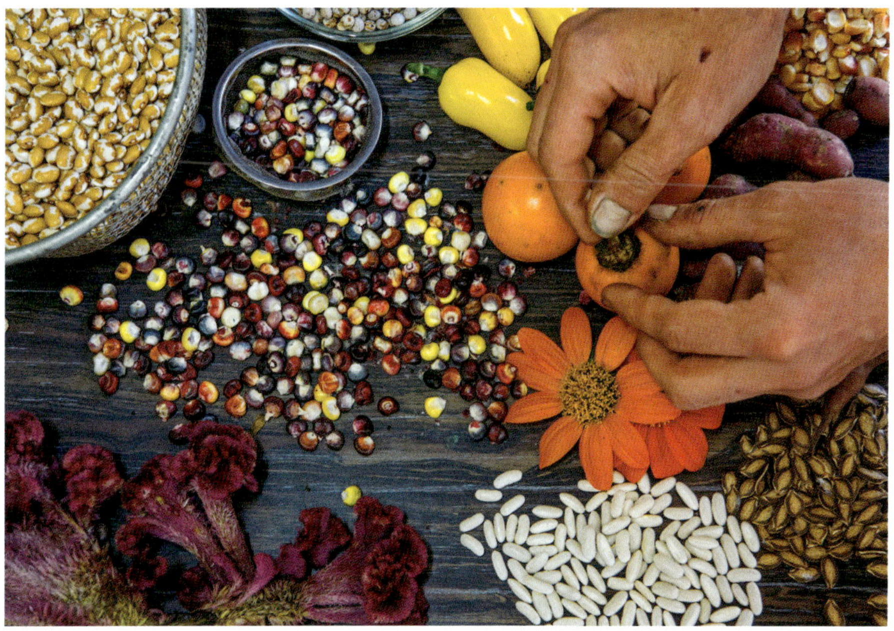

THAT FIRST NIGHT
WE HAD LIGHT WAS
MAGICAL

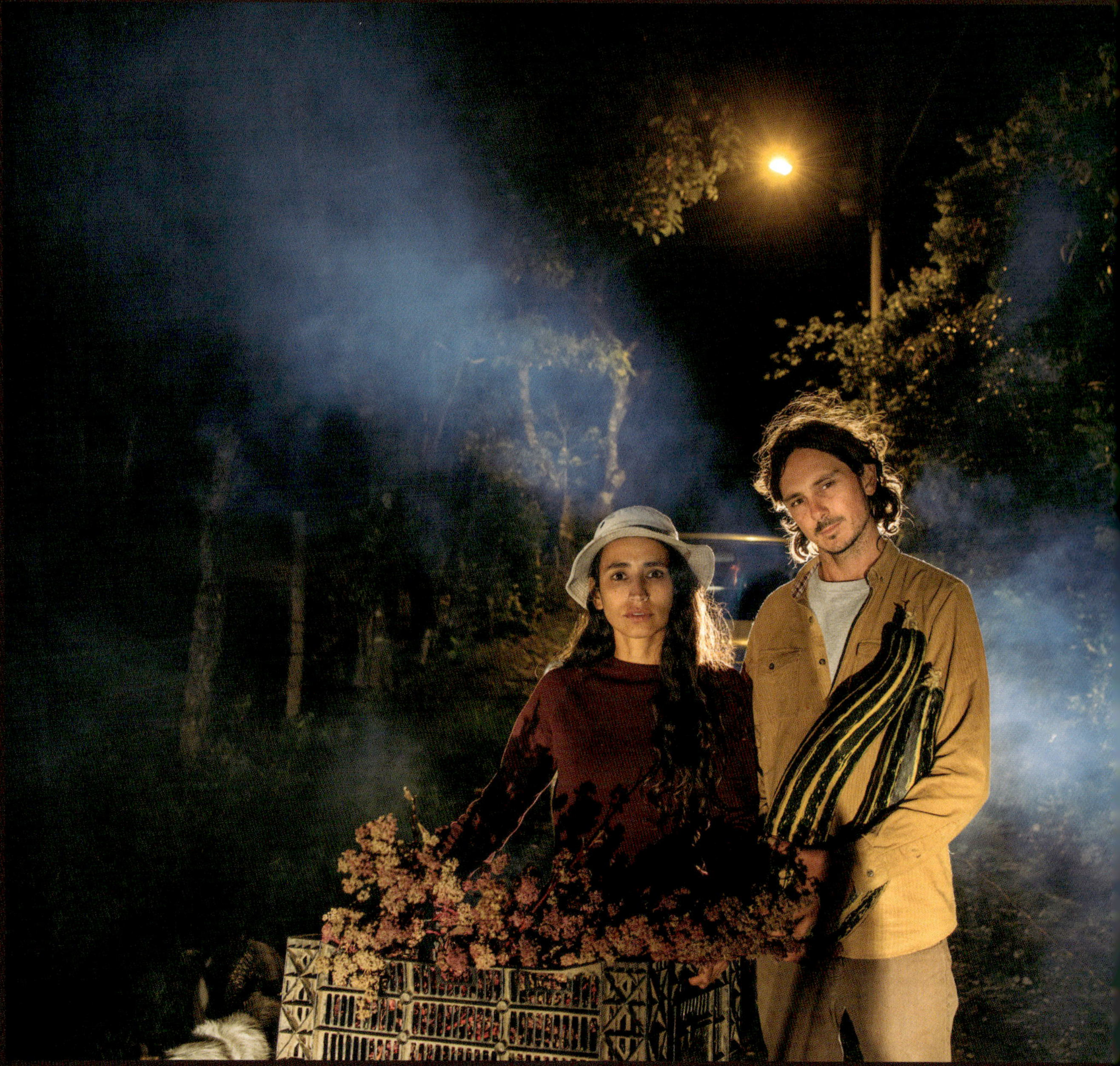

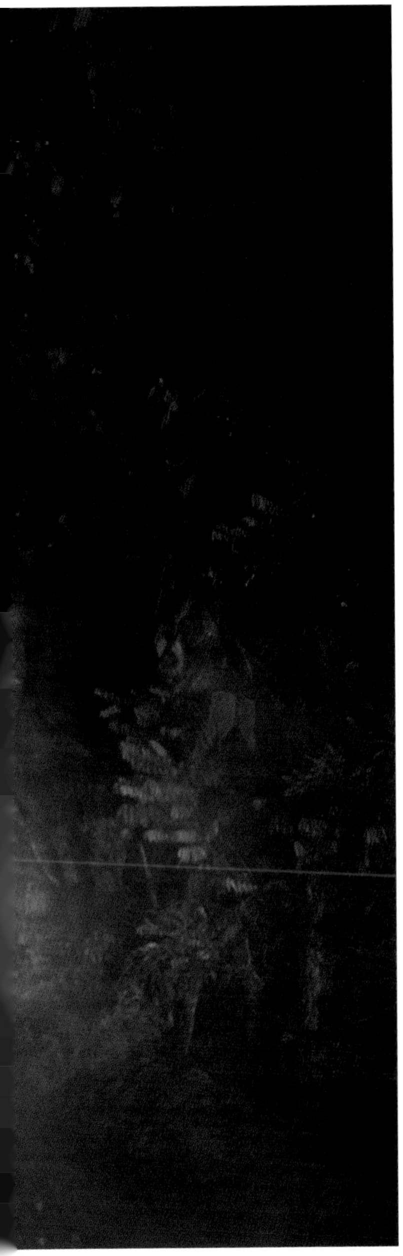

Weeks went by and we started to doubt, until one morning our doorbell rang. There were several young men there with poles and cables. Within a week, we had a transformer in front of our house, all for 600,000 colones. That first night we had light was magical. We went out in the middle of the field with a blanket and stayed there for hours, looking out on the land. There was a lot of fog, but we could see our dreams very clearly.

Now we're operating at full capacity, giving it everything we have. And although it's tiring, I always tell Gabo that those fruits and vegetables are our children. Watching this farm grow is like watching ourselves grow, as if each square meter were an extension of ourselves.
We've arrived at this place because of our daily effort, because we're stubborn and we don't give up. But also thanks to the confidence of people like Don Fructuoso. One day we're going to invite him to eat a good salad so that he can taste our produce, although who knows if he'll remember us.

**Written by: Sofía Quirós**

**Gabriel Bravo Pacheco y Jemima Picado**
San Miguel de Desamparados
Born Feb. 21, 1986, and Feb. 3, 1987

Gabriel is 35 years old and Jemima is 34. "Mima" grew up in San Ramón de Alajuela, studied anthropology at the UCR and natural resources management at UNED. Gabriel grew up right in the middle of Desamparados. They met at UNED. Mima worked at the Rafael Ángel Calderón Museum, and Gabriel, who is a guitarist, had a practice and recording studio. They moved in together, and in time they founded the El Tablazo Agro-Ecological Farm (www.fincaeltablazo.com). For eight years, they've been growing seeds and delivering vegetables house to house. They consider themselves "neo-rural" farmers. They rescued a hectare in Desamparados, where they manage agricultural practices, farm animals, and forested areas. Theirs is an alternative development project, and they're excited about being an example, proving that there are different ways to produce food and collaborate in the country's rural areas. Together, they seek to generate a more sustainable culture as a way of life. Devoted to working the earth, they manage educational projects about agricultural and cattle farming and organic fertilizer, for children and youth. They are also pioneers in the sale of seeds (semillasplantae.com).

# THE SOUND OF MARCHING BANDS MOVING AWAY

usted se pone la máscara y usted se transforma

"The first time I saw a mask parade was from the porch of my house in Barva de Heredia. What was I, seven years old? It scared me so much that I ran off to hide under my bed. The size of the masks, and the music that drew you out of your house, were impressive."
"Don Luis Fernando, what you have are symptoms of malaria."
"OK ... Thanks, Doctor, but call me Bombillo." His nickname means "light bulb."

Bombillo fixes his gaze on one of the windows of the hospital, waiting, increasingly resigned, for at least one of his co-workers from the news station to come visit him.
"You know, Doctor, I'm really explosive, I'm accustomed to violence, in this job as a cameraman you become hardened. What haven't I seen? Shoot-outs, police raids, dismemberments, everything."
"Try to stay relaxed, it's not good to get agitated. Do you have any idea where you could have become infected?"

"They sent me to cover the kidnapping of the two German women in Boca Tapada de San Carlos. Am I in real trouble, Doc? This isn't the first time I've risked my neck for the news, you know? And nobody has come, they haven't even asked about me at the news station."

Bombillo thinks about his family again, remembering how he once asked the technician Ávila to look after his wife and four sons if anything ever happened to him. He preferred the safety of the news van; if news was happening, he would turn on the generator, extend the antenna, and every man to his post.

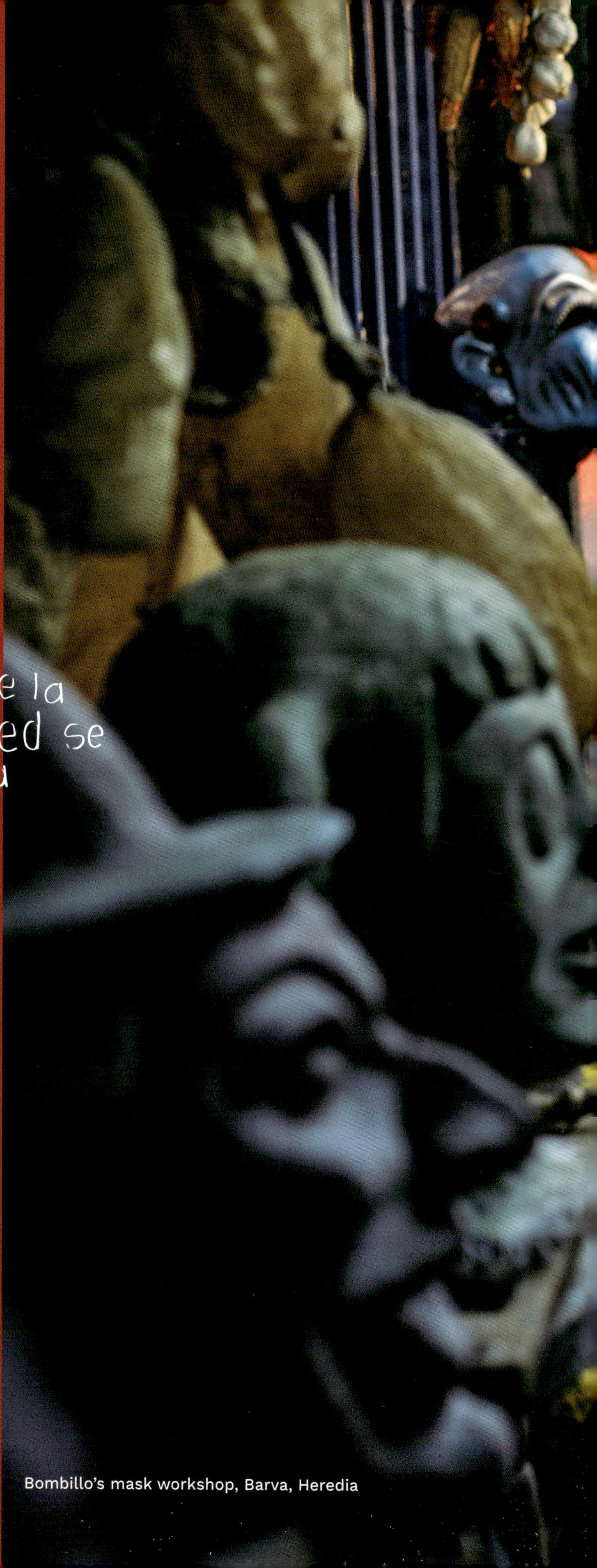

Bombillo's mask workshop, Barva, Heredia

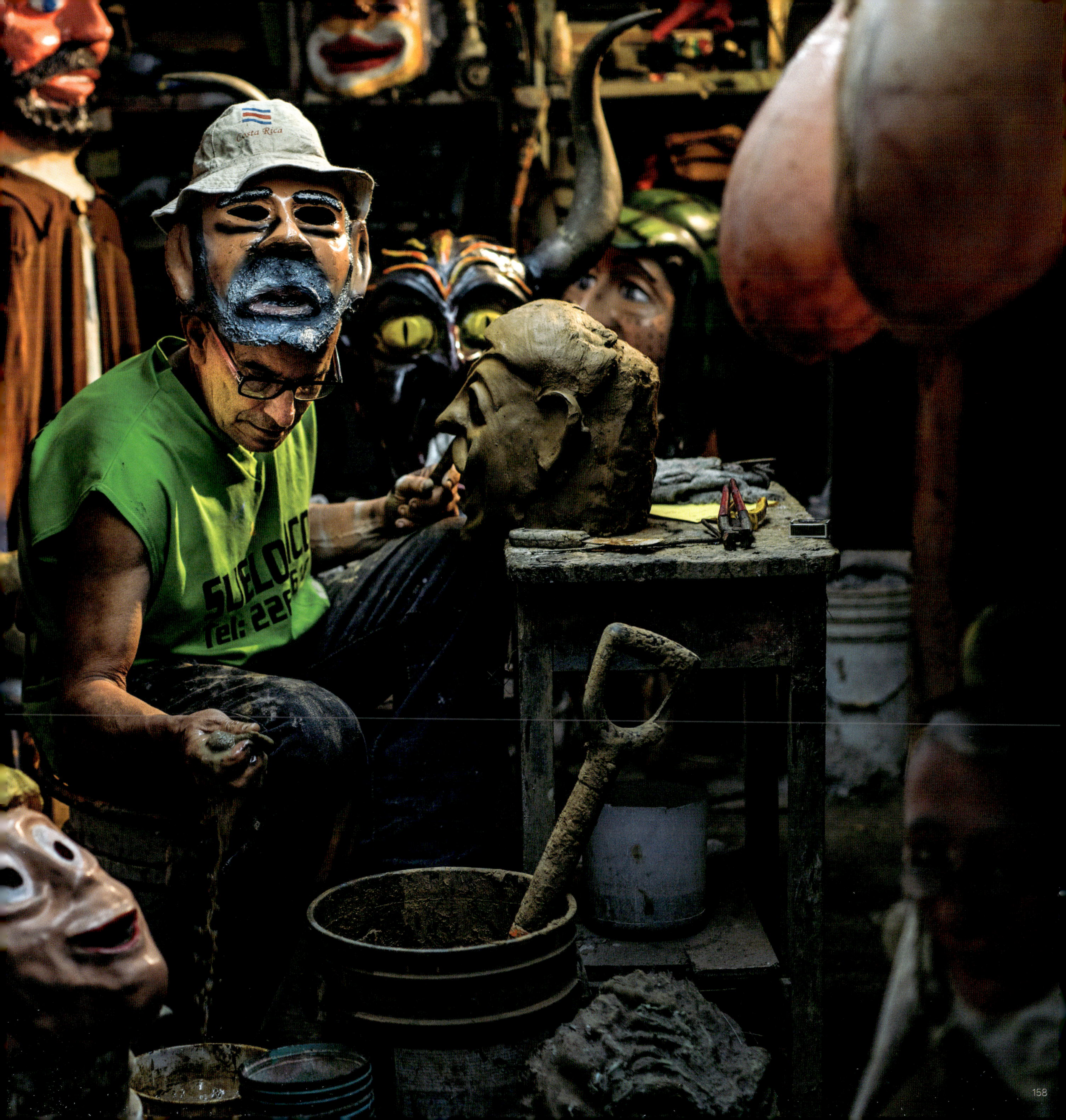
Costa Rica
SUELO
Tel: 22

## THE FIRST TIME I SAW A MASK PARADE

But that morning in 1991, he received direct orders from the news station to go into the mountains beyond the Westfalia River in Limón to cover the biggest manhunt ever. Two hundred armed agents of the Fuerza Pública and the OIJ were moving through a swamp chasing Johnny Monge, an ex-patrolman and a convict, a killer of three civilians and two agents who had him in custody and had saved his life twice, when other agents wanted to kill him.

Bombillo carries the weight of the ENG ¾ camera like he carries the weight of the masks that he learned to make when he was little. He made them out of clay, starch, and paper, and many times they melted on his face, when a downpour decided to join the party. His favorite was the devil, because it was the biggest and it commanded respect.

He was thinking about that when he heard a shout: "Freeze, or you're dead!" He stood the camera on the ground and kept filming the scene. In front of him was Johnny Monge, blinded by the flash and the light of a helicopter overhead. Behind Bombillo was the pack of agents dreaming of revenge, who had prepared a cell where they would show Monge no mercy.

The fugitive looks into the Cyclops of light with the furry microphone, like a demon that's broadcasting his fate. To deny his pursuers the pleasure, he opts to put a bullet through his own temple, and he's lost on the Limón beach. A projectile that jolts him out of his complexes and miseries, and from an entire month of being pursued in the jungle.

Bombillo watches from the ground while the police go up to kick his corpse. This time there are no beds to hide under, nor the sound of marching bands moving away. Evil stops being a fiction.

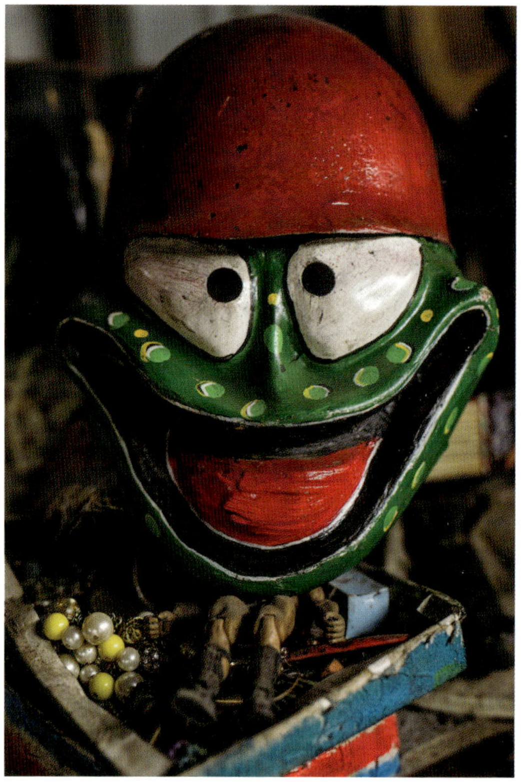

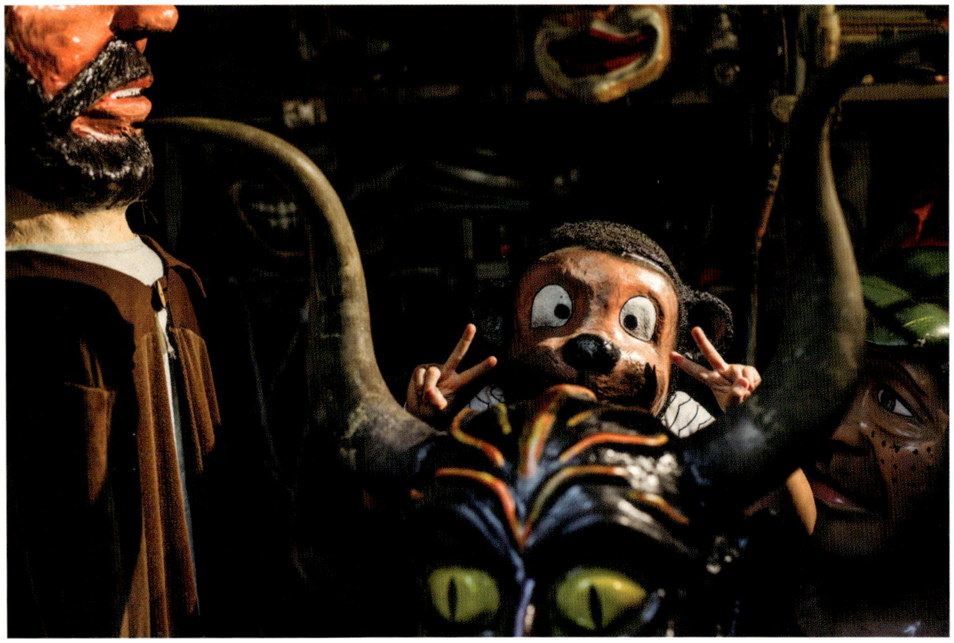

Now in the hospital room, the doctor talks about treatments and Bombillo interrupts him:

"I think I'm going to go back to making clay masks like before. I don't want the tradition to die with me, even though now people don't understand and they use them to scare people, they act like idiots, swinging their cow bladders, and they drink way too much *guaro*. Before, when there was a fight, we'd form a circle on the soccer field and they would come to blows. Now they take out a dagger, they take out a revolver."

"But if things aren't like they were before, can't that cause you problems?"

"Hell, Doc, at least it's a devil I know."

**Written by: Luis Salazar**

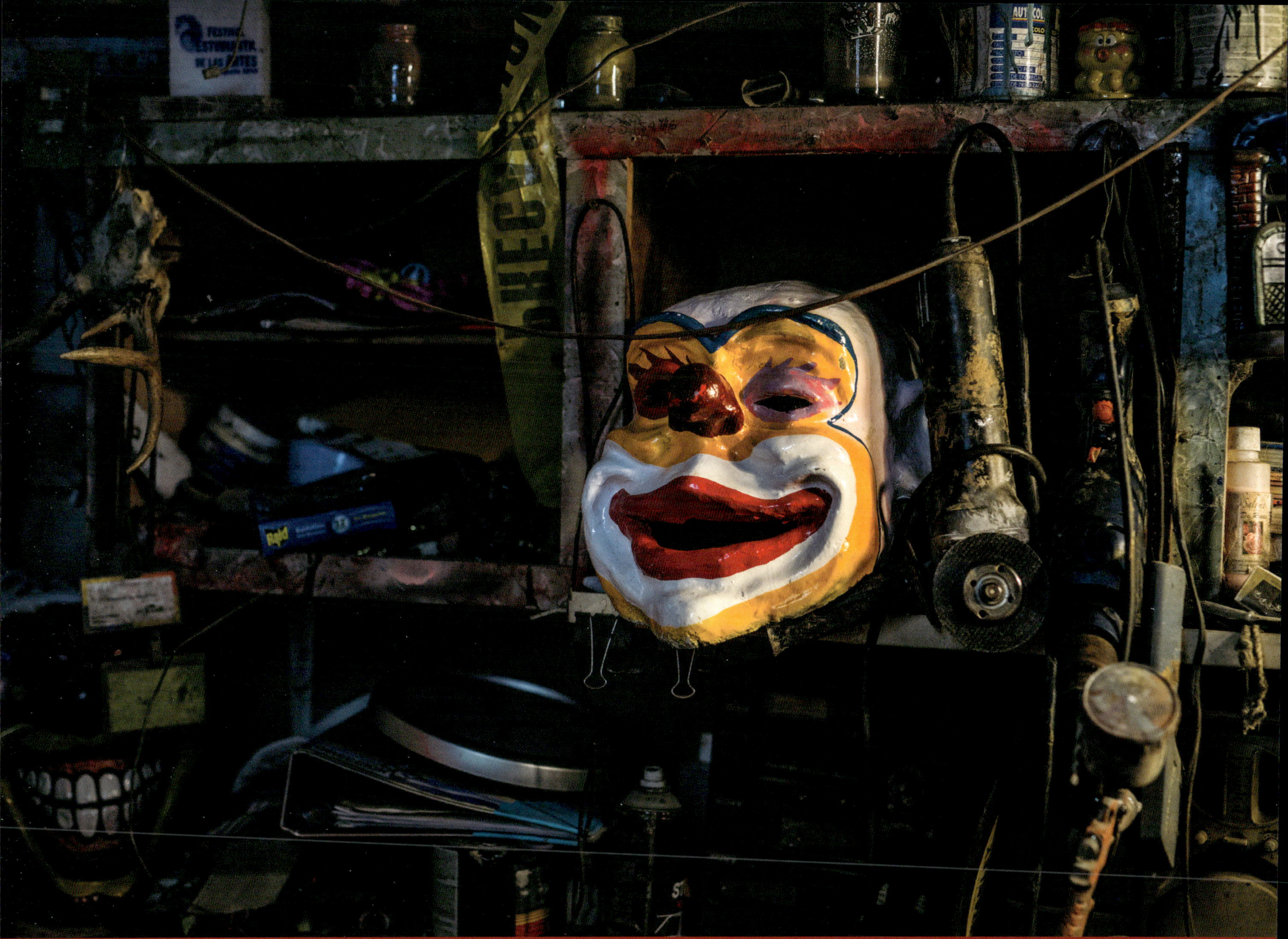

**Luis Fernando Vargas Cascante, "Bombillo"**
Barva
Born Nov. 14, 1961

For 50 years, Luis Fernando has transformed clay and paper-mâché into masks that look like devils, skulls, witches, clowns, TV personalities, and other products of his imagination. Besides being recognized in Barva as an expert mask maker, he also teaches and is a champion of the tradition of using cow bladders. "In Barva, you put the mask on and you're transformed into whoever is depicted on the mask," he says. He's a local icon, and you'll never see him in a bar, because he doesn't want to give young people that kind of example. He spent 12 years working as a cameraman for Channel 7, and in that time he saw things that marked him forever. He's married and has four children.

- **Parades with masked figures are a tradition that started in Costa Rica in 1824.**

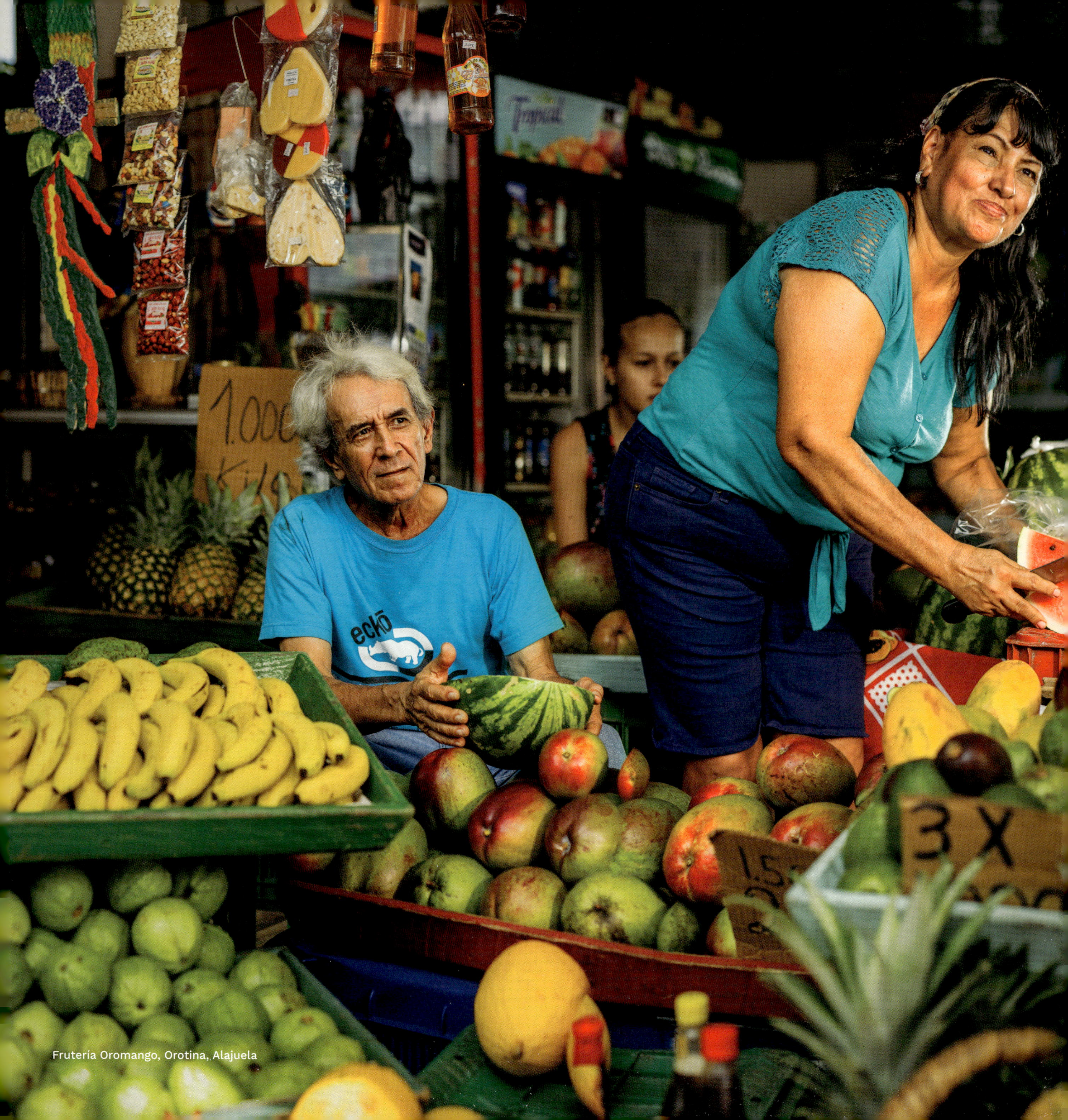


Frutería Oromango, Orotina, Alajuela

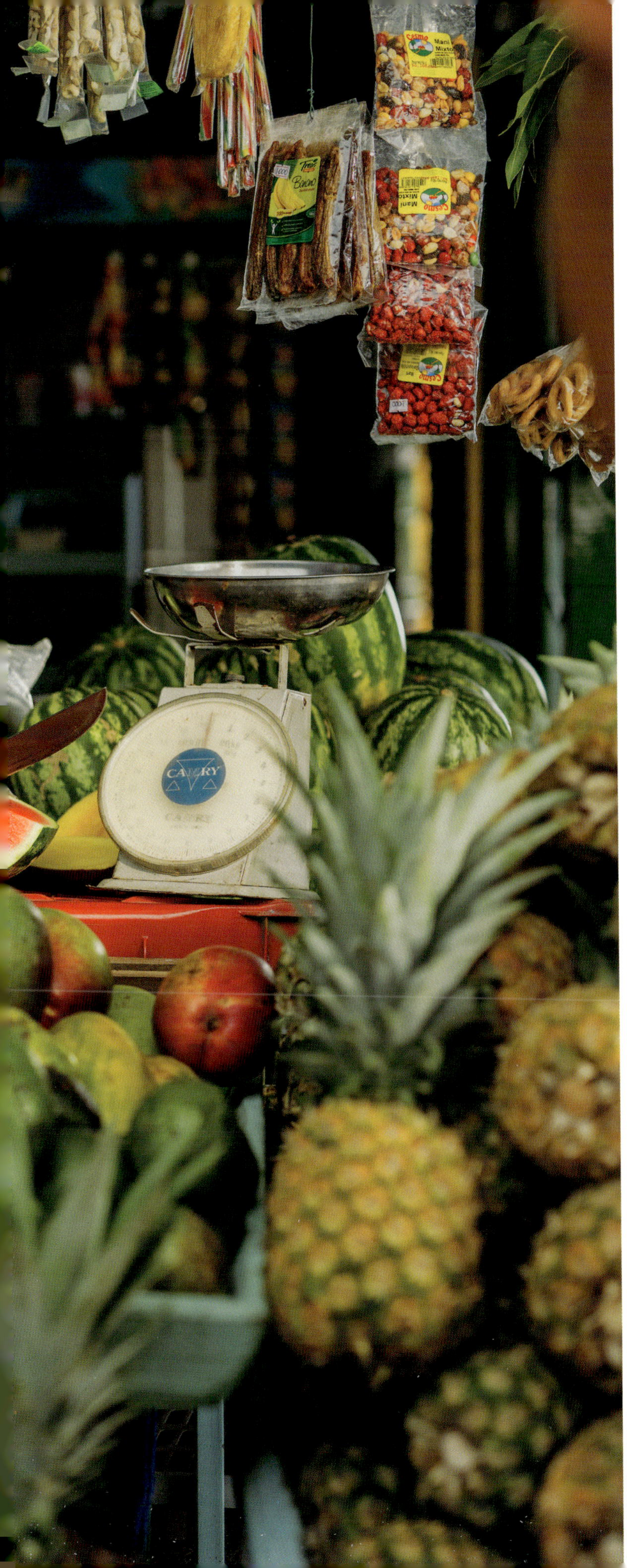

# THE STOLEN DRESS

Floribeth was very accustomed to climbing trees. It was normal for her grandmother, a pioneer of the fruit business in Orotina, to send her out at 5:30 a.m. to pick nances, oranges, star apples, cashews or tamarinds to sell at her shop. That's how the household made money, selling fruit.

That afternoon, the 8-year-old girl climbed a tree, not to pick fruit for sale, but following the bright idea of a neighbor girl that she ran into unexpectedly on her return home.

"Come and climb with me to pick *zapotes*," she said, tempting her with the thought of this oval, orange, fleshy fruit.

The idea sounded like too much fun to pass up. Floribeth dropped what she was carrying — a bag with a loaf of bread that her grandmother had asked her to buy, the small amount of change she got back, and an umbrella.

She thought nothing of climbing the tree in the elegant dress her grandmother had made for her with remnants of her own wedding dress. It was a special garment, the only dress she had because there was no money for dresses. She wore it every time they said her father was coming to Orotina from San José. Floribeth didn't know him and wanted to be sure that she looked really nice the day they finally met.

So she was up in the tree with the famous dress, when suddenly the skies opened and a downpour fell. There was no time to escape the pouring rain.

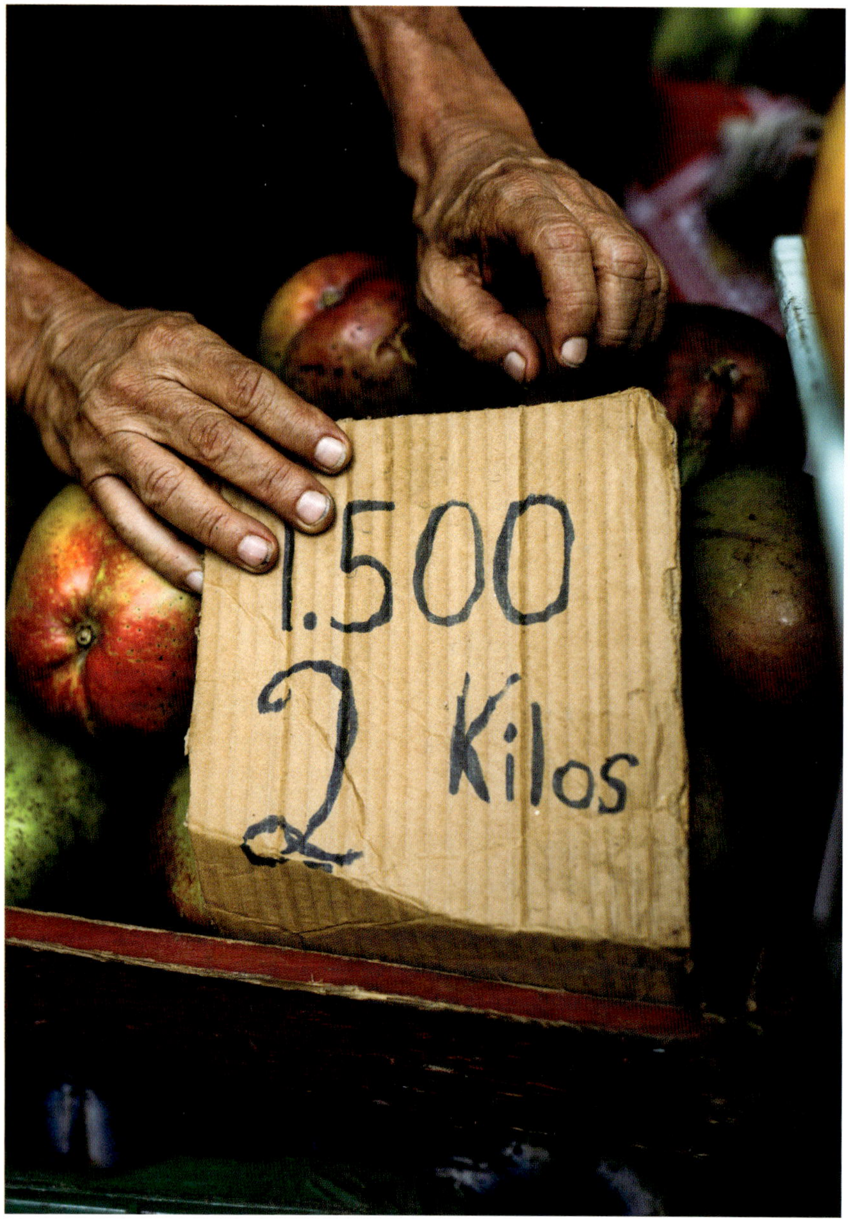


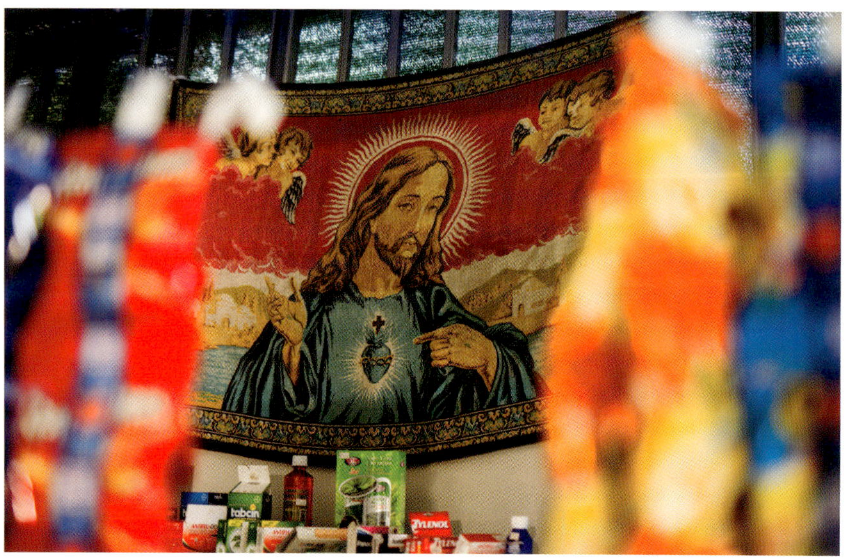

## "GOSH, TAKE OFF YOUR DRESS BECAUSE IT'S TOTALLY SOAKED"

"Gosh, take off your dress because it's totally soaked," the other girl proposed when the rain had lightened a bit.

Floribeth did as suggested without thinking twice. The idea seemed sensible. She took it off and turned around for a moment to check how many *zapotes* she had picked — and when she turned around again, the neighbor was gone, and so were her belongings!

The other girl had taken off like a bullet, having stolen not just her dress, but also her change, her umbrella and the bag of bread.

In flip-flops and a white T-shirt, Floribeth went home crestfallen, her face now wet from the tears streaming out of her eyes. She walked home crying in the middle of the street until she reached the home of her grandmother, who was furious — not just because of the missing bread, but because someone had taken advantage of her granddaughter's innocence.

A police report was filed, and the dress was returned to the girl a while later, but by now it was worn and stained. Those *zapotes* left a bad taste in her mouth.

**Written by: Arturo Pardo**

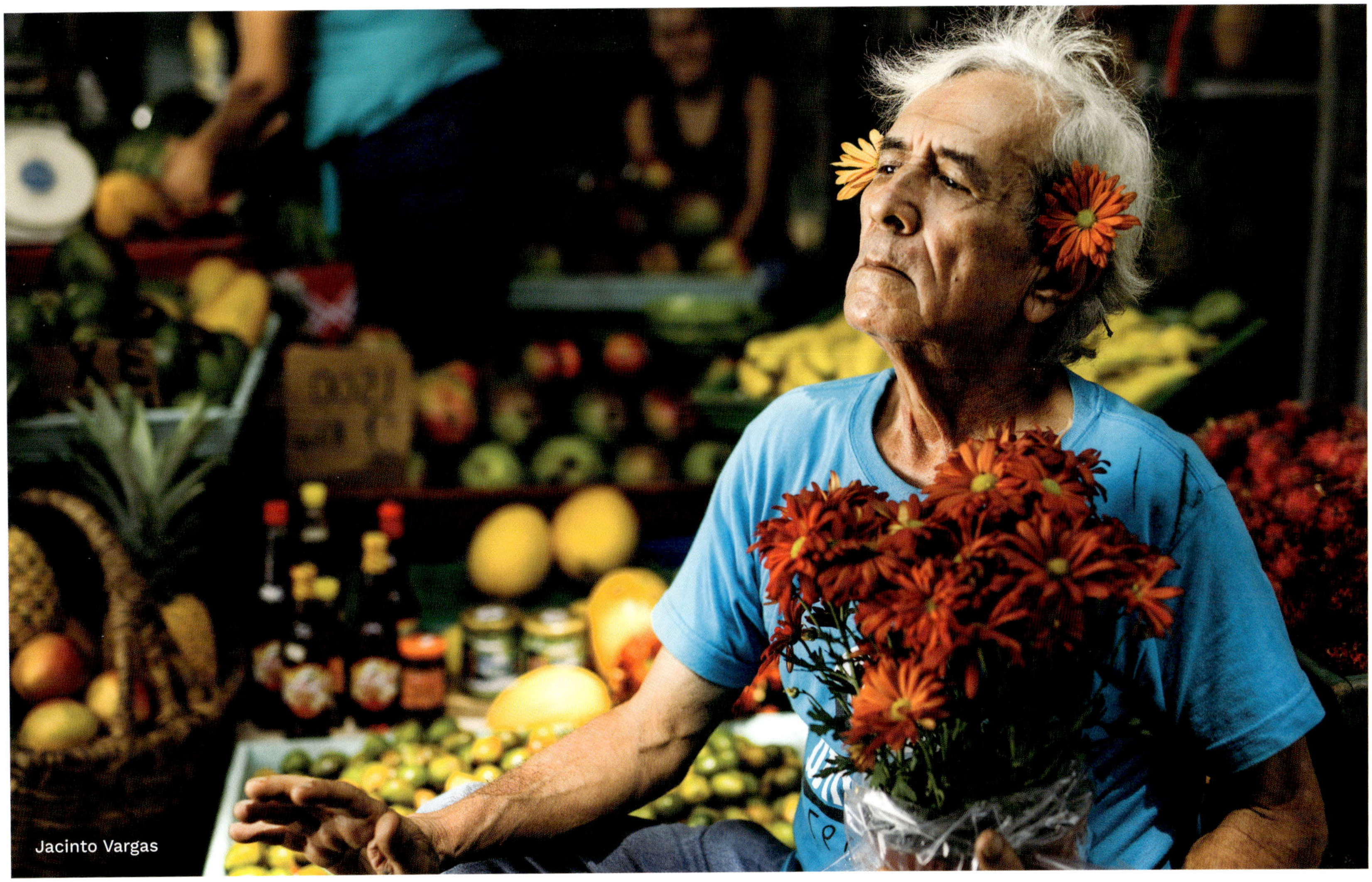

Jacinto Vargas

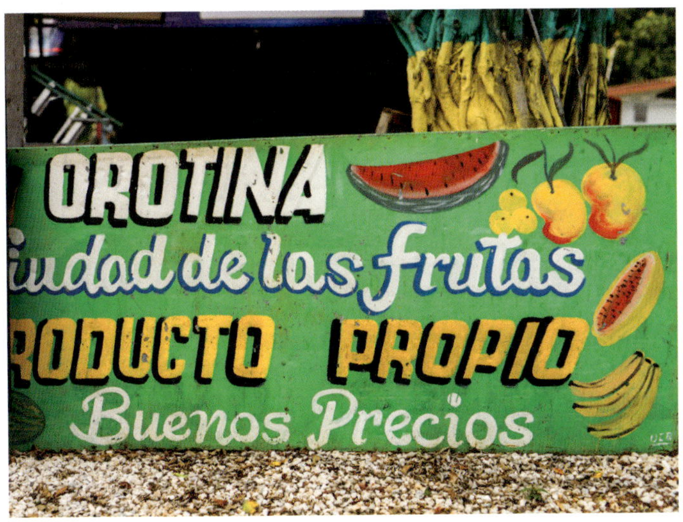


**Floribeth González Vargas**
Orotina
Born Dec. 13, 1958

When Floribeth was born at home with a midwife, she developed an infection. The doctor who visited told her mother that the baby would not survive. But she knew that sometimes it's not medicine, nor the doctor, that a person needs to survive — it's love that keeps us moving forward. "Flori" lives in Orotina, known for "the world's best climate," and works in Oromango, a fruit shop that has been the family business for years. She also has experience in the mango export business.

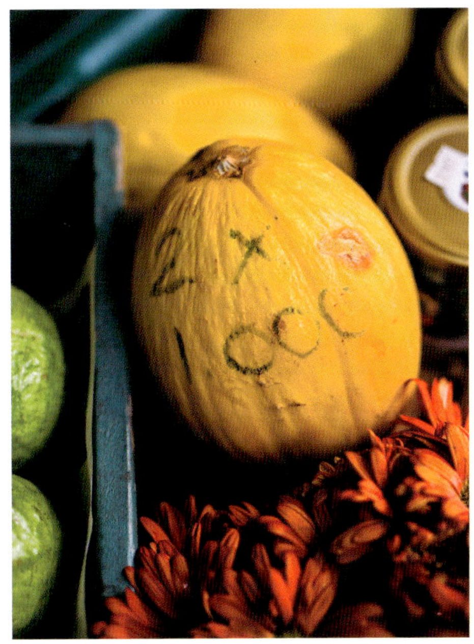

# "THE MAGNET OF HONE CREEK"

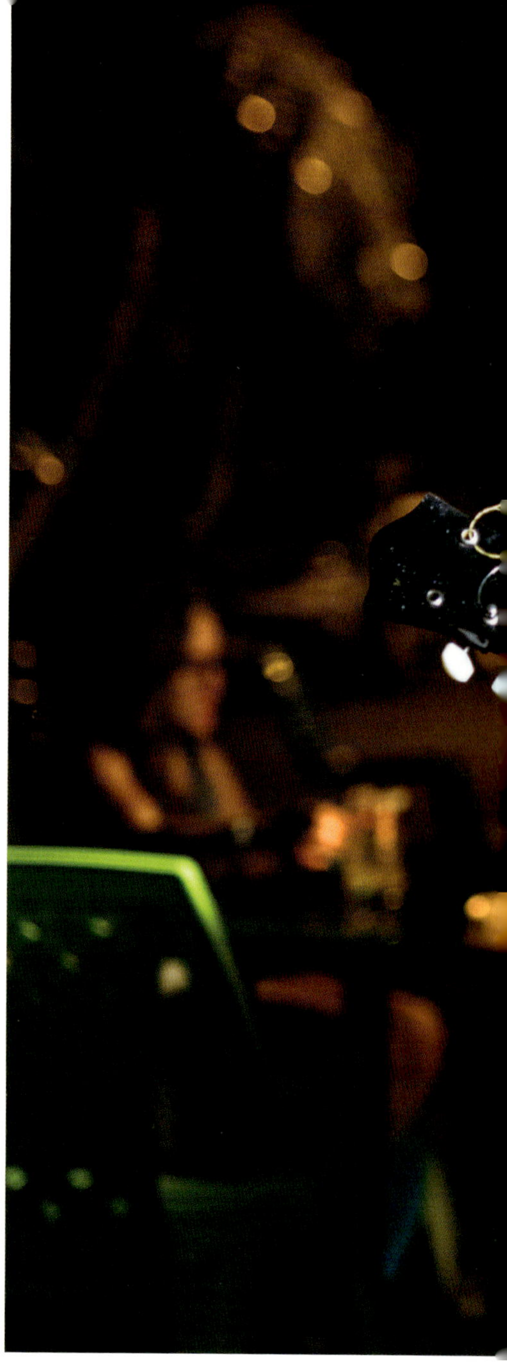

In the mid-2000s, the sun boiled while the waves called to Don Junior, humming between his teeth, dividing his day between fishing and music. Danny, his younger son, never stopped daydreaming. He saw him on his way to the sea and wanted to go with him, wanted to take his toy guitar and wanted to strike chords that would cut through the air like his father did. Their relationship was so close that when his father traveled to perform, Danny didn't eat or play, but only threw tantrums in his absence. Danny wanted to go to the concerts and be part of his band!

In the days when they were preparing the big project *Calypso Limón Legends*, Danny was about five years old. The members of this great band were Don Junior, Cyril Sylvan, Manuel Monestel, Reynaldo "Shanty" Kenton, Herberth "Lenki" Glinton, José Antonio "Momo" Valverde, Roberto "Congoman" Watts and on piano Manuel Obregón, who was also organizing their trip to Guanacaste, to a big concert that would take place in Playas del Coco.

It was morning in Hone Creek and they were about to pick up Don Junior when little Danny came out of his room in a beautiful flowered shirt, saying, "Papa, where are you going? I'll go with you." To which his father responded, "No, you can't come, I'm going very far." Danny insisted and started crying inconsolably, so much so that Don Junior called Manuel Obregón to cancel the trip. To which Obregón replied, "If it's because of your son, bring him. He's going to be the new musician in the family."

And that's how Danny traveled with his father on that dusty trail to the Pacific, a road captured forever in his photographic memory. In Guanacaste, he didn't leave his father's side for a minute. When it was time for the concert, Don Junior picked him up and put him on the stage. With a radiant smile the boy played alongside them! And that's how it became clear that his soul needed to share the magic of music, to recognize in his DNA his father's bass notes, the primordial element of calypso, the national rhythm, the patrimony of the Caribbean people.

This event was Danny's baptism in calypso, the inauguration of his life as an artist. How does a desire get lodged in our soul? How do we attract what we desire? You have to vibrate like a magnet, and that's what Danny did.

At first, life put a gourd instrument called a *guiro* into his hands, with which he started to polish his rhythm, learning that ability to connect and link up. A bit later, his father's band had a bassist who didn't take his responsibilities seriously. All of this Danny understood from a very young age, and he told his father: "We're going to have to look for a bassist, because he doesn't know how to play calypso." His father answered: "Unless you play the bass instead." After that, it was pure magnetism. A girl from the barrio was the mother of a boy who lived in San José and had a bass. The boy returned to Limón and met Danny. Everyone noted immediately that Danny loved the instrument, and without another thought they decided to give him one for his birthday.

One day, Don Junior was returning from the sea. He entered his house and heard a bass playing in the distance, he asked Doña Grace, Danny's mom, "Who's playing?" "It's Danny!" Doña Grace replied. "How can that be Danny?" "Yes, it's Danny playing the bass." It sounded incredible.

That was a Tuesday. The next Saturday, Danny told his dad "Let's take the bass, I want to play!" Danny was 15, and he practiced constantly, with the concentration of someone who is doing what he loves. The rest of the story you already know, or you'll know it soon. Danny is the bassist for his father's band, always going here and there sharing melodies, flavor, and rhythm. Calypso, reggae, and groove. His very soul.

**Written by: Fabrizio Walker**

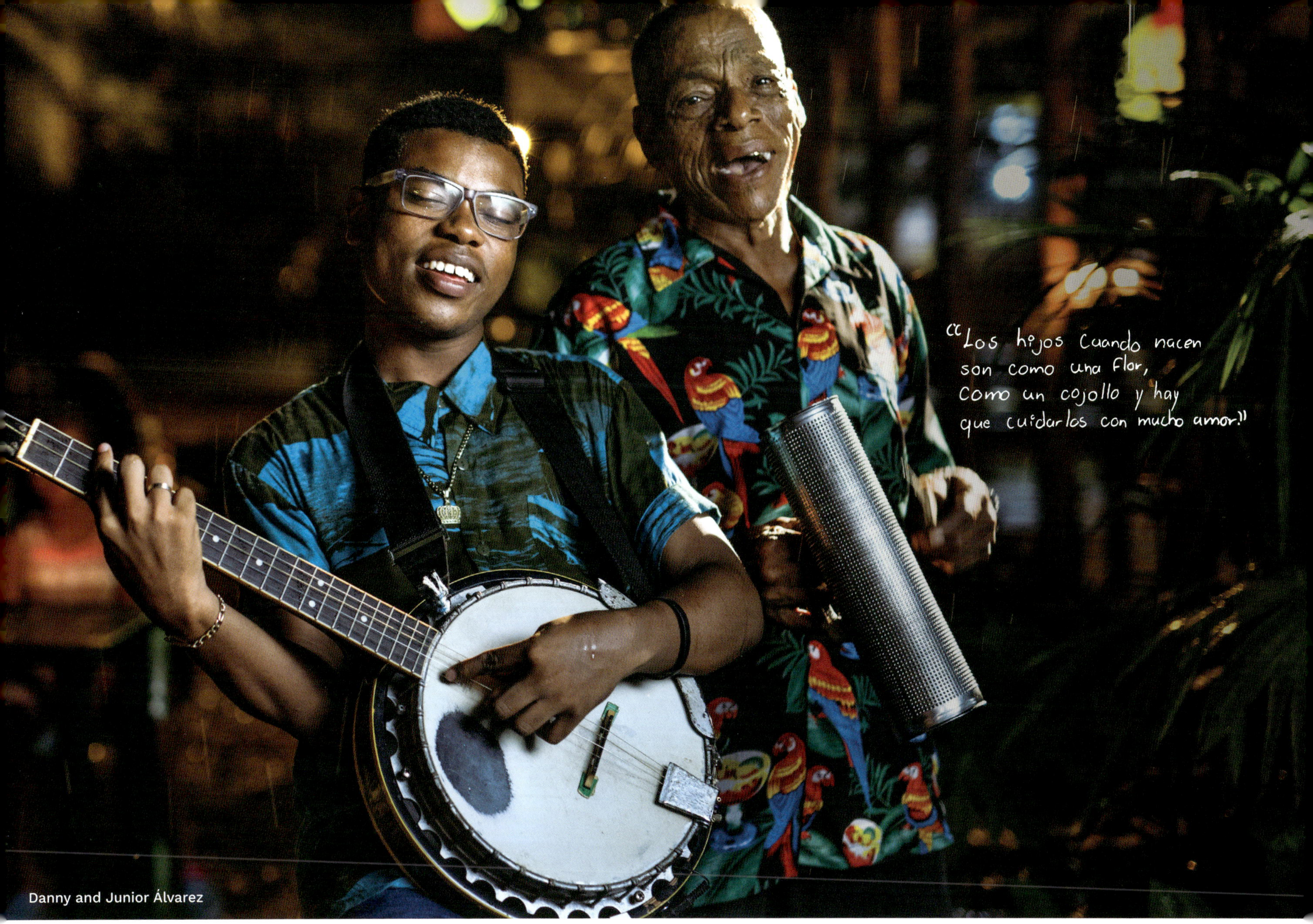

Danny and Junior Álvarez

**Danny Álvarez González**
Hone Creek
Born March 13, 2002

He's the only young musician from the Caribbean who plays calypso with the veterans. His aspiration is to become a great musician and professor (of music and English). He grew up surrounded by adults and influenced by "the other Danny," a Canadian musician whom he was named after, who eventually became his mentor, best friend, and confidant. Danny has an exceptional ear. You could say he's a musician by osmosis, passion, and heritage. His father, Junior Álvarez, is known in Limón as "Sweet Fingers" because of his talent on the banjo, guitar, and bass. Junior was a member of the Bárbaros del Ritmo ("Barbarians of Rhythm") in his native Bluefields, Nicaragua. He's lived in various Caribbean cities and is one of the greats of African/Central American music, someone in whom the past and present converge. Currently he's a member of Kawe Calypso, favorite sons of Cahuita, the capital of Calypso Nation. And everything he knows is now in the hands of his younger son, Danny, the future, or "Ñoco," as his parents call him. The bond between Junior and Danny is very special: They share their music, their life by the sea, and their talent for playing bass.

**• In 2012, the Calypso music of Limón was declared an expression of the intangible patrimony of Costa Rica of African origin.**

# FOREST ESSENCE

The journey to myself was long and full of uncertainty.

Pérez Zeledón, Houston, Belgium, Qatar.... Both on my personal trips and during my three years as a flight attendant, I visited dozens of countries and took hundreds of photos of iconic places. I experienced sleeplessness, poor diet, luxury, modern slavery, inequality, wastefulness.... I couldn't anymore. I got tired. I went to Nepal to search for happiness. That's where I had my first crisis. I wanted to do business and fix the world at the same time. Chairs, chairs, I need chairs! To put them in a circle. The people at the hostel looked at me a bit fearfully. In each one I seated someone who had to resolve a difference with another person: Nicolás Maduro and Leopoldo López, two friends who had grown apart, parents and children.... If people engage in dialogue, they can reach agreement — how can they not understand that? World peace depends on dialogue, it depends on ... me. Kathmandu. All the colors and smells of the world, the snowy peaks of the Himalayas, the little streets full of cars, motorcycles, bicycles, tuk-tuks, of people coming and going who didn't understand me. I couldn't stop. Endless nights, compulsive messages to my family about my plans to fix everything that was wrong with the planet.

News from Costa Rica: My grandmother was ill. I didn't sleep, I was always alert — they were chasing me. Confusion. My grandmother was sick. In one store they gave me a piece of paper with a message on it and a gold chain like my grandmother had. It was her handwriting -- I knew her handwriting well! "Gabriela, let them do what they want." So should I stop fighting against everything that's wrong? I have to get my message out to the world. I look in the mirror, a selfie: I just want to be heard! They wanted to deport me. Fear. I painted my passport and cut up my credit cards. Why are these men pursuing me? Don't touch me, don't tie me up, no! They tried to give me an injection. I didn't allow it. The police picked me up, took me to an asylum. They want to drug me, they want to kill me! NO, NO, No, No, no, no, no, n...! Sleep, silence, nothingness.

One day my father opened the door. Dad, my travel partner, my accomplice in so many adventures. He traveled 1,000 miles to find me. Daddy. He slept with me that night. Pa, I want to leave this place. The return was interminable — anxiety, long waits, impatience, eternal flights, layovers, desperation, layovers, cancellations, layovers, anguish, Costa Rica. Psychiatrists, denial, more psychiatrists — nothing is wrong with me! — another mania, injections — leave me alone, I'm fine! — pills. I break out in a rash, my body reacting — why me? — I get fat, I'm not happy, who am I? Empty, I don't want to see my friends, empty, my grandmother died. Empty.

I returned to the Osa Peninsula to live and work. Jim, my friend who took me to the forest and showed me the infinite types of leaves there are. My vision sharpened, as from the undifferentiated greens I zoomed in on a universe of distinct shapes and tones, seeing details that were invisible before. I started to bathe myself with the forest. To relearn, to see, and to listen. I understood that to be heard, first I had to listen. Breathing, meditation, consciousness, presence, peace, ESSENCE. The forest cured me.

I read, read, and read. My mission of saving the planet and helping as many people as possible depends on knowledge. I want to leave my mark, a carbon-free footprint. I joined the environmental leaders of the country, the first March for the Planet, the power of one person, no more single-use plastic, to raise awareness, to educate for change, my blog Cero Plas Tica. All or nothing. In a bipolar world, surviving between the grays can become a real challenge. I still take pills. Today, I understand that everything is a process and it takes patience.

**Written by: Abril Gordienko**

• **Corcovado National Park is home to 2.5% of the world's biodiversity.**

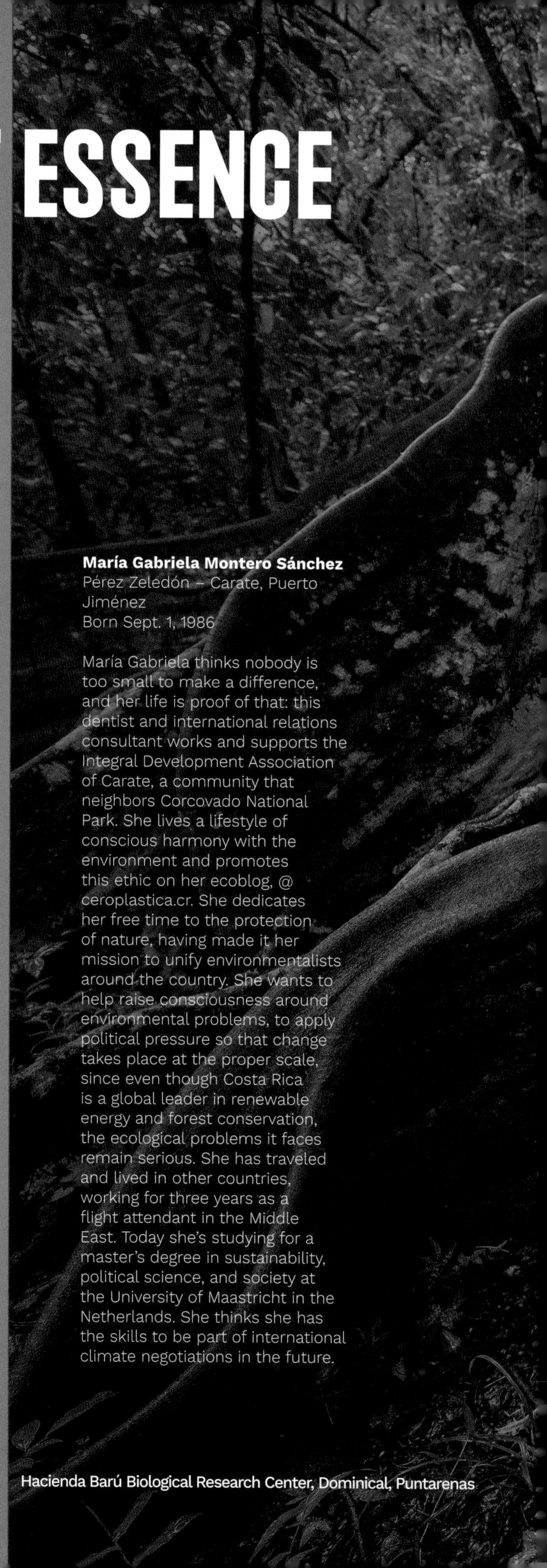

**María Gabriela Montero Sánchez**
Pérez Zeledón – Carate, Puerto Jiménez
Born Sept. 1, 1986

María Gabriela thinks nobody is too small to make a difference, and her life is proof of that: this dentist and international relations consultant works and supports the Integral Development Association of Carate, a community that neighbors Corcovado National Park. She lives a lifestyle of conscious harmony with the environment and promotes this ethic on her ecoblog, @ ceroplastica.cr. She dedicates her free time to the protection of nature, having made it her mission to unify environmentalists around the country. She wants to help raise consciousness around environmental problems, to apply political pressure so that change takes place at the proper scale, since even though Costa Rica is a global leader in renewable energy and forest conservation, the ecological problems it faces remain serious. She has traveled and lived in other countries, working for three years as a flight attendant in the Middle East. Today she's studying for a master's degree in sustainability, political science, and society at the University of Maastricht in the Netherlands. She thinks she has the skills to be part of international climate negotiations in the future.

**Hacienda Barú Biological Research Center, Dominical, Puntarenas**

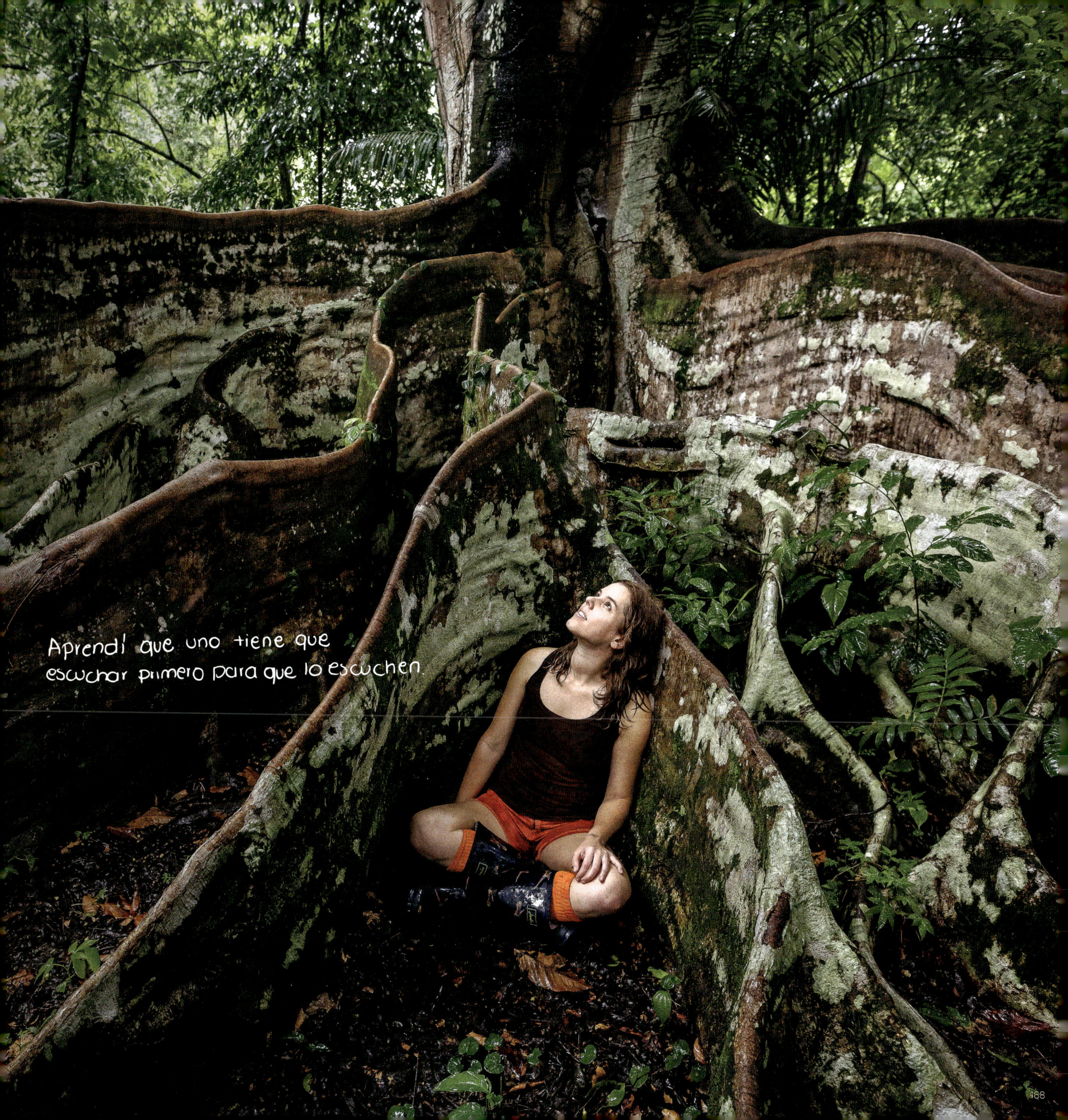

Aprendí que uno tiene que escuchar primero para que lo escuchen.

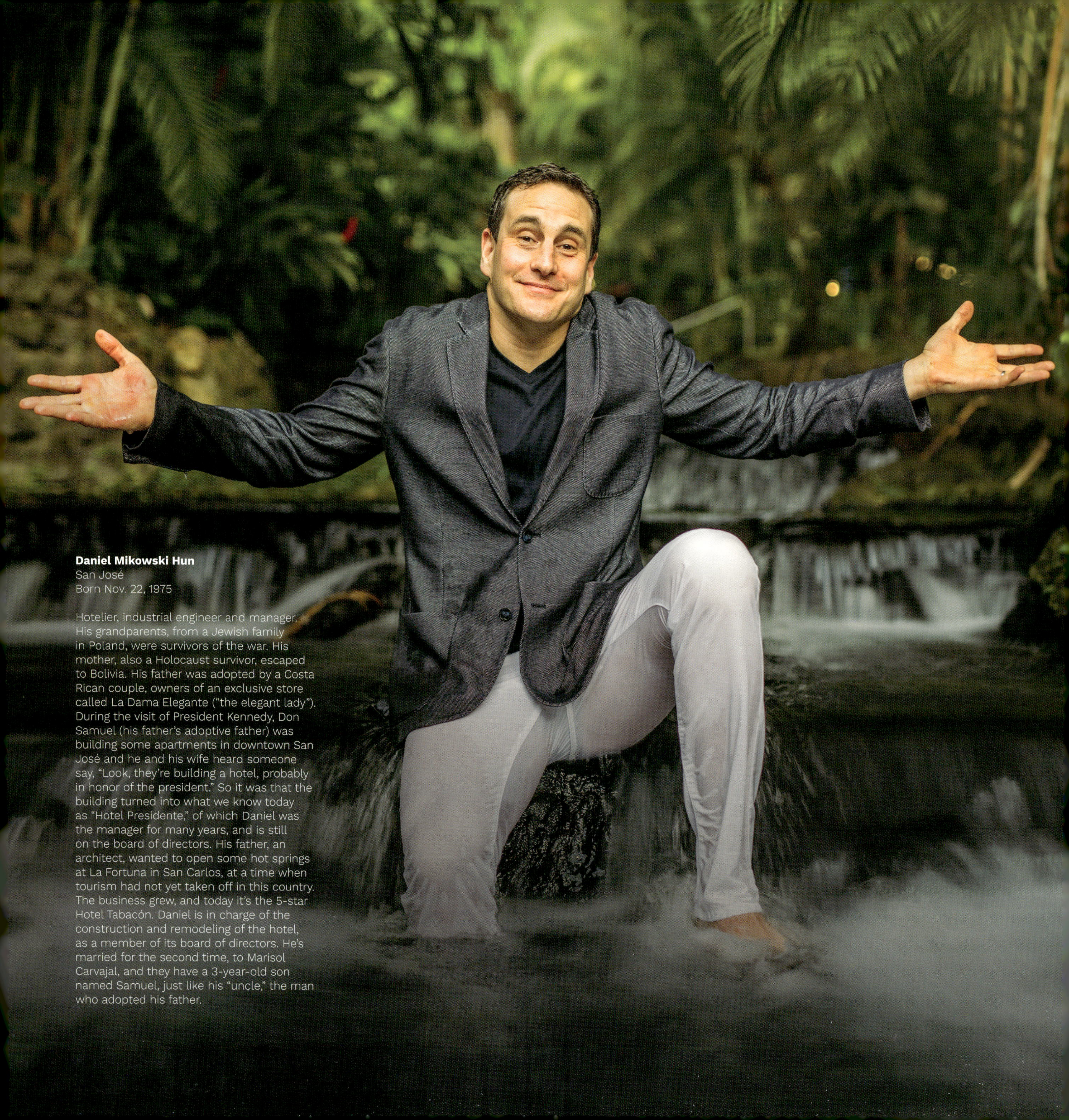

**Daniel Mikowski Hun**
San José
Born Nov. 22, 1975

Hotelier, industrial engineer and manager. His grandparents, from a Jewish family in Poland, were survivors of the war. His mother, also a Holocaust survivor, escaped to Bolivia. His father was adopted by a Costa Rican couple, owners of an exclusive store called La Dama Elegante ("the elegant lady"). During the visit of President Kennedy, Don Samuel (his father's adoptive father) was building some apartments in downtown San José and he and his wife heard someone say, "Look, they're building a hotel, probably in honor of the president." So it was that the building turned into what we know today as "Hotel Presidente," of which Daniel was the manager for many years, and is still on the board of directors. His father, an architect, wanted to open some hot springs at La Fortuna in San Carlos, at a time when tourism had not yet taken off in this country. The business grew, and today it's the 5-star Hotel Tabacón. Daniel is in charge of the construction and remodeling of the hotel, as a member of its board of directors. He's married for the second time, to Marisol Carvajal, and they have a 3-year-old son named Samuel, just like his "uncle," the man who adopted his father.

# INDEPENDENCE TURNED UPSIDE DOWN

That enormous house had been left isolated in the middle of La Sabana. In the '90s, the neighboring houses had started making space for vertical projects and businesses. One way or another, this area kept becoming more unpopulated.

Nevertheless, this residence, which was starting to grow gray hairs and wrinkles, was about to embark on an unprecedented episode.

Daniel, then 25, resisted the idea of abandoning the house and his mother. "Move out, it's time!" said his mother, who had seen the independent streak of her progenitors when, at 16, she had studied microbiology in Israel.

"I'm not going to leave you alone in such a big house," he replied, thinking he wanted to care for her while she mourned her husband, who had recently died. "Do like your siblings," she insisted, referring to Mario and Patricia, who had flown the nest to study abroad as soon as they graduated from high school. "Mom, I'm not going to leave you in this old house, so full of memories."

Apparently, for her and her late husband, it was important that the children blaze their own trail. When they were young, they had done that, and with all the love in their hearts they believed that their children should do the same. Still, Daniel rarely did what was normal.

One day, the mother came home and delivered some unexpected news. She had signed a contract to rent a condominium in Escazú. The one who would be moving out would not be him, but her.

"You stay here!" she said, as decisive as her smile. For the second act, she packed her belongings, including all the appliances, and in a flash the entire house was left with nothing but old furniture, a smelly dog and a sole human inhabitant looking to party.

The young man, who had just begun his working life, brought a little minibar refrigerator from the Hotel Presidente, his family's property, and that's how he lived for a few years, with the basics, with a minibar in a house of 5,400 square feet. That dwelling, up to now sober and serious, turned overnight (literally) into a party house.

Trying to account for all the parties he threw in that deserted house, the mathematics becomes a bit complex. The number 120, nevertheless, is a calculation of the maximum number of people he was able to squeeze into his bacchanals. And if a quorum was lacking, he went with a friend to the hotel to meet and recruit male and female backpackers who wanted to experience a less touristy side of the country. Sometimes they came in groups, and some stayed after the party, lodging there for weeks.

In 1963, his great uncle and his wife, Estanislao, had built the hotel beside the store they opened, La Dama Elegante. By the '90s, this place wasn't in the best condition, and even if Daniel had a party spirit that wouldn't quit, he also had the confidence of his inner circle that he was capable of rescuing the family legacy, which was on the point of bankruptcy.

Today it's obvious that he moved forward with his mission, giving another face to what is today one of the best-known hotels in the capital. By contrast, his bachelor pad was in a sorry state, unattractive and poorly maintained. The host, between laughs, describes it today: "Sometimes that place was a hostel and sometimes it was a zoo."

At 45 years of age, he's living a very different episode of his life now, and he points with admiration to the spirit of his parents, ahead of their time, who motivated each of their children to spread their wings early. The search for independence is in the DNA of this family.

**Written by: Arturo Pardo**

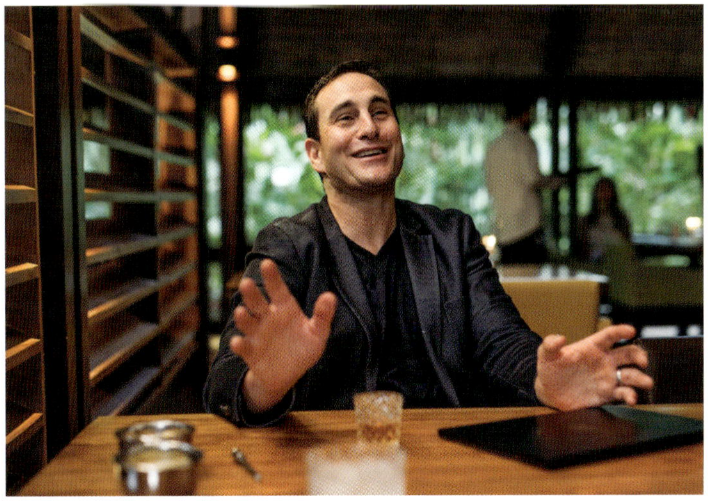

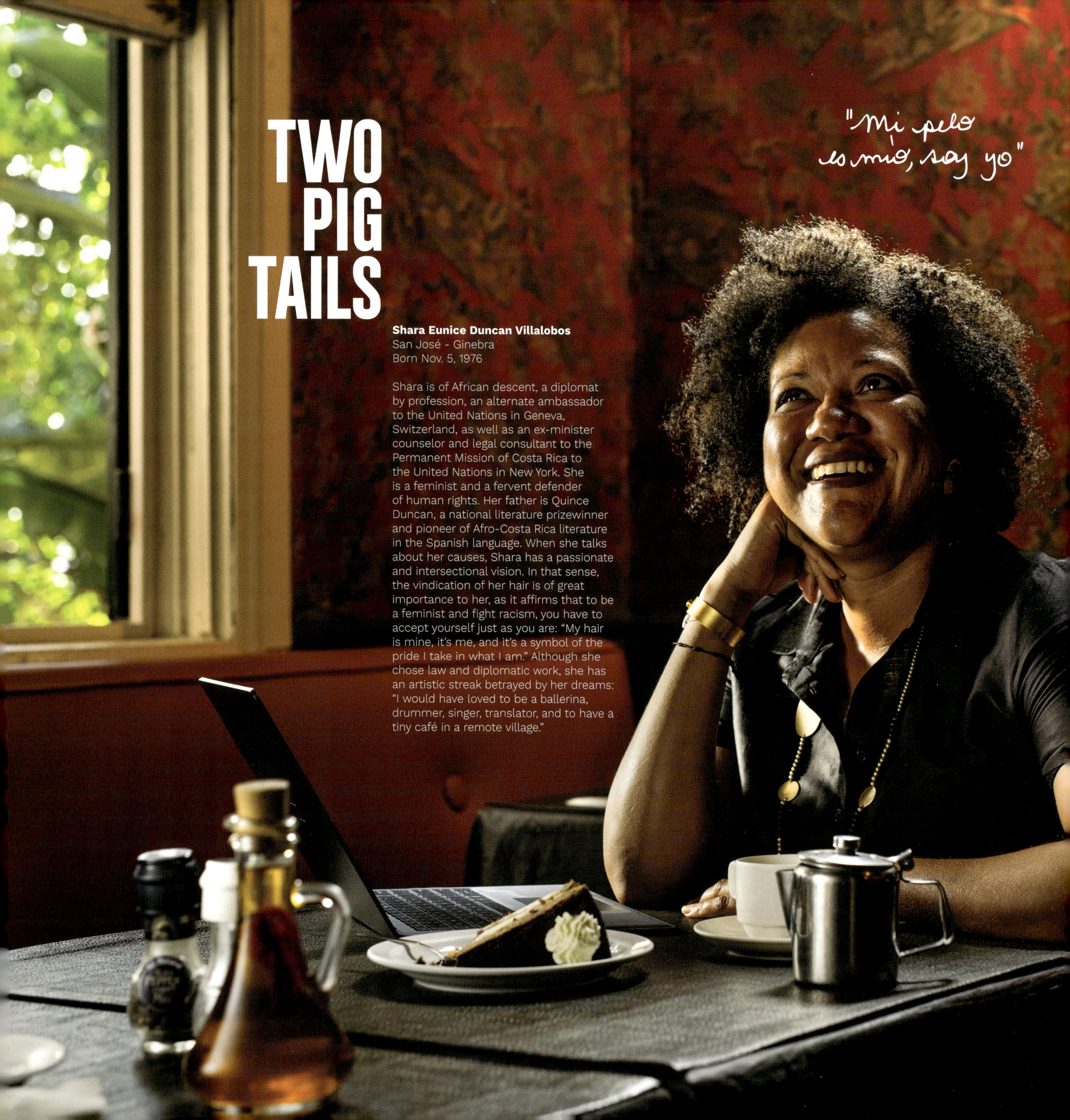

# TWO PIG TAILS

"Mi pelo es mío, soy yo"

**Shara Eunice Duncan Villalobos**
San José - Ginebra
Born Nov. 5, 1976

Shara is of African descent, a diplomat by profession, an alternate ambassador to the United Nations in Geneva, Switzerland, as well as an ex-minister counselor and legal consultant to the Permanent Mission of Costa Rica to the United Nations in New York. She is a feminist and a fervent defender of human rights. Her father is Quince Duncan, a national literature prizewinner and pioneer of Afro-Costa Rica literature in the Spanish language. When she talks about her causes, Shara has a passionate and intersectional vision. In that sense, the vindication of her hair is of great importance to her, as it affirms that to be a feminist and fight racism, you have to accept yourself just as you are: "My hair is mine, it's me, and it's a symbol of the pride I take in what I am." Although she chose law and diplomatic work, she has an artistic streak betrayed by her dreams: "I would have loved to be a ballerina, drummer, singer, translator, and to have a tiny café in a remote village."

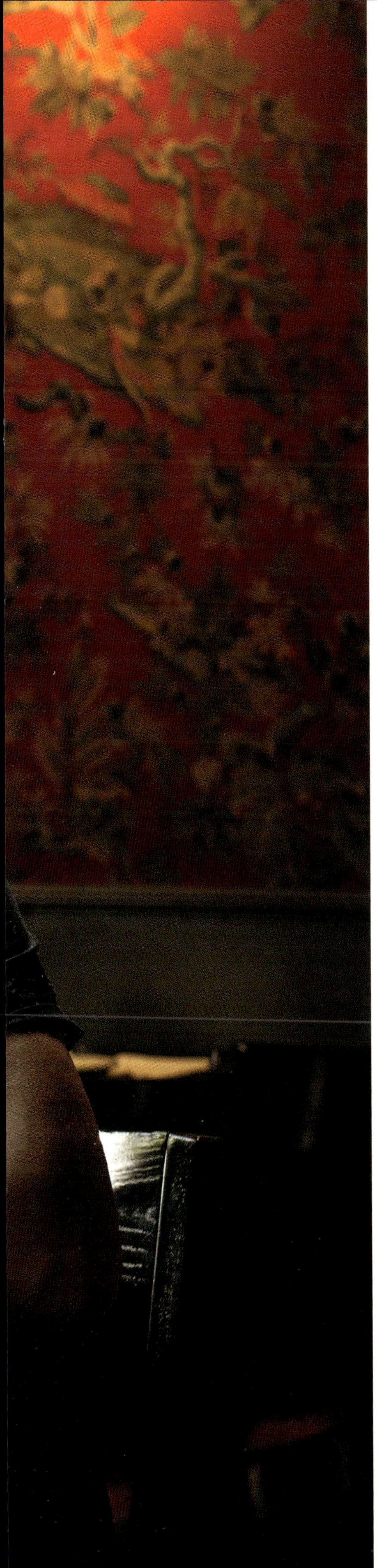

A girl with two pigtails walked quietly down the streets of Heredia. "Black girl!" they shouted at her. "Yeah, I know, and so what?" She slipped away among the stares and shouts of those who were uncomfortable with her differentness. She wasn't born in Limón and never lived there. The great majority of people from the Central Valley are white, including her mother, who, lacking experience with afros, only managed to make two pigtails of her spongy and defiant hair in an attempt to tame it, although on another occasion she simply chose to partially shave it.

She pretended to be blonde, at a school where only she, her sister and the famous soccer player Wanchope were black, tossing her head from side to side with a yellow scarf tied around her hair. In the afternoons, when she drank coffee with her father, she told him about her naive childhood dreams. "Ambassador," she said one day, playfully. "You can be whatever you want," replied Quince, a pioneering Afro-Caribbean writer and national literature prizewinner. "Whatever I want?" With those words and a warm embrace, he gave her the power of confidence. Shara found in her mother, her grandmother and her sister other little pieces of confidence, all very necessary to relate to the other side of the family. Her maternal grandfather, little accustomed to her differentness, stopped seeing her entirely, and when she would approach curiously, he would whistle at his wife and say, "Nany, this little girl is watching me again — take her away." The grandfather never spoke to her.

Little surprise that Shara grew up feeling that she didn't belong, not to her school, to Heredia or to Costa Rica ... not even to her own family.

Once in high school, those two pigtails turned into straight hair with the help of a blow-dryer, a hair iron and some chemicals. One time in Nicaragua, she was transported to her disheveled childhood when her hair collapsed because of a botched alisette treatment.

## ONE DAY SHE WENT OUT ALL DOLLED UP

All grown up and living in Europe, her hair required a lot more effort, yet she found time in her busy schedule as diplomatic to travel an hour and a half by train, submit to a three-hour *alisette* treatment, and spend an hour and a half getting home with her hair stiff and her purse 250 euros lighter.

One day she went out all dolled up and — why not? — it's not every day you sit next to Queen Beatrix of the Netherlands. Among carriages, pages and horses, they paraded down the streets of The Hague, Netherlands and walked the red carpet in front of the palace and the honor guard. But it was when the band struck up the national anthem of Costa Rica that she got goosebumps and almost choked up while she sang along. With a superhuman effort to avoid falling apart with tears of pride, breathing deeply, she noticed that the rest of the Tica delegation was suffering from the same predicament. Maybe the crowd didn't notice, but she recognized the grimaces of her compatriots, trying to hold back tears. At that moment she had a revelation. She wasn't just from Costa Rica, she was its representative.

After 20 years of chemicals, she finally went to the hairdresser and told him, "Cut off everything that's straight." She cut away the sadness and the shame. She took hold of her fears and went back to the origins of her identity, her footprints, her roots. That free little girl, that fearless dreamer, was awakened again. The embrace of her father, and the laughter of her grandmother.

Years later she can say that her uncontainable afro is a symbol of her pride in who she is. Today she's an alternate ambassador for Costa Rica to the United Nations.

**Written by: Berenice Jimenez**

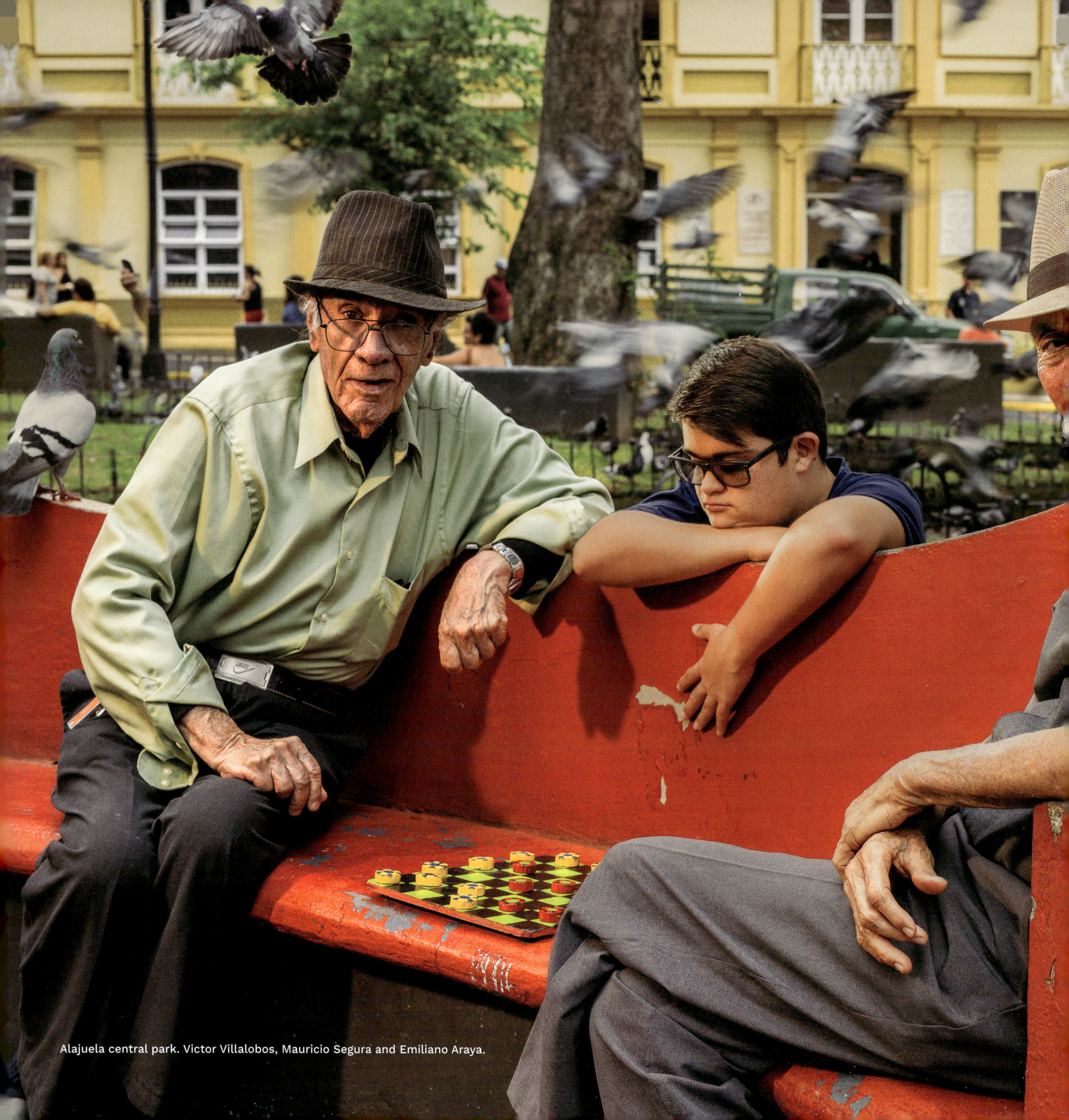

Alajuela central park. Victor Villalobos, Mauricio Segura and Emiliano Araya.

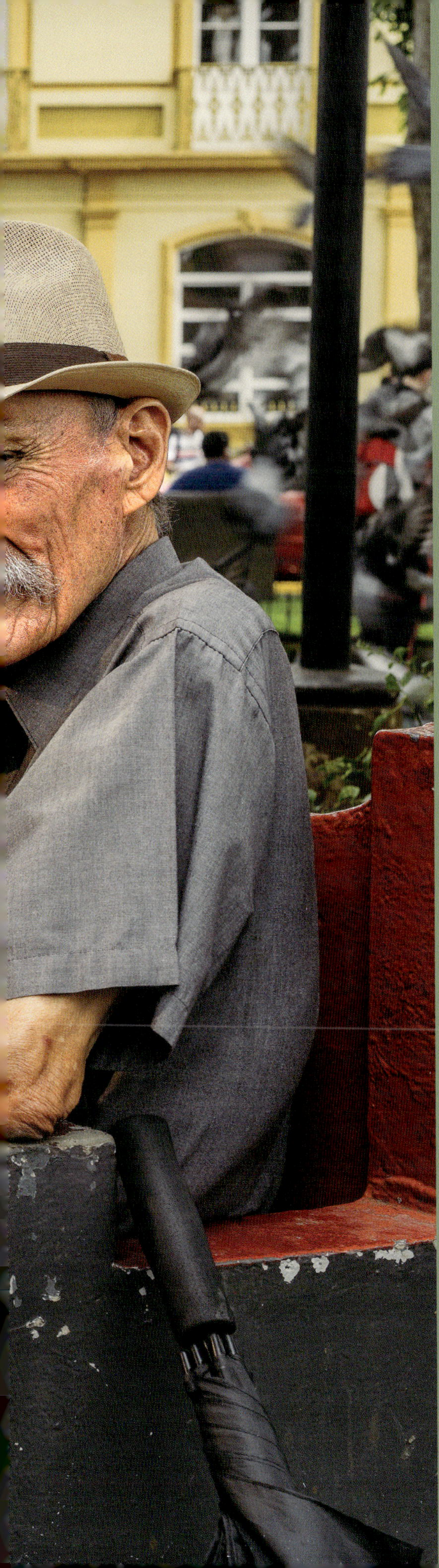

# GATO AND TOTÓ

Seventy years ago, Don Victor "Gato" Villalobos and Don Emilio "Totó" Araya used to play at the same park, among the pigeons, parrots, and mango trees. But although they got along fine, they didn't play together. They couldn't be friends because Gato's parents were "Figueristas" — followers of José Figueres Ferrer, leader of the 1948 civil war — and Totó's parents were "Calderonistas" — followers of Rafael Calderón, Figueres' primary rival. But Totó held out hope that someday his parents would let him play with the famous Gato, who was both mischievous and hilarious.

Another "mariachi" — meaning a Calderonista — was "Perfumitos," the priest of the cathedral, to whom Gato gave that name because of a story he told that one day the priest had fallen into a pit toilet and perfumed himself for days afterwards to remove the odor — a story that the priest, of course, denied.

One Sunday in the 1950s, the bells announced that the 7 p.m. Mass was about to start. The priest was ready, with his cassock adjusted just the way he liked it, and the beautiful mosaic floor of the cathedral was shining and ready for worshippers to arrive. In a few

## THEY WERE WALKING QUIETLY DOWN THE STREET, LIKE A COUPLE OF INNOCENT STRAY DOGS

minutes the wooden pews were filled with parishioners dressed in their finest clothes. Among them were the parents of Gato and Totó.

In front of his house, just two blocks from the church, Gato was sitting alone, bored, looking to find some way to pass the time.

Inside the church, on the packed pews, the grown-ups listened attentively to the Mass. Father Hidalgo combed his hair again, as usual, during the second reading from the Gospels.

But that Sunday evening, as luck would have it, when Gato was bored and looking for action, a pair of bulls wandered down the street that had escaped from a nearby bullring, where the Institute of Alajuela is today. They were walking quietly down the street, like a couple of innocent stray dogs. Upon seeing them, a light bulb turned on over Gato's head, and without another thought, he corralled them toward the cathedral, as if to encourage them to celebrate Mass with everyone else.

They say that Perfumitos totally lost his composure — and his hairdo — upon seeing two big bulls walk down the aisle in the middle of 7 o'clock Mass, crapping all over the polished floor and terrifying the parishioners, who ran out of the church screaming, as if the Devil himself had just walked inside.

Gato, 12 years old, took off running, while the bulls sat down calmly, as if waiting for communion, until they were finally shooed away, who knows how or by whom.

While the priest was hyperventilating with fury, Gato was dying of laughter as he ran home. The laughter lasted until his parents gave him a whipping for having turned a solemn Sunday Alajuela Mass into a Pamplona-style running of the bulls.

It took several years before Totó could make friends with Gato. Nowadays, you see them all the time playing checkers in the park, telling stories about the past and laughing about the mischief they caused and the nicknames they made up.

**Written by: Irene Gutierrez**

**Emiliano "Totó" Araya García**
Alajuela
Born June 19, 1941

Emiliano is one of the "veterans" of the Parque de los Mangos in Alajuela, and a member of one of the most recognized urban tribes of yesteryear: the checkers players of this famous park. There is a very curious fact about Toto, which is also a nice coincidence: Don Juan José Pucci (the father of the creators of this book) operated on his heart several years ago, and they found out by chance when they were taking the picture for this book. As someone who says, "everything is connected."

**Víctor Eduardo "Gato" Villalobos**
Alajuela
Born Feb. 22, 1941

Don Victor Eduardo, known as "Villalobos the Cat" because of the color of his eyes, is one of the "most spoken languages in Alajuela." It's common to see him in the Alajuela park, meeting up with his pals. He's super-famous because since childhood he has made up nicknames for everyone, and Don Victor is a big joker. He named the Alajuela priest Perfumitos ("little perfumes") because he was always dressing up, grooming, and preening. He named the infamous kidnapper of the Negrita de los Ángeles religious icon from a cathedral in Cartago the "Monster of the Basilica." His word games are funny and intelligent, and it was he who named his friend Emiliano "Totó."

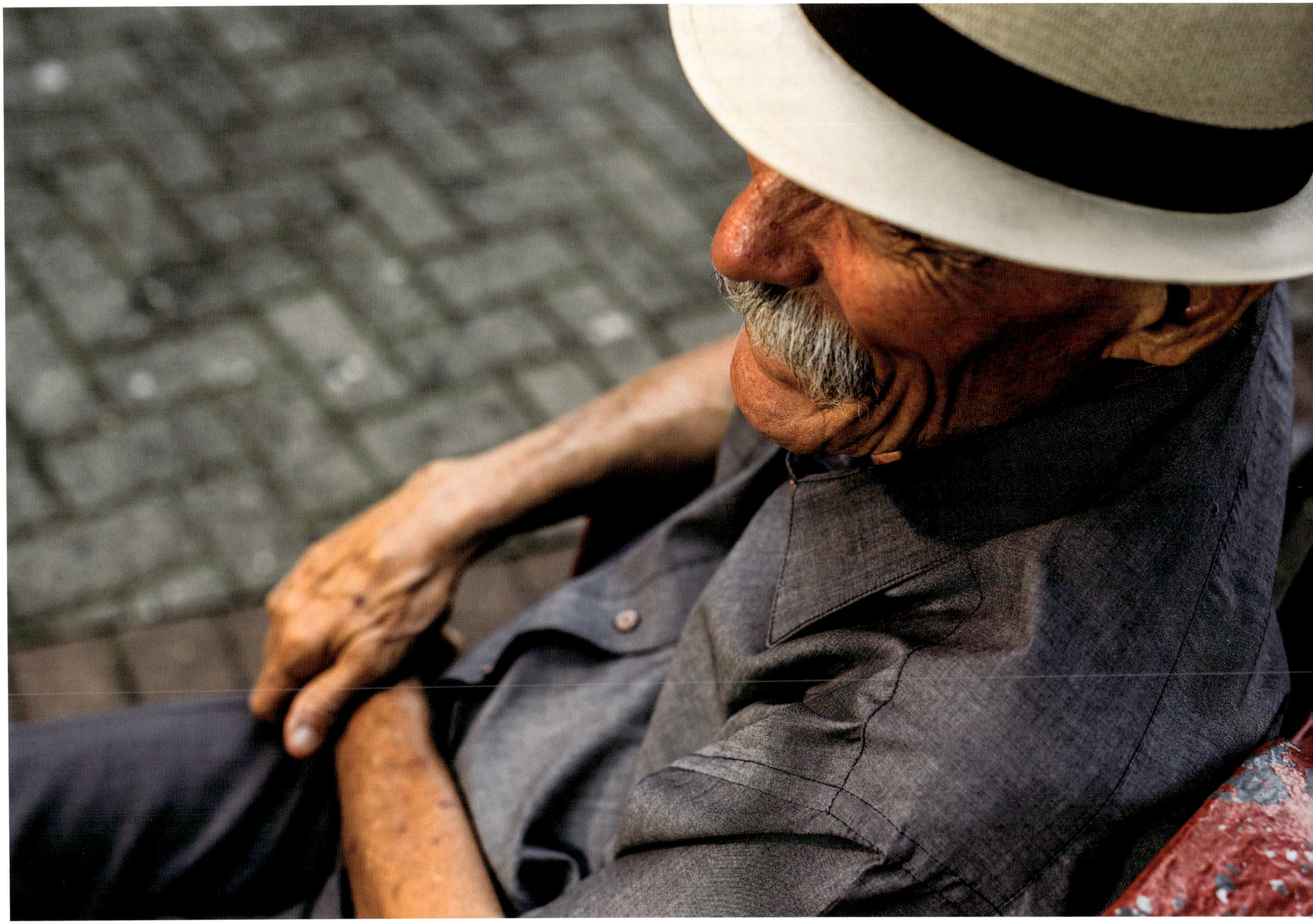

# THAT FIRST DRINK

"Lo que diga mi mamá es santa palabra"

If there's one thing Andrea Leiva enjoys, it's that first drink of beer that bubbles into her mouth and refreshes all the way down. The fact is, she doesn't like the rest of the bottle all that much — you know how it is, the flavor starts getting old, the smell grows a bit stale, and many of us leave the warm "ass end" of the beer at the bottom of the bottle. Oh, if only everything was as perfect as that first swallow.

One day, when Andrea was still getting used to living in Hojancha, she went to the little store in the middle of town. She made a habit of walking there to air questions about her recent move: Her longtime boyfriend and now-husband Jose had an opportunity to open a dental clinic there, and she decided to move with him. For some reason, that day she wanted to drink a beer to beat the heat, and she started thinking. She thought about her years in school, when she had decided to become a doctor, with the full support of her family and the backing of her good grades. She had been at the top of her class her whole life, yet here she was in Hojancha, thinking about dedicating her life to making soaps, creams or perfumes.

With the first swallow came memories of her grandmother Jovita, drinking beer with the whole family, boiling a beef stew or sometimes making

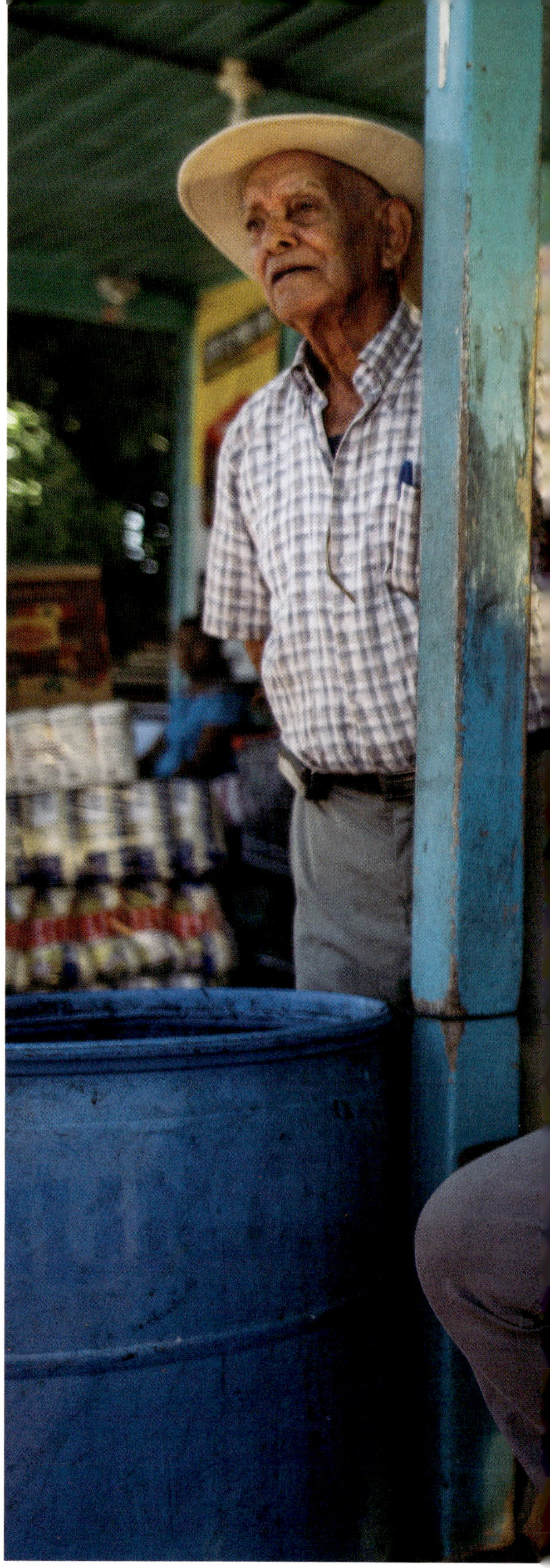

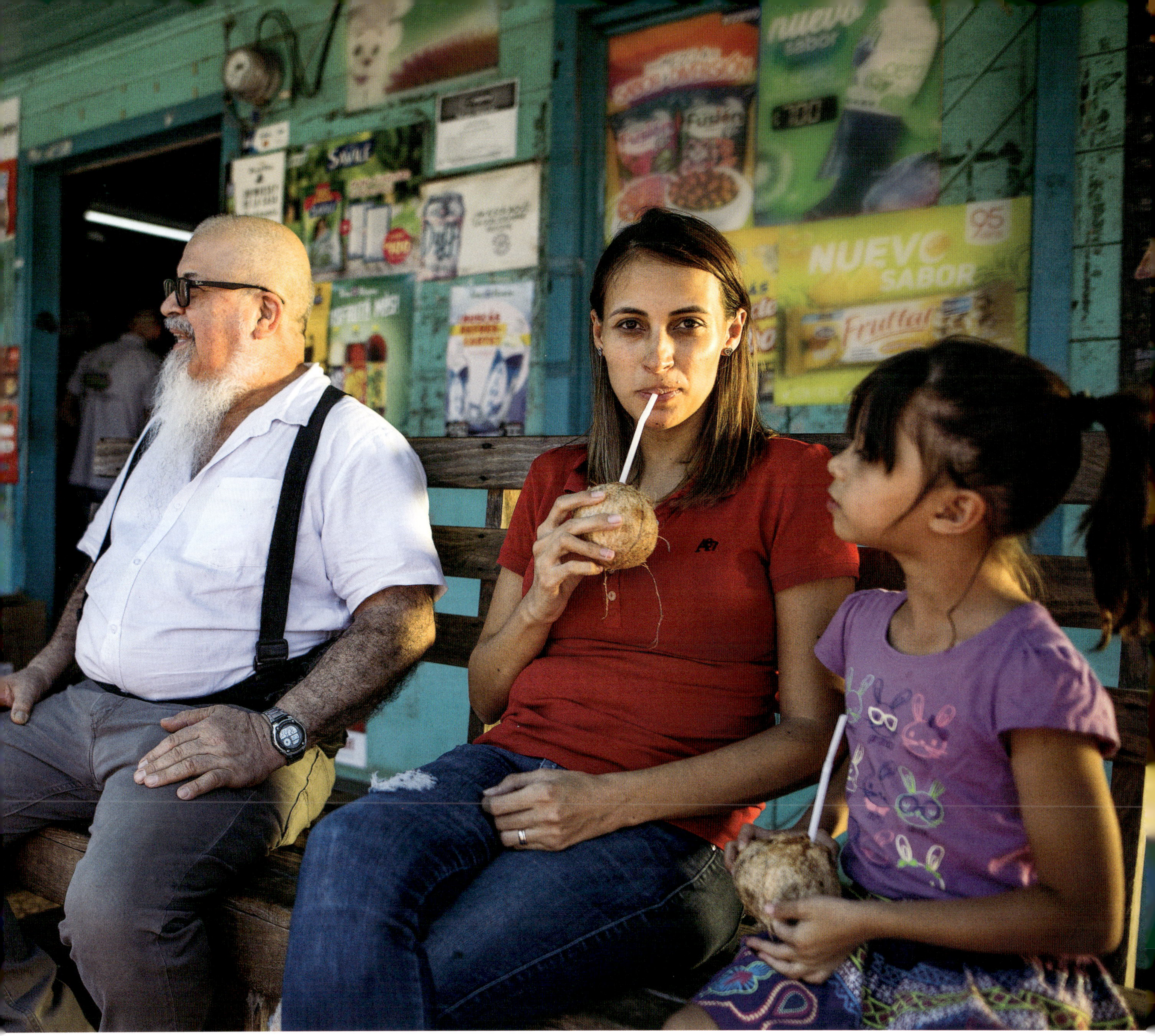


Grocer's shop in Hojancha, Guanacaste. Luis Ángel Pérez, Manuel Pineda, Andrea and Victoria Gutiérrez

tamales. Andrea used to go to the beach with all her cousins, when everyone piled into one car and she told the same jokes over and over. Jovita would laugh nonstop and say, "Oh, you're such a funny drunk!" Jovita, "Grandma," the maternal grandmother who took her every summer to Pérez Zeledón, where Andrea would play to the point of exhaustion at the end of the day.

She also remembered how she couldn't stop praying or crying when she learned that Jovita had cancer.

When Andrea was 16 and was about to start her journey in med school, Jovita was diagnosed with breast cancer.

## A STRANGE ERROR IN TREATING THIS CONDITION WITH A "COBALT BOMB"

A strange error in treating this condition with a "cobalt bomb" caused dozens of cancer patients a premature death. Jovita was one of them. She was given a lethal dose of radiation that created a health problem impossible to cure. This heartbreaking image from the hospital room drove Andrea away from medicine forever.

Eighteen years later, with a daughter and a husband, not knowing what she would do with the rest of her life in Hojancha, that first drink filled her with sadness, joy, fear, love, and a great idea...

And so, GuanaBeer was born, which started producing 48 beers a week, to sell to friends and family, and later some 6,000 bottles a month were distributed to restaurants and hotels.

Sometimes they grill meat or make deep-fried pork in her yard in Hojancha, plus they bottle five liters of Guanacas (their original brand), and they invite the whole family. So, Guanaca is not just the citrous notes that bubble down the throat, but decades of memories, of a united family, and of the certainty that Jovita is still with them, laughing out loud.

**Written by: María Fernanda Cruz**

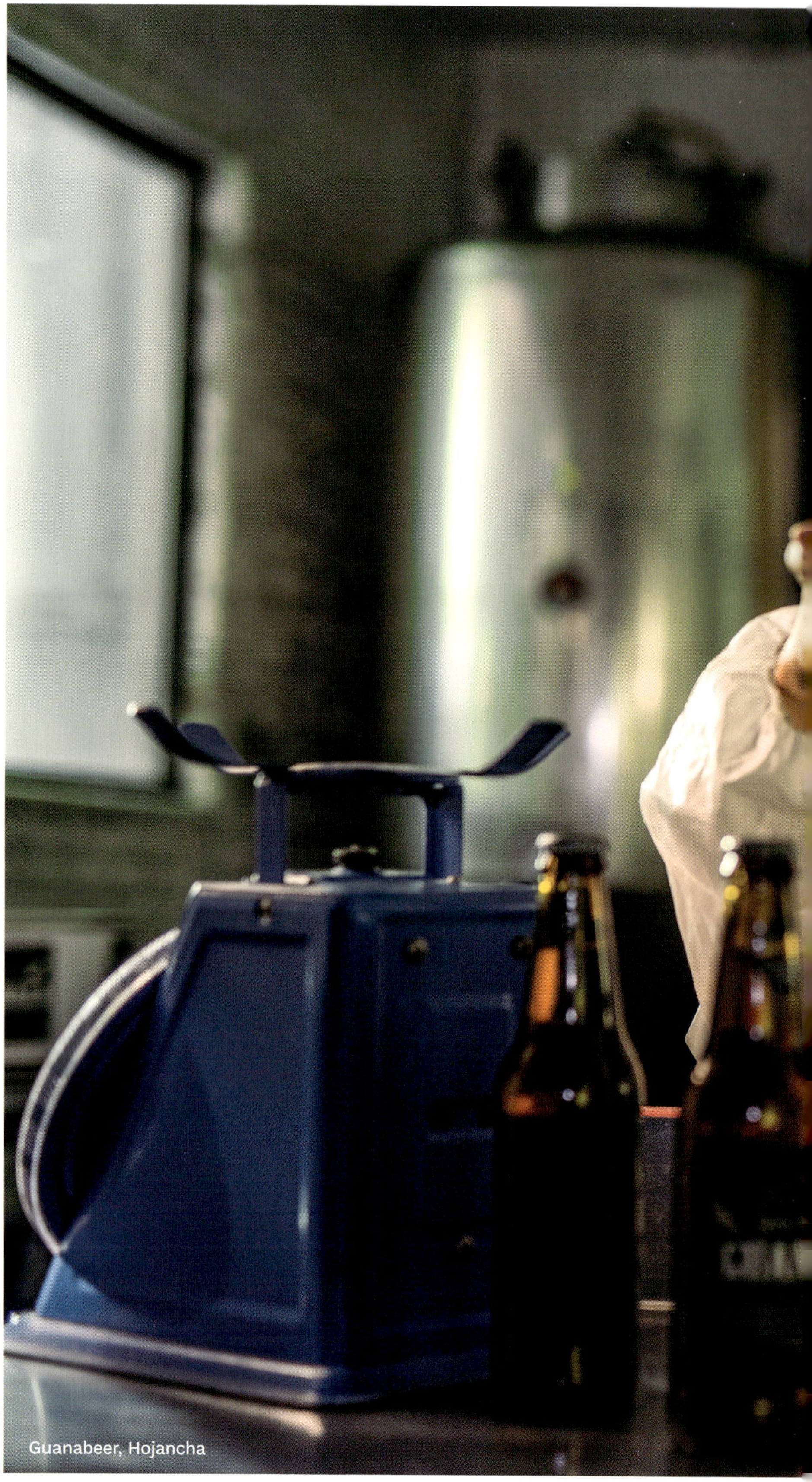

Guanabeer, Hojancha

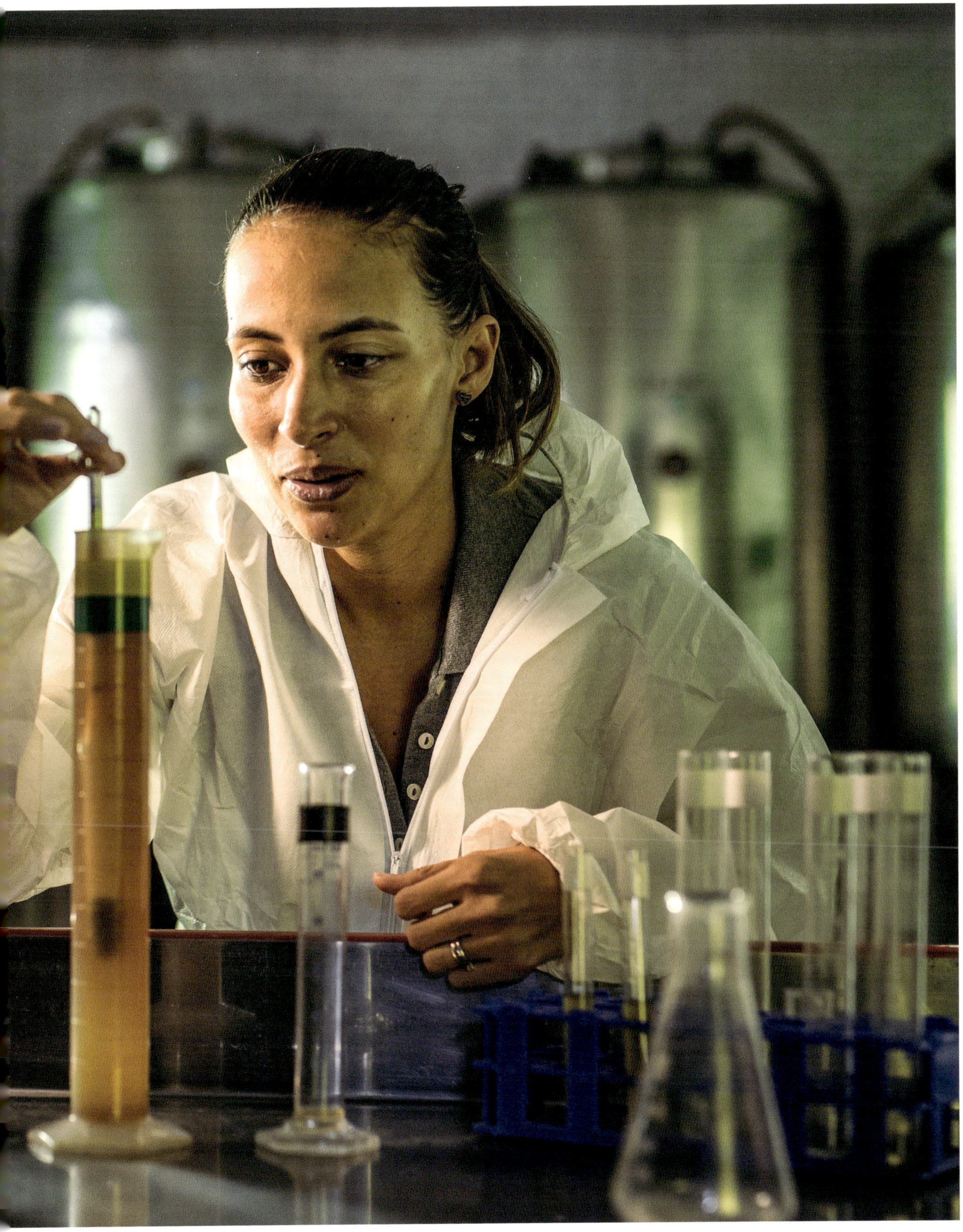

• Outside the Central Valley, Hojancha is the canton with the highest score on the Social Progress Index.

**Andrea Leiva Saborío**
Pérez Zeledón – Hojancha,
Born Sept. 1, 1985

A chemical engineer, an environmental manager for the Municipality of Hojancha, and a brave businesswoman. She was born in Pérez Zeledón, but nine years ago she moved to Hojancha with her husband. In 2016, she founded GuanaBeer, a company that makes craft beer. Andrea is a nascent beer baron, with a growing business born of necessity and willpower, now creating jobs and distributing suds all over the country. "The last words of my grandmother were that I should never stop studying and I should always listen to my parents."

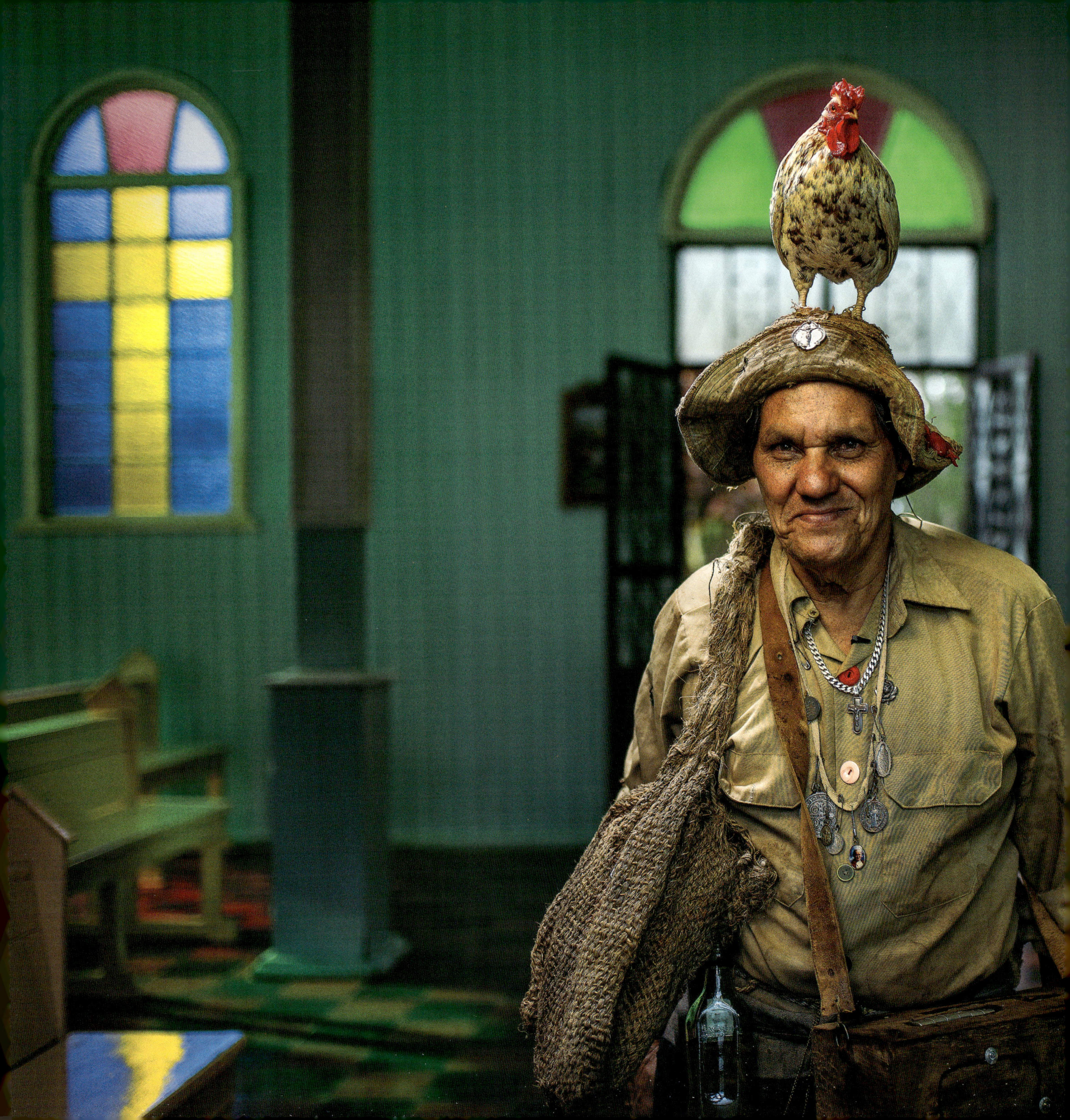

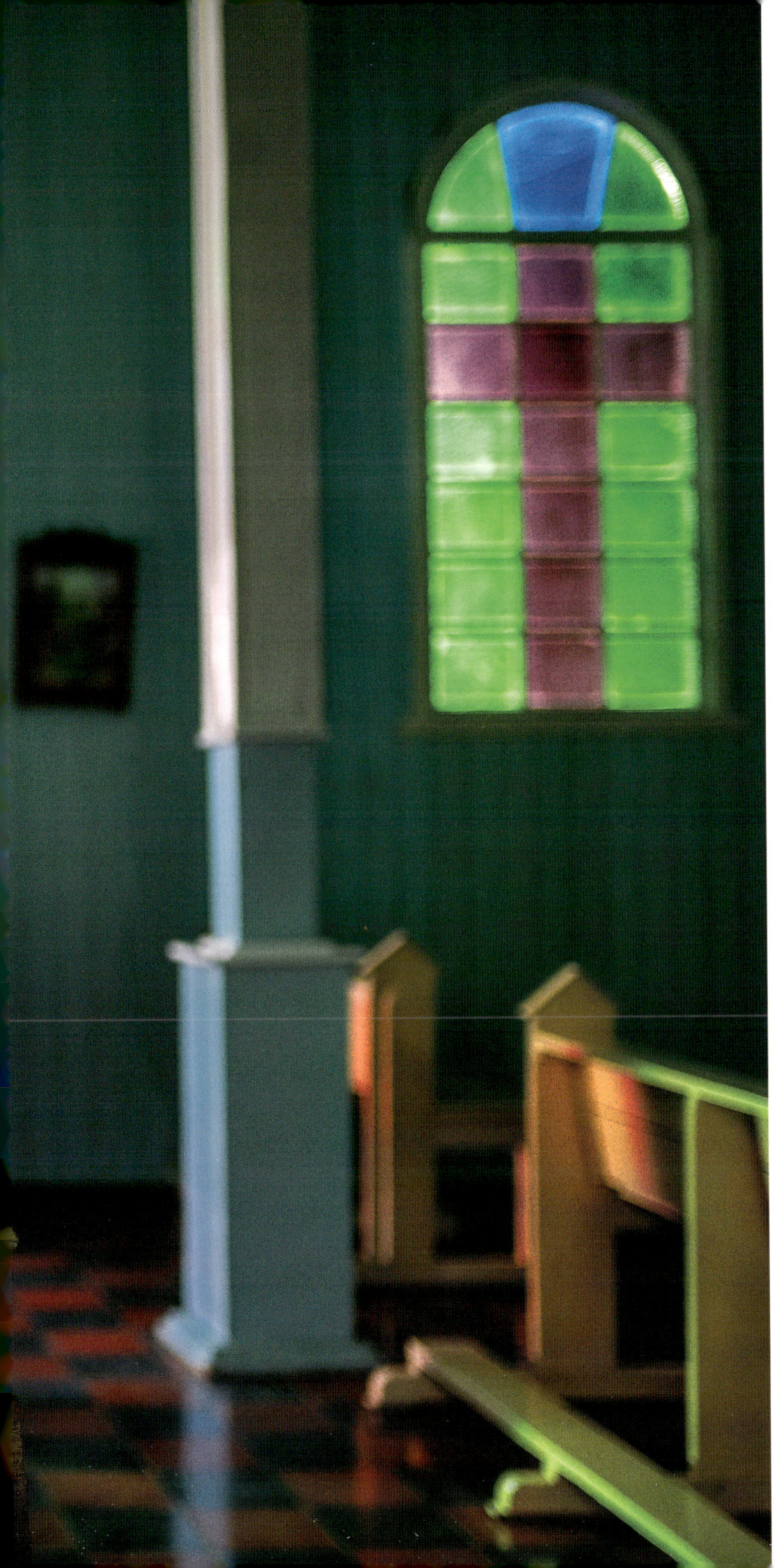

# WITH NEW EYES

Like anyone from the country, Carlos grew up in a close relationship with cows. Maybe closer than normal. "As a little kid, I was really sickly. They say I started to walk when I was about three and a half years old." At that time, the remedy for his ailments came by way of the ancestral wisdom of a friend of her mother's, who suggested bathing him in colostrum, the first milk of a cow that had just given birth. "They put me in a bucket, they bathed me all over with that colostrum, and they say that within two days I was walking. God is good!"

From childhood, he learned to herd cattle. Very early, sometimes in the rain or in the inclement cold of San José over 50 years ago, he spent his working day without a jacket or shoes, but very cleverly. Every day he opened the gate of the corral and lifted up the first cow he found lying there, taking its place on the ground to take advantage of the heat it left behind while all the cows wandered out of the corral. His punishment was ticks everywhere.

# "THE OLD MAN OF THE MOUNTAIN"

**Carlos Guadamuz Hidalgo**
Brasil de Mora
Born Nov. 4, 1949

As a child, Carlos and his siblings slept next to the cows, as his family had few resources. He had to start working on the field when he was very young. As a child he made an unforgettable mistake, accidentally burning down the shack in which he lived with his family. He is proud to be a "country boy," a simple farmhand. He dresses up in traditional country clothing to go to horse parades and local festivals, and although his family doesn't support him in this, these are activities that make him very happy.

He also did his first communion barefoot. On that occasion, blinded by the impeccable shoeshine of the boy in front of him, he noticed that the candle in his hand started melting rapidly. Between his distress and his recognition that the candle of the boy in front was still intact, he had to sit down in a shirt soaked with paraffin, shoeless, with one hand that looked more like an old candelabra than a hand, and the feeling of embarrassment that was hard to absorb.

His first pair of shoes finally arrived one Christmas when he was 12, and since growing up in poverty always meant sharing, the gift wasn't just for him but also for his brother. That night they went out excited to sing Christmas carols and pray at the Nativity displays in front of all the homes, amid the smell of cypress, sawdust, and wax paper typical of the time. Each time they left a house, they would fight to see who would wear the shoes to the next house. That experience, with the blisters from his first shoes, led to one of Carlos' happier memories.

Still, the shame of who he was, where he came from, and what he didn't have was rooted in the deepest part of his soul.

In 1998, on the eve of the San José Carnival, Don Carlos got an idea that he would participate by building a float. On the bed of a truck he replicated scenes from his childhood. He dressed as always, like a peasant from the country. He took a dirty mare, put on a straw hat, wore a dirty shirt and pants smeared with red clay, and to complete his costume he went barefoot. Arriving at La Sabana, he was intercepted by journalists and photographers who fought among themselves to interview him and take his picture. He couldn't believe what he was seeing. That year he won second place in the competition and came out in all the newspapers.

Reliving that story from the perception of how people value what's authentic was like a salve on the wounds he had carried for so long. He was so overwhelmed with gratitude for eyes that saw him as he had never seen himself, that from that day forward he never missed another carnival or horse parade. They christened him "The Old Man of the Mountain," a personality who connects with the common people, which touched him deep in his soul.

"What I love is going around telling people what life is like for country people, and things like that."
With the passage of the years, he developed a different perception of the way he grew up. He says poverty doesn't exist — sometimes he brought poverty on himself. "You may not have money, but you do have happiness, you want to work, to eat, and if there's no food ... you can eat an orange."

**Written by: Valeria Murillo**

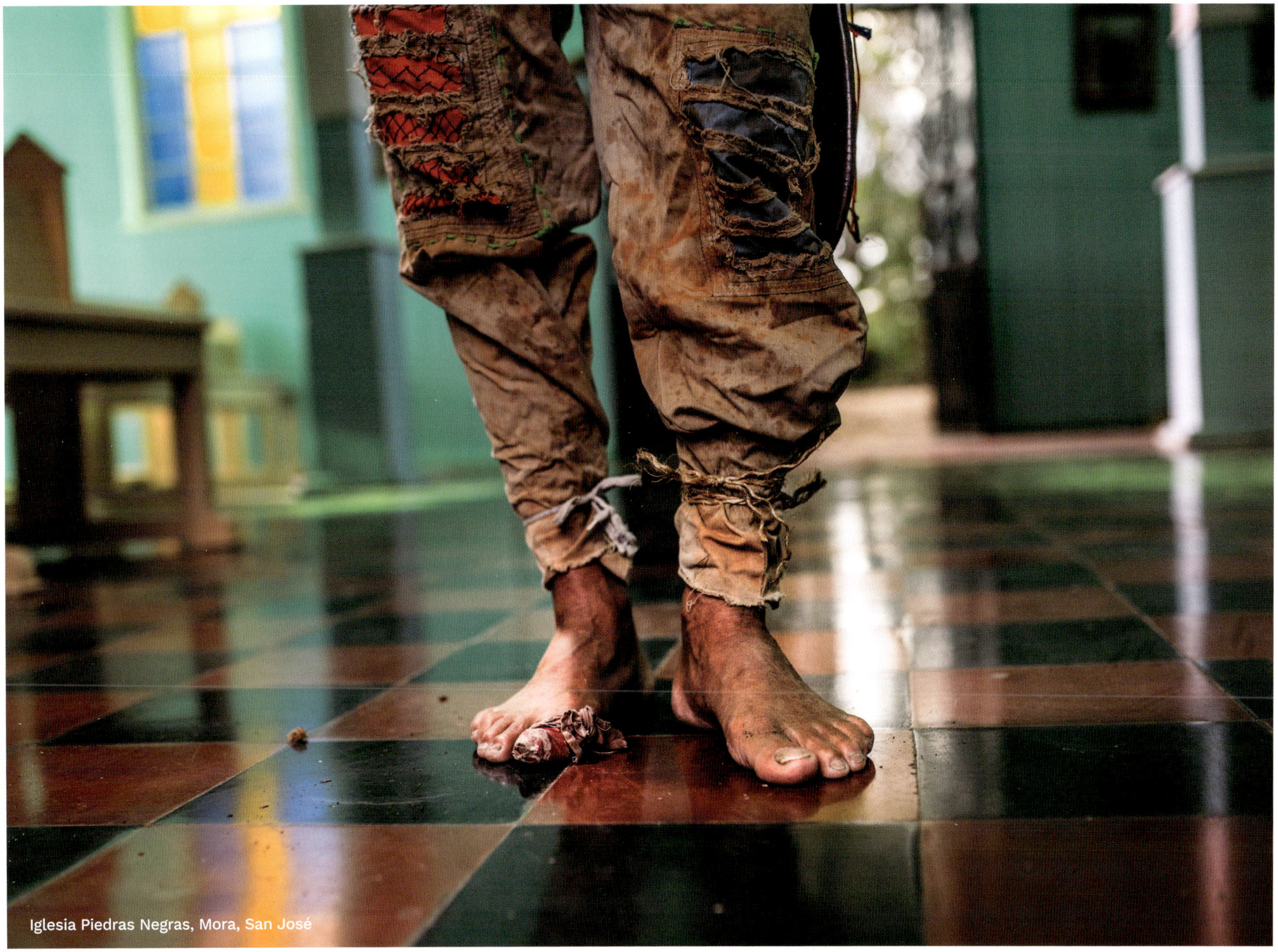
Iglesia Piedras Negras, Mora, San José

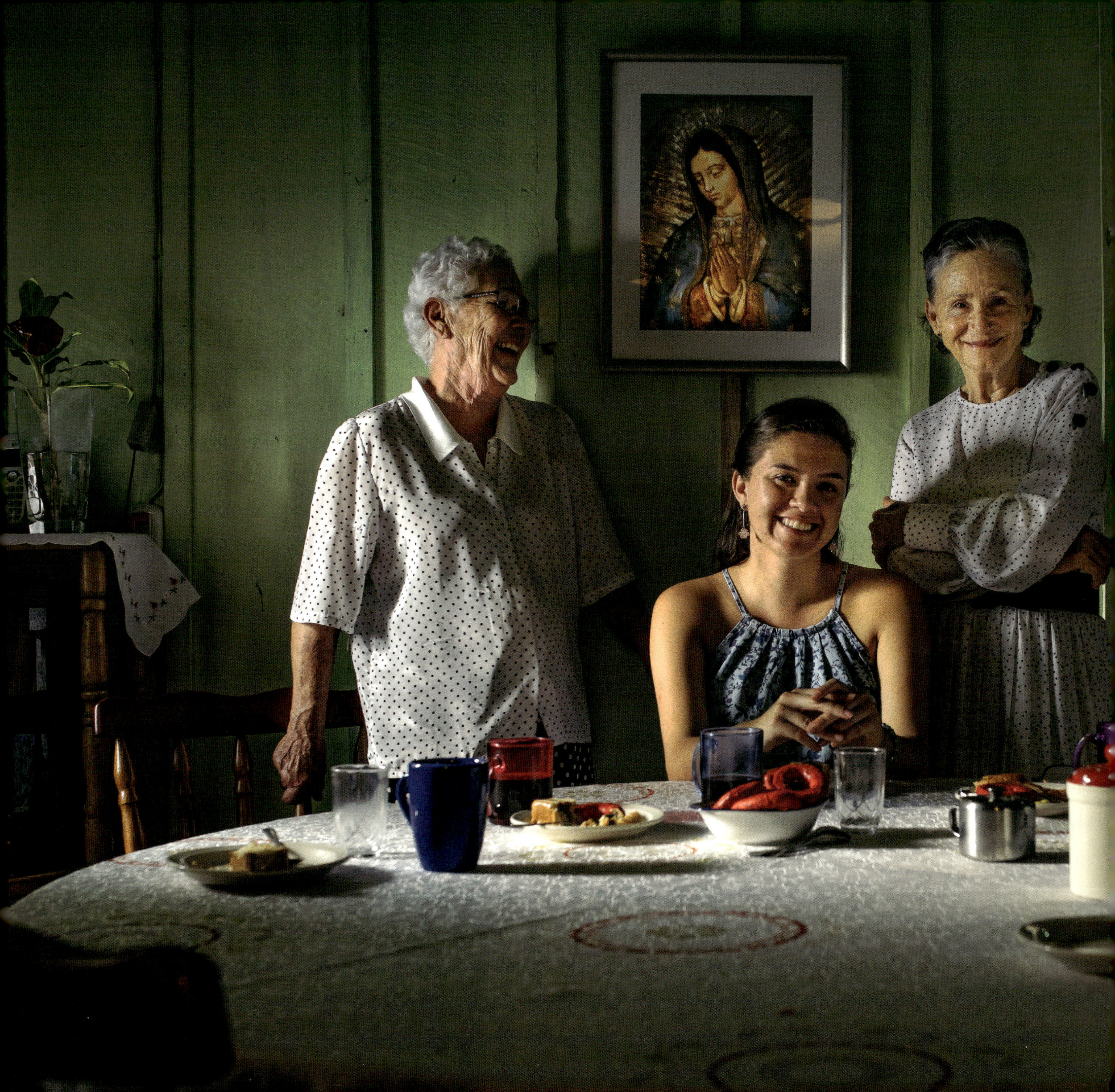

Marta Mora, Guadalupe and Alba Rojas

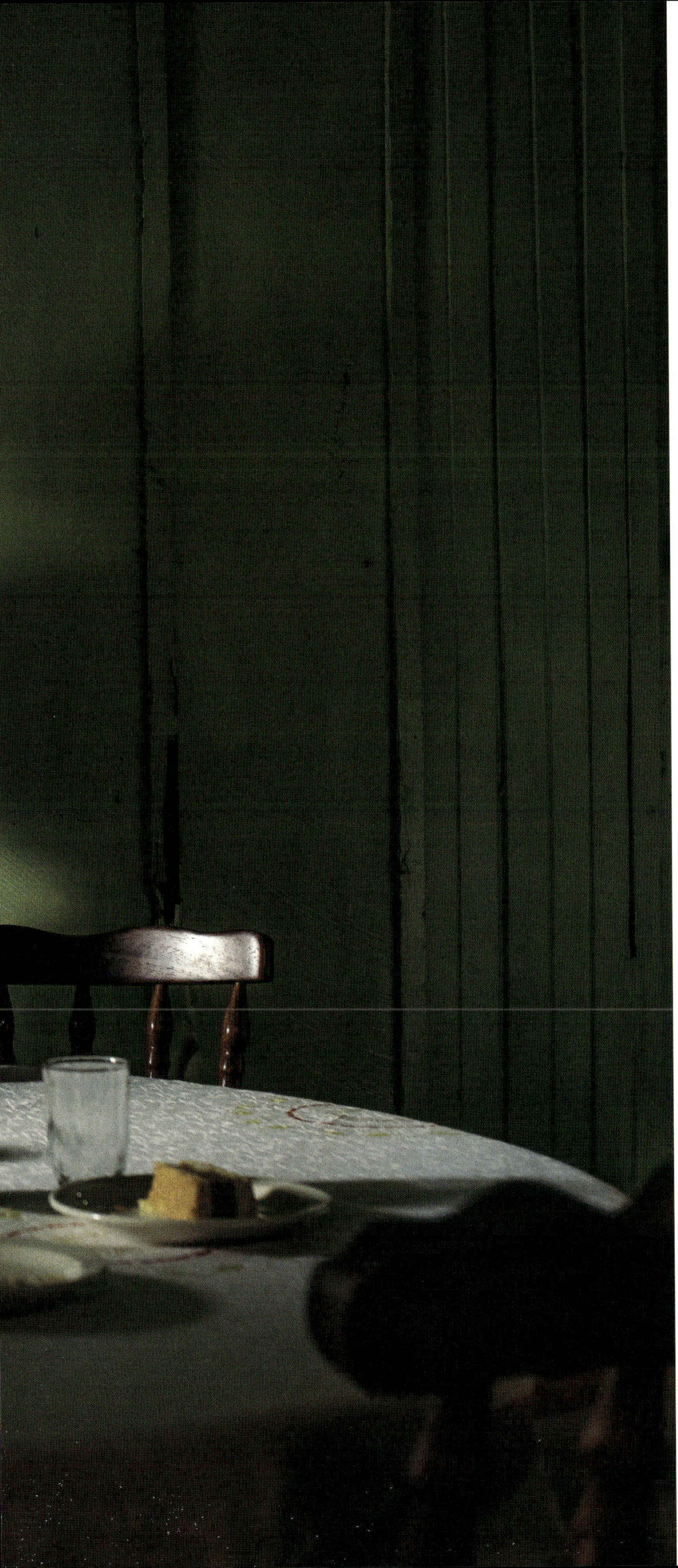

# GUADALUPE'S HAND

As the doctors came out of the operating room, their diagnosis was not the least bit encouraging. "She has a dead hand — we've going to have to amputate," they told her mother.

In the hospital room, while they tried to explain this to Guadalupe, the little girl wouldn't let them talk. In tears, just 4 years old, the girl was not prepared to lose her hand.

Amputation was the only option after a case of medical malpractice that followed an accident at home. Even though her mother had warned her not to carry that glass plate to the kitchen, she had dropped it, and a fragment of glass severed her tendons.

"I don't want them to cut off my hand, Mom! It will get better!" she shouted, inconsolable. The decision was very hard for her mother. With her limited knowledge, she had to trust the doctors' advice. They warned that if she didn't agree to amputate the hand, she would have to sign a waiver clearing them of responsibility.

## GUADALUPE KNEW FROM THE BEGINNING THAT THIS DAY WOULD ARRIVE

But Guadalupe cried so much that her mother ended up trusting her daughter's instincts. Facing a possibly fatal outcome, she would have to bear sole responsibility for not following the doctors' advice. The girl returned home with her hand in a cast, bound to her chest to prevent sudden movements.

The immobilized hand had more consequences than were foreseen. Weeks passed and, little by little, her friends abandoned her. They were afraid because of her hand - they didn't want to play with her and they preferred to avoid her. Guadalupe was left all alone.

With her hand bandaged and her spirits low, eight months of therapy followed. The hand remained immobile, useless, exactly the same as the first day. Once while she was praying, she promised God that if he would heal her, she would use both of her hands to serve.

But she started fulfilling her promise long before that. First she participated in a charity group of child models, and then she joined other charitable causes, with activities in the community and at school. Whenever somebody needed help, Guadalupe was there.

One Sunday, at a sports complex in Desamparados, the girl attended a prayer of healing with her mother. The priest presiding over the activity summoned all the people with ailments down to the soccer field. Guadalupe went with them.

"Here among us there's a girl whose hand stopped moving eight months ago, and she's being healed at this moment," the priest said over a microphone, so that his voice could be heard all over the grounds. "Whoever is next to her, tell her to move her hand. We want her to lift her left hand at this moment," said the voice over the loudspeakers.

A heavyset man lifted the girl onto his shoulders, and hundreds of eyes turned her way. That hand was accustomed to being clutched to the chest, by way of protection, as if to hide itself. Nevertheless, Guadalupe dared to lift her arm little by little. "The priest said I could open it, so I believed him," she says.

She stretched her hand up high, and suddenly her fingers started moving. Little by little, each one separated from that fist that had gone so long without moving. The seconds grew long as her fingers separated.

Guadalupe knew from the beginning that this day would arrive, that her hand would live again. She became popular again in her neighborhood, and even people from other towns would come because they wanted to meet her. By the age of 22 she was studying social work and dedicating her life to helping older adults, women and children.

Medical specialists have offered her ointments to heal her wound, but she prefers to keep the memory visible. "For me it's like a kind of tattoo, and at difficult times I see it and I remember that everything is going to be all right."

**Written by: Arturo Pardo**

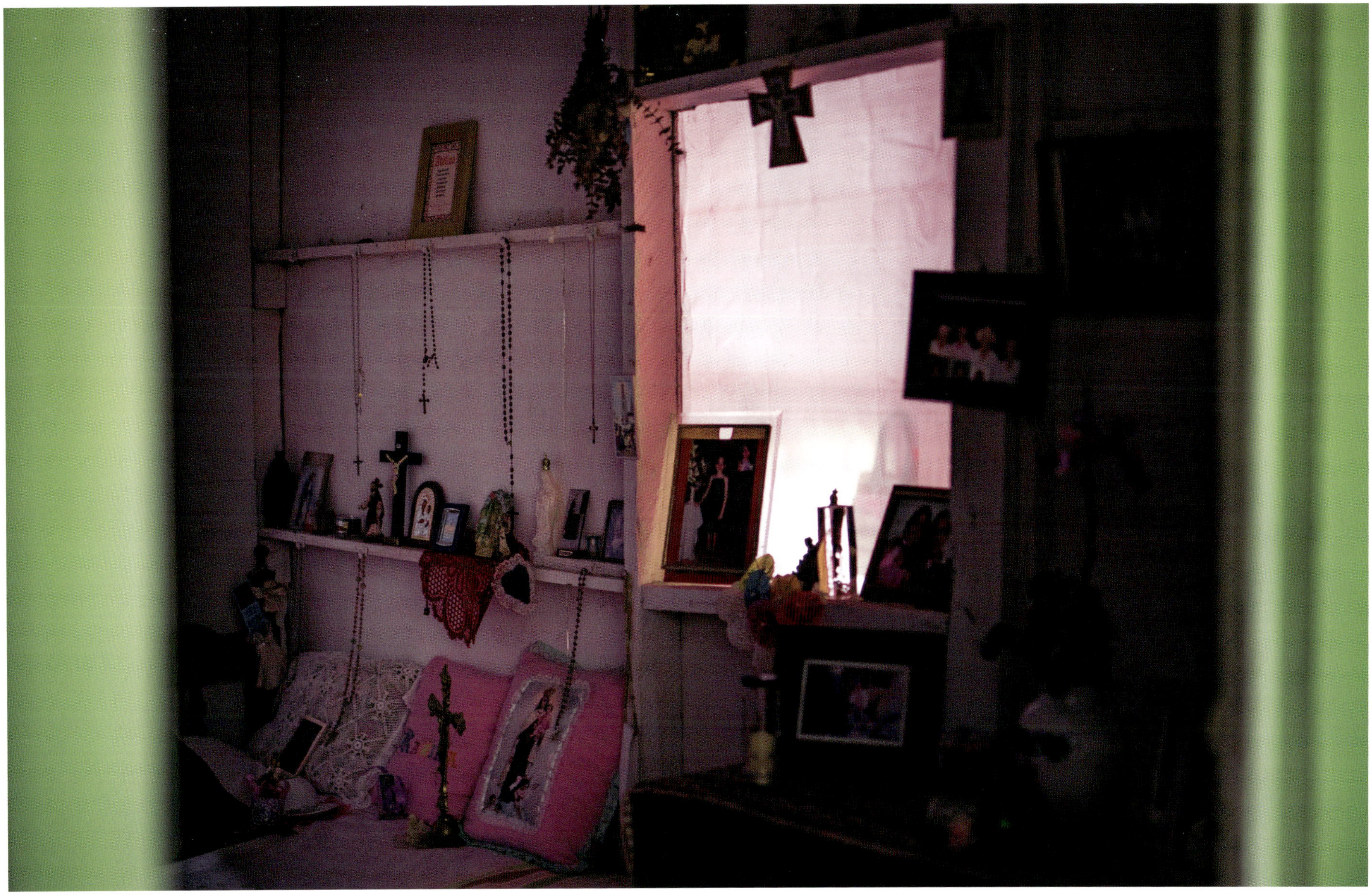

San Ramón, Alajuela.

**Guadalupe Hernández Ramírez**
San Ramón
Born Jan. 3, 1997

Guadalupe is a young feminist, community leader and student of social work at the University of Costa Rica. She's an ambassador of Costa Rica to the Global Union for Democracy. Ever since she was very young, she's been a leader in community development, and she's noted in the canton of San Ramón for her leadership. She's a member of the local Committee for Young People, and she's worked with children, youths, women, and older adults through various organizations and institutions. She was one of the organizers and speakers at a recent Women's Convention in San Ramón. She has a social initiative called "Metamorphosis" in which she assists the rural population and women. As a child, she suffered an accident that changed her life: "My vow was that my two hands would be used to serve, to help others." And she has a good source of inspiration, as her mother is a "doer," a woman who knocks on doors and works hard to make things happen.

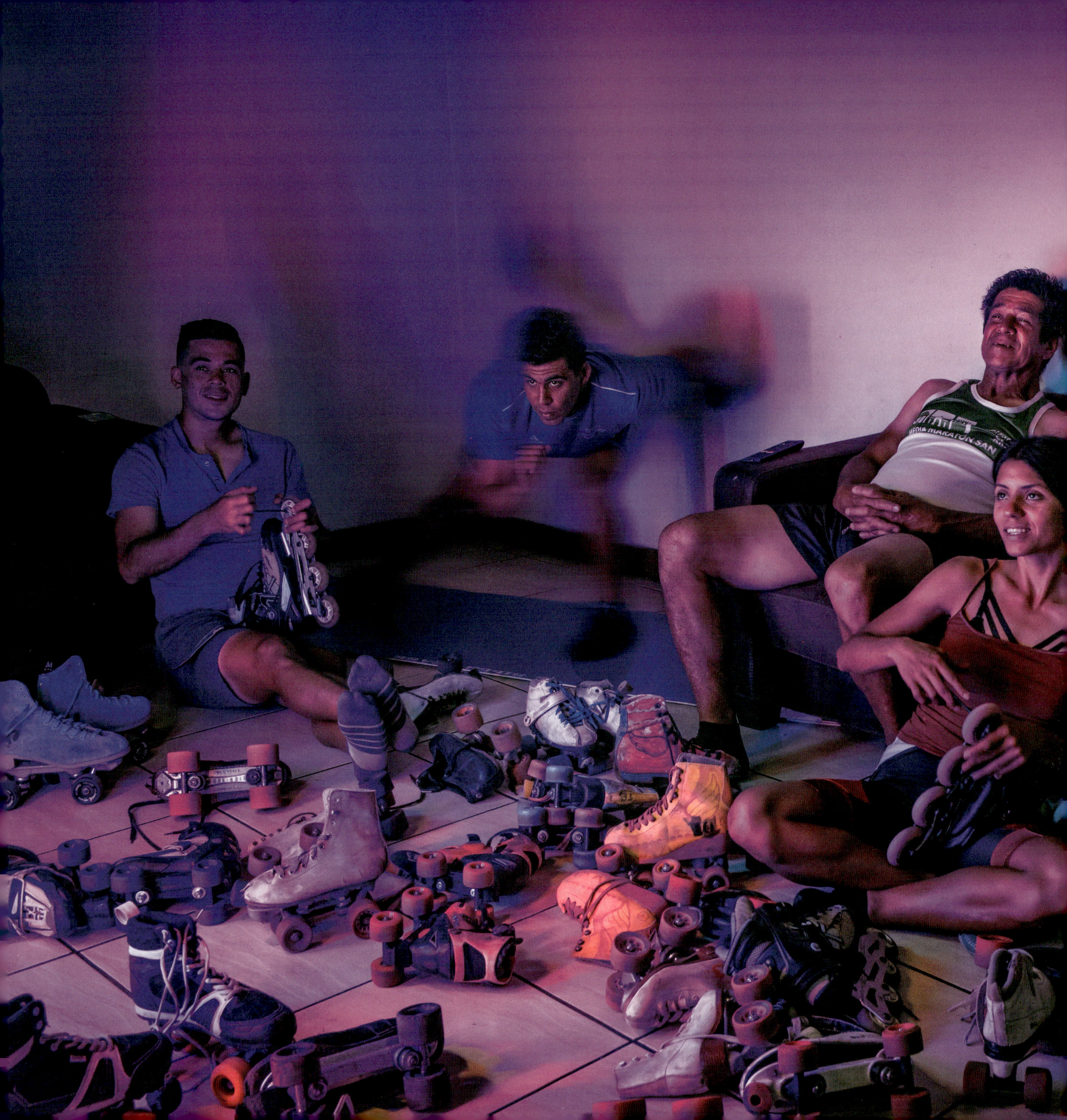

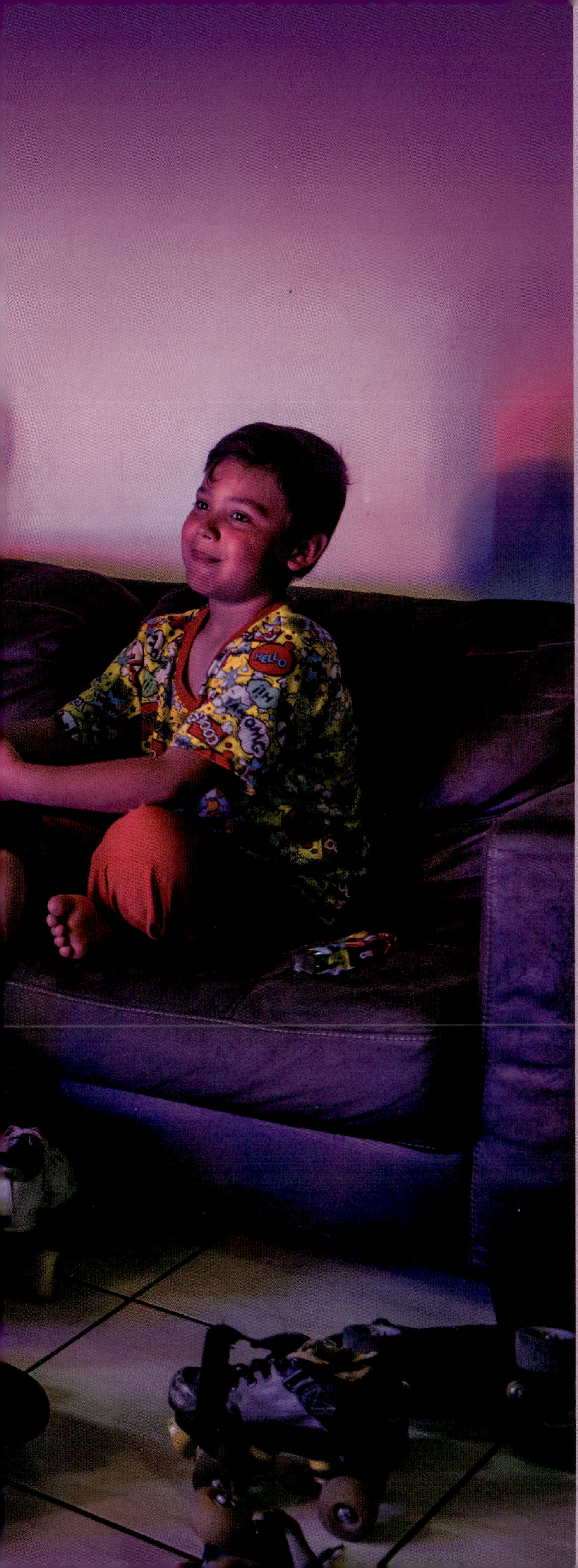


# LUCKY SKATES

"Gooooooold! Medal for Costa Rica! Siles for the gold with the Ticos!" ... Guatemala, Central American Skating Championship, 2019. Fortune can take many forms. This story is a case in point.

Let's talk about skating. Human beings, bored of walking on their legs, decided to create feet on wheels, resulting in speeds the ordinary person cannot achieve. There are families that live from and for this. That's the case with the Siles family.

Where it all began. The decade of the '70s.... "Man, after school, let's go skating, you want to?" "Go do what?" responded a youth who still had the features of a child, a new arrival in the city of Alajuela. "Gosh, man, skating," "I don't know what that is." An outbreak of laughter from the teenagers.... "Man, the Guanacastecos don't skate?" A while later, those who once invited him to skate had already retired their wheels forever. But not Don Enrique, who in his premature version of adulthood started dreaming of skates.

At the same time, his father dreamed of another kind of wheel, in this case that of fortune. "Come on, kids, we're going to sit down and watch 'The Wheel of Fortune'."
(In the Costa Rican version of this show, participants are chosen through a raffle using actual lottery tickets.) "I activated this damned sheet of lottery tickets and again, nothing.... Can you imagine me spinning that wheel?" He talks to his grandchildren, who are like elusive wraiths propelled by skates, moving around everywhere.... "Grandpa, but how many lottery sheets have you already activated?" ... "Oh, my boy, you hadn't been born yet when I started doing this." Destiny is also random, and the grandfather didn't know this yet. Life doesn't always reward us at the moment we want it to.

One that knows nothing about destiny is the rain, which decades later decided to inundate the San José metropolis. In 2018, the Siles family had seen how their rental skates in La Sabana had nobody to roll with. Difficult times.

An ordinary office in the capital. "Don Enrique, here's the lottery sheet that the boss gives away each year. Good luck."

Two dreams, three generations and one television. All in one act. We'll call it lottery and skating. An incoherent combination, it would seem at first glance.

“Enrique Siles?” “Yes, speaking.” “We’re calling from the Social Protection Board. Your lottery sheet has been chosen, and we’d like to invite you to be on the next ‘Wheel of Fortune’ program.” Luck isn’t good or bad. Luck falls where it falls.

A television studio.... “On the air in 3, 2, 1.”

“Good evening, Don Enrique! Welcome to ‘The Wheel of Fortune.’ Who’s here with you in the audience today?” “My father,” says the smiling, hopeful protagonist. The grandfather, sitting in the audience, is all nerves, all happiness. “Let’s do Dicemania!” says the presenter, his face bronzed with makeup and his mane of hair covered in hairspray, appropriate for this world of spectacle.

Our protagonist started throwing dice until he reached the number 18, one point on two impassable routes. “Don Enrique,” the presenter says, “do you want to stick with what you have or throw again? Last chance. If you roll a 3 you win it all; higher than that, you lose everything. What’s your decision, sir?” The face of the grandfather is shouting “Stay!” and the public is too, but it’s worth remembering that the one who’s always had luck on his side is his son.... “I’m ready, I’m going to roll. I’m going for everything,” Enrique says.

A few miles away, a group of people is using the skating rink as a test tube for making their dreams come true. “Coach, my father is on

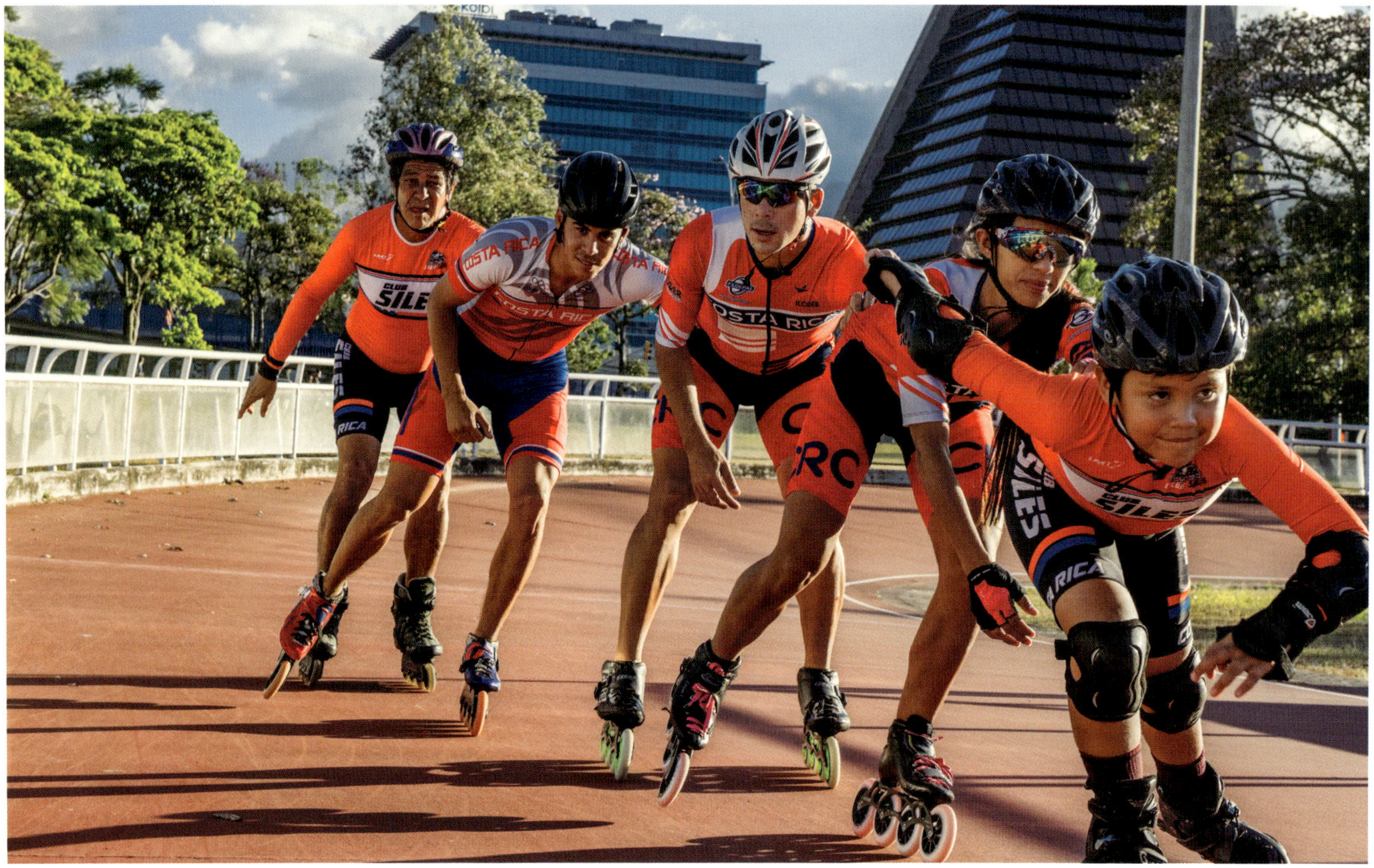


La Sabana Park. Enrique, Byron and Joseph Siles, Yuliana Salazar and Jeicob.

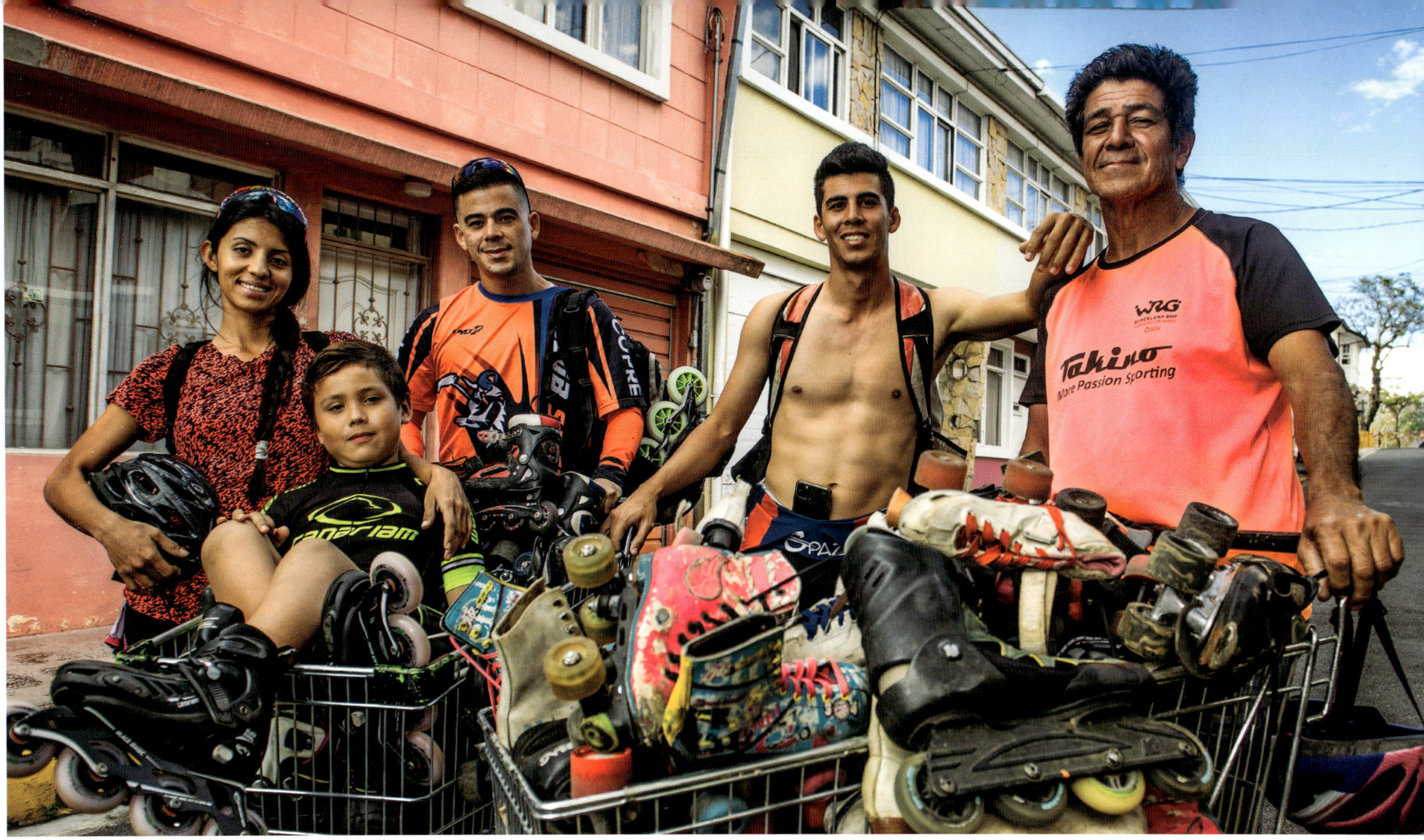

national TV right now, live on 'The Wheel of Fortune'." "What did you say?" The training turned into a public annex by means of a cellphone screen. A father, with one roll of a die, had the possibility of sending his son to the Central American Skating Championship ... if only luck would cooperate.

The big die started spinning infinitely and as it landed it bounced ... 4, 3, 6, 2, 1....

For a moment the world stands still for the roll of the die, each bounce full of uncertainty, the air full of expectation for how it will stop, until the auditorium grows silent for the first time: 3. The die decides to be a 3, and the Siles family celebrates the grand prize with the smile of the grandfather, his crystal eyes shining; in the impulsive, mad embrace between Don Enrique and the TV presenter; in the living room of a house that witnesses the family rejoicing in front of the television; and in the hullaballoo of a skating team that celebrates someone else's victory like it was their own. All was happiness on different planes united by chance. It turns out, big surprise, that fortune has the power to unite souls that love each other. Luck dressed in the shape of a skate. Ever unpredictable.

**Written by: Fernando Alvarado**

**Siles Family**
Alajuela – La Sabana

Don Antonio Enrique Siles, 59, is the father of Joseph, 33, and Byron, 27. All are skaters. They grew up in Alajuela, traveling from there to La Sabana to train. Joseph started training at 6 and Byron at 3. They've been national and Central American champions, they work as trainers and they rent skates. Byron sums up the values of the family well: "I'm a very positive person and I'm extremely disciplined. I'm always willing to work harder to surpass my own ability as an athlete, as well as being grateful and committed because of the great support I've received." Their accomplishments are many. Joseph's wife, Yuliana, and their son Jeicob have also been national champions.

# WHEN SOMEONE COMES IN EARLY TO DRINK

"And that one?" asks Nancy. A gray-haired man sits at the bar, way too early for a Tuesday. He has a thick mustache that doesn't appear to move any more than his smile, plus a rectangular suitcase that's not so much big as inconvenient.

"Maybe he's waiting for someone," replies Giorgio, jotting something in the notebook that he uses as an accounting system.

"A woman? I doubt he's able to get a woman aroused," says Nancy. She takes a rag, turns to the bar and mutters between her teeth, "At best, he arouses suspicions."

"What can I get you, buddy?" asks Nancy. "Straight guaro," says the gray-haired man, in a hurry. "And can you turn up the TV? I have a full sheet of lottery tickets."

Giorgio turns up the volume, without looking away from the TV. When they announce the winner, the guy puts away his tickets, making a smacking sound.

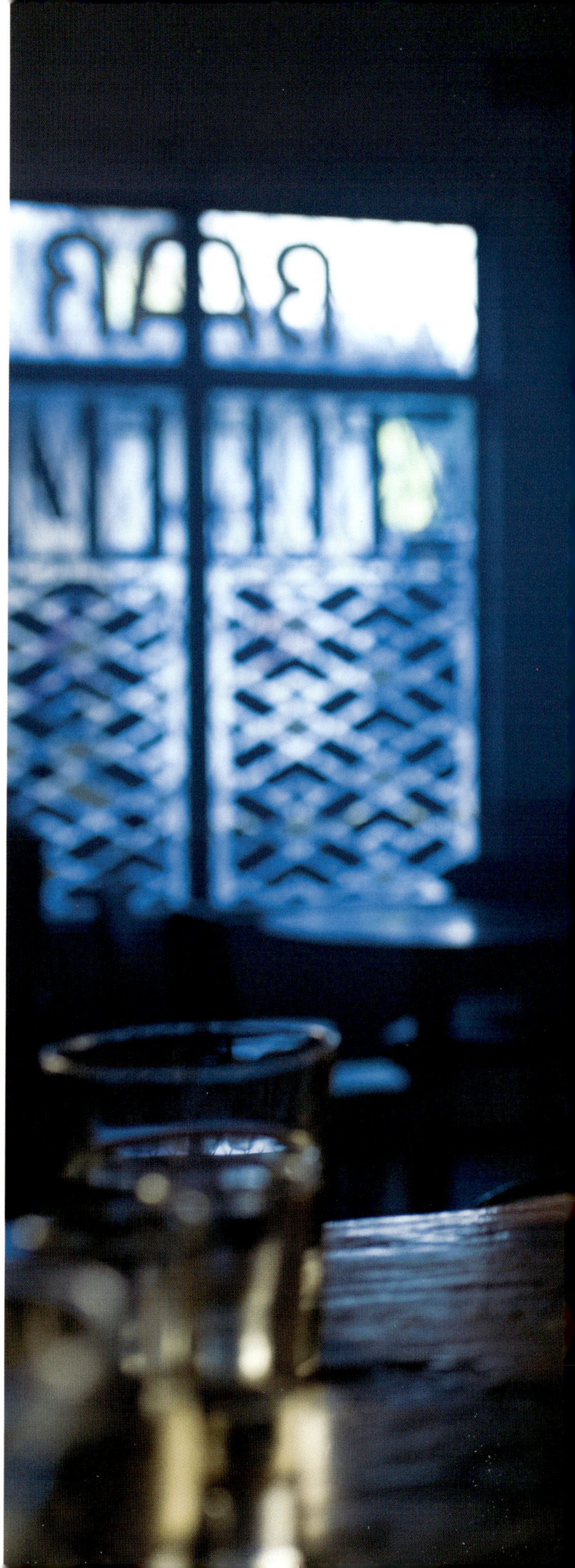

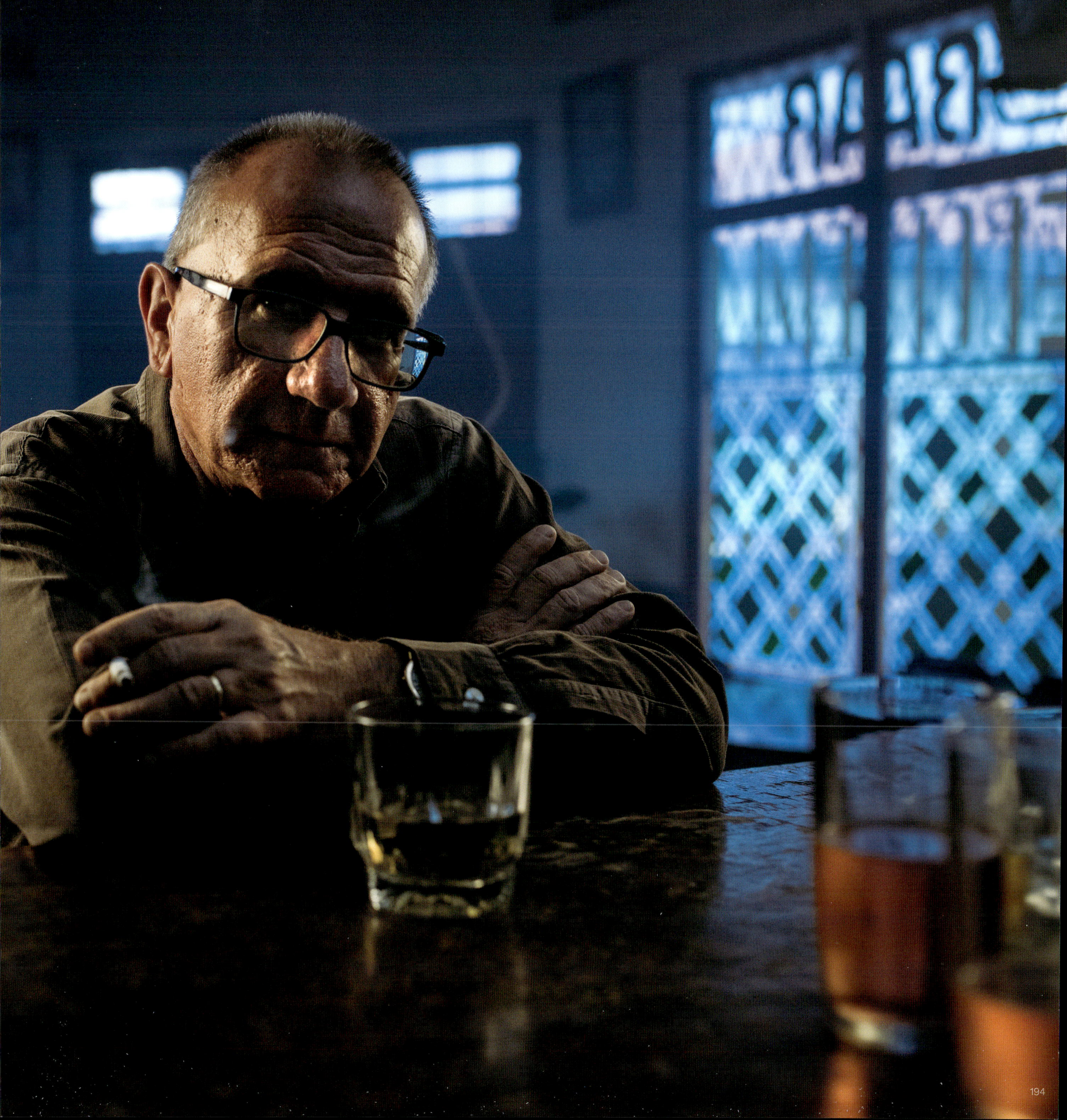

**IT'S EASY TO READ SOMEONE WHO EXAGGERATES**

"Damn, I didn't even have one number right!" he exclaims.

"It's hard to win the lottery," says Giorgio sympathetically. "I've never seen anyone here win."

"Don't believe it," says the gray-haired man. "Life is a lottery. I've seen it all." Giorgio looks at him and nods. The man is excited to see that he has someone's attention.

"Seen it all! If you can believe it, one time right here in downtown San José, what was it? Maybe ... 40 years ago ... we ran into an elephant," he relates euphorically. "Some people were chasing it, in the wee hours after midnight, and they cornered it at this bar ... La Nueva Lira, it was called. I was inside when I heard this commotion, so I threw back a drink and jumped on top of the elephant. I jumped right on his back, and we held him there until the Muni arrived!"

Giorgio offers him his drink on the rocks. "No way!" he says instinctively.

The man takes the glass and smiles nervously. His enthusiasm dissipates with his first sip. "Amigo, sorry, but do you have any odd jobs I could help out with around here?" he asks, without letting go of the drink. Giorgio pauses, looks him in the eyes and without saying a word shakes his head.

"Oh, well, look, I've got this little painting." The gray-haired man takes a rectangle out of his suitcase. "Really nice, with this lion and this girl making love under these rocks, at Stonehenge, that crazy place. I'll sell it to you." Giorgio declines again.

"Or, look, I'm really sharp," says the man, rising from his stool. "I don't think you're from here, and I'll bet you one of those collectible bottles that I can guess your nationality — I know a guy who pays good money for those. If I'm wrong, you don't give me the bottle, but let me do some work for you, I'll wash your windows tomorrow." Giorgio lowers the volume on the TV, looks at the man, and says, "OK, but if you're wrong, you wash them tomorrow."

"Absolutely, boss! OK, so with those features and hand gestures of yours, I'm going to say your ancestry is ... German!" the man says, taking a wild shot. Don Giorgio smiles, nods and hands him a fancy bottle from the shelf.

The man puts it in his suitcase, slides his stool under the bar and hands him the painting. "Keep it, man, it's going to look good here, in a German tavern," he says, and walks out of the bar smiling, without paying for his drink.

Giorgio's grandfather arrived in Costa Rica in 1927 from Calabria, Italy, and opened La Bohemia bar in 1936. The bar was passed down through the generations until, in the 1980s, it was Giorgio's. Meanwhile, his family opened other bars, including La Nueva Lira.

Nancy approaches the bar and asks, "Why did you let him win?"

"He wasn't going to come tomorrow, and besides, those bottles are worthless. Hang the painting there, above the cash register."

"How do you know?" asks Nancy.

"It's easy to read someone who exaggerates," says Giorgio.

"Of course, with that story about the elephant," says Nancy.

"The elephant story is true," says Giorgio. "I saw it that night, it had escaped from a circus."

"And so?" Nancy asks.

Don Giorgio, picking up the glass the man left behind, says, "La Nueva Lira has never been open in the wee hours."

**Written by: Luis Salazar**

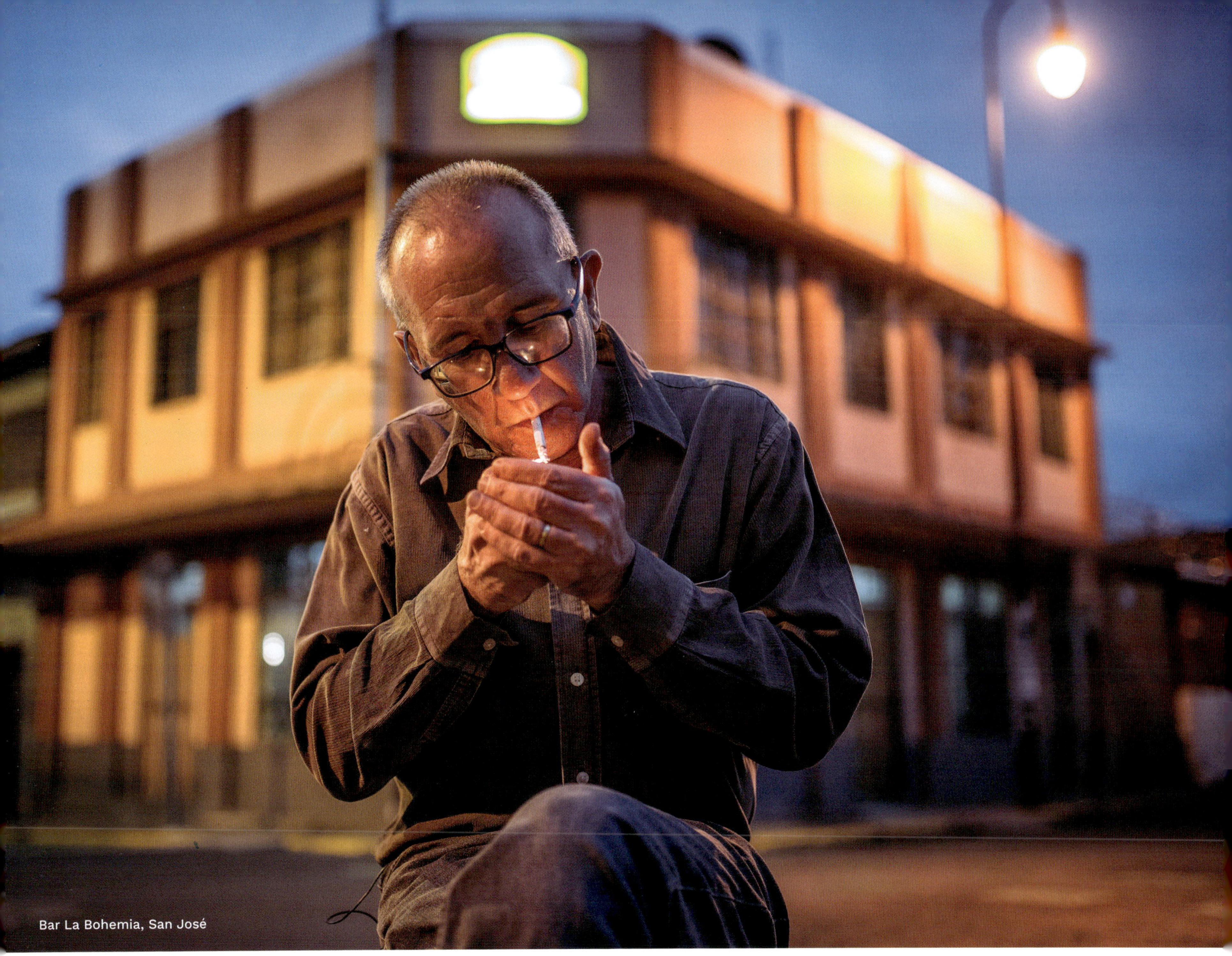

Bar La Bohemia, San José

**Jorge Motta Aronne**
San José
Born Nov. 21, 1958

Don Jorge (Giorgio) is the owner of La Bohemia, a famous cantina in downtown San José, one of the few that's still run like in the old days: with a bartender who knows his customers by name and by drink, with one of those heavy wooden bars occupying the central space. In the years he's run this family business he's seen it all: Even presidents have sat at this bar to drink a beer. Thanks to so much contact with people, he's developed a special ability to detect lies, since he's heard so many stories at this bar that he knows how to tell which ones are real, which ones are exaggerations and which ones are pure baloney.

# THE PATH OF THE COWBOY

Look, a cowboy is someone who knows how to saddle, lasso, herd cattle, braid rope, and *chucarear*. ... Don't tell me you don't know what *chucarear* is! The word is self-explanatory: *chu-ca-rear*, meaning you grab a horse and you take the *chúcaro* [wildness] out of him, but to do that you have to know how, you have to be a cowboy.... Me? No way! I'm not a cowboy, not yet, I've got a ways to go. I do know a few things, but I still have a lot to learn, and then yes, I can say I'm a real cowboy. But what I really like is working with oxen. Oh, you don't know what an ox driver is either? It's someone who teaches oxen to pull a cart, the one who prepares them, patiently, putting the yoke on them a little bit at first, then a little longer, until they get used to it, and then to teach them to haul the cart as if they were one animal, until they learn not to get ahead of each other, meaning they haul the cart together so it doesn't fall over and they don't get hurt. That's a beautiful job, because every ox driver has his own way, the words he says, the way he whistles or uses his switch to help them without hurting them. When I'm older, more than a cowboy, I want to be an ox driver. Even though I come from a family of cowboys. My grandfather, he was, well, they say he was one of the best cowboys ever. A man through and through, see: loyal to his friends, ready to take on anything in the field. He knew about everything and he was brave, but not brave like ... how do I explain? He was brave because he

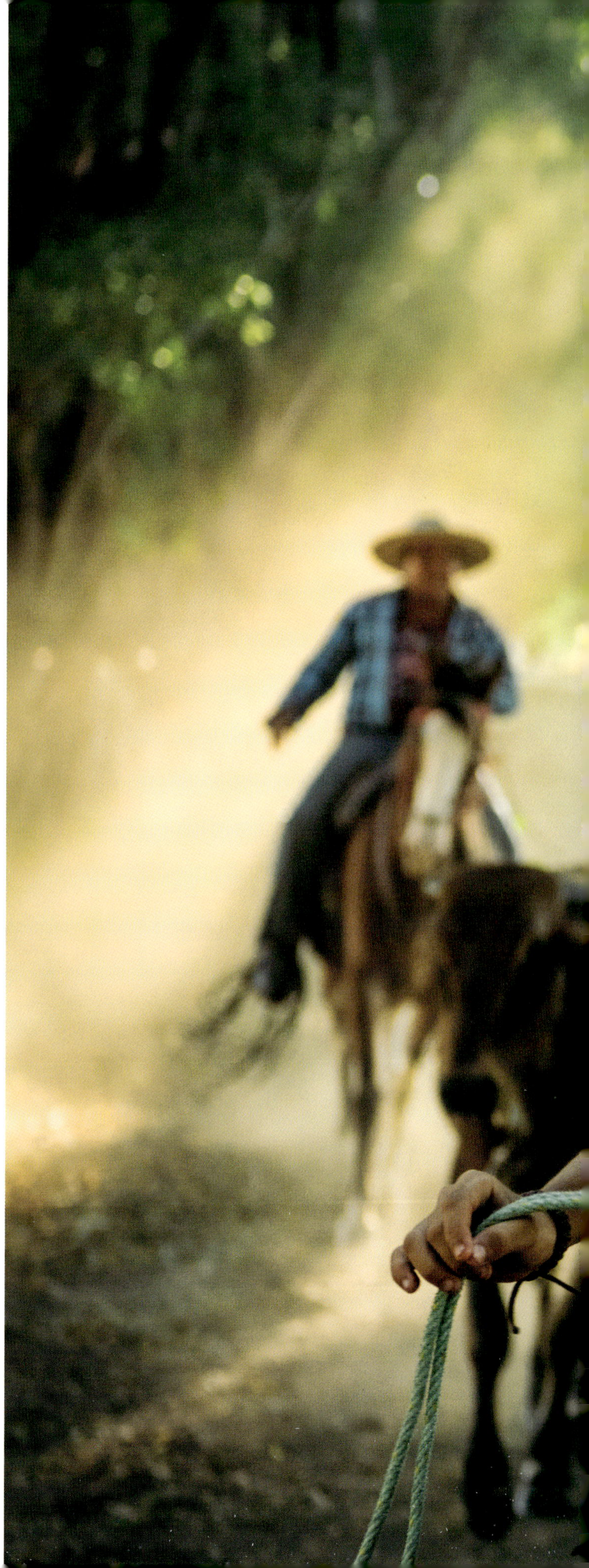

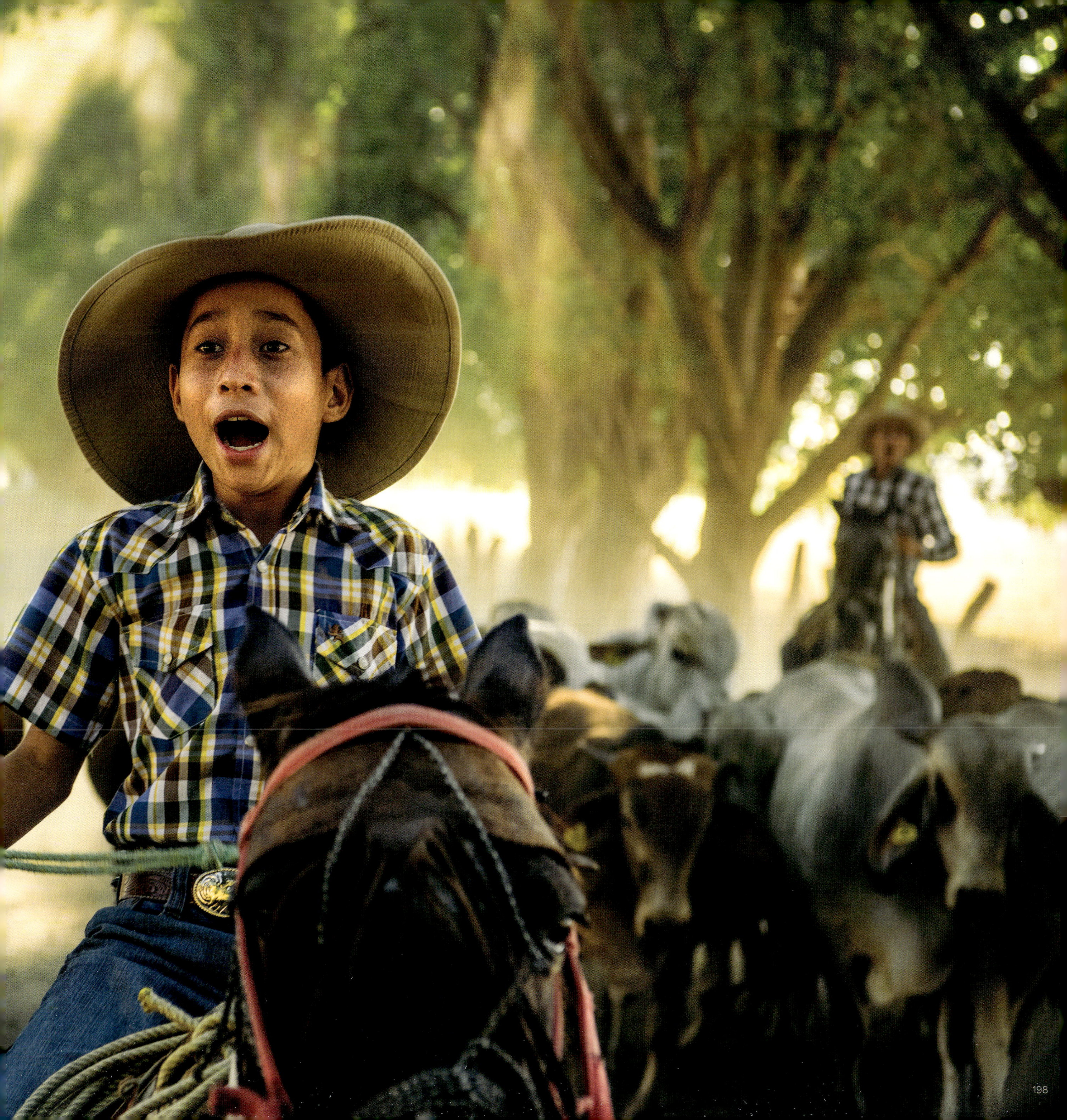

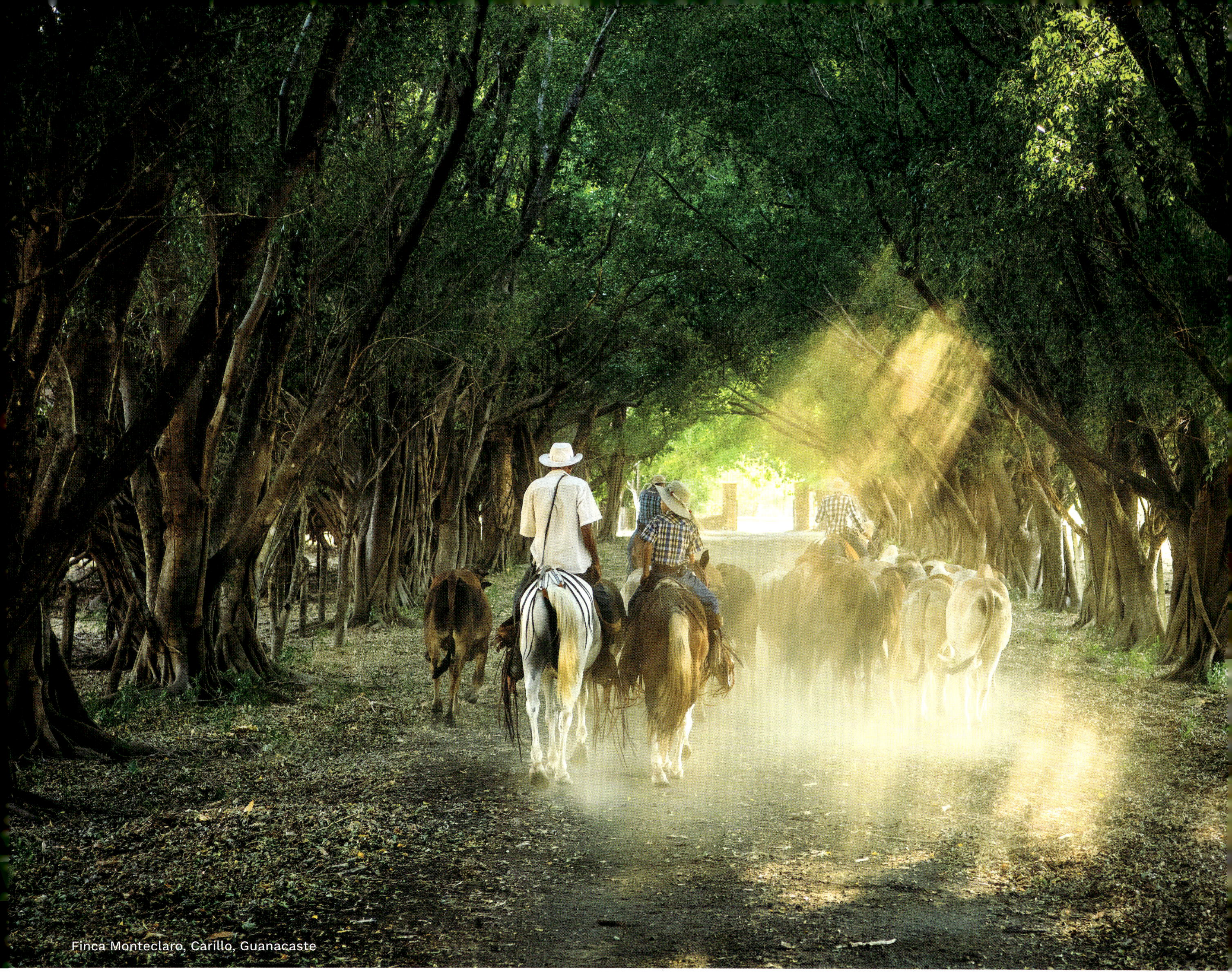

Finca Monteclaro, Carillo, Guanacaste

**Antony Daniel Coronado Cortés**
Liberia
Born Nov. 30, 2008

Born and raised in Liberia, Antony is the cowboy of the future, a young representative of the traditions of his people. At his young age, he already knows how to saddle, lasso, herd cattle, braid rope, and bust broncos. He's a polite boy, simple and intelligent, and he works hard with great enthusiasm. He learns from his Uncle Aquiles, with whom he has a very special relationship. One moonless night, Antony was riding really close to his uncle so as not to get scared, and Aquiles told him, "You'd better hurry up, or a witch monkey could jump on top of you." Antony is not satisfied with being a cowboy, and some day he hopes to become a *boyero*, an ox driver, a job that takes great dedication and effort, in which you dedicate your life to taming young bulls from an early age and training them to work wearing yokes.

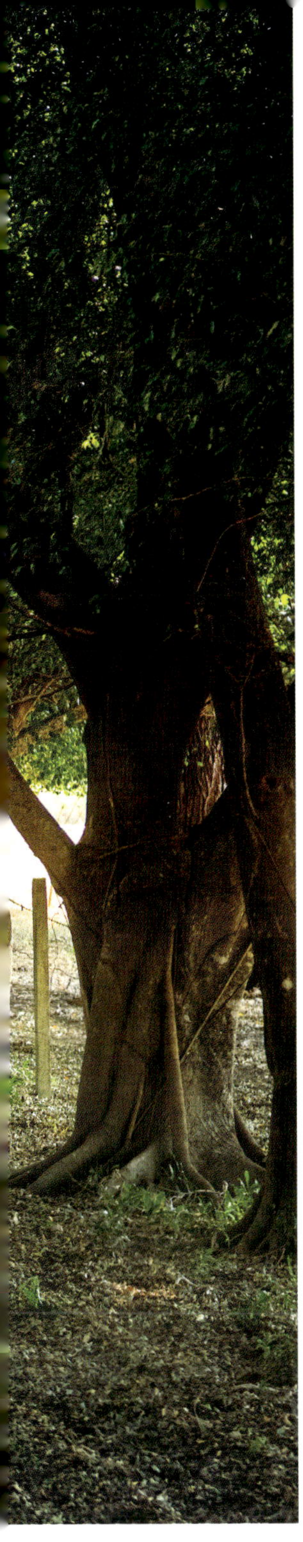

# IN FACT, THANKS TO HIM I BECAME A TV STAR

was a good man, the kind that never has to hit anybody, much less a woman, to prove he's a man. Those others aren't men, they aren't cowboys, they aren't anything. My dad always hit my mom. And I had to see that since I was little, until one day, I was, I don't know, now I'm 12, but then I was about 9, and I stood up and told him he wasn't a man or anything, and I threw a bottle at him, and to my mother, God forgive me, I told her: If you keep being a dumbass with that man, I'm leaving, and so she, I don't know what she did, but she found the courage to throw him out of the house, and so I said to that man I called my father, you know what, don't come looking for me because I'll go to the police. And he left and I've seen him around a few times, drunk, but my mom is better now. At first, I didn't like her new husband. He would approach me to talk, and I treated him badly. But later an aunt talked to me and said Antony, look, that's a good man and he treats your mom well, give him a chance and you'll see. And so I did. One day we went out and I saw that he was a great guy and he did love us, and since that day we've gotten along well. And now I call him dad, and I say it gladly, because he really is a dad, not like that other man, may God forgive him, because I won't. That's why I don't like to talk about him, but I do like to talk about my new dad and my Uncle Aquiles who ... he's a real cowboy, through and through. I've gone riding with him until it's so late at night you can't see the palm of your hand. With my uncle, I'm not afraid of anything. In fact, thanks to him I became a TV star, because one time someone uploaded a video of mine on YouTube telling a *retahíla* [a type of loudly recited verse], and Max Barberena saw it, and he called my uncle to see if I wanted to go to the Zapote rodeo to tell my *retahíla* on TV, in front of 2,000 people, at the end of the year. You wouldn't believe what that was like. Unforgettable. The second one I dedicated to [the model] Marcela Negrini, and later everyone here teased me by saying I had found a new girlfriend over there. But definitely not, because I'm faithful to my girlfriend, the one from over here, and I treat her well, because that's how real men are.

**Written by: Jaime Gamboa**

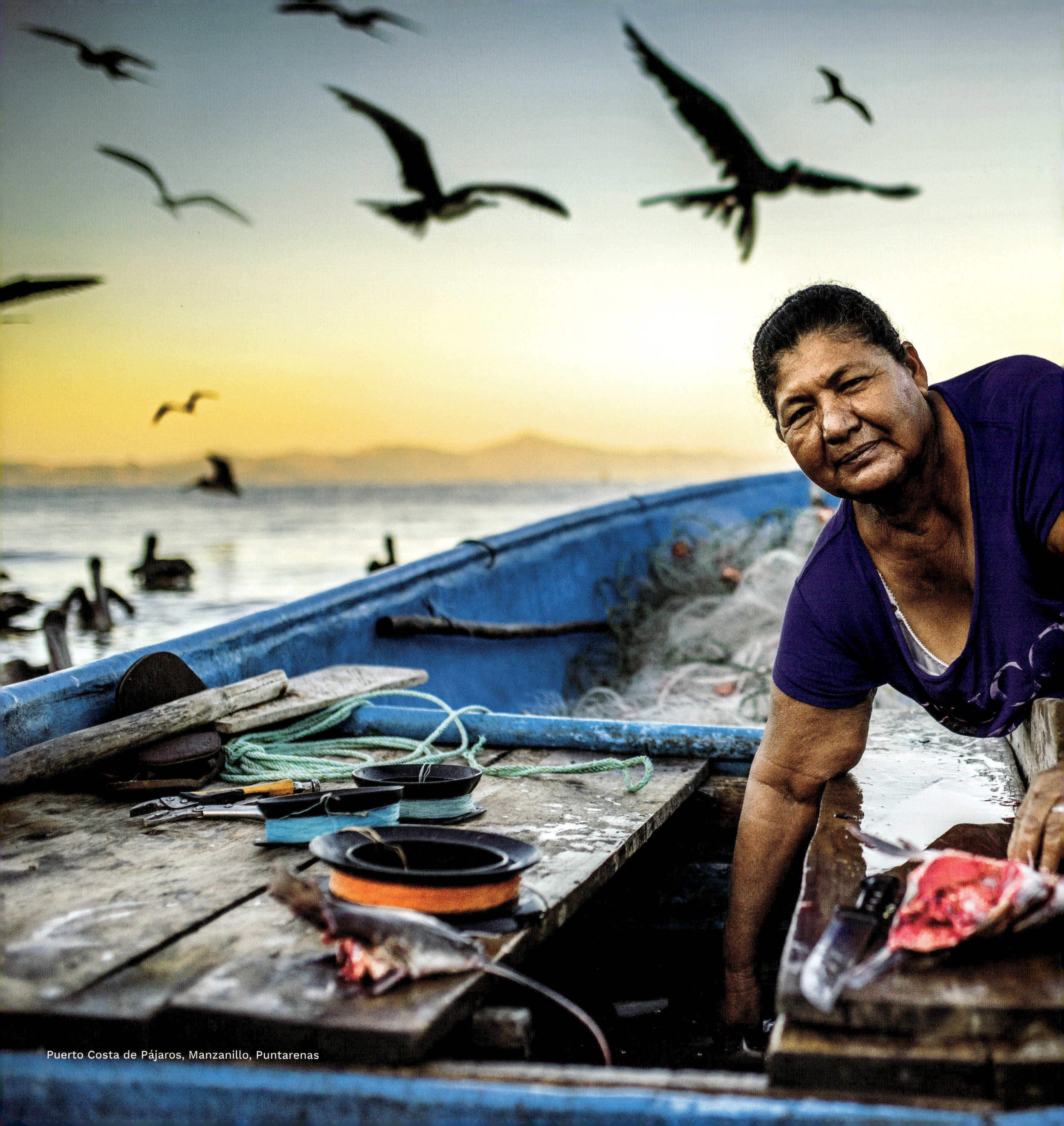

Puerto Costa de Pájaros, Manzanillo, Puntarenas

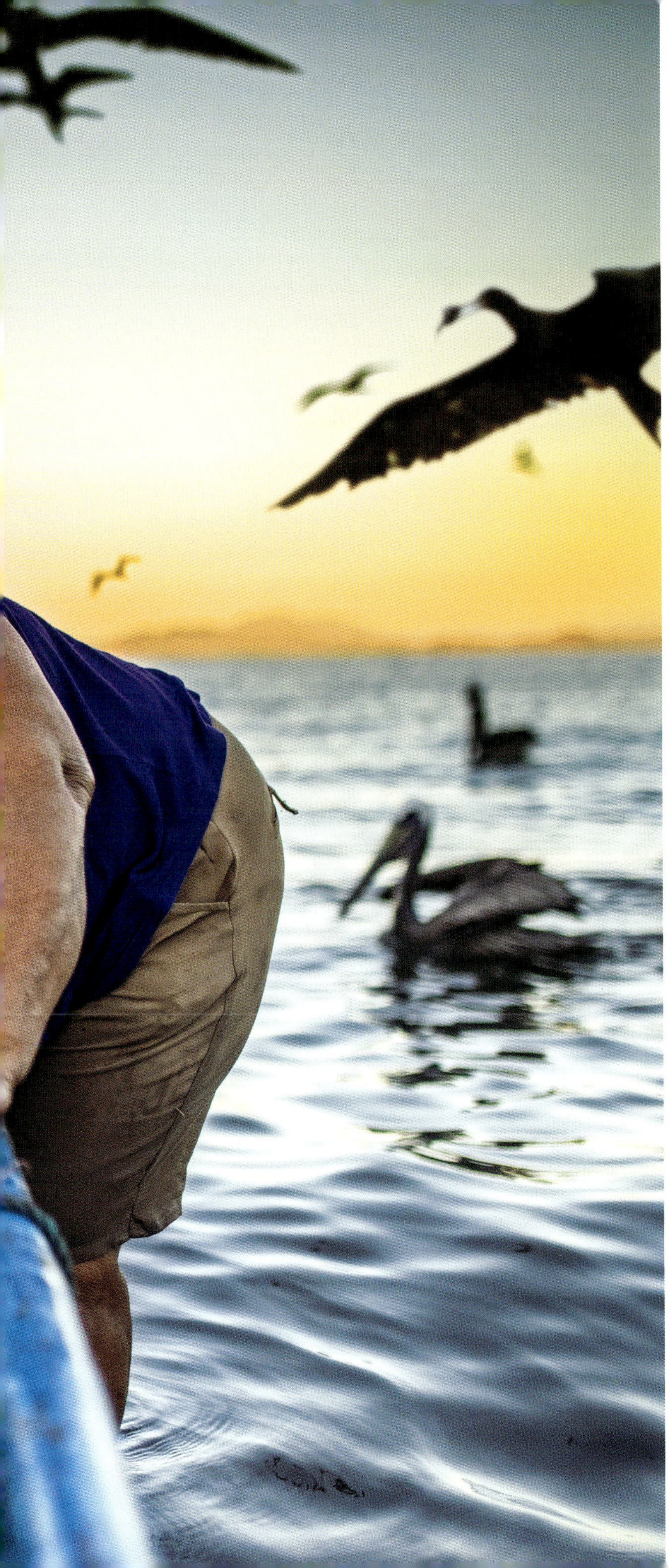

# SEA OF LOVE

"Auntie, do you know how to swim?"

The boat, buffeted furiously by the waves, started filling with water. When the buoy and the lead weight slipped through a crack in the bottom, Estebana knew they were going to sink.

She wasn't afraid of the sea. When she threw out her gillnet earlier, it got stuck on some rocks and she couldn't get it loose, even with the help of some other fishermen who passed by. And now this. She thought about her two kids waiting for her at home, and her brother, who was counting on her to bring both his son and his boat home safe and sound. They had to make it back.

Within minutes, the boat disappeared into the dark underbelly of the Gulf of Nicoya, and she swam and prayed with all her strength, without letting go of the little boy. She told him to hold onto a piece of wood, which she tried to tow toward the island, hoping someone would rescue them. An eternity later, she saw a boat from afar. The sea was still furious; she raised her exhausted arms and screamed, the waves hitting her in the face. What if they don't see us? Those fierce waters that gave birth to her 16 years before seemed to want to swallow her whole.

Finally, they were spotted and rescued. As soon as she set foot on land, Estebana ran to embrace her little children, crying and crying until her tears became a stream that reached the ocean. That day, she and the sea made a truce. The next months she would dedicate to working until she had her own boat and fishing equipment.

For countless generations of these bronzed women, like Estebana and the Princess Chira — the first inhabitant of the island, according to Chorotega legend — the world is 43 square kilometers of earth and 2,500 square kilometers of water. There they fish, suffer and love. "If you fall down, you get up even stronger, by the grace of my Lord Jesus Christ," who has given strength every day to Estebana and her six children. They are all from the same man, who married another woman and never lived with her, but he gave her 29 years of abuse and mistreatment. She raised the kids alone, gave them an education and taught them her trade. When the oldest of them had to get a kidney transplant, she said "Enough," and broke up forever with her abuser.

Later she met Jesus.
They are made for each other. She knew it before him and went looking for him at his house. "I asked his mother for him, I asked her to let me come in to visit him." She pulled him onto her ample, generous lap and told him, "Papi, I'm going to take care of you, my love." A little later, she was told that he was in the hospital; he had been thrown by his horse and had injured two vertebraes. She took care of him for two months. They got married.

Jesús Peralta is also from Chira. They go out together to throw out gillnets, fish with lines and collect clams, *pianguas* (blood cockles) and chora mussels; and they raise pigs and chickens for Christmas. He loves her with a single lung, as he lost the other one in a work accident. "He supports me in everything, and I do the same for him. We keep going, hand in hand, always moving forward. If things didn't work out well today, maybe they will tomorrow." In the bloom of maturity, he taught her to love and to love herself. She, who felt worthless, who had never been loved by anyone, with Jesús felt loved "just because I am a woman."

At 56 years old, Estebana Pérez thinks "life is wonderful." Her resounding laugh rises above the song of the birds in the dry tropical forest, above the whistle of the refreshing, salty wind. Afar off, the sea washes up at Chira's feet, offering its daily bounty of fish and mollusks.

**Written by: Abril Gordienko**

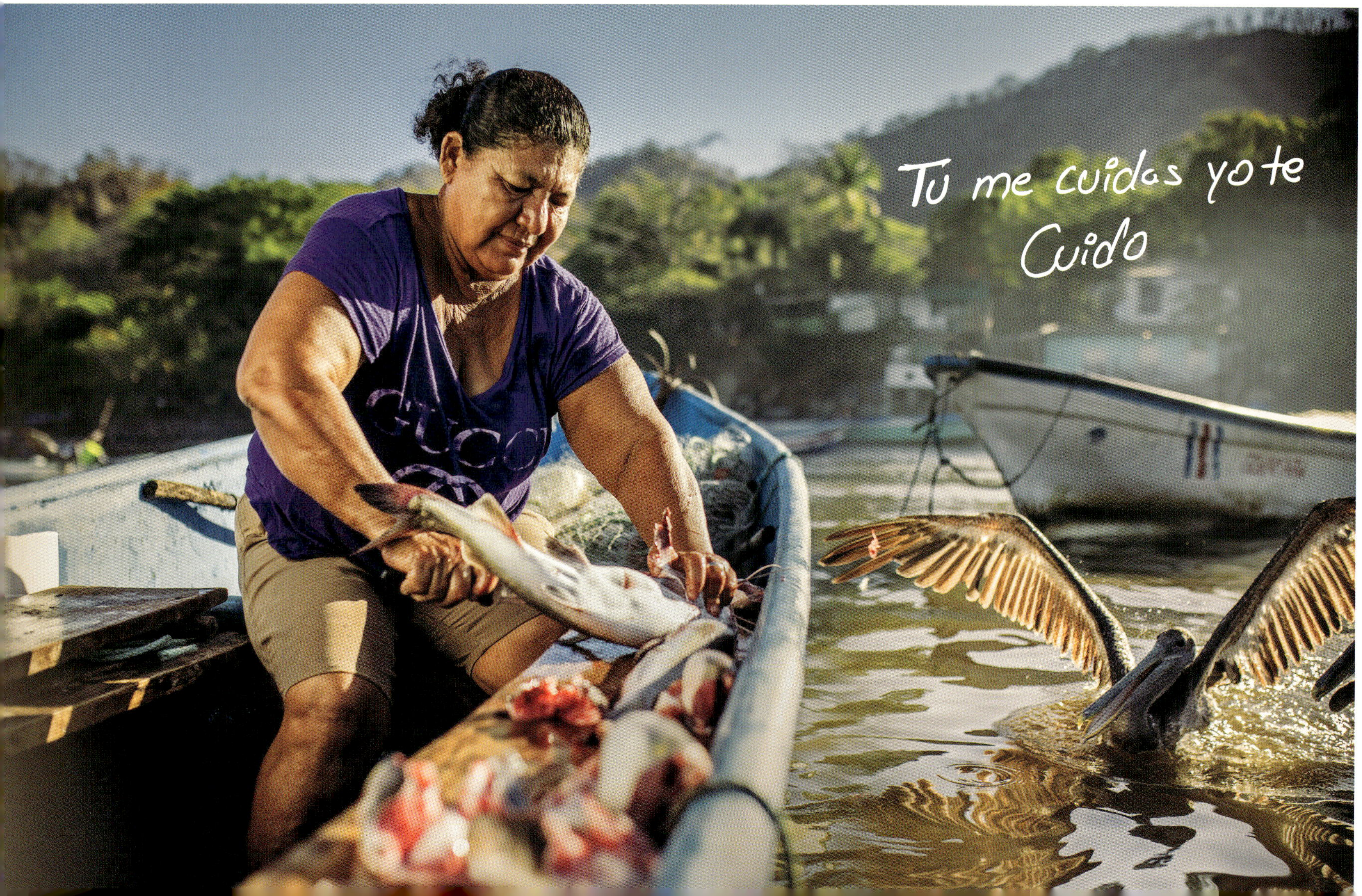

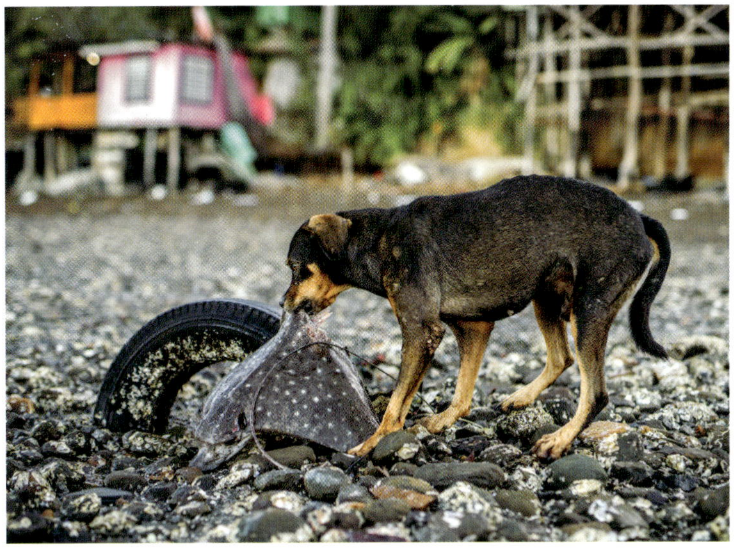

Puerto Costa de Pájaros, Manzanillo, Puntarenas

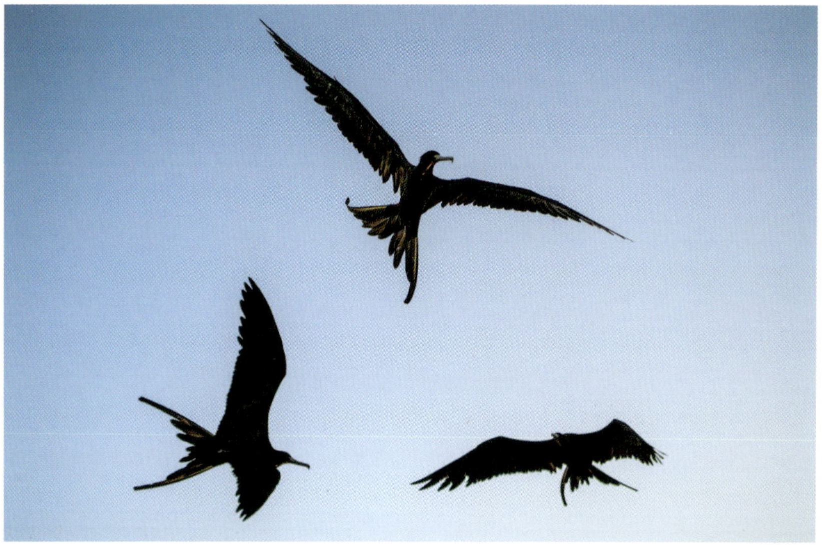

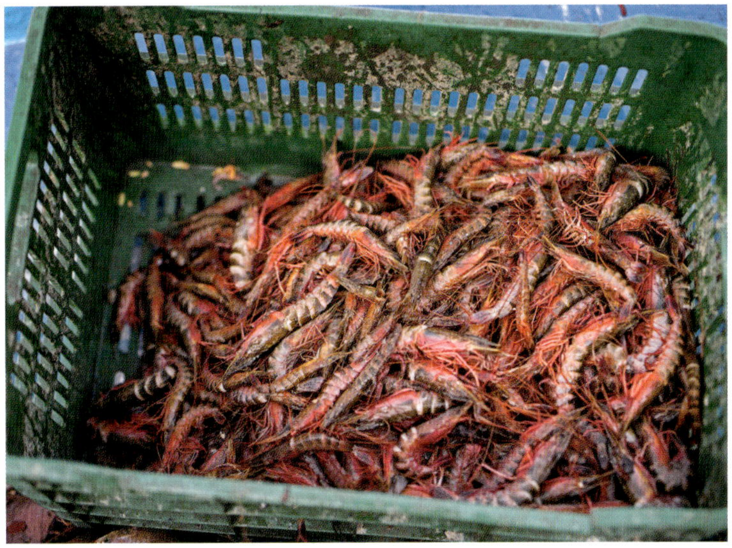

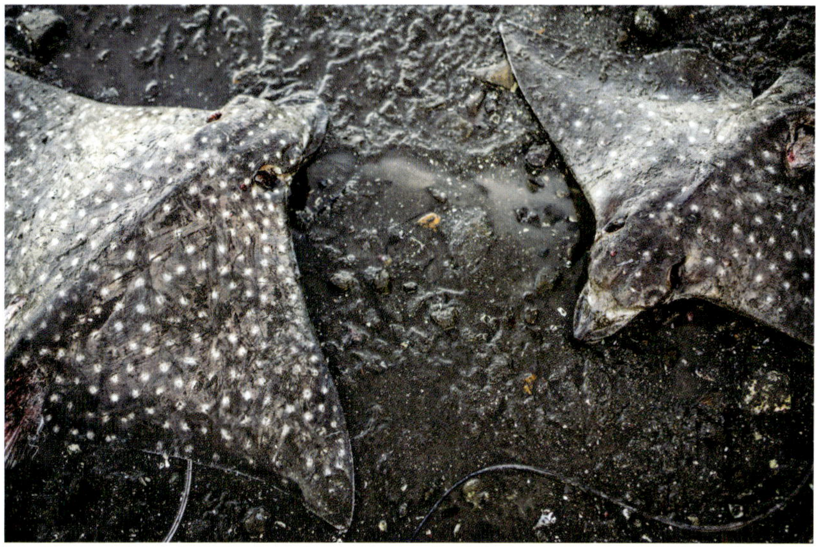

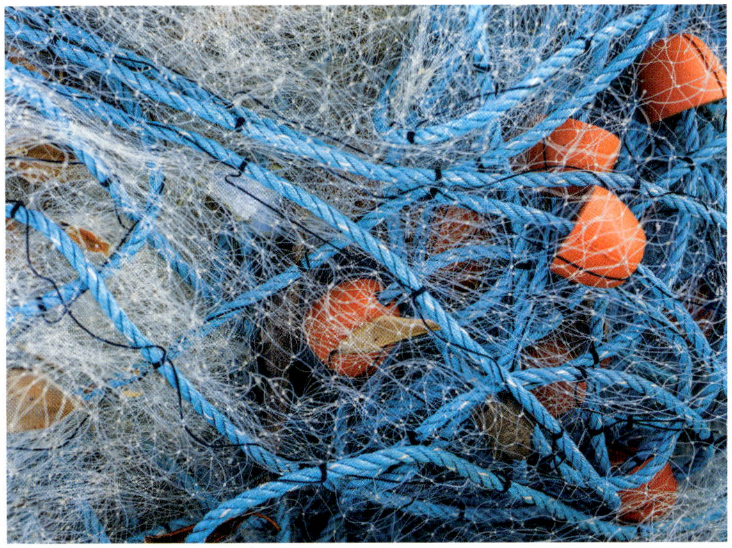

• Some 10,000 people in Costa Rica rely on fishing to support their families.

**Estebana Pérez Martínez**
Golfo de Nicoya
Born Dec. 30, 1963

Estebana is an artisanal fisherwoman. She was born and has spent her entire life on Chira Island, where this occupation is pursued in a sustainable manner by many women. Her father taught her the fishing trade, which she's been doing forever. A single mother of six children (Marlon, Elizabeth, Cristofer, Carol, Ana Lujeidi and Vladimir), she worked very hard for many years to support them. "I always found the courage to keep moving forward. A person falls down, but you get up even stronger to keep going. I don't look back, always forward." Estebana knows what she's talking about, because in her life nothing has been easy. That's how fishing is: some days yes, some days no; no matter how hard you work, the sea decides. Six years ago she married Jesús, her current partner, and they help each other to keep moving forward. They walk around town holding hands. Estebana says of him, "I found love when I was old; he taught me that you can be loved just as you are."

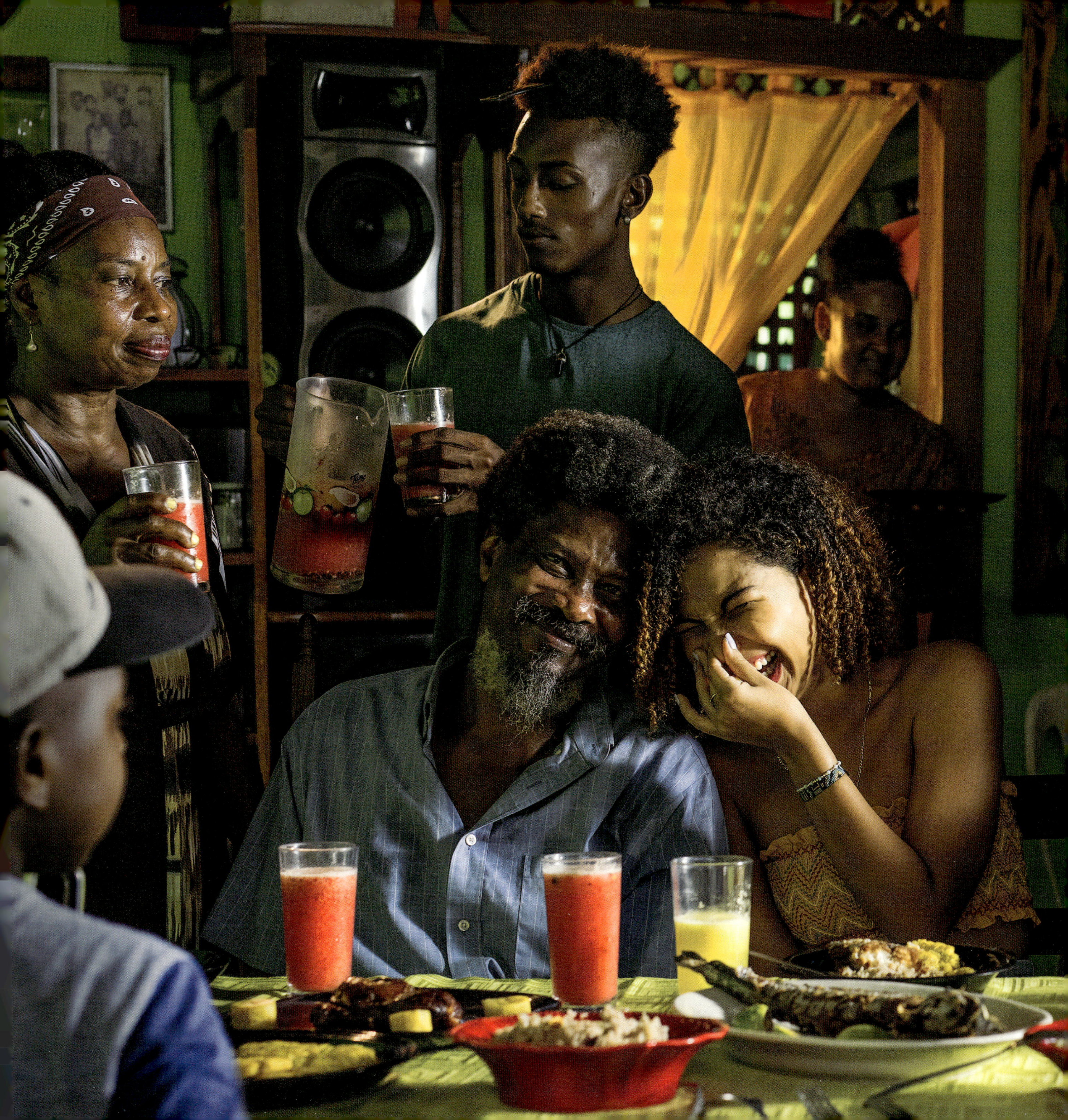

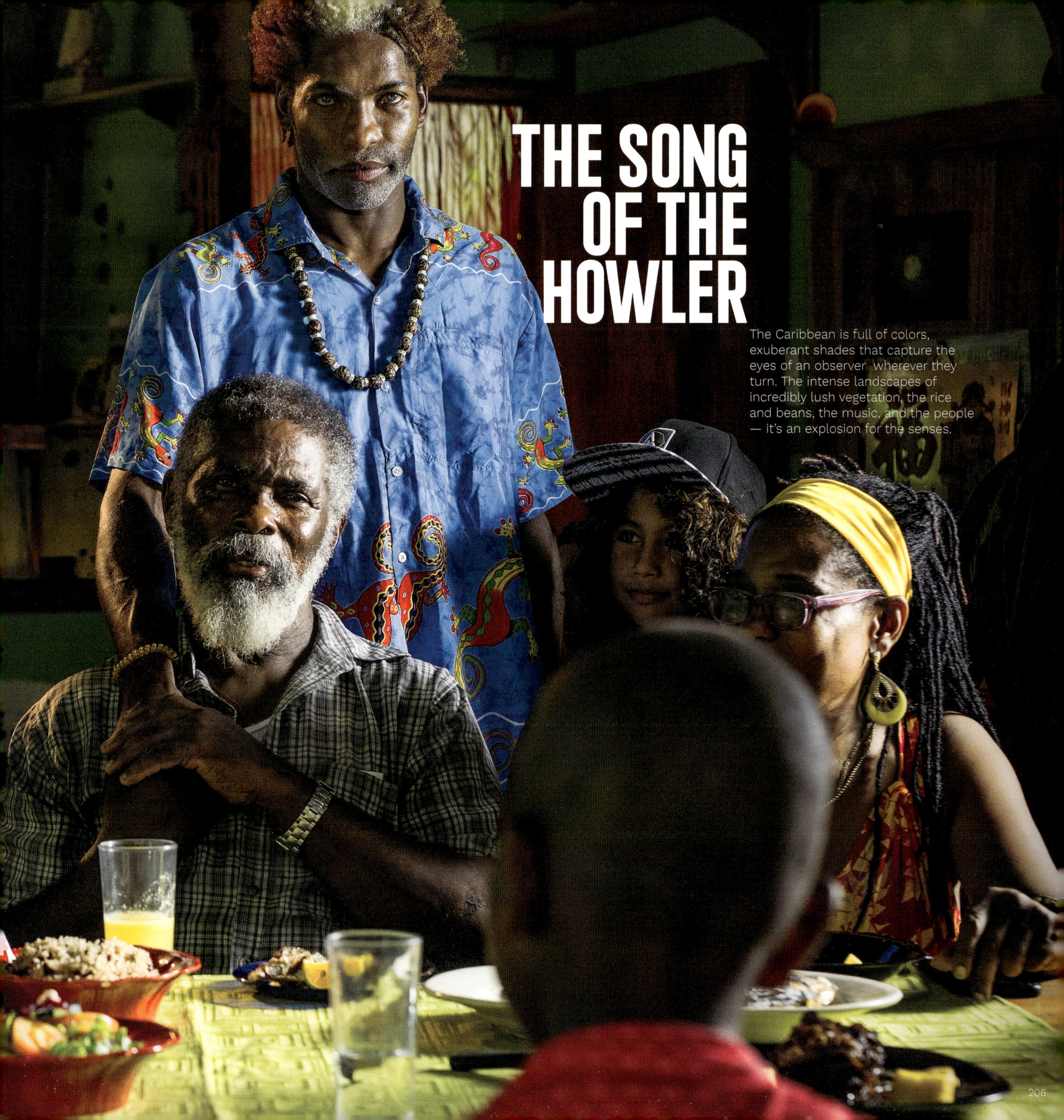

# THE SONG OF THE HOWLER

The Caribbean is full of colors, exuberant shades that capture the eyes of an observer wherever they turn. The intense landscapes of incredibly lush vegetation, the rice and beans, the music, and the people — it's an explosion for the senses.

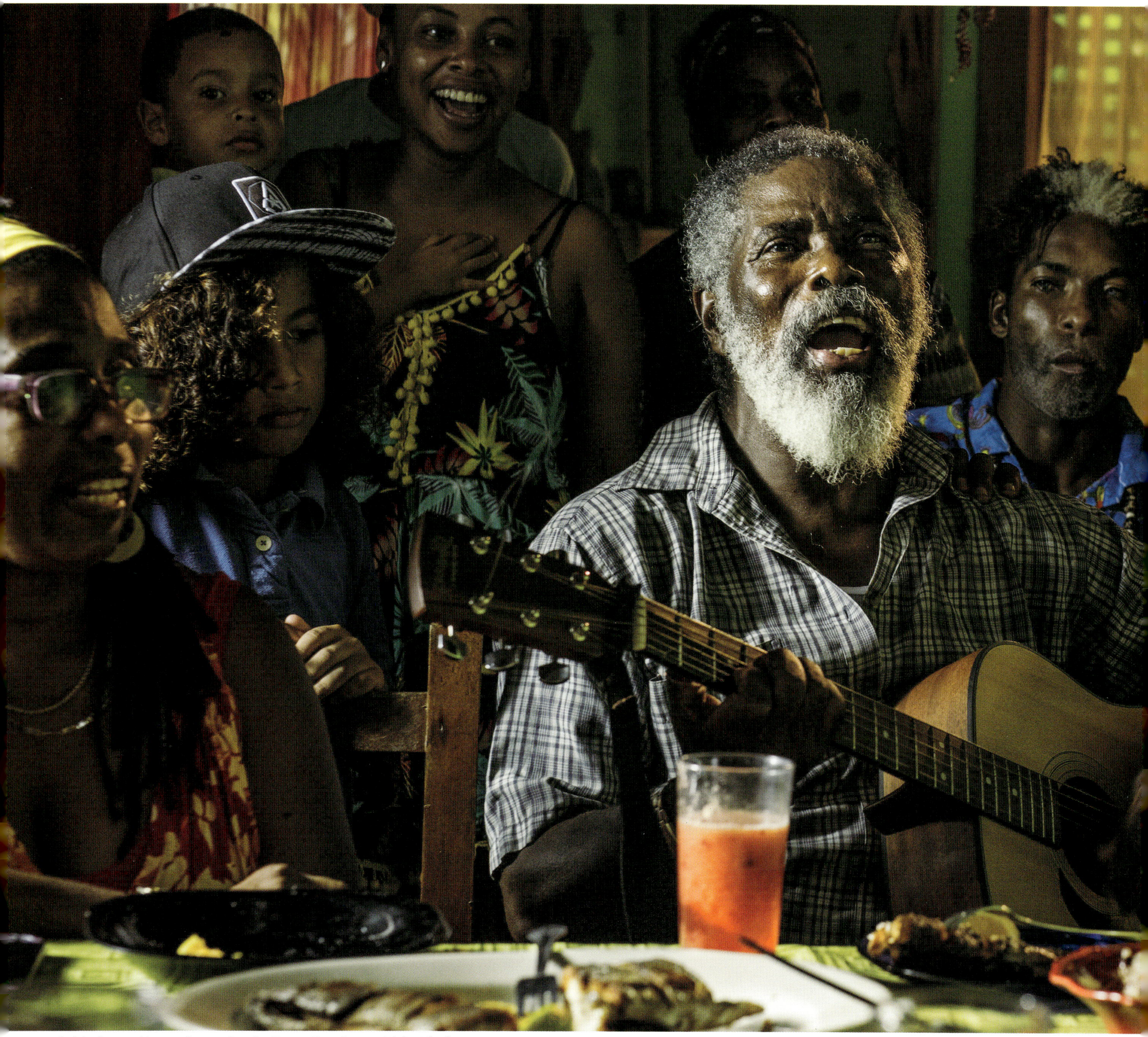

Selvin Brown House, Brown Family. Punta Uva, Puerto Viejo, Limón.

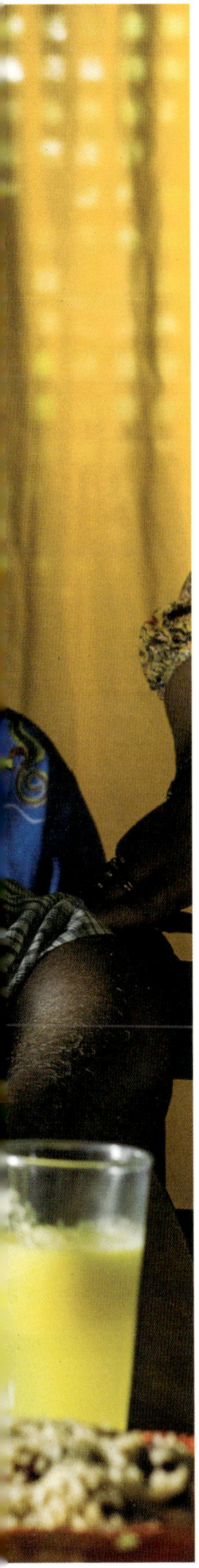

One night in October, immersed in this beauty, I was walking with my friend through Puerto Viejo, like a lot of city people who migrate to the south Caribbean at that time of year to escape the storms that occur on the other side of the mountains. Suddenly some crystalline blue eyes, like the sea at Playa Chiquita, called to us. A man with an impressive body got up and started moving his arms enthusiastically, gesturing for us to approach. It was Carl Brown. That same day we had met at his Uncle Selvin's restaurant. His attractive, almond-shaped body, his odd white lock of hair, his incandescent irises, his tenderness for his family, and his charisma, capable of communicating so much while saying so little, made an impact on us. Excited and in unison, we crossed the street to greet him on the edge of the beach. Soon, we were laughing loud together, and with that, I dared to ask him about his life. His teeth were shining, and he nodded his head in agreement. He loves to tell stories.

Within minutes, we were immersed in his world. First, he picked up a little branch from the ground that he used to point out places and objects. He made hand gestures in the air to express himself, and from time to time he drew in the sand as if it was a big blackboard, and his foot was the eraser. He had us mesmerized. Without words. We forgot about the raucous Friday night dance floor at Stanford's bar, or the nocturnal party creatures dancing around us. At that moment, all that existed was Carl and the sea breeze breathing at our feet.

*It's still not dawn, the sky is dark but clear, and Carl is pedaling his bicycle because he has to get to his construction job very early. Relaxed, on his way to a normal day, he looks ahead in case he runs into anyone to greet: maybe a night owl who hasn't made it home yet, some surfer who can't wait to hit the water, maybe a fisherman friend left behind by one of the boats missing from the shore. At his side, the tropical rainforest begins to wake up, subtle rays of light start to penetrate the tangled jungle, the insects become less active, the birds come to life — seed eaters, oropendolas, and even a few mammals.*

*Puum.... Puum.... Suddenly he feels this drumming in his chest. (His pupils dilate as he tells this part.) He keeps pedaling, trying to decipher that "puum" that keeps shaking him. The closer he gets to the forest, the more he feels it. He stops, lays the bike down and goes in. His heels get wet from the leaves he brushes against, with the immensity of the forest all around him, his senses on full alert. Puum ... it starts hitting him harder and harder. Puum ... no pain, but he can feel the impact. Puum ... stronger. He looks up, and there they are, between the jobo and the trumpet trees: The howler monkeys are no longer sleeping, the troop greets the day, Carl understands what's happening, and he's astonished.*

He opens his eyes and stares at us as if we had been there. It isn't the first time he sees the monkeys howl. That frequency that attacks the entire body, it's nothing more or less than the song of the howlers. Yes! It is the first time that he hears them.

*After contemplating the scene in a state of total surrender and admiration, he runs, jumps on his bike, rides to his father's house, and throws himself into his arms. They smile, deeply moved.*

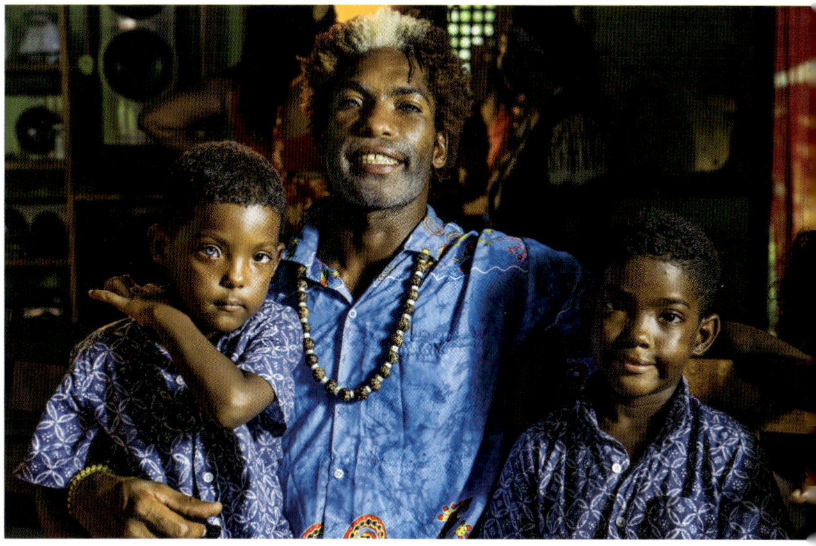

We lowered our feet to the sand to go back, while Carl used his to erase the doodles he'd made. I looked at my friend, both of us hiding teary eyes. Can nature really be so powerful? Giving this gift to a man born deaf, who transported us to that place without speaking a word. With a big hug we said goodbye to Carl, with the feeling in our chests of those howlers that we heard and felt but didn't see.

**Written by: Maria Teresa Brenes**

**Carl Cunningham Brown and the Brown family**
Punta Uva
Born April 19, 1988

Carl is deaf and has heterochromia, meaning his eyes are different colors (and he also has one lock of hair that's white and one that's red). He has a son who lives outside the country, whom he misses very much. He also lived abroad for a while, but he returned to the Caribbean because he doesn't like the cold. He has a large family, in which good food is very important. In fact, his Aunt Elena and Uncle Selvin are well-known in Punta Uva and Puerto Viejo, where they have little restaurants that are famous for their delicious food. They're a loving family that, thanks to a simple lifestyle and a leisurely rhythm, know how to be present and enjoy each moment, without thinking much about the future. Of the Brown siblings, several are deaf, some have heterochromia and some were born with a white lock of hair.

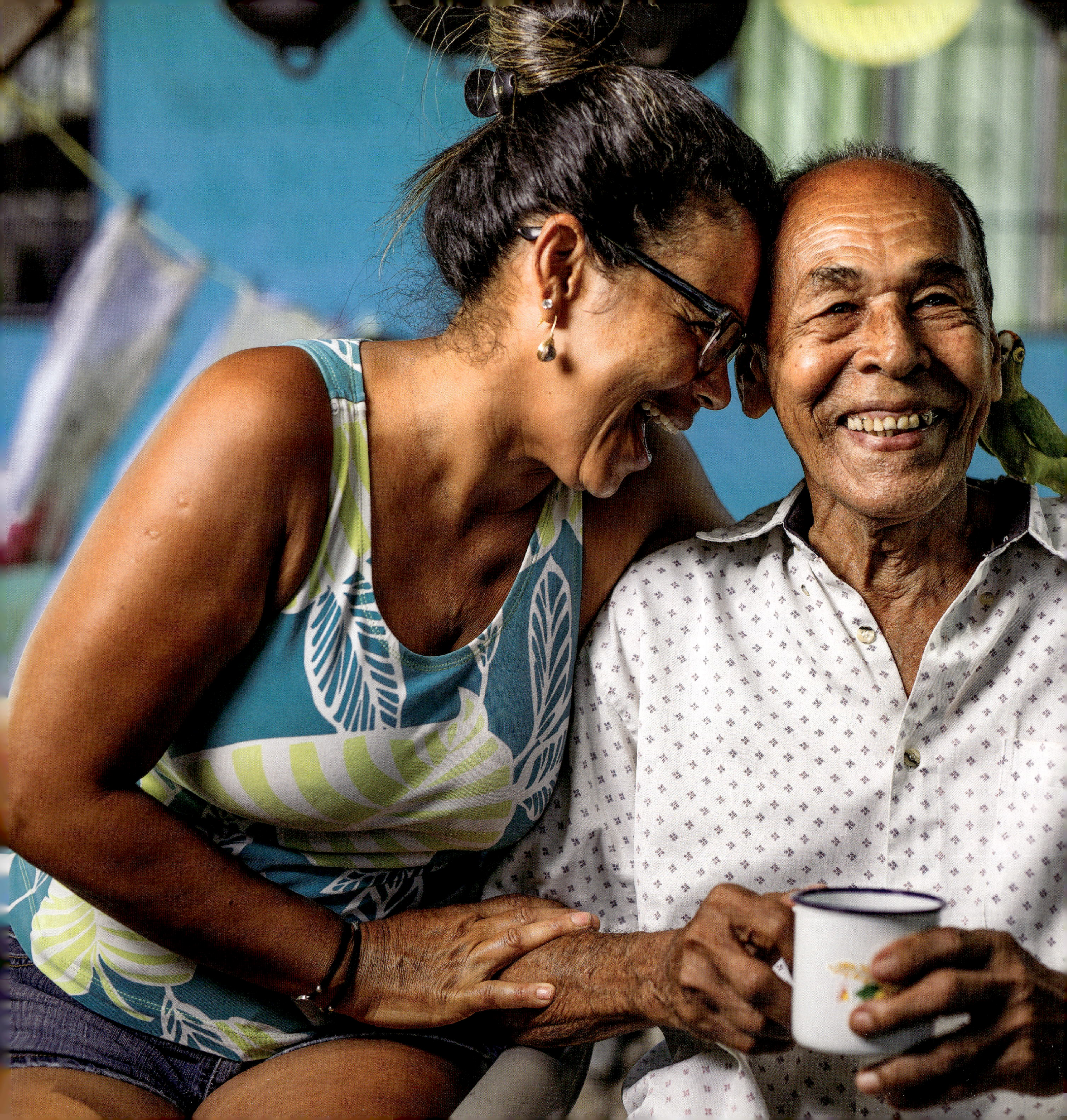

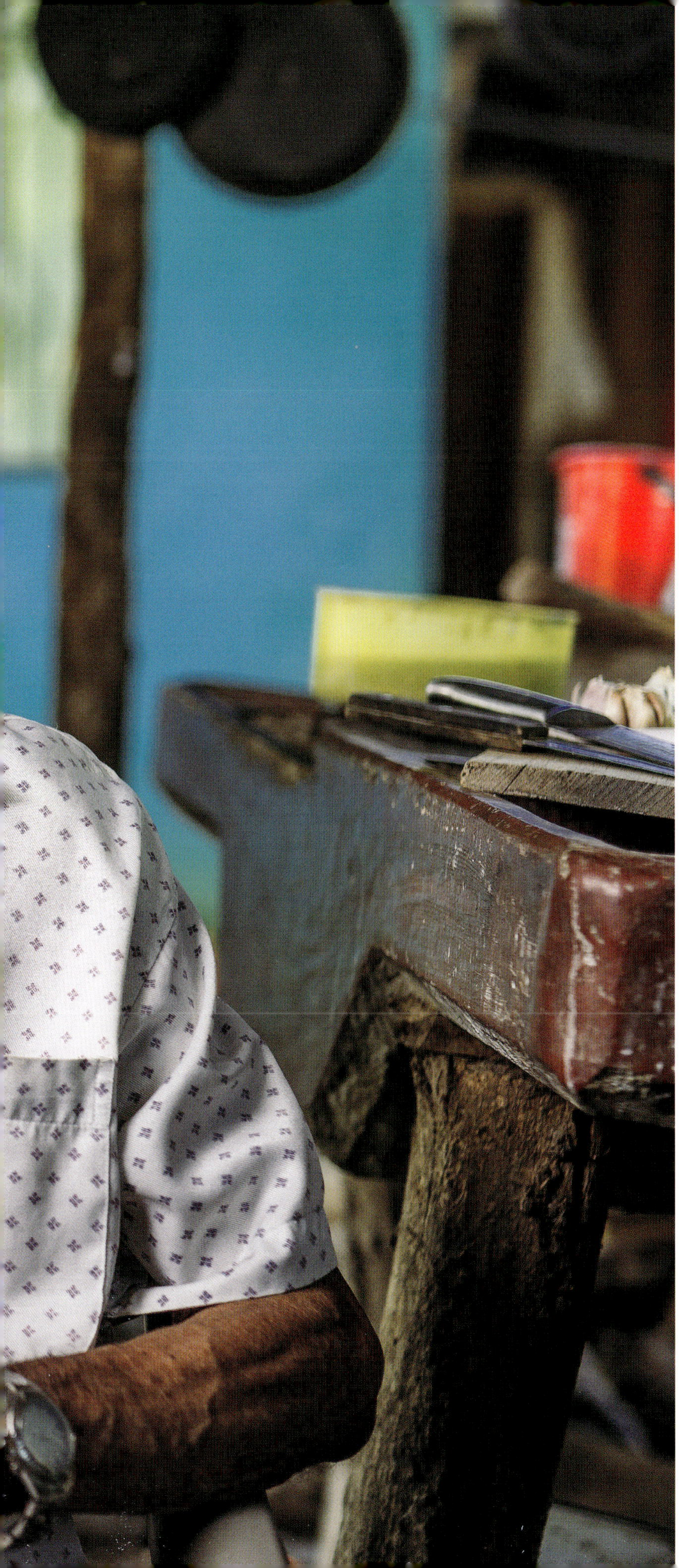

# A TOWN GOES UP IN DUST

Manuel Zamora was born in a place where the sun burns your pupils, in Villarreal, Santa Cruz, Guanacaste. As if from a typical Costa Rican painting, his youth unfolded amid the dust clouds of the endless gravel roads, cutting firewood, the tireless search for dances, finding all the wrong lovers, and playing soccer on the field downtown.

Although the soccer championships seemed like battlefields more than mere games, that was where he started a friendship with the man who would become the owner of the first hotel in Tamarindo. Their friendship, almost a brotherhood, turned Manuel into the man in charge of placing the cornerstone for the construction of the hotel. There he worked as a bartender, cashier, and waiter.

Dancing didn't just move his body, it moved his soul. "I loved dances, I rode a horse to wherever they were. We danced to cowboy music, drank *guaro* straight and said when we ordered it: 'Bring me a bottle, a handful of salt and a woman to sit beside me!" The partying and dancing went on and on, and so did the shots of firewater.

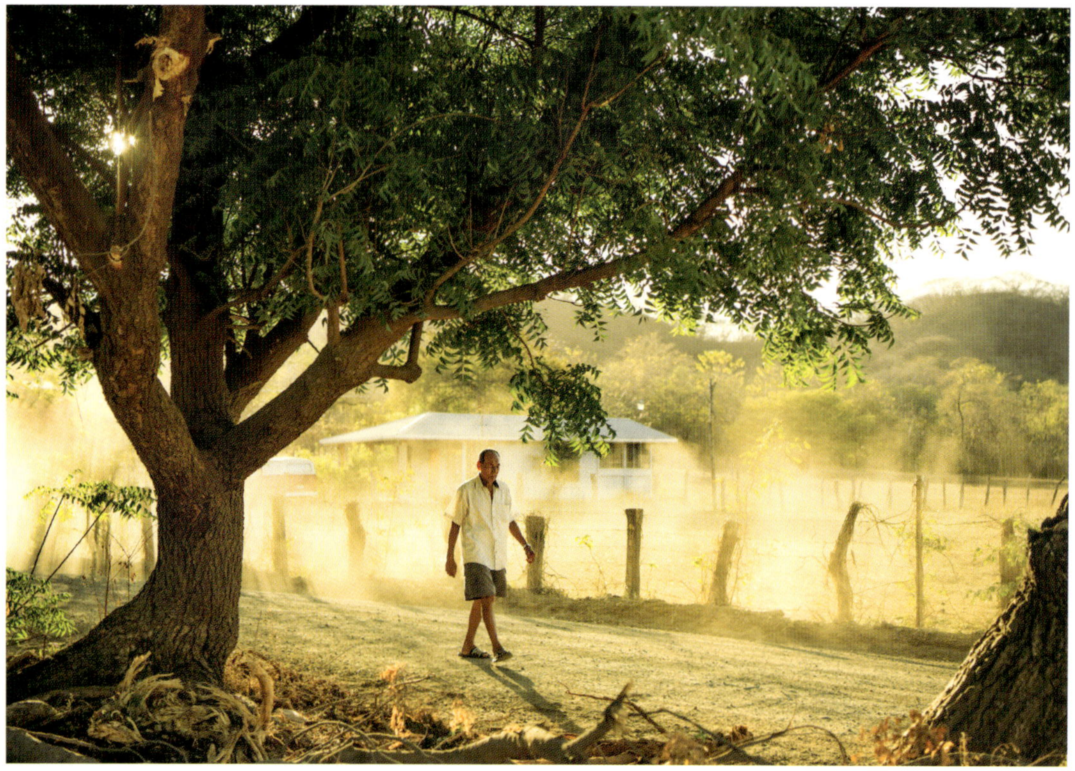

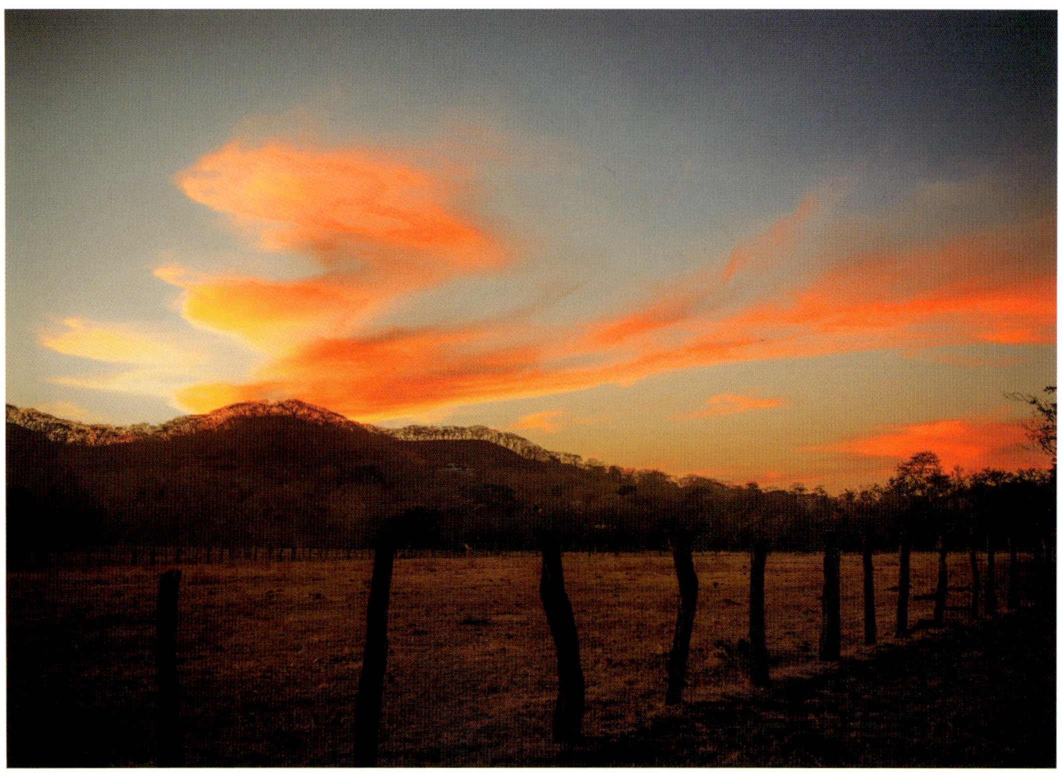

As for the dry, dusty soccer field that Manuel knew when he was young and partying, he never imagined that one day, in addition to bulls, horses, and people taking shortcuts across it, it would become the location for an event that wouldn't leave anybody's shoes clean.

It was in March of 1994, in honor of its patron saint San José, that Villarreal organized the big festival. As was common, the construction of the bullring was the responsibility of the townspeople. With the suffocating heat, the dry ground, the dusty field, and the racket orchestrated by hammers, nails and boards, Manuel crossed the road to the iconic cantina Villa Costa and asked for a donation of a liter of guaro for the workers to share.

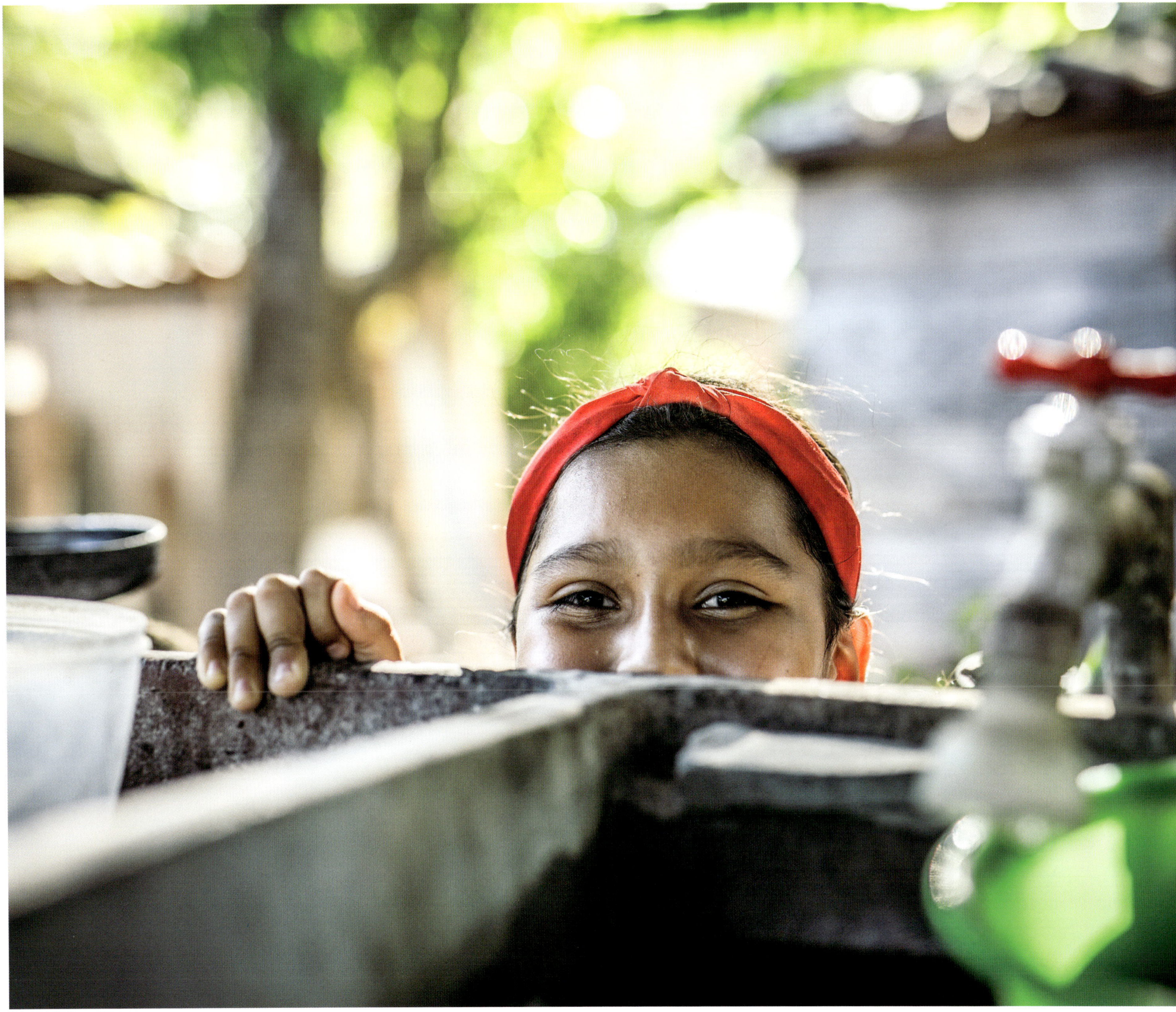

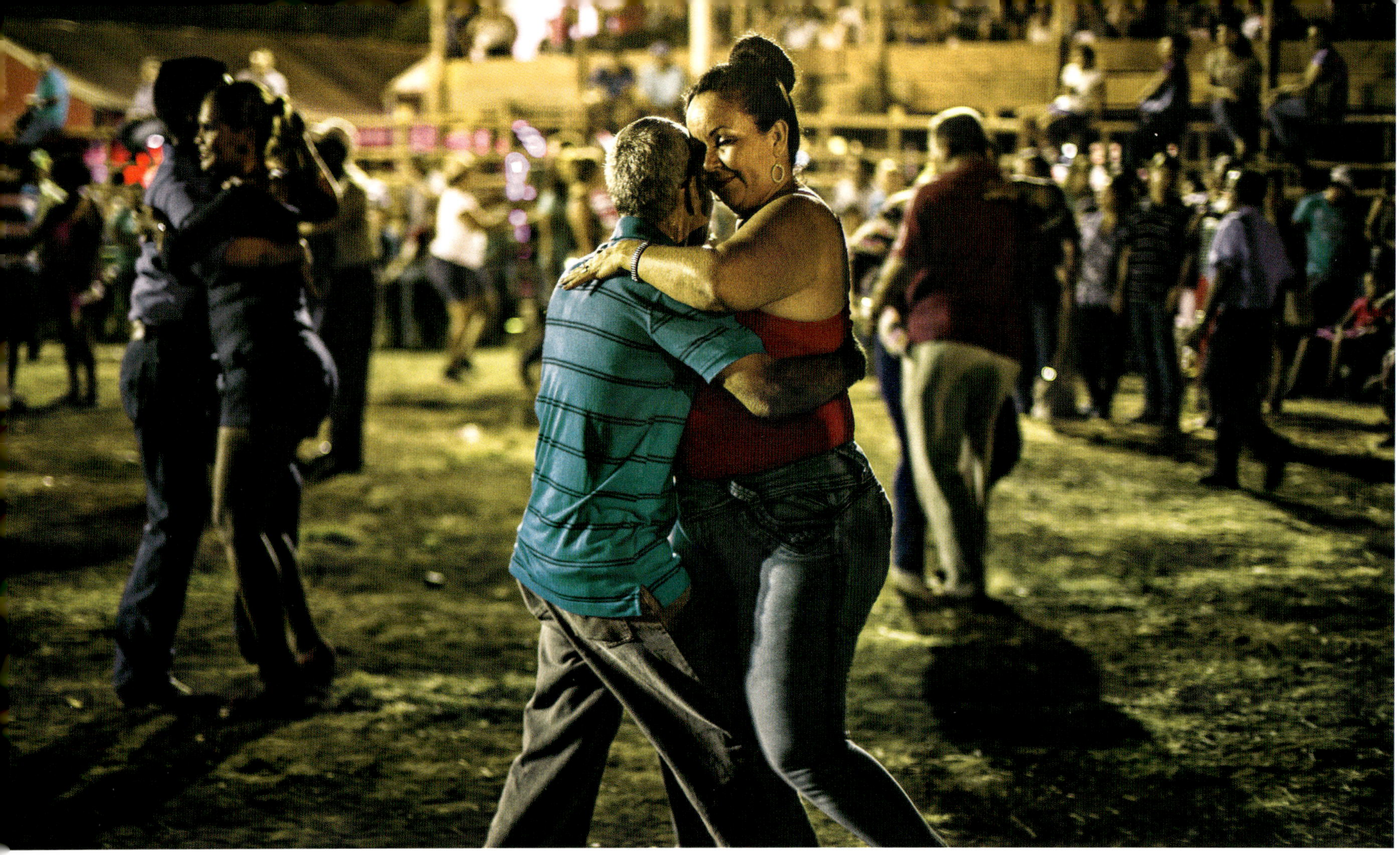

Dust dance, Villareal, Santa Cruz, Guanacaste

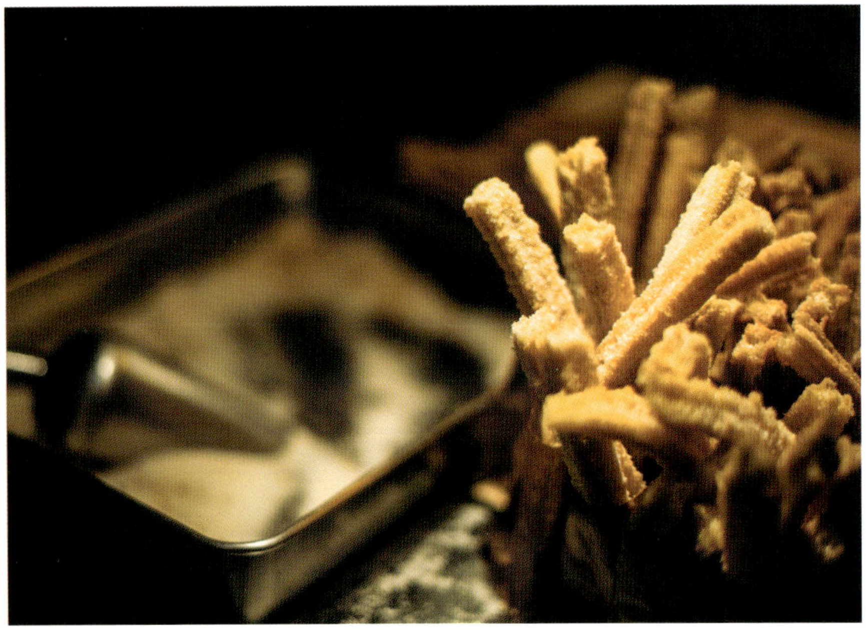

On the final day the drunken comrades were assembling the bullring, they also started assembling the party. New people were approaching, and others were already part of what was developing. "Brother-in-law, brother-in-law," Manuel said to his friend Santiago Rosales, with good foresight amid all the racket, "let's ask Marcial García to bring his marimba."

He managed to convince his friend to go to Tamarindo and borrow a marimba from García, the owner of a restaurant who had one. Marcial, his wife and the marimba ended up at the bullring that night, knowing little that they were inaugurating the first, unofficial edition of the "Dust Dance," a gathering that has been raising dust clouds for 27 years now.

The next year, curious people gathered asking about a second edition. Manuel, Marcial, and other organizers went around asking people for money to pay the musicians. As the years went by, the event got better — they built a little bar and put in tables. Eventually, by popular demand, they brought in a band, loudspeakers, and fireworks.

**Manuel Zamora Contreras**
Villareal
Born March 20, 1938

Don Manuel was born and raised and has always lived in Villarreal. From a young age he worked at clearing brush, and later he worked for a while on a banana plantation. Once while playing soccer, he met the owner of the Hotel Diriá, and they became friends. He participated in the construction of that hotel, where he continued to work for many years. In fact, when they began work on the expansion of the hotel, his new friend told him, "I want you to lay the first stone," and so he did. He worked as a bartender, cashier, and waiter. He's been married for 40 years and he loves to dance. He's the creator of the well-known "dust dance," which was born on the day they were finishing the construction of a bullring for a local festival.

Written by: Valeria Murillo

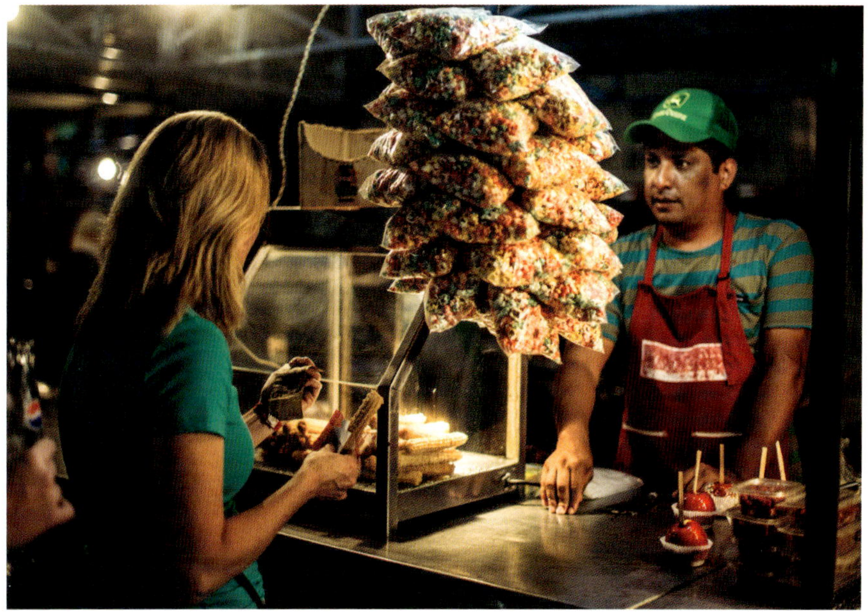

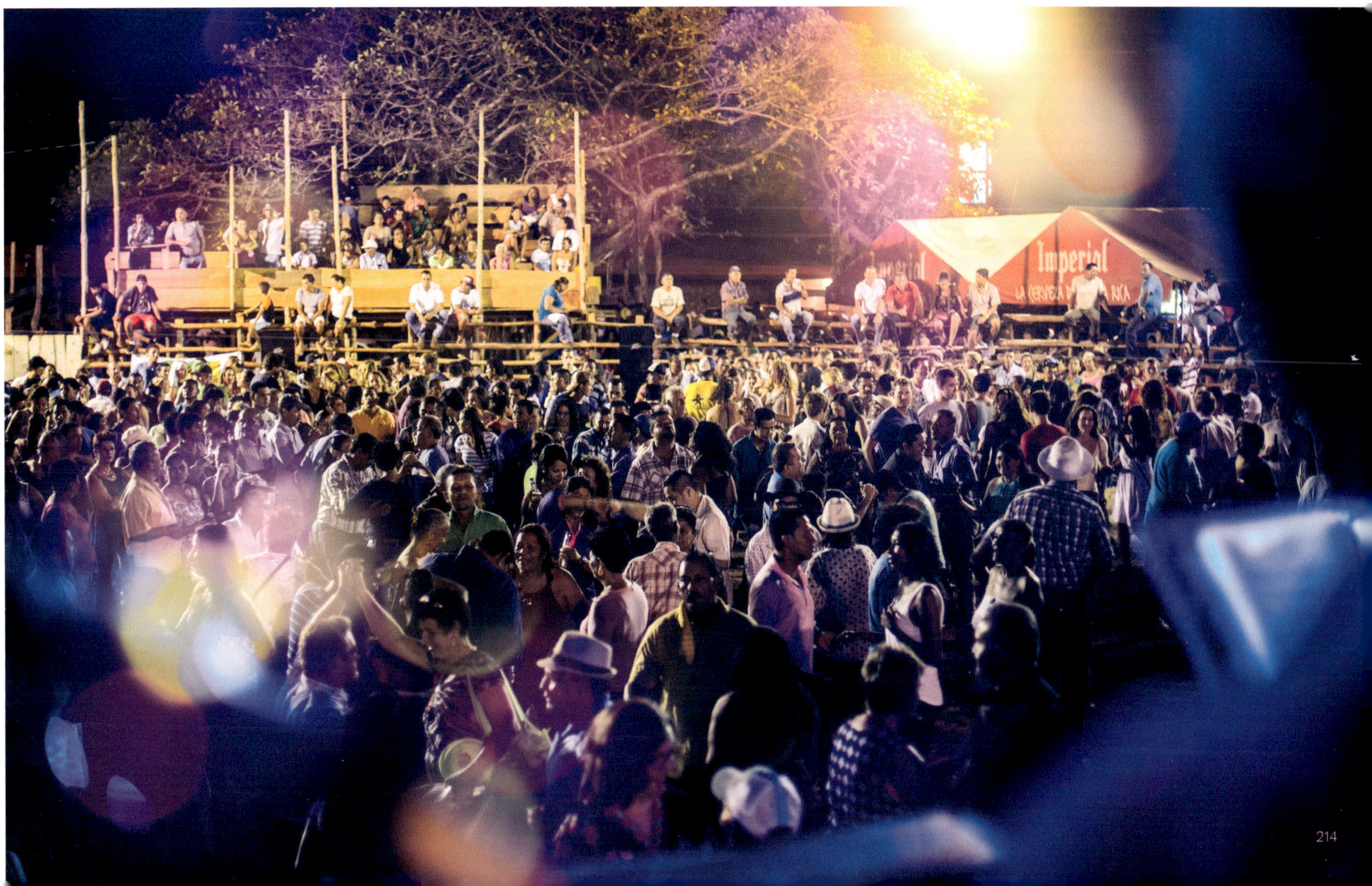

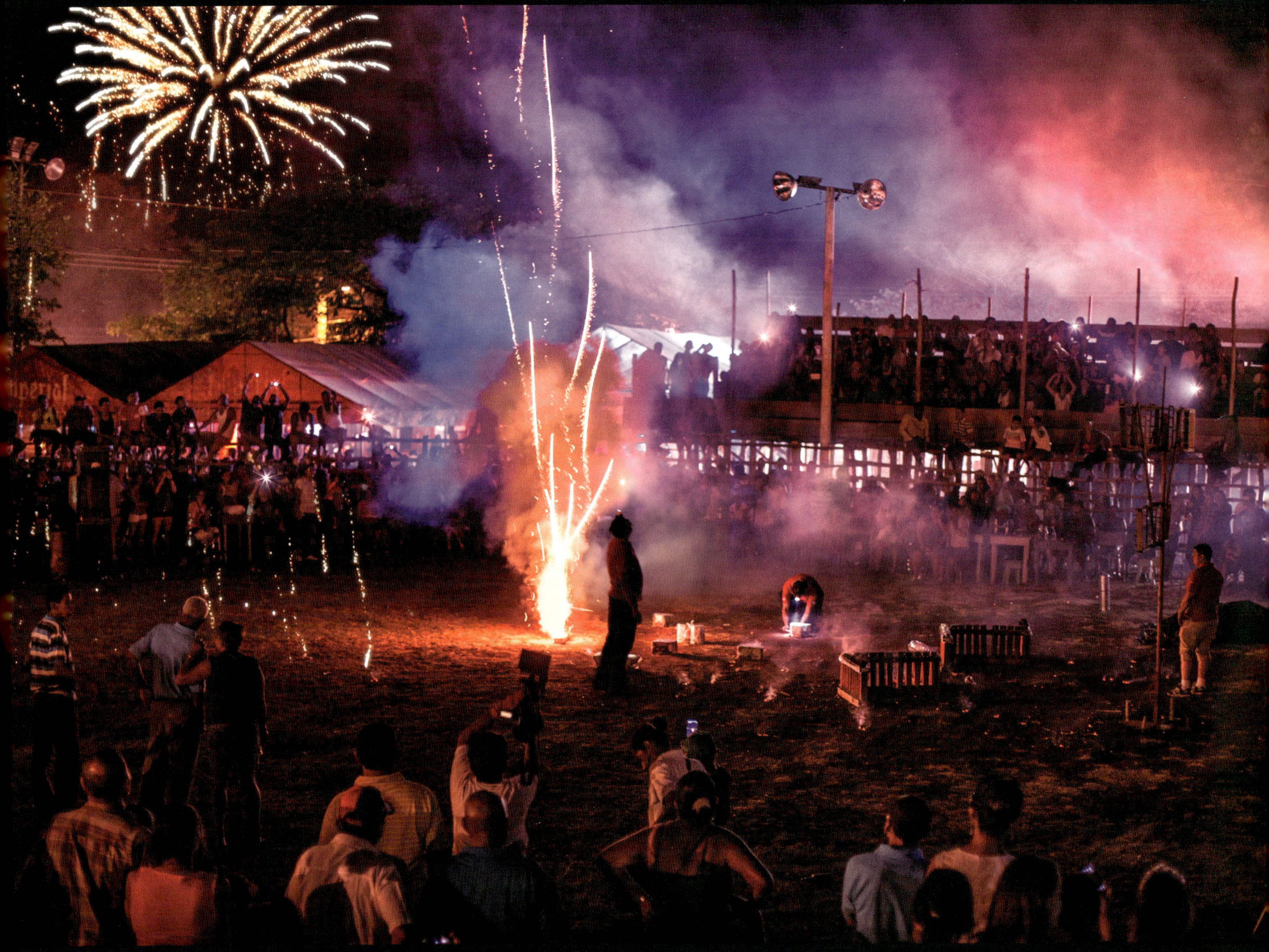

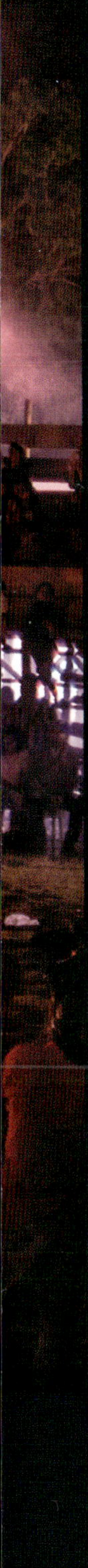

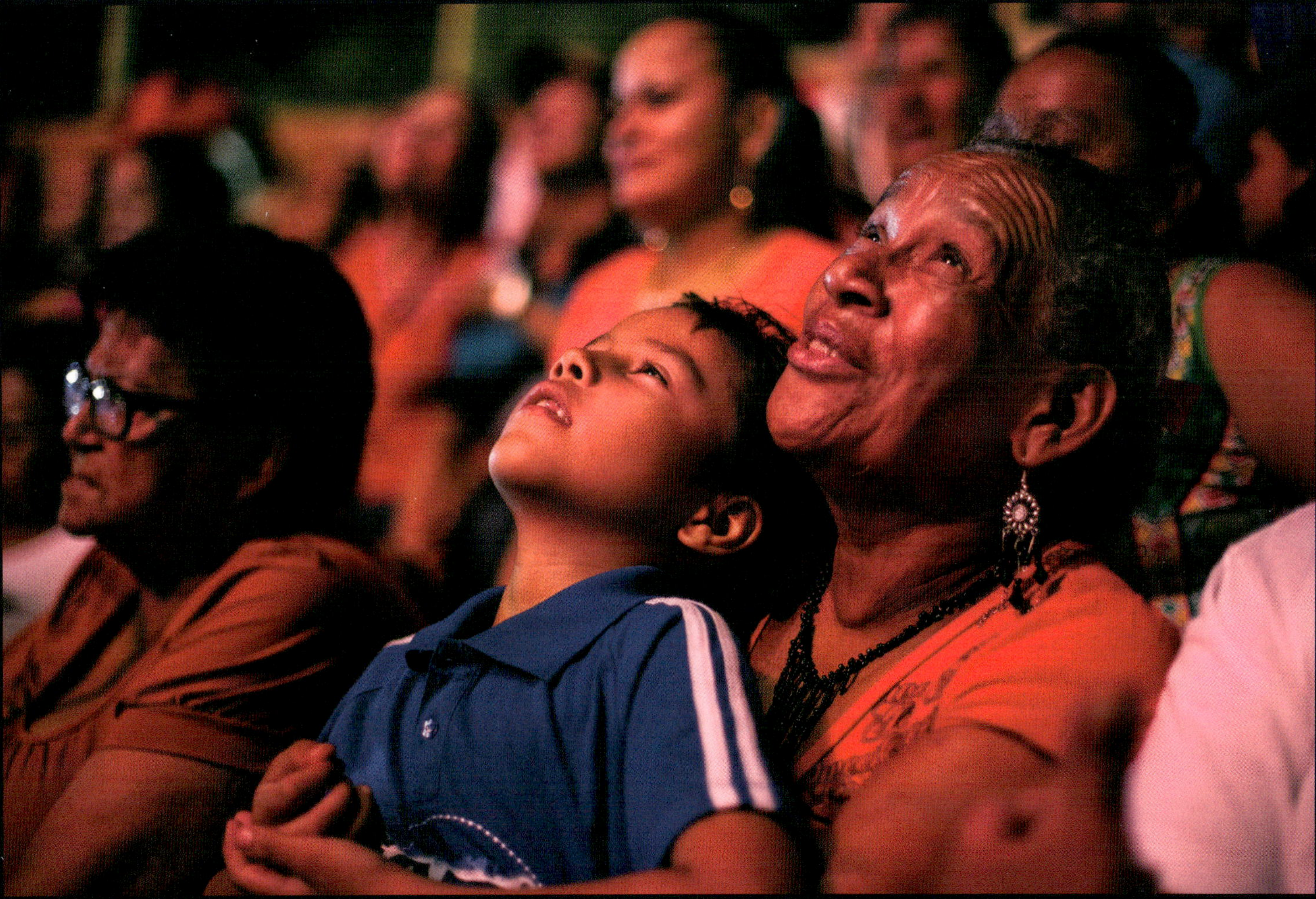

Don Manuel says he doesn't like to be in the middle of it all. He doesn't participate in many of the activities, saying he prefers to see bulls from afar, although one year the president of the association chose him to crown a queen chosen from among the senior citizens of the town.

With 2,000 people in attendance, this dance became so renowned that a couple of years ago Santa Cruz wanted to organize its first dance of the same name. They brazenly invited the organization of the Dust Dance of Villarreal, but they were obliged to rename their dance because of a torrent of criticism that they didn't foresee. When you ask Don Manuel if he accepted the invitation, he responds with a categorical no, saying, "I don't eat pudding off of anyone's finger."

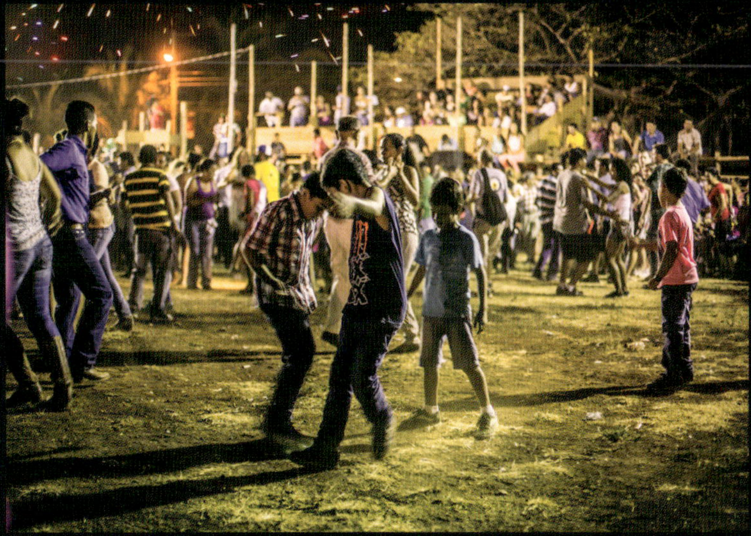

pura gente

# STORY *tellers*

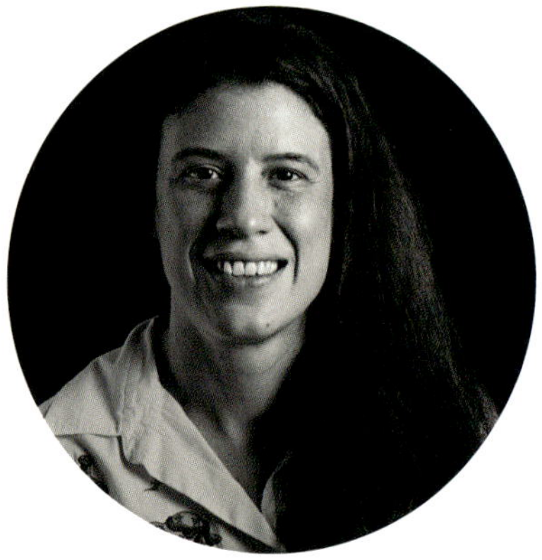

Adriana Sánchez González, San Isidro de El General, 41

Cook, writer, jiu-jitsu practitioner and facilitator. Daughter of Doris and Melvin, sister of Cristina, Antonio and Angélica, aunt of Manuel and Alexa. She's a philologist and a cook by vocation. She's worked on several rural development projects, and for nearly eight years she's been cooking at her restaurant, Manos en la Masa ("hands in the dough"). A feminist and a women's rights activist, a published writer and a developer of projects that involve cooking with a vision for development and social change. She loves Bahía Ballena de Osa, a place that holds treasured childhood memories.

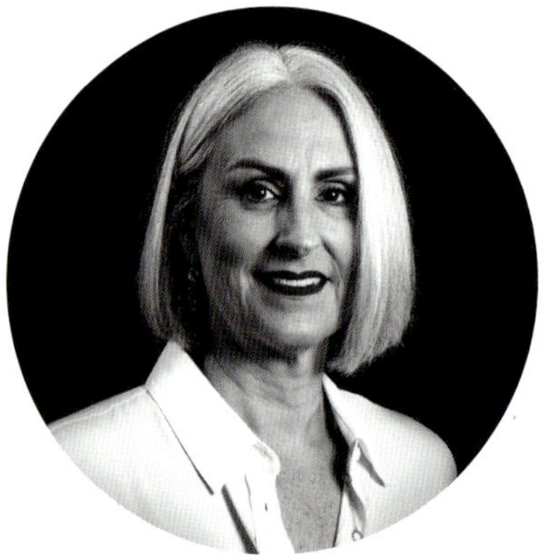

Abril Gordienko, San José, 53

Community activist, professor and writer. Mother, wife, grandmother and daughter. She loves the beaches of the central Pacific and Guanacaste. She has a law degree from UCR and she's a notary public; she has a master's in public administration from Harvard University and she's the cofounder of People Power Now!, a promoter of election reforms. She participated in government reform commissions in 2014-2017 and 2018-2019. She's published a novel and a book of short stories, and in 2015 she received the Alborada Prize for Professional Woman of the Year.

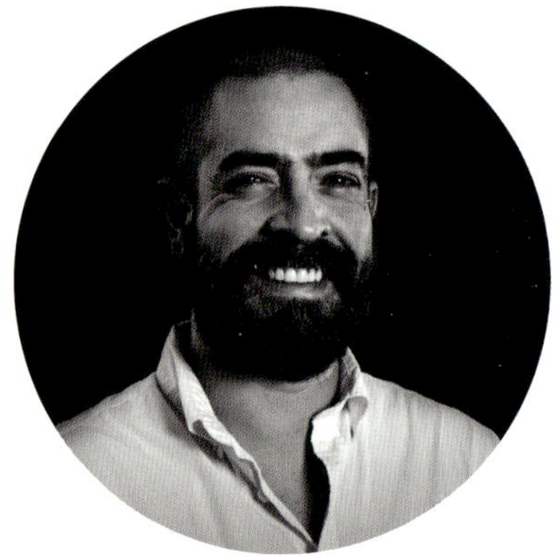

Arturo Pardo Vargas, Montes de Oca, 34

Arturo is a musician and a communicator, an ex-asthmatic, a specialist in jigsaw puzzles, Chinese checkers and nacho tasting. He loves Monteverde because it feels to him like an idyllic place to be at one with nature and with oneself. This project reminded him of the value of the richness behind human stories, because one person's life story will never be repeated, and his identity is built on very personal details — this is what makes every person unique.

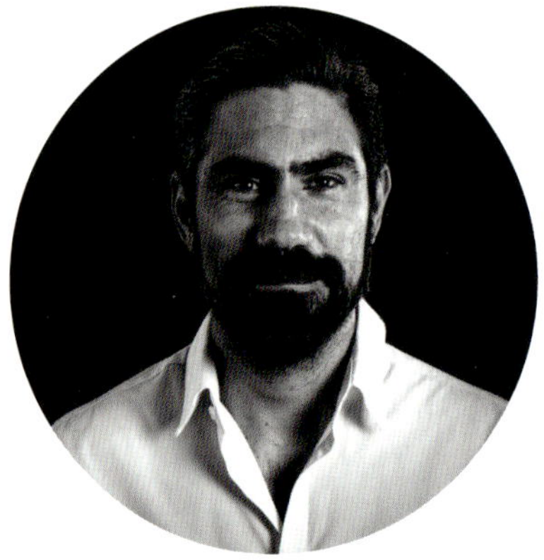

Alonso Muñoz Solís, Escazú, 40

Alonso is a professor of sustainable development at the University of Peace. This project interested him from the start because it offered the possibility of working collectively and of transforming a story in text. He felt like a sculptor finding the statue hidden inside.

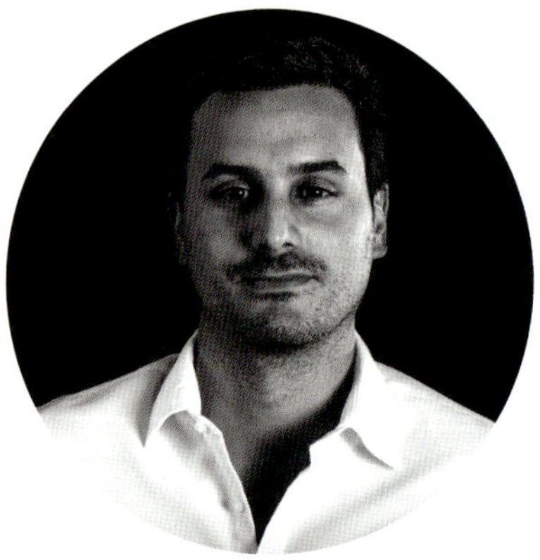

Adrián Castro Baeza, La Sabana, 34

Cinematic and theatrical producer and director. Graduated in business administration from UCR, with a degree in film direction from the University of Buenos Aires. He's written and directed films and plays, including "Chicago el musical" ("Chicago: The Musical") and "Nido de Águilas" ("Nest of Eagles"), both of which were recognized with national culture awards. His favorite place in the country is Platanares de Moravia, the source of childhood memories in which he visited his cousins in the mountains and ran through the pastures — and once they even saw a chupacabra! To Adrián, imagination is more important than knowledge.

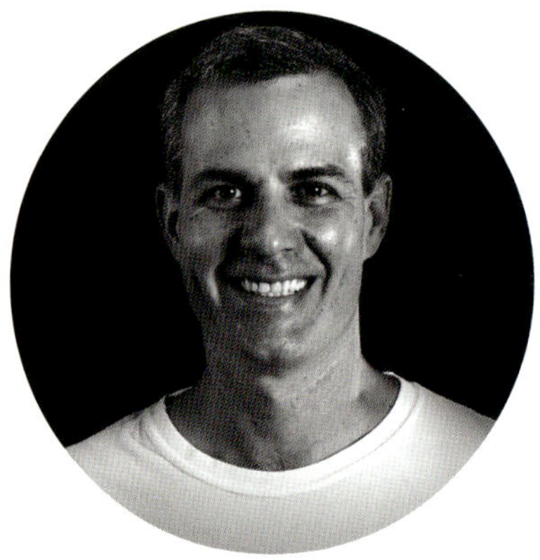

Álvaro Cedeño Molinari, Pinares, 46

Álvaro is a specialist in corporate diplomacy, a leader in the convergence between climate action and the fourth industrial revolution. A manager of processes that make life flourish on earth. A facilitator of peace and a family man. The place he holds closest to his heart is Nosara, Guanacaste, and he embraces the challenge of producing well-being from the biosphere. He found this project to be a job based on empathy, a matter of developing the ability to put yourself in other people's shoes to be able to tell their stories.

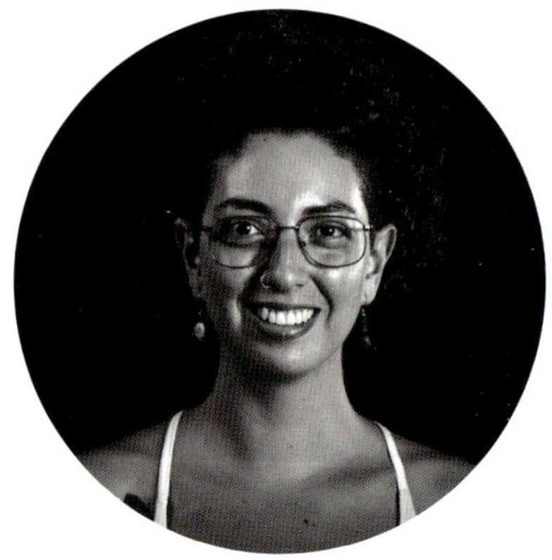

Berenice Jiménez Murillo, Llorente, Tibás, 27

Composer, singer and social psychologist, Berenice is a promoter of cultural and community development. In 2017 she represented Costa Rica at the Second International Singers Festival. She's sung in Argentina, Uruguay, Mexico, Cuba and Guatemala through her own independent efforts. She works as a producer at the Festival Madremonte in the community of Longo Maï in southern Costa Rica. In 2020 she used digital platforms to launch her first live recording production, called Muchas Miradas.

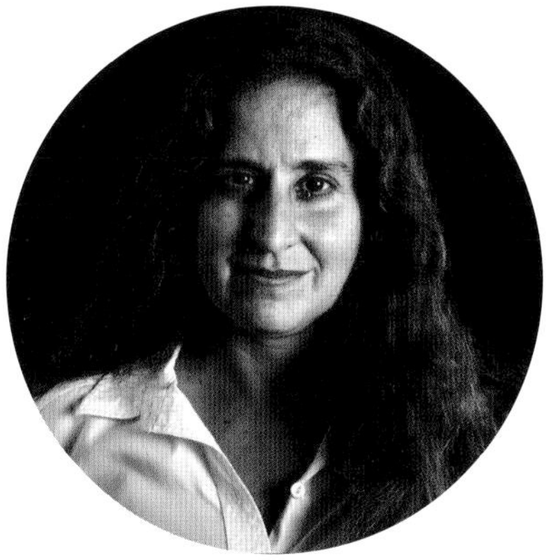

Carla Pravisani, Argentina, 44

Carla has a master's in creative writing from the University of Pompeu Fabra, with a postgraduate degree in digital literature from the University of Barcelona. She manages projects at the Escuela de la Nada y Casa de Escritura ("school of nothing and house of writing"), and she runs creative writing workshops at the San José Cultural Center. She's published eight books, two of which have won the Aquileo Echeverría National Prize: *La piel no miente* ("Skin Doesn't Lie"), 2012, and *Mierda* ("Shit"), 2018. She loves the community of Mata de Plátano: the climate, the rural nature, the coffee farms keeping the condominiums out. Carla believes that a country is the sum of all its differences.

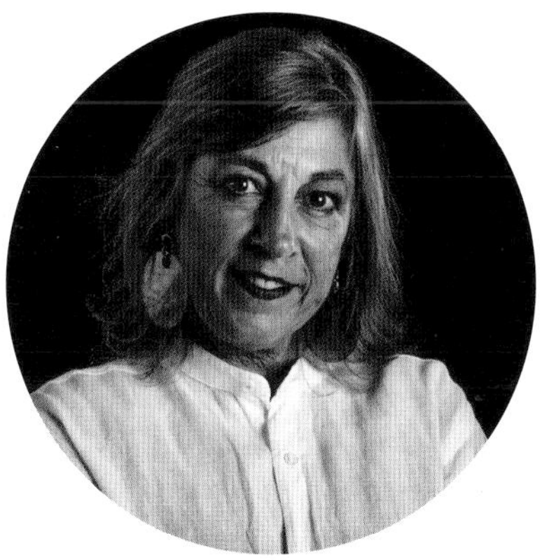

Claudia Barrionuevo, Curridabat, 60

Claudia is a playwright, film and television scriptwriter, opinion columnist, theater director and screenwriting teacher. She loves to meet different people, giving her material to construct different characters. She lives on the east side of the city with her daughters, Manu and Vale, and her three cats. She's won two playwriting prizes in Spain and three in Costa Rica, and she's published six books. With this project, she enjoyed the creative challenge of hearing the stories of people she didn't know, listening to them carefully and trying to be faithful to what they had to say.

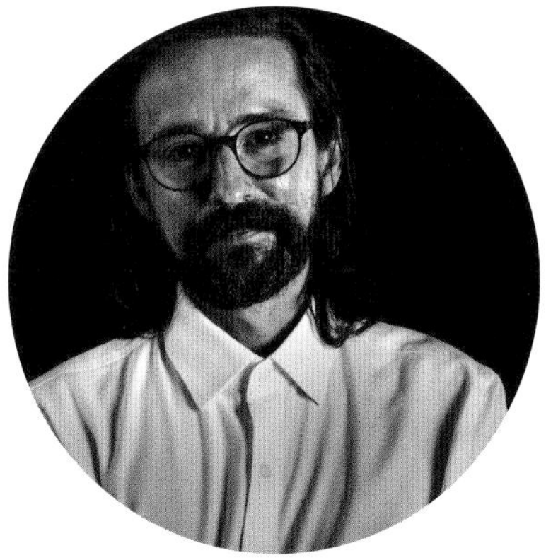

Diego van der Laat, San José, 41

Diego is a writer and architect, a graduate of the Architectural Association School of Architecture in the United Kingdom. He's published four books of short fiction: *Reparticiones* ("Sharings"), *11*, *Veintidós* ("Twenty-two") and *666*. He's currently working on a book of short stories titled Whisky, on a false atlas called Nit, and on his first film, cowritten with Neto Villalobos, *Amor es el Monstruo* ("Love is the Monster").

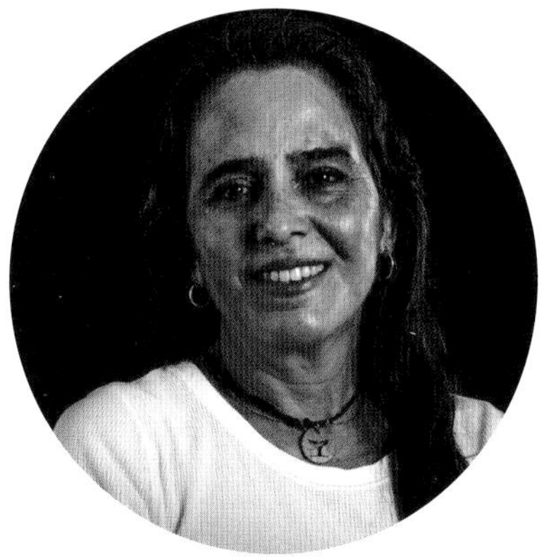

Dorelia Barahona, Moravia, 62

Dorelia Barahona Riera studies fine arts and philosophy. She has a degree in philosophy and a master's in art theory, both from the UCR. A writer of essays and novels. A professor of aesthetics and the philosophy of art at the Universidad Nacional, where she also pursues her research in the field of aesthetics. Also a scriptwriter, feature writer and painter. Her first novel, *De qué manera te olvido* ("How Do I Forget You?"), received the Juan Rulfo prize in 1989. She's published eight novels, four books of short stories, two of poetry, two of theater and three of essays.

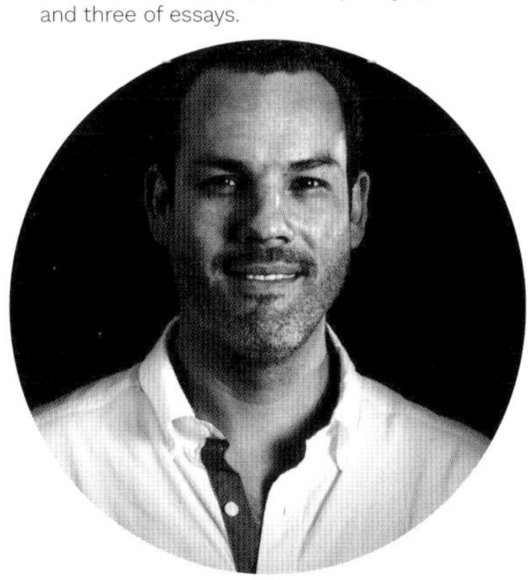

Eugenio Desanti Jerez, Escazú, 40

Eugenio started out studying law but ended up with a master's degree in creative publicity. He's convinced that good ideas resolve almost everything. He has a study of copywriting called *Once Upon*, and the fortune of collaborating with talented people and clients who have become friends. This project allowed him to put himself in someone else's shoes, if only for a moment, and he feels that if we did this type of exercise more, the world would be a very different place. His heart is scattered in every corner of Costa Rica.

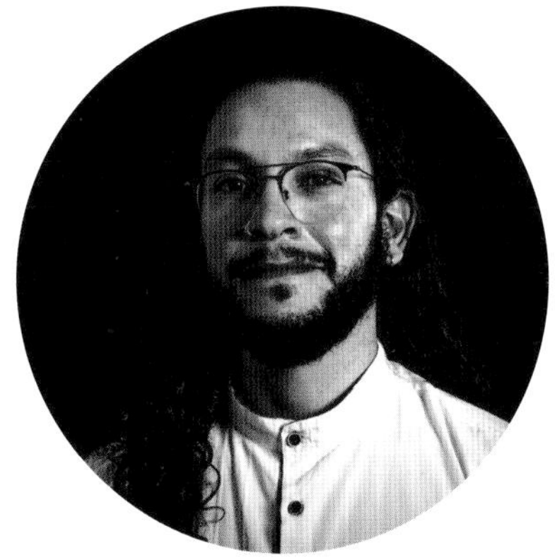

Fabricio Walker Morera, El Guarco, Cartago, 34

Fabri is a musician, composer, interpreter and geographer's apprentice. He was born into a family of musicians and artists and started singing at a very early age. In 2009 he started singing with the collective Infibeat, with whom he has won two Acam prizes, and on a parallel track he's developed his own career as a soloist. He's released two records: "La Cola del Pescado" ("The Tail of the Fish") and "Leirundé." In 2019 he started an interdisciplinary project with Sol Pardo (dancer) and his first audiovisual production, "Párpado" ("Eyelid"), collaborating with Eloy Mora (cinematography) and Andrés Cervilla (musical production), which will premiere soon.

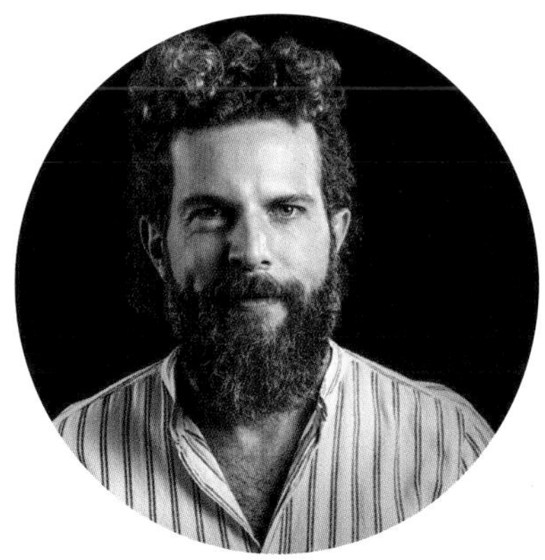

Fernando Alvarado Saborío, San José, 36

Photography, writing and contemplation are Fernando's favorite activities. He's a consultant on subjects having to do with psychology and project development, and he currently lives in Puerto Viejo de Talamanca. A lover of nature, he has a heart that's anchored equally in the mountains and in the sea. A traveler and a dreamer. He liked this project for the challenge of taking on the responsibility of telling someone else's story, which though it may seem commonplace, might be the most fascinating of all.

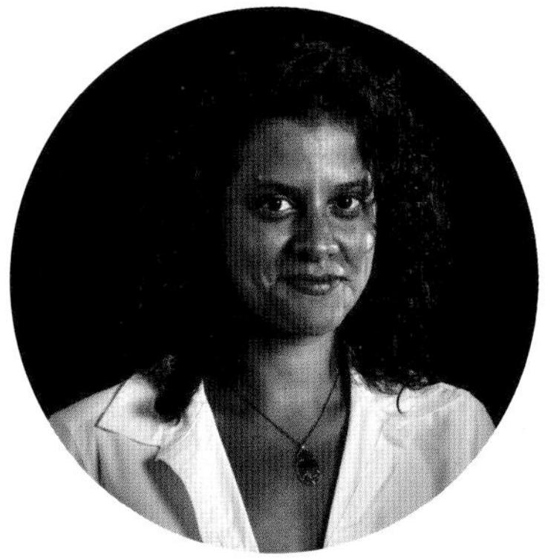

Irene Gutiérrez Valverde, Zapote, 33

Born and raised in San José, she's a social anthropologist at the UCR. In 2021 she earned a master's in dance with an emphasis in training from the National University. She's been practicing yoga since 2009 and currently teaches classes. Her curiosity has led her to experiment and learn different languages, places and disciplines, from public education to feminism to independent political collectives — and she's even a clown, singer and performer. She's part of the collectives Mujeres Libres Riendo ("Free Women Laughing") and Viajo Sola ("I Travel Alone"), and she's a project manager for Manada ("Herd"), a feminist initiative focused on research and gynecological education.

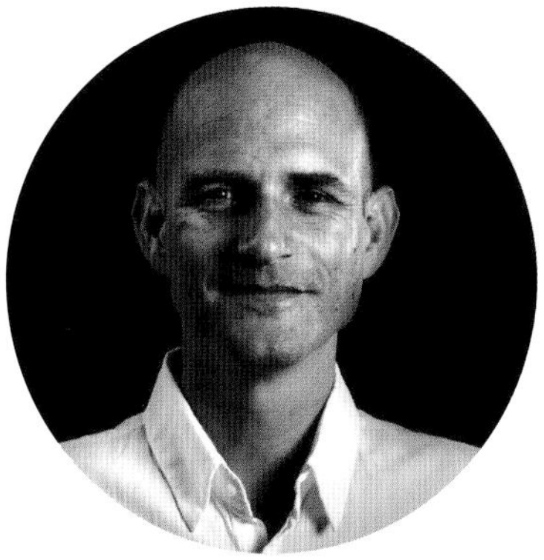

Giancarlo Pucci Golcher, Santa Ana, 45

Father of Aurora and Clara. Responding to an internal calling to regenerate collective presence through vulnerability, beauty and the wisdom of the body. Ten years ago, he took a leap of faith on an uncertain path, driven by a sense of purpose that led to a master's degree in strategic leadership for sustainability in Sweden. To found Árboles Mágicos ("Magic Trees"). To fly over Costa Rica and take its portrait from a fresh perspective. To facilitate transformative group processes with social technologies like Art of Hosting, U Theory, Empathetic Communication and Flow Game. Serves on the faculty of the Presencing Institute.

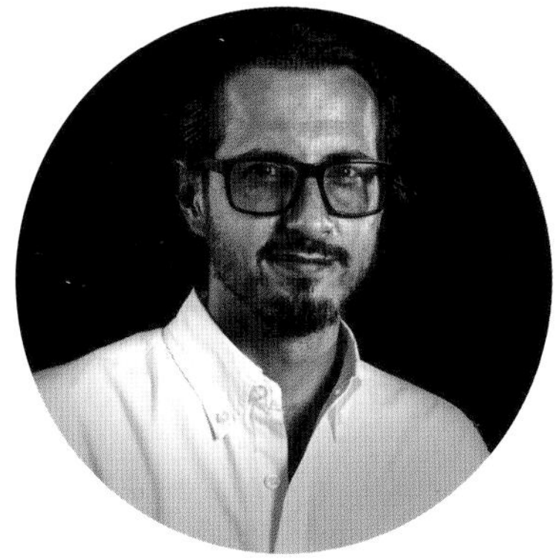

Luis Salazar Gómez, Hatillo, 36

Luis is an architect (a graduate of UCR), researcher, illustration teacher and columnist. Occasionally he creates humorous vignettes, and he has published several pieces in print and digital magazines. He has worked on creating new initiatives in vulnerable communities and instigating change in public spaces. His first book, *Te vas a acordar de mí* ("You're Going to Remember Me"), 2020, is the authorized biography of Carmen Morales Jenkins, the first person with Down's syndrome in this country to retire because of old age. His favorite place is Lagunilla de Heredia, where he lives with his family.

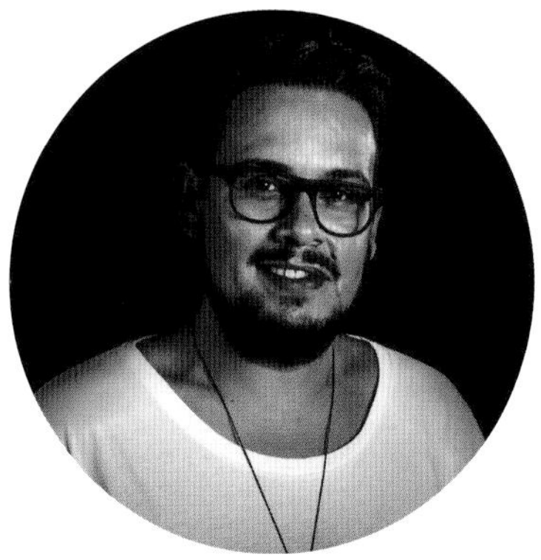

Jeison Herrera Chacón, Pérez Zeledón, 34

Jeison is an English professor and a writer. He's entered several literary contests in the Brunca region, and in 2015 he published his first book of stories, *Sobre todos la misma lluvia* ("The Same Rain Falls on All"). He loves Quepos, where he works, a canton of great beauty. Jeison believes you can't know a country without knowing its people.

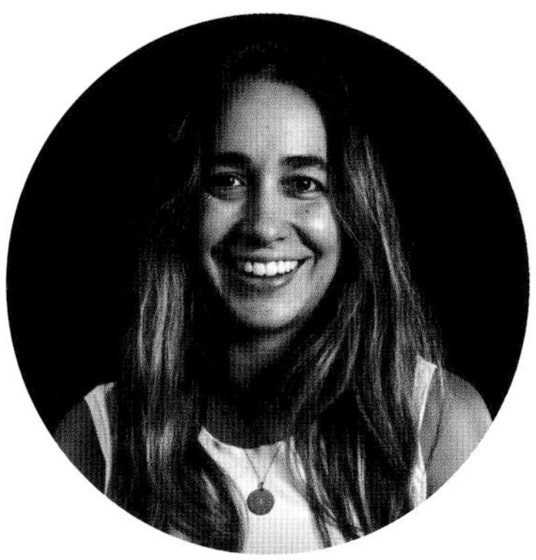

Gloriana Sojo Lara, Escazú, 29

With a master's degree in international relations and journalism from George Washington University, she's spent five years working for the Inter-American Development Bank as a leader in project development for the prevention of violence and more recently in strategic communications. Mount Chirripó is her favorite place in the country because the calm she has experienced there allowed her to understand and see things that wouldn't be possible anywhere else. Her favorite part of this project has been remembering, through the stories of its people, how extraordinary Costa Rica truly is.

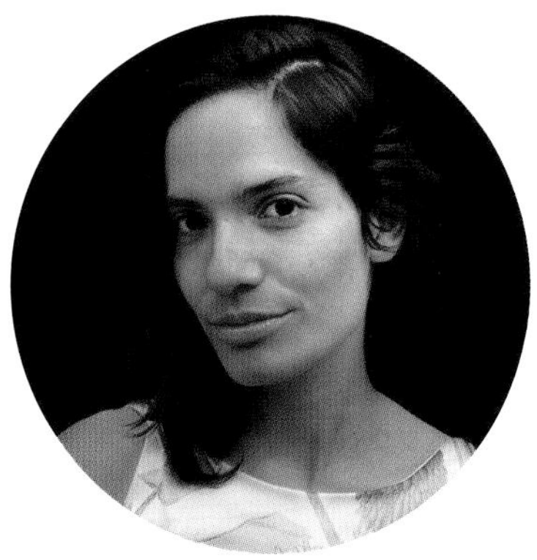

Libertad Sobrado, Carmen de Guadalupe, 23

Libertad was born in Caracas. She's been a multidisciplinary artist forever, and not long ago she became an urban planner. Her heart lies in the blue mountains you can see beyond the power lines on any street in the Central Valley, Monteverde or Punta Uva. Her greatest inspiration is the power of beauty, which she has explored through photography and painting. She also writes, and she studied urban planning in France, as she dreams of more cities where girls can pedal bikes without fear.

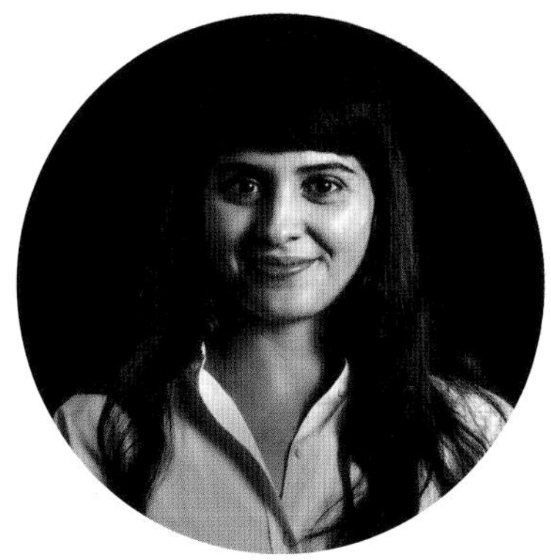

María José Sosa Guzmán, San José, 28

María José is an astrologer, playwright and yoga teacher. She inherited an entrepreneurial spirit from her family and started experimenting in theater when she was 12 through courses in improvisational drama. She wrote and directed her first play before she graduated. She taught herself astrology as part of her path to self-knowledge. This project allowed her to face the challenge of bringing to life unknown people through their words, feeling their essence through the stories they told.

María Teresa Brenes Mata, San José, 32

Tere is a doctor of pharmacy, currently studying for a master's degree in phytotherapy. She is the project leader and producer for Editorial Pucci. A lover of Costa Rica, music and dance. She's poured her heart into this project, which has left its mark on her as a Costa Rican and a human being, for the opportunity to meet so many people through their gazes, their expressions, their stories and their authenticity, as well as the connection she's formed with each one of them.

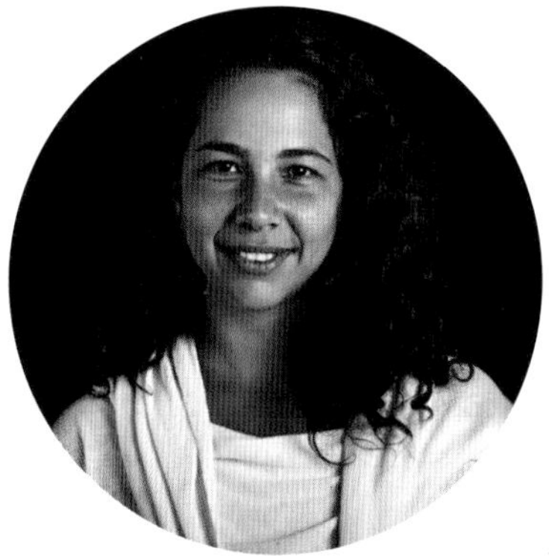

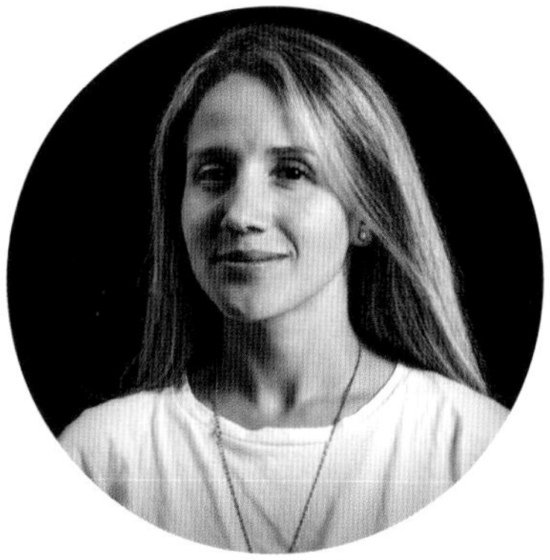

Michelle Macluf Vargas, San José, 29

A designer and seller of clothing, an entrepreneur and a family therapy facilitator. She's a lover of life and the people who live it, and she's fascinated by the stories we're made of. She has a son who teaches her self-observation and compassion. She has a line of clothes born of the remnants from her father's factory, founded by her Lebanese grandfather, and she says that with those genes it's no surprise that she has a gift for both fabrics and business. She loves Uvita, the community she lives in, where she has found a lifestyle that's both authentic and healthy.

Sofía Quirós Ubeda, Guayabos, Curridabat, 31

Sofía is an Argentine-Costa Rican film director and acting coach. She graduated with a degree in image and sound from the University of Buenos Aires. Sofía has focused on working with natural actors and actresses, creating personal stories with a poetic and sensory vision. Her first film, Ceniza Negra ("Black Ash"), premiered at the 58th Critics' Week of 2019, becoming the first feature-length Costa Rican film to appear in a competitive portion of the Cannes Festival and the first to compete for the Caméra d'Or award.

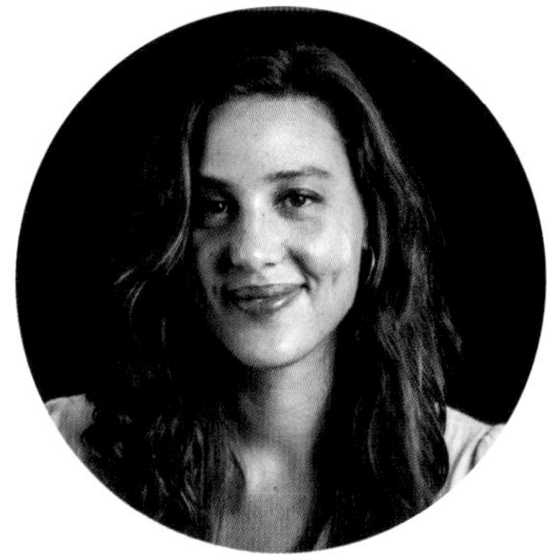

María Fernanda Cruz Chaves, San Ramón, 32

She's a student of corruption and government at the University of Sussex in the UK. For 10 years she's been a journalist, writer, reporter and editor in various media inside and outside the country. She worked on the international investigations into the "Panama Papers" and "Transnationals of Faith." For more than four years, she was the editor of the newspaper The Voice of Guanacaste, to which she hopes to return when she finishes her studies. Her love for Guanacaste developed during that time, and she says her heart is buried in Cerro de la Cruz. Her favorite beer is Guanaca, a product of GuanaBeer.

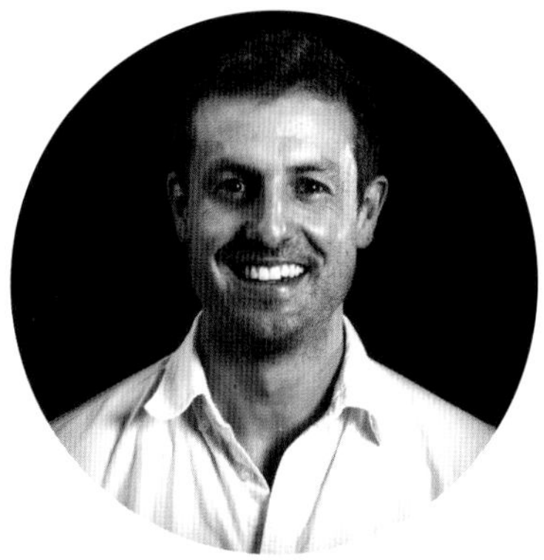

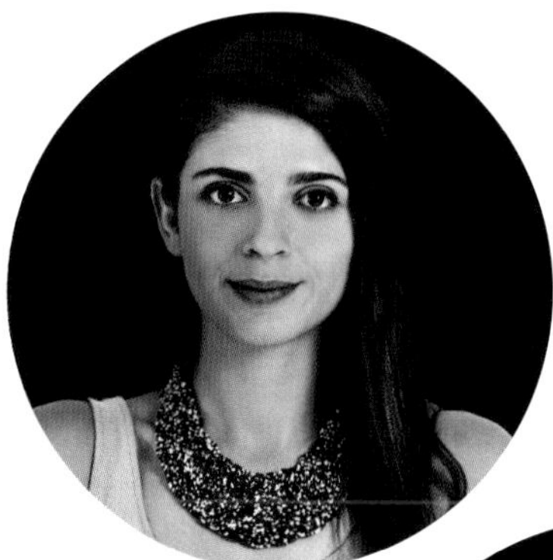

Sebastián Castro Sasso, Tres Ríos, 33

Adventure director for Wondermore and chauffeur for "Subite al Chunche" ("Climb Aboard the Whatchamacallit"). He's a born explorer. Whether it's as a reporter for CNN or driving a strange car to a world soccer championship, his passion is telling stories. He's the cofounder of Wondermore.org along with his wife, Christine Raine. His heart is wrapped up in Monteverde, looking toward the ocean from the mountains.

Valeria Murillo Paniagua, Sarchí, Alajuela, 34

Valeria is motivated by beauty and words, lost between communication, flowers and lychee fruit. She's dedicated the past 10 years to content creation, but lately she writes more, dances more and feels more. She holds the Caribbean in her heart as the place that cures all ills. This project allowed her to reconnect with her ancestors to appreciate and admire their story, as well as to rediscover writing.

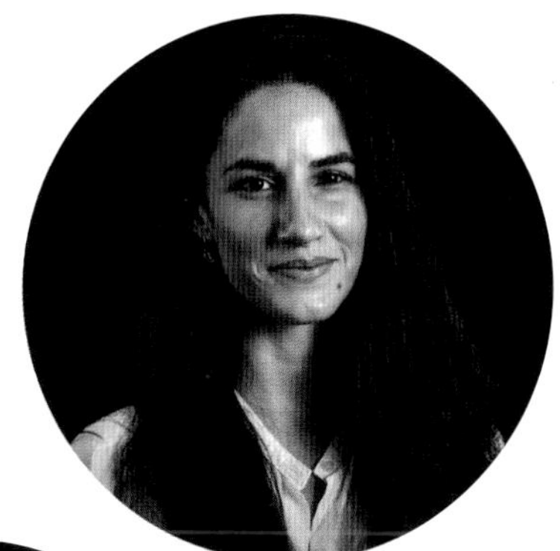

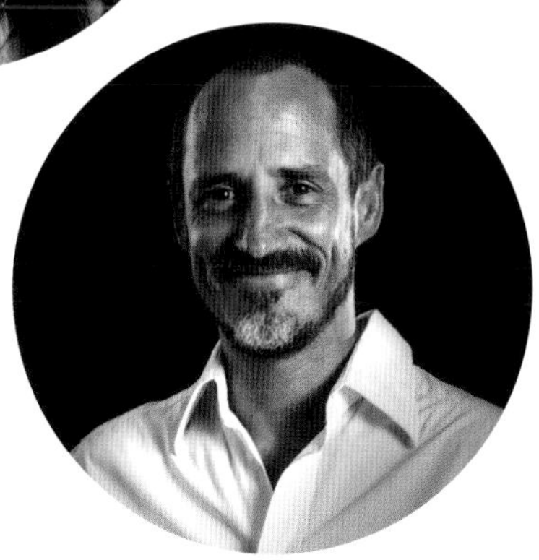

Sergio Pucci Golcher, Escazú, 41

A restless spirit since childhood: All his grades were red except in theater and poetry. He earned a degree in business administration because he didn't know what to study. Later he studied photography for a year, but he spent the money for the last quarter on a safari. For 25 years, his love of nature threw him headlong into the world of photography, and he's been through every branch of the discipline: architecture, weddings, sports, publicity.... He's been honored by the BBC and has recorded for National Geographic. Without being a director, he directed the film Güilas ("Kids"). Even though he's afraid to fly, he made Costa Rica Aérea with his brother Gianca.

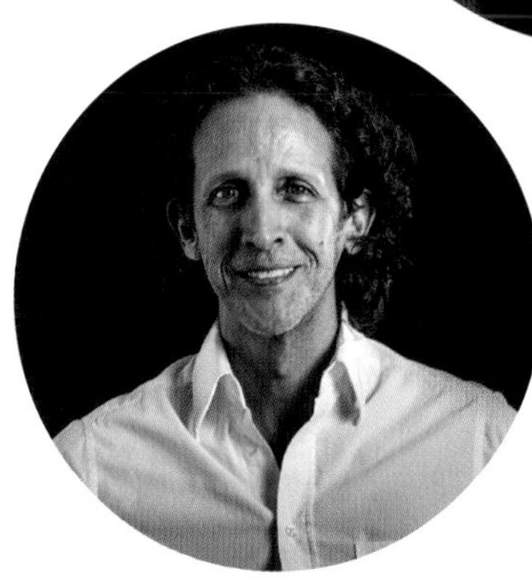

Jaime Gamboa, Liberia, 53

A writer, musician, publicist and member of the band Malpaís, for which he has composed songs and written most of the lyrics. He's helped to record dozens of records and written some 20 children's books (*El Cuento Fantasma*, "The Ghost Story," *Alma del Mar*, "The Soul of the Sea," *Corazón de Marimba*, "The Heart of Marimba"); stories (*La orquesta imposible*, "The Impossible Orchestra"); and works in other genres (*Árboles y Bosques Mágicos*, "Magical Trees and Forests," and *Costa Rica Aérea* ("Costa Rica from Above," among others). He currently divides his time between creating new communication projects in support of sustainability and writing stories, songs and scripts for film and television.

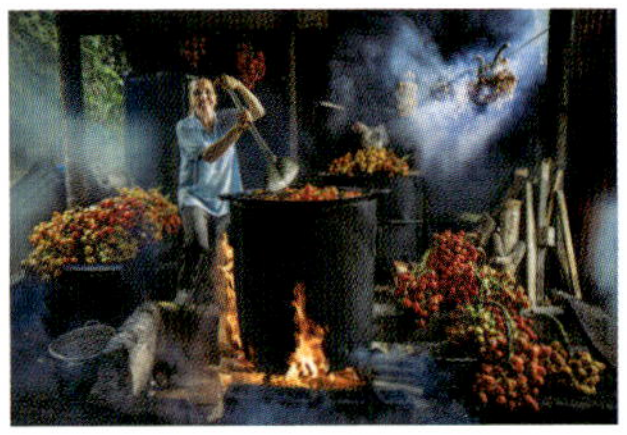
Magda Araya Brenes
Page 7

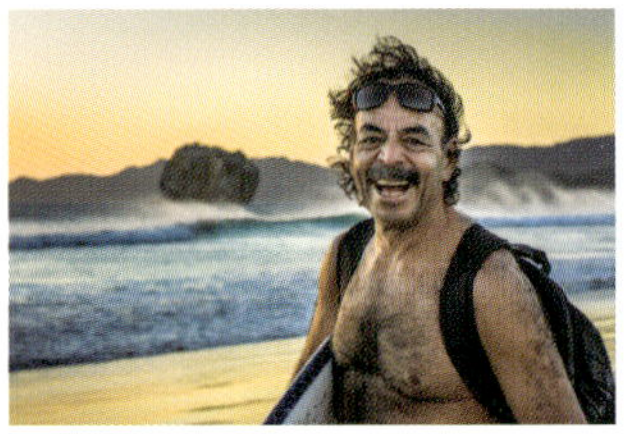
Eladio Castro Mora
Page 11

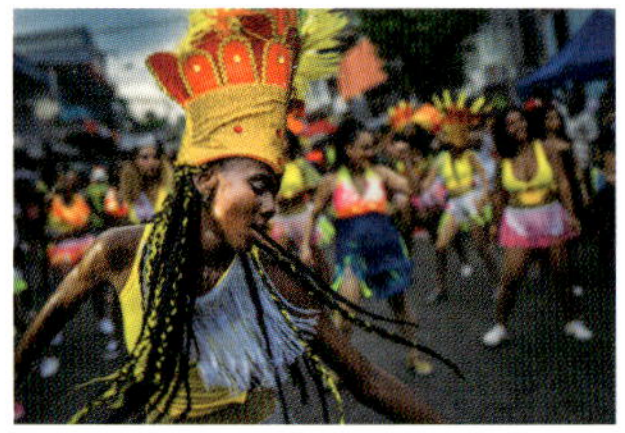
Angeline Pondler Estrada
Page 17

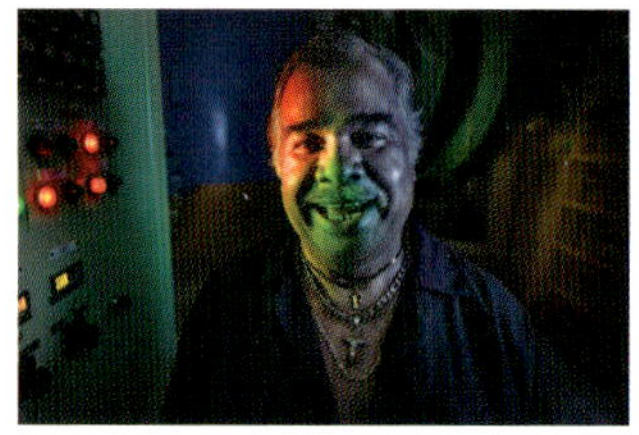
Francisco Edwin Hernández
Page 25

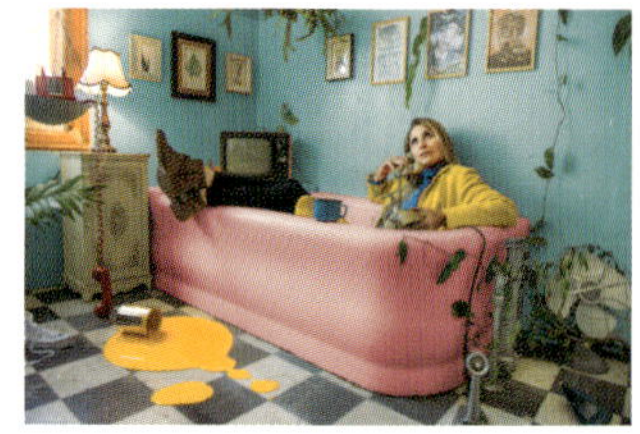
Elizabeth Arguello Miranda
Page 27

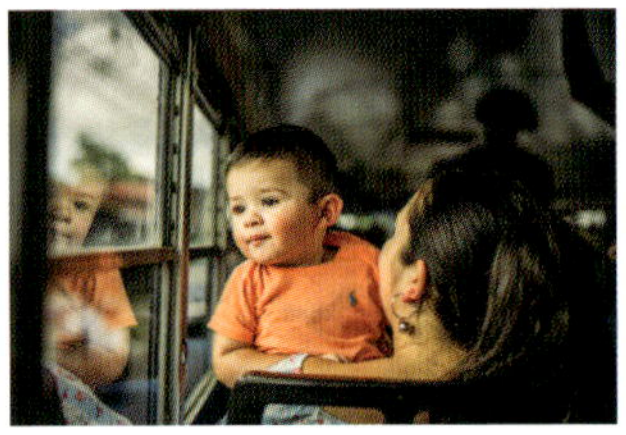
Eithan de Jesús Brenes
Page 31

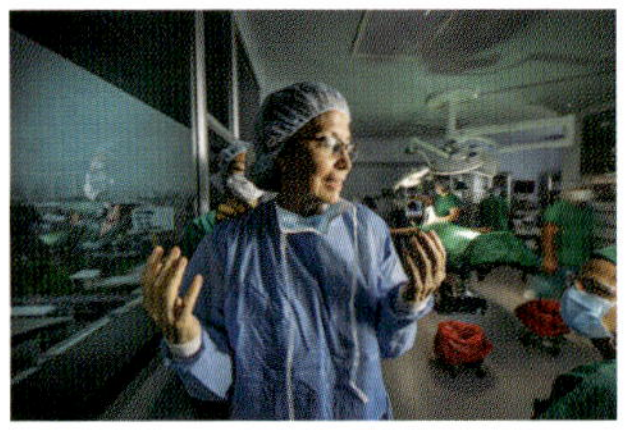
María Amalia Matamoros Ramírez
Page 35

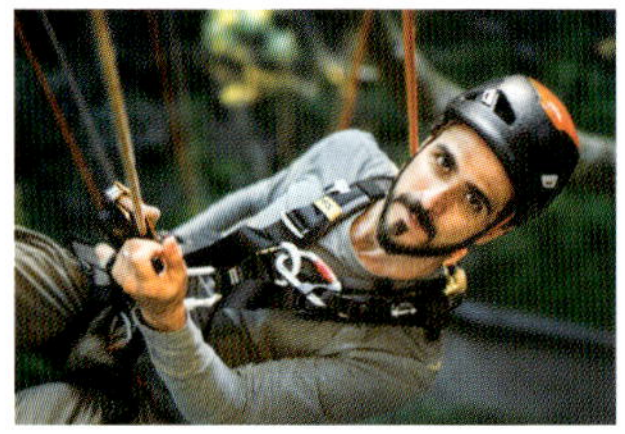
Andrés Valverde
Lizano Page 39

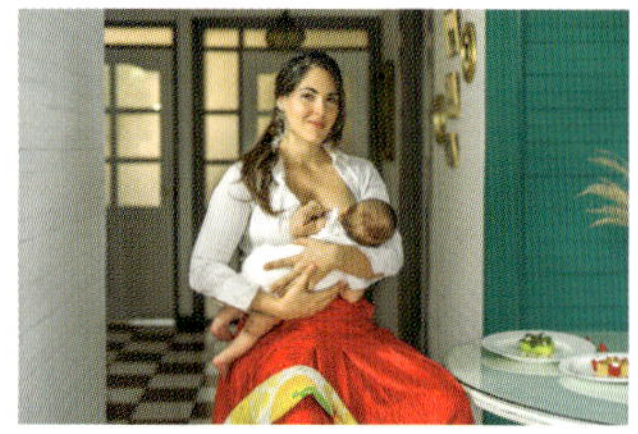
María Laura Zamora
Page 41

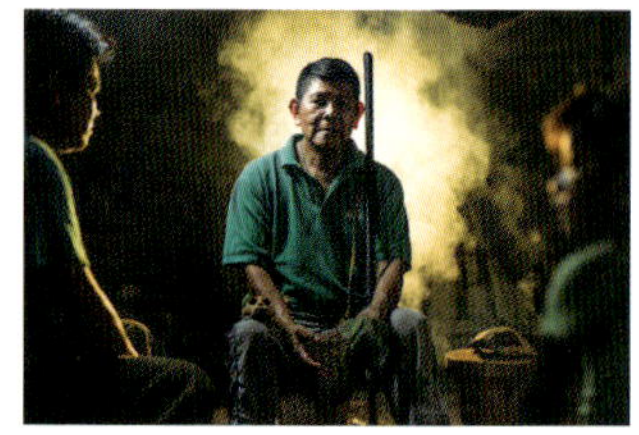
Lisandro Porras
Page 45

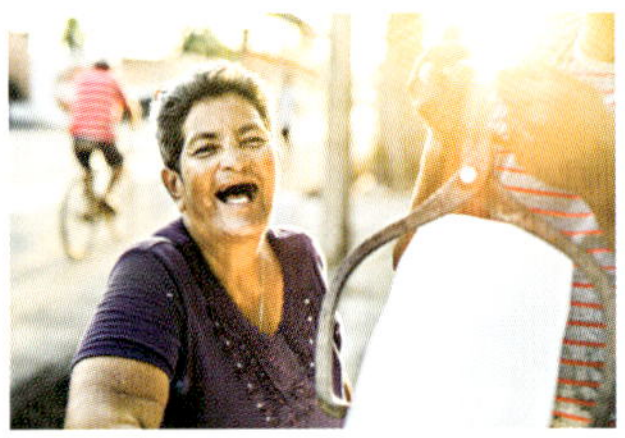
María Cecilia Cantillo Cantillo
Page 49

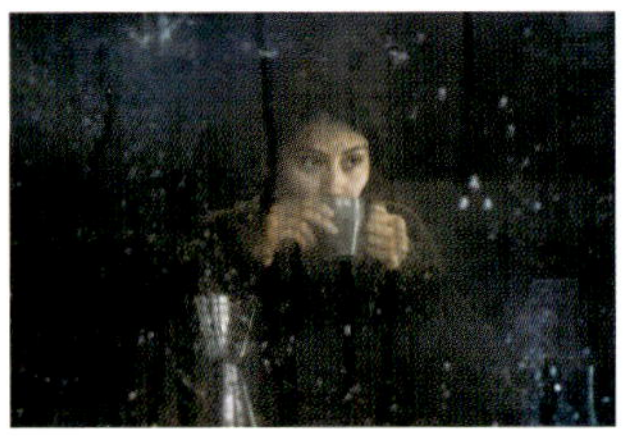
María Elena Rivera Garita
Page 51

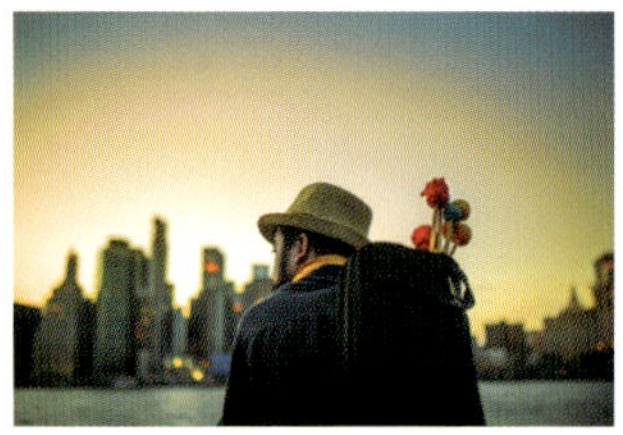
Felipe Fournier Soto
Page 53

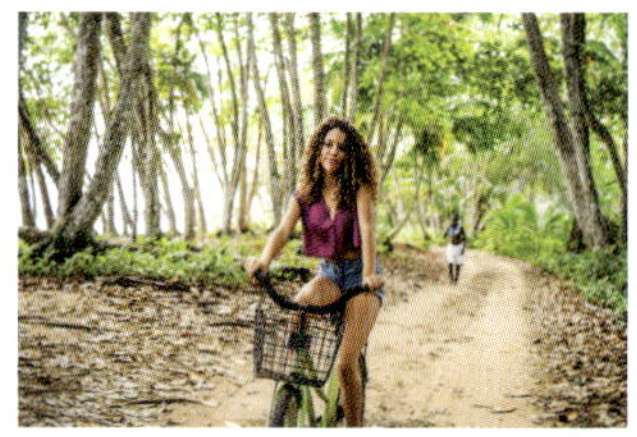
Jubanel Taylor Larrauri
Page 57

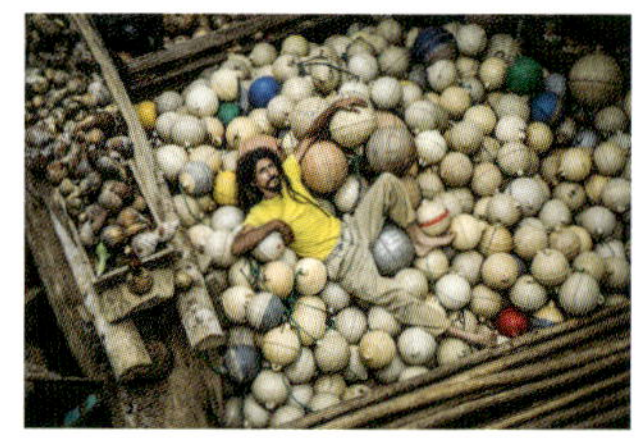
Javier Francisco Pancho Quesada
Page 59

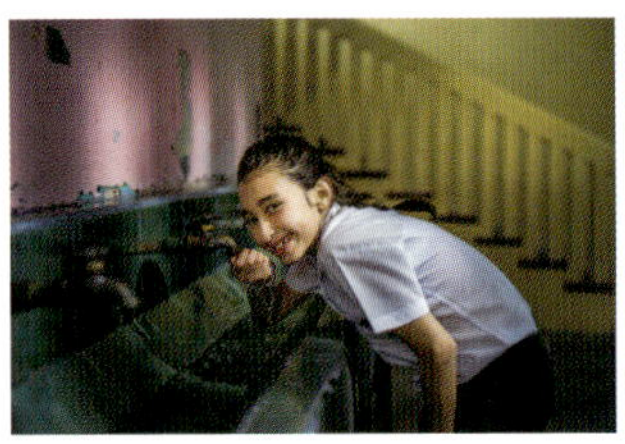
Mariam Leiva Delgado
Page 65

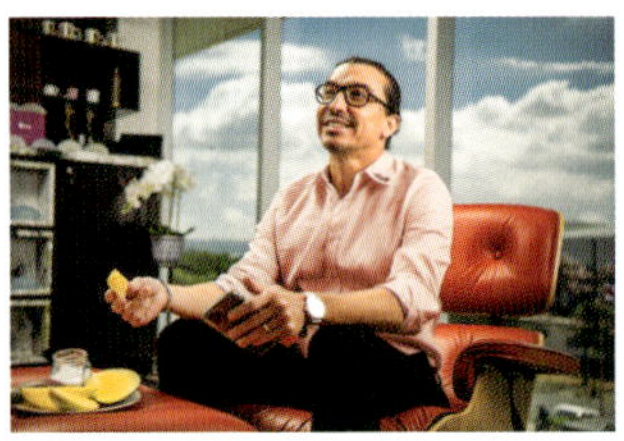
Juan José Chacón Quirós
Page 69

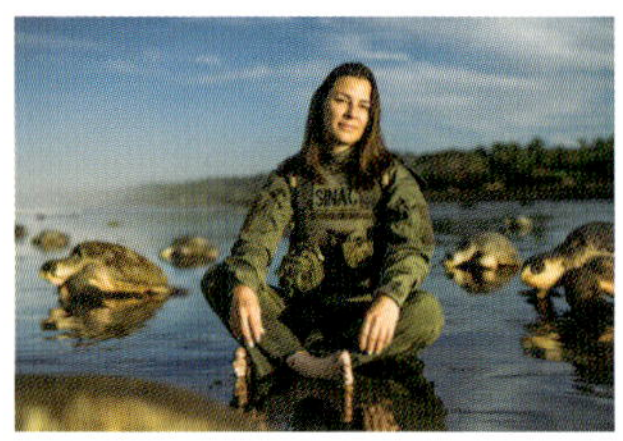
Yeimy María Cedeño Solís
Page 73

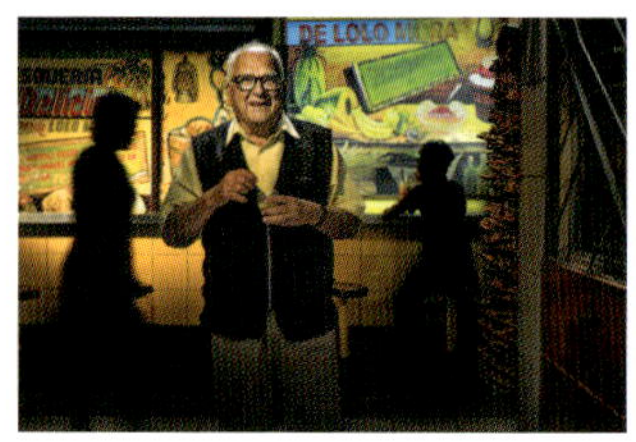
Lisímaco Chavarría Trejos
Page 79

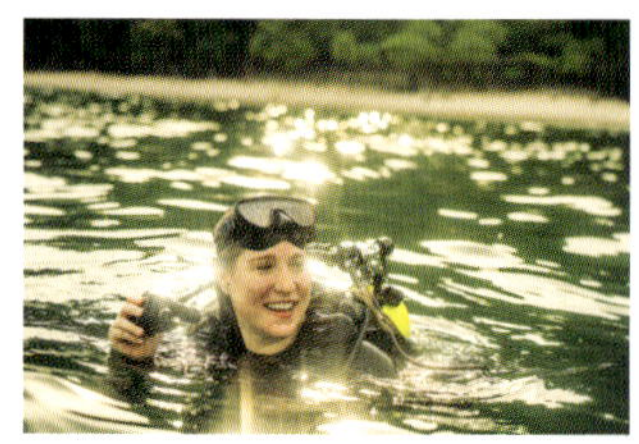
Melania Guerra
Carillo Page 81

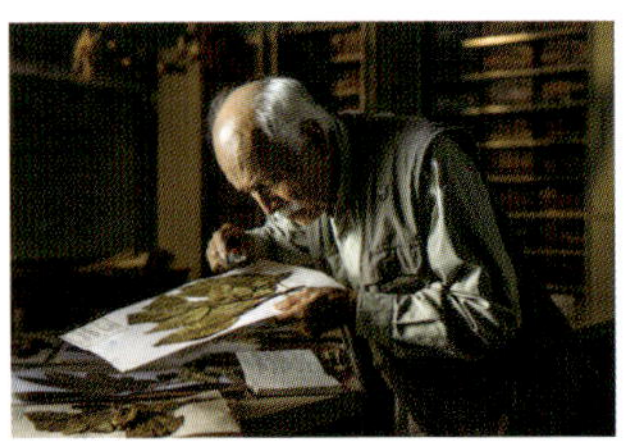
Luis Jorge Poveda Alvarez, “Pove”
Page 85

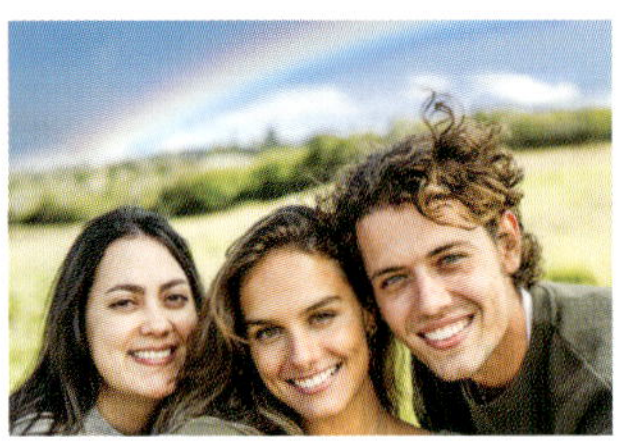
Luciana Koberg Garrón
Page 89

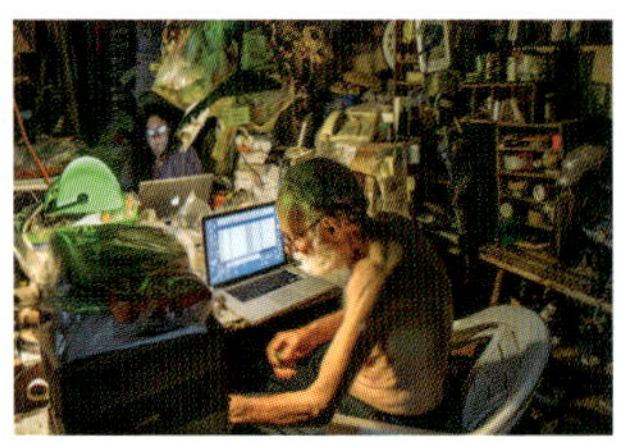
Winifred Hallwachs and Daniel
Janzen Page 93

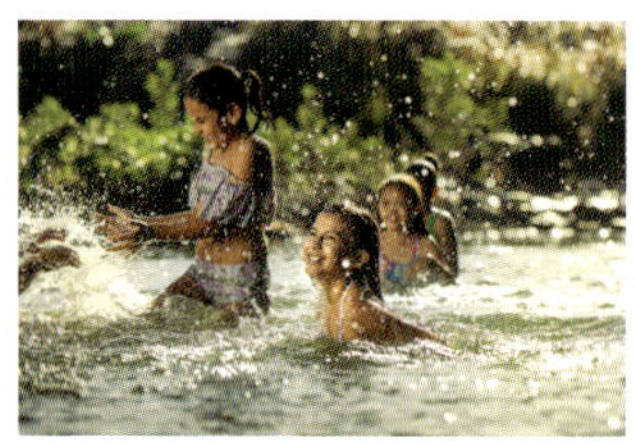
Jimena Amador.
Page 95

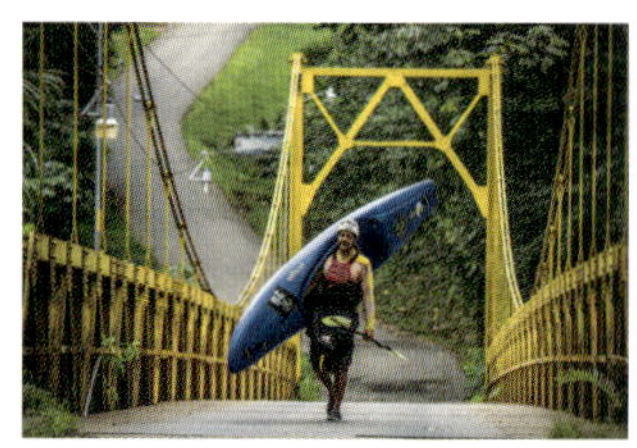
Leonardo Vásquez
Boza Page 99

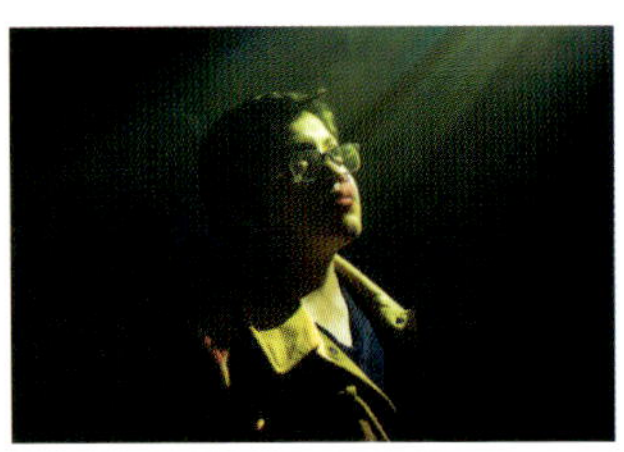
Jackeline Villalobos Morales
Page 103

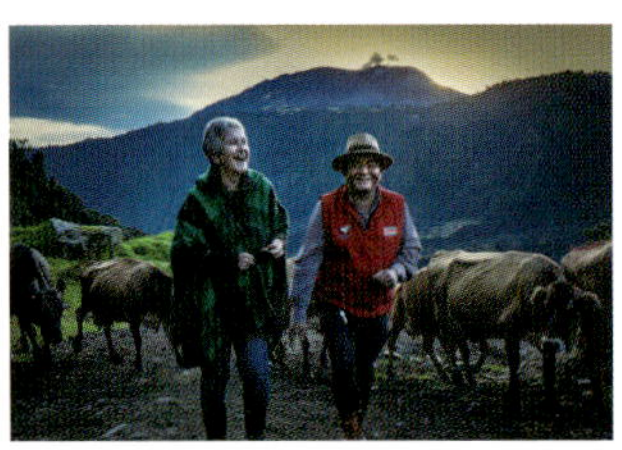
Eduardo Robert Ureña and
Marlene Robert Rohrmoser
Page 105

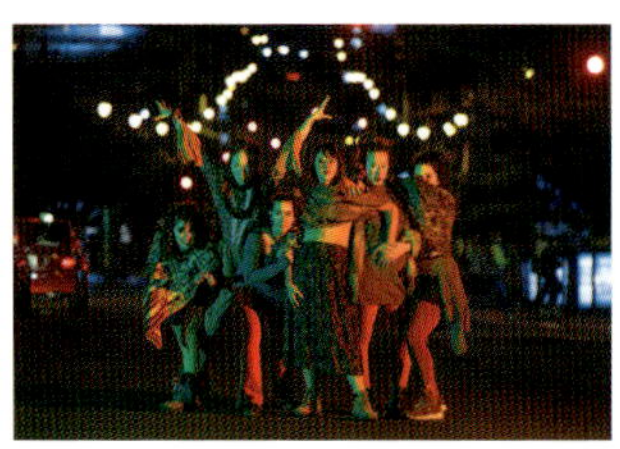
Colectiva Viajo Sola - Daniela
Quesada Page 109

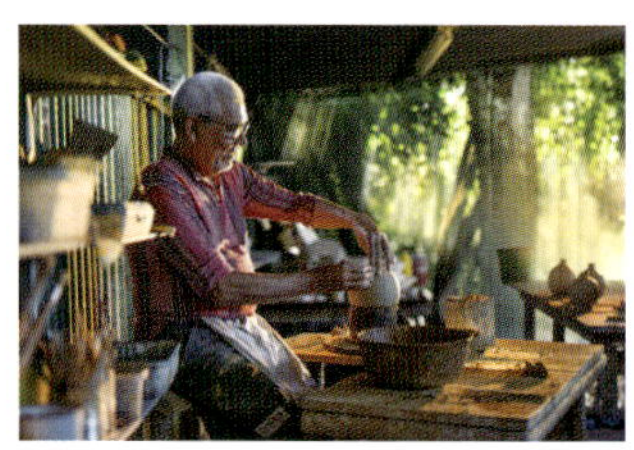
Gerardo Selva Godoy
Page 113

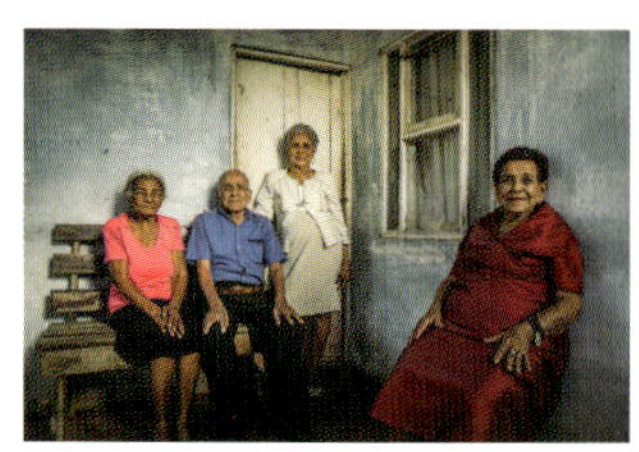
Dora Amparo Bustos
Duarte Page 117

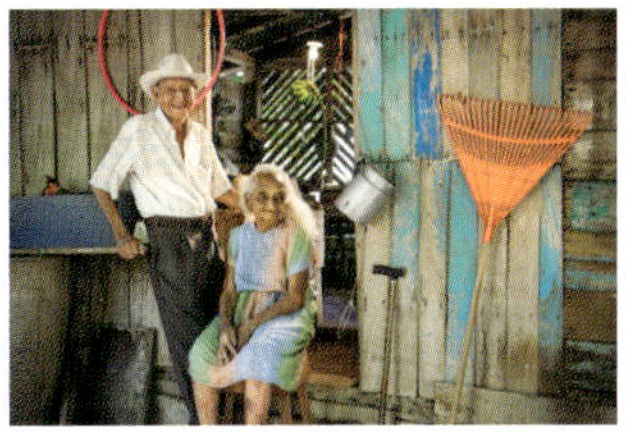

**José Bonifacio Villegas Fonseca, "Pachito"**
Page 123

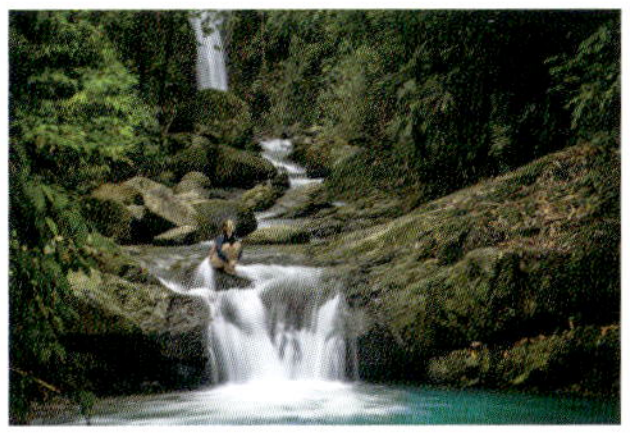

**Pilar Salazar López**
Page 129

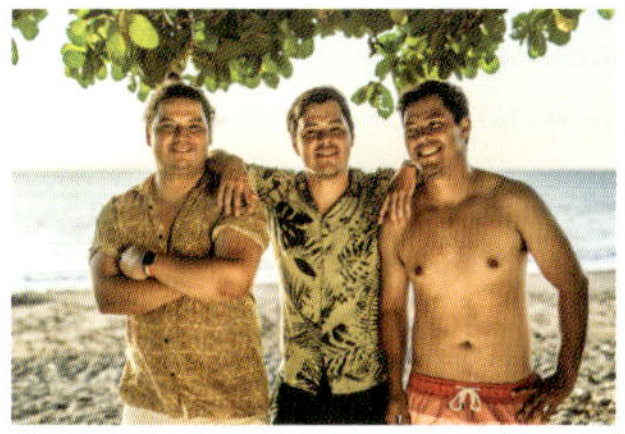

**Róger Alonso and Alonso José Durán Hernández**
Page 133

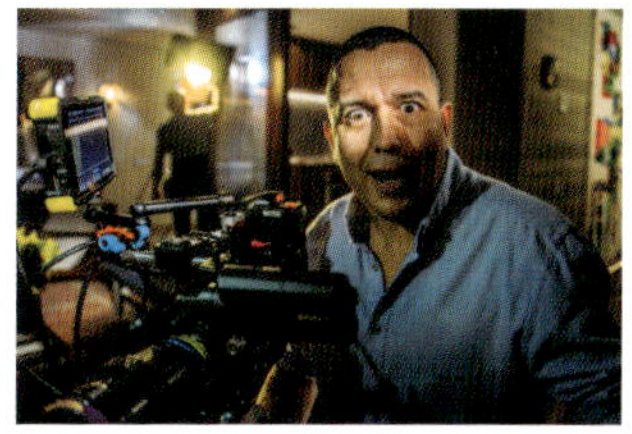

**Sebastián Vega Fernández**
Page 137

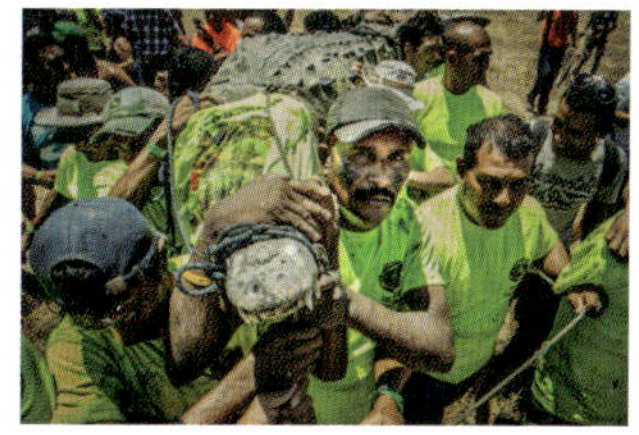

**Humberto Miguel Angulo Piña**
Page 139

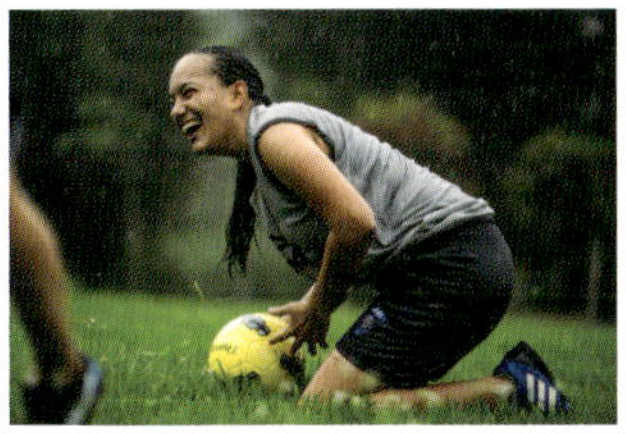

**Verónica Acuña Navarro** Page 143

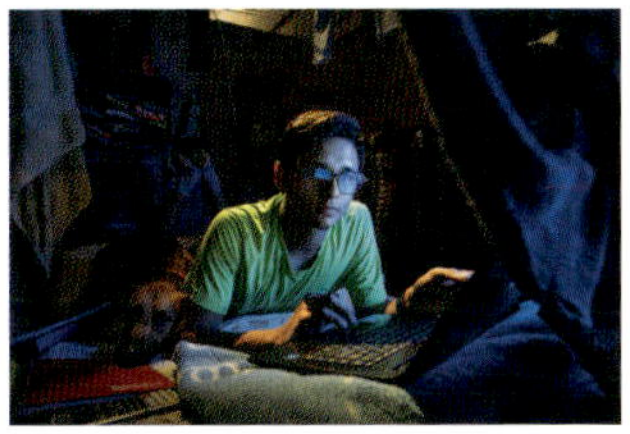

**Yilmer López Lacayo**
Page 145

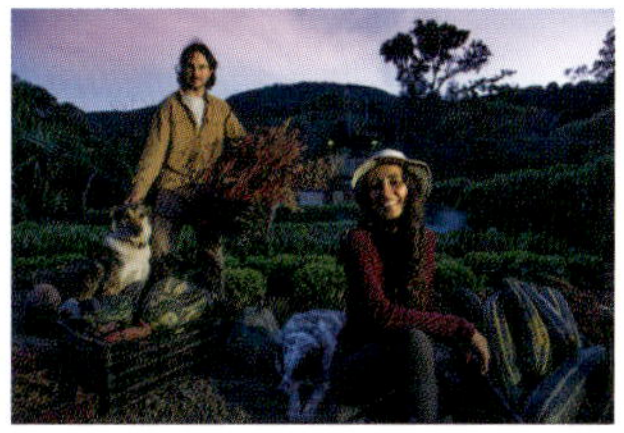

**Gabriel Bravo Pacheco and Jemima Picado** Page 151

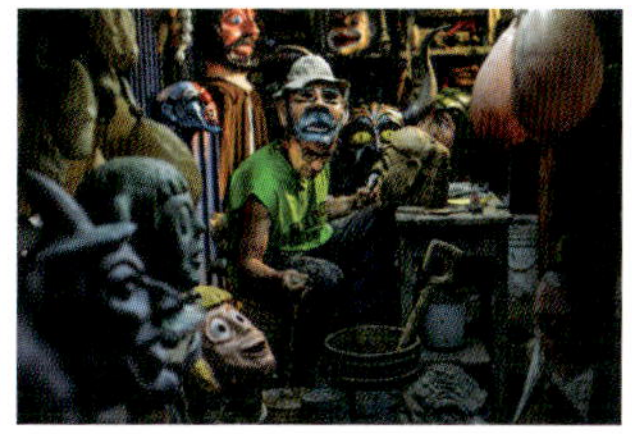

**Luis Fernando Vargas Cascate**
Page 157

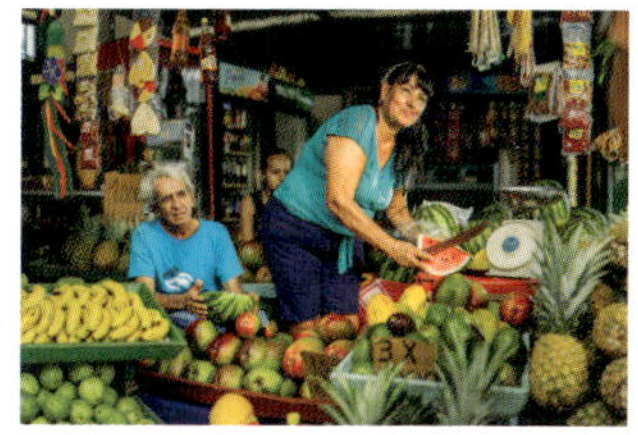

**Floribeth González Vargas**
Page 161

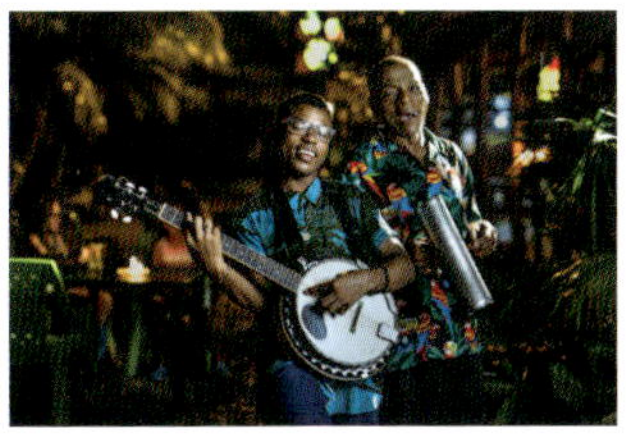

**Danny Álvarez González** Page 165

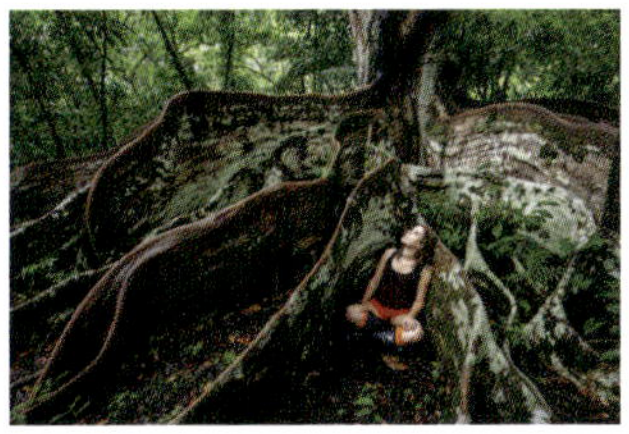

**María Gabriela Montero Sánchez** Page 167

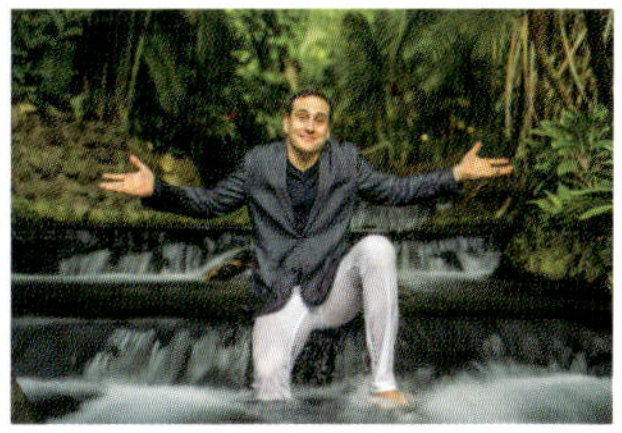

**Daniel Mikowski Hun**
Page 169

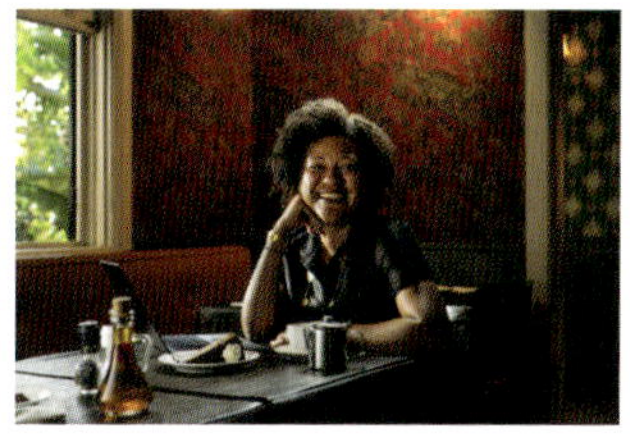

**Eunice Shara Duncan Villalobo** Page 171

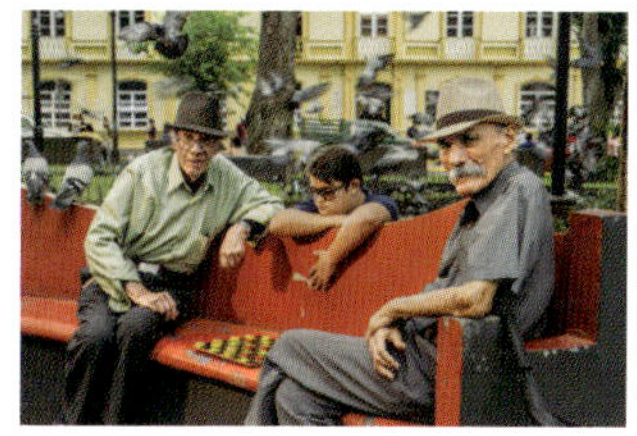

**Emiliano "Totó" Araya García** Page 173

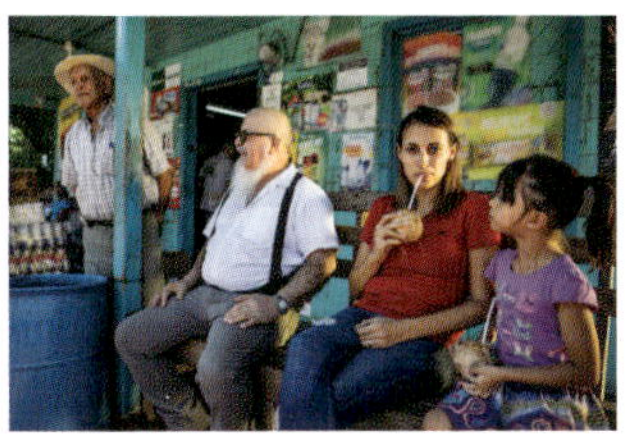

**Andrea Leiva Saborío**
Page 177

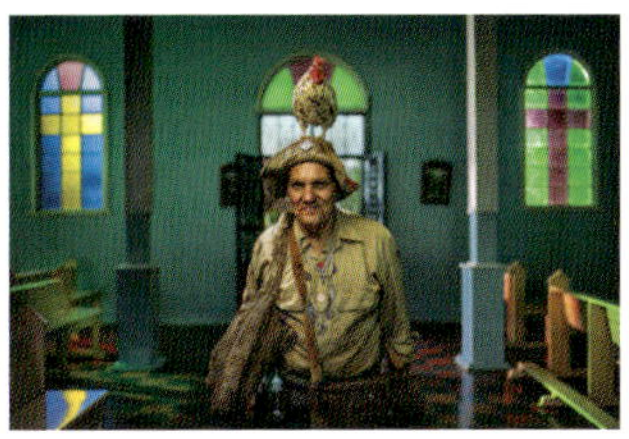

**Carlos Guadamuz Hidalgo**
Page 181

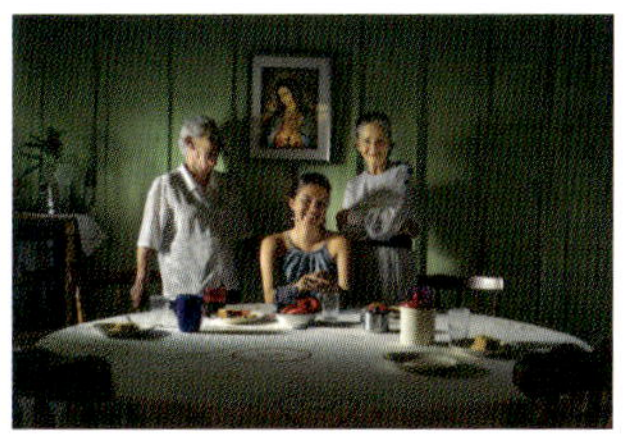

**Guadalupe Hernández Ramírez** Page 185

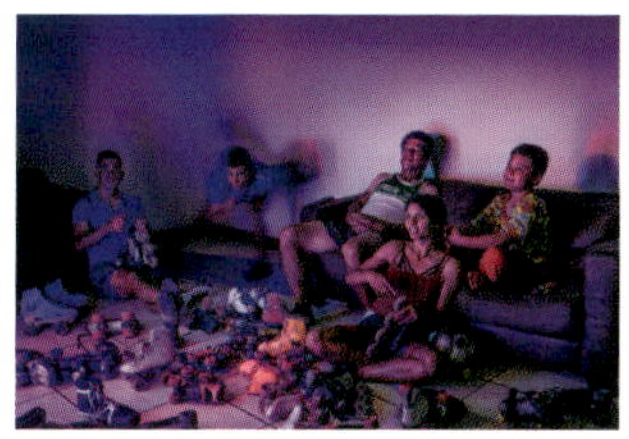

**Siles Family**
Page 189

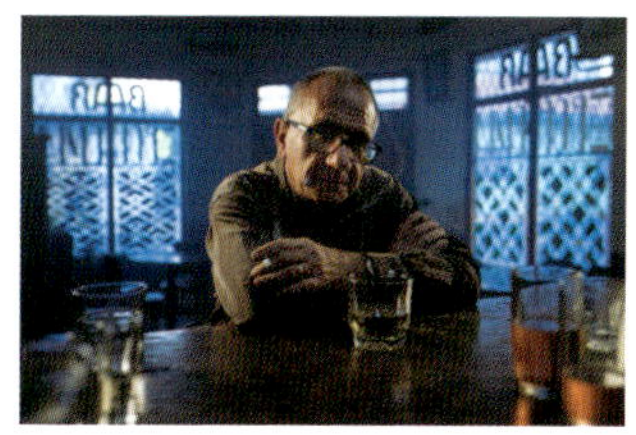

**Jorge Motta Aronne**
Page 193

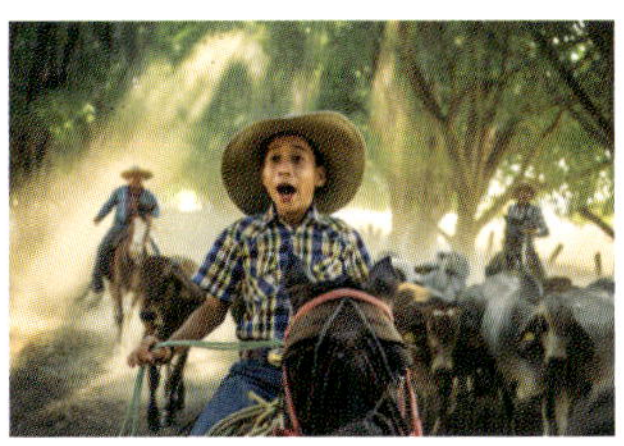

**Antony Daniel Coronado Cortés** Page 197

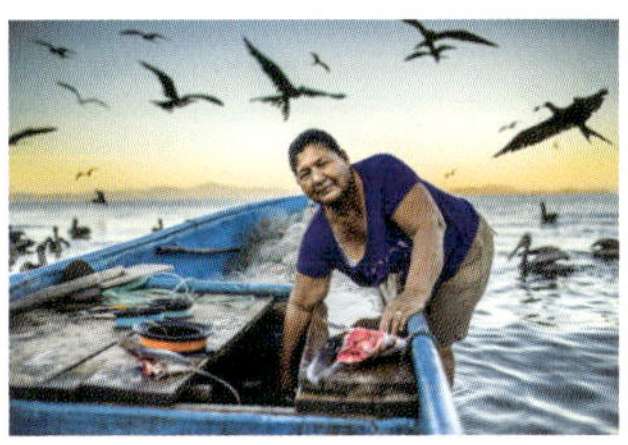

**Estebana Pérez Martínez**
Page 201

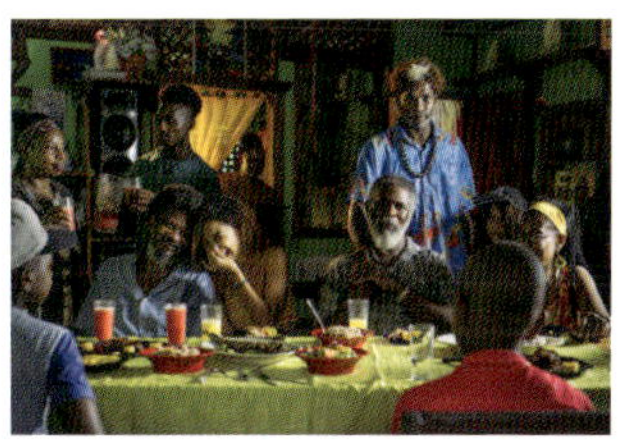

**Carl Cunningham Brown and Brown Family**
Page 205

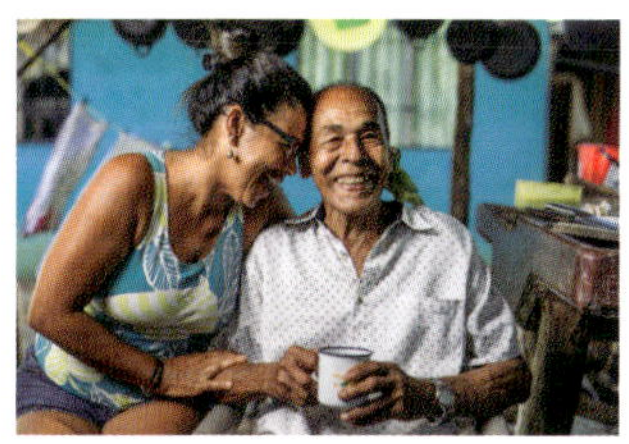

**Manuel Zamora Contreras**
Page 209

# DEDICATION

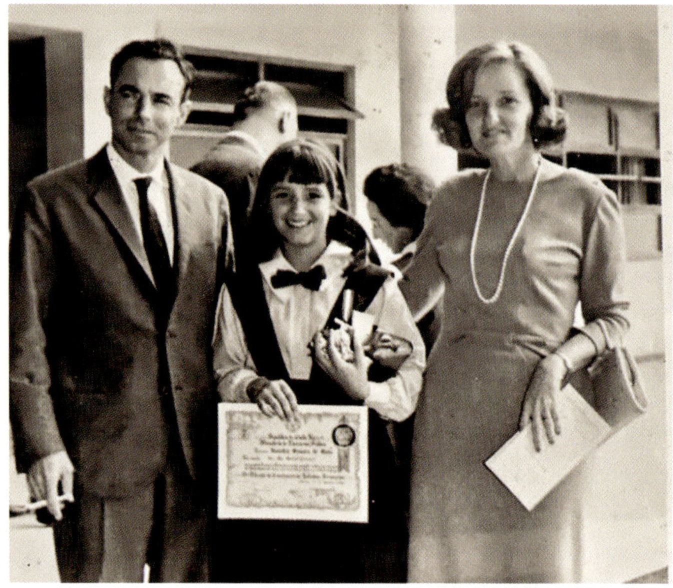

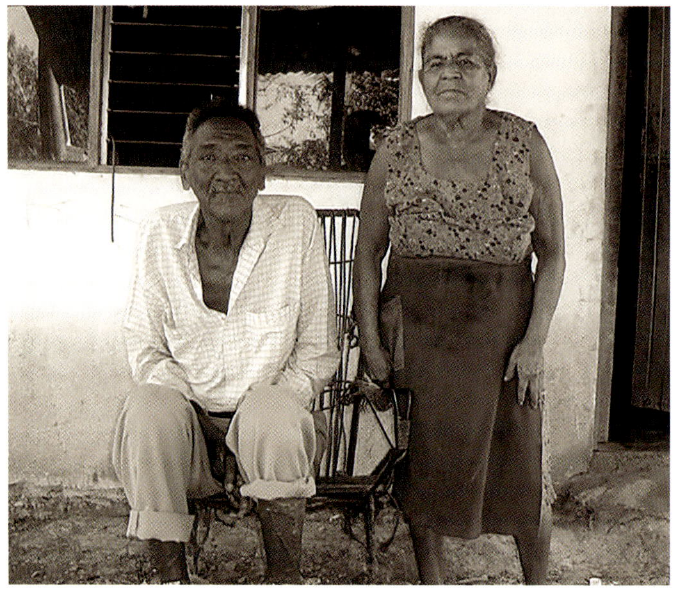

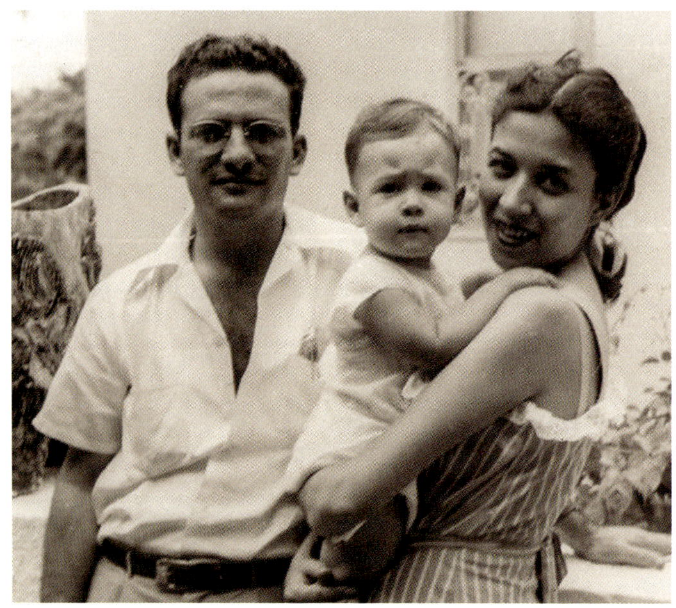

**To the people who honored us with their trust and agreed to share their stories and be featured here**

Don Giorgio, Carlos, María Amalia, Lisímaco, Doña Alba and Doña Marta Eugenia, Shara, Sebas, Jackeline, Mela, Yilmer, Verónica, Gabriel and Jemima, Enrique, Joseph, Byron, Yuliana and Jeicob, Juan José, Luciana, Mateo, Caro Lao, Colectiva Viajo Sola, Blu, Amanda, Ximena, Laura and Ana María, Karol, Luis, Rita, Josué, Roger, Mari and Sergio, Gerardo Selva, Guadalupe, Floribeth, Emiliano "Totó," Victor Eduardo "Gato," Jimena, Francisco Edwin, Elizabeth, Doña Carmen, Mariam, Magda, Eduardo, Marlene, María Elena, Angeline, Lisandro, the Brown family, Carl Brown, Jubanel, Danny, Junior Álvarez, Pove, Luis Fernando "Bombi," Eithan, Reinier, Madeley, María Laura and Antonia, Estebana, María Cecilia, Andrés, María Gabriela, Pili, Pancho, Leonardo, Daniel M., Andrea, Anthony, Aquiles, Eladio, Yeimy, Bonifacio "Pachito," Trini, Dora, Humberto, Manuel, Felipe, Winnie and Daniel.

To all the people who were born or live in Costa Rica, who for obvious reasons couldn't be included in the book, but we hope they feel somehow represented in this project.

To Dad (Juan José), for the loving guidance in the world of photography and for so much more.

It also feels important in this project to thank our ancestors. Origin and creation. There have been many generations of Ticas and Ticos, of mixed blood, of stories, of mourning, of struggles, of healing. To those who passed this way but whose bodies are no longer here. Without the history that precedes us, we wouldn't be here. We hold you close.

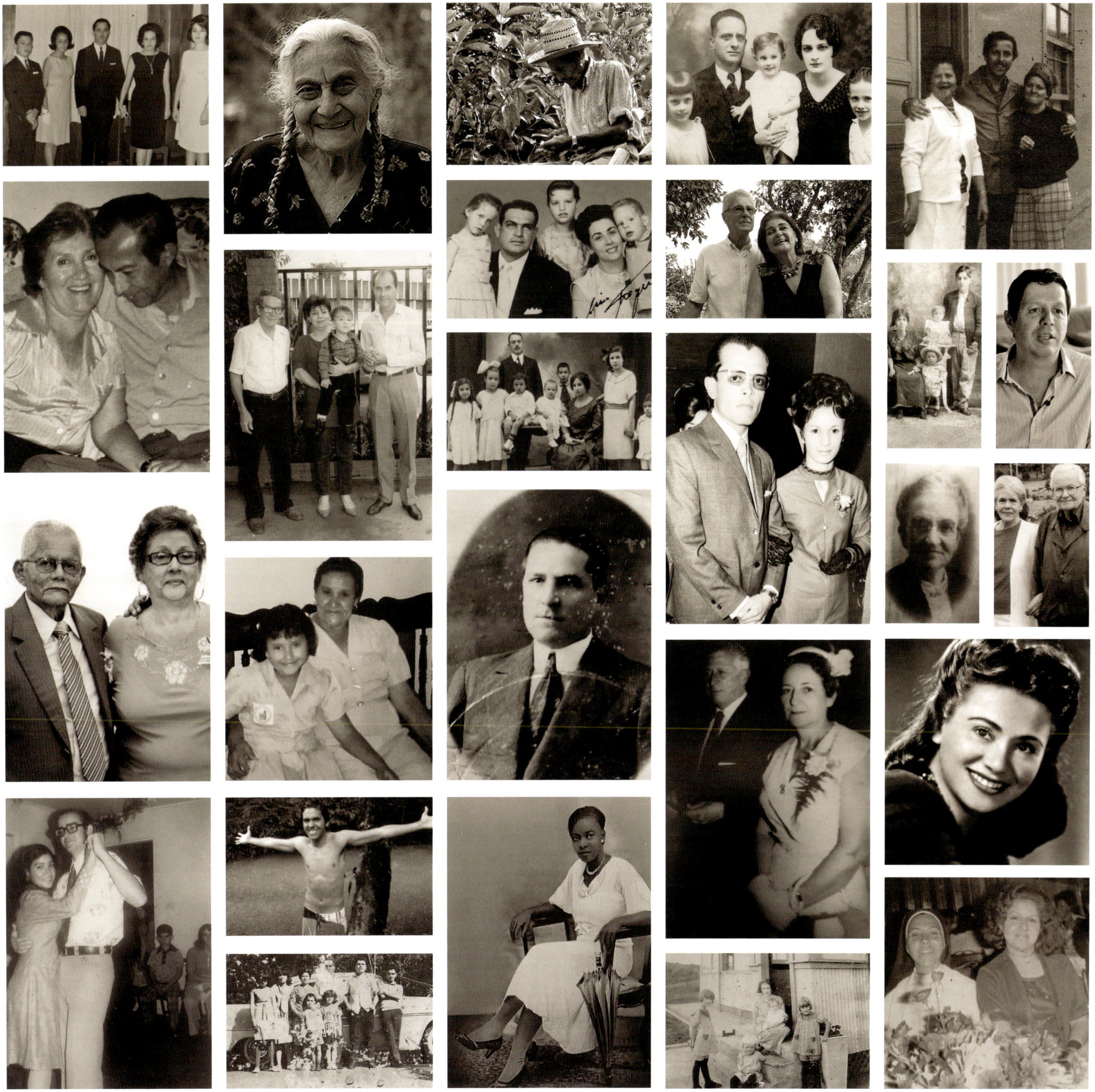

# ACKNOWLEDGMENTS

Ilse Golcher Carranza - To Mom, for life, courage and love
María José Trejos
Aurora and Clara
Priscilla Hine
Alvaro Brenes
Victoria Mata
Matías Brenes
Sergio Brenes
Sor Carmen Brenes
Maria Angélica Vargas
Marcela Sotela
Yusafín Jarquín
Michelle Macluff
Daniel Rescio
Ana Javier Quintero
Melissa Zuñiga
Ximena Guardia
Carolina Quirós
Andrés Cervilla
Kevin Durán
Mónica Hidalgo

**Contributors**

Gabriela Bruna
Karol Méndez
Lucía Vasquez
David Ramirez
Camilo Villegas
Marielos Cordero
Esteban Zabala
Pablo Acuña
Natalia Díaz
Mohamed AlShammari

**Team**

Enrique Camacho
Carolina Quirós
Daniel Montiel, Cindy Montero, Marcelo Rosales, Guillermo Vargas

**Sponsors**
Nisa Sanz
Marcela Sandoval
María José Rodríguez
Anabelle Calderón
Laura Moreno
Gustavo Guerrero
Sergio Morales
Marco Agüero
Greivin Badilla
Nicolás Marín
The Marca País team

**Genuine and spontaneous assistance**

Blue Zone: Jorge Leiva, founder and presidente of the Asociación Península de Nicoya Zona Azul
Villegas family: Paulina Villegas Reyes, Ingrid Villegas Reyes, Alexa García Villegas
and Mateo Fonseca García
Ma. Trinidad Espinoza, Martha Beatriz García, Zuri Valeska Suárez
Bustos family: Filemón, Encarnación, Ninfa, Rodrigo, Zeidy, Marta, Sugeilyn and Santiago
Hojancha: Luis Ángel Pérez, convenience store; Manuel Pineda, José Gutierrez, Guanabeer
Cowboys: Carlos Martínez, Jose Gerardo Martínez, José María Cruz, Aquiles Vargas,
Federico Apestegui Pacheco, Finca Monteclaro
Ostional: José Pablo Baltodano Díaz
Puntarenas: Olman Jorge Shedden Cerna Sr., Olman Ricardo Shedden Quiros Jr.
Shedden ice factory: Jose Pérez, Lisseth Sánchez, Walter Calderón, Victor Espinoza, Augusto Rojas
Centro de Investigación Biológica Hacienda Barú
Santiago Montero
Esteban Solano
Francini Hernández, Julizxa Salazar, Pamela Jiménez, Valentina and Monserrat Bonilla, Mariela and Jimena Amador, Joshua Zuñiga, Tatiana Castillo,
Fabiola Madrigal, Génesis and Avril Mora, Saray Acosta, Sarah Rodriguez, Arley Montoya, Kevin and Kiane Salazar, Ma. Fernanda Méndez and Joab Araya
Frutería Oromango, Ma. Carolina Fernández García, Jacinto Vargas
Carmen Miranda, Ana Rita Arguello
Jose María Álfaro, Amón Solar
Johana Delgado
Escuela Jesús Jimenez Zamora
Cesar Madriz, Cafetería Franco
Comparsa Los Brasileiros
Carolina Lao, Mateo Esquivel
Leila Garro
Juan José Delgado
Mickey Ryan Castillo
Maitena Larrauri
Junior Álvarez, Grace González
Laura Pacheco, CETAV, Parque La Libertad
Alejandro Masis, Área Conservación Guanacaste
Octavio Durán, Kevin Durán
Colectiva Viajo Sola
Saunak Shah
Vanessa Arley Villalobos
Jaime Rouillon
María Pérez, La Esquina
Hotel Tabacón
Jorge Rosales
Tatiana Berger

And to two people who have been an important source of growth during the process of this book.

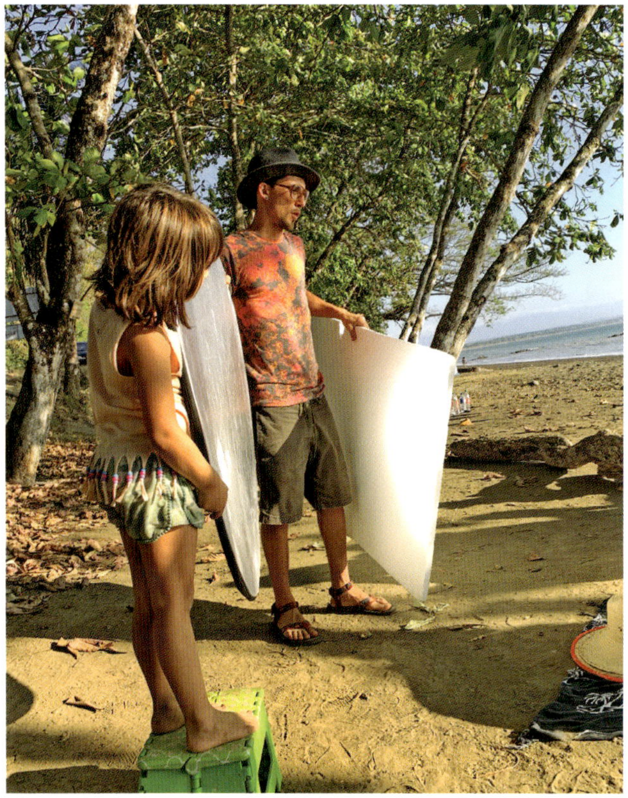

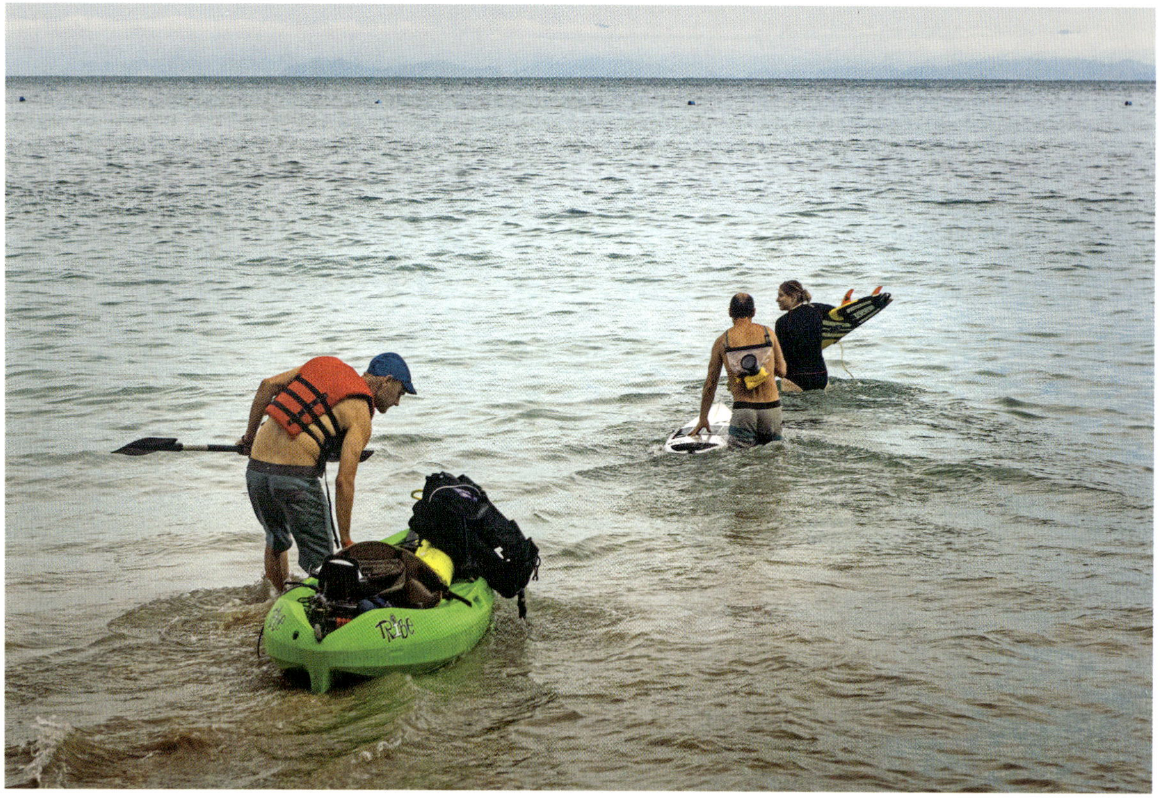

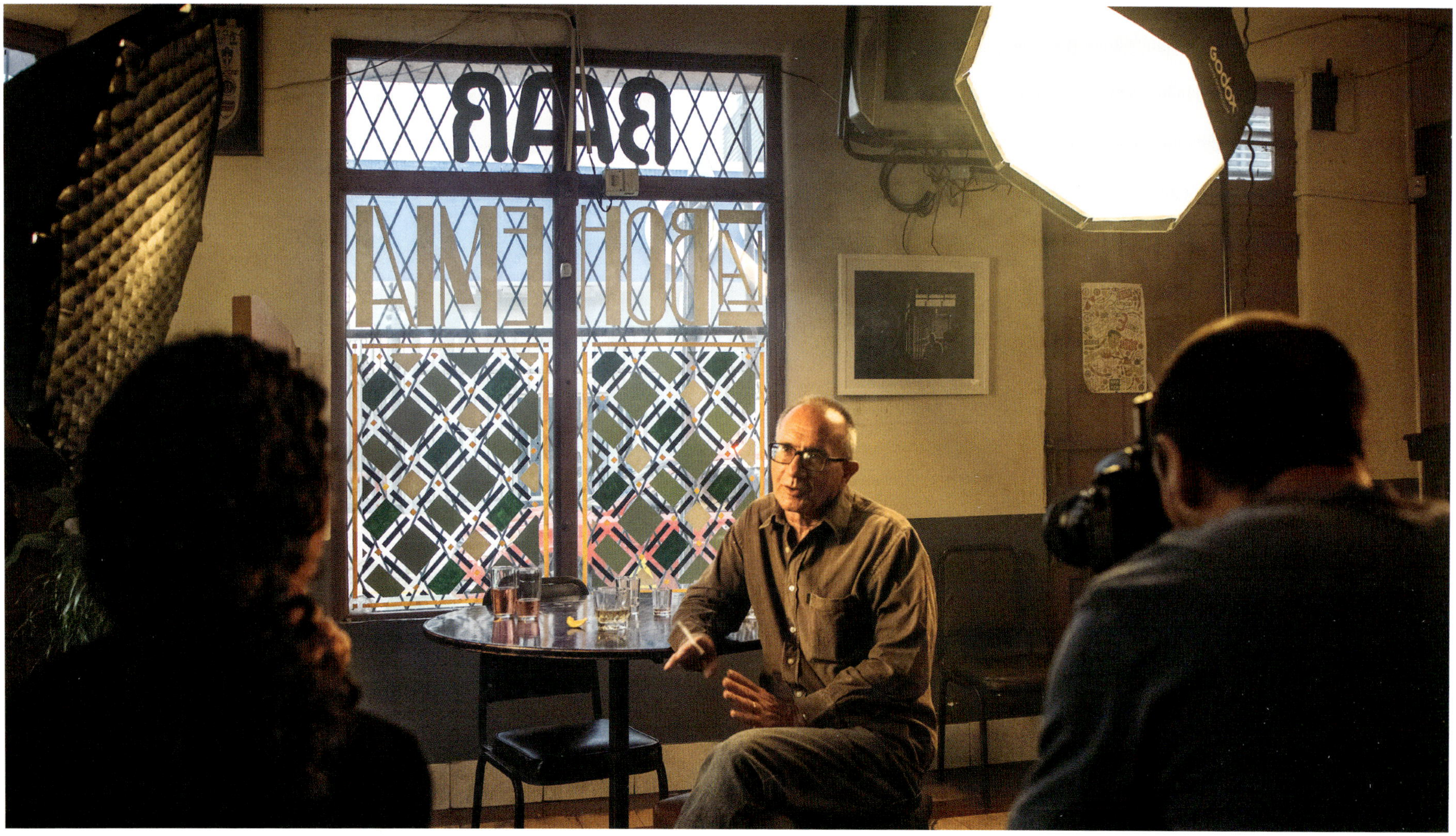
BAR

# CREDITS

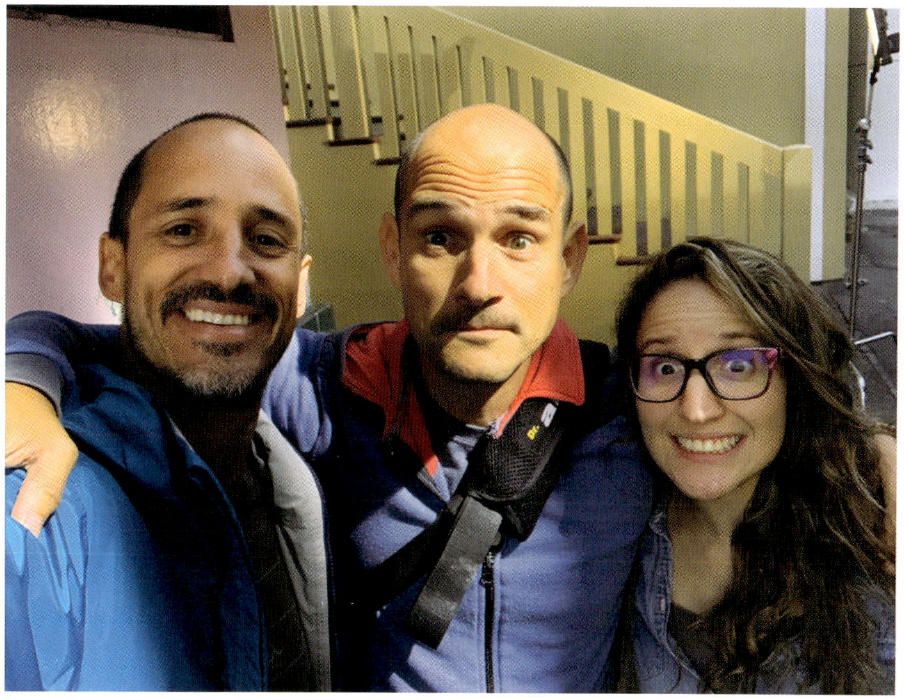

**Editorial committee:** Sergio and Giancarlo Pucci, María Teresa Brenes
**Photos:** Sergio and Giancarlo Pucci. (Except page 54-55 Saunak Shah)
**Concept:** María Teresa Brenes, Gabriela Bruna, Sergio Pucci, Giancarlo Pucci, Juan José Pucci
**Photo curator:** Juan José Pucci
**Photography production:** María Teresa Brenes, Sergio Pucci, David Ramírez, Tremendo
**Lighting:** Sergio Pucci, Gaffers Roberto Valerio, Willy Fuentes
**Photo editing:** Sergio Pucci
**Photo calibration:** Kenneth Naranjo
**Project management:** María Teresa Brenes
**Introduction text:** Jaime Gamboa
**Additional text:** Giancarlo Pucci
**Story selection:** Sergio Pucci
**Story editing:** Jaime Gamboa
**Story collection:** Fernando Bolaños
**Biographies:** Adriana Sánchez
**Translation:** Karl Kahler
**Identification of subjects:** Editorial committee in collaboration with Tremendo and Comuna Producciones
**Demographics researcher:** Pablo Acuña
**Graphic design:** Gitanos
**Communications:** Giancarlo Pucci, Gloriana Sojo, Sergio Pucci and María Teresa Brenes
**Video production:** Camilo Villegas

---

398.097286
P977p Pucci, Sergio, fotógrafo
Pura Gente: Sergio Pucci, Giancarlo
Pucci ; edición de Sergio Pucci. – 1 ed. – San José, C.R. : Inversiones
GSPG Internacional, 2021.
248 p. ; fotógrafos. : 27 X 27 cms.

ISBN: 978-9930-503-08-9

1. Personas– Fotografías - Costa Rica. 2. Personas – Vida Social y
Costumbres – Costa Rica. I. Pucci, Giancarlo. II. Título.

# HOW DID WE TAKE THE PHOTOS?

We didn't set out to do documentary photography, but real-life portraits of 54 individuals. They were photographed in their world and their real context in an effort to accent their authenticity. This map shows the locations where the photographs were taken.

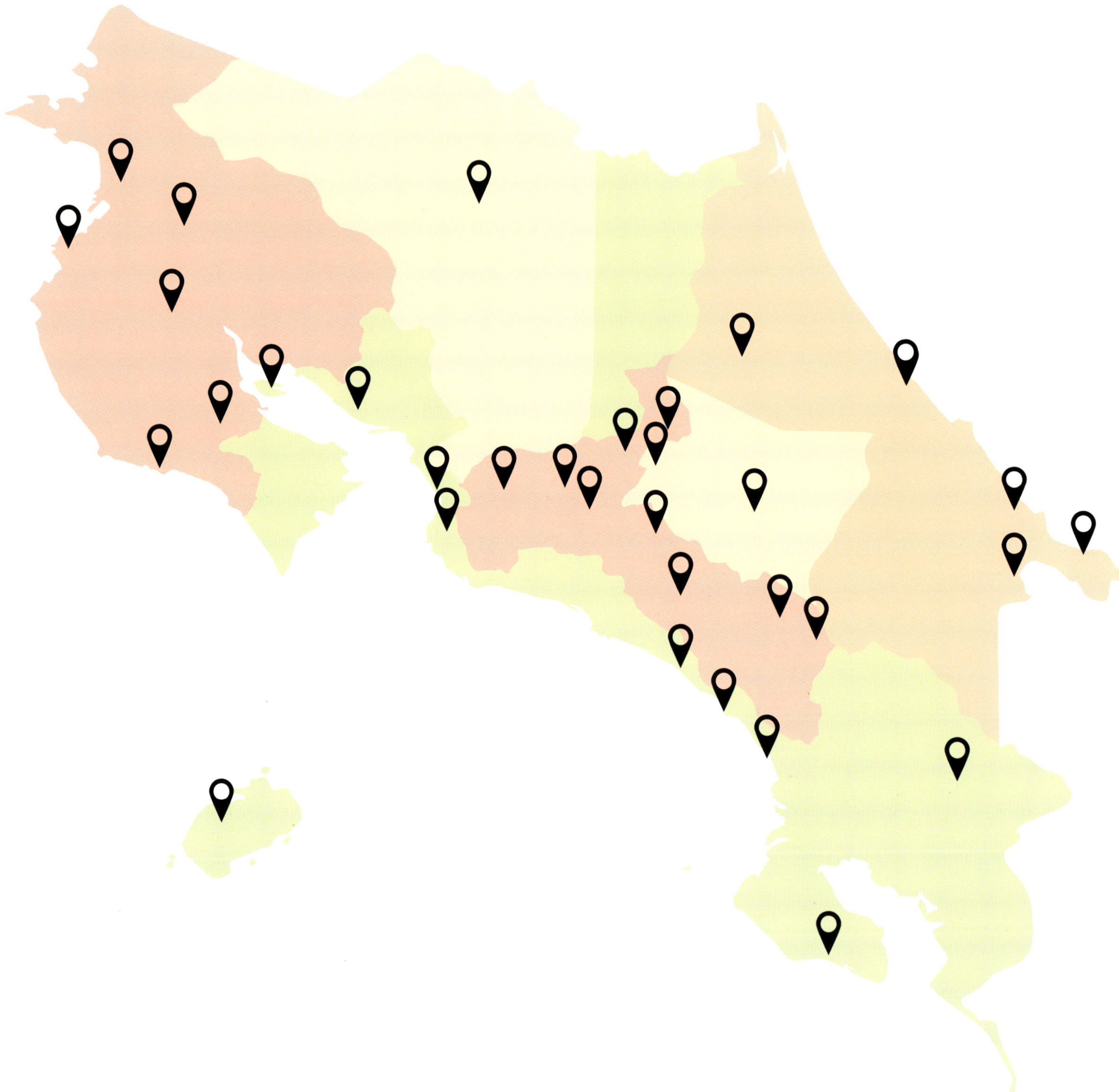

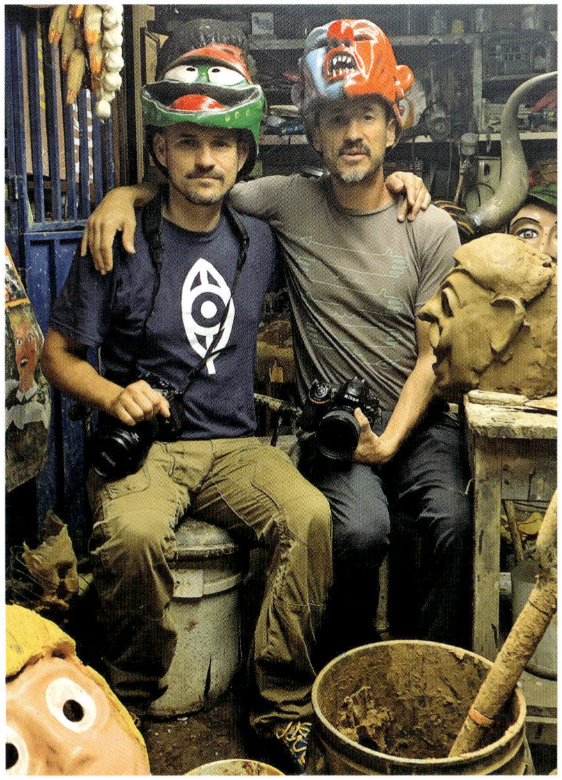

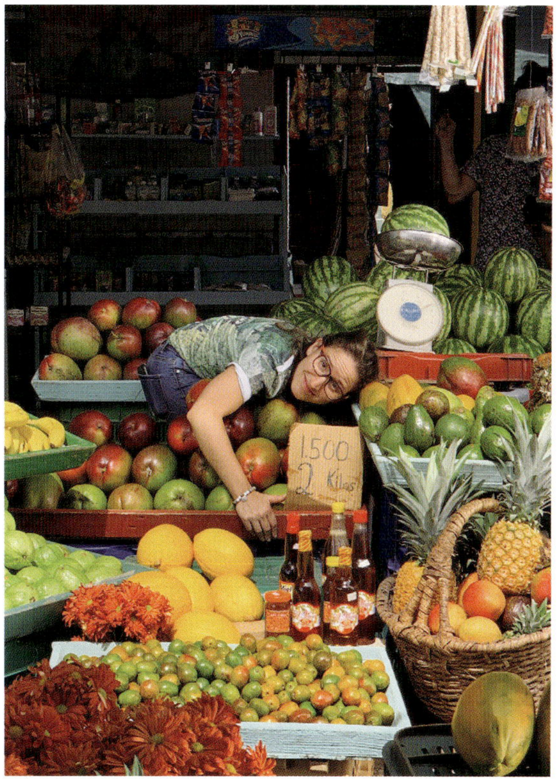
1500
2 Kilos

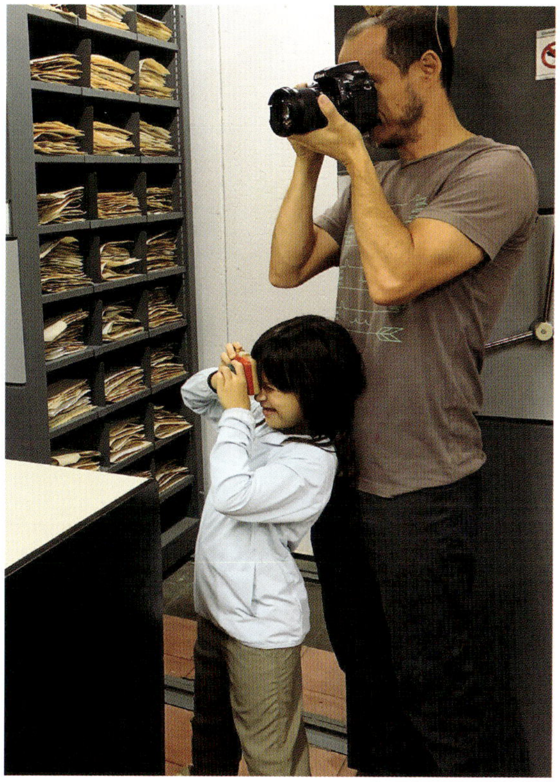

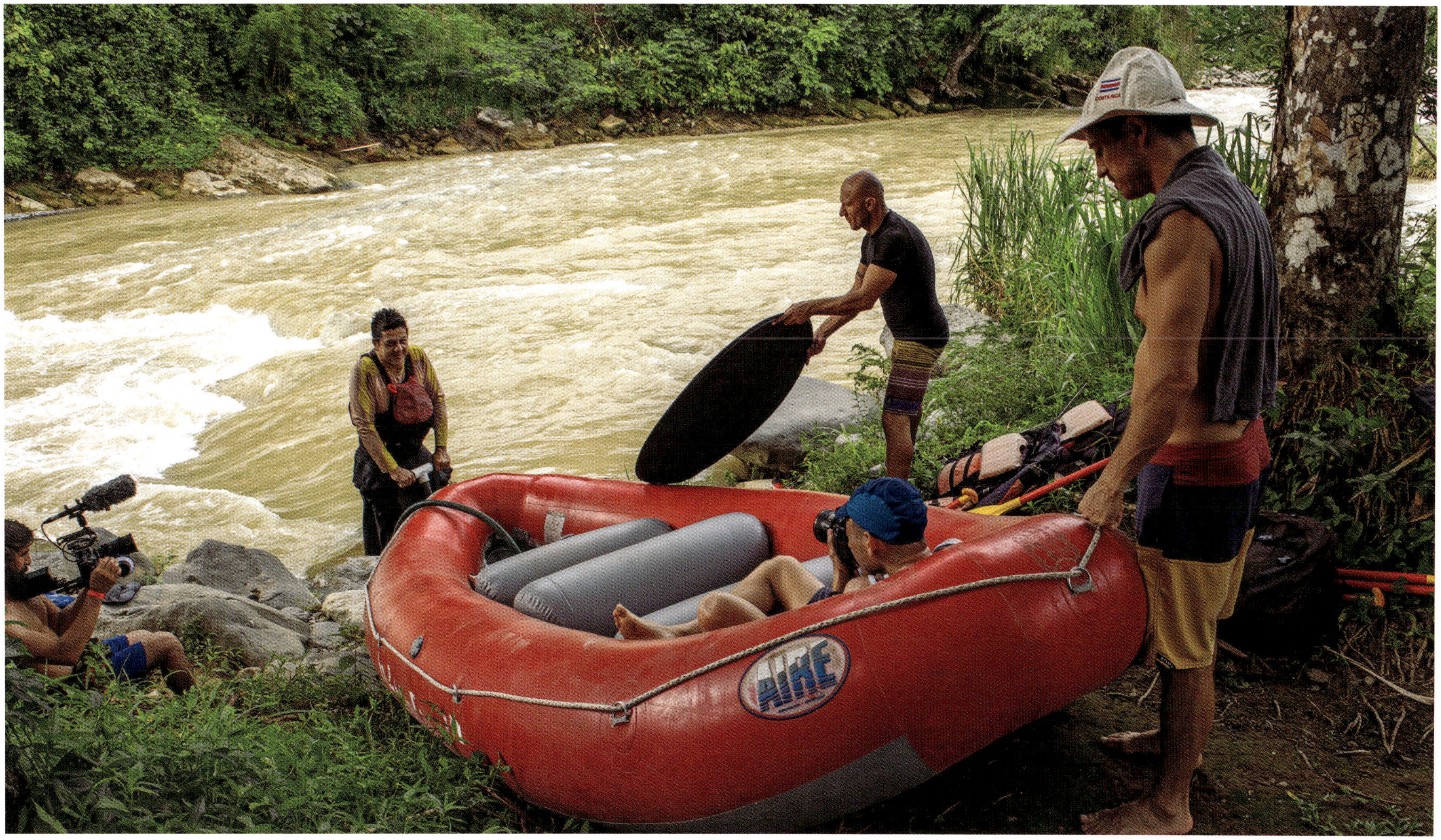
AIRE

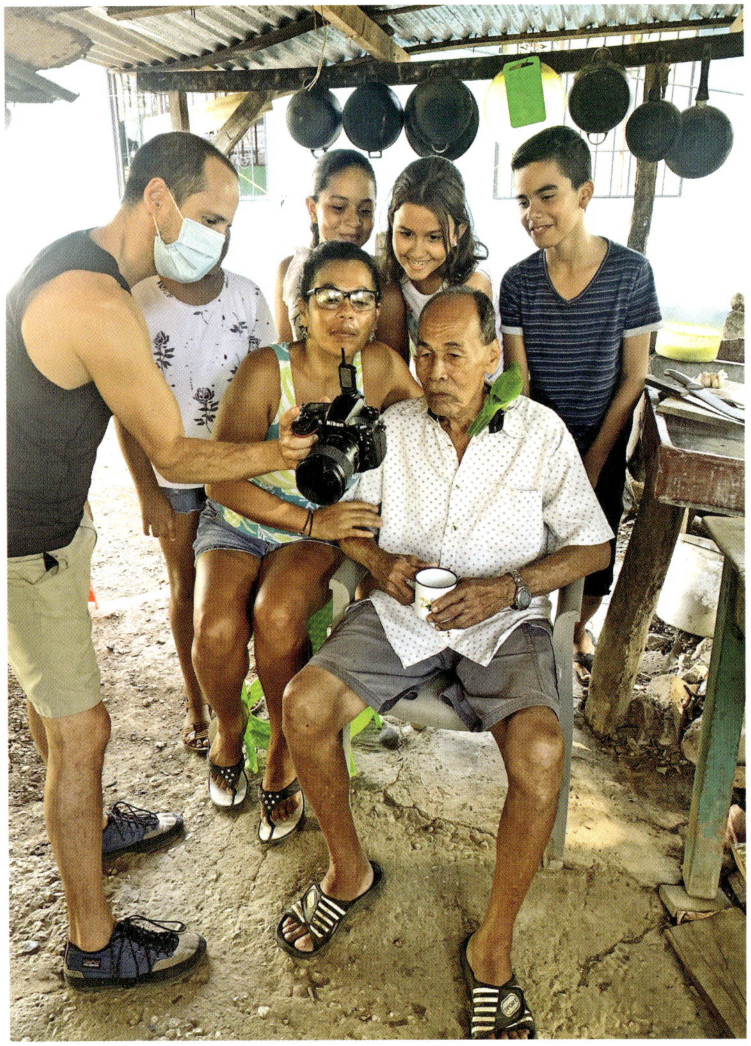

## OUR PROCESS

Although it sounds cliché, our process here has been as important as the result. We'll share a bit here about the path we traveled for more than two years.

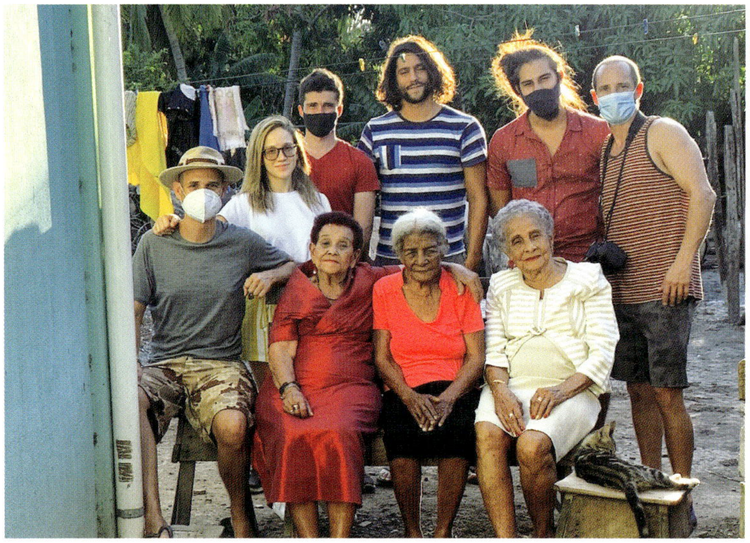

## HOW DID WE CHOOSE THE PEOPLE?

It was important to put the country's diversity on display. The people of this country are a mirror of its biodiversity.

We approached this task, along with our good friend, the researcher Pablo Acuña, of consolidating statistics from the State of the Nation, INEC and other sources, to gather representative profiles in a matrix, considering factors like province, gender, ethnicity, income, occupation and others. For example: a professional woman from the central canton of Heredia, head of household, between 30 and 35 years old, middle class, entrepreneur. We still hadn't put a face or name to her. Based on these profiles, we searched for people that met the parameters. It took more than two years to find, evaluate and choose these individuals. This matrix and these profiles, far from being rigid, were a guide that never pretended to be a visual census, but more of a demonstration of the diversity that exists in Costa Rica.

We know that there are many more we could have chosen, but we thought this could be the beginning of a showcase that could lead to many other stories.

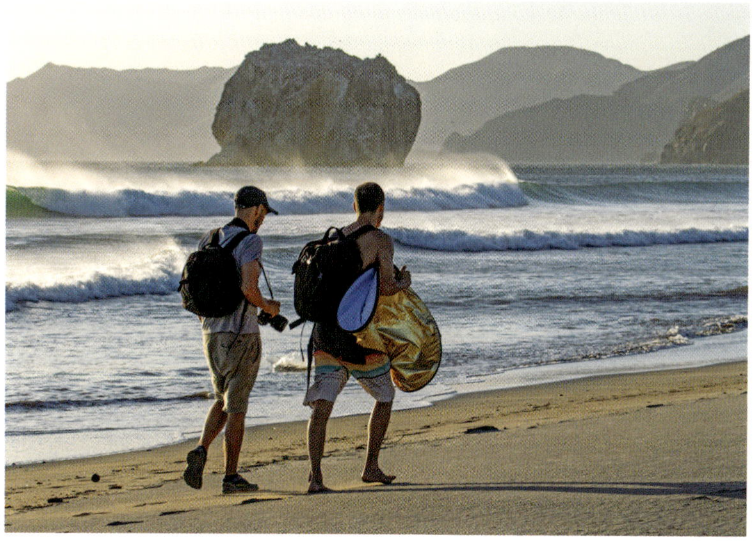

## HOW DID WE WRITE THE STORIES?

We looked for stories that would generate connection, empathy and above all, that would honor the lived experience of these people.

The stories are an intimate part of each person, and we've treated them with great care and affection. When we photographed each one of them, a member of the team sat down to talk, to listen, to ask questions. This person recorded audio and took notes. As a team, we discussed the possibilities of each story, to dig deeper and ask more detailed questions. This process took several hours and involved a good deal of both randomness and authenticity, recording everything the person shared with us that day.

The next stage was to shape, synthesize and write the story on one page. For this task, we decided to include many outlooks and styles, turning to several writers, some with a lot of experience and some with less, but all with great sensitivity and narrative skills.

We matched stories with writers, and then through one or more rounds of recommendations, the selected versions were edited by Jaime Gamboa.

It felt like a risky venture to create a book with so many different pens. It wasn't about forcing them into some predetermined style, but more about discovering the inspiration and creativity of each writer.

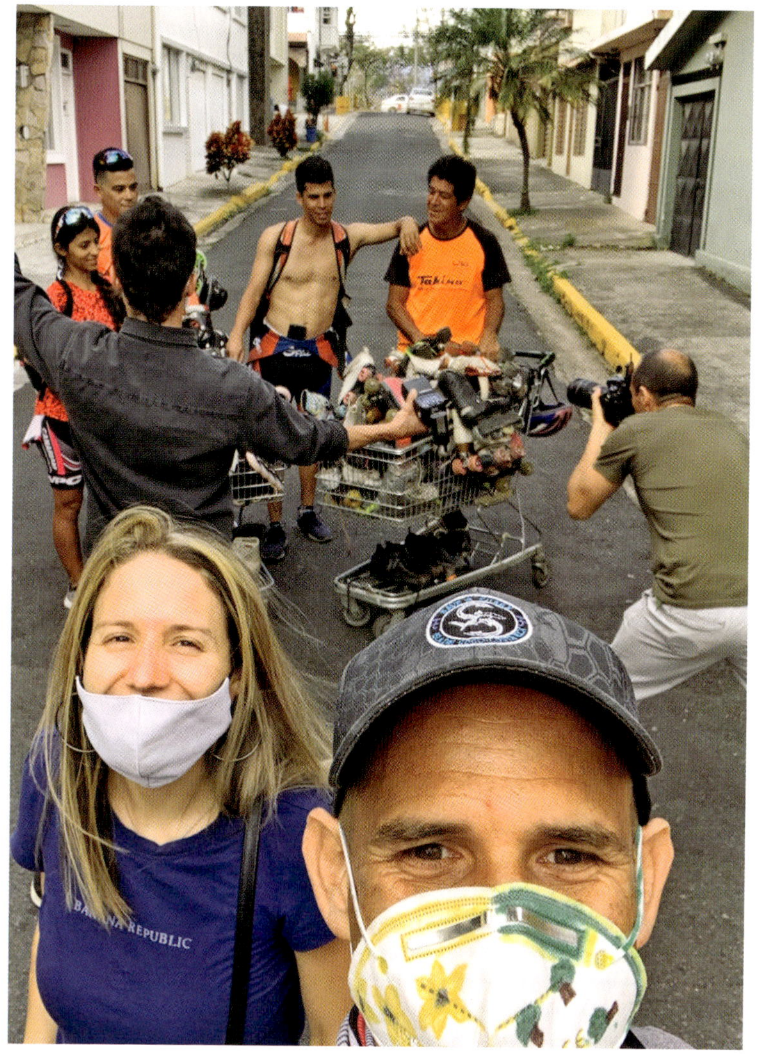

# 200 YEARS OF DEMOCRACY

**1814**
On April 24, the first public school was founded, named Casa de Enseñanza Santo Tomás.

**1820**
Costa Rican coffee is first exported, to Panama.

**1821**
On October 13, the Act of Independence of Central America arrived and was signed on October 29, granting Costa Rica independence from Spain.

**1824**
On July 25, the annexation of Nicoya was signed. The fundamental law of the Republic of Costa Rica was officially announced.

**1848**
On August 31, the independence from the Federal Republic of Central America was signed.

**1869**
On April 15, education for both sexes was officially declared compulsory and free, fully subsidized by the state.

**1884**
San José was the first city in Latin America to install electric streetlights, and the third in the world after New York and Paris.

**1940**
The University of Costa Rica was officially founded.

**1941**
On November 1, the Costa Rican social security system was founded (Caja Costarricense de Seguro Social).

# POPULATION IN 200 YEARS

**1821**
POPULATION: 65,393

CENTRAL VALLEY
**55,484** | 85% CENTRAL

COASTS
**9,909** | 15% COASTS

From independence to the 100-year anniversary, the population grew seven times larger.

**1945** The term "national park" was mentioned for the first time in Decree 197 and the first corps of park rangers was created.

**1948** The motion to abolish the army was signed.

**1949** A new constitution was announced, and the Second Republic was proclaimed.

Women's voting rights were approved and were exercised for the first time on June 30.

**1956** First wildlife conservation law, No. 2093.

**1977** On August 17, law No. 6084 was signed. The law of the creation of the National Park Service.

**1998** Biodiversity law No. 7788, the creation of SINAC (National System of Conservation Areas).

**2012** Law 9106 prohibited sport hunting.

**2020** On June 5, law No. 9849 was amended to recognize and guarantee the human right of access to water.

**2021** On May 25, Costa Rica became the first Central American country and the fourth in Latin America to join the OECD (Organization for Economic Cooperation and Development).

**1921**
**POPULATION:**
**476,581**

CENTRAL VALLEY
**382,530** | 83% CENTRAL

COASTS
**82,031** | 17% COASTS

From the 100th to the 200th anniversary, the population grew 11 times larger.

**2021**
**POPULATION:**
**5,163,038**

CENTRAL VALLEY AND OTHER NON-COASTAL
**3,793,905** | 73.5% CENTRAL

COASTS
**1,369,116** | 26% COASTS

In 200 years, the population grew 78 times larger.

# DEMOGRAPHICS OF COSTA RICA

## BY SEX

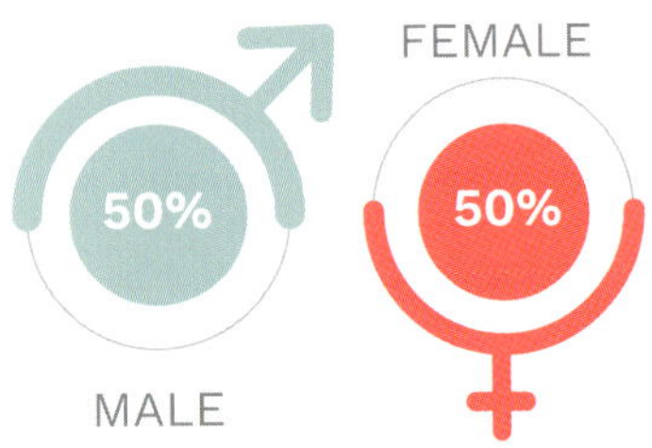


## BY AGE

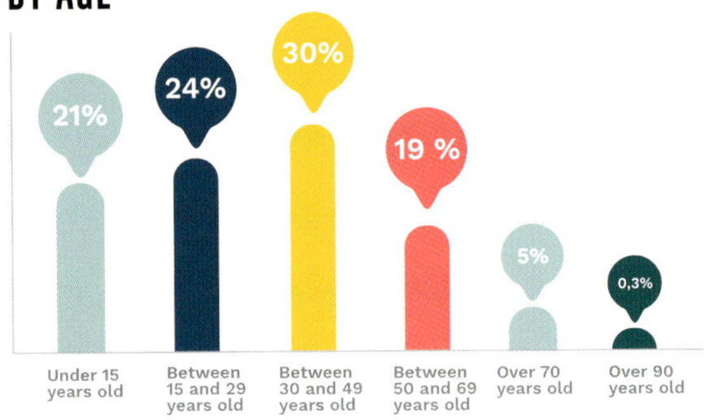


## BY PROVINCE

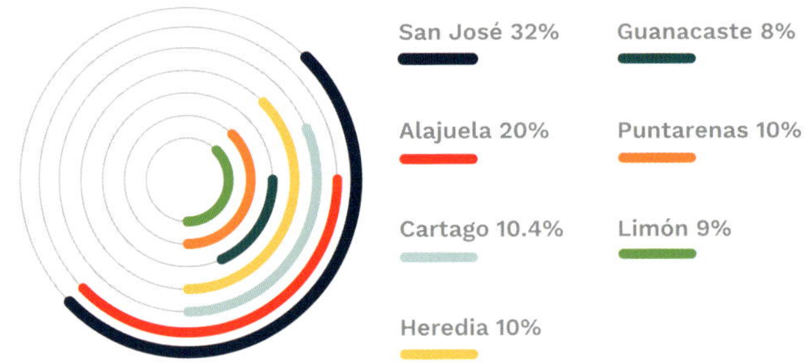


## AVERAGE TOTAL MONTHLY INCOME PER HOUSEHOLD BY QUINTILE

% of people

| | % of people |
|---|---|
| ₡ 200,314 ( I Quintile) | 23% |
| ₡ 381,426 (II Quintile) | 21% |
| ₡ 601,068 (III Quintile) | 20% |
| ₡ 998,549 (IV Quintile) | 19% |
| ₡ 2 278,895 (V Quintile) | 16% |

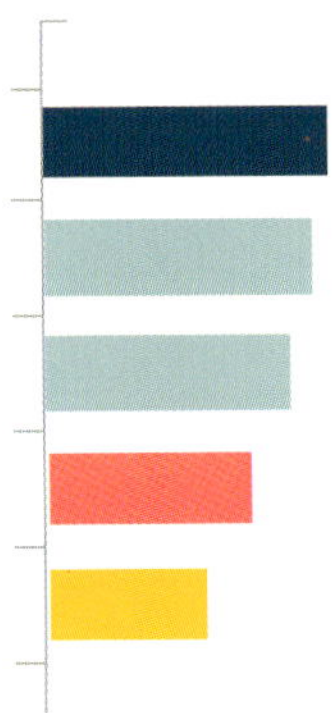

***The number of people per quintile varied 1-2% during 2020

## BY ETHNIC GROUPS (SELF-IDENTIFIED)

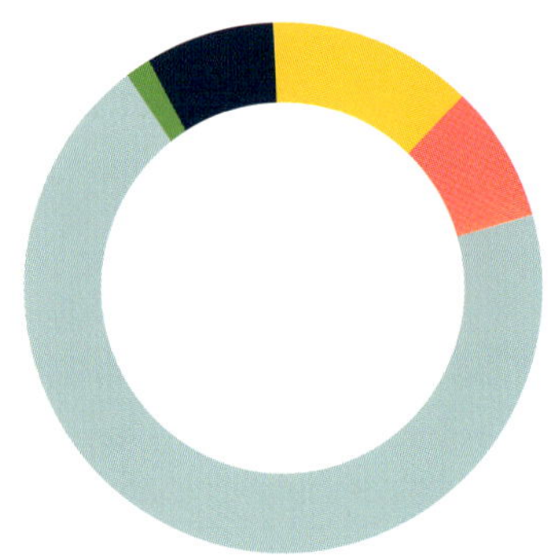

81%*
White or mixed population

7.6%**
African descent

1.2%*
Indigenous communities

1.2%**
Chinese origins

5.9%*
Other/not declared

*2011 census
**Other sources

## IMMIGRANTS (8.3%)

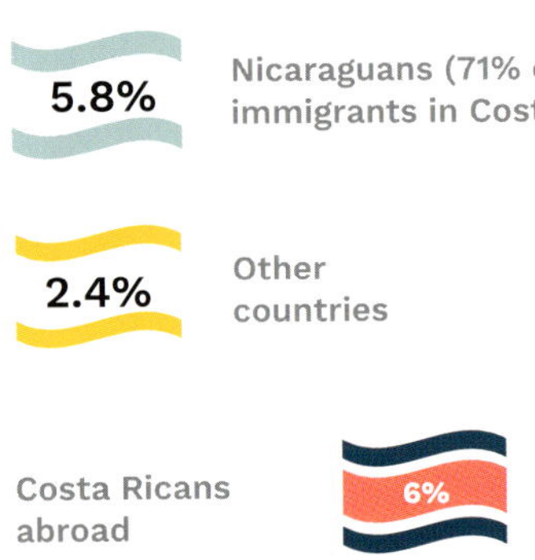


5.8% Nicaraguans (71% of immigrants in Costa Rica)

2.4% Other countries

Costa Ricans abroad 6%

## EMPLOYED AND UNEMPLOYED POPULATION

Workforce (people over 15 years of age with possibility of actively seeking paid work)

Female 40%

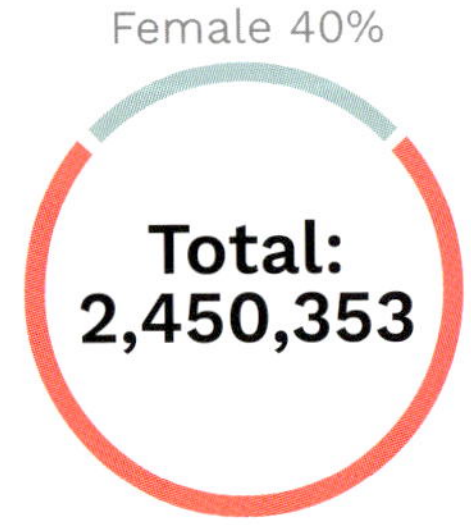


Male 60%

**Employed**

81.3%

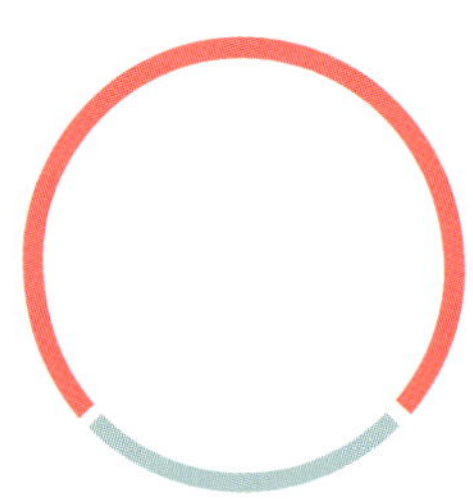

Unemployed 18.7%

**Unemployed population**

Female: 56.5%

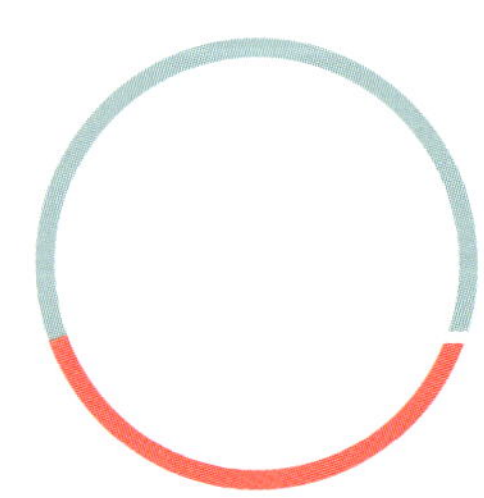

Male: 43.5%

***This data includes an increase in the unemployed population from 2020 to 2021 of more than 6% due to the pandemic.

# PRODUCTIVE SECTORS

## PRIMARY SECTOR (5%)

|  | ♂ | ♀ |
|---|---|---|
| Agriculture, livestock and fishing | 3% | 2% |

## SECONDARY SECTOR (7%)

| % | Sector | ♂ | ♀ |
|---|---|---|---|
| 5% | Manufacturing industry | 2.5% | 1.4% |
| 3% | Construction | 3% | 0% |

## BUSINESS AND SERVICES SECTOR (26.7%)

***Decreased by around 2% due to the pandemic

| % | Sector | ♂ | ♀ |
|---|---|---|---|
| 7% | Trade and repair | 4% | 3% |
| 2% | Transport and storage | 2% | 0.2% |
| 3% | Hotels and restaurants*** | 1% | 2% |
| 1% | Financial and insurance services | 0.5% | 0.5% |
| 3% | Professional services and administrative support | 2% | 1% |
| 2% | Public administration | 1% | 1% |
| 3% | Communication, entertainment and other | 2% | 1% |
| 4% | Education and health | 1% | 3% |
| 2% | Employed in homes | 0.3% | 2% |

# BY TYPE OF EMPLOYMENT

(POPULATION WITH PAID WORK)

- 5% Public workers
- 34% Private sector workers (***decreased about 3% during 2020)

## BY JOB POSITION

- 28% Wage earners (decreased by 3% in 2020)
- 9% Entrepreneurs, independent workers (increased 1% in 2020)
- 1% Employers, business owners

## FORMAL AND INFORMAL WORK

- 21% In formal work
- 18% In informal work

# BY SEX

60% ♂ 40% ♀

# OTHER DATA

**41.2%** Households in which women provide the primary income.

The economic value of unpaid domestic work was estimated in 2017 at **25.6%** of gross domestic product.

**71%** of domestic work is done by women.

- By 2020, the 330 multinational companies attracted by CINDE had generated 134,026 jobs, representing about 5.5% of the workforce and 6.75% of the employed population.
- 13%, or 1 in 10, of those who work are public workers.
- 22% of working people did not finish high school.
- 78% of the population is in the workforce age (over 15 years old).

# SOCIAL CONDITIONS

There is more poverty concentrated in urban areas, but rural areas and the coasts are the poorest in the country.

**1 IN 5**
**Ticos lives in poverty**

# BY AGE

**The population is largely concentrated in the 20-44 age group (more than 2 million)** → **41%** OF THE POPULATION

**FERTILITY RATE:**
1.7 is the average number of children per woman.

# BY GENERATION

Born after the year 2000 **30%** Digital natives

They will live throughout the 21st century

Those between **59 YEARS** **89 OLD** Lived through the crises of the ’40s and ’50s

# DISTRIBUTION

**1 IN 3 TICOS LIVES IN SAN JOSÉ**

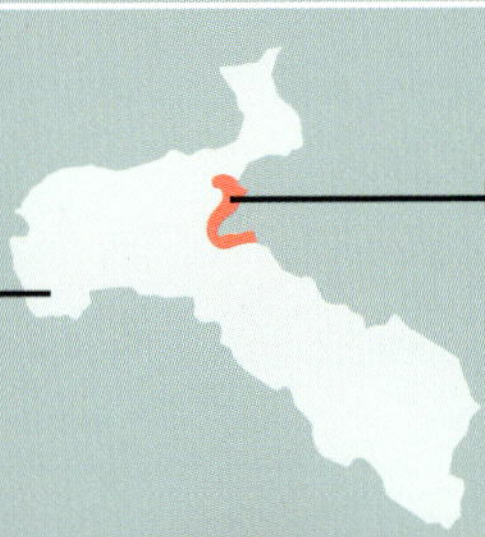

**5%** of the country’s population lives in Desamparados

**TALAMANCA** is the canton with the lowest rating in the Social Progress Index (SPI)

**SAN JOSÉ** **32%** is the province where the majority of the population lives (32%)

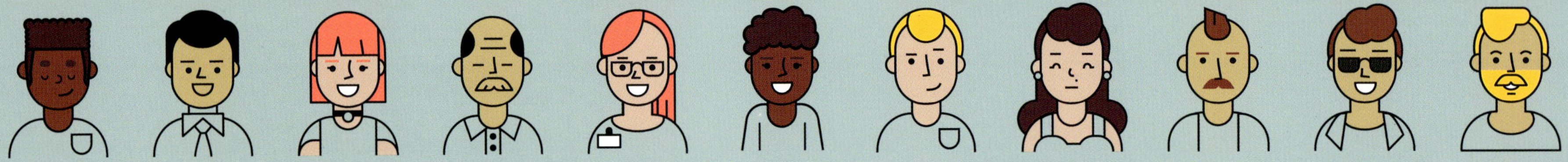

## 97.5% OF THE POPULATION BELIEVES IN A GOD, DEITY OR A HIGHER POWER

**1940** Creation of the Symphonic orchestra

**1942** Creation of the National Conservatory of Music

**GALLO PINTO** is the most recognized food

# CULTURE, TRADITIONS AND CUSTOMS

# RELIGION

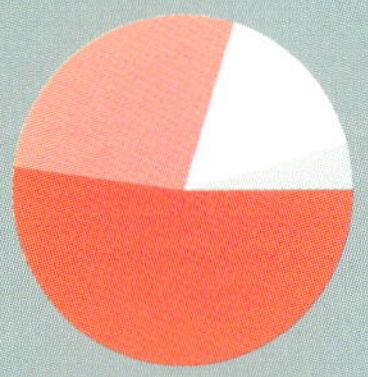

- **52%** Catholics
- **22%** Evangelicans
- **17%** No religion specified/other beliefs
- **9%** Other religions

**INDEPENDENCE DAY** is the most recognized celebration

**FAVORITE LEGENDS:**
- **LLORONA** 45%
- **CADEJOS** 43%
- **CEGUA** 34%

# SPORTS

**75%** of the population is a fan of a soccer team

- 36% Saprissa fans
- 30% Alajuelense fans
- 6% Herediano fans
- 4% Cartago fans

# PEOPLE WITH DISABILITIES

12% of the population has some kind of disability — 1 in 10 Ticos

# OTHER

- More than 60% of the population suffers from obesity
- Cultural activities represent 2.2% of the GDP
- **13,600 doctors** in the country; 60% work for the CCSS
- **15% of the population** drives a motorcycle
- **8% of the population** are entrepreneurs or independent workers. This number rose to 9% during the COVID-19 pandemic
- **82,502** teachers in the country work in the MEP
- **1,200,000** students
- **59%** of young people between 15 and 24 years of age do not finish high school
- **10%** of the population speaks English

## ARTISTIC SKILLS

(Population over 5 years of age)

2.1% OF THE POPULATION PLAYS AN INSTRUMENT

1.2% ♂ 0.9% ♀

3.2% OF THE POPULATION DANCES

0.9% ♂ 2.3% ♀

## RECREATION AND LEISURE

**44%** of Ticos attended traditional local festivals

**1 IN 3** is a cinema-goer

**64%** of men play pickup soccer

**SINCE 1993** the Pejibaye Fair has taken place in Tucurrique, annually attracting around 25,000 people

**72%** of Ticos enjoy telling stories, jokes and anecdotes

## SEXUAL ORIENTATION

**In Costa Rica an estimated of 300,000 people (6% of the population) identify as LGBTQIA+**

## MARITAL STATUS

(over 10 years of age)

**30%** Married **40%** Single **14%** Living with partner
**4.4%** Divorced **7.2%** Separated **4.1%** Widowed

# MISCELLANEOUS

- Costa Rica has exported **coffee** since before gaining independence.
- **Bananas** represented the most exported agricultural product.
- 98% of **pineapples** grown in Costa Rica are exported.
- **Oxcarts** were very important for coffee export during the 20th century.
- Costa Rica's three top **exports** are medical equipment, bananas and pineapple.

- In 2019, the country emitted 8,979 kilotons of $CO_2$, ranking #74 out of 184 countries.
- In 2020, Costa Rica reported six consecutive years of using 98% renewable energy.
- **The distribution of renewable energy was**: hydroelectric 71.95%, geothermal 14.90%, wind 12.39%, biomass and solar 0.54%.
- **The vehicle fleet** grew between 1990 and 2016 by 435%.

- Most marijuana and cocaine seizures occur in the coastal provinces of **Limón and Puntarenas**. Seizures of crack occur predominantly in San José.
- **The leading causes of death in Costa Rica** are: acute myocardial infarction, mellitus diabetes and cancer (surpassed in 2020 by COVID-19).
- Almost 80% of Ticos have **easy access to marijuana.**

- Nearly 60% of women over the age of 16 have experienced at least one incident of physical or **sexual violence**.
- An average of **133 measures of protection** are requested **per day** due to domestic violence.

- As of 2015, the **country's forested areas** represented about 54% of the national territory.
- Costa Rica conserves more than **27% of its territory under a system of protected areas**.
- **Manuel Antonio** is the most visited national park.
- As of 2018, the percentage of waste was 6.6%.
- **4,000 tons of waste** are produced daily. Of these, some 3,120 are collected and 880 are not collected. Of those collected, 2,456 go to landfills, 400 to dumps and 64 are recycled.
- As of 2015, the country uses the largest amount of **pesticides per crop** in the world.

**Author's note: The people who live in Costa Rica are much beyond these figures. Some of the data may fall short from reality. We wanted to lightly touch on these topics to generate curiosity and conversation. The data is approximate and rounded, and of course dynamic, that is to say today, as you read this, a lot has changed. For sources, scan the code.**

# OUR TITTLES

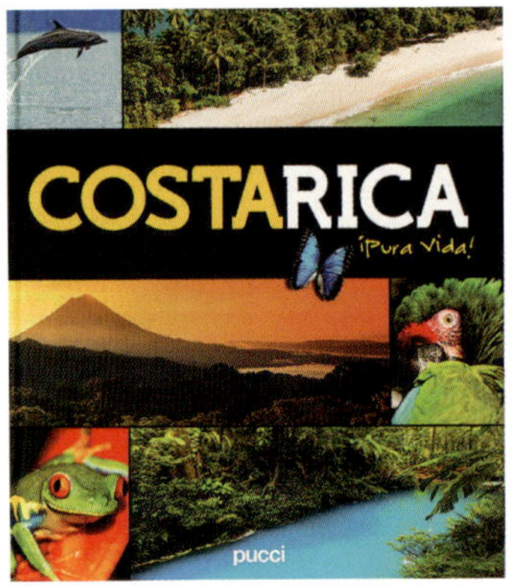


Costa Rica Pura Vida
Costa Rica Pura Vida (2011)

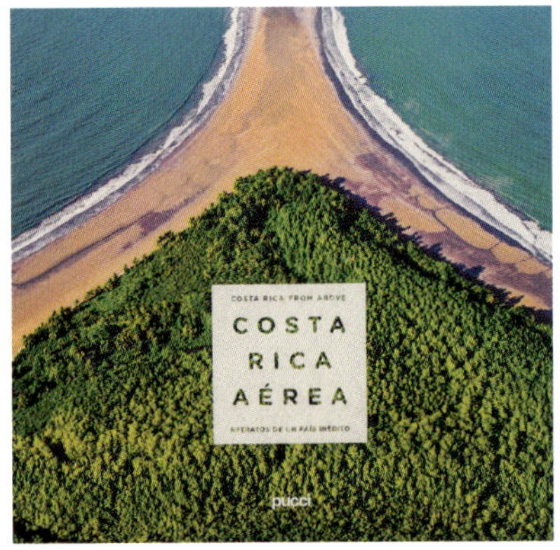


Costa Rica Aérea
Costa Rica From Above (2015)

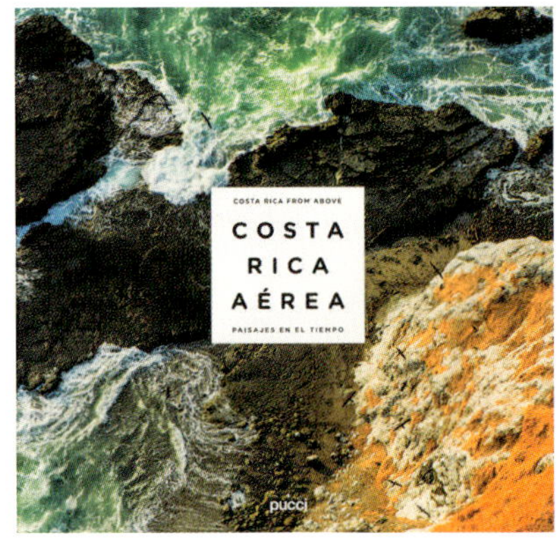


Costa Rica Aérea 2
Costa Rica From Above (2018)

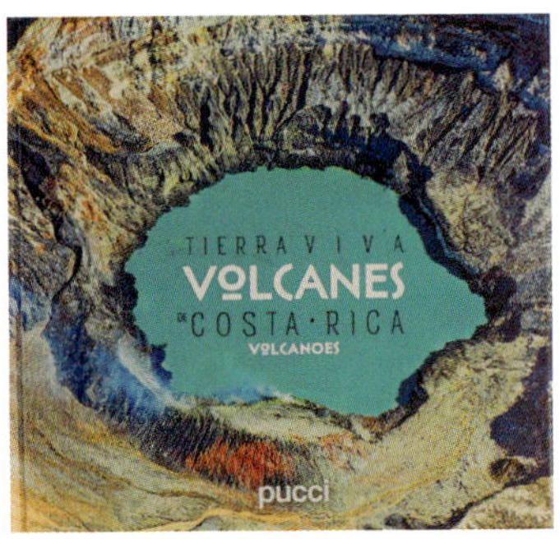


Volcanes de Costa Rica
Costa Rica Volcanoes (2017)

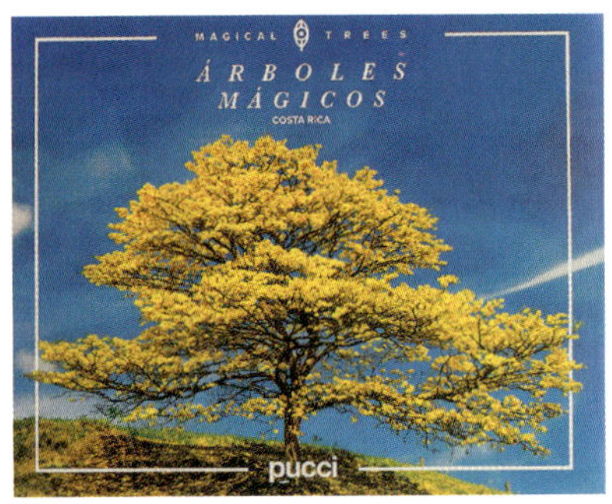


Árboles Mágicos
Magical Trees (2016) - 3rd Edition

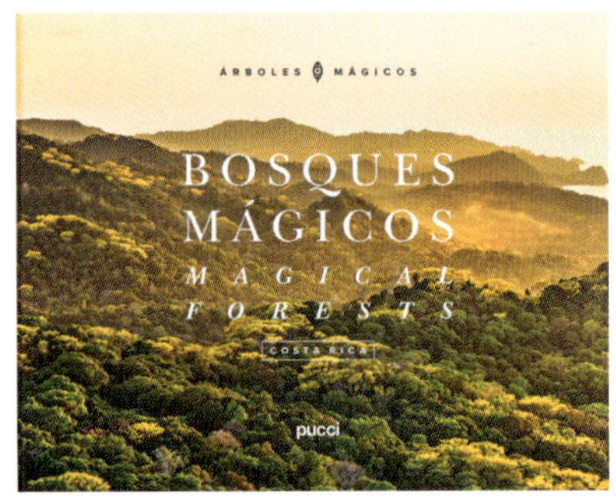


Bosques Mágicos
Magical Forests (2016)

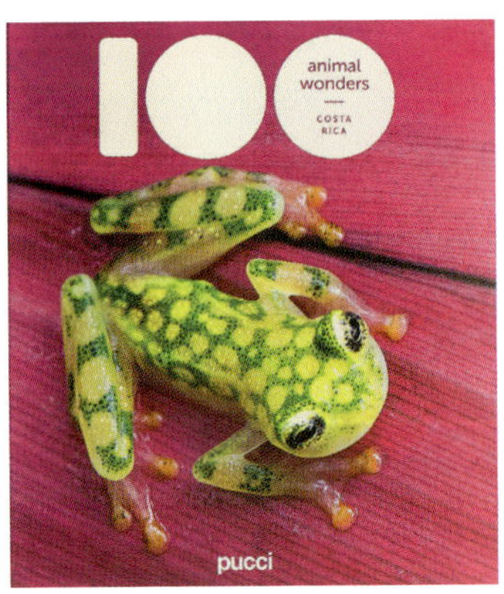


100 Maravillas Animales
100 Animal Wonders (2018)

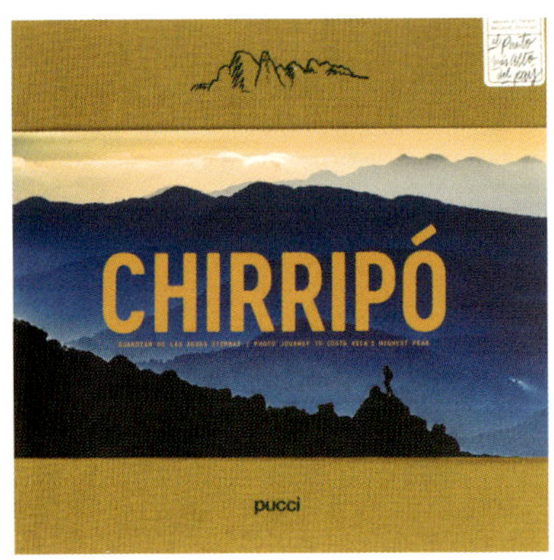


Chirripó
Chirripó (2018)

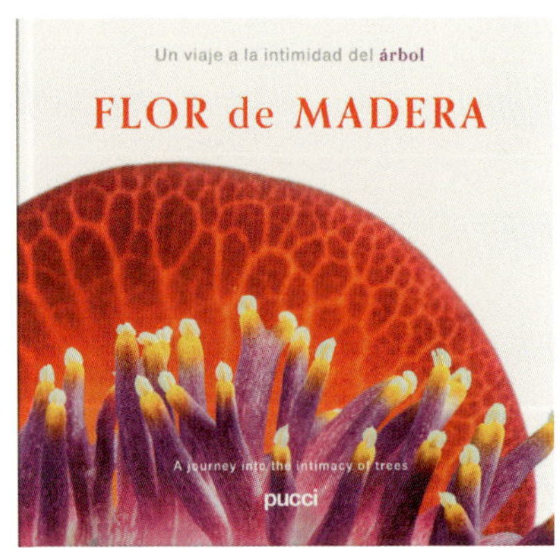


Flor de Madera
Flor de Madera (2019)

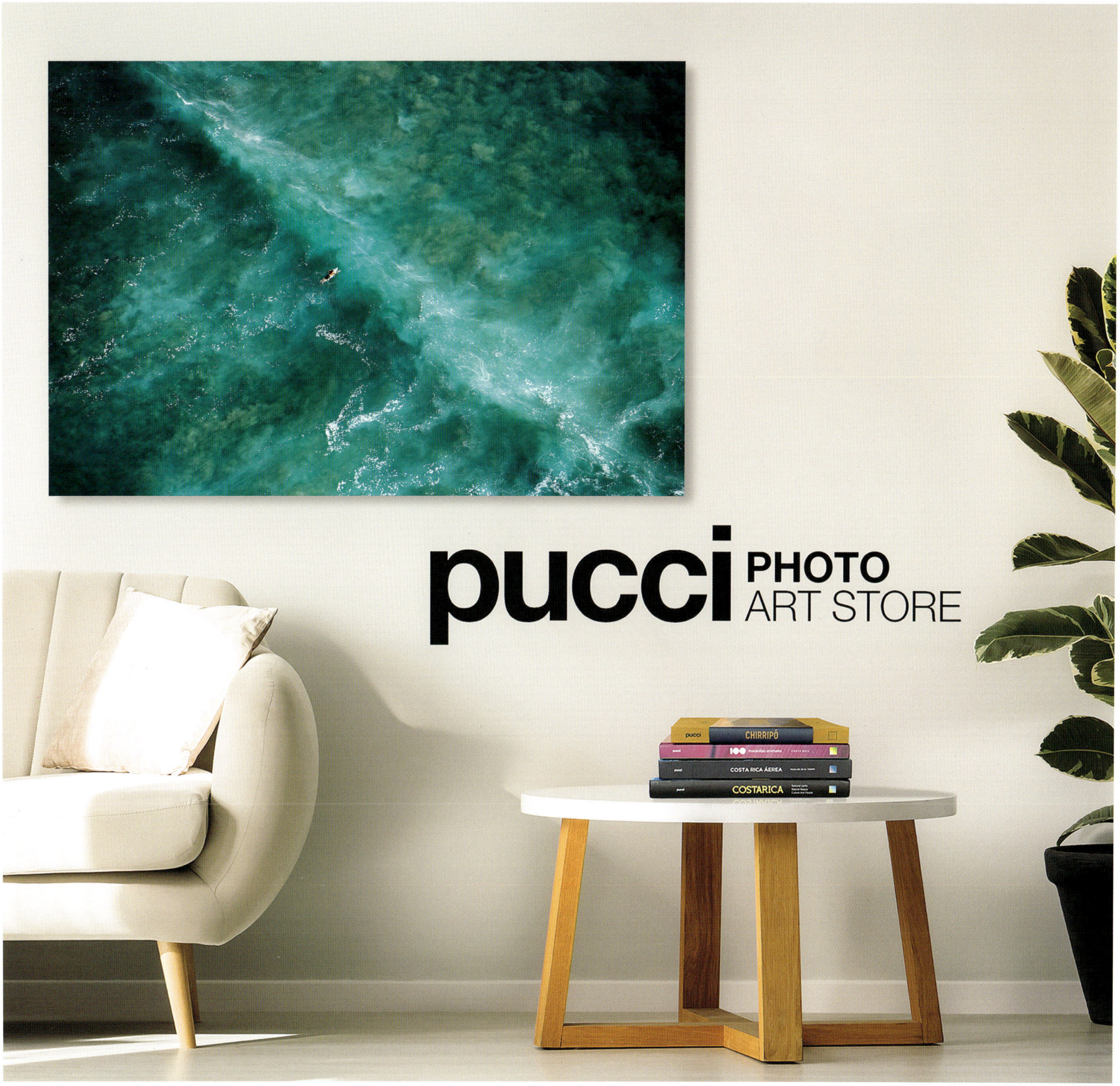
pucci PHOTO
ART STORE
CHIRRIPÓ
COSTA RICA AÉREA
COSTARICA

In this project there were many reasons to stop moving forward — brotherly quarrels, painful breakups, confusion, exhaustion, lack of funding. But there has also been great intention, heart, happiness, openness, creativity, curiosity, reconciliation, new friendships, collaboration, unity among allies, a serene struggle and love. We've come to see this as a mirror on ourselves — to grow, to keep recording our own humanity. There's been grief and there's been celebration. Life expressing itself through people. More than a book, this is a collective creation.

**pucci**

gente GENTE gente gente

gente gente gente

Gente Gente

GENTE gente

Gente gente gente

gente

GENTE gente gente

Gente gente

Gente

gente Gente

Gente GENTE

gente gente

gente

Gente gente gente

GENTE

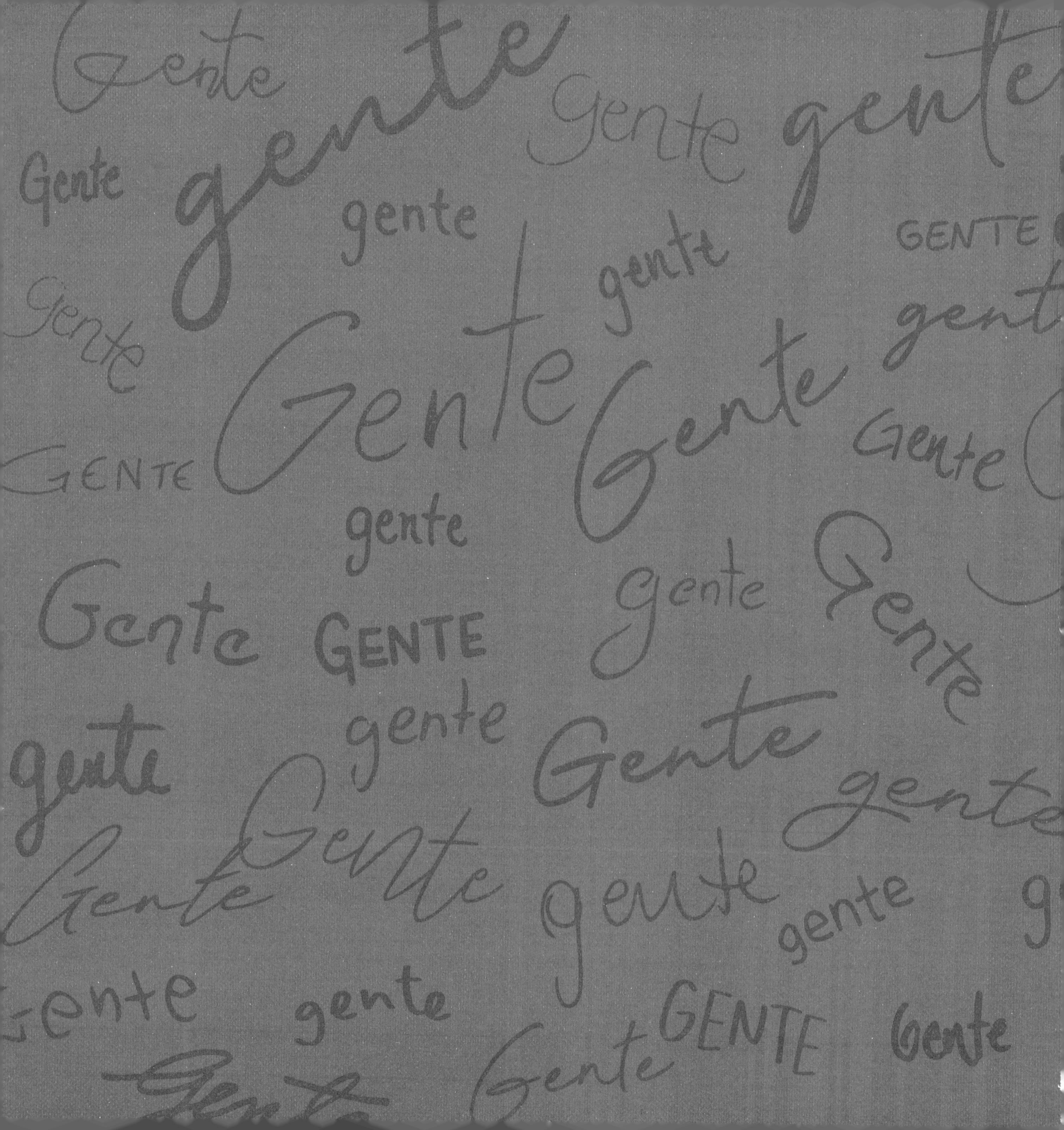